D1481741

School Learning

AN INTRODUCTION TO EDUCATIONAL PSYCHOLOGY

David P. Ausubel
The City University of New York

Floyd G. Robinson
The Ontario Institute for Studies in Education

HOLT, RINEHART AND WINSTON, INC.

New York · Chicago · San Francisco · Atlanta
Dallas · Montreal · Toronto · London · Sydney

PREFACE

THIS BOOK IS INTENDED FOR THOSE WHO WILL BE RESPON-
sible for the facilitation and guidance of learning in the classroom. For the
most part our readers will be teachers-in-training, although the ideas presented
here should prove helpful as well to practicing teachers and administrators
who wish to update or deepen their understanding of the teaching–learning
process.

Why do the authors presume to put forward yet another introductory
educational-psychology textbook? Certainly it cannot be argued that the
prospective reader is constrained by a lack of alternatives to choose from.
A fair answer requires some explanation of the genesis of the book and
the central premises upon which it is based.

For almost a decade, D. P. Ausubel has been working toward a systematic theory of classroom learning. This work culminated in *Educational
Psychology: A Cognitive View* (1968), a text considered appropriate for
graduate or senior students of considerable theoretical sophistication. During the same period the second author found himself in a variety of situations
—as classroom teacher, consultant to instructional improvement projects, and
instructor in educational psychology—which required the application of
educational psychology to classroom practice.

These experiences tended, on the whole, to shake this writer's initial
belief that educational psychology could be a substantial force in the improvement of public education. It is easy enough to have a group of teachers respond favorably on the evaluation questionnaire at the end of an educational-
psychology course, but the behavior of these same teachers observed later in
the classroom has typically shown distressingly little influence of the principles
and theories which they have presumably learned. Too quickly, it seems, they

cast off their thin layer of theory and are soon operating by the procedural rules learned in methodology courses (which are by no means always consistent with psychological theory), by imitation of their own teachers, by intuition, or by the dictates of educational mythology and its current fads. Many surveys of teacher opinion on the long-term value of educational-psychology courses, and observations of classroom transactions by learning theorists, attest to the fact that this phenomenon is widespread.

Here we have a paradox of great and alarming proportions. For on the one hand it is intuitively obvious that a teacher's effectiveness *should* be related to his ability to conceptualize and measure learning outcomes and to fashion valid hypotheses as to how to manipulate classroom factors to produce these outcomes. And yet the subsequent behavior of teachers who have been exposed to a course which purportedly develops these very skills is far from encouraging.

In our opinion, the root of the contradiction lies in the fact that the introductory educational-psychology course has too slavishly followed the eclectic orientation of contemporary liberal arts programs. Typically the student is given an overview or synopsis of a variety of essentially irreconcilable theories of learning, development, personality, attitude change, and motivation—to which are added innumerable details of physical, emotional, and ego development. Such extensive coverage, excellent as it may be from the liberal arts point of view, precludes the possibility of pursuing anything in depth and, more important, of showing how sustained application might be made to the teaching of particular subjects. Thus, as may be predicted from the learning theory advanced in this text, such theoretical structures—lacking consolidation and integration with the teacher's subject-matter knowledge—are readily supplanted in classroom practice by the concrete, rehearsed procedures which the teacher has acquired in his methodology courses.

It was with this set of speculations that the present writer first encountered the Ausubel theory which, on the basis of his own experience, seemed to have many attractive features insofar as classroom teachers are concerned. In the first place, the theory begins with, and continually focuses upon, *classroom* teaching and learning. That is to say, it is concerned almost exclusively with building a theoretical model of learning that will explain how students acquire the concepts and generalizations that are taught *in school,* and how they solve problems inherent in school learning tasks. In this approach, the theory stands apart from the widespread tendency to extrapolate from laboratory studies of learning which involve much simpler concepts and problems of artificial learning situations.

A second strength of the Ausubel theory is its *comprehensiveness.* The theory begins by describing the conditions for meaningful learning and by deducing from this a hierarchy of learning processes. In brief, *meaningful learning* takes place when an idea is related in some "sensible" fashion to ideas that the learner already possesses. When we discuss *forgetting,* we use the same model but extend it slightly to include a "strength of separation" (dissociability strength) between the established idea and the newly learned one. If we postulate that this dissociability strength spontaneously declines with time, then stages in the course of forgetting can be charted and explained. Next we encounter *transfer,* and here the model—focusing now on the structure of the material to be learned—shows the importance of providing the learner in advance with highly general ideas to which the new ideas can be anchored. Another small elaboration allows us to deal with *practice,* which we conceptualize as a process of repeated presentations of a set of ideas such that on each trial some of these new ideas are anchored, while the dissociability strengths of those already anchored are increased. An account of cognitive *development* follows from the model by postulating a sequence of stages of decreasing dependence on concrete props for the incorporation of new ideas into cognitive structure. *Motivation,* a topic typically treated as though it were at far remove from cognitive considerations, can be handled by the model by assuming that drive states (aroused by motives) have their chief effect in energizing the initial anchoring process. In brief, it would seem that the theory developed by a progressive expansion of the initial model can embrace most of the aspects of learning commonly thought to be the concern of educational psychology. And since the teacher is not required to shift mental gears at every turn, opportunity for consolidation and application is clearly enhanced.

Of course, comprehensiveness in a theory is a virtue only if the theory is a valid one. In this writer's experience, a remarkable feature of the Ausubel system is its overall congruence with the intuitions, insights, and gleanings from experience of teachers of acknowledged competence. While the danger in making such an assertion is that it invites criticism that the theory is merely "glorified common sense," it is not difficult to show that there is a vast difference between "congruence" and "identity." For example, most teachers have reflected upon the loss in memory which has occurred in subjects which they studied years before, and thus recognize that ideas become fuzzy and confused with concepts to which they were originally related. In this case the theory goes beyond these introspections to provide an abstract *model* of the learning and forgetting process, a model that provides a descriptive history of this memory loss and indicates the factors that are responsible for it. In like manner, all elementary-school teachers recognize that young children depend upon concrete examples in learning concepts; but here again, the theory provides a general model which indicates the *exact nature* of this dependence at each stage of development, and which suggests the means of facilitating the transition from one stage to the next. In these and many other instances, the theory provides a set of concepts which are more general and comprehensive than the teacher's "native" ideas and which, because of their generality, allow the assimilation of the latter's class-room experience. What results from this congruence of theory and practical insight is a teaching–learning cognitive structure of considerable sophistica-tion, flexibility, and permanence.

The value of such a structure of ideas is that it acts as a conceptual filter, that is, as a means of classifying the otherwise overwhelming mass of data by which the teacher is incessantly bombarded, and as an ideational matrix for generating hypotheses as to how classroom variables should be manipulated to produce specific learning outcomes. Not only does it sug-gest specific pedagogical practices, but it allows its possessor to evaluate arguments which are presented for or against specific educational proposals. In this text, for example, evaluative comment is offered on discovery learn-ing, the mental health emphasis, the proposition that creative behavior is amenable to training, the assertion that learning should be anxiety-free and devoid of aversive motivation, and so on.

Finally, the Ausubel exposition is not content to present pros and cons, but states its convictions about desirable practice in unequivocal terms. It asserts, for example, that the school can—on the basis of present knowledge —vastly improve the learning of organized subject-matter content (a task that should not be denigrated), as well as increasing problem-solving abili-ties. At the same time, it takes issue with the extravagant claims concerning the discovery approach, the value of discussion, the possibility of basing education on intrinsic motivation, and the feasibility of generating creativity in all children.

These desirable characteristics of the Ausubel theory are balanced by what some will regard as negative features. First, depth of treatement is attained only by concentration on the *cognitive* domain, while treating affec-tive factors only insofar as they relate to cognitive outcomes; thus the student who is primarily concerned with the shaping of attitudes, the inculcation of values, or the enhancement of the child's mental health must look elsewhere for guidance. Second, it must be admitted frankly that certain aspects of the theory have yet to be validated by long-term research studies; in this con-nection, it is assured that the products of reasoning within a comprehensive theoretical system are to be preferred as guidelines to classroom practice to extrapolations from research studies which, at best, relate tangentially to the critical elements in classroom learning.

Finally, an integrated, sequentially developed theory makes heavy demands on the reader in that the arguments in later chapters depend upon comprehension of the conclusions of earlier ones. This means that the student must develop, from the very outset, an intent to master each set of ideas as they are presented, to relate his concurrent classroom experience to these ideas, and to think through their implications in his own subject-matter field by constructing appropriate examples and illustrations when the text does not provide them. For it is only by these means that the theory will become firmly established, particularized to fit into the learner's own subject field, and internalized to the point where it becomes second nature for the teacher to view ongoing classroom learning from the perspective which it provides.

By what criteria shall this theory be judged? All learning theories, including the present one, must be subjected to the standard requirements of internal consistency, explanatory and predictive power, and degree of parsimony in the use of concepts and undefined terms. But if it is to aspire to pedagogical *usefulness,* the theory must face the more severe criterion of substantially changing the classroom behavior of the teacher who has internalized it.

Like other authors, we can offer no definitive evidence on this point, and we have to fall back here upon the opinions and completed assignments of the teachers with whom we have worked, and to the projects which they have on their own initiative subsequently carried out in their classrooms. Ausubel's theory will no doubt be revised and extended as more evidence accumulates; but in this writer's opinion its basic outline is so deeply rooted in an intuitive understanding of the teaching–learning process that, in the long run, it will not be found to be greatly in error.

We would like to express gratitude to those who have provided critical comments and suggestions and otherwise facilitated the production of this book. These include Nancy Johnston and Ira Brooks, doctoral candidates at the Ontario Institute for Studies in Education, Drs. D. Brison, E. Sullivan, and S. Miezitis of the Institute; Dr. S. Avital of the University of Jerusalem, and Harriet Dawes of the Central Midwestern Regional Educational Laboratory. Finally, a special word of thanks is due Jane Hill, who displayed sufficient confidence in the merit of the project to devote her evenings and weekends to the typing and editing of the manuscript.

The authors also wish to acknowledge the courtesy of those publishers who permitted the use of material from previously published articles and books.

All of the above contributed materially to the merit of this text, but the authors themselves must be held to account for its demerits. We will welcome and appreciate comments and suggestions from our readers.

F. G. R.

Toronto, Ontario
January 1969

CONTENTS

PART THREE   COGNITIVE VARIABLES IN LEARNING

PART ONE

THE DOMAIN OF EDUCATIONAL PSYCHOLOGY

The objectives of this opening section are to induce the mental set and introduce the preliminary ideas necessary for a proper consideration of the theoretical constructs and empirical results reported in later chapters. An important initial conception, which should be retained throughout the reading of the book, is that educational psychology may be envisaged as a set of empirically or logically derived relationships between factors (variables) in the school situation and desired outcomes (measured in terms of student behaviors). While there is no serious dispute concerning this definition, Chapter 1 shows that there *is* controversy concerning how such educational principles should relate to psychological generalizations derived from research in the laboratory. Our contention is that the direct extrapolation of psychological generalizations into educational principles (the *extrapolation* viewpoint), or the translation of psychological generalizations into educational hypotheses requiring further testing in the classroom setting (the *translation* viewpoint), is not likely to be as productive as direct concentration on learning as it occurs in the classroom (the *first principles* viewpoint).

The educational psychologist's attempt to fashion the principles underlying school learning may be thought of as *basic research,* an activity contributing to the subsequent *design* of new educational programs, which are in turn *tested* for their actual performance under real classroom conditions. Chapter 1 elaborates this basic research/design/testing sequence and indicates that it is paralleled by the teacher's actions as a classroom decision-maker, except that the teacher *uses* rather than *creates* learning principles (that is, uses the products of basic research).

Educational psychology is concerned with relationships between school factors and desired behavioral outcomes; therefore a first consideration in studying this discipline is to analyze these two classes of variables. The more important of these tasks, the subject of Chapter 2, is the classification of outcomes along some dimension of increasing complexity. By means of specific examples, it is shown that the taxonomy proposed by Bloom is useful in sensitizing the prospective teacher to the existence of such a behavioral hierarchy. But at the same time the consistent use of a taxonomy requires that its user possess an underlying *theory* which explains the psychological processes involved in the different kinds of behavior represented in the hierarchy. The way is thus prepared for the study of the central theoretical concepts of Part Two.

CHAPTER 1

THE NATURE, SCOPE, AND VALUE OF EDUCATIONAL PSYCHOLOGY

For the teacher-in-training the present year will be a time of preparation for his first professional role. Many specific and often anxiety-laden questions will be in his mind—how will he be able to manage large learning groups; how will he present the material to be learned; how will he handle discipline problems? It is, of course, understandable that many of the questions pertain to the young teacher's current anxieties about stepping into an ongoing class and keeping it moving forward as a learning unit.

Teacher-training institutions anticipate these immediate needs and try to provide the prospective teacher with the skills necessary to meet them. Thus the neophyte teacher is given "practice" teaching opportunities that allow him to assume a temporary teaching role with reduced responsibility, under the guidance of a regular teacher. In addition, "methods" courses provide detailed knowledge of many of the skills involved in presenting specific ideas in the subject-matter field in which the new teacher will be working. And by "observing" live classes in natural settings, the beginner will discern how the accomplished teacher deals with a variety of day-by-day problems.

However, the training institution recognizes that while the possession of the initial set of skills required to function with confidence in a real classroom is important to the teacher, such confidence does not in itself constitute the mark of a professional. To be considered a professional a teacher must, to start with, possess a clear notion of the objectives of his teaching; in other words, he must have a way of conceptualizing the outcomes of education which, in some respects at least, surpass in clarity and sophistication the commonsense notions of the layman. But even more important, the professional must manifest *adaptability,* born of an understanding of the phenomena of his field, an adaptability that allows him to deal with the unexpected, with problems not specifically discussed in his training, and with new factors and problems resulting from the continuous change inevitable in educational practice.

The beginning teacher will not be long in the classroom before problems requiring such professional competencies will begin to crowd in upon him. New teaching aids and new curricula are appearing with increasing frequency, and the teacher will have to decide what relevance and usefulness they might have in his particular classroom. He cannot ignore them; he must evaluate the evidence on the learning outcomes they produce and judge how this evidence relates to the goals of his teaching.

The new teacher will also soon find out that while it is relatively easy to teach facts and organized bodies of knowledge to motivated students, encouraging these students to solve complex intellectual problems is a more demanding and less frequently successful venture. Since it is no longer acceptable to assume that the child "lacks problem-solving capacities," the teacher must continuously improve his skill in analyzing the processes called for in solving particular kinds of problems and in diagnosing learning failures. Another common problem which challenges professional competence is that involving slow learners and students of average ability who exhibit little motivation toward school learning. Both of these groups, however carefully the lesson plan is contrived, will fall increasingly behind unless the teacher is sufficiently ingenious in devising effective ways of capturing their interest and dealing with their gaps in knowledge.

It is important to note that none of the problems cited can be solved merely by the teacher's possession of a high degree of subject-matter knowledge. While it is assumed that he must understand mathematics, for example, before he can effectively teach problem-solving skills in that field, it by no means follows that subject-matter sophistication in itself is sufficient to insure that the teacher will have such capacities. In fact, it is a commonplace that many learned people are abominable teachers of their own specialties. And in more general terms, the correlation between subject-matter knowledge and teaching outcomes is rarely very high.

Also, it is fallacious to assume that the solution to these problems can be derived intuitively from the "common sense" which all teachers are supposed to possess. Many commonsense "truths" are plausible in the sense that they could be true but just do not happen to be. Moreover, incorrect theories, especially if backed by the weight of authority, tradition, or persuasive logic, often masquerade as commonsense truisms. Some truisms in educational practice—such as the traditional placement of subject matter, the traditional methods of teaching arithmetic, science, reading, and foreign languages, the traditional elementary- and secondary-school curriculums, and postponement of the lecture method of instruction until the student reaches university age—tend, because of their seeming "naturalness" and familiarity, to impress us as eternal verities. Actually they are merely particular products of time-bound educational conditions and objectives, based on the prevailing commonsense notions of the day. In short, commonsense principles are not necessarily wrong but neither are they necessarily correct and, in themselves, they are an inadequate guide to the professional teacher.

Other solutions to the problems facing the beginning teacher are recollection of his own teachers' behavior, of the practices of "model" teachers observed during his training, and of the prescriptions of methodology specialists. Many of these models have much to offer, and the accumulated wisdom of a seasoned teacher can certainly benefit the novice in many ways. It has to be remembered, however, that what constitutes masterful teaching is closely tied to the particular objectives stressed and to the material, technological devices, and student population available at any given time. Such factors change with time, and with them the nature of outstanding teaching. Merely to imitate what is considered excellent, without comprehending the theoretical principles involved, may be a poor guarantee for coping with novelty or change.

What kinds of knowledge and competencies then, in addition to subject-matter mastery, can the teacher acquire in order to develop the adaptability and resourcefulness that is the mark of the professional? Certainly an ability to analyze educational objectives in terms of specific student behaviors, an understanding of how learning takes place and how the child's mode of thinking changes as he grows older, and an appreciation of the factors underlying school motivation would all be useful to any teacher facing the kinds of problems cited. Other kinds of knowledge are relevant, but we are limiting ourselves to areas of concern to educational psychology.

When we claim that the possession of certain kinds of facts and theoretical knowledge can help the teacher to cope with educational problems, we do not mean to imply that the "master teacher" can be created by subjecting someone to the right courses, no matter how excellent these courses might be. Obviously the outstanding teacher must be intelligent and must possess such qualities as sensitivity, flexibility, and the ability to empathize— qualities which are, in part at least, inborn. The contention is, rather, that a knowledge of principles will interact with the nonteachable intellectual and personal qualities of the teacher and will hasten and facilitate the attainment of high-level classroom skill which we characterize as the "teaching art."

It is an assumption of teacher-training institutions that educational psychology, along with other disciplines included under the general rubric of educational theory, will buttress and support competent teaching. In order to examine this proposition more critically, and to provide a general orientation to the field, it is necessary to define in more detail the domain of educational

psychology, and the kind of research and development which is undertaken
therein. The remainder of this chapter is devoted to this task. Specifically,
the following important matters will be discussed:

(a) how educational psychology fits into the general field of educational theory;
(b) how educational psychology is related to the study of pure psychology which takes place in university psychology departments;
(c) how educational psychology relates to the current large-scale programs of educational research and development which are aimed at
producing continuous and systematic improvement in education;
(d) how educational psychology benefits the decision-maker in education, whether this decision-maker be a teacher, administrator, or curri-
culum-builder.

EDUCATIONAL PSYCHOLOGY AS AN AREA OF
SPECIALIZATION WITHIN EDUCATIONAL THEORY

We begin with the simple assertion that the function of the
school is to change or develop behavior. Although the prospective teacher
may not be accustomed to viewing the learning of concepts, the development
of desirable attitudes, or the acquisition of physical skills as changes in student
behavior, analysis of what actually takes place suggests that the concept of
behavioral change is appropriate. For example, formal statements of the
objectives of the school—found in the preambles to "official" courses of
study and in the prospectus or statement of purposes accompanying new
curricula—describe the desired outcomes in terms of change in pupil behavior, that is, in terms of what the student should be able to do after completing
the course that he could not do before.

One may find, for example, that one of the stated objectives of the
elementary-school mathematics program is "to develop the ability to use
quantitative methods in solving real-life problems." Similarily, it is the stated
intent of many language programs at the same grade level to "develop the
child's ability to produce written communications which employ correctly the
grammar, spelling, and word meanings of the English language." In each of
these areas it is clear that an objective or goal has been stated in terms of an
ability (behavior) to be developed or improved (that is, changed).

In order to produce changes in behavior, public-education agencies
systematically create or devise a sequence of *educational experiences*. Of
course other educational agencies, such as the home and community, also
create experiences intended to produce behavioral changes in children. But
they usually do this in a less systematic and self-critical fashion than the
formal school system. The crux of the problem of any educational science is

to ascertain methods of providing educational experiences which are relatively more effective than existing methods in producing the desired educational outcomes.

Educational Theory

In order to facilitate the study of the production of desired behaviors, we conceptualize both these behaviors and the educational programs intended to produce them in terms of their constituent variables.[1] Educational theory refers to empirically or logically derived statements of general relationships between variables in the educational environment and those behavioral outcomes reflected in the school's aims. The "educational environment" can, of course, include the home and community as well as the school. However, educational theory tends to concentrate on the school because it is here that we have the greatest opportunity to systematically manipulate the educational environment variables (which are, therefore, commonly referred to as "independent" variables) and observe the outcomes ("dependent" variables).

Examples of such general statements of relationship are very numerous. For one, it has consistently been found that the level of aspiration and school achievement of middle-class children tends to exceed that of lower-class children. For another, it has been found that the optimal level of "drive" (that is, motivation or state of arousal) for problem solving lies somewhere between the highest and lowest drive levels that the student typically manifests in the school setting. And still another would be that in the elementary school there is a positive relationship between teacher "warmth" and student achievement.

These three statments are "general" in the sense that they define trends or tendencies which hold over broad groups of children, but which may be overridden by other factors in any particular case. For example, if we were to pick any two children at random from a classroom, we would not always find that the child with the higher socioeconomic status out-performed the child of lower socioeconomic status, for in any particular case the latter child might possess a compensating higher level of motivation. The problem of how the teacher is to utilize such general statements in the specific context of his classroom is one that will be discussed in a later section.

It is clear from the preceding comments that the purpose of educational theory is to make more precise our understanding of the relationship between

---

[1]A variable is a quantity or quality associated with each element of a defined set (that is, a collection of entities) which changes in value from element to element within the set. For example, IQ is a measurable quantity which varies from student to student within the classroom. Similarly, the rate of presentation of material, the type of rewards and punishments employed, and the type of grouping of students utilized can be conceptualized in terms of their component variables.

educational environment (independent) variables and behavioral outcome (dependent) variables, so that the former can be manipulated to produce optimum values of the latter. In other words, by understanding which characteristics of educational programs produce which outcomes, we become able to change our programs to produce behaviors more consistent with the school's goals.

Educational Psychology

Educational psychology may be thought of as the subdiscipline within educational theory that is concerned with such independent variables as intellectual ability, the structure of ideas in the learner's mind,[2] and motivation, which are *directly psychological* in nature. In addition, however, educational psychology investigates the effect on behavioral outcomes of variables which, on some theoretical basis, are postulated to be *directly related to psychological variables*. Examples here would include the size and composition of the learning group, the logical structure of subject matter, and the instructional "style" of the teacher.

Educational psychology differs somewhat from such sister disciplines as educational administration and educational sociology in the way it obtains evidence which serves as the basis of its generalizations. Because of the nature of the variables with which they deal, educational psychologists are more frequently able to actually manipulate independent variables than colleagues in the other branches of educational theory. Thus the *experimental method* has become the most frequently used research technique in educational psychology, while other educational theory disciplines often have to rely on *correlational analysis*.

Perhaps some simple examples will clarify the difference between these approaches. For instance, one might wish to investigate the relationship between "size of school district" (an independent variable) and "school achievement" (a dependent variable), with a view to creating school districts of optimum size. Since existing school districts cannot be readily changed in size for research purposes, one might have to be satisfied with a correlational analysis. In this approach one would plot "size" and "achievement" values on a two-dimensional graph (Figure 1.1) and would then compute a correlation coefficient between them. While the magnitude of this coefficient indi-

---

[2]Cognitive structure variables have been classified here as independent variables because, as we shall find later, they particularly influence the learning of new ideas. We have to recognize, however, that these same variables can in some circumstances be regarded as dependent variables because, taken together, they describe the learner's total organization of knowledge in a field, which is certainly an important outcome of instruction. Because of their intervening position between instructional variables on the one hand and such behavioral outcomes as problem solving on the other, some theorists would classify cognitive structure as "intervening" variables.

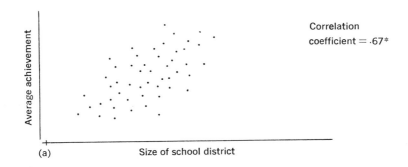

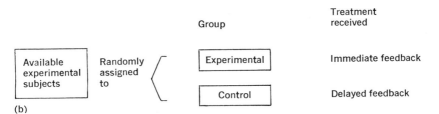

FIGURE 1.1 *Examples of correlational and experimental methods: (a) scattergram illustrating relationship between size of school district (independent variable) and average achievement (dependent variable), data hypothetical; (b) simple experimental arrangement for determining the effect of immediacy of feedback (independent variable) on acquisition of arithmetical skills (dependent variable).*

    *The Pearson product moment correlation coefficient, most typically used to measure the degree of relationship between two variables, produces numbers which range from +1 to −1. The absolute value of the coefficient indicates the degree or strength of the relationship. The sign of the coefficient represents the direction of the correlation. Positively related variables are such that the high values of one tend to correspond with high values of the other. Negatively related variables tend to have high values of the first variable associated with low values of the second.

cates the degree of relationship between the variables, it is extremely difficult to rule out the possibility that some third uncontrolled variable, such as the average intelligence in school units, is primarily the *causal* variable in school achievement. If this were the case, one could not then deduce that increasing the size of the school unit would necessarily increase the average level of achievement.

The experimental method, on the other hand, provides more assurance that one is getting at the variables that are really causal in producing a particular result. For example, let us suppose that we wish to determine the effect of immediate "feedback" (that is, being told immediately whether an answer is correct or incorrect) on the learning of mathematical skills. In this case we would create two "treatment" groups—the first receiving immediate feedback, the second, delayed feedback. The groups would otherwise receive identical treatment. Moreover, to insure that an uncontrolled variable such as intelligence does not influence the outcome, we would assign children randomly to one or the other of the treatments (See Chapter 18). This procedure would tend to equate the groups not only in intelligence but in such other relevant variables as socioeconomic level and previous knowledge. In this case we could reasonably conclude that any difference in the scores obtained could be attributed to the treatments themselves (the immediacy of feedback) rather than to the effect of some uncontrolled variable. Consequently we would be considerably more confident about acting on the results than if we had merely observed that a correlation existed between these variables.

Difficulties with the Definitions

It is admitted that the definitions offered above will necessarily present some problems and ambiguities. In the first place, the student of educational theory will find that since each subdiscipline is sufficiently ambitious in its definition there tends to occur some overlap in the content presented, particularly in the research results that are reported. For example, educational psychology must obviously be interested in the relationship between IQ (a psychological variable) and educational achievement. However, educational sociology also deals with this relationship because IQ is correlated with socioeconomic level (a sociological variable). While these "boundary disputes" might be somewhat confusing to the beginner, they pose no real problems in practice.

A second problem, of a rather more technical nature, has to do with the fact that the definitions do not indicate the optimum level of analysis for the variables involved in educational theory. For instance, educators frequently make statements such as: "discovery learning is more effective than traditional methods in teaching arithmetical skills." The difficulty with this statement, aside from its dubious validity (Chapter 16), is that it is stated at too high a level of generality. The principal terms involved ("discovery method," "traditional method," "arithmetical skills") describe entities which are, in fact, comprised of numerous variables. Consequently, there may be a considerable amount of variation between the different approaches which are called "discovery" method. Considerably more precision would seem to be required if the statement is to convey any specific meaning to the teacher.

On the other hand, it would be possible to describe educational procedures in extremely specific detail. For example, in an attempt to analyze "educational experiences" in terms of the most elementary stimuli to which the learner is sensitive, one might describe a specific episode in a teaching procedure (the teacher addressing the question "how" to a student) in such terms as these: "a 2.4 decibel, 5000 cycle per second sound of 1.8 seconds' duration, emitted 8.2 feet from the student." Obviously this level of detail in the analysis of variables, common in rigorous experiments conducted in psychological laboratories, contains far more information than the educational researcher is able to cope with or incorporate into viable generalizations. It is easy to say that there is an "optimum" level in the degree of generality at which educational theory should be formulated, and that this level will vary somewhat depending upon the purposes to which the generalization is to be put. However, as we shall see, this will be a continuing problem in reporting research results in attempting to apply the generalizations of educational psychology at the classroom level.

A third group of difficulties inheres in the formulation of the aims themselves. To begin with, official statements of aims are usually vague in that they do not spell out objectives in precise behavioral terms. A second difficulty is that there is considerable lack of agreement as to what the aims of education really are. Finally, some would maintain that some of the loftier goals of education cannot be expressed in behavioral terms.

It is sometimes concluded that these difficulties in dealing with dependent variables actually preclude the possibility of an empirically based educational theory. The initial apparent cogency of the argument that "if you can't define (agree upon or state in precise terms) educational objectives, then you cannot find general relationships between independent and dependent variables" does not stand up to detailed scrutiny. In the first place, the fact that the objectives of specific courses are typically cast in imprecise terms does not in any way suggest that this is a necessary state of affairs, but rather that curriculum-builders have had insufficient experience in attempting more precise formulations. Although it is true that from time to time there is considerable disagreement concerning aims (and that some goals of education may indeed be indefinable in precise behavioral terms), the fact remains that there is widespread agreement on many goals. One such goal is that children should develop their language abilities or their quantitative abilities to the fullest degree possible within the time and ingenuity available to the school. Consequently, educational psychology at least has a clear sanction to proceed in these and many other noncontroversial areas. Moreover, even though there exist such controversial areas as the influencing of attitudes, educational psychology does not purport to be *prescriptive* (that is, to say what *should* be done), but rather to find out what *can* be done. In many such areas the decision to actually employ or not to employ a given technique must rest with a higher authority than the researcher, an authority which is responsible to the public for the behavioral changes that the school is attempting to make.

EDUCATIONAL PSYCHOLOGY AS AN APPLIED SCIENCE

Since pure psychology is typically thought of as "the science of behavior," it is appropriate to inquire how educational psychology relates to that discipline. In a general sense, one might think of educational psychology as lying within the proper domain of pure psychology since the latter discipline is interested, in theory at least, in relationships between all possible genetically determined and environmental variables and all conceivable behavioral outcomes. Certainly any psychologist housed in an academic psychology department would be free to undertake studies in educational psychology (as we have defined it) while maintaining his position within the broad confines of his discipline. For example, there seems no reason why a psychologist could not study the effects of grouping in classrooms, say, on achievement in secondary-school mathematics.

However the university psychologist has, historically, evinced considerably less interest in educational problems than one might at first expect. Although some of the prominent figures in early North American psychology (particularly Thorndike and James) were very much interested in educational processes, psychologists were soon to adopt the position that the study of simple behavior must precede the study of complex behavior. Consequently, it has become customary for the experimental psychologist to formulate and test his theories in the psychological laboratory on data derived largely from the behavior of animals. Animals can be studied intensively and subjected to experimental treatments that cannot be used with children in a publicly supported educational system. Moreover, by removing the animals from complex social environments, the pure psychologist is able to study behavior uncontaminated by social variables which, while extraneous to his theory, normally operate in school situations. The intent of these studies is to yield general scientific laws as ends in themselves quite apart from any practical utility.

Psychologists have, of course, studied human learning as well. The typical approach has been to use college students (the most readily available subjects) and to concentrate on rote learning and other tasks which are relatively simple in comparison with what the school attempts. Although primarily interested in advancing knowledge about the control of behavior in general, most psychologists still believe that their research will *ultimately* make some contribution to school learning, but they quite properly do not see it as their responsibility to make an *immediate* application (for example, Spence, 1959).

One way of epitomizing the difference between the two disciplines is to say that *general* aspects of learning interest the psychologist, whereas *class-room* learning is the special province of the educational psychologist. The subject matter of educational psychology, therefore, can be inferred directly from the problems facing the classroom teacher. The latter must generate interest in subject matter, inspire commitment to learning, motivate pupils, and help induce realistic aspirations for educational achievement. He must decide (within limits) what is important for his pupils to learn, ascertain what learnings they are ready for, pace instruction properly, and decide on the appropriate size and difficulty level of learning tasks. He is expected to organize subject matter expeditiously, present materials clearly, simplify learning tasks at initial stages of mastery, and integrate current and past learnings. It is his responsibility to arrange practice schedules and reviews, to offer confirmation, clarification, and correction, to ask critical questions, to provide suitable rewards, to evaluate learning and development, and, where feasible, to promote discovery learning and problem-solving ability. Finally, since he is concerned with teaching groups of students in a social environ-ment, he must grapple with problems of group instruction, individualization, communication, and discipline.

Thus the scope of educational psychology as an applied science is exceedingly broad, and the potential rewards it offers in terms of the social value of facilitating the subject-matter learning of pupils is proportionately great.

The Extrapolation Viewpoint

Although we can distinguish between pure psychology and educational psy-chology in this somewhat abstract way (that is, by pointing out differences in emphasis in both the independent and dependent variables), the problem still remains of how the applied psychologist is to utilize the knowledge produced by pure psychologists. This problem is of particular importance when the educational psychologist attempts to enlighten teachers on princi-ples of learning underlying classroom practice or to advise curriculum-developers. It is perhaps not too erroneous to say that the different view-points of educational psychologists in North America form a continuum defined by the intensity of association which they envisage between these disciplines.

To begin with, there is what might be called the "extrapolation" viewpoint. This is the notion that much of pure psychology can be "extrapolated" from the psychological lab to the classroom situation; in other words, this viewpoint holds that the observed relationship between two variables in the laboratory setting can be used to predict outcomes in an ostensibly analogous educational setting.

For example, B. F. Skinner, a well-known American psychologist, has conducted a great deal of research on the manipulation of pecking responses in pigeons. In the typical Skinner experiment, a hungry pigeon was placed in a box and "rewarded" by receiving grain pellets for pecking on a bar. While Skinner found that the pigeons' pecking behavior could be systematically controlled and predicted from the "schedule of reinforcement" employed (that is, the relative frequency of reward to response), the pecking rate of the pigeon was invariably increased by any kind of reinforcement. Some of the more extreme advocates of programmed instruction have attempted to extrapolate many of the concepts and predictions from this laboratory research into the classroom situation in which, say, a student is required to give responses to a sequence of arithmetic questions of the type "2 + 3 = ___ , 2 + 4 = ___ , ..." One prediction made by such extrapolationists was that the child, like the pigeon, would continue to respond as long as rewards were forthcoming (in the child's case, the reward was the knowledge of being correct). Data bearing on this prediction are reviewed in Chapter 11.

The Translation View

A second viewpoint on the relationship between pure and educational psychology can be described by the term "translation." This approach is considerably more cautious in that it suggests that many empirically demonstrated principles of pure psychology, although they cannot be directly extrapolated to the educational situation, may yield *educational hypotheses*. That is, on the basis of laboratory findings, such generalizations suggest what might happen to an analogous dependent variable if an analogous independent variable in the educational setting were manipulated. According to this view, however, such hypotheses may have to be modified from the form which they take in the psychological laboratory to take into account the more complex situation in which they are being applied. Moreover, whether reformulated or not, these hypotheses must be empirically tested in the educational setting to determine their validity.

An example of this approach can be found in current attempts to apply theories of "arousal" (Berlyne, 1960) to educational practice. It has been found in the laboratory, for instance, that when an organism (human or animal) is faced with a situation that elicits conflicting responses, curiosity is engendered and the organism will seek further information to reduce this conflict. In the translation phase it is hypothesized that a similar information-seeking (motivational) effect might be induced in school children if material or ideas to be learned were preceded by devices (for example, statements) which generate conflicting conceptual responses. Although a seemingly reasonable hypothesis (see Chapter 12 for further discussion) it has not yet been thoroughly tested in classroom settings.

The First Principles View

The third view on the relationship of educational psychology to pure psychology might be described as the "first principles" approach. This approach, which characterizes the present text, begins with the observation that there are enormous differences in the complexity of the tasks which the school is attempting to teach and those from which most psychological principles are derived. Thus, it is argued, it is frequently advisable to focus on educational phenomena as they are actually found in schools: the complex learner facing a complex learning task. Indeed, this viewpoint goes further and asserts that not only is such an approach more economical in terms of effort, but that the alternate approaches (particularly the extrapolation viewpoint) may lead to erroneous predictions and applications.

A case in point has to do with the phenomenon of "retroactive inhibition." This refers to the situation in which an individual first learns material "A," then similar but not identical material "B," then is retested on "A." Typically it has been found that the intervening learning ("B") leads to poorer performance in recalling "A" than one would expect on the basis of the passage of time alone. Moreover, the "inhibiting" effects of "B" have usually been found to be large and to increase with an increase in similarity between "B" and "A." These results have been found with simple learning materials such as lists of words or paired nonsense syllables. But such materials differ greatly from the highly structured, hierarchically organized, and extended subject matter found, for example, in arithmetic, algebra, or geometry—to which the child is subjected in school. In contradiction to the phenomenon of retroactive inhibition, the theory advanced in this book—which takes into account this complex structure as well as the organization of ideas in the learner's mind—makes a considerably different prediction. In fact, as will be seen later, it is predicted that learning "B" will occasionally *facilitate* the retention of "A" rather than impair it.

The "first principles" viewpoint, then, tends more than the other views to regard educational psychology as a separate discipline which must expect to develop its own concepts and theoretical structures. It recognizes that the complexity of classroom learning will pose many problems in designing experiments from which clear-cut results may be obtained, but it maintains that such experiments are possible, provided that sufficient ingenuity is brought to bear upon them.

EDUCATIONAL PSYCHOLOGY IN A BASIC
RESEARCH AND DEVELOPMENT CONTEXT

It is important that the student of educational psychology appreciate how this discipline, as one of the specialties within educational theory, contributes to large-scale programs for educational change. In most of the advanced countries of the world there has occurred within the last decade an increasing awareness of the need to revitalize education, to base its practices as much as possible upon empirical research, and to build into the educational system a systematic means of generating needed change. Further, it has been increasingly realized that educational reform on a large scale is a complex phenomenon, involving agencies at various levels in the education hierarchy.

The concrete response to this sensed need for rational intervention in educational change has been the creation of new institutes for educational research, development, and implementation. The nature of the institute, and its relationship to the established decision-making powers in education, varies considerably from place to place. Undoubtedly the best known to readers of this text will be the research and development centers and the regional laboratories in the United States (Holzner, 1966), the Ontario Institute for Studies in Education in Canada (Jackson and others, 1966), and the Schools Council in England (Taylor, 1966).

The prospective teacher's interest in these developments stems from the fact that teachers will be increasingly involved in educational reform. They will be exposed to the reports of research undertaken and the implementations proposed, and they will be required periodically to take additional training to become familiar with new content and approaches. Moreover, large-scale research and development processes exemplify the relationship obtaining between educational theory in general and educational practice in particular. Thus the relationships which are visible on the large scale suggest steps that teachers-in-training will have to follow as they attempt to translate the content of an educational psychology course into actual practice in their classrooms.

Basic Research

The functional relationship between the various phases of the research and development process are illustrated diagrammatically by Figure 1.2. The region designated "Research and Development Institute" indicates the functions normally undertaken by these bodies. To begin with, the research and development institute undertakes *basic research*, whose function is to produce the statements of general relationship between the independent and the dependent variables comprising educational theory. As explained in the

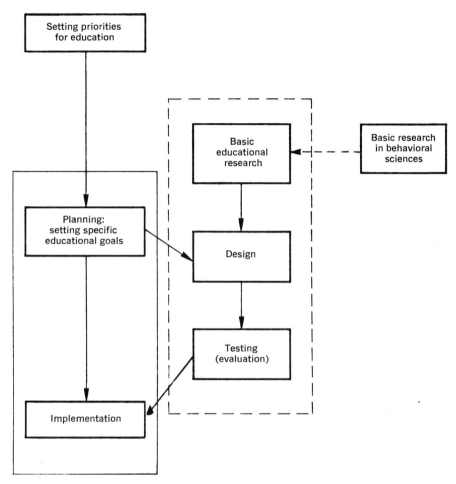

FIGURE 1.2 *Functional relationships in plan for educational change.*

previous section, a person engaged in basic research in education will relate more or less directly to a "pure" behavioral science (such as psychology), depending on his understanding of the relationship between these disciplines.

Development

The second major function of the research and development institute is typically described as "development," and may be analyzed into two further subfunctions. In the first or *design* phase, a team comprising subject-matter specialists, teachers, and educational psychologists is brought together to create an educational "package"—that is, a new curriculum sequence, teaching technique, or administrative arrangement for use in the school. Such a group might be constituted to design a new mathematics program for the primary grades of the elementary school. The educational psychologist will contribute to the design phase his knowledge of the general principles of classroom learning, and of the levels of learning which children are capable of at various stages of development.

The second or *testing* phase of the development function is to try out the new "package" (in our illustrative case, a new mathematics program) on a sample of the proposed "target population" (that is, the group of students with which it is ultimately hoped that the material will be used). At this stage the new program will be subjected to extensive *evaluation*, and careful measures will be taken to determine the extent to which the behavioral outcomes produced by the program measure up against the goals set for it. Frequently the new package will be found deficient in some respects and will be returned to the design unit for further work.

Integration with Decision-Making Bodies

It seems clear that a research and development institute cannot, in and of itself, effect educational change. What is required in addition is a working relationship with the principal decision-making body in education, namely the state or provincial department of education or, in many instances, the regional or local school board. The actual arrangements that have been worked out vary from institute to institute so that Figure 1.2 constitutes a theoretical model rather than an illustration of any specific case. It is clear, however, that an important participant in effecting educational change would be a *planning agency* in the department of education, whose task it would be to formulate specific plans for producing new educational packages and implementing them in classrooms within a specified period of time. For example, the planning agency might decide to implement a new mathematics program in the primary grades within a period of five years. This intention, together with adequate financial support, would then be directed to the design section of the research and development institute, which would hire the necessary staff to undertake the project. After the field-testing phase of the development program had been completed, the results of the evaluation would be made available to senior decision-makers in the department, who would decide whether or not the program should be implemented. If so, a large-scale program of teacher re-education and preparation of textbooks and supporting materials would be undertaken.[3]

---

[3] It is also suggested that an extra-departmental structure is necessary to determine the general priorities which shall be followed in public education. Such an agency, designated in Figure 1.2 as a *goal-setting* agency, would attempt to synthesize informed public opinion on the relative merit of the many claims for reform or change which are continually being put forward by those interested in the improvement of public education.

Application to the Classroom Teacher

The sequence of stages envisaged for the research and development institute are paralleled by the steps which a teacher must take in applying educational psychology to classroom practice. The student of educational psychology, although not undertaking basic research himself, is acquainted with the results of research as they are formulated into the general principles of that discipline.

When the teacher attempts to apply these principles in the context of a specific classroom situation, he will, in effect, undertake to design a new educational experience, probably involving primarily a change in instructional procedures. However modest this change may be, the teacher must nevertheless bring to bear the same kinds of skills that are represented in the design phase of the research and development process. He must take into account not only the general principles of classroom learning and readiness, but also the specific nature of the subject matter he is teaching and other circumstances particular to his classroom situation.

Finally, the teacher should be expected to try out his proposed innovations on a sample (for example, a class) of his "target population" (all the groups of children with whom he will utilize the new material over a period of years), prior to incorporating it into his permanent repertoire of instructional techniques. In this process he will also determine by measurement the actual outcome of his innovations and the extent to which they seem worthwhile in light of his teaching goals.

THE VALUE OF EDUCATIONAL PSYCHOLOGY TO THE PROFESSIONAL EDUCATOR

The previous section indicates in a general way the steps through which the teacher might proceed in utilizing the results of an educational-psychology course. This section attempts to make a further analysis and clarification of the outcomes of these procedures.

The Educator as Decision-Maker

Implicit in the previously discussed total structure for educational change is the assumption that educational practice changes as a result of decisions made at every level in the educational hierarchy. To begin with, at the highest administrative level the state or provincial authority may decide to improve mathematics instruction (make a planning decision). In more general terms, the highest educational authority typically decides what subject areas will be studied in the school, the total time to be allotted to instruction, the level of qualification which teachers must possess to teach in the schools, and so on.

These decisions at the highest level provide a series of constraints or limitations within which decisions at the next lowest administrative level must be made. At this level the superintendent of a large school system, the board itself, or the principal of a school, will make further decisions concerning the acceptance or rejection of the proposed new mathematics program, how much time will be allotted to mathematics instruction within the system, what resources would be made available in the way of audio-visual aids, how classes will be scheduled, and so on. Finally, at the classroom level the teacher, although constrained by the limitations imposed by the two previous decision-making levels, is free to make many further decisions concerning actual instructional techniques. For example, the teacher is usually completely free to determine how new material will be sequenced, what schedule of practice will be allowed, what the method of presentation will be, what kind of reviews will be given and how they should be spaced, and how instructional groupings will be employed in his class.

It is instructive, therefore, to think of the teacher as making decisions which would improve educational practice in the sense of bringing actual outcomes closer to stated aims. If educational psychology is to have an impact, this impact must occur at all points where decisions are made.

An Illustrative Example

For purposes of illustration we may consider a grade 6 teacher who, in common with many other teachers, has found that while his students acquire a high mastery of mechanical arithmetical skills (such as, the ability to provide the answer "63" to the question "What is 9 times 7?"), they have great difficulty in solving problems posed in verbal form. The teacher, therefore, wants to improve the problem-solving ability of his students. Also, as a result of previous experience, pedagogical training, or intuition, our "typical" teacher will have numerous hypotheses as to how he might manipulate the variables at his disposal to produce the desired effect. It is our experience that teachers will frequently hypothesize that problem-solving abilities could be improved by:

> (a) providing specialized language training to facilitate translation between verbal and arithmetical statements;
> (b) providing the child with concrete materials;
> (c) providing more experience in discovering generalizations; or
> (d) providing the child with opportunities to work in a group problem-solving situation.

Now each of these hypotheses defines a possible course of action, so that the teacher finds himself in a decision situation—that is, in a situation where he must choose one of these alternatives as a basis for his own subsequent design of a new procedure.

We must now return to our initial question as to how educational psychology can facilitate this decision-making process. In the first place, it seems a prerequisite that if the teacher is genuinely interested in producing better "problem solving," he should have a clear conception of what this ability is, and how it differs from such subordinate abilities as concept acquisition or the discovery of generalizations. Without some clear behavioral definition in mind, and an appropriate instrument with which to measure this behavior, the teacher would be in the position where he would be unable to determine precisely the degree to which the alternative he chose led to the attainment of his stated goal. It has been our observation that many of the controversies concerning which of two competing instructional techniques produces "superior problem solving" (or other kinds of abilities) stem from the fact that the disputants have different conceptions of the ability involved.

In a more direct way, the research studies reported in educational psychology texts provide empirical data on many of the alternative paths of action considered by the teacher in our example. Thus, research has been undertaken on the effect of language training on problem solving, the effectiveness of group problem solving, the effectiveness of the discovery method, and on the effectiveness of concrete props. The generalizations resulting from research on these specific hypotheses refine the teacher's subjective estimate of the likely success of any alternative in a particular situation. In other words, if the empirical results suggest that one alternative is superior to the others in the sense of producing a closer approximation to the desired behavior, then such information will reduce the teacher's uncertainty as to which alternative is the correct one in his situation. Of course, after the teacher has made this preliminary decision, he will still have to design in specific detail the procedure he will use, and will also have to test its effectiveness in his classroom.

The third, and perhaps the most important contribution of educational psychology comes through providing the teacher with a *theoretical structure* from which he may formulate his own hypotheses as to how to cope with new problems arising from day to day. It is the possession of a sophisticated, integrated theory—a mesh of coordinated propositions concerning how independent variables relate to dependent variables—which provides the teacher with that degree of flexibility which we earlier described as characterizing the way a professional approaches his work.

The importance of such flexibility lies in the fact that educational psychology does not provide a set of specific prescriptions as to how the teacher should proceed in the particular situation in which he operates. For example, on the basis of existing research, our "typical" teacher may decide that the best approach to the improvement of problem-solving skills in his classroom may be a program of specialized language training. He must then proceed to design such a program, and will have to take into account, in addition to relevant research, such specific local conditions as the kind of subject matter he is dealing with, the age level of his class, its general motivational level, its previous experience in problem solving, and a host of other variables. And while it may have happened that the research literature will deal fairly specifically with his problem (for example, he might encounter research results on the use of language training in elementary arithmetic), it is not conceivable that any research study could have been conducted which exactly duplicates his situation.[4] Consequently, the teacher will have to go beyond the generalizations given and, in the process of his "design," formulate more refined hypotheses which better fit the precise conditions which prevail. It is a fundamental belief of the authors of this text that the possession of a comprehensive, unified theory will help the teacher immeasurably in the refining process.

The discussion in the previous paragraph has referred to the value of a theory in elaborating and modifying hypotheses which the teacher—through some unspecified means—already possesses. Of course, the theoretical structure will frequently suggest alternatives which would *not* have occurred to the teacher. For example, as we shall see later (Chapter 17), our analysis of problem solving suggests that the way to improvement in that skill may lie in: (1) organizing the relevant propositional knowledge; (2) providing training in rules of inference; and (3) teaching "strategies." Again, these are global hypotheses requiring adaptation—via the total theoretical structure—before they can serve as the basis of classroom procedures.

Typically then, the classroom teacher must regard the generalizations derived from the research literature as *hypotheses* to be modified, elaborated, and extended to fit local conditions. While the degree of ingenuity which the teacher will display will depend on such factors as his knowledge of subject matter and personal inventiveness, he can also be helped by a knowledge of how to proceed systematically with the *testing* of his refined hypothesis. Because of its importance, this latter process is discussed in some detail in Chapter 18.

TOPICS FOR DISCUSSION AND FURTHER STUDY[5]

1.* The notion of manipulating learning variables to produce behavioral outcomes strikes many educators as being ultra-mechanistic. Discuss other possible conceptualizations of the educational process and their appropriateness for the

---

[4]For one thing, the teacher himself constitutes a set of critical variables in any instructional method, and his presence itself makes his own situation unique.
[5]Questions marked with an asterisk (*) in this and subsequent chapters will require outside reading for their adequate discussion. Appropriate sources are indicated in parentheses.

study of empirically derived generalizations about school learning. (See, for example: Aiken, 1966; Green, 1964; Komisar, 1967.)

2. Many educators point to the conflict between present learning theories as evidence that educational psychology cannot be relied upon for guidance and that the educator must, therefore, improve education through a trial and error process. Examine the adequacy of this argument.

3. It is a contention of this book that a knowledge of educational psychology principles should contribute to the teacher's effectiveness. At the same time, some studies have found little correlation between the teacher's knowledge of such principles and the results produced in the form of student learning. How would you explain this apparent contradiction?

4. Cite some "commonsense" assumptions about children and learning that are presently being acted upon in the schools. Trace, if possible, the origin of these assumptions and determine the extent to which they are supported or contradicted by objective evidence.

5. Cite educational objectives that are commonly agreed upon and those that are a matter of controversy. In respect to the controversial objectives, discuss kinds of evidence which the educational psychologist might provide which would help to clarify the issues involved.

6. Make a list of specific decisions which are within the classroom teacher's jurisdiction. Identify the independent variables inherent in these decisions.

7. To what extent does the school have an obligation to cooperate with other educational agencies in promoting the growth of desired forms of pupil behavior? What concrete means are available for facilitating cooperation between these agencies? In what ways may these agencies hinder the work of the school?

8.* Investigate and make a report on the controversy concerning the relationship of theories of learning to theories of instruction. (Ausubel, 1968; Carter, 1967; Engelmann, 1967; Gage, 1964; Scandura, 1966; B.O. Smith, 1960) In what respects is this disagreement of concern to teachers? How can these differences be related to the view put forward in this chapter?

9.* In this text and in other conceptualizations of the teaching process (McDonald, 1963; Ryans, 1963; Travers, 1966) the teacher is regarded as a decision-maker who systematically manipulates classroom variables to produce desired outcomes. Other writers (Cronbach, 1967; Jackson, 1966) assert that the rapid interaction between teacher and pupil severely limits rational or formal decision making by the teacher. Examine the merits and limitations of the arguments put forward on both sides.

10. Some educators hold that the plan for educational change inherent in Figure 1.2 represents too "centralist" or bureaucratic a position. They advocate in its place the "decentralist" view that important decisions should be made by those who must implement them, that is, local administrators and teachers. List types of decisions for which each model would, on logical grounds, seem to have merit.

SUGGESTIONS FOR ADDITIONAL READING

Ausubel, D. P. *Educational psychology: A cognitive view.* New York: Holt, Rinehart and Winston, Inc., 1968, Chapter 1.

Cronbach, L. J. How can instruction be adapted to individual differences? In *Learning and individual differences* (Robert M. Gagné, Ed.). Columbus, Ohio: Charles E. Merrill Books, Inc., 1967, pp. 23–39.

Englemann, S. Relationship between psychological theories and the art of teaching. *J. sch. Psychol.,* 1967, *5*(2), 93–100.

Gage, N. L., and W. R. Unruh. Theoretical formulations for research on teaching. *Rev. educ. Res.,* 1967, *3,* 358–370.

Green, T. F. Teaching, acting and behaving. *Harvard educ. Rev.,* 1964, *34,* 507–524.

Hilgard, E. R. A perspective on the relationship between learning theory and educational practices. In *Theories of learning and instruction: 63rd Yearbook.* Nat. Soc. Stud. Educ., Part I. Chicago: University of Chicago Press, 1964, pp. 402–415.

McDonald, F. J. The influence of learning theories on education (1900–1950). In *Theories of learning and instruction: 63rd Yearbook* Nat. Soc. Stud. Educ., Part I. Chicago: University of Chicago Press, 1964.

Newman, F. M. Questioning the place of social science descriptions in education. *Teachers Coll. Rec.,* 1967, *69* (1).

The Ontario Institute for Studies in Education. *Emerging strategies and structures for educational change: Conference proceedings.* Toronto: The Institute, 1966.

Robinson, F. G. Academic psychology and educational practice: A new attempt at fusion. *Ontario Psychol. Assn. Quart.,* Summer 1966.

Travers, R. M. W. Towards taking the fun out of building a theory of instruction. *Teachers Coll. Rec.,* 1966, *68,* 49–60.

CHAPTER 2

CLASSIFICATION OF VARIABLES IN SCHOOL LEARNING

IN THE FIRST CHAPTER IT WAS POINTED OUT THAT EDUCA-tional psychology attempts to formulate general principles relating education-al environment (independent) variables to behavioral outcome (dependent) variables. The present chapter attempts to come to grips somewhat more directly with the actual content of the field by: (1) identifying the broad categories of behavioral outcomes usually considered in educational psychol-ogy, and (2) specifying the classes of educational environment variables usually related to them.

CLASSIFICATION OF BEHAVIORAL OUTCOMES

For purposes of easy categorization psychologists have tra-ditionally divided the realm of human behavior into three general domains. Keeping in mind that the interest of the educational psychologist is limited to behavioral outcomes that have social utility, we will define each domain as it relates to the goals of school instruction. Thus the first or *cognitive domain* can be thought to deal with such phenomena as the recall or recognition of knowledge and the manifestation of intellectual abilities and skills. The second or *affective domain* deals with interests, attitudes, and values. The third or *psychomotor domain* deals with such complex skilled behaviors as handwriting, typing, and other manual or motor skills developed in the shop or in the school's athletic program.

Emphasis on Cognitive Outcomes

As stated in the preface, this book deals exclusively with ways of developing behaviors that fall in the cognitive domain. Affective factors such as atti-tudes, values, and the broader aspects of personality are considered only insofar as they relate to cognitive outcomes. Thus, for example, we are interested in a student's general level of anxiety because of its known or postulated relationship with problem-solving ability, rather than as a phenomenon of interest (dependent variable) in its own right.

Despite this strong emphasis on cognitive outcomes, we do not mean to imply that the school has no responsibility for, nor interest in, developing affective and motor behaviors. Our choice of emphasis springs rather from our assessment of the traditional role of public education and the direction of current reform movements.

To begin with, there can be little doubt that public education, since its inception, has been regarded as the institution whose unique responsibility is the training of the mind. Other institutions such as the home and church share this responsibility to some extent, but the school is the only agency which has deliberately created systematic and long-term programs of instruction to transmit organized bodies of knowledge and to foster such intellectual skills as reasoning and problem solving. Studies of public opinion concerning the role of the school have justified this emphasis (Andrews, 1959; Robinson, 1959). Certainly the layman regards the "training of the mind" to be primarily the school's responsibility, while the development of desirable attitudes and values is seen to be a joint responsibility of the home, the church, the community, and, to a lesser extent, the school.

The traditional emphasis on cognitive outcomes has been dramatically intensified throughout the world since the end of World War II. It is quite clear from the statements of aims of the many new curriculum projects (Goodlad and others, 1966) that the chief objective of these programs is to present to the child a more accurate conception of the current structure of such disciplines as mathematics and physics (by an emphasis on the central concepts of the discipline), and to do this at a much earlier age than was formerly attempted. Such programs vary in the "acceleration of learning" that they advocate, but perhaps the most dramatic set of proposals to date were those put forward by a group of professional mathematicians (Cambridge Conference on School Mathematics, 1963), which advocate that the entire content of the undergraduate college mathematics course be taught by the end of high school.

To what may we attribute the recent upsurge and interest in cognitive acquisitions? It is sometimes argued that the current emphasis represents, in part, a reaction against prevailing "life adjustment" theories advocating that organized subject matter should not be taught to young children for its own sake, but rather that the child should acquire such knowledge as he needs it in the solution of "real life" problems. While it is doubtful whether many schools actually implemented the extreme form of this proposition, the general thesis it embodied became the target of many critical attacks beginning in the late 1940s, when articles and books began to appear with such provocative titles as "The Failure of American Education," *Quackery in the Public Schools* and *Educational Wastelands* (Jennings, 1957).

We would have to admit that invidious comparisons between the school performances of North American and European children, comparisons which seem to indicate that European children—particularly in the earlier grades— were subjected to a much more content-laden curriculum, led to the conclusion that the cognitive demands made upon children on this continent were relatively light.[1] This suspicion became almost a public outcry when European technology, particularly that of the Soviet Union, began to achieve spectacular successes which were attributed in large measure to the demanding nature of its school programs.

Whatever the causes, there can be no doubt that both curriculum reform and much of the present research effort in educational psychology is directed toward attempts to lead children to acquire bodies of knowledge and intellectual skills at much earlier ages. There are some who seriously question whether we may not be going too far in this direction, and the arguments and counter-arguments in this area will be discussed in Chapter 7.

With these considerations in mind, there seems not only ample justification but a logical necessity for an educational-psychology text that purports to represent the current thrust of knowledge in the field to put considerable emphasis on the cognitive domain.

Taxonomy of Educational Objectives in the Cognitive Domain

Although there have been a number of attempts by psychologists (for example, Melton, 1964; Gagné, 1966; Tyler and others, 1967) to construct formal behavioral classification systems, the one most directly relevant to education is found in the *Taxonomy of Educational Objectives [Handbook I: Cognitive Domain]* (Bloom and others, 1956). Work on the classification

---

[1]Perhaps the most sensational of these has been the recent International Study of Achievement in Mathematics (Husén, 1967) which indicated, for example, that Japanese thirteen-year-olds outscored American thirteen-year-olds on a specially prepared mathematics achievement test by a ratio of almost two to one, the mean scores being 31.6 and 16.2 respectively. (See also: Sato, 1968). Some caution in interpretation is required because of differing selection ratios, course emphasis, and learning conditions (Fattu, 1967; Carnett, 1967). Nevertheless, it is difficult not to conclude that the results for the thirteen-year-olds—an age group marking an important transitional point of compulsory education in the countries studied—represent sizable differences in mathematics achievement of comparable youth.

Canada, although invited to participate in the study, did not do so; apparently some of the responsible provincial education officials felt that the test was too difficult for Canadian children.

system was initiated in 1948 by a group of college entrance examiners who were looking for a theoretical framework for the test scores utilized in their daily work. This group originally planned to produce a set of behavioral objectives for the school in each of the three classical subdivisions of human behavior, though plans for a taxonomy in the psychomotor domain were later dropped (Bloom, 1956). The taxonomy for the cognitive domain was published in 1956 after four years of preliminary work, and the taxonomy for the affective domain did not appear until 1964 (Krathwohl and others, 1964). While not part of this same series, psychomotor taxonomies have been proposed by other investigators (Guilford, 1958; Simpson, 1966).

There are a number of reasons why the cognitive taxonomy should be brought to the attention of the prospective teacher. In the first place, this categorization system is increasingly being used to construct achievement tests which teachers are likely to encounter in their subsequent work, and it therefore seems essential that they should understand something of its principles and potential. Again, the teacher-in-training will find references made to the taxonomy in courses on curriculum development and the pedagogy of individual subjects, so that the instrument provides a point of contact with the theory to be developed in this book.

The Nature of the Taxonomy

In their attempts to classify objectives, Bloom's committee distinguished between a "classification system" and a "taxonomy." A classification system can be merely nominalistic, as would be, for example, the system that arbitrarily divided the children in any particular group into those on the "left side" and those on the "right side." In this case there is no "real order" among the classes so that, for example, one cannot say that the phenomenon represented by one class is higher or lower on some scale than that represented by the other.

It is precisely this quality of hierarchical order, however, which characterizes the intended behavioral acquisitions resulting from attendance at school. A child acquires a relatively simple kind of behavior (for example, a concept) which is subsequently used in a higher order behavior (the learning of generalizations) which in turn is used in a still higher order of behavior (problem solving). Thus the committee decided that its classification system should obey the more demanding requirements of a taxonomy in that the "order of the terms employed to describe the categories should correspond to a 'real' order among the phenomena represented by these terms" (Bloom, 1956, p. 17).

In addition to the primary criterion concerning the hierarchical nature of the taxonomy, certain other guiding principles were employed in its construction (Bloom, 1956, pp. 13–14). First, it was felt that the labels used to describe the different categories of behavior should "reflect, in large part, the distinctions which teachers normally make among student behaviors." Second, it was considered important that the total system of definitions and descriptions be internally consistent. Third, it was felt that the categories proposed should reflect current psychological theorizing concerning the nature of learning. Finally, and perhaps most ambitiously, it was felt that the taxonomy should be comprehensive to the extent that it would allow one to incorporate "the kinds of behavioral changes emphasized by *any* institution, educational unit, or educational philosophy." In other words, one should be able to include any objective in any subject-matter field at any grade level.

Use of the Taxonomy

The major category descriptions are included in Table 2.1, together with a representative item. In practice, one of the difficulties that arises in trying to assess the accuracy of the classification is that the level at which an item should be placed will depend upon what the student has been taught. For example, if the item classified as "comprehension" in the accompanying table has been specifically taught, and therefore could be recalled rotely by the student, it would really only reflect "knowledge," as Bloom defines it.

It is instructive, therefore, to examine a related series of items in a subject matter area in which the student's previous learning is known specifically. The examples employed will also be useful in subsequent chapters in illustrating various concepts, and reference will be made to them from time to time.

We will consider, then, a student who has recently begun to receive instruction in the "modern" approach to Euclidean geometry, currently advocated for the junior high-school grades. After a week or so has elapsed, the student will have been taught such basic skills as the correct naming of a point, a line, and an angle and will, further, have been introduced to the elementary results depicted in Figure 2.1. The student will not have been offered formal "proofs" for these results, but will either have been encouraged to discover them through measurement or will have had them enunciated and illustrated by the teacher. We now construct a series of items reflecting behavioral outcomes of increasing complexity, which conform generally to the descriptions of the taxonomy.

The first item (Figure 2.2) unmistakably fits the "knowledge" category. It requires the student merely to reproduce a result (generalization) which he already has been taught. No more would be required here than mere recall of the second proposition in Figure 2.2.

In the second item (Figure 2.2), the student is required to produce a conclusion based on the second proposition in the learned series, but in this case a verbatim reply will not suffice because the triangles have been

TABLE 2.1

OUTLINE OF BLOOM'S TAXONOMY OF EDUCATIONAL OBJECTIVES IN THE COGNITIVE DOMAIN

CATEGORY	GENERAL DESCRIPTION OF CATEGORY	ILLUSTRATIVE ITEMS
I Knowledge (a) of *Specifics* (terminology, facts) (b) of *Ways and Means of Dealing with Specifics* (conventions, classifications, criteria, methodology) (c) of *Universals and Abstractions* (principles, generalizations, theories)	*Recall* of specifics and universals, methods and processes, pattern, structure of setting. Knowledge objectives emphasize most the psychological processes of *remembering*.	About what proportion of the population of Canada is living in cities? 1. 10% 2. 20% 3. 40% 4. 50% 5. 60% (Knowledge of specific fact) The volume of a given mass of gas varies directly as the _____ and inversely as the _____ . 1. pressure and temperature 2. temperature and pressure 3. atomic weight and pressure 4. temperature and atomic weight (Knowledge of principles and generalizations)
II Comprehension (a) Translation (b) Interpretation (c) Extrapolation	Lowest level of understanding of what is communicated. Can use idea being communicated without necessarily being able to relate it to other ideas or see all its implications.	Four less than three times a certain number equals eight. In algebra this may be expressed as: 1. $4 - 3X = 8$ 3. $3X - 4 = 8$ 2. $4X - 3 = 8$ 4. $4 + 3X = 8$ (Translation)*
III Application	The use of abstractions in particular and concrete situations.	Two basic laws governing an electrical circuit are: Voltage = (Current) × (Resistance) Power = (Voltage) × (Current) If an electric iron develops greater resistance (rust, etc.), its power will: 1. increase 2. remain the same 3. decrease

CATEGORY	GENERAL DESCRIPTION OF CATEGORY	ILLUSTRATIVE ITEMS
IV Analysis (a) of *Elements* (b) of *Relationships* (c) of *Organizational Principles*	Breakdown of a communication into its constituent parts, such that relative hierarchy of ideas is made clearer and/or the relations between the ideas expressed is made clear.	The given figure represents a hoop of 28 in. diameter. If the hoop is rolling without slipping in the indicated direction, how many inches has point A moved horizontally when the hoop has finished half a turn? ($\pi = 22/7$) (Analysis of Relationships)*
V Synthesis (a) Production of a unique communication (b) Production of a plan (c) Derivation of a set of abstract relations	Putting together of parts to form a whole; analyzing and combining pieces in such a way as to constitute a pattern or structure not clearly there before.	Without adding all items, find the sum of: $$\frac{1}{1\times 2}+\frac{1}{2\times 3}+\frac{1}{3\times 4}+\frac{1}{4\times 5}+\cdots$$ $$\frac{1}{98\times 99}+\frac{1}{99\times 100}\ *$$
IV Evaluation (a) *Judgments in terms of internal criteria* (b) *Judgments in terms of external evidence*	Making judgments about the value of material and methods for given purposes. Judging extent to which material and methods satisfy given criteria.	The ability to indicate logical fallacies in arguments (Internal Evidence) Ability to compare a work with highest known standards in its field. (External Criteria)

*Illustrative items from Avital and Shettleworth, 1968.

Source: Adapted from B. S. Bloom and others (Eds.). *Taxonomy of educational objectives: The classification of educational goals. Handbook 1: Cognitive domain.* New York: David McKay Company, Inc., 1956. Reprinted by permission of David McKay Company, Inc.

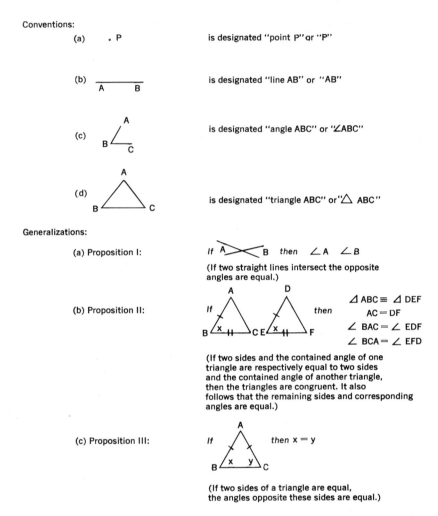

Conventions:

(a)   • P   is designated "point P" or "P"

(b) ‾‾‾‾‾‾‾‾‾   is designated "line AB" or "AB"
       A   B

(c)   is designated "angle ABC" or "∠ABC"

(d)   is designated "triangle ABC" or "△ ABC"

Generalizations:

(a) Proposition I: If A ⟩⟨ B then ∠ A ∠ B

(If two straight lines intersect the opposite angles are equal.)

(b) Proposition II: If   then   △ ABC ≡ △ DEF
                                              AC = DF
                                           ∠ BAC = ∠ EDF
                                           ∠ BCA = ∠ EFD

(If two sides and the contained angle of one triangle are respectively equal to two sides and the contained angle of another triangle, then the triangles are congruent. It also follows that the remaining sides and corresponding angles are equal.)

(c) Proposition III: If   then x = y

(If two sides of a triangle are equal, the angles opposite these sides are equal.)

FIGURE 2.1 *Set of relevant concepts and propositions assumed known.*

reoriented and relettered. Consequently the student must be at least capable of transposing the general idea embedded in this result to a new set of figures: thus the item fits the category of "comprehension" quite clearly.

In the third item (Figure 2.2), the task is more difficult because the student must recognize that the composite figure can be divided into two triangles and that line *PT* is a common line in these two resulting triangles. This item involves more than straightforward comprehension and seems to meet the criteria for "application," that is, the application of a learned generalization to a specific situation not encountered before.

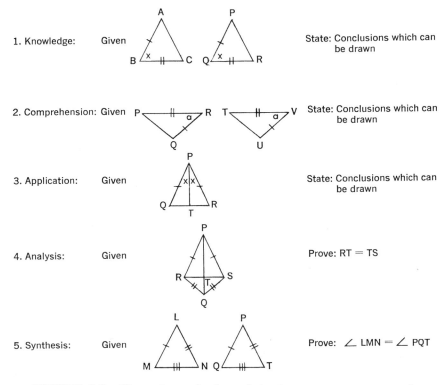

1. Knowledge: Given ... State: Conclusions which can be drawn

2. Comprehension: Given ... State: Conclusions which can be drawn

3. Application: Given ... State: Conclusions which can be drawn

4. Analysis: Given ... Prove: RT = TS

5. Synthesis: Given ... Prove: ∠ LMN = ∠ PQT

FIGURE 2.2 *Illustrative tasks from deductive geometry corresponding to taxonomy categories.*

Item 4 (Figure 2.2) is manifestly more complex than those preceding it. Here the student is required to prove that *RT* equals *TS,* and there is nothing in his set of learnings up to this point which would allow him to do this directly. Obviously, then, we are dealing here with something more than a direct case of application. The means by which children can be taught "strategies" for dealing with such "problems" will be discussed in considerable detail in the chapter on problem solving. We need only say now that the appropriate strategy in this case takes the form of the student's continually asking himself the following three sequentially related questions:

1. What sort of fact am I to prove (for example, one line equals another, one angle equals another, or one triangle is congruent to another)?
2. Which of the results (propositions) that I already know might be utilized to establish this fact?
3. What additional facts would I need (or what other conditions must hold) before I could use this proposition?

The repeated application of this strategy yields a solution, as is shown in Figure 2.3. At the termination of the extensive analysis, the student merely reverses the steps and writes down a formal "proof" as shown in the table. This kind of item, which has been traditionally termed a "problem" by mathematics teachers, evidently calls for a considerable amount of analysis. If synthesis is involved, it is of a rather routine kind and involves primarily a

Given: Prove RT = TS

Analysis:

Q$_1$: Kind of fact?   : Line = line (RT = TS)
Q$_2$: What existing proposition   : Proposition II (with $\angle$ PRT and $\triangle$ PST)
    can be used?
Q$_3$: What additional fact is   : ($\angle$ RPT = $\angle$ SPT)
    needed to use Proposition II?

Q$_1$: Kind of fact?   : ($\angle$ RPT = $\angle$ SPT)
Q$_2$: What existing proposition   : Proposition II; others, I and III.
    can be used?   obviously not applicable
Q$_3$: What additional   : Need two triangles containing $\angle$ RPT
    conditions needed to use   and $\angle$ SPT respectively; choose
    Proposition II?   (by elimination) $\triangle$ PRQ and $\triangle$ PSQ

Q$_1$: Kind of fact?   : $\triangle$ $\equiv$ $\triangle$ · ($\triangle$ PRQ $\equiv$ $\triangle$ PSQ)
Q$_2$: What existing proposition   : Proposition II
    can be used?
Q$_3$: What additional facts are   : $\angle$ PRQ = $\angle$ PSQ
    needed to use Proposition II?

Q$_1$: Kind of fact?   : $\angle$ = $\angle$ ($\angle$ PRQ = $\angle$ PSQ)
Q$_2$: What existing proposition   : Proposition III
    can be used?
Q$_3$: What additional required?   : Apply Proposition III twice

End of Analysis

Proof:

$\angle$ PRT = $\angle$ PST (by Proposition III)
$\angle$ QRT = $\angle$ QST (by Proposition III)
∴ $\angle$ PRQ = $\angle$ PSQ (by addition)
$\triangle$ PRQ $\equiv$ $\triangle$ PSQ (by Proposition II)
∴ $\angle$ RPT = $\angle$ SPT
∴ $\triangle$ PRT $\equiv$ $\triangle$ PST (by Proposition II)
∴   RT = TS

FIGURE 2.3 *Analysis of problem by repeated application of strategy.*

gathering together of the various pieces of the analysis in reverse order from that in which they were generated.

The final item (Figure 2.4) presents a task that students would find even more difficult than the previous one. If the student attempts to apply the strategy that led to the solution of the previous problem, he would ascertain that the only way he knows to prove triangles congruent is to demonstrate that they have two sides and that they contained angles (respectively) equal. Consequently the congruence of the two triangles in question would depend upon proving the equality of two corresponding angles such as *M* and *Q*. At this point, however, there is nothing in his repertoire which the student can employ to establish this equality. Actually the solution requires that, on the basis of intuition, analogy with some situation encountered elsewhere, or by some other means, the student realize that if he were to place *QT* along *MN* and allow point *P* to fall opposite point *L* (Figure 2.4) then the equality of angles *P* and *L* would follow by repeated application of proposition 3; the congruence of the triangles follows.

It is evident then that the student must reach beyond what he has been specifically taught or, putting it otherwise, must synthesize knowledge beyond that specifically given. For this reason, the label "inventive synthesis" might be appropriately used to describe the behavior required for a correct solution. Some educators would be tempted to employ the term "creativity" here. We will reserve comment on the wisdom of such a choice to Chapter 3.

In summary, it can be seen that in this particular field of traditional and current interest to educators it is possible to construct a series of items corresponding generally to the descriptions of the taxonomy and increasing in complexity from item to item. However, we note that no item was found for the "evaluation" category (in mathematics the skills required for evaluation would seem to be classifiable under "analysis").

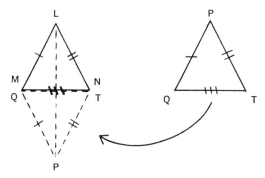

FIGURE 2.4 *Solution of problem involving synthesis. Apply Proposition III twice, proving $\angle L = \angle P$. Apply Proposition II.*

Value and Limitations of the Taxonomy

Many studies have been conducted which have attempted to use the taxonomy either for theoretical and research purposes or as a basis for constructing new tests (Cox and Gordon, 1965; Cox, 1966). Despite the difficulties encountered in any particular subject area, there is widespread feeling that the taxonomy can serve to sensitize teachers to the variety of possible behavioral outcomes in the cognitive domain, and to suggest means (test items) by which they might be measured. For example, since teachers frequently employ a constricted taxonomy—in mathematics, distinguishing only comprehension and problem solving—some practice in devising items will probably be a worthwhile experience.

The taxonomy should also be useful in allowing one to appraise critically the somewhat exaggerated claims made for many of the new curricula and teaching aids. For example, some recent research on the effect of the "modern" mathematics programs (Avital, 1967; Russell, 1966) suggests that students in the new programs are no more proficient in problem solving than students who have studied traditional mathematics. It would appear that those who hold that the new content should facilitate the child's ability to apply mathematical ideas in a variety of settings and problems—and this is frequently stated in the proposed aims of new courses—may be deceiving themselves on the outcomes actually attained.[2]

Despite the merits of the taxonomy cited above, certain reservations must be entertained in any realistic assessment of it (Cronbach, 1963; Kropp and others, 1966; Stoker and Kropp, 1964). We have already noted the apparent necessity of modifying the general format to accommodate the unique characteristics of intellectual performance in a particular subject-matter field (Avital, 1967; Scriven, 1965). A more central difficulty, in our opinion, is that how any experimenter or teacher will classify a particular item will depend upon his conception of the *psychological processes* involved in its completion. Differences in such conceptualizations will be particularly important in dealing with those items which lie in marginal areas, as for example between comprehension and application, or between application and problem solving (analysis and synthesis).

---

[2]This is not in any way to suggest that the comprehension of the new concepts and generalizations embedded in these courses is not in itself a worthwhile objective, but rather to raise a question as to whether claims for improvement in the "higher mental processes" have any basis in fact. Moreover, it seems clear from such evaluations that if these higher mental processes are to be attained in any worthwhile degree, a better understanding of their underlying psychological processes must be had and their appearance in both students and teachers-in-training will have to be recognized and rewarded to a far greater degree than they presently are (Avital, 1967).

The teacher's initial sensitization to a range of possible behavioral outcomes must, therefore, be followed by a detailed search for a consistent learning theory which illuminates the hierarchical distinctions inherent in a taxonomic description of behavior. The formulation of such a theory is the central task of this text, which postulates as behavioral outcomes: *representational learning* (naming), *concept formation, concept assimilation, proposition learning, problem solving,* and *creativity.* While this system of outcomes is hierarchical in nature and can be put into rough correspondence with the Bloom taxonomy (Chapter 3), our categories are derived from the assumed processes underlying the acquisition of knowledge and the development of mental abilities rather than from a predetermined classification of abilities.

CLASSIFICATION OF EDUCATIONAL ENVIRONMENT VARIABLES

How may we classify the variables in the educational environment (the independent variables) which we wish to relate to behavioral outcomes? One way that suggests itself would be to group the independent variables according to whether they are *intrapersonal* (representing intellectual ability, motivation, and so on), or *situational* (representing such things as practice, instructional materials, and social variables). Another way might be to categorize the independent variables in terms of their assumed potency in accounting for changes of behavior. Still another way might be to arrange them in order of the degree to which they can actually be manipulated in the school situation.

The classification decided upon for the book divides the learning environment variables into two classes, the *cognitive* (relatively objective intellectual factors) and the *affective-social* (including subjective and interpersonal determinants of learning). The cognitive category includes:

(a) *Cognitive structure variables*—substantive and organizational properties of previously acquired knowledge in a particular subject-matter field that are relevant for the assimilation of another learning task in the same field. Since subject-matter knowledge tends to be organized in sequential and hierarchical fashion, what one already knows in a given field, and how well one knows it, obviously influences one's readiness for related new learnings in this field;

(b) *Developmental readiness*—the particular kind of readiness that reflects the learner's stage of intellectual development and the intellectual capacities and modes of intellectual functioning characteristic of that stage. The cognitive equipment of the fifteen-year-old learner obviously makes him ready for different kinds of learning tasks than does that of the six- or ten-year-old learner;

(c) *Intellectual ability*—the individual's relative degree of general scholastic aptitude (general intelligence or brightness level) and his relative standing with respect to particular more differentiated or specialized cognitive abilities. How well a pupil learns subject matter in science, mathematics, or literature obviously depends on his general intelligence, verbal and quantitative abilities, and on his problem-solving ability;

(d) *Practice*—its frequency, distribution, method, and general conditions (including feedback or knowledge of results);

(e) *Instructional materials*—in terms of amount, difficulty, step size, underlying logic, sequence, pacing, and the use of instructional aids.

The affective and social factors include:

(a) *Motivational and attitudinal factors*—desire for knowledge, need for achievement and self-enhancement, and ego-involvement (interest) in a particular kind of subject matter. These general variables affect such relevant conditions of learning as alertness, attentiveness, level of effort, persistence, and concentration;

(b) *Personality factors*—self-consistent individual differences in level and kind of motivation, in personal adjustment, in other personality characteristics (for example, open-mindedness), and in level of anxiety. Subjective factors such as these have profound effects on quantitative and qualitative aspects of the learning process;

(c) *Group and social factors*—such as classroom climate, cooperation and competition, social class stratification, cultural deprivation, and racial segregation;

(d) *Characteristics of the teacher*—his cognitive abilities, knowledge of subject matter, pedagogic competence, and personality.

Organization of the Book

The problem of organizing a textbook in educational psychology in a logical manner presents difficulties which should be acknowledged at the outset. Essentially the problem is that we have a two-dimensional table (with educational environment variables along one dimension and outcome variables along the other) and, after developing the integrating theoretical concepts, we must then attempt to describe the empirically derived relationships between the two classes of variables. Logically, a decision should be made concerning which dimension (independent or dependent) is to receive first priority. Thus, if chapters were to be organized according to learning outcomes (for example, problem solving), one would then summarize in such chapters all the known relationships between the various kinds of variables in the learning situation and that particular behavioral outcome. On the other hand, if the chapters were organized by independent variables (for example, practice), one would relate that particular manipulable variable to each kind of behavioral outcome.

Actually there is no way to resolve this problem and, as we shall see, there are good reasons for devoting separate chapters both to each class of independent variable and to each class of behavioral outcome. Although this may result in a certain amount of duplication in the reporting of empirical results, we believe that this cross-indexing will help consolidate the material in the learner's mind.

The general outline of this text is as follows: Part Two is devoted to the main theoretical concepts and their preliminary application to each category of behavioral outcomes; Part Five gives more detailed accounts of discovery learning, problem solving, and creativity—phenomena of particular significance to the educator. Parts Three and Four deal systematically with independent variables, Part Three covering cognitive factors in learning and Part Four, affective and social factors. Finally, Part Six deals with essential concepts of measurement and experimentation as they apply in the classroom setting.

TOPICS FOR DISCUSSION AND FURTHER STUDY

1. Construct a related series of items in some content field familiar to you which reflects the hierarchial structure of Bloom's taxonomy in the cognitive domain. Justify your classification of each item in terms of what the student is assumed to know and what he is expected to do.

2.* Study the taxonomy in the affective domain (see reference below) and cite particular educational goals which would fall in each of its categories.

3.* Investigate Guilford's or Simpson's proposed classification of psychomotor abilities and learning outcomes (see reference below) and list particular educational outcomes which could be classified in its terms.

4. Examine the course of studies in the area in which you will be teaching and attempt to classify its cognitive objectives in terms of taxonomy levels.

5. We have suggested that the "new" curricula may not be improving student performance above the level of simple comprehension. To what might these short-comings be attributed? Is the time and effort required to produce the new curricula justified if these results and findings are generally true?

6. What counterarguments may be brought against our contention that the school's function and, therefore, the emphasis of an educational-psychology course, is properly cognitive in nature?

7. Although psychologists classify behavior in the three major domains of thinking (cognitive), feeling (affective) and acting (motor), it is commonly recog-

nized that any particular instance of behavior may fall partly in two or more of the domains. Illustrate this with examples drawn from students' school behavior.

8.* Examine the variety of item formats illustrated in any standard text on educational measurement and evaluation. For a given behavioral objective, construct a series of items employing different formats.

SUGGESTIONS FOR ADDITIONAL READING

Bloom, B. S., M. D. Englehart, E. J. Furst, W. H. Hill, and D. R. Krathwohl (Eds.). *Taxonomy of educational objectives: The classification of educational goals. Handbook I: Cognitive domain.* New York: David McKay Company, Inc. 1956.

Cox, R. C., and J. M. Gordon. *Validation and uses of the taxonomy of educational objectives: Cognitive domain. A select and annotated bibliography.* Pittsburgh School of Education, University of Pittsburgh, 1965. (See also, *Addendum* by R. C. Cox, December 1966.)

Gagné, R. M. Educational objectives and human performance. In *Learning and the educational process.* (J. D. Krumboltz, Ed.). Skokie, Ill.: Rand McNally & Company, 1965, pp. 1–24.

Goodlad, J. I., Renata Von Stoephasius, and M. Frances Klein. *The changing school curriculum.* New York: The Fund for the Advancement of Education, 1966.

Guilford, J. P. A system of the psychomotor abilities. *Amer. J. Psychol.,* 1958, *71,* 164–174.

Karplus, R., and H. D. Thier. *A new look at elementary school science.* Skokie, Ill.: Rand McNally & Company, 1967.

Klausmeier, H. J., and W. Goodwin. *Learning and human abilities: Educational psychology* (2nd ed.). New York: Harper & Row, Publishers, 1966, Chapter 1.

Krathwohl, D. R., B. S. Bloom, and H. B. Masia. *Taxonomy of educational objectives: The classification of educational goals. Handbook II: Affective domain.* New York: David McKay Company, Inc., 1964.

For particular applications of the taxonomy within specific fields, the reader should consult:

MATHEMATICS

Avital, S. M., and Sara J. Shettleworth. *Objectives for mathematics learning: Some ideas for the teacher.* (Bulletin No. 3). Toronto: Ontario Institute for Studies In Education, 1968.

PHYSICAL AND BIOLOGICAL SCIENCES

Dressel, P., and C. Nelson. Questions and problems in science, *Test Folio No. 1.* Princeton: Cooperative Test Division, Educational Testing Service, 1956.

Lombard, J. W. Preparing better classroom tests, *The Science Teacher,* 1965, pp. 33–38.

SOCIAL SCIENCE

Scriven, M. *The methodology of evaluation.* Paper written during author's tenure as director of the Evaluation Project of the Social Science Education Consortium, supported by a developmental grant from the U.S. Office of Education, 1965. (mimeo) (Annotated in Cox and Gordon, 1966.)

HEALTH EDUCATION

Ellis, J. K. The application of the "taxonomy of educational objectives" to the determination of objectives for helath teaching. (unpublished Doctoral dissertation). University of Michigan, 1963.

SOCIAL STUDIES

Jarolimek, J. The taxonomy: Guide to differentiating instruction. *Social Educ.,* 1962, *26,* 445–447.

GEOGRAPHY

Lessinger, L. M. Test building and test banks through the use of the taxonomy of educational objectives, *California J. of educ. Res.,* 1963, *14*(5), 195–201.

ENGLISH

Forehand, G. A. Problems of measuring response to literature, *Clearing House,* February 1966, *40,* 369–375.

MEANINGFUL LEARNING AND RETENTION

Essential to the theory to be developed in Part Two is the postulation of two dimensions representing fundamental distinctions between types of learning processes. The first distinction deals with the means by which the knowledge to be learned is made available to the conscious mind of the learner (the reception learning/discovery learning dimension). The second distinction deals with alternate ways in which the learner may incorporate such knowledge into his existing structure of ideas (the meaningful learning/rote learning dimension). It is assumed that these two dimensions are relatively independent, so that the following four basic kinds of learning may occur: (1) meaningful-reception; (2) rote-reception; (3) meaningful-discovery; (4) rote-discovery.

THE RECEPTION/DISCOVERY DIMENSION OF LEARNING

In *reception learning,* the entire content of what is to be learned is presented to the learner in its final form. For illustrative purposes, we may consider a teacher who is attempting to have his students learn the generalization that "the sum of the angles in a triangle equals 180 degrees." In pure reception learning, the teacher would enunciate the generalization and perhaps illustrate it with one or more particular triangles drawn on the board. The important point, however, is that the learning task does not involve any independent discovery on the part of the learner. The generalization is presented to him and he is merely required to learn and remember it.

In *discovery learning,* on the other hand, the principal content of what is to be learned is not given in its final form but must be discovered by the learner. In the example under consideration, the teacher might employ a form of "guided" discovery learning by asking each child to measure the angles in a number of triangles to see if he can formulate some generalization concerning their sum. The likely result of this exercise would be the discovery, by many of the pupils at least, of the generalization concerning the sum of the angles.

The first phase of discovery learning, therefore, involves a process quite different from that of reception learning. The learner must rearrange a given array of information, integrate it with his existing knowledge, and reorganize or transform the integrated combination in such a way as to generate a desired end product, (typically, a new concept or proposition).

THE MEANINGFUL/ROTE DIMENSION
OF LEARNING

Up to this point we have discussed only the first stage in the learning process, namely that stage in which the concept or preposition to be learned actually becomes available to the learner in its final form. Now the learner must relate this new idea to the knowledge which he already possesses (that is, to his cognitive structure).

In the second stage the learner consciously acts upon this concept or preposition in an attempt to remember it so that it will be available at some future time. He may do this in either of two quite distinct ways. If the learner attempts to retain the idea by relating it to what he knows, and thereby "make sense" out of it, then *meaningful learning* will result. On the other hand, if the learner merely attempts to memorize the idea, without relating it to his existing knowledge, then *rote learning* is said to take place.

It should be made clear at the outset that the reception/ discovery and meaningful/rote dimensions *do not* describe simple dichotomies, but instead are more in the nature of continua. For example, insofar as educational settings are concerned, one rarely finds a pure discovery approach, but rather, varying degrees of "guided" discovery. Similarly, on the other dimension, the meaningfulness or roteness of the learning depends on a number of factors, some of which are variable quantities. Consequently, although we may abridge our description for convenience, any learning that occurs is not simply either meaningful or rote; it is, instead, *more or less* meaningful or *more or less* rote.

With these qualifications, it seems evident that in the instance under consideration we may obtain learning exemplifying all four combinations of the meaningful/rote, reception/discovery dimensions. Thus *meaningful reception learning* will take place when the teacher presents the generalization in its final form, and the learner relates it to his existing ideas in some sensible fashion. On the other hand, *rote reception learning* would take place if the teacher presented the generalization, and the student merely memorized it. Again, *meaningful discovery learning* will occur if the student formulates the generalization himself and subsequently relates it in a sensible way to his existing ideas. Finally *rote discovery learning* could occur if the learner, having arrived at the generalization himself (typically by trial and error), subsequently commits it to memory without relating it to other relevant ideas in his cognitive structure.

In each case the degree of relative meaningfulness (or roteness) will depend in part on the extent of the interaction between the final form of the new idea and the existing ideas in the learner's cognitive structure. While in the present instance it seems unlikely that the learner, once having discovered the generalization himself, would subsequently *not* relate it to his cognitive structure (thus yielding relatively meaningful learning) the degree of relationship which results may vary considerably. Moreover, one can find instances in which the solution is not embodied in a set of propositions and has little chance of being related to cognitive structure, for example, the trial and error solution to a mechanical puzzle. In this case, it must be said that although the learner has discovered a solution, it could not be said to be learned in a very meaningful fashion.

In summary, then, learning tasks can be found which exemplify all combinations of the meaningful/rote and reception/discovery dimensions. The independent nature of the two dimensions in question must be stressed because of the tendency to confuse them, and to assume that all reception learning must be rote in nature, and, conversely, that all discovery learning must be meaningful.

CONTENT OF PART TWO

In keeping with the school's interests, Part Two proceeds to elaborate the basic notions underlying the meaningful acquisition of ideas and their subsequent retention in memory. A first prerequisite for meaningful learning is that the *material* presented to the learner be capable of being related in some "sensible" fashion. Second, the *learner* must possess relevant ideas to which this new idea can be related or anchored. Finally, the learner must actually *attempt* to relate, in some sensible way, the new ideas to those which he presently possesses. To the extent that any of these conditions fail to exist, subsequent learning will be relatively rote. And even though meaningful learning is much more efficient than rote learning—in the sense that larger quantities of material can be learned at a single encounter—students will frequently resort to rote learning, as for example when they are under heavy pressure to exhibit the appearance of comprehension, or when the teacher insists upon a verbatim recounting of the ideas presented in class.

Chapter 3 also develops a hierarchy of behavioral outcomes of interest to the educator. At a primitive level, the child comes to understand at an early age that verbal symbols (for example, the spoken word "horse") are used by adults to designate objects which the child apprehends directly through his senses. In time, and with continued pairing, the verbal symbol will come to elicit the meaning which the real object has for the child. Another process characteristic of the child's first learnings is that of *concept formation,* in which he demonstrates the ability to abstract essential qualities of a class of objects (for example, "cats"). These criterial attributes of the concept are embedded in a composite image which constitutes the child's meaning of the concept. It seems clear that the child will frequently acquire concept meanings through the process of concept formation even though he has no specific name for the concept in question. Indeed, one of the early tasks of the school is to provide *concept names* for many of the primitive concepts which children have developed prior to their admittance to school. Concept formation must be distinguished from *concept assimilation,* a process by which older children and adults learn the meaning of a concept by being exposed to its verbal definition or by encountering it in a particular verbal context. Both concept formation and concept assimilation have their counterparts in the formation and assimilation of *propositions.* In the latter process the learner combines the meanings of existing concepts to acquire new propositional meanings, utilizing for this purpose his intuitive knowledge of the syntax of the spoken language.

Problem solving and *creativity* stand at the highest levels of the behavior hierarchy, being characterized by very complex cognitive processes. In problem solving, the learner is faced with a "gap" between what he knows (in terms of his existing concepts and generalizations) and the solution which he is to produce. In order to close the gap—thus attaining a solution—he must recombine or transform this existing knowledge in some fashion. Frequently he will be aided in this transformation by a *strategy,* a set of verbal rules which guides his selection and manipulation of relevant background information. *Creative behavior* is envisaged as an extreme form of problem solving in which the learner draws upon knowledge which has not been specifically taught as relevant to the problem, and which utilizes strategies which are not formally stated.

The final concern of Chapter 3 is to examine the structure of ideas which is gradually built up in the learner's mind. The resulting structure in any substantive subject-matter field is thought to be pyramidal in nature, with the most general ideas forming the apex, and more particular ideas and specific details subsumed under them. Given this organization, the principal mode of incorporating a new idea into the learner's cognitive structure is to *subsume* it under an existing *high-level* idea. When the new idea constitutes a special case of an existing idea, the relationship is one of *derivative subsumption;* when the new idea involves some transformation of existing ideas, we speak of *correlative subsumption.* While subsumption is the typical mode for learning new concepts, the learner will occasionally encounter a new idea which is more general than those presently existing in his cognitive structure. Such ideas are related in a *superordinate* fashion to existing ideas, and derive their generalized meaning from the specific ideas subsumed under them. Finally, some ideas cannot be *specifically* related in either a subordinate or a superordinate fashion to *particular* existing ideas but are consistent with, or generally congruent to, a broad background of relevant ideas. Such concepts are said to bear a *combinatorial relationship* to existing ideas in cognitive structure.

Chapter 4 applies the meaningful learning model to the

areas of reading, second-language learning, and mathematics learning. The principal tasks in reading are seen to be: (a) the acquisition of rules for converting unknown written symbols (printed words) into known spoken symbols, and (b) utilizing an intuitive understanding of the syntax of spoken language to reconstruct the individual words into a meaningful sentence. The learning of a second language can similarly be envisaged as a problem of translating new verbal symbols into the already meaningful symbols of the learner's native tongue. Because of the nature of these tasks, methods which emphasize translation rules (for example, the phonetic method in reading, and the translation—as opposed to the audiolingual—approach to second language) would appear to have theoretical advantages in facilitating rapid comprehension of the meaning of the "foreign" symbols.

Arithmetic learning is seen to begin with a primitive (probably rote) counting process, progressing then to the acquisition of the ordinal and cardinal properties of numbers and the comprehension of basic arithmetical operations. Each of the latter phases can be understood as the acquisition of "kinetic" images which constitute the meanings of the properties and operations in question. It would seem that algebra is initially comprehended by the student much as he comprehends a second language, that is, by a process of translation into an equivalent (arithmetical) form.

Mathematics learning presents the paradox that while it is amenable to easy comprehension—since its basic operations are related to clearly specifiable concrete operations which can be performed in the physical environment—many children and adults exhibit great confusion and fear when confronted with mathematical arguments. The apparent difficulty in learning mathematics can be explained by the fact that this subject-matter content, more than any other taught in the school, is highly *sequential* in nature. Consequently, a failure to learn each link in its development jeopardizes subsequent understanding and forces the student to fall back on rote learning.

Chapter 5 follows the history of a new idea in the learner's mind from the point when it is first related to an existing (anchoring) idea to the time when it is completely forgotten. When first introduced, the new idea forms an interactional complex with its anchoring idea(s), and the latter provides the anchorage that permits the new idea to be retained. At first, the two ideas are clearly *dissociable,* but in time the new idea is progressively reduced in meaning to the meaning of its more stable anchor. As the degree of dissociability declines with time, the learner passes through various stages in his recollection of the idea. Initially he will be able to *recall* the meaning of the idea; later he will not be able to recall it but will *recognize* the idea when it is presented with a plausible alternative. Later still, he will not recognize it but could *relearn* it in less than the original learning time. Finally, the new idea will be completely assimilated by the existing idea, and no residue of the previous learning will exist.

The theoretical principles of remembering and forgetting are then applied to explain a variety of memory phenomena of interest to the educator. For example, the stability provided by anchoring ideas explains why meaningfully learned material is retained much more permanently than rotely learned material. In effect, the latter is *arbitrarily* associated with existing ideas and thus lacks firm anchorage. The same concept of anchorage also explains why the recollection of meaningful material, unlike that of rotely learned material, is not interfered with by the subsequent learning of similar material. A major pedagogical implication of Chapter 5 is that the teacher should take steps to insure the existence of clear and stable ideas to which subsequent material can be anchored, while at the same time clarifying the distinguishing characteristics (thus increasing the dissociability strength) of the newly learned idea.

CHAPTER 3

MEANING AND MEANINGFUL LEARNING

IN THIS CHAPTER WE BEGIN THE DEVELOPMENT OF THE theoretical ideas that are central to an understanding of later topics. Since this text differs from others in its much heavier emphasis upon theory, it may be well to offer reasons why a comprehensive theory is attempted at the outset, rather than proceeding directly with an analysis of the relationships between independent and dependent variables.

In the first place, a comprehensive theory provides a means of assimilating the particular research results which follow. Without the ideational framework provided by such a theory, the student is reduced to retaining a large number of empirically derived results virtually as separate items of information. In addition, presenting the theory at the start—rather than abstracting it from the research results—helps direct our search for relevant empirical studies. By the same token, it can help us weed out the large proportion of research studies that are not relevant. Finally, the most potent and valuable aspect of a comprehensive theory is that it will allow its possessor to fill in the gaps in empirical knowledge—and these gaps are considerable both in number and size—by predictions (that is, by formulating hypotheses) where no evidence exists.

THE MEANINGFUL LEARNING PARADIGM

The theory of meaning and meaningful learning propounded in this book takes as its starting point two phenomena which are well known to classroom teachers. First, a primary assumption which is central to the theory is that the most important factor influencing learning is the quantity, clarity, and organization of the learner's present knowledge. This present knowledge, which consists of the facts, concepts, propositions, theories, and raw perceptual data that the learner has available to him at any point in time, is referred to as his *cognitive structure.*

The second important focus is the nature of the material to be learned. For illustrative purposes, we have set out in Table 3.1 a variety of tasks which have confronted learners in the psychological laboratory or in the classroom. In each case an item of material is presented to the learner, who is required to learn it for recall at some later point in time.

The Relatability of Material to be Learned

It seems clear that the items in Table 3.1 may be distinguished from each other on the basis of one very important variable. These items vary in the extent to which they could be related in some sensible or understandable way to the most completely developed cognitive structure which one could envisage existing in any individual mature human being. Another way of putting this is to say that the items differ in respect to the degree of relationship which they could exhibit to ideas that lie within the realm of human learning capability.

TABLE 3.1

ILLUSTRATIVE LEARNING TASKS

ITEM	CONTENT	NATURE OF ITEM
1.	"lud"	Nonsense syllable
2.	strong–pliable	Paired associates (task is to recall second word when the first is given)
3.	Mr. Jones	Name of specific object
4.	they went out slowly together when it came with her check	4th order approximation to English*
5.	The cat climbed the plum tree.	Simple declarative sentence (proposition)
6.	An equilateral triangle is a triangle with three equal sides.	Definition of a concept
7.	The sum of the three internal angles of any plane triangle equals 180°.	Generalization (proposition) which is true in plane Euclidean Geometry

*A 4th order approximation to English is achieved in the following manner. A number of persons contribute one word each to a chain, of which they see only the four immediately preceding words, with the additional requirement that the word which they contribute must make sense in the context of the preceding four words.

For example, the first item (a nonsense syllable) contains letters which are individually identifiable, but taken together the collection makes no sense, and it would be difficult to imagine how this particular syllable could be sensibly related to anything that the learner might already know. Consequently, when the learner attempts to remember the item for future recall, there is really little he can do but remember it in a literal (that is, letter by letter) fashion.

A completely different situation prevails with respect to the sixth item, which is the definition of the concept "equilateral triangle." The fact is that the learner to whom this item is presented has probably already encountered and can recognize and define the general concept of triangle, so that the item to be learned is merely a specific instance of something which he already knows. In this case he is able to relate the new item to his existing knowledge and therefore to make sense of it.

We could examine each of the items in turn, and we would probably conclude that they are arranged roughly in an order of increasing strength of relatability, where the strength of the relationship depends in large measure upon the number of items in cognitive structure to which the new material can be related and on the kind of relationship (a matter to be discussed later). However it will suffice at this point to note that the kind of relatability that leads to *meaningful learning* must possess two particular qualities. The first, called the quality of *substantiveness*, means that the relationship is not altered if a different, but equivalent, form of wording is used. This quality is apparent in item 6, for example, because the relationship of an equilateral triangle to a general triangle is not changed in any way if one were to reword the definition of the former to read "an equilateral triangle is a triangle that has all of its sides equal." On the other hand, the nonsense syllable "lud" is not capable of substantive relationship with any item of existing knowledge, so that if any of the letters are changed a completely new learning task emerges.

The second quality which is necessary for meaningful learning is that the relationship between the new item to be learned and relevant items in cognitive structure be *nonarbitrary*. The equilateral triangle example again illustrates this property, in that the relationship between "equilateral triangle" and "triangle" is the relationship of specific instance to general case and is certainly nonarbitrary. The last item also exhibits this property quite clearly, since it can be derived from a more general proposition (which could well exist in the cognitive structure of the learner) that "the sum of the angles in a quadrilateral (that is, two triangles) equals 360 degrees." On the other hand, it would be difficult to conceive of a possible nonarbitrary relationship between the nonsense syllable "lud" and any items in existing cognitive structure. Or to take the second item, since the particular members of the given pair of adjectives are linked together in purely arbitrary fashion, there seems no possible basis for nonarbitrarily relating the learning task to anyone's cognitive structure.[1]

These two specified properties of relatability (nonarbitrariness and substantiveness) invest the material to be learned with what we call *logical meaningfulness*. It seems evident that the material will vary in logical meaningfulness to the degree that it possesses these two underlying qualities.

Meaningful Learning

Logical meaningfulness, as stated above, is clearly a property of the material to be learned, and is not sufficient to guarantee that it will be meaningful to the learner (that is, that it will possess *psychological meaning*). In order for it to be meaningful to the learner, two additional conditions must be met.

In the first place the fact that the material is logically meaningful means only that it *could* be related to ideas that lie within the realm of human learning capability. In order for the material to be understandable by a *particular* individual, that individual must himself possess these necessary relevant items. If a particular learner does possess ideas in his cognitive structure to which the new learning material can be related in a substantive and nonarbitrary fashion, then we say that the material is *potentially meaningful* to him, or that it possesses *potential meaningfulness*.

We say that the material possesses potential meaningfulness at this point because the learner could make it meaningful if he wanted to. That is, the material itself can be related to some hypothetical cognitive structure, and the particular individual possesses the necessary ideas to which to relate this material. All that is lacking at this point is the *intent* of the learner to do so. If this intent is present or, in other words, if the learner has a *meaningful learning set* (that is, if he has the intent to relate this material in a nonarbitrary and substantive fashion to relevant items in his cognitive structure) then *meaningful learning* results. In sum, meaningful learning requires that these three conditions hold:

(a) The material itself must be relatable to some hypothetical cognitive structure in a nonarbitrary and substantive fashion.

(b) The learner must possess relevant ideas to which to relate the material.

(c) The learner must possess the intent to relate these ideas to cognitive structure in a nonarbitrary and substantive fashion.

The conditions are summarized in Figure 3.1.

---

[1]In the typical laboratory study, the learning task requires that the subject, when presented with the first number of a pair, recall the second (arbitrarily related) member. In both this and the "lud" example, the subject may, to facilitate his recall, invent a relationship to some existing idea in cognitive structure. In the latter case, for example, he may think of "lud" as a distortion of "lid" or as a word that rhymes with "mud". This strategem, while perhaps necessary for making sense of the learning task, by no means removes the arbitrariness from the associations (that is, from the "lid-lud" or "mud-lud" coupling).

Meaning

Meaning itself is the product of a meaningful learning process. It is the differentiated cognitive content, or content of awareness, which emerges when potentially meaningful material is incorporated into cognitive structure in a nonarbitrary and substantive fashion. It can also be said that meaning is an *idiosyncratic phenomenon* in that it is a particular content of awareness evoked in a particular learner who has a unique cognitive structure. Consequently the meaning elicited by any particular symbol or group of symbols will depend upon the ideas that exist in a particular learner's mind. In some instances, such as that illustrated by item 6 (Table 3.1), one might suppose that the ideas in cognitive structure to which the notion of an equilateral triangle could be related would be roughly similar in individuals with the typical training in geometry. In this case, it would be reasonable to say that the meanings emerging in these different cognitive structures would be approximately equivalent. On the other hand, a concept such as "democracy" might evoke considerably different states of awareness in different cognitive structures, even when their possessors had somewhat similar educational backgrounds. In most cases, however, the meanings which emerge are usually sufficiently similar across broad cultural subgroups to permit interpersonal communication and understanding.

An alternate way of representing relationships between meaningful learning, potential meaningfulness, logical meaningfulness, and psychological meaning is set out in Figure 3.2. The reader is advised at this point to reread this section and relate the verbal descriptions to each of the diagrams.

Meaningful versus Rote Learning

Having now set out more completely the conditions which must pertain if meaningful learning is to take place, we can immediately deduce which factors in the learning situation will lead to rote learning. Remembering that rote learning and meaningful learning are not true dichotomies (but that a particular instance of learning can be more or less meaningful), we can say that learning will be increasingly rote to the extent that:

(a) the material to be learned lacks logical meaningfulness;
(b) the learner lacks the relevant ideas in his own cognitive structure;
(c) the individual lacks a meaningful learning set.

Any one of these conditions by itself will produce learning that is relatively rote. For example, completely arbitrary material (such as nonsense syllables) cannot be learned with any real degree of meaning no matter what the state of the learner's cognitive structure or what his intent. Again,

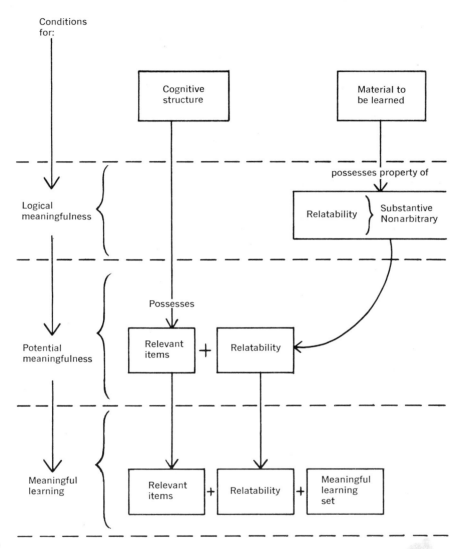

FIGURE 3.1 *Schematic representation or requirements for logical meaningfulness, potential meaningfulness, and meaningful learning.*

material which has logical meaningfulness (for example, our equilateral triangle example) cannot be meaningfully learned if the learner lacks appropriate ideas to which to relate this material, and it could only be retained by rote memorization. Finally, even if the material is logically meaningful and the learner has the appropriate ideas in cognitive structure, rote learning will still take place if the learner is set (intends) simply to memorize it.

		(1)		(2)
A MEANINGFUL LEARNING or THE ACQUISITION OF MEANINGS	requires	Potentially Meaningful Material	and	Meaningful Learning Set
B POTENTIAL MEANINGFULNESS	depends on	*Logical Meaningfulness* (the nonarbitrary and substantive relatability of the learning material to correspondingly relevant ideas that lie within the realm of human learning capability)	and	The availability of such relevant ideas in the *particular* learner's cognitive structure
C PSYCHOLOGICAL MEANING (IDIOSYNCRATIC, PHENOMENOLOGICAL MEANING)	is the product of	Meaningful Learning	or of	Potential Meaningfulness and Meaningful Learning Set

FIGURE 3.2 *Relationships between meaningful learning, potential meaningfulness, logical meaningfulness, and psychological meaning.*

The Power of Meaningful Learning

This book concentrates on meaningful, as opposed to rote, learning because the school itself is primarily interested in the teaching of materials that can be meaningfully incorporated into cognitive structure. This emphasis is rather fortunate because of the enormous difference in human capacities to absorb and retain meaningful, as opposed to rote, material. For example, many psychological investigations have determined that the typical adult can remember approximately seven random digits presented sequentially on one occasion (Miller, 1956). Moreover, the capacity for memorizing lists receiving multiple presentations is notoriously limited both over time and with respect to the length of the list, unless this list is greatly overlearned and frequently reproduced. Both of these limitations can no doubt be attributed to the rather frail human capacity for sheer memorization, a capacity in which man is vastly exceeded by the computer.

The potency of meaningful learning can be gauged when we compare with this the acquisition and retention of large bodies of subject matter and the ability to comprehend and retain complicated arguments at a single hearing. The tremendous efficacy of meaningful learning as an information processing and storing mechanism can be largely attributed to its two distinctive characteristics, that is, to the nonarbitrariness and substantiveness of the learning task's relatability to cognitive structure. First, by *nonarbitrarily* relating potentially meaningful material to relevant established items in his cognitive structure, the learner is able to effectively exploit his existing knowledge as an ideational and organizational matrix for the incorporation, understanding, and fixation of large bodies of new ideas. It is the very nonarbitrariness of this process that enables him to use his previously acquired knowledge as a veritable touchstone, for internalizing and making understandable vast quantities of new meanings, concepts, and propositions, with relatively little effort and few repetitions.

Because of this factor of nonarbitrariness, the potential meaning of new ideas *as wholes* can be related to established meanings *as wholes* to yield new meanings. In other words, the only way it is possible to make use of previously learned ideas in the processing (internalization) of new ideas is to relate the latter *nonarbitrarily* to the former. The new ideas, which become meaningful in turn, also expand the base of the learning matrix.

When, on the other hand, learning material is *arbitrarily* related to cognitive structure, no direct use whatsoever can be made of established knowledge in internalizing the learning task. At the very best, already meaningful *components* of the learning task can be related to existing *unitary* ideas in cognitive structure, thereby facilitating indirectly the rote learning of the task as a whole.[2] This in no way either makes newly internalized arbitrary associations *themselves* relatable to established content in cognitive structure or makes them usable in acquiring new knowledge. And because the human mind is not efficiently designed to interiorize and store arbitrary associations, this approach permits only very limited amounts of material to be internalized and retained, and then only after much effortful repetition.

Also, the very fact that a new idea becomes *meaningful* (that is, becomes a clear, differentiated, and sharply articulated content of awareness) after it is meaningfully learned presumably makes it less vulnerable, than are internalized arbitrary associations, to interference from other arbitrary associations, and hence makes it more retainable. In addition, as will be pointed out later in discussing the assimilation process, the maintenance of the same "nonarbitrary relatability" advantage (through the "anchorage" of the new meaning to its corresponding established ideas during the storage period) further extends the span of retention.

Second, the substantive (or nonverbatim) nature of relating new material to and incorporating it within cognitive structure circumvents the drastic limitations imposed by the short item and time spans of rote memory on the storage of information. Much more can obviously be apprehended and retained if the learner is required to assimilate and retain only the substance of the ideas rather than the precise words used in expressing them.

In view of all these advantages of meaningful learning, one might well ask why it is that students frequently learn in rote fashion. One reason why pupils may develop a rote learning set in relation to potentially meaningful subject matter is because they have learned from sad experience that substantively correct answers, which are, however, lacking in verbatim correspondence to what they have been taught, receive little credit from certain teachers. If we require verbatim answers and judge others to be inaccurate, then rote memorization obviously is being encouraged and rewarded. Another reason for a rote learning set may be that because of a generally high level of anxiety, or because of chronic failure in a given subject, some students lack confidence in their ability to learn meaningfully and hence perceive no alternative to panic, apart from rote learning. Finally, some pupils may develop a rote learning set if they are under excessive pressure to exhibit glibness, or to conceal rather than admit, and gradually remedy, an original lack of genuine understanding. Under these circumstances it seems easier and more important to create a spurious impression of facile comprehension by rotely memorizing a few key terms or sentences than to try to understand what they mean.

---

[2]Similarly in learning the nonsense syllable DAC, the learner recognizes each of the letters involved and therefore can make sense of the individual components of the word even though the total word makes no sense. See also first footnote in this chapter.

KINDS OF MEANINGFUL LEARNING

In the previous section it was pointed out that psychological meaning is the *product,* or *differentiated cognitive content,* which results when potentially meaningful material is incorporated into cognitive structure. This section will look more closely at the process of incorporation and will attempt to describe the kinds of differentiated cognitive content which result. In doing this, we look at a hierarchically organized set of psychological processes, ranging from representational learning (naming) at the lowest level to creativity at the highest.

Representational Learning

One of the first major intellectual tasks for the child is to learn the meaning of individual symbols. Initially these symbols take the form of words spoken by parents to the child, and they typically refer to objects to which the child happens to be attending. Our task is to understand how the child comes to attach meaning to these symbols, and the nature of the differentiated cognitive content which constitutes the meaning of the symbols.

Let us imagine, then, that a young child is watching a particular dog, perhaps the family pet. While he is doing this the parent says the word "dog," which initially has no meaning to the child. In the child's cognitive structure there are simultaneously active two patterns of internal stimulation (or items of differentiated cognitive content). One is the visual image of the dog, the second is the pattern of internal stimulation resulting from the child hearing the spoken word "dog" (Figure 3.3).

Through his manner of speaking and his gestures (for example, actually pointing at the dog), the parent indicates to the child that the spoken word "dog" is to represent the actual dog. Consequently, the meaning which the child attributes to the word "dog" is that differentiated cognitive content (that is, the visual image) elicited by the actual dog. Moreover, after one or more pairings of the symbol (word "dog") and object, presentation of the symbol by itself will reliably elicit the visual image of the dog which constitutes its meaning.[3]

In time, the child will notice that different objects in his environment are given different names and that different exemplars of the same class of objects (that is, different dogs) are given the same name ("dog"). By about

---

[3] An image may result either from a direct sensory experience (the child looking directly at the dog) or from a revival of a direct sensory experience (the child recalling to mind a dog which is no longer present). In the second stage of the naming process the image elicited is of the second kind; that is, it is a "reduced" or less intense image than that which would result from the direct perception of the dog.

Early stage

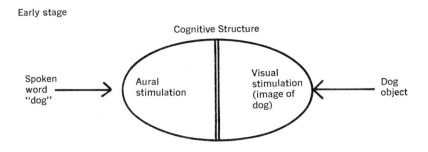

Later Stage

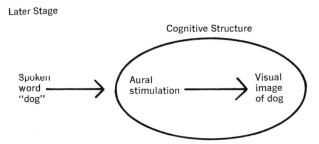

FIGURE 3.3 *Stages in naming process.*

the end of the first year the child is able to generalize from these experiences and acquire the insight that it is possible to use a symbol to represent *any* object. By this we mean that the child comes to understand intuitively that every object has a "name" which takes the form of a verbal symbol and that the meaning to be attached to the symbol is the image evoked by the object. This general understanding is called the *proposition of representational equivalence.*

After the child has grasped this general notion, the learning of names will henceforth not be a completely arbitrary kind of learning for him. For if the child subsequently hears the word "cat," in the presence of an actual cat, he will realize that this particular act of attaching a verbal label to a physical object is an instance of the more general proposition that "things have names." Moreover he will understand that the meaning to be attached to the word "cat" is the image evoked by the real cat. Consequently, even though the verbal symbol employed bears no intrinsic relationship to the object (it is, rather, an arbitrary pattern of sounds), this instance of naming is not completely arbitrary, and so satisfies at least one of the criteria for meaningful learning. Thus it can be argued that while representational learning is relatively near the rote end of the meaningful/rote continuum, it does not contain the virtually complete arbitrariness (and therefore roteness) involved in the learning of paired associates or lists of randomly selected digits.

Non-Noun Names It would seem that the naming process illustrated in our example could also explain how the child acquires the meaning of prepositions like "in" or "on," or of verbs like "run" or "eat." For example, the word "on" would be used by a parent when the child is perceiving the *relationship* between objects. Thus, he might be observing the "on" relationship between dog and floor (that is, the dog is on the floor). As in the earlier case the verbal symbol (the spoken word "on") can, with repeated pairing, come to elicit an image of the relationship pertaining between these objects. This image, the differentiated cognitive content elicited by the word "on," could constitute the meaning of that symbol.

It would be interesting to speculate as to whether the meanings of all words can be interpreted in terms of concrete images. The theory advanced in this book does not take a position on the related and ancient philosophical question as to whether all thinking is accompanied by images. We do, however, attempt to clarify the discussion by making reference to images when they may be assumed to be present.[4]

Concept Learning

In line with our earlier discussion, it will be apparent that a concept can have both logical and psychological meaning. Logically, a concept refers to phenomena in a given field that are grouped together because of their common characteristics. For example, the word "triangle" refers to a unique class of objects which are manifestly distinct from rectangles or circles. We might speak of the *criterial attributes* of the concept to refer to the set of properties that each member of the concept class has in common and, moreover, that distinguish members of that particular class from members of other classes. In other words, once the criterial attributes of a concept are known, the individual would be able to judge whether any particular instance which he encounters is an exemplar or nonexemplar of the concept in question.

Concept Formation It will be evident from the previous discussion that the chief problem for the young child in concept learning will reside in ferreting out the criterial attributes of a class of stimuli to which he is exposed. It is clear that at any stage in the child's development there may be a considerable discrepancy between the criterial attributes that he has discovered, and which give psychological meaning to his concept, and the

---

[4]It seems clear that the child's early thinking is dominated by fairly concrete images. It should be remembered that although our examples refer only to visual images, the term "image" can refer to a present or revived sensory experience from any of the sense modalities including sensory feedback from overt physical actions. It also seems clear that as humans mature their reliance upon concrete images declines. The point at issue is whether vague and diffuse images are at play even in such abstract concepts as "democracy," "love," and so on.

criterial attributes that define the logical meaning of a concept. For example, a young child may have a very limited and imprecise concept of "triangle," which, as a result of experience and feedback, will become progressively more similar to the logical concept.

To illustrate concept learning, we will consider a young child who, left for long periods in his playroom or playpen, manipulates a variety of cubes. These cubes, we will suppose, differ in size, color, and texture. As a result of this concrete experience, the child discovers inductively the criterial attributes of the cube. Moreover, these attributes are embedded in a representative image of a cube, an image that the child has developed from his experience and can recall in the absence of real cubes. This process of inductively discovering the criterial attributes of a class of stimuli is called *concept formation.* When it is complete the child is said to possess the concept of a cube, and the meaning of this concept is the representative image comprising the criterial attributes of this class of objects. At this stage, although the child has acquired a concept, he has as yet no name for it (Figure 3.4).

Stage I
Concept has meaning

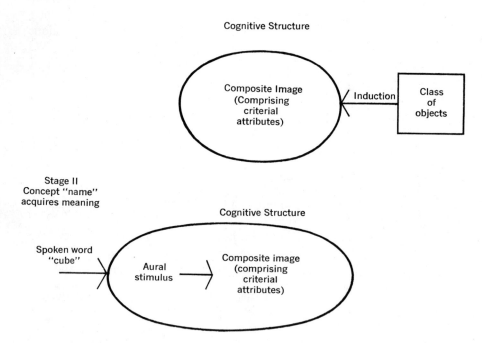

FIGURE 3.4 *Two stages in learning of concept names.*

At a later stage, perhaps when the child enters school, he will learn the formal *concept name,* or *concept word,* "cube." Learning a concept name is a kind of representational learning in that the child learns that the spoken or written symbol "cube" is to represent the concept that he has already acquired. In this process, then, he equates the word "cube" in meaning to the representative image which represents the meaning of the concept (Figure 3.4). The concept word has now acquired *denotative* meaning and, on subsequent presentations, will elicit differentiated cognitive content which consists of the representative image comprising the criterial attributes of the concept.

In addition to denotative meaning, the concept name may also have *connotative* meaning. This refers to the idiosyncratic, personal, affective, and attitudinal reactions that the term elicits in each child, depending upon his particular experiences with that class of objects. It would seem that the word "cube" would have relatively little connotative meaning for most children, although there may be individual differences in that playing with blocks may have been a relatively happy experience for some children and a relatively unhappy experience for others. However, it is clear that concept names like "country" or "friend" will have a heavy connotative overtone, and that the particular emotions elicited by these terms will vary considerably from individual to individual.

This two-stage process, comprising (1) the formation of the concept and (2) learning the meaning of the concept name, occurs in a large proportion of the instances in which children learn concepts. However, in other instances (such as our dog example) the concept name is present from the beginning so that the child may retain this symbol as its meaning changes from the image of a specific object to a representative image comprising the criterial attributes of a class of objects. In any case the distinction between the concept formation and concept-naming processes is an important one. It frequently happens, for example, that we may forget a concept name while remembering the meaning of the concept itself. On the other hand, we may remember the concept name but forget the concept meaning.

It is also apparent that learning what the concept word means demands a more sophisticated knowledge of the corresponding referents than do other forms of representational learning (the initial dog example). In the latter case, the appropriate image is immediately available to the learner; in the former case, the prior development of the representative image (the concept meaning) involves a long process of abstraction.

Concept Formation versus Concept Assimilation The concept formation process described above is typical of the learning of young children. However, after the preschool years the meanings of most concept words are learned by definition or by being encountered in appropriate contexts. A definition furnishes for the learner the criterial attributes expressed in already meaningful terms. Since a definition is a form of "proposition," the process by which the meaning of a new concept name emerges will be better understood after the reader has read the section on propositional learning below. At this point we need only remark that when the criterial attributes of a concept are presented to the learner by definition, rather than being discovered by him (as in concept formation), the concept learning involved is referred to as *concept assimilation*.

Proposition Learning

A proposition is a sentence such as "Crocodiles eat children." The sentence cited is illustrative of an important class of propositions called *generalizations,* which are statements of relationship between two or more concepts. The proposition "The neighbor's alligator ate Billy Jones" is not a generalization, since the principal terms involved are the names of specific objects. In either case, however, the task in proposition learning is to apprehend the meaning of the composite idea expressed by the sentence. Although this composite idea depends upon the individual words in the sentence, it is more than just their sum and involves some reconstruction of their individual meanings.

Learning of Syntax   In order to understand how the child comes to apprehend the meaning of the proposition cited, we must make a preliminary reference to the learning of the syntactical rules that are used by the speakers of a language for inflecting words and combining them into sentences. Linguistically these rules, which collectively might be called the *syntactic code,* consist of (a) *connecting words* (prepositions, conjunctions); (b) *designative words* (articles, demonstrative adjectives); (c) *inflections* indicating number, gender, case, tense, mode and mood; and (d) *word order rules* adding relational meaning to connected discourse.

From a psychological standpoint, however, syntactic rules primarily serve the *transactional* function of bringing verbally expressed ideas (images and concepts) into relationship with each other for the purpose of generating and understanding new ideas. Although the learning of syntax is not completely understood, it would appear that the functional mastery of the syntactic code of one's native language is acquired inductively through extensive practice in decoding the meaning of sentences. We have already considered how a child might come to acquire the meaning of a preposition such as the word "on." Although the image initially evoked by this verbal symbol would refer to the perceived relationship between specific objects, it would seem reasonable to believe that after the child has encountered a variety of such specific instances he will develop a composite image inductively through a process quite similar to that of concept formation.[5]

Moreover, it seems that the child could learn word order rules through a process of decoding complete sentences. For example, let us suppose that the child is watching the family dog which is sitting near him, and that the words "dog" and "sitting" already evoke meaning for him. If the parent now says "dog sitting," the child will compare the temporal sequence of individual images generated in cognitive structure by this condensed sentence with his perceived representative image (a sitting dog). From repeated experiences of this kind he would come to understand that the symbol for the agent of the action (the subject) tends to precede the symbol representing the action (the verb). Despite the fact that the learning of the complete syntactic code is an enormously complex process, the child appears to master this task approximately two years before entering school.

We may now turn to consideration of how the child comes to understand the proposition "crocodiles eat children," that is, how he comes to acquire the meaning of the composite idea expressed by the proposition. To begin with, the child understands the individual terms so that he has appropriate images for them. Moreover, from his intuitive knowledge of syntax the child understands that the word "crocodile" represents the subject or thing doing the eating, and that the word "children" represents the object or the thing eaten. Thus, he has a set of rules for transforming the individual images resulting from the verbal message into a representative image (that is, a crocodile eating a child) which constitutes the meaning of the proposition.

Types of Relationships   When the meaningful learning of propositions takes place, the sentence to be learned is related to existing ideas in cognitive structure. It is now possible to elaborate and describe somewhat more precisely the various kinds of relationships which can hold between the new material and established ideas.[6]

Subordinate Relationships   The most common kind of relationship between new material and existing ideas is a *subordinate* one, in which the new material is subsumed under existing and more inclusive ideas in cognitive structure. Subordinate relationships can be of two kinds. *In derivative* subsumption, the new propositional material is merely illustrative of, or directly

---

[5]One might say, in fact, that the child acquires a concept of "on" in that he develops a composite image which comprises the criterial attributes of the relationship it expresses.
[6]Although these relationships are discussed under proposition learning, they describe equally well the possible relationships between new concepts and concepts already established in cognitive structure.

derivable from, an already established and more inclusive proposition. For example, if a child has already meaningfully learned the proposition "cats climb trees," then the specific proposition, "The neighbors' cat is climbing our tree," may be subsumed under it. In this case, the representative image comprising the meaning of the general proposition need only be modified in slight detail (actually need only be *particularized*) to yield the meaning of the new proposition, and it would seem that this specific proposition would be relatively easy to learn. In other words, the meaning of the general proposition is adequate to convey the meaning of its derivative, and little cognitive activity is required to apprehend the meaning of the latter.

A second type of subordinate relationship, called *correlative subsumption,* occurs when the new material is an extension, elaboration, modification, or qualification of previously learned propositions. Suppose, for example, that a child understands the meaning of the concept name "parallelogram" (defined as a closed four-sided figure whose opposite sides are parallel). We might then define the term "rhombus" (the meaning of which is assumed, for the present discussion, to be unknown to the learner) by means of the proposition "A rhombus is a parallelogram in which all the sides are equal." In this case of correlative subsumption the term "parallelogram" has been qualified to yield a "rhombus." Moreover, it is clear that assimilating the meaning of the new concept (developing a representative image) requires a *transformation* of the image constituting the meaning of the original concept (parallelogram). Again, the learner's knowledge of the syntax of the defining sentence indicates to him how the individual images (of "parallelogram," "sides," "equal") are to be combined to form the representative image representing the meaning of "rhombus."

Superordinate Relationships New learning material bears a *superordinate* relationship to ideas in cognitive structure when one learns an inclusive new proposition under which several *established* ideas may be subsumed. This type of propositional learning is relatively rare since textbooks and teachers typically introduce more general and inclusive propositions first and then present examples, corrollaries, qualifications, extensions, and elaborations.[7] However, in establishing these general and inclusive ideas, we frequently must present the learner with a proposition which *cannot* be subsumed under any existing idea, so that its meaning must be developed by induction from particular instances.

---

[7]This is probably more true of organization within a specific course (for example, Grade 10 biology) than between related courses within a subject-matter field. In the latter case, gross exceptions to desirable practice are not hard to find. For example, as geometry has traditionally been organized in our schools, *Euclidian* concepts (the most specific) are taught first *projective* concepts (more general) at a considerably later stage, and *topological* concepts (the most inclusive) only to those few who survive to graduate programs in mathematics.

For example, the teacher may wish to have students learn the general proposition that "the sum of the angles of any quadrilateral equals 360 degrees." (We assume that they already know that the respective sums of the angles of a square, rectangle, and parallelogram equal 360 degrees.) By generalizing from these specific cases of the general quadrilaterals, the learner may inductively arrive at the general proposition. In this process he will also develop a new representative image representing the meaning of the proposition. Of course, once the general proposition has been established in cognitive structure, the more specific propositions concerning parallelograms, squares, and rectangles could be subsumed under it in a derivative fashion.

Combinatorial Relationships   The meaningful learning of new propositions that bear neither a subordinate nor a superordinate relationship to *particular* relevant ideas in cognitive structure gives rise to *combinatorial* meanings. The learning of many new propositions, as well as concepts, yields this category of meaning. They are potentially meaningful because they consist of sensible combinations of previously learned ideas that can be nonarbitrarily related to a *broad background* of *generally* relevant content in cognitive structure.

A very common kind of combinatorial relationship can be found in the notion of a *model*. We might suppose, for example, that an instructor is attempting to explain the derivation of the formula for the period of a pendulum[8] to a group of students who have previously studied both geometry and Newtonian mechanics. He points out that the pendulum might be considered to be *structurally equivalent* to the line segment and the Newtonian particle shown in Figure 3.5. Because of this structural similarity, known propositions relating to the movement of Newtonian particles can be used to explain the newly encountered phenomenon. In particular, the formula for the period (a formula is a proposition) derives its meaning from the meaning possessed by these original propositions.[9]

In a more literary vein, metaphors provide meaning to a phenomenon at hand by making an implied comparison between it and some idea already existing in the cognitive structure of the learner. For example, in the metaphor contained in the line, "Life's but a walking shadow," Shakespeare compares an abstract idea (life) to a concrete object (a shadow in motion), thus conveying the notion of life's ethereal, fleeting, and essentially somber qualities. It is typical of the human mind, particularly when attempting to

---

[8]The period of the pendulum is the time required for it to complete one cycle. The formula for the period is $t = 2\pi \sqrt{\dfrac{l}{g}}$
where l is the length of the pendulum and g is a gravitational constant.
[9]The actual procedure by which this happens will be better understood after the reader has reviewed the section on the learning of algebraic symbolism.

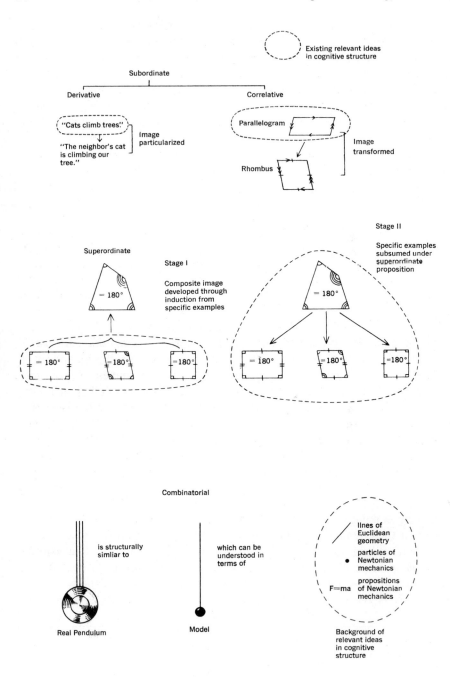

FIGURE 3.5 *Possible relationships between new and existing ideas.*

invest enormously abstract or profound concepts with specific meaning, to turn to the imagery elicited by the metaphor. Such comparisons invest the ideas concerned with temporary meaning (images) that seem appropriate to the situation, and thereby enhances the understanding the writer wishes to convey at that moment.

Discovery Learning

We may recall that discovery learning refers to the situation in which the material to be learned is not presented to the learner in final form (as it is in reception learning) but requires that he must undertake some kind of mental activity (rearrangement, reorganization or transformation of the given material) prior to incorporating the final result into cognitive structure. It is clear, therefore, that discovery learning cuts across the whole range of processes we have discussed to this point. In particular, discovery learning is very much in evidence in concept formation and in the inductive learning of superordinate propositions. In the final two kinds of processes to be discussed, problem solving and creativity, discovery by the learner is usually the predominant activity.

Problem Solving Compilations of definitions of "problem solving" (Berlyne, 1964) make it clear that different authors attach different meanings to that term. However if it is to have much usefulness, "problem solving" should indicate psychological processes distinctly more complex than those involved in simple *application* of meaningfully learned propositions. In addition to the minimal requirement that a "problem" must involve discovery learning, we would add that there should be no clearly defined or frequently practiced procedure leading from the student's existing knowledge to the solution of the problem. In other words, there should be a gap between where the student now is and where he has to get in order to attain a solution.

A teacher might, for example, ask students to discover (by measurement) the generalization involving the sum of the angles of a triangle. While this certainly involves guided discovery (to the extent that the student would actually arrive inductively at the proposition himself), the process involved (adding up of the angles for a number of triangles and generalizing the result) is straightforward and would not, according to our criteria, qualify as problem solving. Similarly the student who knows that the area of a triangle may be expressed by the formula "Area $= \frac{1}{2}$ (Base $\times$ Height)" may be required to find the area of a particular triangle that he has never seen before. Although this might be classified as "application," the "solution" should follow immediately for any motivated student who has meaningfully learned the proposition, that is, who has grasped the meaning of the concepts involved and their relationship. If the student is unable to find a solution in any particular case, we must conclude that he either does not understand the meaning of the concept names "base" or "height," or that his arithmetical skills are deficient.[10]

An example satisfying our criteria for "problem solving" was provided in Figure 2.3. In this case the student was required to "prove $RT = TS$." As we found in our preliminary analysis, there was a considerable gap between the background propositions which the student had already learned and the result to be proved. In analyzing the processes involved in problem solving, it would seem that the first step will be for the student to apprehend the meaning of the problem-setting propositions. These include (in our example) the formal statement of what is to be proved and the meanings of the markings on the triangles, which together define the problem situation. It is obvious that unless the student can understand these propositions he will make no progress with the problem.

After the student has grasped the meaning of the problem-setting proposition, he must then transform the propositions that he already knows in such a way as to yield the desired results. For example, in the instance cited the student first attempts to transform proposition II (that is, to mentally manipulate the image representing the meaning of this proposition) until it fits triangles PRT and PST. Having done this, he can then see (by comparing the direct image of the given figure to the images resulting from a transformation of proposition II) that certain pieces of needed information are not yet available (that is, that angle RPT = angle SPT). In the next phase the student attempts to transform proposition II to fit the triangles PRQ and PSQ. Again he discerns that needed information is not available. The transformation of background propositions continues in this way until all the necessary information has been derived.

The crux of the educator's problem is whether a general set of teachable principles can be derived which, if followed by the student, will generate the transformations that lead systematically to a solution. In Chapter 2 we referred to such a set of principles as a *strategy,* and outlined in relatively crude terms one that was appropriate to the present class of problems. In a later chapter we will analyze the geometry strategy further to determine its limitations and the steps which can be taken to overcome them.

Creativity Any discussion of the processes underlying creative behavior is bedeviled by the lack of agreement on what the criteria for that

---

[10]We might also say, in this case, that the image representing the meaning of the formula must be transformed to fit the specific triangle under consideration. Again this constitutes a straightforward transformation which should be expected from adequate comprehension of the formula.

behavior shall be. By definition, creativity must refer to the production of something new; but the question remains as to whether the product shall be new to the individual, or new in the sense of making a contribution to human knowledge.[11] In this book we shall adopt the view that while both kinds of products should be described as *creative behavior*, only those individuals who are able to produce the latter kind of products should be regarded as truly *creative persons*.

Creative behavior itself, if it is to have any useful meaning as a separate concept, should indicate a level of synthesis (a bringing together of elements to form a new product) beyond that found in problem solving (Figure 3.6). Actually, there is no adequate explanation of the psychological processes involved in creative performance. However, it is possible to describe, in a general way, how such performance is related to the processes that we have discussed to this point. It was observed earlier that one of the kinds of relationship between propositions to be learned and existing cognitive structure may be described by the term "combinatorial." In the meaningful reception learning of material that has a combinatorial relationship to existing ideas in cognitive structure, the *teacher* would point out the somewhat remotely related existing knowledge which is being utilized to explain the new phenomenon (for example, in the pendulum problem). In creative behavior, on the other hand, the *individual* himself, in some unknown fashion, perceives the relationship of a phenomenon to be understood to some remotely related idea in cognitive structure.[12] Thus the model-builder and the metaphor-constructor are exhibiting creative behavior; in both cases a new product or idea is created (that is, the formula for the period of the pendulum, and the new comparison).

In Figure 2.4 we examined a problem whose solution might be said to involve a certain amount of creative behavior. In order to solve this problem the individual has to perceive a relationship between the existing problem and some hitherto unrelated idea in cognitive structure. For example, it might occur to the learner that the second triangle might be thought of as the mirror image of the first, or as the result of rotating the first about its baseline through 180 degrees.

---

[11]In keeping with the cognitive emphasis of this book we are concerned exclusively with that kind of creativity which results in extensions of existing knowledge, that is, in which the underlying psychological process is primarily cognitive and for which the possession of propositional knowledge is a prerequisite. We do not, however, deny the importance of creative behavior in the fine and performing arts, nor do we argue that the underlying psychological processes necessarily differ in these cases.

[12]This may be rephrased by saying that creative behavior, unlike problem solving, draws upon a set of propositions which are not specifically taught (or otherwise known in advance) as being relevant to the problem at hand. And also, unlike problem solving, the strategies employed in creative behavior to manipulate the relevant background ideas are usually not explicitly formulated (or taught).

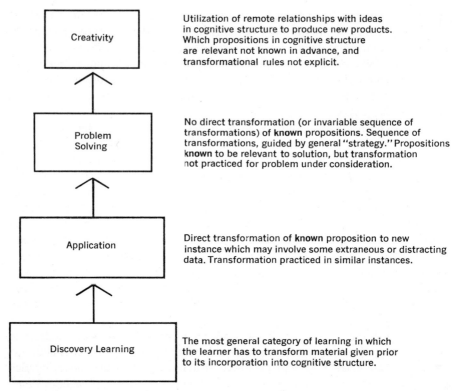

FIGURE 3.6 *Relationship between application, problem solving, and creativity.*

RECONCILIATION OF THE PRESENT CHAPTER AND BLOOM'S TAXONOMY

Teachers will likely encounter the Bloom taxonomy in their subject-matter fields. Therefore some attempt to reconcile it with the behavioral hierarchy outlined in the present chapter will be offered at this point. Since *knowledge* in Bloom's system depends chiefly on memory, most of the tasks assigned to that level could be accounted for by rote learning. On the other hand, *comprehension,* and performance at all superior levels in Bloom's system, clearly call for meaningful learning.

Our taxonomy, derived strictly from the hypothesized underlying psychological *processes,* introduces two additional considerations at the comprehension level. First, it is recognized that the learning of propositions (or generalizations) should be considered a more complex process than the learning of concepts, for the former typically involves the combination of concepts to form more comprehensive ideational units. Second, an important process distinction, with both psychological and pedagogical implications, can be made between *discovery* and *reception* learning. In other words, it is thought important that we not only test the *product* of the student's learning (whether he has acquired the meaning of a concept or proposition) but that we recognize the *process* (reception or discovery) by which the product is generated. Thus it is necessary—from a psychological and pedagogical point of view—to separate the inductive *formation* of concepts and generalizations from their *assimilation* through reception learning.

Application presents difficulties in both systems, primarily because the precise boundary between it and comprehension is exceedingly difficult to ascertain. Theoretically it could be held that applying a principle (rule, algorithm, and so forth) in a context not previously encountered requires that one go beyond the minimal criterion for comprehension (that is, restating the principle in one's own words, correctly identifying variant forms of its verbal expression, or recognizing exemplars and nonexemplars presented in concrete embodiments). While, for the sake of theoretical consistency, we adopt this position, we recognize that any given task might be thought to require "adequate" comprehension by some, and application by others. This is not, in our opinion, a very important discrepancy.

We employ the term *problem solving* rather than *analysis* to describe the next level in the hierarchy, largely because we find the latter term too restrictive. For while it is true that a form of analysis may be seen in the geometry problem (and is even more in evidence in the pendulum problem cited in Chapter 5), we believe that performance at that level is best conceptualized as the transformation of existing relevant propositions to produce some required end, and that this total process is not adequately described by the label "analysis."

Here we come to a fundamental difference in viewpoint between students of mathematics and science on the one hand (who use the "problem-solving" label freely), and students of the humanities on the other (who seem to find the term "analysis" more congenial to their way of conceptualizing the phenomena of their field). An essential query, examined in detail in Chapter 17, is whether intellectual tasks that might be described as "problems" exist in history or English literature, to cite two examples from the humanities. Certainly, teachers in these fields do not tend to use the terms "problem" or "problem solving." Nevertheless, granting that the content of such fields exhibits fewer formal propositions and less clearly defined transformational rules (strategies), our contention will be that it is still useful to think of problem-solving tasks in these areas—tasks which fall within the general criteria we have set for problems.

Finally, Bloom's *synthesis* and our *creative behavior* are clearly similar in that both involve the emergence of a product that is unique in terms of the individual's past experience. However it is necessary to stipulate an additional requirement for creative behavior which distinguishes it clearly from problem solving. In our system this requirement is that the background propositions and strategies that are brought to bear to produce the solution have not been taught as specifically relevant to the task at hand.

In summary, the taxonomy outlined above seems generally compatible with Bloom's so long as certain important process distinctions are admitted. Consequently, it should not prove difficult for subject-matter oriented teachers to adapt themselves to our system, even while encountering the Bloom analysis in other courses.

TOPICS FOR DISCUSSION AND FURTHER STUDY

1. For the grade level and subject matter areas that you will be teaching, list concepts and propositions which would be potentially meaningful, but which cannot be psychologically meaningful to the child (at that level) because he lacks an appropriate subsuming idea in cognitive structure.

2.* In your subject specialty construct a sequence of ideas whose learnings range from the relatively rote end of the meaningful/rote continuum to the highly meaningful. What ways exist, if any, for making the potentially rote learning more meaningful?

3. Under what circumstances will students learn potentially meaningful material in rote fashion? What may the teacher do in these circumstances to encourage more meaningful learning of this material?

4.* Construct examples of concepts and propositions that bear derivative, correlative, superordinate, and combinatorial relationships to ideas in the learner's cognitive structure. In each case make clear the nature of the particular anchoring ideas in cognitive structure.

5. Make a list of concepts whose meaning children normally acquire by a process of concept formation and another list of concept meanings acquired by concept assimilation. To what extent can a similar distinction be made for the learning of generalizations?

6. Is it possible to cite ideas to be learned which possess either substantiveness or nonarbitrariness (in relation to ideas in cognitive structure), but not both? If so, give some examples.

7. Cite examples of problem solving and creative behavior which might be expected of children in the elementary and secondary-school grades.

8.* Contrast the theory of meaning put forward in this book with the neo-associationist viewpoints of Mowrer and Berlyne (see references below).

9. How can the teacher be certain that meaningful rather than rote learning is taking place? Describe an appropriate test for the meaningfulness of learning.

SUGGESTIONS FOR ADDITIONAL READING

Ausubel, D. P. *Educational psychology: A cognitive view.* New York: Holt, Rinehart and Winston, Inc., 1968, Chapter 2.

Bellugi, Ursula, and R. W. Brown (Eds.) The acquisition of language. *Monogr. Soc. Res. Child Develpm.*, 1965, *29* (I), 1–129 (Whole No. 92).

Berlyne, D. E. *Structure and direction in thinking.* New York: John Wiley and Sons, Inc., 1965, Chapter 1.

Harré, R. Formal analysis of concepts. In *Analysis of concept learning* (H. J. Klausmeier, Ed.). New York: Academic Press, Inc., 1966, Chapter 1.

McNeill, D. Developmental psycholinguistics. In *The genesis of language: A psycholinguistic approach.* (F. Smith and G. A. Miller, Eds.). Cambridge, Mass.: The M.I.T. Press, 1966.

Mowrer, O. H. The psychologist looks at language. *Amer. Psychol.*, 1954, *9*, 660–692.

CHAPTER 4

MEANINGFUL LEARNING
IN MAJOR SCHOOL SUBJECTS

THE CONCEPTS DEVELOPED TO THIS POINT ARE APPLICABLE to various subject-matter areas of concern to the school. Specifically, we will consider in this chapter the psychological processes involved in: (1) learning to read; (2) learning a second language; (3) learning arithmetic, and (4) learning algebra. We will then conclude with some general comments on meaningful reception learning.

The discussion which follows is not intended as a detailed set of prescriptions of the kind found in methods courses. Rather, our purpose is to show that the theory helps to explain the nature of the learning tasks in each of these areas, and that it provides us with a perspective on the relative merits of alternate approaches to instruction.

LEARNING TO READ

Let us consider the beginning reader who has encountered for the first time the *written* proposition, "The dog is in the garden." When the child begins to read, he is already able to understand (apprehend the meaning of) this proposition in spoken form. That is (in the language of the last chapter), he is able to *perceive* the *potential meaning* of the spoken sentence (awareness of the meanings of such individual words as "dog" and "garden," and of the syntactical relationships between them), and then is able to convert this potential meaning to *actual* meaning by relating the resulting composite idea to relevant ideas in cognitive structure.

It would seem, then, that the essential problem in learning to read will be to reconstruct the written message into a spoken message, so that the ability to understand spoken messages may be utilized. Learning to reconstruct written into spoken messages involves at least two major component steps. First there is the problem of converting individual written words to individual spoken words. This problem is rendered less difficult, however, by the alphabetic basis of structuring most written languages. Thus written words are not just configurations of visual symbols that arbitrarily represent their auditory counterparts. Rather, there is a more or less lawful relationship between the combination of distinguishable sounds (phonemes) constituting a spoken word (such as "dog") and the analogous combination of letters (graphemes) constituting the corresponding written word. The beginning reader must, therefore, learn how to convert graphemes and combinations of graphemes into their phonemic equivalents and then learn how to put together several graphic combinations and reconstruct them into spoken words. In this latter process of word recognition he is aided by such cues as knowledge of commonly occurring graphemic combinations (for example, prefixes and suffixes) and an awareness of the wider context in which the written message is presented.

The second step in reconstructing the written message is learning how to combine and convert *groups* of written words into spoken phrases and sentences. By so doing, knowledge of the syntactic code of the spoken language can be utilized in perceiving the potential meaning of the written message. The beginning reader, in other words, is unable to apprehend *directly* the syntactic functions of the words in the written message. In order to perceive its potential propositional meaning, therefore, he translates it into a spoken message, relying on his intuitive knowledge of the syntax of the spoken language.

Once a facility in reading is acquired, it seems reasonable to suppose that the spoken language no longer plays a mediating role in the perception of meaning from written messages. In other words, a skilled reader perceives directly both the denotative meanings of words and their syntactic functions without reconstructing component words and phrases into their spoken counterparts. Once the reconstructive process is dispensed with, word meanings emerge as an immediate (perceptual) content of awareness. It goes without saying, however, that the directly perceived denotative meanings and syntactic functions do not in themselves yield propositional meaning. The individual meanings must first be combined into a composite idea and related to cognitive structure. The product of this interaction constitutes actual propositional meaning.

In light of the foregoing discussion it is obvious that in learning to read the child is not learning a completely new symbolic code, but rather a written equivalent of the familiar spoken code whose basic vocabulary and syntax are known to him. Thus, while learning to read represents an extremely important development, it is not as impressive a cognitive accomplishment as the original learning of the spoken language.

Phonetic versus Wholistic Methods of Teaching Reading

In terms of the foregoing analysis of the steps involved in learning to read, the so-called phonetic or phonic method of teaching reading (that is, initial emphasis on letter recognition and grapheme-phoneme correspondences before reading whole words) makes more psychological sense than teaching children to recognize written words as wholes from the outset (the "look-say" method). The phonetic approach makes the problem of recognizing written words less arbitrary by giving the child a lawful code with which to reconstruct currently meaningless but potentially meaningful written words into their already meaningful spoken equivalents.[1] Word recognition thus becomes more a matter of rational problem-solving than of random guessing. That is, it becomes a process of lawfully decoding the unknown written word by applying existing knowledge of grapheme-phoneme correspondences with the aid of such additional cues as context. The "look-say" method, on the other hand, renders written English, based for the most part on regular and learnable correspondences between graphemes and phonemes, into a pictorial, non-alphabetic written language like Chinese. It is true, of course, that children who learn to read by the "look-say" method tend spontaneously to develop some impressions about grapheme-phoneme correspondence, and to use these impressions in deciphering unfamiliar words. But this haphazard, incidental, and unguided discovery learning of grapheme-phoneme correspondences can hardly be considered a defensible instructional procedure when such knowledge can be transmitted much more efficiently on a systematic, suitably programmed, and guided reception basis.

The learning of grapheme-phoneme correspondences does not imply that pupils must learn a complete set of formal or explicitly verbalized rules, a task which would hardly be practicable at the age of initial reading instruction. Rather, it means providing guided practice in responding phonically to the more frequently encountered letter combinations in words so that the child acquires an *intuitive* grasp of grapheme-phoneme correspondences, together with an *explicit* awareness of such simple rules as that governing the transition from short to long vowel pronunciation through the addition of a final *e*. He thus eventually becomes capable of responding automatically with the correct phonemic equivalents of the different graphemes and graphemic combinations.

---

[1]For example, one such rule consists in recognizing that a vowel generally takes its "short" pronunciation when it occurs before a final consonant (c*a*p, d*u*n, m*a*t), but takes its "long" pronunciation when a final "e" is added (c*a*pe, d*u*ne, m*a*te). For a current compendium of grapheme-phoneme relationships see Venezky (1967).

Wholistic methods of teaching reading are sometimes defended on the grounds that mature readers perceive whole words and even phrases at a time, rather than individual letters or syllables. This, of course, is true but totally irrelevant to the point at issue. What applies to skilled readers does not necessarily apply to pupils who are first learning to read. The techniques employed by an expert in performing a complex skill can hardly be recommended as suitable practice exercises for the novice. The beginning student of Morse code, for example, thinks in terms of letter units, not in terms of the larger word and phrase units characterizing the transmitting and receiving operations of the skilled telegraphist.

Finally, it is important to bear in mind that phonetic and wholistic approaches need not be mutually exclusive procedures, either in theory or in practice. Advocates of the phonetic method ordinarily teach whole-word recognition of some of the more common words as a means of making possible earlier reading of simple meaningful text, and of thereby enhancing the beginning reader's interest, self-confidence, and motivation. "Look-say" advocates typically introduce varying degrees of phonic analysis *after* their pupils acquire some reading fluency. While the difference between the two schools of thought today is thus largely one of timing and relative emphasis, this difference is still important both theoretically and practically. Although definitive empirical evidence is still lacking, Chall's recent analysis of fifty years of research (Chall, 1967) strongly supports a phonetic approach. This is not surprising since the arguments of the phonetic school, in our opinion at least, rest on more tenable theoretical ground.

The Augmented Roman Alphabet The use of the augmented Roman alphabet (also called the Initial Teaching Alphabet) in teaching reading (Pitman, 1961), now in the experimental try-out stage, represents a further attempt to capitalize on grapheme-phoneme correspondences in helping children to derive meaning from written messages. This method seeks to overcome the ambiguities and inconsistencies inherent in the fact that some English graphemes, particularly vowels, have several phonemic equivalents. It accomplishes this aim by using instructional materials based on an alphabet of 46 graphemes, one for each recognizable phoneme in the English language (Figure 4.1). An hypothesis of this method, apparently supported by early research (Sebasta, 1964) was that, once children acquired initial facility in reading material written in the augmented alphabet, they would experience little difficulty in reading text employing the conventional alphabet. This would not be surprising, however, when one considers that the use of supplementary cues to simplify the learning process during early stages of acquiring a new cognitive skill does not necessarily create dependence on these same cues after the skill is partially acquired. The beginning reader is much better equipped to cope with irregularities in grapheme-phoneme cor-

sum birdſ in a trεε sau ſhem. ſhæ had tω laf.

ſhe turtl wonted tω tauk tω ſhe birdſ about hiſ trip, but hεε nuε hεε cωd not œpen hiſ mouſh.

5

FIGURE 4.1 *A page printed in Pitman's Initial Teaching Alphabet (from a beginning reader of the Early-to-Read series published by Initial Teaching Alphabet Publications, Inc., N.Y.). Reprinted from The Story of i/t/a. New York: Initial Teaching Alphabet Publications, Inc., 1965, p. 3.*

respondence after mastering the regularities and acquiring a basic vocabulary of written words.

Despite the theoretical advantages of the augmented Roman alphabet, recent research has by no means unequivocally demonstrated its superiority over teaching methods employing traditional orthography (see, for example: Fry's 1967 summary of six studies conducted in the United States during the past few years). On the other hand, Downing (1967) reports generally encouraging results from Britain and argues that misconceptions concerning the nature of i/t/a have invalidated most American research studies. He admits, however, that problems have arisen in the transition from i/t/a to traditional orthography which have, to some extent, offset the early advantages of this method (see also references in Kerfoot, 1967). Downing also suggests that a re-examination is needed of the basic writing system employed, and that the merits of other possible "simplified and regularized writing systems" be looked into.

SECOND-LANGUAGE LEARNING

Until quite recently second-language learning in North American schools was conducted chiefly in the secondary school. It concentrated mainly on reading the second language, translating the second language into the native language, and writing prose in the second language. The language of instruction was the native language, and there was a tendency to neglect oral comprehension and speaking ability in the second language. In the past few years, however, the so-called audiolingual method has become popular, particularly as new second-language programs have been introduced in the elementary-school curriculum. In this approach the learner is treated as though he were learning a first language. Thus objects are named in the second language, syntax and grammar are learned inductively, the spoken form of the second language is presented before the written form, and the beginner is exposed to the "natural speed of rendition" of the second language. In short, the audiolingual method completely avoids any possible mediational role for the native language.

The respective merits of the two approaches undoubtedly depend upon the behavioral outcomes required. If a major objective is to acquire accurate pronunciation or the ability to think in the second language, then present evidence (Scherer and Wertheimer, 1964) suggests that a well-defined audiolingual component is warranted. However, there appears to be a tendency to believe that because children learn their native tongue the "natural" or audiolingual way, this approach must be the most effective way of acquiring new languages and should be used by older learners in second-language learning, even where the principal intent is the comprehension of the written form and the understanding of grammatical generalizations of the second language. Because of these assertions, it is worthwhile to examine some of the characteristics of the audiolingual approach in the light of the postulated processes involved in second-language learning.

Psychological Processes in Second-Language Learning

According to W. Bernard (1951), "learning a foreign language consists fundamentally in the acquisition of an additional *set of symbols* for old familiar meanings." Just as the child learns to read by establishing equivalence between new written symbols and familiar (already meaningful) spoken symbols, and by reconstructing written into spoken messages, so we learn a new language by establishing equivalence between new foreign language symbols (both spoken and written) and their already meaningful native-language counterparts, and by reconstructing the foreign language into native-language messages.

It is evident, therefore, that the second language learner is in a different psychological position from that of a native-language learner. In the first place, he has already mastered the basic vocabulary and the syntactical code of one language. Secondly, he is generally able to read this latter language. Lastly, he is capable of comprehending and applying formally stated syntactical propositions. Thus ". . . the learner . . . approaches the second language with the mechanism of a first language already fixed in his thought and speech, and he is by no means expected to discard or even neglect his native language" (W. Bernard, 1951).

Critique of the Audiolingual Approach

In this section we discuss certain features of the audiolingual approach which, in the light of the postulated processes in learning a second language, seem incompatible with effective language learning by adolescents and adults.[2]

Avoidance of the Native Language The audiolingual method seeks in all possible ways to avoid the mediating role of the native language in second-language learning. It attempts to accomplish this objective through the rote learning of phrases and through the inductive learning of syntatic rules, through direct association of second-language words and phrases with objects, pictures, and situations rather than with native-language words; by giving second-language instruction in the target language itself; and by proscribing translation practice.

Actually, it is both unrealistic and inefficient for the learner to try to circumvent the mediating role of his native language when learning a second language. In the first place, after early childhood, even the . . .

> . . . greater part of our own language is learned . . . not by the direct method, i.e., not by the direct association of words and things, but *indirectly* through old, known symbols, e.g., by way of synonyms, antonyms, definition, or context in speech or reading matter. . . . Hence it is clear that . . . the direct association of . . . [new] symbols with their respective objects is, of necessity, totally inadequate for the learning of a new language. . . . Indeed . . . even where the possibility is offered for a direct association between the new symbol and the object, the old symbols at first always involuntarily intervene (W. Bernard, 1951, pp. 91–92).

---

[2]For a more complete discussion of these issues the reader should consult Ausubel (1968).

In addition, it is important to recognize that we learn the new syntactic code by using native-language syntax as a model and then noting similarities and differences between the two codes. This type of analysis is also best conducted in the native language. Thus numerous aspects of first-language knowledge—the meanings of most concepts, the understanding of syntactical categories and functions, facility in using many structural patterns that are nearly identical in two languages—are directly transferable to second-language learning. It would, therefore, be impracticable as well as impossible not to make use of this knowledge in acquiring the second language.

Rote Learning of Phrases The audiolingual approach unwarrantedly tends to assume that second-language learning, both in children and adults, is largely a process of rote verbal learning. Both in "pattern practice" drills and memorized dialogue practice,[3] there is either no awareness of phrase meaning whatsoever, or at the very best, awareness of *total* phrase meaning. Thus the learner understands neither the syntactic functions of the component words nor the denotative and syntactical contributions of the *individual* words to the total meaning of the phrase. A purely arbitrary (rote) rather than lawful or meaningful relationship prevails between phrase meaning and component elements of the phrase.

However, the principal transferable objective which truly *meaningful* pattern practice should aim to achieve is precise knowledge of the syntactical function of each word and of its semantic contribution to total phrase meaning. When the learner manifests this knowledge, it is possible for him (1) to construct a structurally comparable phrase expressing an entirely different idea, in which each component word bears a syntactical relationship to total phrase meaning that is analogous to the set of relationships prevailing between component words and total phrase meaning in the learned model phrase; and (2) to recombine familiar words and known syntactic functions in the learning of new grammatical patterns.

The remedy, therefore, is not to eliminate pattern practice drills but to make them more meaningful. Second-language learning obviously requires overlearning of the basic and characteristic structural patterns of the language. But unless the learner appreciates the precise relationship between the verbal manipulations he practices and the changes in meaning that he induces by such manipulation, the practice is not very transferable.

Inductive Learning of Grammatical Rules Pattern practice drills seek to duplicate in second-language learning the process whereby children attain

---

[3] Pattern practice drills consist of practice in repeating phrases illustrating a particular grammatical construction, and in making simple substitutions and transformations in such phrases that further exemplify the same construction with only slight changes in meaning. In memorized dialogue practice, students rotely learn and practice the phrases they use in carrying out a conversation.

syntactical mastery of their native language. What is primarily striven for is a functional, intuitive grasp of syntax after inducing much manipulative experience with the major structural patterns of the language. Grammatical generalizations are provided, if at all, only after the principles in question are acquired on an inductive, intuitive basis and are rendered virtually automatic.

This type of discovery learning, however, is exceedingly wasteful and unnecessary when we deal with older learners who are perfectly capable of comprehending abstract syntactic propositions. It takes a long time to discover grammatical rules autonomously and inductively; and until the correct discovery is made, practice is not transferable. Furthermore, as long as these rules are known only intuitively and implicitly, their transferability to comparable situations is restricted to what is analogically quite similar and obvious.

Deductive use of grammatical generalizations, on the other hand, is decidedly more efficient in second-language learning. No time is wasted in discovery, and both the generalization and the experience of applying it to appropriate exemplars are transferable from the very beginning of practice. As a precisely, explicitly, and abstractly stated proposition, a grammatical generalization also has wider transferability to new situations.

Prior Presentation of Materials in Spoken Form   A cardinal principle of the audiolingual approach is that instructional materials should be presented in their spoken form before they are presented in their written form, and that listening and speaking skills should be acquired before reading and writing skills.

The major rationale offered for this order of skill acquisition is that it is the "natural" order in which children learn their native language. But because a child *has* to learn how to speak and understand his native tongue before he can read it, it does not necessarily follow that *once he knows how to read,* he has to observe the same sequence of events in learning a second language. Once any new skill such as reading is learned, it can obviously be used as a tool in acquiring new knowledge. It is *un*natural to expect that after an individual becomes literate, he will learn in the same way as when he was illiterate.

Cogent reasons can also be advanced for presenting written and spoken materials in the second language both alternately and concomitantly. Perhaps the most obvious is that, in our culture, adolescents and adults are habituated to learning most new ideas and subject-matter content by reading rather than by listening. Thus a pure audiolingual approach deprives the older learner of his principal learning tool and of the instructional medium in which he feels most comfortable and confident. This is particularly unfortunate during the early phases of instruction, when learning stresses tend to be greatest.

"Natural Speed Rendition" of the Spoken Language In the audio-lingual approach, beginners are typically exposed to the "natural speed rendition" of the spoken language—presumably to accustom them to the "natural rhythm" of the language. It is pointed out that children eventually learn to understand their native tongue under comparable circumstances. In terms of gain per unit of learning time, however, it should be self-evident that practice in listening improves oral comprehension ability primarily insofar as what is heard is also understood. Thus, if the sample of speech to which the learner listens is too rapid for him to understand, it does little to enhance his ability to comprehend the spoken language. Furthermore, even if he is able to understand the material in a general way, he may still not be able to distinguish the major structural patterns well enough to transfer them to speaking and other listening situations.

Since learning to comprehend the spoken language is a very gradual process, it should undoubtedly be assisted in the beginning by means of a slower rate of speech that is progressively accelerated as oral comprehension improves. Artificial simplification is always justifiable during the early stages of any learning process. When any given passage of material is presented to the beginner, he can, of course, be exposed first to a slowed-down version and then to a normal speed rendition.

THE LEARNING OF ARITHMETIC AND ALGEBRA

Although the theoretical concepts developed in this book deal explicitly with the learning of verbally expressed symbols, concepts, and propositions, it will be clear from the examples provided that mathematics learning can be adequately accounted for within this general framework. In fact, the learning of mathematics is sometimes regarded as the acquisition of a special formalized language, lying within the native language of the learner. It is true, however, that mathematics learning differs in certain respects from other kinds of learning, which depend more heavily upon purely verbal formulations. In the first place, mathematics—at least in its early stages—deals with concepts whose meanings can be adequately conveyed by very explicit and simplified images. For example, the images corresponding to the meaning of the concepts "line" and "triangle" are very explicit compared to whatever images might exist for concepts like "beauty" and "democracy." Another feature of mathematics learning is that its "operational" terms (for example, add and subtract) again have explicit images, although in this case these dynamic (or kinesthetic) images are derived from the child's experience in manipulating objects (or in observing others, for example, the teacher, manipulating them).

Both of these distinguishing features of mathematics would, at first sight, suggest that it should perhaps be the most easily comprehended of all the subject matters with which the school deals. It is well known, however, that many students do not comprehend mathematics, and that there is in fact a widespread fear among children and adults, sometimes referred to as "number anxiety," concerning their inability to cope with its subject matter. One reason for the evident lack of comprehension can be found in a third characteristic of mathematics learning: more than any other discipline studied in the school, mathematics requires that the learner understand long, sequentially related, and hierarchically organized systems of propositions. Failure to comprehend any step in this sequence invariably means that the student will find comprehension from that point onward impossible, and that he virtually will be reduced to rote learning, with its inevitably disastrous results. Further discussion of these characteristics of mathematics learning is contained in the sections which follow.

Number Learning

It seems clear that children progress through a series of stages in their learning of number concepts. At a very early age, and well before the time children enter school, parents teach the child to recite a few number names. At this stage the child does not associate these verbal labels with any particular collection of objects, and the process involved in their acquisition is essentially one of rote learning.

At a later stage, the child begins to count collections of objects, such as his fingers. In this process the child learns to attach a verbal symbol to a particular position in a sequence; thus the first finger in the sequence is called "one," the second "two," and so on. In the early stages this process probably involves a form of sequential representation learning (naming), in which the child learns that each finger is to have its own name. However as soon as the attachment of one symbol to one object is made, the child begins to observe that "three" is not only the label for a particular finger, but that it describes a position in a series of objects (that is, third from the beginning Figure 4.2). As the child begins to count other sets of objects he gradually abstracts the notion of a "third" object in a series, this being the object lying between the "second" and "fourth" objects. This more generalized notion (referred to as the *ordinal* property of the number "three") has the characteristics of a concept, whose meaning is the representative image the child has of a third element in a series. This image undoubtedly involves an awareness of movement, from the first position in a representative series, through the second, and on to the third.

Another important concept which the child must develop, and which probably emerges at the same time as ordinal concepts, is that of the *cardinal* property of number. As a result of experience with sets containing three elements, the child—as in the normal process of concept formation—

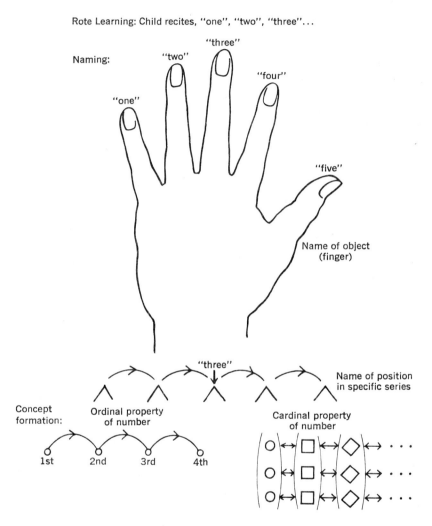

Rote Learning: Child recites, "one", "two", "three"...

Naming:

"three"

"two"

"four"

"one"

"five"

Name of object
(finger)

"three"

Name of position
in specific series

Concept
formation:

Ordinal property
of number

Cardinal property
of number

1st   2nd   3rd   4th

FIGURE 4.2 *Stages in number learning.*

abstracts the criterial attribute of these sets (its "threeness" or cardinal number), and this criterial attribute is embedded in a representative image which constitutes the psychological meaning of the symbol "three." When the concept of number has reached full maturity, the child will realize that all sets which can be represented by the cardinal number "three" can be put into one-to-one correspondence and, moreover, that this correspondence is maintained even when the elements of one of the sets is physically translated (moved) so that the perceptual basis for the one-to-one correspondence disappears (Figure 4.3). According to Piaget, this ability (described as the ability to "conserve number") is a relatively late development, typically appearing in most children approximately at the age of six or seven years (See also Chapter 7). When the child reaches this stage he is apparently able to visualize the inverse translation, that is, the translation which would carry his directly perceived image of the elements of the second set back to their original position, a position in which the one-to-one correspondence was perceptually obvious.

Number Operations

It would seem that the child comes to understand the meaning of the "operational" terms in arithmetic (add, subtract, multiply, and divide)

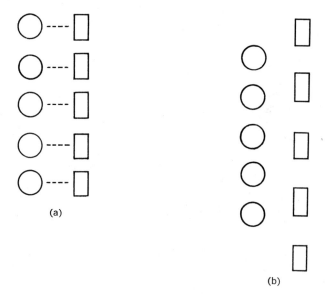

FIGURE 4.3   *Piaget "conservation of number" task. (A) Step 1: Circles and squares are set out in obvious 1:1 correspondence. When asked, "Are there more circles or more squares?," the child replies, "They are the same." (B) Step 2: Experimenter now separates the squares. When asked, "Are there more circles or more squares?," the nonconserving child typically replies, "There are more squares."*

through a process similar to that of acquiring the meaning of action words represented by the verbs in ordinary verbal propositions (non-noun names). In other words, the verbal symbol "add" is used by the teacher when the child is observing, or actually performing, the process of physically adding elements to a set. Through a number of experiences of this kind, the symbol "add" acquires a meaning which is represented by a representative (kinesthetic) image of the adding process. In other words, we might say that the child acquires the meaning of the symbol "add" through a process of concept formation (see Chapter 3). The meaning of the other operations can likewise be learned through generalization from concrete operations performed upon a set of objects.

There is a considerable emphasis in present-day arithmetic instruction upon providing children with the opportunity to manipulate concrete objects. Thus arithmetic teachers use such devices as sets of counters, number lines, and sets of sticks (for example, the Cuisenaire rods) produced by many commercial companies. This reliance upon an early exposure to concrete manipulative experience certainly seems consistent with the inductive process of concept formation in general and the need to develop kinesthetic images as the basis of the comprehension[1] of arithmetical ideas in particular.

Arithmetical Symbols

When the child begins formal instruction in arithmetic, the auditory symbols (spoken words) employed to that point are replaced by the more convenient arithmetical symbols (for example, "3," "+," and others). Of course, learning the meaning of the concept name "3" is merely a form of representational learning, in which the mathematical symbol is paired with its spoken equivalent and is equated in meaning to the latter. Similarly the symbol "+" is given the meaning of the spoken symbols "add" or "plus."

Number Combinations

The learning of number combinations (sometimes called the number "facts") is one of the first formal tasks attempted by the school and actually extends over quite a portion of the primary grades. Learning, for example, that "2 + 3 = 5" is a form of propositional learning (If 3 is added to 2 the

---

[1]While there is widespread agreement on the desirability of providing the child with concrete manipulative experiences in the *early* stages of mathematics learning, the field is not without controversy. Two current issues are: (a) the extent to which the teacher should rely on an individual "package" or set of manipulative materials (for example, the Cuisenaire rods) as opposed to providing a *variety* of materials (see: Nelson 1964; chap. 10), and (b) the point at which *systematic* use of concrete models can be abandoned in favor of the *incidental* use of models for illustrating the criterial attributes of concepts and relationships (see Chapter 7).

result is 5). In line with our earlier discussion of propositional learning, the child comprehends (apprehends the meaning of) this proposition because he is able to combine the images representing the meaning of the elements ("3," "2," and so on) to obtain a composite image which, having in the process been related to his cognitive structure, now constitutes the meaning of the proposition as a whole. Typically, the image constituting the propositional meaning may take one or both of the forms shown in Figure 4.4, or any of the possible representations (embodiments) of these basic forms. In the early stages, (prior to the time that the child has acquired stable meanings for the component terms of the proposition and is able to combine them meaningfully to form a representative image) such arithmetical propositions may have to be enacted with sets of concrete objects if they are to be understood. However, with practice and increasing age, the child will acquire the ability to comprehend the meaning of such statements by performing the operations mentally.

In the learning of number combinations the child is not only required to comprehend a proposition such as "3 + 2 = 5," but *overlearn* it to the extent that he can instantaneously provide the sum ("5") when the numbers to be added are given.[5] Consequently a very large amount of practice is required before the child will have acquired the number facility necessary if these arithmetical propositions are to be used for computational purposes. Such "drill" should not be regarded as rote learning, but rather as the overlearning

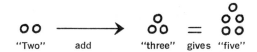

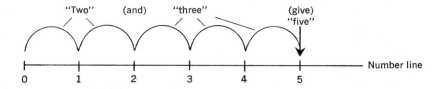

FIGURE 4.4   *Number combinations.*

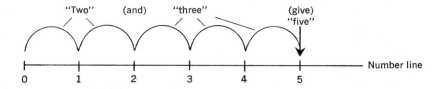

[5]It might also be said, on the basis of an earlier discussion, that with repeated appearance, the meaning of the proposition "3 + 2 = 5" is perceived directly by the child, without the necessity of intervening cognitive processes. Also in line with our earlier discussion, with overlearning and increasing maturity the specific dependence upon concrete images undoubtedly declines. In particular, it is a matter of theoretical debate whether an arithmetical proposition (for example, "5 + 4 = 9") elicits any well-defined image in an adult using it routinely for computational purposes.

of propositions which are already meaningful to the learner. In undertaking such practice the learner is in a somewhat similar position to the actor who is memorizing lines, the meaning of which he has already apprehended.

Simple "Problem Solving"

It is virtually universal experience that the child who has learned the number combinations still has difficulty with such "problems" as the following: "If a certain number is added to 6 the result is 10. What is the number?" Since we are assuming that the child can already comprehend the proposition "6 + 4 = 10" (that is, can mentally perform the operation to yield the composite propositional image), how do we explain his difficulty? To begin with, when the child first encounters this type of question, he will have difficulty understanding the *problem-setting proposition;* he will not realize that he is to translate the given statements into the incomplete proposition which can be written symbolically as follows:

$$6 + [\quad\quad] = 10$$

where some unknown quantity is to be placed in the box [ ]. In other words, there is a comprehension (or translation) difficulty here which goes beyond the prior comprehension of number combinations. Once the child is able to recast the problem-setting proposition, he can be taught a simple rule ("start by putting the number "1" in the box and work up through 2, 3, and so on until the correct combination is found") which would generate the sequence of propositions required to solve the "problem."[6] Later, when the child encounters simple algebra he will learn a formal process for solving this "equation."

---

[6]The word "problem" has been put in quotation marks throughout to acknowledge some doubt about the proper designation of the processes involved. For the young child, when first introduced to this activity, the situation presents both the need for discovery and a "gap" between the learner's existing knowledge and the solution, and so might properly be said to involve problem solving as we have defined this process earlier. However, once the simple rule for filling the box is taught, the solution requires merely a straightforward application of an existing proposition (algorithm), and would perhaps be better labeled as "comprehension" or "application."

It is likely that the difficulties encountered in many such "problems" could be counteracted in advance if the child were taught the inverse relationship holding between the operations of addition and subtraction and between multiplication and division (Avital, 1967). Thus from the outset the child would learn that "6 + 2 = 8" implies that "8 − 2 = 6" and that "8 − 6 = 2," multiple relationships which are easily demonstrated in either of the concrete representations shown in Figure 4.4. Similarly the child would be taught from the outset that "5 × 4 = 20" implies that "20 ÷ 4 = 5" and that "20 ÷ 5 = 4."

The Learning of Algebraic Symbols and Syntax

The learning of algebraic symbolism and syntax poses the same problems to a child as learning a second language. Initially algebra, like the second language, is understood by translating it back into the "native tongue" (in the case of algebra the native tongue is arithmetic). Moreover in attempting to understand the syntactical relations in algebra, the learner initially makes use of his existing knowledge of the syntax of arithmetic; thus the fact that $X + Y$ means that Y is to be added to X can be understood by the student by translating the algebraic statement into a particular arithmetic statement (for example, $2 + 3$).[7] Finally, as in second-language learning, with experience the student of algebra no longer depends upon the mediational role of the native tongue but can directly perceive the meaning of the algebraic statement. The major difference between the learning of algebraic symbolism and the learning of a second language is that the symbols in algebra are generic rather than particular, so they do not bear a $1:1$ relationship with the corresponding symbols in arithmetic. Consequently, in the "translation" process an algebraic symbol (such as X) can be translated into a whole class of arithmetical symbols (for example, the natural numbers).

Acquisition of Algebraic Skills

We can acquire some notion of the dependence of mathematics learning on the understanding of long-integrated sequences of propositions by analyzing how a learner comes to understand the procedure for obtaining the solution of the equation $2X + 3 = 11$. A number of preliminary propositions must be understood before the learner is able to comprehend the solution typically offered. In the first place, he must know the meaning of such concepts as "$2X$" and "equation." Second, he must understand the proposition that "if equal amounts are added to, or subtracted from, each side of an equation the equality remains (even though the numerical value of each side changes)." Finally, he must understand the related proposition that "if both sides of an equation are multiplied or divided by the same amount the equality remains." Each of these notions can be meaningfully learned (appropriate propositional images developed) in a variety of ways, as, for example, by induction from concrete experience with a physical balance. Once the learner has acquired these meanings (and assuming that he has already learned the symbolism and syntax of algebra), he is then capable of comprehending the process of solution which proceeds as follows:

---

[7] At this point $x + y$ has also acquired more general meaning as a superordinate concept abstracted from a large number of its specific exemplars.

$$2X + 3 = 11$$
$$(2X + 3) - 3 = 11 - 3$$
$$2X + 3 - 3 = 11 - 3$$
$$2X + (3 - 3) = 11 - 3$$
$$2X + 0 = 11 - 3$$
$$2X = 11 - 3$$
$$2X = 8$$
$$2X \div 2 = 8 \div 2$$
$$X = 8 \div 2$$
$$x = 4$$

Understanding the transition from line to line requires that the student recognize each stage in the transition as a particular instance of an already meaningfully learned proposition. For example, in progressing from the first line to the second line the student need only apprehend the meaning of the proposition "if 3 is subtracted from both sides of an equation, then the equality remains." This proposition is easily understood because it is a derivative of a more general proposition ("if equal amounts are subtracted from both sides and so on") which the learner already possesses in cognitive structure.

After the learner has had some experience with this kind of equation solving, the procedure may be simplified by the formulation of *rules* which will eliminate steps. One such rule would read: "Bring all the number terms to the right-hand side of the equation and change their signs if they cross the equals ($=$) sign." This rule condenses or coalesces a number of meaningful steps into a single step (in our example it allows one to proceed directly from the first to the sixth step). The meaning of the rule derives from the meaning of the sequence steps which it replaces. The composite image constituting the psychological meaning of the rule involves a transformation of the original equation (that is, moving the number items to the right-hand side and changing their signs) which is logically equivalent to the *product* of the individual transformations represented by the deleted steps.

The general proposition constituting the rule may be learned by induction from numerous specific instances (discovery learning), or—more likely—may be explained and exemplified by the teacher (reception learning). In either case, once it is meaningfully incorporated into cognitive structure it greatly simplifies the solution of simple equations. For example, the student may subsequently encounter the following solution to the given equation:

$$3X - 2 = 13$$
$$3X = 13 + 2$$
$$3X = 15$$

and so on.

He can now recognize the transition between the first and second lines as an instance of the general proposition embodied in the rule, already meaningfully learned. Thus he can be said to understand the abridged solution.

Problems in Mathematics Learning

We may now profitably return to our initial inquiry as to why mathematics learning has posed seemingly insurmountable obstacles for countless students and teachers. Despite the precision possible in the meaning of its initial concepts and action terms, mathematics stands at one end of a continuum defined by the *degree of sequentiality* found in the material to be studied. As shown in Figure 4.5, the comprehension of the "transposition" rule discussed in our example represents the culmination of a long sequence of prerequisite learnings which stretch back over a period of years. Failure to learn any of these prior tasks (indeed, most of them must be overlearned) means that the learner will find himself in the position of being unable to comprehend what follows in the sequence. The learner might survive for a while thereafter by pure rote learning, but he will become increasingly confused and unable to undertake even the most simple applications.[8]

The material of other school subjects possesses this quality of sequentialness to a lesser degree. At one extreme the learning of English–foreign language equivalents is markedly nonsequential, since failure to learn that "chien" means "dog" in no way impedes the subsequent learning that "porte" means "door." In history, an understanding of the early period of exploration and settling of North America would not be hampered by an ignorance of ancient Greece and Rome, but it would suffer from a lack of comprehension of developments in Europe at that time. In physics, an understanding of Newtonian mechanics is not prerequisite for understanding the phenomena of electromagnetic field theory, but it is prerequisite for an understanding of many branches of engineering.

---

[8]While a critical factor, the high degree of sequentiality is by no means the only difficulty inherent in the learning of this discipline. For example, some students (particularly slow learners) seem to have difficulty in distinguishing different concepts whose symbolic representations are perceptually similar (for example, "$2x$" and "x^2") and in recognizing the identity (in meaning) of two representations of the same concept which are perceptually dissimilar (for example, "$a/4$" "$a \div 4$", "$1/4a$"). Once recognized by the teacher, however, these problems should be readily overcome by careful instruction.

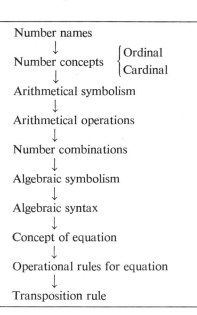

Number names
↓
Number concepts ⎰ Ordinal
⎱ Cardinal
↓
Arithmetical symbolism
↓
Arithmetical operations
↓
Number combinations
↓
Algebraic symbolism
↓
Algebraic syntax
↓
Concept of equation
↓
Operational rules for equation
↓
Transposition rule

FIGURE 4.5 *Sequence of tasks prequisite to meaningful learning of "transposition" rule.*

In one respect the school stands in a favorable position in mathematics learning, unlike its position in such areas as language learning. For in the first field the parent usually does not teach the child much beyond rote counting, and the school can readily build from the experiential base which the child has acquired from his normal experience with the physical environment. On the other hand, the parent's verbal interaction with the child is critical in the latter's acquisition of an intuitive understanding of syntax and general vocabulary, and the many children who come to school severely retarded in these respects will experience extreme difficulty in learning to read or even in comprehending the language of instruction. In view of mathematics' favored position, it seems all the more regrettable that we presently fail to develop the mathematical competencies of so many of our students.

In summary, mathematics learning illustrates clearly the possibilities for meaningful learning which inhere in school subjects and, conversely, the difficulties which must be overcome if the child is not to revert to rote learning. In particular, it makes clear the great care which must be taken to insure that the material to be learned is potentially meaningful to the child, and that in highly sequential material the new ideas must be sufficiently overlearned to provide a stable basis for further comprehension. Failure to appreciate the problems inherent in the meaningful learning of mathematics has no doubt contributed to extensive failure and feelings of frustration in that subject, and the widespread fear of mathematics which is all too apparent in the adult population.

THE ADEQUACY OF RECEPTION LEARNING IN SCHOOL SUBJECTS

We have described in the preceding section of this chapter the learning tasks which the child encounters in approaching four major areas of study in the school. It was understood throughout that the school's intent is to foster the highest degree of *meaningful* learning that is possible in any particular situation. It was also assumed that a large part of the child's time will be spent in *reception* learning or, conversely, that a large part of the teacher's time will be spent on *expository* teaching. In other words, it was assumed that where feasible it would be in the interests of economy to present new content to the learner in more or less final form; the latter's task, subsequently, will be to incorporate this material into his cognitive structure in order for it to be available for later reproduction, related learning, or problem solving.

In view of these assumptions, it seems necessary at this point to acknowledge that few pedagogic devices in our time have been repudiated more unequivocally by educational theorists than the method of expository instruction.[9] It is fashionable in many quarters to characterize reception learning as parrot-like repetition and rote memorization of isolated facts, and to dismiss it disdainfully as an archaic remnant of discredited educational tradition. In fact, quite apart from whatever intrinsic value they may possess, many educational innovations and movements of the past three decades— activity programs, project and discussion methods, various ways of maximizing nonverbal and manipulative experience in the classroom, emphasis on "self discovery" and on learning for and by problem solving—owe their origins and popularity to the widespread dissatisfaction with the techniques of expository instruction. It is frequently argued today, for example, that meaningful generalizations cannot be presented or "given" to the learner but can be understood only as a product of problem-solving activity (Brownell and Hendrickson, 1950), and that all attempts to master concepts and

---

[9]Typically, expository instruction is conducted through the medium of symbols which may be either words or the highly specialized symbols of mathematics and science. Again, these symbols may appear in spoken or written form. Nevertheless, taking the child's education as a whole, the most frequently encountered form of expository instruction involves spoken verbal symbols, and it is this particular form of expository instruction which has come under the heaviest criticism.

propositions are forms of empty verbalism unless the learner has recent prior experience with the realities to which these constructs refer (Brownell and Hendrickson, 1950; Brownell and Sims, 1946).

There are good reasons, of course, for some of the disenchantment with expository teaching and reception learning. The most obvious of these is that, notwithstanding repeated declarations of educators to the contrary, potentially meaningful subject matter is frequently presented to pupils in such a way that they can learn it only rotely. Another less obvious but equally important reason why meaning is perceived as an exclusive product of problem solving and discovery techniques of learning stems from two serious shortcomings of prevailing learning theory. In the first place, psychologists have tended to subsume many qualitatively different kinds of learning processes under a single explanatory model. As a result, widespread confusion exists concerning basic distinctions between reception and discovery learning and between rote and meaningful learning. It has not always been sufficiently clear, for example, that such categorically different types of learning as problem solving and the understanding of presented material have different objectives, and that conditions and instructional techniques facilitating one of these learning processes are not necessarily relevant or maximally effective for the other. Second, in the absence of an appropriate theory of meaningful learning, many educational psychologists have interpreted long-term subject-matter learning and forgetting in terms of the same concepts (for example, retroactive inhibition) used to explain laboratory forms of rote learning. It is hardly surprising therefore, that reception learning has been widely perceived as a rote phenomenon.

Is Reception Learning Meaningful?

How valid is the contention that abstract concepts and generalizations are forms of empty, meaningless verbalism unless the learner discovers them autonomously from his own concrete, empirical, problem-solving experience? Careful analysis of this proposition reveals that it rests on three logical fallacies: (1) the prevailing tendency to confuse the reception/discovery dimension of the learning process with the rote/meaningful dimension; (2) a straw-man representation of the method of reception learning; and (3) unwarranted generalization of the distinctive developmental conditions of learning and thinking during childhood to adolescence and adult life.

The first of these fallacies has already been considered in some detail. As to the second, the use of the straw-man technique was, of course, the simplest and most effective way of discrediting the method of verbal exposition. Instead of describing this pedagogic procedure in terms of its essential characteristics, it became fashionable to picture it in terms of its worst abuses. Examples of such abuses were naturally not very difficult to find, since an appreciable number of teachers still rely on rote verbal learning in teaching potentially meaningful subject matter. Some of the more flagrantly inept practices include premature use of purely verbal techniques with cognitively immature pupils; arbitrary presentation of unrelated facts without organizing or explanatory principles; failure to integrate new learning tasks with previously presented materials; and the use of evaluation procedures that merely measure ability to recognize discrete facts or to reproduce ideas in the same words or in the context originally encountered.

Although it is entirely proper to caution teachers against these frequent misuses of expository teaching, it is not legitimate to represent them as inherent in the method itself. An approach to instruction which, on logical and psychological grounds, appears appropriate and efficient should not be discarded as unworkable simply because, like all pedagogic techniques in the hands of unskilled teachers, it is subject to misuse. It would seem more reasonable to guard against the more common misapplications, and to evaluate the expository method against relevant theoretical principles and research findings that actually deal with the long-term learning and retention of large bodies of potentially meaningful, symbolically presented materials.

Some representatives of the Progressive Education Movement speak with disdain about the school's role of imparting knowledge, contrasting it with the allegedly more desirable role of helping children learn by themselves. They assert that the former role is a paltry one and that it invariably results in the learning of glib and meaningless verbalisms. This is not necessarily true, provided that the obvious abuses of expository instruction are avoided. Symbolic exposition is actually the most efficient way of teaching subject matter and leads to sounder and less trivial knowledge than when pupils serve as their own pedagogues. Thus the art and science of presenting ideas and information effectively—so that clear, stable and unambiguous meanings emerge and are retained over a long period of time as an organized body of knowledge—is really one of the principal functions of pedagogy. This is a demanding and inventive rather than a routine or mechanical task. The job of selecting, organizing, presenting and translating subject-matter content in a developmentally appropriate manner requires more than a rote listing of facts. If it is done properly it is the work of a master teacher, and it is not a task to be disdained.

Finally, it is important to appreciate that various developmental considerations limiting the meaningfulness of reception learning during childhood do not apply during adolescence and adult life. We have seen, for example, that the child acquires concepts through a gradual process in which the criterial attributes of the concept are abstracted from concrete exemplars. We have also seen that an understanding of propositions requires the ability to use the "transactional power of language." It is understandable therefore that in his learning the child must rely more heavily upon concrete experience than the adult. At the same time, however, there will be continual progress, as the learner matures, in his ability to learn new concepts and propositions without direct reference to concrete exemplars. The adult reader of this text will undoubtedly be able to understand the proposition that "a surface of genus one is a surface which has exactly one hole in it." He can do this without the aid of a concrete model because he is able to apprehend directly the meaning of the words in the definition and the syntactical relations between them, and from these is able to construct an image whose criterial attributes comprise the meaning of this defined concept.

In the later discussion of developmental growth in cognitive processes (Chapter 7), it is shown that children progress through a regular sequence of stages in their transition from dependence upon concrete material to the ability to apprehend the meaning of abstract propositions presented symbolically. The point which needs to be made here is that while the young child is manifestly dependent upon concrete experience in his learning, it does not follow (as is sometimes argued) that in the higher elementary-school grades the child can learn *only* by making his own discoveries with concrete materials. Certainly, as every elementary-school teacher knows, meaningful reception learning—without any problem-solving or discovery experience whatsoever—is perhaps the most common form of classroom learning, provided that the necessary concrete props are made available.

Moreover, beginning in the junior high-school period, students can acquire most new concepts and can learn most new propositions by *directly* grasping relationships between abstractions. To do so meaningfully, they need no longer depend upon current or recent concrete empirical props, and hence are able to bypass completely the limited type of understanding inherent in such dependence. In large measure this development reflects the availability of an adequate body of higher-order abstractions and transactional terms. Expository instruction therefore becomes much more feasible. Through reception learning, students can proceed directly to a level of abstract understanding that is qualitatively superior to the intuitive level in terms of generality, clarity, precision, and explicitness. At this stage of development, therefore, properly arranged reception of symbolic material is highly meaningful; and hence it is unnecessary to *routinely* introduce concrete props or time-consuming discovery techniques in order to make possible or to enhance *intuitive* understanding of abstract propositions.

This is the point at which some of the more zealous proponents of Progressive Education took a disastrously false turn. John Dewey had correctly recognized that the understanding of abstract concepts and principles in childhood must be built on a foundation of direct, concrete, empirical experience, and for this reason advocated the use of project and activity methods in the elementary school. But he also appreciated that once a firmly grounded foundation of abstract understanding was established, it is possible to organize secondary and higher education along more abstract and verbal lines. Unfortunately, however, perhaps because Dewey himself never elaborated or implemented this latter conception, some of his disciples took precisely the opposite position. They rashly generalized childhood limiting conditions, with respect to meaningful abstract-reception learning, broadly enough to encompass learning over the entire life span. And this unwarranted extrapolation, frequently but erroneously attributed to Dewey himself, provided an apparent rationale for, and thus helped perpetuate the seemingly indestructible myth that, under any and all circumstances, abstractions cannot possibly be meaningful unless preceded by direct, empirical, discovery experience.

Is Meaningful Reception Learning Passive?

The acquisition of meanings through meaningful reception learning is far from being a passive kind of cognitive process. Much activity is obviously involved, but not the kind of activity characterizing discovery. Activity and discovery are not synonymous in the realm of cognitive functioning. Merely because potential meanings are presented, we cannot assume that they are necessarily *acquired* and that all subsequent loss reflects forgetting. Before meanings can be retained they must first be acquired, and the process of acquisition is typically active. Neither can we assume that reception learning is necessarily more passive and mechanical than independent data-gathering and interpretation. The unmotivated student who gathers and interprets routine data need manifest no greater intellectual activity than the unmotivated student who receives expository instruction. The motivated student, on the other hand, reflectively considers, reworks, and integrates new material into his cognitive structure irrespective of how he obtains it.

Thus meaningful reception learning involves more than the simple cataloguing of ready-made concepts within existing cognitive structure. In the first place, at least an implicit judgment of relevance is usually required in deciding which established ideas in cognitive structure are most relatable to a new learning task. Second, some degree of reconciliation between new ideas and similar established ideas is often necessary to differentiate between them, particularly if there are discrepancies or conflicts. Third, new propositions are customarily reformulated to blend into a personal frame of reference consonant with the learner's experiential background, vocabulary, and structure of ideas. Lastly, if the learner, in the course of meaningful reception learning, cannot find an acceptable basis for reconciling apparently or genuinely contradictory ideas, he is sometimes motivated to attempt a degree of synthesis or reorganization of his existing knowledge under more inclusive and broadly explanatory principles. He may either seek such propositions in more recent or sophisticated expositions of a given topic or, under certain circumstances, may try to discover them himself.

All of this activity (except for the last-mentioned), however, stops short of actual discovery or problem solving. Since the substance of the learning task is essentially presented, the activity involved is limited to that required for effectively assimilating new meanings and integrating them into existing cognitive structure. This is naturally of a *qualitatively* different order than that involved in independently discovering solutions to new problems, that is, in autonomously reorganizing new information and existing ideas in cognitive structure in such a way as to satisfy the requirements of a given problem situation.

The extent to which meaningful reception learning is active depends in part on the learner's need for integrative meaning and on the vigorousness of his self-critical faculty. He may either attempt to integrate a new proposition with *all* of his existing relevant knowledge or remain content with establishing its relatedness to a single idea. Similarly, he may endeavor to translate the new proposition into terminology consistent with his own vocabulary and ideational background, or remain satisfied with incorporating it as presented. Finally, he may strive for the acquisition of precise and unambiguous meanings or be completely satisfied with vague, diffuse notions.

The main danger in meaningful reception learning is not so much that the learner will knowingly adopt a rote approach, but rather that he will delude himself into believing that he has *really* grasped precise intended meanings when he has grasped only a vague and confused set of empty verbalisms. It is not so much that he does not want to understand, but that he lacks the necessary self-critical ability and is unwilling to put forth the necessary active effort in struggling with the material, in looking at it from different angles, in reconciling and integrating it with related or contradictory knowledge, and in reformulating it from the standpoint of his own frame of reference. He finds it easy enough to manipulate words glibly so as to create a spurious impression of knowledgeability, and thereby to delude himself and others into thinking that he truly understands when he really does not.

A central task of pedagogy, therefore, is to develop ways of facilitating an active variety of reception learning characterized by an independent and critical approach to the understanding of subject matter. This involves, in part, the encouragement of motivations for and self-critical attitudes toward acquiring precise and integrated meanings, as well as the use of other techniques directed toward the same end. For example, precise and integrated understandings are, presumably, more likely to develop if the central unifying ideas of a discipline are learned before more peripheral concepts and information are introduced; if the limiting conditions of general developmental readiness are observed; if precise and accurate definition is stressed, and emphasis is placed on delineating similarities and differences between related concepts; and if learners are required to reformulate new propositions in their own words. All of these latter devices come under the heading of pedagogic techniques that promote an active type of meaningful reception learning. Teachers can help foster the related objective of assimilating subject matter critically by encouraging students to recognize and challenge the assumptions underlying new propositions, and to distinguish between facts and hypotheses and between warranted and unwarranted inferences. Much good use can also be made of Socratic questioning in exposing pseudo-understanding, in transmitting precise meanings, in reconciling contradictions, and in encouraging a critical attitude toward knowledge.

TOPICS FOR DISCUSSION AND FURTHER STUDY

1. In terms of the concepts employed in this book, outline the major cognitive learning tasks in a subject-matter area other than those treated in this chapter (for example, science, social studies, literature, or music).

2. In terms of the students with whom you will be dealing, what would you consider to be the chief objectives of second-language learning? For each of these objectives, discuss the relative merits of the audiolingual and traditional methods of instruction.

3. Select ideas which would be presented to students in your grade level and subject area, and determine the antecedent ideas upon which the understanding of each depends (that is, the relevant ideas in cognitive structure to which the new idea can be related). To what extent is sequential dependence in evidence in these examples? Is the degree of meaningfulness of the learning related to the degree of sequential dependence in a subject area?

4. It is suggested in this chapter that students may relate new ideas to one existing idea in cognitive structure or to numerous established ideas. Select ideas to be learned in different subject fields, and for each one indicate the range of relationships possible with existing ideas in cognitive structure.

5. A grade 6 teacher observes that a certain student suffers from "number anxiety" and suspects that the cause may be attributed to faulty previous learning. How would the teacher proceed to remedy the situation?

6. What advantages and disadvantages might be cited for the use of a variety of concrete exemplars in teaching number combinations rather than a single model? How does this bear upon the present controversy concerning the use of the Cuisenaire rods?

7.* What conclusion can be drawn from the present controversy concerning the possibility of interference with the acquisition of native language when the child is introduced to a second language at an early age? How should these conclusions influence the type of second-language program offered and the age at which children are subjected to second-language instruction? (References: C. Anderson, 1966b; T. Anderson, 1960; Dickinson, 1961; Gaarder, 1965; Penfield, 1964; Potts, 1967.)

8.* By examining current research evidence (Fry, 1967; Downing, 1967) ascertain the criteria on which i/t/a has performed well, and the criteria on which it has shown to poor advantage. Discuss the actual details used in a relatively successful and a relatively unsuccessful use of i/t/a.

9.* Review the evidence on the relative effectiveness of "phonetic" and "look-say" methods contained in Chall's (1967) analysis. Does clear evidence exist, in your opinion, favoring heavy concentration on one method, to the relative exclusion of the other, during the early stages of reading?

10.* It is traditional that beginning readers (and many educational-psychology textbooks) are studded with "explanatory" or "motivating" pictures. In view of the learning task involved, what contribution might be expected from such pictures? Under what circumstances might they be detrimental? (See Samuels, 1967.)

SUGGESTIONS FOR ADDITIONAL READING

Bernard, W. Psychological principles of language learning and the bilingual reading method. *Mod. Lang. J.,* 1951, *35,* 87–96.

Birkmaier, E., and D. Lange. Foreign language instruction. *Rev. educ. Res.,* 1967, *37,* (2), 186–199.

Brooks, N. Language learning: The new approach. *Phi Delta Kappan,* 1966, *47* (7).

Carnegie Corporation of New York. Learning to read: The great confusion. *Carnegie Quarterly.* 1967, *15*(3).

Carroll, J. B. Psychology: Research in foreign language teaching: The last five years. In *Language teaching: Broader contexts* (R. G. Mead, Jr., Ed.). Northeast Conference on the Teaching of Foreign Languages, Reports of the Working Committees. New York: The Conference, 1966, pp. 12–42.

Dickinson, E. Foreign languages in the elementary schools? *New York State Education,* 1961, *49,* 25–27.

Dienes, Z. P. The growth of mathematical concepts in children through experience, *Educ. Res.,* 1959, *2,* 9–28.

Downing, J. What's wrong with I/T/A? *Phi Delta Kappan,* 1967, *48*(6).

Fry, E., I/T/A: A look at the research data, *Education,* 1967, *87*(9), 549–553.

Kerfoot, J. F. Reading in the elementary school. *Rev. educ. Res.,* 1967, *37* (2), 120–133.

Pitman, I. J. Learning to read. *J. Royal Soc. Arts,* 1961, *109,* 149–180.

Venezky, R. L. Reading: Grapheme-phoneme relationship. *Education,* May 1967. *87* (9).

Williams, J. D. Teaching arithmetic by concrete analogy I. Miming Devices. *Educ. Res.,* 1961, *3* (2 & 3).

——— Teaching arithmetic by concrete analogy II. Structural Systems. *Educ. Res.,* 1962, *4*(3).

——— Teaching arithmetic by concrete analogy III. Issues and Arguments, *Educ. Res.,* 1963, *5*(2).

CHAPTER 5

RETENTION AND FORGETTING

In THE PRECEDING CHAPTERS WE HAVE CONSIDERED THE conditions which must prevail for meaningful learning to take place and have examined a series of meaningful learning tasks of increasing complexity. A problem still to be considered is the ubiquitous human phenomenon of forgetting, for one of man's most widely acknowledged shortcomings is his tendency to forget what he learns. Obviously this is a problem of particular importance in education, where we are attempting to establish a large part of the ideational framework upon which the student will build for the rest of his life.

Examples of the forgetting of subject matter learned in school are not hard to come by; the reader need only try to recall ideas with which he was once sufficiently familiar to pass examinations and solve related problems. If we consider chemistry, for instance, what remains of the detailed knowledge of this subject which we once firmly possessed? Perhaps we can still recall such general ideas as that the union of elements to form compounds is governed by the number of electrons in the outer ring of the elements. Similarly, we can probably remember that the volume of an ideal gas varies directly with its temperature and inversely with the pressure to which it is subjected. But at the same time we are likely to have forgotten (depending on how long ago we studied chemistry) the exact number of electrons possessed by a carbon atom, or the atomic weight of sodium.

Psychologists have long been intrigued by the phenomena of memory and forgetting, and have put forward many conflicting theories to account for them (Ausubel, 1968). Generally speaking, these theories have been rather pessimistic about the long-term possibilities for retention. But this pessimism, in our view, stems mainly from the fact that, the material to be remembered in the typical psychological experiment is learned in rote fashion. The important task for the educator is that of explaining the processes of retention and forgetting as they occur in the *organized bodies of knowledge* which the school transmits and which possess sufficient logical meaningfulness to be learned in a *meaningful* (rather than rote) fashion. The theory of retention advanced in this text is concerned specifically with the latter task.

Learning, Retention, and Forgetting

We begin this discussion by offering some preliminary definitions. In terms of the theory advanced to this point, *learning* refers to the process of acquiring meanings from the potential meanings presented in the learning material. Once these new meanings are acquired, they are, of course, available to the learner for subsequent additional learning or for recall and utilization at some later point. *Retention* refers to the process of maintaining the availability of the new meanings or some part of them. It seems sensible to suggest that the amount of the original meaning that will be retained at any given point in time is a variable quantity. Finally, *forgetting* represents a decrement in the availability of an acquired meaning. That is, it describes the loss in availability that occurs between the original establishment of the meaning and its later reproduction; again it seems reasonable to suggest that forgetting is not an all-or-none process but one that proceeds by stages.

THE ASSIMILATION HYPOTHESIS

We will now describe in detail what is postulated to happen when a new idea is learned by an individual, retained for a time, and subsequently forgotten. This process occurs in two principal stages: (1) initial acquisition and immediate post-learning, and (2) retention and forgetting.

The Initial Learning and Immediate Post-Learning Stage

As an illustration, let us reconsider the case in which the concept *parallelogram* is established in cognitive structure and in which a new idea (*rhombus*) is subsequently learned in a meaningful fashion. For simplicity we will refer to the established idea (parallelogram) as A^1, and to the concept to be

---

[1] *A*, an item of cognitive content, is a *meaning* in the sense in which that term has been used previously. Thus the term "idea," as used in this discussion, is synonymous with the word "meaning."

learned (rhombus) as *a*. You will recall that we have previously described how such learning takes place.[2] Briefly, the new concept *a* is related to the established idea *A*, and, as a result of their interaction, *a′*, the meaning of *a*, emerges. In the case in question, *a′* is the representative image of a rhombus, comprising the criterial attributes of that class of objects.

What has been said to this point is merely a recapitulation of previous discussions. However, to explain the phenomenon of forgetting, it is now necessary to extend these preliminary notions. In the first place, we must recognize that when *a* interacts with *A*, the latter idea (*A*) may itself be changed. In the example under discussion[3] it is not likely that the change in *A* would be large, since learning that a rhombus is a special form of parallelogram would not normally change the learner's representative image of a parallelogram. In some instances, however, the relation of a new concept a′ to the established idea *A* would change the criterial attributes (and therefore the representative image) of the latter. For example, the child might initially classify as "ball" objects which are not balls (for example, an egg-shaped object). When he is later presented with similar items which he thus classifies, but is immediately told that his classification is faulty, he would then modify the meaning which he attributes to the word "ball." For convenience we will say that *A* is always changed to *A′*, although we recognize that the amount of change may be virtually or actually zero in some cases.

A second addition to the previous theory is the assumption that both interactional products (*a′* and *A′*) *remain* in relationship to each other as linked co-members of a new composite ideational unit or ideational complex, *A′a′*. In other words, it is assumed that the fact that *a′* was derived from *A* means that these ideas (actually *A′* and *a′*) will remain closely linked in cognitive structure. In a more complete sense of the term, therefore, the actual "interactional product" of the meaningful process is not just the new meaning *a′*, but the entire new ideational complex *A′a′*.

Now even though *a′* and *A′* remain linked in the interactional product *A′a′*, it is a matter of common observation that both meanings are

---

[2] The definition of *a* (rhombus) is presented to the learner as follows: "A rhombus is a parallelogram in which all the sides are equal." The learner, utilizing his knowledge of the meaning of the individual words in the proposition, as well as the transactional function of the syntax of the sentence, transforms the meaning (image) of parallelogram to obtain a new meaning (image) for "rhombus."

[3] In considering the following section the reader should work through the steps in the example provided. Since our rhombus illustration deals with a very specific image, it may be useful to take an example in which images (if present at all) are much more vague and diffuse. For this purpose *A*, the anchoring idea, may be taken to represent the concept "disease" and *a* the concept "pellegra" (defined as: a clinical deficiency syndrome manifested in the skin, alimentary tract, and nervous system, and due to a deficiency of niacin, the administration of which reduces or entirely eliminates most of the symptoms.)

independently retrievable, at least immediately after learning has taken place. In other words, once a has acquired meaning, one can recall its meaning and utilize it for further cognitive operations. Consequently it is necessary to assume that immediately after learning has taken place, and indeed for some time thereafter, both a' and A' are *dissociable* from $A'a'$. Borrowing some symbolism (which seems to fit the case) from chemical theory, the dissociability of a' and A' from $A'a'$ is represented by the symbolic statement:

$$A'a' \rightleftarrows A' + a'$$

For purposes of clarification, these steps have been set out graphically in Stages I and II of Figure 5.1. In brief, what has happened to this point is that a has interacted with A and has acquired its meaning a, which is subsequently "anchored" to A' in the ideational complex $A'a'$. It is postulated that anchorage to a stable or established idea provides the possibility for a to be retained over long periods of time. In other words, a' shares vicariously, as it were, in the long-term retention of the idea to which it is linked.

We have pointed out that a' enjoys a degree of dissociability from $A'a'$, and it is convenient to refer to this degree of dissociation as the *dissociability strength* of a'. Clearly, the dissociability strength of a immediately after learning will depend upon such factors as the degree of relatedness of A and a', the stability and clarity of the anchoring item, and the degree to which the new ideas can be discriminated from the anchoring idea. For example, if the anchoring idea A is itself unclear, then the dissociability strength of a' could hardly be great. This would be equally true if a' represented a minor variation or modification of A, that is, if a' was barely discriminable from A, in which case representative images comprising the meanings of the two ideas would be virtually identical.

It should be pointed out further that the concept a (a rhombus) is related not only to A (parallelogram) but can also be related, perhaps to a lesser extent, to established ideas B (rectangle), C (quadrilateral), D (square) and so on (Figure 5.2). In other words, we have to envisage a number of ideational complexes involving a' and established ideas in cognitive structure and, correspondingly, that a would possess a number of dissociability strengths in relation to each of these ideational complexes. However, for purposes of simplifying the discussion we shall subsequently consider only the association of a' with A'.

Later Retention Phase

It is assumed that, during the retention phase, a' remains anchored to A' (Figure 5.1) and that this anchoring to a stable idea facilitates the retention

	New, Potentially Meaningful Idea	related to and assimilated by	Established Idea A in Cognitive Structure		Interactional Product
I	MEANINGFUL LEARNING OR ACQUISITION OF SUBORDINATE MEANING a'			$\longrightarrow$	$A'a'$
	a	related to and assimilated by			
II	POST-LEARNING AND EARLY RETENTION OF MEANING a'	New meaning a' is dissociable from $A'a'$	$A'a' \rightleftarrows A' + a'$ (high dissociability strength)		
III	LATER RETENTION OF MEANING a'	Gradual loss of dissociability of a' from $A'a'$	$A'a' \rightleftarrows A' + a'$ (low dissociability strength)		
IV	FORGETTING OF MEANING a'	a' is no longer effectively dissociable from $A'a'$	Dissociability of a' from $A'a'$ is below the threshold of availability: a' is reduced to A'		

FIGURE 5.1 *Stages in the learning and retention of a subordinate idea in relation to its dissociability strength.*

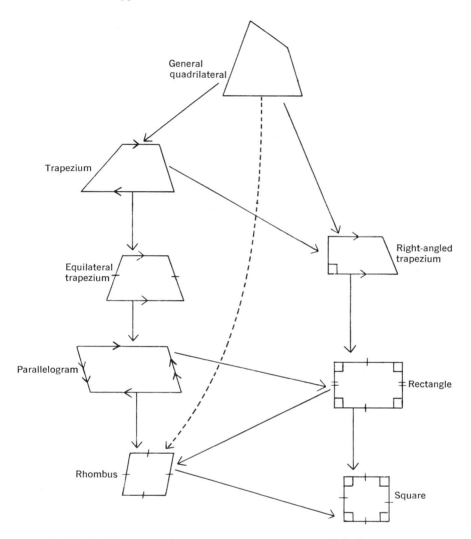

FIGURE 5.2 *A family of geometrical shapes to which the concept of rhombus might be anchored.*

of a'. Nevertheless, a' is still subject to the general "reductionist" trend in cognitive organization. In other words, because it is more economical and less burdensome merely to retain the more stable established anchoring concepts and propositions than to remember the new ideas that are related to them, the meaning of the new concept tends to be *assimilated* or *reduced* over the course of time to the more stable meanings of the established anchoring ideas. Immediately after learning is complete, when this second or *obliterative* stage of assimilation begins, new ideas become spontaneously and progressively less dissociable from their anchoring ideas, as entities in their own right, until they are no longer available and are said to be forgotten.[4] It should be noted that the same cognitive structure factors (for example, the relevance, stability, clarity, and discriminability of the anchoring ideas) determining the dissociability strength of the new meaning immediately after learning (initial interaction) also determine the rate at which dissociability is subsequently lost during retention (later interaction).

When the dissociability strength of a' falls below a certain critical level (called the *threshold of availability*), it is no longer effectively dissociable from $A'a'$ (that is, it is no longer retrievable). Actually, there are two critical levels, which depend upon the type of retrieval attempted. The highest of these levels would be associated with the *recall* of a'. When the dissociability strength falls below the threshold of availability for recall for a learner, he would not be able to recall the meaning of a', which would mean (in our example) that he would be unable to provide a definition describing the criterial attributes of a rhombus. In other words, the image of "rhombus" has been reduced to the point that it is no longer retrievable as a separate entity embodying the criterial attributes of this class of objects.[5] Even though the dissociability strength has fallen below this particular level, it may still be higher than the threshold of availability for *recognition*. In this case, the learner, although he could not provide a definition, could correctly pick out a rhombus from a number of geometrical figures which were somewhat similar to the rhombus.

If the dissociability strength falls even further so that it is now below the critical level for recognition, we cannot yet conclude that there is no residue in memory from the previous learning of a'. It might still happen that although the learner could not recall the meaning of, nor recognize, a rhombus, he might relearn its definition with considerably less effort than was required in the original learning. It is postulated that eventually a state of zero dissociability is reached in which $A'a'$ is further reduced to A' itself, the original anchoring idea (Figure 5.1). At this point no vestige remains of a prior acquisition of a' insofar as the learner's cognitive structure is concerned.

It is also necessary to assume that the threshold of availability is a

---

[4]Since, in our rhombus example, the meaning takes the form of a well-defined image, the *reduction* of a' to A' implies that a' (the representative image of a rhombus) is progressively transformed until it is indistinguishable from A' (the image of a representative parallelogram).

[5]At this point the learner might recall vaguely that a rhombus is related (somehow) to a parallelogram, but without being able to specify the nature of this relationship.

variable quantity. This assumption is necessary to explain transitory fluctuations in availability that can be attributed to general cognitive or motivational factors (for example, increased attention, anxiety, change of set or context, release of repression) without any change in dissociability strength (the intrinsic strength of the item in memory) itself. By the same token the notion of a variable threshold of availability explains why items of low dissociability strength that are ordinarily not available under typical conditions of consciousness become available under hypnosis (Rosenthal, 1944).

One factor that causes fluctuations in the threshold of availability warrants special mention. This is the phenomenon of "learning shock," a postulated type of resistance and general cognitive confusion which occurs when unfamiliar ideas are introduced into cognitive structure. It is assumed that learning shock is gradually dissipated as new ideas become more familiar and less threatening. In this conception, the initial resistance and confusion and their gradual dissipation are paralleled respectively by a corresponding initial elevation and subsequent lowering of the threshold of availability. This latter phenomenon is traditionally referred to as "reminiscence."

The term *assimilative process* is used to describe the events that occur between the formation of the ideational complex $A'a'$ and the complete obliteration of a'. In general it designates the tendency of a less general idea to become associated with a more general idea in cognitive structure and to be reduced in meaning to the latter through a gradual process of loss of dissociability. In this conception, forgetting constitutes a continuation or later temporal phase of the same process underlying the availability of newly learned ideas. Paradoxically, the same nonarbitrary relatability to a relevant established idea in cognitive structure that is necessary for the meaningful learning of a new idea, and leads to its enhanced retention through the anchoring of the emergent meaning to that of the established idea, provides the mechanism for most later forgetting.

Assimilation in Superordinate Learning

The previous discussion and Figure 5.1 applied to learning in which the new idea bears a subordinate relationship to the anchoring idea. We could invoke a similar explanation to account for the forgetting of ideas learned in a combinatorial manner. Here the less stable (and more specific) meaning of a combinatorial idea is incorporated within or reduced to the more stable (and more generalized) meanings of the wider, less specifically relevant body of ideas in cognitive structure to which it is related. Thus in our pendulum example the progressive deterioration in the dissociability strength of the meaning of the model would result in a decline in the retrievability of its meaning, until this meaning is assimilated entirely by a general background of knowledge about Newtonian mechanics.

We are left then to explain the forgetting of *superordinate* concepts and propositions which, by definition, are more generalized and inclusive from the very beginning than the established *subordinate* ideas in cognitive structure that assimilate them. Here the process of obliterative assimilation must obviously conform to a somewhat different paradigm, since in this case the more stable anchoring ideas in cognitive structure are less inclusive than the new superordinate meanings they assimilate.

We might consider as an example that a particular child knows the meanings of "corn," "peas," and "carrots" and subsequently learns the meaning of the more general concept "vegetable." In the beginning, while the new superordinate meaning is relatively unstable, it can be reduced to its less inclusive (subordinate) anchoring ideas during the process of obliterative assimilation. Later, however, if and when the new superordinate idea is overlearned, it would tend to become more stable than the subordinate ideas it originally assimilated, inasmuch as the stability of an idea in memory, everything else being equal, tends to increase with its level of generality and inclusiveness. Thus, at this point the direction of obliterative assimilation is reversed. The less inclusive, and now less stable, meanings of the earlier learned subordinate ideas tend to be incorporated in, or reduced to, the more generalized meaning of the later learned, and now more stable, meaning of the superordinate idea (see Figure 5.3). It will sometimes happen, as in our present example, that these subordinate ideas are themselves overlearned, and are therefore able to maintain a high degree of dissociability from the superordinate idea, and do not tend to be assimilated by it.

Summary

On the basis of the previous discussion, we can now summarize the factors influencing the retrievability of an idea from memory at any given point in time (Figure 5.4). The first factor is the *dissociability strength* at the time of retrieval, which is a function of the strength of the *initial anchorage* and the *time* which has elapsed since this anchorage took place. The first variable in this function (strength of initial anchorage) is itself dependent upon the stability and clarity of the anchoring idea, the kind of relationship it has to the new idea, and the discriminability of the new idea. The second factor influencing retrievability is the *threshold of availability*, which may be elevated by competition of alternative memories, negative attitudes, bias, or set not to remember (commonly called repression), change of context, high anxiety, and learning shock, and may be lowered by hypnosis or acute concentration. The third factor influencing retrieval is the *type of retrieval* required (recall or recognition).

		New Potentially Meaningful Idea A	related to and or assimilated by	Established Ideas a and α	$\longrightarrow$	Interactional Product $a'\ \alpha'\ A'$
I	MEANINGFUL LEARNING OR ACQUISITION OF SUPERORDINATE MEANING A'	A	related to and or assimilated by	a and α	$\longrightarrow$	$a'\ \alpha'\ A'$
II	POST-LEARNING AND EARLY RETENTION OF A'	New meaning A' is dissociable from $a'\ \alpha'\ A'$		$a'\ \alpha'\ A' \rightleftarrows a' + \alpha' + A'$		
III	FORGETTING OF A'	A' is no longer effectively dissociable from $a'\ \alpha'\ A'$		A' is reduced to $a' + \alpha'$		
IV	OVERLEARNING OF A'	a' and α'	subsumed under	More Stable and Established Idea A'	$\longrightarrow$	Interactional Product $A'\ a'\ \alpha'$
V	LATER RETENTION OF a' and α'	a' and α' are dissociable from $A'\ a'\ \alpha'$		$A'\ a'\ \alpha' \rightleftarrows A' + a' + \alpha'$		
VI	FORGETTING OF a' and α'	a' and α' are no longer effectively dissociable from $A'\ a'\ \alpha'$		a' and α' are reduced to A'		

FIGURE 5.3 *Stages in the learning and retention of a superordinate idea in relation to dissociability.*

Retrievability of Idea at Any Time → depends upon →

Dissociability Strength + Level of Threshold of Availability + Type of Retrieval Required

Dissociability Strength

which is a function of
1. elapsed time, *and*
2. *strength of the initial anchorage,* which depends upon:
   (a) stability of anchoring idea
   (b) clarity of anchoring idea
   (c) type of relationship between new idea and established idea
   (d) discriminability of new idea from established idea

Level of Threshold of Availability
which can be raised by
1. competition with alternative memories
2. repression
3. learning shock

and can be lowered by
1. hypnosis
2. acute concentration

Type of Retrieval Required

Recall or Recognition

FIGURE 5.4 *Factors determining whether an idea can be retrieved at some given time.*

APPLICATION OF THE THEORY

The reader should recognize that notions like dissociability strength, interactional products, and ideational complexes are purely hypothetical constructs and do not purport to represent "real" or observable processes. In other words, the theory says in effect, "Let us suppose that some such postulated (but unobservable) mechanisms were in operation; what results would one expect to follow?" The reasonableness of the postulated mechanisms, and of the theory as a whole, can only be ascertained by determining their potency in explaining and predicting phenomena in the field. It is to this task that the present section is devoted.

Tendency toward Hierarchical Organization

We observed at the beginning of the chapter that we usually can recall only the more general ideas of a subject matter area studied some time ago. Obviously the progressive obliteration of less general ideas (their assimilation by more general ideas) explains this phenomenon quite adequately. According to the theory, the only ideas of low order of generality which remain in one's memory for a lengthy period of time are those which are overlearned or subsequently rehearsed or utilized.

Extending this idea, the assimilation hypothesis also helps explain how knowledge is organized in cognitive structure. New ideas are stored in linked relationship to relevant existing ideas in cognitive structure. And if it is also true that (1) one member of the linked pair is typically superordinate to the other and that (2) the superordinate member is the more stable of the pair, then it necessarily follows that the cumulative residue of what is learned, retained, and forgotten (the psychological structure of knowledge or cognitive structure as a whole) conforms to the organizational principle of progressive differentiation. In other words, if the principle of assimilation were actually operative in the storage of meaningful ideas, it could then be seen why an individual's representation of a particular subject matter discipline in his own mind exemplifies a hierarchically ordered pyramid in which the most inclusive and broadly explanatory ideas occupy a position at the apex of the pyramid, and subsume progressively less inclusive or more highly differentiated ideas, each linked to the next higher step in the hierarchy through assimilative bonds.

Superiority of Meaningful Learning and Retention

The theory and supporting illustrations presented so far have dealt with material relatively near the meaningful end of the meaningful/rote learning dimension. Of course, material can also be learned rotely, either because it is not potentially meaningful or because the learner does not manifest an appropriate set to learn it in a meaningful way. Whatever the reason, convincing arguments can be advanced which would lead one to expect that meaningfully learned material will be retained much longer than rotely learned material.

Meaningful learning is more efficient because of the advantages inherent in a substantive and nonarbitrary relatability of new ideas to relevant established ideas in cognitive structure. As a consequence, a greater quantity of material can be incorporated into cognitive structure in a given period of learning time and made more available immediately after learning (that is, more learning occurs in an equal period of time). Further, this same relatability to established ideas provides meaningfully learned material with anchorage that continues throughout the retention stage and helps to insure its longevity in memory. Rotely learned material, on the other hand, enjoys no such anchorage and is incorporated into cognitive structure only in the form of arbitrary associations that is, as discrete, self-contained entities organizationally isolated, for all practical purposes, from the learner's established ideational systems.

Much research testifies to the transitory retention of rotely learned materials. In fact, in one of the earliest and best-known studies of memory, Ebbinghaus (1913) found that memorized lists of nonsense syllables (CAC,

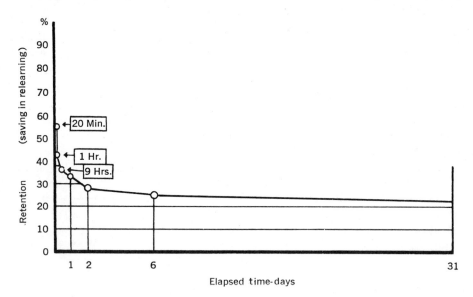

FIGURE 5.5 *Rate of retention for rotely learned material. From Ebbinghaus, 1913.*

FAU, and so on) were retained only for brief periods of time. The rapid loss of this material is shown in Figure 5.5, which exemplifies the typical rate of decline found in many experiments of this kind.[6] Where learning must be of rote fashion—and this is fortunately not characteristic of the tasks learned in school—the teacher's only recourse must be to over-learning, that is, to having the student rehearse the material beyond the point at which it can be accurately recalled. A study by Krueger (1929) indicates the enormous amount of overlearning that would be required if rotely learned material were to be retained for any period of time (Figure 5.6).

Several lines of evidence point to the conclusion that meaningful learning and retention are more effective than their rote counterparts. First, Jones and English (1926) and Briggs and Reed (1943) demonstrated that it is much easier to learn meaningfully and remember the substance of potentially meaningful material than it is to memorize the same connected material in rote, verbatim fashion. Second, Avital and others (1968) found that the use of cues to facilitate stable anchorage of potentially meaningful material, thus increasing its actual meaningfulness, led to superior retention

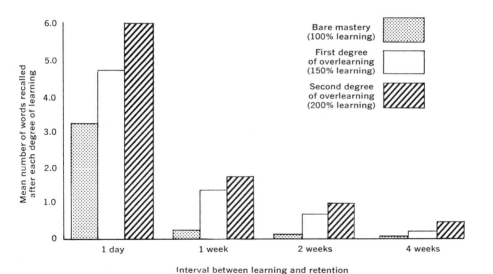

FIGURE 5.6 *Effects of overlearning on retention. From: W. C. F. Krueger, "The effect of over-learning on retention," J. exp. Psychol., 12, 1929, 71-78.*

---

[6]A sophisticated treatment of Ebbinghaus's data, as well as experiments on the rote learning of longer connected passages of prose, can be found in Alin (1964).

when initial learning time was controlled. Third, material that can be learned meaningfully, (poetry, prose, and observations of pictorial matter) is learned much more rapidly than arbitrary series of digits or nonsense syllables (Glaze, 1928; Lyon, 1914; H. B. Reed, 1938); moreover, an increase in the amount of material to be learned also adds relatively less time to meaningful learning than to rote learning tasks (Cofer, 1941; Lyon, 1914).

A fourth type of experimental evidence is derived from studies demonstrating that various problem-solving tasks (card tricks, matchstick problems) are retained longer and are more transferable when subjects learn underlying principles than when they rotely memorize solutions (Hilgard, and others, 1953; Katona, 1940). In one of Katona's studies, two groups of subjects were to learn the following series of numbers:

$$5\ 8\ 1\ 2\ 1\ 5\ 1\ 9\ 2\ 2\ 2\ 6$$

$$2\ 9\ 3\ 3\ 3\ 6\ 4\ 0\ 4\ 3\ 4\ 7$$

One group learned the numbers by rote, following the experimenter's suggestion that they group the numbers in sets of three (581, 215, and so on). The second group was encouraged to look for a *principle* underlying the sequence of numbers (the principle becomes obvious when the numbers are grouped 5, 8, 12, 15, and so on). A test of recall was administered soon after the experiment and repeated three weeks later. The results demonstrated that while the initial retention scores were similar, the group attempting to find the principle retained much more on the delayed test. Indeed, for those who actually discovered the principle (and thus had only to retain a meaningfully learned rule) there was little actual loss in the three-week interval.

Many classroom studies have obtained similar results. In general, they show that principles, generalizations, and applications of principles studied in such courses as biology, chemistry, geometry, and physics are remembered much better over periods of months—and even years—than are more factual items such as symbols, formulas, and terminology (Eikenberry, 1923; Frutchey, 1937; R. W. Tyler, 1930, 1934b; Ward and Davis, 1938). A second type of classroom evidence demonstrates that knowledge of number facts (addition, subtraction, multiplication, and division) learned with understanding is retained more effectively and is more transferable than when learned in mechanical, rote fashion (G. L. Anderson, 1949; Brownell and Moser, 1949; T. R. McConnell, 1934; E. J. Swenson, 1949; Thiele, 1938).

In Tyler's study (Tyler, 1934b), the superiority of retention of principles, as well as the ability to apply these principles to interpret new experiments was actually increased over a period of a year (Table 5.1), a result which can be explained by the general long-term retainability of meaningfully learned material coupled with the fact that these principles might have

TABLE 5.1

IMMEDIATE AND LONG-TERM RECALL
FOR MEANINGFULLY LEARNED MATERIAL

TYPE OF EXAMINATION EXERCISE	*Beginning of Course*	MEAN SCORES AT: *Time of Course Examinations*	*One Year Later*	PERCENT OF GAIN LOST ONE YEAR LATER
1. Naming animal structures pictured in diagrams	22.2	61.8	31.4	76.8
2. Identifying technical terms	19.7	83.1	66.5	26.2
3. Recalling information (a) Structures performing function in type forms	13.3	39.3	33.9	20.8
(b) Other facts	21.4	62.6	54.1	20.6
4. Applying principles to new situations	35.2	64.9	65.1	Gain 0.7
5. Interpreting new experiments	30.3	57.3	64.0	Gain 24.8
Average for all exercises in the examination	28.7	74.4	63.3	21.9

Source: R. W. Tyler, 1934b.

been recalled in other contexts in the interval. As usual, the factual material, which is capable of very limited and specific (derivative) anchorage, suffers considerable loss.

Retroactive and Proactive Inhibition

The chief cause of forgetting in meaningful learning is the progressive reduction of meanings to the meaning of their anchoring ideas. In rote learning, however, the retention of rotely learned material is explained on the basis of the continuation of the associations established at the time of their initial learning. Consequently, theories derived from experiments employing rote learning tend to explain forgetting in terms of factors which can disrupt the existing associations. Thus the so-called *interference theory* argues that forgetting occurs in paired associate learning tasks because the original response R_1 in the paired associate S-R_1 is replaced by a new

120 *Retention and Forgetting*

response, R_2; consequently, when this occurs, S_1 will evoke a response other than the one it originally elicited, and the original association is thus destroyed. Many experiments have been conducted to investigate the conditions under which this kind of "response substitution" occurs.[7]

In Chapter 1 we indicated that one of these experimental arrangements, designed to study the phenomenon of *retroactive inhibition*, exists when the student first learns material "A," then material "B," and is subsequently retested on his knowledge of material "A." If the loss of retention which occurs is larger than would be expected as a result of the mere passage of time (as determined from a control group), then retroactive inhibition is said to have occurred and is attributed to the effect of the interpolated material. In another arrangement *proactive* inhibition is studied by presenting material "B" prior to "A," and subsequently retesting on "A." Again, if the loss in retention on "A" is greater than that obtained in a control group not exposed to the prior material "B," proactive inhibition is said to have occurred and is attributed to the prior learning of "B." The experimental arrangements involved in both kinds of study are shown in Table 5.2.

Studies of retroactive inhibition employing rotely learned material have shown that the degree of inhibition is directly related to the amount and similarity (to the original material) of the learning activities interpolated during the interval between original learning and recall. When interpolated activity is reduced by such conditions as sleep (Jenkins and Dallenbach,

TABLE 5.2

EXPERIMENTAL MODELS
FOR RETROACTIVE AND PROACTIVE INHIBITION

	RETROACTIVE		PROACTIVE	
	Experimental Group	*Control Group*	*Experimental Group*	*Control Group*
First learning task	$S_1 - R_1$ (A)	$S_1 - R_1$ (A)	$S_2 - R_2$ (B)	Rest
Second learning task	$S_2 - R_2^*$ (B)	Rest	$S_1 - R_1$ (A)	$S_1 - R_1$ (A)
Recall task	$S_1 - R_1$ (A)	$S_1 - R_1$ (A)	$S_1 - R_1$ (A)	$S_1 - R_1$ (A)

*S_2 and R_2 may have varying degrees of similarity to S_1 and R_1 respectively. Similarly, B may possess varying degrees of similarity to A, short of complete identity.

[7]For a recent statement concerning the present situation in this field, see E. R. Hilgard and G. H. Bower, *Theories of Learning*. New York: Meredith Publishing Co., 1966.

1924; E. B. Newman, 1939; Van Ormer, 1932; Ekstrand, 1967), hypnosis (Nagge, 1935; Rosenthal, 1944), and anesthesia (Summerfield and Steinberg, 1957), retroactive interference decreases; and when the amount and similarity of interpolated activity increases, retroactive interference correspondingly increases (McGeoch, 1936; McGeoch and McGeoch, 1937; Melton and Irwin, 1940; Underwood, 1945).

Underwood (1957) reinterpreted the data from many such studies (Figure 5.7) and observed that most of the forgetting involved in laboratory studies of retroactive inhibition might better be attributed to proactive inhibition resulting from the subjects' previous involvement in similar studies. The trend reported in Figure 5.7 indicates again the generally high magnitude of the loss when the learner is exposed to successive lists of weakly anchored words. Within this general result, however, considerable variation in loss may be anticipated depending on the specific characteristics of the material to be learned (Underwood and Ekstrand, 1967).

The inapplicability of behavioristic principles of proactive and retroactive interference to meaningfully learned verbal materials becomes evident when we study retention after meaningful learning has occurred. As already

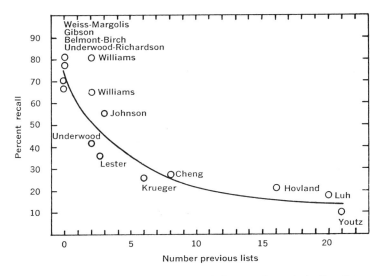

FIGURE 5.7 *Recall as a function of the number of similar lists previously learned by the subject. This curve was constructed by combining data from several different investigations, the authors of which are indicated by the names beside the circles. From: B. J. Underwood, "Interference and forgetting,"* Psych. Rev., 64, *1957, 53. Copyright 1957 by the American Psychological Association, and reproduced by permission.*

pointed out, it has been found that verbatim but not substance items are forgotten after a period of normal waking activity (E. B. Newman, 1939). Other experiments have shown that the explicit study of a long passage about Christianity, immediately before or after the learning of a comparable passage about Buddhism, does not significantly impair the immediate or delayed Buddhism retention scores of college students in comparison with those of matched control subjects not exposed to the Christianity material (Ausubel and Blake, 1958; Ausubel, Robbins, and Blake, 1957). Similar findings were obtained by Hall (1955) and Rao (1966) with meaningfully learned material. Moreover retroactive interference is generally found only when verbatim recall of the potentially meaningful material is demanded (Jenkins and Sparks 1940; King and Cofer, 1960; Slamecka, 1959, 1960, 1962).

The short-term interference of similar elements, so crucial in rote forgetting, becomes relatively insignificant when potentially meaningful materials are related to established anchoring concepts and progressively interact with them to the point of obliterative assimilation. Under these conditions the *discriminability* of the new material from the anchoring material, and the *clarity* and *stability* of the anchoring concepts, are the significant determining variables (Ausubel and Blake, 1958; Ausubel and Fitzgerald, 1961; Ausubel and Youssef, 1963) in the subsequent retention of the new material. The same studies also showed that retroactive learning of material with the same ideational import as the learning passage (but differing in specific content, sequence, and mode of presentation) not only has no inhibitory effect on retention, but is just as facilitating as repetition of the learning passage (Ausubel, Robbins, and Blake, 1957). Meaningfully (unlike rotely) learned materials obviously have a general substantive content that is transferable or independent of specific verbatim form and sequence.

TABLE 5.3

Effects of Interpolation and Overlearning
on Retention of Original Material

	ZEN BUDDHISM PASSAGE	
	Overlearned	*Not Overlearned*
Buddhism passage interpolated	M = 16.08 (N = 38)	M = 11.36 (N = 39)
Buddhism passage not interpolated	M = 14.55 (N = 42)	M = 9.89 (N = 37)

Source: D. P. Ausubel, Mary Stager, and A. J. Gaite, "Retroactive facilitation in meaningful verbal learning," *J. educ. Psych.*, 59, 1968, 250–255. Copyright by the American Psychological Association, and reproduced by permission.

A similar retroactive facilitation effect was found in a recent study (Ausubel, Stager, and Gaite, 1968) in which a passage on Buddhism was interpolated between the original learning of a Zen Buddhism passage and its later recall. The experimental design employed allowed the effects of over-learning of the original passage to be ascertained as well. The results (Table 5.3) indicated that both the interpolated material and the overlearning of the original material facilitated retention of the latter. In view of the importance of the possible inhibition effects for public education, and the pessimistic views resulting from an extrapolation of irrelevant research results, it is sobering to reflect on the authors' conclusions:

> These findings, if replicated and given greater generality, would have far-reaching implications for classroom teaching practice. Instead of suggesting (as do the classical retroactive interference findings in the case of rote learning and retention) that teachers scrupulously avoid introducing similar and conflicting material after a typical lesson involving meaningful learning, they imply that such material should be introduced deliberately. This recommendation would be based on the expectation that conflicting interpolated material would encourage the learner to compare related ideas in the original and interpolated sets of material, and thus facilitate retention of the original material through the influence of such intervening variables as rehearsal and clarification (p. 254).

In a recent attempt at replication, Gaite (1968) varied the time intervals between the Zen Buddhism and Buddhism passages and between the Buddhism passage and the recall test (both intervals varied from zero to two or three days' duration). Irrespective of the size of the interval, however, he found neither facilitation nor inhibition. Apparently, facilitation is far from a routine expectation, and one might hypothesize that whether or not it will occur would depend upon such factors as the degree of initial learning and the nature and degree of the relatedness of the passages in question.

Reminiscence

Reminiscence refers to an apparent increment in the retention of learned material over a period of several days without any intervening practice. Since retention cannot possibly exceed original learning under these conditions, this phenomenon probably reflects a spontaneous recovery from the threshold-raising effects of initial learning shock. It is postulated, in other words, that the confusion and resistance characteristic of learning shock causes a temporary rise in the threshold of availability. When learning shock subsequently dissipates, the threshold is correspondingly lowered.

This interpretation of reminiscence is strengthened by a number of lines of experimental investigation. In the first place, reminiscence occurs only when the material is partially learned or not overlearned and when practice trials are massed, that is, when an opportunity exists for immediate confusion and later clarification. Again, reminiscence has been convincingly demonstrated only in elementary-school children (Sharpe, 1952; Stevenson and Langford, 1957) and declines in older subjects (Sharpe, 1952; O. Williams, 1926). This is consistent with the notion that initial "learning shock" should decrease as cognitive structure becomes more stable and better organized with increasing age.

Discrepancy between Presented and Remembered Content

In addition to outright forgetting, it will frequently happen that the learner will be able to reproduce information presented to him, but that this information (as for example, a factual account of some occurrence) may suffer considerable distortion in the learner's later reproduction of it. Such discrepancies may be readily accounted for by the assimilation theory that has been proposed.[8] Thus during the learning phase, vague, diffuse, ambiguous, or erroneous meanings may emerge from the very beginning of the learning process because of the unavailability of relevant anchoring ideas in cognitive structure, because of the instability or unclarity of these anchoring ideas, or because of a lack of discriminability between the learning material and the anchoring idea. This unfavorable outcome is extremely likely if the learner's need for, and self-critical attitude about, acquiring adequate meaning is deficient.

Another source of discrepancy between presented and remembered content is attributable to this first phase and reflects the selective emphasis, omission, and distortion that takes place as a result of initial interpretation of the presented material. Since each individual possesses an idiosyncratic array of established and relevant anchoring ideas (which include personal biases) in his cognitive structure which assimilates new material, the resulting meanings in each case are a function both of the *particular* assimilations that occur and of the selective distortion, discounting, dismissal, and reversal of the intended meanings that are influenced by this particular set of biases.

During the retention phase itself, newly learned meanings tend to be reduced to the established ideas in cognitive structure that assimilate them. That is, they tend to become more similar in import to the anchoring ideas. Consequently, if a message was initially distorted by the learner's idiosyncratic cognitive structure, this distortion will be maintained or even strengthened during the obliterative assimilation phase.

---

[8]For a critical discussion of other explanations of this phenomenon, see Ausubel, 1968.

Finally, errors and distortions can occur when the stored meaning is retrieved and reformulated into a verbal statement. For example, available meanings may be altered in the process of being reconstructed in accordance with the requirements of the current reproductive situation (for instance, the tendency to exaggerate or dramatize certain incidents in the act of retelling a factual account of an occurrence). Again, it is conceivable that a momentary rise in the threshold of availability could inhibit the recall of ordinarily available meanings.

Leveling and Sharpening

The terms "leveling" and "sharpening" refer to two familiar phenomena of Gestalt psychology (Wulf, 1922; Allport and Postman, 1947). Both of these phenomena may be regarded as special instances of a discrepancy between material presented and the learner's reproduction of it (see previous section). In "leveling" a somewhat irregular form of an existing idea is reduced to a more familiar form of that idea; in "sharpening" some salient characteristic of the idea presented is accentuated (Figure 5.8).

In terms of the present theory, the process of leveling occurs when a new idea a, which is a specific derivative or illustration of A or a slightly asymmetrical or incomplete variant of (A), becomes a' after it is learned and is simply reduced to A' in the course of forgetting. Thus in the example illustrated, a slightly distorted circle would presumably be subsumed under the learner's representative image of a circle, and in the course of forgetting its meaning (image) would be reduced to that of the circle.

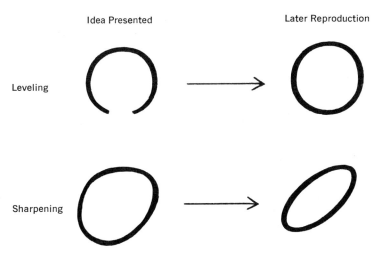

Idea Presented   Later Reproduction

Leveling

Sharpening

FIGURE 5.8 *Examples of leveling and sharpening.*

In the process of sharpening, a striking aspect of the new idea (*a*) becomes its criterial feature and is remembered in accentuated form because it is subsumed under and is eventually reduced to a pre-existing representation of this feature in cognitive structure. Thus in the example in Figure 5.8, the slightly distorted circle may be subsumed under the concept "oval" and eventually be reduced to this meaning in obliterative subsumption.

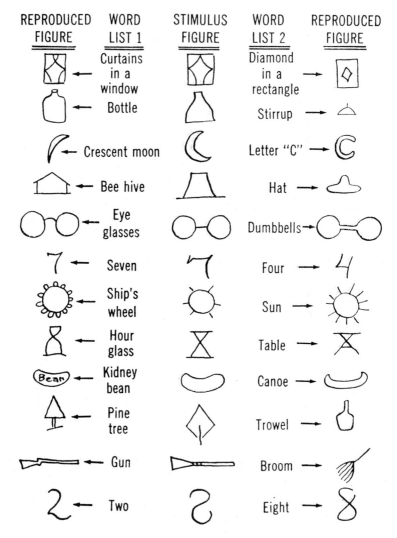

FIGURE 5.9 *Influence of words upon classification and recall of images. From: L. Carmichael, H. P. Hogan, and A. A. Walter, "An experimental study of the effect of language on perceived form," J. exp. Psychol., 15, 1932, 78-86.*

A somewhat more complicated form of leveling and sharpening occurs when the learner is presented with an *ambiguous* stimulus to which the experimenter arbitrarily attaches a name. In one well-known experiment by Carmichael and others (1932), two groups of subjects were presented with the same series of stimulus pictures, but each group was given a different word with each of the pictures. After viewing the stimulus pattern and reading the words, the subjects were asked to reproduce the pictures from memory. As shown in Figure 5.9, the changes in the reproduced figure indicate a kind of "sharpening" movement in the direction of the stimulus word provided. The explanation of this phenomenon is similar to that provided earlier for simpler cases of sharpening. To take the third item, for example, the learner who hears the words "crescent moon" for the ambiguous stimulus is encouraged, in effect, to subsume the stimulus under the concept defined by that term. On the other hand, the student who is provided with the phrase "letter 'C' " would subsume the stimulus under this concept. In both cases, the ambiguous meanings (images) presented are quite unstable and are rapidly reduced to the meaning of the subsuming concept.

This same effect can be observed when a vague stimulus is presented to the learner, who tends to categorize it by providing a verbal label himself. For example, the stimulus in Figure 5.10 might be subsumed by the learner under the concept "bird," and again be rapidly reduced in meaning to the subsuming idea.

THE EDUCATIONAL CONSEQUENCES OF FORGETTING

It is natural, of course, that the educator should be concerned with the forgetting of material taught in school and that he should do everything possible to counteract this tendency. It is not always appreciated,

Stimulus presented   Reproduced as

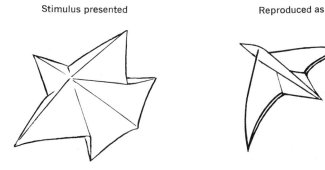

FIGURE 5.10 *Distortion in recollection of a vague stimulus.*

however, that forgetting has a positive as well as a negative side and that the actual loss which results from forgetting varies according to the kind of relationship which the forgotten material has with established ideas in cognitive structure.

On the positive side, the general reductionist trend in cognitive organization effects a kind of cognitive economy, since it is less burdensome to retain the more stable and established anchoring concepts and propositions than to remember all the new ideas that are assimilated in relationship to them. This process of reduction of the meaning of new ideas to the least common denominator capable of representing them (to their relevant established ideas) is very similar to the reduction process characterizing concept formation. A single abstract concept is more manipulable for cognitive processes than the dozen diverse instances from which its commonality is abstracted; and, similarly, stable established ideas in cognitive structure are also more functional for future learning and problem-solving operations when stripped of the less stable meanings they have assimilated.

The advantages of obliterative assimilation are gained, of course, at the expense of losing the differentiated body of detailed propositions and specific information that constitute the flesh, if not the skeleton, of any body of knowledge. However, in considering the loss incurred as a result of forgetting, it is necessary to distinguish between the two basic kinds of subsumption that occur in the course of meaningful learning and retention, that is, between derivative subsumption and correlative subsumption. Derivative subsumption, as we saw earlier, takes place when the learning material constitutes a specific example of an established concept in cognitive structure, or supports or illustrates a previously learned general proposition. In either case, the new material to be learned is directly derivable from an already established and more inclusive proposition in cognitive structure. Under these circumstances, the meaning of the derivative material emerges quickly and relatively effortlessly and, unless greatly overlearned, tends to undergo obliterative subsumption relatively rapidly. The reason for the rapid obliterative subsumption is simply that the meaning of the new material can very adequately be represented by the more general and inclusive meaning of the established subsumer, and that this latter process of representation in memory is more efficient and less burdensome than the actual retention of supporting or illustrative data. If such data are needed, they can sometimes be synthesized or reconstructed from specific elements of past and present experience. For example, in recounting a long past incident one ordinarily retains the ideational substance of the experience and from this reconstructs or invents plausible details that are consistent with its general import or setting.

More typically, however, new subject matter is learned by a process of correlative subsumption. Here the learning material is an extension, elaboration, modification, or qualification of previously learned propositions. It is incorporated by and interacts with relevant and more inclusive subsumers in cognitive structure, but its meaning is not implicit in and cannot be adequately represented by these latter subsumers. Nevertheless in the interests of economy in cognitive organization and of reducing the burden of memory, the same trend toward obliterative subsumption occurs. This trend is particularly evident if the subsumers are unstable, unclear, or insufficiently relevant, or if the learning material is lacking in discriminability or is not overlearned. But in this instance the consequences of obliterative subsumption are not as innocuous as in the case of derivative subsumption. When correlative propositions lose their identifiability and can no longer be dissociated from their subsumers, a genuine loss of knowledge occurs. The subsumers cannot adequately represent the meaning of the new correlative proposition, and hence the mere availability of the subsumers in memory does not make possible a reconstruction of the substance of the material forgotten. The same situation exists when new superordinate and combinatorial meanings are forgotten. The acquisition of knowledge, therefore, is largely a matter of counteracting the trend toward obliterative assimilation and retaining correlative, superordinate, and combinatorial learnings.

TOPICS FOR DISCUSSION AND FURTHER STUDY

1. Try to recall a subject matter area which you studied a number of years ago and make a diagram showing the relationship between the ideas you have retained. Does the cognitive structure remaining in this field exhibit properties of pyramidal organization? Is the tendency to forget specifics and remember general ideas in evidence?

2. Make a list of superordinate and subordinate ideas in the subject area in which you will be teaching. What means will be provided for retaining necessary factual (that is, low order) items?

3. In relation to an actual account of some real event, discuss the kinds of discrepancies that might occur between the facts as presented and the learner's reproduction of them. Relate these distortions to the assumed idiosyncratic nature of particular cognitive structures, the tendency toward obliterative assimilation, and distortions produced at the time of reproduction.

4. Cite instances of leveling and sharpening which may take place in school learning. What may the teacher do to prevent occurrence of this phenomenon?

5. Make a mental inventory of your recollections of the first chapter in this book. After checking your recollections against the original material, account for the loss of retention in terms of the concepts presented in this chapter.

6. What scheduling of subjects studied by the child in the course of the school day might lead to retroactive or proactive inhibition? What arrangement of subjects might provide retroactive or proactive facilitation? On the basis of these two con-

siderations, draw up a timetable, covering a school day, indicating the optimal placement of subjects to facilitate retention.

7. Consider some concept names that could be introduced to students at the grade level at which you will be teaching. For each new term, what ideas in the student's cognitive structure will be utilized for anchorage? What recollections of the idea would you expect the student to have at a number of points over the course of the year?

8. Under what circumstances might reminiscence take place in school learning? Cite examples.

9. A chief pedagogical implication of this chapter is that the teacher should insure that clear, stable anchoring ideas exist and that a new idea is adequately discriminated from the assumed anchor. Using specific examples, discuss how the teacher might determine whether these conditions prevail.

10.* Investigate alternate theories of memory (see Ausubel, 1968). In what areas, if any, would predictions based on these theories differ from predictions made on the basis of the theory indicated in this text?

11.* Study Krech's (1968) article on the chemical basis of memory. What long-range implications does this research hold for public education? What obstacles would exist in respect to utilizing these findings?

12.* Mehler (1963) has hypothesized that an individual retains the broad general sense of a sentence by incorporating (within cognitive structure) both its logical kernel and a "mental tag" indicating the particular transformation of this kernel (declarative, passive, interogative, and so forth) which it represents. How can this explanation be reconciled with the concepts offered in this chapter?

SUGGESTIONS FOR ADDITIONAL READING

Ausubel, D. P. *Educational psychology: A cognitive view.* New York: Holt, Rinehart and Winston, Inc., 1968, Chapter 3.

Bartlett, F. C. *Remembering.* Cambridge: Cambridge University Press, 1932.

Broadbent, D. E. The well ordered mind, *Amer. educ. Res. J.*, 1966, 3(4).

Katona, G. *Organizing and memorizing.* New York: Columbia University Press, 1940.

Krech, O. The chemistry of learning, *Sat. Rev.*, January 20, 1968.

PART THREE
COGNITIVE
VARIABLES
IN
LEARNING

In the previous chapters we have outlined a theoretical model for meaningful learning and retention. This theory takes as its starting point the existence of a cognitive structure which, for any particular school subject, comprises a hierarchically organized system of facts, concepts, and generalizations. In the first stage of the meaningful learning process a new idea is related in a nonarbitrary and substantive fashion to one or more of the existing ideas in cognitive structure, most commonly to an idea of higher generality. The new idea is not immediately assimilated by the old one but remains distinguishable from it, a measure of this distinguishability being the new idea's dissociability strength. Progressively the dissociability strength declines until it falls below the threshold of availability, at which point the idea can no longer be recalled.

This learning-retention model can now be extended and applied to a variety of standard classroom learning problems. First, we recognize that most integrated sets of ideas are not learned in a *single* presentation; thus the reader of this text will probably read individual sections more than once, each time adding to the completeness of his understanding of the material. Consistent with the theory, *practice* may be viewed as a sequence of repeated presentations of new material to cognitive structure, each presentation obeying the basic rules of meaningful learning, except that on each successive presentation more of the ideas in the material will have been incorporated into cognitive structure, so that they now facilitate the learning of the remaining ones. The question of how tasks are to be divided for efficient learning, how early practice sessions should begin after initial learning, the kind of practice (for example, overt, covert, rereading or recall) and "feedback" required for optimum practice schedules are discussed in Chapter 10.

A second extension examines the conditions under which the ideas presently existing in cognitive structure facilitate or *transfer to* the learning of new ideas. While transfer can occur between the learning acquired in school and tasks encountered outside school, or between one level in the taxonomy (for example, understanding of generalizations) and another (solving problems), the commonest form arises in a sequentially related series of learning tasks, for example: A,B,C,D,E, . . . where the learning of B depends in some way upon the learning of A (and C depends upon B, and so on). From the previous theory one can predict that a facilitating effect (positive transfer) from A to B would occur to the extent that A (coupled with already existing ideas in cognitive structure) provides relevant anchoring ideas for B. Consequently it would seem pedagogically sound to attempt to insure that there will invariably exist anchoring ideas in the student's cognitive structure for all substantial bodies of new learning; in Chapter 6 the proposal is made that each major new passage be preceded by a short statement called an "organizer" which either activates *existing* ideas in cognitive structure to serve as anchoring concepts, which introduces *new* high-level concepts for this purpose, or more commonly does both of these things.

The learning-retention-practice-transfer model describes an integrated sequence of events which can be identified in the learning of students from the preschool to the university level. Nevertheless it is clear that *qualitative differences* exist in the thinking processes (and therefore in the learning) of the child and the adult. For example, while we saw earlier that the acquisition of concepts by young children is tied closely to inductive generalization from *concrete experience,* common observation informs us that adults are capable of learning ideas which have no immediate reference to real objects at all. Chapter 7 takes up this question and argues that there are three qualitatively different stages in *cognitive development*—covering roughly the preschool (pre-operational), elementary-school (concrete operational) and adult (abstract) levels—each marked by a distinctive mode of utilizing concrete experience. In explaining these stages in terms of cognitive structure, it is suggested that the child acquires an increasing stock of abstract concepts, and that he becomes progressively better able to mentally manipulate these concepts without the aid of concrete props. The existence of stages would have implications for such important questions as when children can be effectively taught an idea at a particular level of abstractness (the question of *readiness*) and what degree of dependence on concrete props is appropriate to instruction at a given grade level.

The developmental stage theory (pre-operational, concrete operational, abstract) provides a label to attach to the child's existing *mode of cognitive operation,* a label which indicates the degree of his dependence on concrete props in learning new ideas. Another useful notion, particularly when making predictions as to how well children will do in particular streams or courses, is that of the child's *general level of cognitive ability,* or *mental age,* at a given point in time. Mental age is calculated by ascertaining the student's *present* ability to perform a variety of intellectual tasks and by then determining to what chronological age group his total performance score can be equated. Typically, the student's mental age is divided by his chronological age to yield an index of "relative brightness" or IQ. Although IQ and innate capacity are frequently confused, it should be kept in mind that intelligence (measured by the present ability to perform intellectual tasks) is a product of *both* innate capacity *and* relevant experience. Chapter 8 deals with such questions as the stability of IQ, its relation to achievement, and its various uses in the school setting.

Both developmental stage and relative brightness (IQ) describe dimensions on which the performance of children of the same chronological age may be located. Thus, taking any two children in a given classroom with a chronological age of 10, it might be found that the first has an IQ of 90 and the second an IQ of 120, and that the first is in the stage of "concrete" operations while the latter is in the stage of "formal" operations. Despite the fact that these children have the same chronological age, their modes of learning and their abilities to cope with intellectual problems are obviously so different that any single method of presentation could hardly maximize the learning of both. The problem of coping with such *individual differences* between children has long been of interest to educators, although mass instructional methods have prevented very much being done

133

about it. This situation has improved somewhat in the past few years with the increased emphasis on nongraded instruction, various "homogeneous" ability grouping plans, and self-instructional materials. Chapter 9 describes this problem in general and its specific application to culturally deprived children.

Although we have set out the topics in this section in a linear fashion, it is clear that they are highly interrelated. In general, since all the topics relate to the central principles of meaningful learning and retention we can expect a nucleus of ideas to reappear in different contexts. For example, when we speak of the transfer from A to B, we are simultaneously discussing the initial learning and retention of B, so that the factors involved in initial learning and retention (for example, existence, clarity, stability, and discriminability of anchoring ideas) may be expected to be influential in transfer as well. Again, one would expect that mental age and "stage of cognitive development" would be related, for in both cases a central criterion of growth is an increasing ability to handle abstractions.

All of these topics (with the exception of practice) are tied together in another way. Educational psychologists differ widely on several fundamental questions concerning the nature of man, one of the more important of these differences being the so-called "nature-nurture" controversy. One extreme position holds that man's abilities are entirely the product of his genic endowment; the opposite extreme view holds that man's abilities are essentially the product of experience. Although most contemporary educational psychologists take a middle position—that is, claim that "nature (genic endowment) sets limits within which "nurture" (experience) will produce individual differences—*how much* can be expected of nurture alone remains a matter of considerable controversy. This unresolved problem occurs in the discussion of transfer when it is asked whether certain intellectual competencies can be developed which will transfer to other learning situations. It is raised again when the question is posed as to whether the appearance of developmental stages can be "accelerated" (that is, made to occur earlier than they normally would) by special training. It is raised a third time when the influence of specific training on IQ is examined. Finally, it is raised (although in a somewhat indirect fashion) when it is asked whether the cognitive deficiencies of culturally deprived children can be overcome by early training. In all of these issues, the central question is not whether special training produces more than normal growth, but *how much* growth it will produce. Related to this problem is the assertion (made by some) that even if extraordinarily rapid intellectual development is possible, it is not always desirable or worth the time, effort, increased probability of failure, and disinvolvement from other worthwhile activities.

CHAPTER 6

•

TRANSFER OF LEARNING

IT IS AN ASSUMPTION OF THE SCHOOL THAT WHAT IS learned there will be used in other contexts when the student leaves to pursue his way of life. This assumption, inherent in the very nature of education, is perhaps more necessary today than ever before. We are constantly reminded that these are times of rapid change, that the future is uncertain, and that we do not know what occupations will exist twenty years from now or what skills and knowledge will be required for their successful performance. Consequently, we must believe that what we teach the student today will somehow enable him to perform more efficiently than he otherwise would in these changing conditions.

The educator's problem is not merely to have the student *retain* what he has learned, but to provide him with the knowledge and intellectual competencies which will allow him to cope with new learning situations. Here we come to the question of "transfer," one of the most ancient and important concerns of the educational theorist. Although well-defined positions on this matter date back to the ancient Greeks, many of the issues involved still provoke spirited debate.

Various Forms of Transfer

In general terms, the word *transfer* refers to the influence of learning in one situation or context upon subsequent learning in another situation or context. Thus we would be concerned with transfer when we studied the effect of learning in one school subject on later learning in another school subject, the effect of learning in school on performance outside school or, more generally, the effect of past learning on present learning.

136

The experimental paradigm for measuring transfer requires the conditions shown in Table 6.1. Since we are attempting to determine the degree of transfer between prior learning *B* and the subsequent learning of *A*, the experimental group would first learn *B* (the control group would not), both groups would then learn material *A*, and the measure of transfer would be the extent to which the learning of *A* has been facilitated for the experimental group. The reader should notice the similarity between the arrangements for proactive facilitation and transfer. Theoretically, a distinction can be made by observing that the test for transfer would require a measure of the *ease of learning A*. Practically, this would probably take the form of a test on the comprehension of *A* at the end of a set learning time (for example, 20 minutes) whereas the proactive facilitation paradigm calls for a test of the *retention* of *A* at some later point in time.[1]

What kinds of transfer are of interest to the educator? To clarify our thinking in this regard, suppose that a child has been taught the addition and

TABLE 6.1

EXPERIMENTAL PARADIGM FOR TRANSFER EFFECT
OF LEARNING *B* ON LATER LEARNING OF *A**

	EXPERIMENTAL GROUP	CONTROL GROUP
First occasion	*B*	
Second occasion	*A*	*A*

Criterial test (1) Speed of learning *A*, or
  (2) Immediate or delayed test of retention of *A* (See footnote 1).

*This is the simplest of several possible designs; for others, and comments on their respective merits, see H. E. Ellis (1965).

[1] One may sometimes make inferences about initial learning even though a "retention" test was used rather than a "rate of acquisition" test. For example, if on a retention test administered three weeks after the initial learning of *A,* the experimental group outperformed the control group, one might assume—under appropriately controlled conditions—that the initial learning had also been greater. Normally, however, a retention test (in the transfer paradigm) would provide evidence of the effect of prior learning *B* on the initial learning *and* subsequent retention of the new material *A*. Since much of the research reported in this chapter is of the latter kind, we are in these instances broadening somewhat the literal definition of transfer.

subtraction "facts" for integers. Certainly, if he can comprehend that $12 - 7 = 5$ in the context of blocks, beads, number lines, and other exemplars employed in the classroom, we would hope this understanding would transfer to other situations (for example, that if the child *at home* removed seven eggs from a carton containing a dozen, he would understand that there would be five eggs left). Such transfer, which involves performance at the *same* level as the initial learning,[2] but in a different context, is frequently called *lateral* transfer; it is the most common kind of transfer to occur when understandings and skills specifically taught in the school are employed by the child in learning situations not under the teacher's control.

While educators collectively must be concerned with the means for enhancing such transfer, a more central responsibility of the individual classroom teacher lies in a different direction. Most of the subject matter taught by the school is organized into broad disciplines, the content of which is taught sequentially. That is, an idea taught today will typically have some relationship to an idea taught tomorrow, and both ideas will have some relationship to the ideas taught the next day. In our arithmetic example, the understanding of addition facts is subsequently drawn upon when the teacher attempts to explain multiplication, and the student's knowledge of multiplication is drawn upon when the teacher attempts to explain division, and so on. In other words, in the typical classroom the teacher's concern with transfer must focus upon the influence of prior knowledge on new learning in a continuous sequential context. It would seem appropriate to refer to this positive facilitation of present learning through past learning as *sequential* transfer. Again, we are dealing with a kind of transfer in which learning at one level of behavior (comprehension of addition facts in our example) facilitates new learning at a comparable level of behavior (comprehension of multiplication facts).

Thus both *lateral* and *sequential* transfer (Figure 6.1) are essentially "horizontal" in that the learner stays within the same behavioral category in making the transfer. Another central concern of the teacher is that the comprehension of addition and subtraction facts should facilitate the subsequent solution of problems utilizing these operations. In this case, which we call *vertical* transfer, learning at one behavioral level (comprehension) facilitates learning at a higher behavioral level (problem solving). Obviously these distinctions are not foolproof, since instances can be found which cannot be placed exclusively in one category. The three primary distinctions nevertheless serve to facilitate classification and subsequent discussion.

---

[2]We refer to the same level of performance on the taxonomy of behavioral outcomes. In our example both performances would seem to be at the level of adequate comprehension.

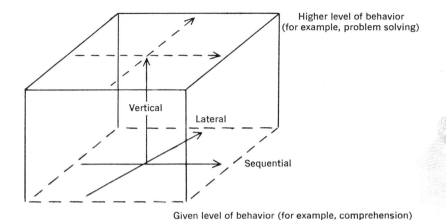

FIGURE 6.1 *Categorization of types of transfer.*

THE HISTORICAL BACKGROUND
OF TRANSFER THEORY

Since we have not dealt with alternative theories or viewpoints, it may seem strange that we now look briefly at theories which are not merely at variance with the one proposed here but which have actually been discredited. The reason for doing this is that notions about transfer are deeply imbedded in philosophical views of man, and some of these ancient ideas are still extant. It seems important therefore for the teacher, who will encounter these ideas in the professional attitudes and opinions of his colleagues, to recognize their origins, to have some knowledge of the experimental evidence which has been collected on them, and to know what present viewpoints exist on these basic matters.

Mental Discipline Theories

Until the early part of the twentieth century public education was dominated by a particular view of transfer known as the theory of "mental discipline."[3] Its basic premise was the notion that there existed a "mind substance" which, although unlike physical substances, was nevertheless trainable. There were, in fact, two forms of mental discipline theory. The first of these, called "classicism," can be traced to Plato and Aristotle, and, as it developed over the centuries, it was argued that the mind was best trained by studying the

---

[3]Also called the "theory of formal discipline." For a more detailed discussion see M. L. Bigge, (1964) chapter 2.

classical languages, philosophy, and other subjects which we would loosely lump together today as the "liberal arts." The second branch of mental discipline theory, termed "faculty psychology," originated with the philosopher Wolff, who, in 1734, enunciated a theory that mind was composed of "faculties" which were somewhat analogous to muscles, in that exercise tended to strengthen them. Given this viewpoint, the essential requirement of the educational program was to provide *hard intellectual work*. It was even advocated that the work should be distasteful as well, so that its enforced study would exercise the faculty of "will." The two forms of mental discipline theory came together in the 19th century when it was argued that the classical languages (Latin and Greek) and mathematics were the best subjects for training minds.

It is clear that the mental discipline theory, if true, would provide a rather neat solution to the problem of transfer. All that would be required would be that the various faculties be exercised, and thus strengthened; transfer would then be automatic. For example, if the faculty of reasoning could be strengthened through exercise, then reasoning in any field encountered thereafter would be facilitated.

Confrontation by Experimental Results   The hold of the mental discipline theory on the school was weakened by experiments conducted in North America and Europe shortly after the turn of the 20th century. Perhaps the most damaging research was that conducted by Thorndike (Thorndike, 1924; Broyler and others, 1927), who studied the gain on intelligence test scores made by students who had or had not studied the supposedly "disciplining" subjects. Contrary to the theory, Thorndike found that there was no greater gain in intelligence by students who had studied Latin and French than by students who had studied physical education. Moreover, he found that there was little overall gain in mental age for any group beyond that which would be expected on the basis of increasing chronological age.[4]

There were a number of immediate consequences of this research and of other investigations along similar lines. In the first place, since the classical languages were found not to have the disciplining value which was their purported main contribution, their study rapidly declined in public secondary schools in North America. A second consequence was that the mental discipline theory was to a large extent replaced by Thorndike's *theory of identical elements* which said, in brief, that if transfer is to take place the new

---

[4]Thorndike was, in effect, testing the validity of the "intellectual discipline" theory except that, instead of measuring the effect of the learning of classical languages on such "faculties" as memory and reasoning, he tested their effect on general intellectual capacity. Again, if such a strengthening of general intellectual capacity were possible then "massive transfer" would ensue, in that the child would tend to learn a great variety of things much more quickly.

learning situation must contain a predominance of elements (Thorndike thought in terms of *S-R* units) which are identical to those found in the original learning situation. For example, according to the theory of identical elements, oral spelling skills would transfer to the learning of written spelling since the grapheme-phoneme code which the subject must utilize in responding is common to the two kinds of responses.

The ensuing pessimism on the possibilities of producing the kind of massive transfer suggested by the mental discipline theory was largely responsible for the so-called "social utility movement" in public education. It was argued that if transfer is limited to the possibilities inherent in identical elements, then there is a need to make school learning as nearly identical to real-life situations as is possible. This thinking led to the practice of basing the arithmetic curriculum upon studies of the arithmetical skills required in various occupations, and of drawing up spelling and reading lists from frequency counts of adult usage of words.

Current Positions

The mental discipline controversy is informative in that it shows how research can change viewpoints and influence education. At the same time it shows how one extreme generalization (mental discipline) can be replaced by another (identical elements). As it turns out, the large amount of research conducted on the problem of transfer since Thorndike's early experiments has led to a much greater optimism about the possibilities of transfer than was expressed in his theory. While few people today believe that there exists a "faculty" of memory which, if strengthened by exercise, will automatically facilitate all subsequent memory tasks, yet there is a resurgence of belief in the possibility of massive transfer. As Bruner (1960, p. 6) puts it:

> . . . Virtually all of the evidence of the last two decades on the nature of learning and transfer has indicated that, while the original theory of formal discipline was poorly stated in terms of the training of faculties, it is indeed a fact that massive general transfer can be achieved by appropriate learning, even to the degree that learning properly under optimum conditions leads one to "learn how to learn."

What evidence is there to support the assertion that massive general transfer is possible? One might cite, first, evidence from studies of what would be called "culturally deprived" groups of children that it is possible to raise the general level of intellectual functioning of such children, thereby leading to massive transfer. For example, studies conducted among primitive West African cultures (Greenfield, 1966) have shown that there is a greater difference in intellectual functioning between children who have attended school and children who have not attended school in these cultures than between the children who have attended school and typical North American children of a comparable age. The implication is clearly that schooling, even of the most rudimentary sort, does have a massive transfer effect.[5]

Closer to home, many studies have been conducted concerning the effects of preschool programs (Operation Headstart and other "intervention" programs) intended primarily for culturally deprived children from slum areas. Typically, these studies report significant IQ gains (Reidford, 1968; Gray and Miller, 1967); and tentative findings from a program designed by Bereiter and Englemann (1966) shows average IQ gains of up to 25 points over a two-year period (Bereiter and Englemann, 1968; Rusk, 1967).

It is true that these results apply to children who have been deprived of the massive language stimulation of the typical middle-class environment and that our expectations for children typically found in our public schools—in respect, for example, to the raising of IQ—must be much more modest.[6] Nevertheless, optimism runs high at the present time that "typical children" can be provided with intellectual skills which, while not raising IQ appreciably, *do* allow them to learn more efficiently in a variety of situations. For example, one promising approach to the attainment of vertical transfer is found in a kind of task analysis, on the basis of which one provides the learner with a *strategy* for solving classes of problems in a given field. Another important contemporary approach, and a major emphasis of this chapter, concerns the increasing awareness of the possibility of enhancing transfer within the mainstream of subject-matter learning by utilizing principles of cognitive organization on the one hand, and the unifying principles of a subject-matter discipline on the other.

SEQUENTIAL TRANSFER
WITHIN SCHOOL SUBJECTS

We now return to the problem of transfer as it most frequently affects the teacher in his classroom. It was previously mentioned that the material within the major disciplines studied by the school is presented within a sequential context. While almost all subject matter areas share this characteristic of *sequential relatedness,* we must recognize that these same areas vary in the degree of *sequential dependence* of their material. At one end of the scale, mathematics learning exhibits such a high order of sequen-

---

[5]The point is sometimes made that the "schooling effect" could not be discerned in the Thorndike experiments because *all* the children in those experiments (high-school students) had already profited from it prior to the commencement of the study.

[6]On the other hand, research on the effects of infant stimulation suggests that even children from "normal" environments can experience exceptional mental growth—presumably with far-reaching permanent effects—if they are subjected to an enriched learning environment *from a very young age* (Fowler; 1962a, 1966). For a neurophysiological viewpoint, see Krech (1968).

tial dependence that unless the student masters each step in the development of the subject, further progress is impossible except on the basis of rote learning. On the other hand, the degree of sequential dependence in the field of history would seem to be considerably less. For example, it seems possible to comprehend ancient history (which comes typically in high school) without comprehending national history (which comes earlier in the sequence). However, closer analysis would reveal that even in this case some sequential dependence exists. For example, a knowledge of the early history of North America (involving primarily the explorers and initial settlements) might be necessary to fully understand the later history of this region.

Importance of Cognitive Structure Variables

It is obvious from the theory presented in previous chapters that the most important factor influencing the meaningful learning of any new idea is the state of the individual's existing cognitive structure at the time of learning. We have seen that if new material is to be learned meaningfully there must exist ideas in cognitive structure to which this material can be related; moreover the strength of the initial anchorage of a new idea depends upon such cognitive structure variables as the relevance of anchoring ideas in cognitive structure, the clarity and stability of these ideas, and the discriminability of the new idea. Thus, insofar as past learning influences present learning, it will do so through its effect upon the same variables that are crucial in providing the *initial anchorage* of any new idea. Consequently, the research evidence to be adduced here will tend to deal with the same cognitive structure variables that have been studied in meaningful retention, the difference being that we are now interested primarily in their influence upon the initial anchorage of *new* ideas rather than in their influence on the long-term retention of the *same* ideas.

It seems important to make another preliminary point. In the more general and long-term sense, cognitive structure variables refer to those aspects of the content and organization of the learner's *total* knowledge in a given subject-matter field at a given time that influence his future academic performance in the same area of knowledge. In a more specific and short-term sense, cognitive structure variables refer to those aspects of the content and organization of the *immediately relevant* concepts and propositions within cognitive structure that affect the learning and retention of relatively small units of related new subject matter.

Availability of Relevant Anchoring Ideas

As mentioned above, the existence of relevant anchoring ideas is the primary prerequisite for subsequent learning and, by definition, for sequential transfer. This claim is so self-evident that it is perhaps not necessary to adduce evidence to support it. Nevertheless such evidence exists in abundance in both long- and short-term studies.

Taking the long-term viewpoint, it is quite clear that the amount of knowledge which a student has at a particular time, as represented for example by grade averages, is highly related to his success in learning sequentially related material. Table 6.2 shows the correlation between high-school grade-point average and subsequent achievement in university. The fact that there is an *initially high* (though rapidly declining) relationship between the general level of knowledge at a given time (for example, grade 13) and the learning of sequentially related tasks (for example, content of courses in successive university years) is partly attributable to constancy of academic aptitude and motivation. However it is reasonable to attribute some of the relationship typically obtained between earlier and later educational attainment levels to the cumulative effect of cognitive structure variables (Garside, 1957; C. H. Swenson, 1957). Swenson, for example, reported that even when academic aptitude is held constant, students from the upper two-fifths of their graduating classes make significantly higher quality point averages in college courses than do students from the lower three-fifths.

TABLE 6.2

GRADE 9 AND GRADE 13 AVERAGES
AS PREDICTORS OF UNIVERSITY GRADES
(MEDIAN CORRELATION COEFFICIENTS)

CRITERION	PREDICTOR	
(*University Grades*)	*Grade 9 Average*	*Grade 13 Average**
First year average	.35†	.65
Second year average	.16	.49
Third year average	.14	.43
Fourth year average	.12	.37

*Grade 13 is the normal secondary school terminating grade for students proceeding to university in the Province of Ontario.
†Correlations are median values computed from product moment correlations from a large number of groups.
Source: Fleming, 1965, pp. 23, 27.

Use of Organizing Concepts or Rules

While the evidence cited above sheds some light on the importance of the availability of relevant anchoring items to subsequent learning, the relationship between these two classes of variables is not direct because the particular anchoring ideas are not identified nor is their strength manipulated in any way. However, there have been studies meeting one or both of the latter criteria. It has been found, for example, that verbal prefamiliarization with the content of films by means of a pretest (Stein, 1952) or by exposure to key words (Weiss and Fine, 1956) also facilitates learning and retention. Moreover, it has been found that concepts are more easily acquired if the specific instances from which they are abstracted are frequently (rather than rarely) associated with their defining (criterial) attributes, and if subjects have had more rather than less relevant information about the nature of these attributes (Underwood and Richardson, 1956).[7] Greenhouse (1967) found that even the temporal grouping of words in a list to be learned led to an increase in the total number of unrelated words recalled and to an increase in the number of categories of related words recalled. Reynolds (1966) found that advance perceptual organization of material by means of a map facilitated the learning of factual material related to the map.

Organizers   The examples cited above demonstrate the importance of what might be termed "organizing" (anchoring) concepts for the facilitation of learning. In this text, however, the term *organizer* is used to describe more complex and deliberately prepared sets of ideas which are presented to the learner in advance of the body of (meaningful) material to be learned, in order to insure that relevantly anchoring ideas will be available.

Generally speaking, advance organizers would be used by teachers when either of two circumstances prevails. In the first instance, *if specifically relevant ideas are not available* in cognitive structure when new, potentially meaningful material is presented to the learner, then the likely consequences would seem to be rote learning, or that tangential or less specifically relevant ideas would be pressed into service. If tangential ideas are used, the outcome would be either a form of combinatorial assimilation or less relevant correlative subsumption. In either case, less efficient anchorage of the new material to congitive structure would occur, giving rise to relatively unstable or ambiguous meaning with little longevity. In a second situation, appropriately or specifically relevant ideas *are* available, *but their relevance is not recognized by the learner.* In both instances it is preferable to introduce suitable organizers in the form of introductory materials at a high level of generality and inclusiveness, presented in advance of the learning material—whose relevance to the learning task is made explicit—to play an anchoring role, rather than to rely on the spontaneous availability or use of less appropriate anchoring ideas in cognitive structure.

Organizers may be of two kinds. If the new learning material (for

---

[7] For a detailed summary of research in this area, see Ausubel 1968; chap. 4.

example, the Darwinian theory of evolution) is entirely unfamiliar to the learner, an *expository* organizer would be used. Such an organizer would include whatever established and relevant knowledge currently exists in cognitive structure that would make Darwinian theory more plausible, cogent, or comprehensible. The organizer itself (a highly general and inclusive statement of Darwinian theory) would thus bear a combinatorial relation to cognitive structure, and its content would make explicit both its relatedness to general relevant knowledge already present in cognitive structure and its own relevance for the more detailed aspects of Darwinian theory. These latter detailed aspects (the learning task per se) would then be subsumed under the organizer (derivative and correlative subsumption). If the new learning material is *not* completely novel (for example, the later presentation of Lamarck's theory of evolution), a *comparative* organizer would be used. This organizer would point out explicitly in what ways the two theories are similar and different. Thus, whether already established anchoring ideas are nonspecifically or specifically relevant to the learning material, the organizer both makes this relevance more explicit and is itself explicitly related to the more differentiated content of the learning task.[8]

Although the number of research studies to date employing organizers is limited, evidence on their effectiveness is quite convincing. In an initial study by Ausubel (1960) an expository organizer was employed in advance of a learning passage on the properties of steel. This organizer emphasized similarities and differences between metals and alloys, their respective advantages and weaknesses, and the reasons for making alloys. Although the organizer provided relevant background ideas, it was known by prior testing that it did not by itself give any advantage on the final test measuring knowledge of steel. The control group studied historical material describing methods used in processing iron and steel. Although such material is typical of introductory passages in metallurgy textbooks, and presumably enhances the interest of the student, it contained no concepts which could serve as an ideational framework for the concepts shown in the steel passage. The results of the experiment are shown in Table 6.3. Although the experimental group outperformed the control group at a statistically significant level, it is believed that the discrepancy in their performances would have been even more pronounced if the subjects had not had some prior knowledge of steel, thus offsetting to some extent the potential advantage of the organizer.

---

[8]Several examples of the use of organizers can be found in this text and the accompanying student workbook (Robinson, 1969). Each major section of the book is preceded by a comparative organizer which attempts to show how ideas in that section are related to (or derived from) the basic conceptions of the meaningful learning process. Further comments on the nature and use of organizers can be found in a later section of this chapter and in Chapter 11.

TABLE 6.3

EFFECT OF EXPOSITORY ORGANIZER
ON LEARNING OF SUBSEQUENT PASSAGE

GROUP	TYPE OF INTRODUCTION	MEAN SCORE
Experimental	Expository organizer	16.7
Control	Historical introduction	14.1

Source: D. P. Ausubel, "The use of advance organizers in the learning and retention of meaningful verbal material," *J. educ. Psych., 51,* 1960, 267–272. Copyright 1960 by the American Psychological Association, and reproduced by permission.

In a later study Ausubel and Youssef (1963) employed two learning passages in sequence, the first on Buddhism and the second on Zen Buddhism. In this study comparative organizers were employed; the first (prior to the Buddhism passage) pointing out the principal similarities and differences between Christianity and Buddhism, the second (prior to the Zen Buddhism passage) making similar distinctions between Buddhism and Zen Buddhism. The control group studied historical and biographical material, prior to the learning of each passage, which related to that passage.

The effects on learning and retention scores are shown in Table 6.4. As predicted, the organizer produced a significant effect on the learning and retention of the Buddhism material; the result for Zen Buddhism, although in the predicted direction, was much smaller. It is believed that the latter result was caused by the fact that the Zen Buddhism material was learned while the Buddhism concepts (which acted as the relevant anchoring ideas) were still firmly fixed in the students' minds so that the potential advantage of the comparative organizer was partly offset.

TABLE 6.4

EFFECT OF COMPARATIVE ORGANIZERS
ON SUBSEQUENT LEARNING AND RETENTION

GROUP	MEAN BUDDHISM TEST SCORE	MEAN ZEN BUDDHISM TEST SCORE
Experimental	19.4	14.8
Control	17.6	14.2
Significance of difference	Significant	Not significant

Source: D. P. Ausubel and M. Youssef, "The role of discriminability in meaningful parallel learning," *J. educ. Psych., 54,* 1963, 331–336. Copyright 1963 by the American Psychological Association, and reproduced by permission.

Other research studies (Ausubel and Fitzgerald, 1961; Merrill and Stolurow, 1966; Newton and Hickey, 1965; Grotelueschen and Sjogren, 1968; Scandura and Wells, 1967) have obtained similar results. However, it has been found in some instances that the facilitating effect of purely expository organizers seems to be limited to learners who have *low verbal* (Ausubel and Fitzgerald, 1962) and *low analytic* (Schulz, 1966) ability and hence presumably less ability to develop an adequate scheme of their own for organizing new material in relation to existing cognitive structure. It should be noted, however, that when the learning task is particularly difficult, organizers may differentially benefit high ability students (Grotelueschen and Sjogren, 1968) and those with more background knowledge (Ausubel and Fitzgerald, 1962) by making it possible for them to learn material that would in any case be beyond the capacity of less able and less sophisticated students.

Organizers probably facilitate the incorporability and longevity of meaningfully learned material in three different ways. First, they explicitly draw upon and mobilize whatever relevant anchoring concepts are already established in the learner's cognitive structure and make them part of the subsuming entity. Thus, not only is the new material rendered more familiar and potentially meaningful, but the most relevant ideational antecedents in cognitive structure are also selected and utilized in an integrated fashion. Second, by making subsumption under specifically relevant propositions possible, organizers at an appropriate level of inclusiveness provide optimal anchorage (see Chapter 5). This promotes both initial learning and later resistance to obliterative subsumption. Third, the use of organizers renders unnecessary much of the rote memorization to which students often resort because they are required to learn the details of an unfamiliar discipline before having available a sufficient number of key anchoring ideas.

Discriminability, Clarity, and Stability

It seems clear that the *degree of discriminability* of new learning material from previously learned concepts in cognitive structure is a major factor in meaningful learning and retention. In the effort to simplify the task of apprehending the environment and representing it in cognitive structure, new learning material that resembles existing knowledge often tends to be interpreted as *identical* to the latter, despite the fact that objective identity does not exist. Existing knowledge, in other words, tends to pre-empt the cognitive field and to superimpose itself upon similar potential meanings.

Under these circumstances, the resulting meanings obviously cannot conform to the objective content of the new learning material. In other instances, the learner may realize that the new propositions differ somehow from established principles in cognitive structure, but yet be unable to specify where the difference lies. When this situation exists, ambiguous meanings emerge, permeated by doubt, confusion, and alternative or competing meanings. In either case, however, the newly learned meanings enjoy relatively little initial dissociability strength. In addition, if new meanings cannot be readily distinguished from established meanings, they can certainly be adequately represented by them for purposes of memory and must tend to lose their initial dissociability strength, or become reduced, more rapidly than initially discriminable meanings. This is especially true for long retention periods. Over short retention intervals, of course, nondiscriminable material can be retained on a purely rote basis.

The discriminability of a new learning task is in large measure a function of the *clarity* and *stability* of the existing ideas to which it is relatable in the learner's cognitive structure. Thus we would postulate that as clarity and stability increase so should discriminability and, therefore, learning and retention. Experimental evidence exists to support this assertion. For example, in an experiment by Ausubel and Fitzgerald (1961), subjects were tested on their knowledge of Christianity and then required to learn a Buddhism passage. Prior to this learning passage, one group of experimental subjects was subjected to a comparative organizer (which pointed out similarities and differences between Buddhism and Christianity), a second experimental group was exposed to an expository organizer (which merely presented Buddhism ideas at a high level of abstraction), and the control group studied an historical and biographical passage on Buddhism.

The most relevant result (Table 6.5) is that short- and long-term retention scores were related to the stability and clarity of the learner's knowledge of Christianity (which provided the anchoring ideas). Presumably relatively clear and stable notions of Christianity allowed a greater degree of discriminability of the sequentially *related* Buddhism passage.[9] In another experiment (Ausubel and Fitzgerald, 1962) it was also found that the degree of knowledge of antecedent learning material is positively related to the learning of sequentially *dependent* passages.

From these and other experiments we may summarize the conditions by which discriminability may be improved, either directly or by increasing the stability and clarity of the anchoring idea. To begin with, one might simply review or rehearse the anchoring idea itself, thereby increasing its stability and clarity. Again, one might use comparative organizers that explicitly delineate similarities and differences between the existing ideas and the new material to be learned. Third, one might follow the newly learned material with additional material which is potentially conflicting but which forces the

---

[9]It is also clear that the organizers had little effect when the subject already possessed suitable anchoring ideas; however when such ideas were lacking both the comparative and expository organizers (but particularly the former) led to greater learning and retention.

TABLE 6.5

EFFECT OF STABILITY AND CLARITY OF ANCHORING IDEAS
ON LEARNING AND RETENTION OF SUBSEQUENT PASSAGE

	KNOWLEDGE OF CHRISTIANITY	GROUP I *Comparative Organizer*	GROUP II *Expository Organizer*	CONTROL GROUP *Historical Passage*
Three-day retention scores	Above median	23.50*	22.50	23.42
	Below median	20.50	17.32	16.52
Ten-day retention scores	Above median	21.79	22.27	20.87
	Below median	19.21	17.02	14.40

*Mean scores: chance score is 9.0 on 45-item multiple choice tests.
Source: D. P. Ausubel and D. Fitzgerald, "The role of discriminability in meaningful verbal learning and retention," *J. educ. Psych., 52,* 1961, 266–274. Copyright 1961 by the American Psychological Association, and reproduced by permission.

learner to review the relationship between the anchoring ideas and the first-learned material. We saw earlier that this may lead to increased retention of the initial learning passage, presumably through increasing its clarity and stability. Finally, we may overlearn the material to be retained.

Subject-Matter Factors in Transfer

In what has preceded, we have been describing cognitive structure variables which are particularly crucial to transfer in the kind of sequential learning which takes place in the school. The general strategy proposed is to provide or activate high-level organizing ideas under which much more specific content can be subsumed. The degree to which the classroom teacher can do this will depend to some extent upon the actual subject-matter area itself. On the one hand, if the objectives of a course call for the absorption of a large amount of low-level factual material, the incentive to introduce high-order ideas and abstractions will be reduced. Fortunately, however, the emphasis in most of the modern curriculum reform movements is precisely to have the student become familiar with the central (organizing or higher-order) ideas of a discipline. In other words, present tendencies in curriculum reform will provide increasing opportunities for the teacher to utilize the high-level ideas of a subject-matter field as organizers for lower-level content. This important consideration is discussed in further detail in a later section.

LATERAL TRANSFER

The kind of transfer situation that we have been describing (involving sequential transfer) is certainly the one over which the educator has the most control. Nevertheless what the student does with the knowledge he has acquired in school when he encounters new situations to which this knowledge is potentially applicable is of concern to the individual teacher and to curriculum-builders collectively. What advice can be offered the teacher about means of facilitating such transfer, other than such self-evident platitudes as that he should "attempt to develop positive attitudes toward transfer"? As it turns out, some reliable advice is available, based both upon logical considerations and empirical evidence.

Teaching Transferable Skills

One obvious thing which schools can do is to train students in skills that readily transfer to new situations. Of course, the school already does this to some extent; thus, the student is taught to write paragraphs, to use proper grammatical constructions and correct spelling, and these skills should apply to the student's subsequent attempts to write prose after he leaves the classroom. Similarly, students are taught methods of obtaining information for themselves, such as consulting encyclopedias or dictionaries, and procedures for locating information in libraries.

At a somewhat higher level of skill, experiments have been conducted to determine the effects of teaching students methods of study. In one investigation (Di Michael, 1943) a group of ninth-grade pupils was given special instruction in study methods and their gains (relative to a control group which received no such instruction) were determined for each of the school subjects. Although there was an overall gain which could be attributed to the special help, the results were not clearcut, since neither very capable students nor students with low ability seemed to profit much from the special teaching. In another study (Salisbury, 1947) students were given training in methods of outlining and summarizing the material covered in the classroom. The results suggest that this training had a beneficial effect both upon study skills and the kinds of reasoning ability measured by the criterion tests administered to the subjects. In a study with college students, Myers and Gates (1966) found that special training in listening skills transferred to the academic setting, resulted in greater retention of information presented.

The Use of Real-Life Situations

The reader will recall that one of the principles of the "identical elements" theory of transfer was that school learning situations should be made as "life-like" as possible; a related idea is that students will benefit from learning in actual field settings. One study (Lorge and others, 1955) found some indications that learning is undertaken more rapidly in a "simulated field situation"—that is, employing a laboratory-housed model of the field problem—than in a comparable classroom setting. Given that the field experience was an infrequent one for the subjects in question, it is conceivable that the effect was due to a short-term enhancement of motivational factors.

Overing (1966, Experiment 2) conducted a more sophisticated study in which children were either trained under "realistic" conditions (in which a good deal of information and visual stimuli irrelevant to the problem were available) or under reduced conditions (where a large part of the irrelevant information was eliminated). The task in question had to do with shooting a target submerged under water (see section below). The real-life situation used targets similar in appearance to real objects (fish, and so forth) and did not attempt to screen out such irrelevant data as the size and shape of the pool or the general stimulation from the surroundings. In the reduced situation schematic targets were used, the students worked in a semi-darkened room, and the contours of the pool were masked, thus stripping the task setting of all extraneous data. One half of each training group was tested for transfer in a real-life setting and one half in a reduced setting.

It was found that students trained under realistic conditions were able to transfer their learning equally well to reduced and real-life settings; on the other hand, students trained under reduced conditions were less able to transfer their learning to real-life situations than to reduced situations. However, in a related experiment Overing (1966, Experiment 1) found that when the training in the reduced situation (in this case using instructional materials with extraneous information eliminated) was preceded by the verbal formulation of a relevant realistic problem, the subject was able to apply the information learned in the training session to the real-life problem as well as if he had been trained in a real-life situation. Apparently the advance problem generated a "set" which induced the student to "discriminate between relevant and irrelevant features of situations in which the principle learned is to be applied."

It would appear that any pedagogical implications to be drawn from such studies would be highly specific to the kind of principle for which transfer was being sought, and the context in which it naturally occurs. Certainly, on grounds of sheer practical utility it seems unthinkable that any sizable proportion of school learning could be undertaken in "real" field settings, although an occasional field experience might have motivational value. Simulated field settings may, however, be appropriate when they are not inordinately time-consuming. With respect to the principles that the school attempts to inculcate, there seems a danger that the complexity of the field situation would obscure central ideas which could be more clearly presented in simplified classroom presentations. Moreover, in the classroom presentation the teacher may select reduced tasks which will rapidly allow the principle to be consolidated, apparently a prerequisite to its successful use in other settings. The need for such consolidation does not, however, rule out the possibility of utilizing Overing's "orienting problem" approach.

Utilizing Subject-Matter Content as a Vehicle for Training Transferable Knowledge or Skills

Another method which the teacher can use to enhance lateral transfer is to use course material, in part, as a vehicle for transmitting transferable knowledge or developing transferable skills. For example, a number of studies have investigated the effect of studying Latin on the improvement of English vocabulary. While it is generally found that there is no *automatic* transfer (Douglass and Kittelson, 1935; Pond, 1938), other studies have shown that some transfer can be expected if the Latin course *emphasizes derivations* (Haskell, 1923).

In another subject area it has been found that the study of geometry in itself does not improve the quality of the student's reasoning in other areas (Clarke, 1943). On the other hand, Ulmer (1939) utilized the content of the geometry course to study principles of reflective thinking and thereby obtained a significant transfer of these skills to problems dissimilar to those studied in class. Other promising attempts to enhance critical thinking ability by utilizing the content of particular subject-matter areas as a training ground for generalized skills have been made by Abercrombie (1960), Suchman (1959, 1960), and B. O. Smith (1960). Abercrombie, for example, tried to improve medical students' ability to reason more effectively by providing them with opportunities for "therapeutic" group discussions in an unstructured, non-authoritarian atmosphere. She found a positive transfer of this training to the analysis of X-rays.

Suchman (1959, 1960, 1962) has been experimenting with what he calls "inquiry training," an attempt to teach general tactics of scientific inquiry to children who learn to apply them in question-and-answer investigations. In this approach children view a film exhibiting some scientific phenomenon. For example, they might be shown how a bimetallic bar alternately bends and straightens out when subjected to heat and then cooled. The children are then encouraged to ascertain the cause of the phenomenon by asking the teacher, who acts as a "responsive environment," a series of questions which can be answered by "yes" or "no." Preliminary findings (1959) indicate that although such training increases the number of valid questions asked in the test (criterion) situation, it does not significantly enhance the quality of the questions or facilitate grasp of concepts. Hence, more definitive evidence of the transfer value of such training to new situations is required, where the criteria of transfer are not only more independent of the particular training procedures used, but also reflect more accurately the ultimate purpose of such training, that is, greater knowledge of the content and/or the method of science.

Smith and Henderson developed instructional materials "designed to develop critical-thinking abilities and . . . helped the teachers learn how to handle these materials in the classroom . . . [they] found wide differences among teachers with respect to improvement of their students in critical thinking" (B. O. Smith, 1960), but refrained from drawing definitive conclusions because they had not as yet devised a technique for describing and measuring what teachers were *actually* doing in this situation. Their next step, therefore, was to devise a method of categorizing the logical operations involved in teaching. The great promise of this approach lies in the attempt to influence critical thinking through the simultaneous teaching of the logic of a *particular* subject-matter field along with its content, rather than on instruction in *general* principles of logic.

Stressing Underlying Principles and Generalizations

It has long been advocated that lateral transfer can be facilitated by teaching students *general principles* rather than *specific solutions,* knowledge, or skills. This position was formally stated by Judd, and was based in part on evidence from his classic experiment on learning to hit targets submerged under water (Judd, 1908). In Hendrickson and Schroeder's later (1941) modification of this study, the target was initially set at a depth of six inches, and one group of boys was instructed to practice until they could perform the task successfully. Prior to commencing practice, the boys in a second group

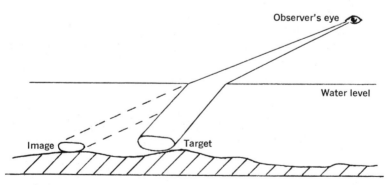

FIGURE 6.2 *Refraction principle used in Hendrickson-Schroeder transfer study.*

were instructed on the principles of the refraction of light, the phenomenon which governs the discrepancy between the location of the target and its image (Figure 6.2). In a third group, the subjects received not only an explanation of principles but the additional information that the "refraction effect" increases with the depth of the water. After the initial task had been mastered, the target was moved to a new depth (two inches) and the number of trials required by each student to master the task was recorded. The results (Table 6.6) indicate that the more complete the explanation of the principle, the greater was the degree of transfer to the "new" situation to which the principle was applicable.

Recently Overing (1966, Experiment 1) modified the Hendrickson-Schroeder experiment to investigate the effect on transfer of methods of presenting the relevant principles. Contrary to his expectations, a visually compressed explanation (line-diagram illustration) of the refraction principle was not found to be superior to a more detailed verbal presentation which contained considerable extraneous information. However, presenting a real-life problem prior to the compressed (visual) explanation did lead to results better than those obtained with the redundant verbal presentation. In fact, this combination ("orienting problem" plus visual representation) was as effective as a realistic demonstration (using a real light beam) coupled with a detailed verbal explanation. Overing suggests that conditions leading to the effective utilization of compressed explanations of principles—a practice

TABLE 6.6

TRANSFER OF PRINCIPLE TO NEW LEARNING SITUATION

GROUPS	MEAN NUMBER OF TRIALS REQUIRED		GAIN IN TRIALS	PERCENTAGE IMPROVEMENT
	at 6"	*at 2"*		
Experimental (principle plus additional explanation)	7.73	4.63	3.10	40.3
Experimental (principle only)	8.50	5.37	3.13	36.5
Control (practice only)	9.10	6.03	3.07	34.1

Source: G. Hendrickson and W. H. Schroeder, "Transfer of training in learning to hit a submerged target," *J. educ. Psychol., 32,* 1941, 205–213.

commonly found in textbooks and wall charts—are not yet understood, at least insofar as the transfer of any resulting learning is concerned.

In another well-known study, Brownell and Moser (cited in Cronbach, 1954) taught subtraction to different groups of grade 3 pupils by two different methods. The first or "decomposition" method (D) is the one commonly used in North American schools, while the second or "equal additions" method (EA) had some following in Britain at the time of the study (Table 6.7). Each method was taught both *mechanically* (D mechanical and EA mechanical groups) *and* with a *meaningful explanation of principles* (D meaningful and EA meaningful groups), and this original learning involved two-digit numbers. The experimenters found that the students taught the underlying principles not only performed better on a retention retest on the original task but did better on a transfer test involving three-digit numbers. The latter result was confined to the D meaningful group, apparently because the decomposition principle was more easily understood (that is, actually meaningful) to students at that grade level.

TABLE 6.7

Two Methods of Subtraction Used
in Brownell-Moser Study of Transfer

DECOMPOSITION (D)	EQUAL ADDITIONS (EA)
$\begin{array}{r} 7\ \ 13 \\ \cancel{8}3 \\ \underline{46} \\ 37 \end{array}$	$\begin{array}{r} 13 \\ 83 \\ \underline{46} \\ 37 \end{array}$
In this case: 10 is "borrowed" from the 80, reducing it to 70 and increasing the 3 to 13.	In this case: 10 is added to the 3 to make it 13. To compensate for this, 10 is added to the 46, making it 56 (the 10 is carried over to the "tens" column).

Attitudes toward Transfer

Obviously the student's desire to apply relevant principles is an important factor in determining whether transfer will actually take place. Potential applications can be missed if the student is too lazy or too indifferent to do so, for—as we have seen—meaningful learning always required a meaningful learning set, irrespective of whether the learning involves reception or discovery. While preaching would probably have little effect, one method which might be employed involves eliciting the student's interest through some form of discovery learning. The evidence concerning the effectiveness of the discovery method suggests that if the students have formulated generalizations as a result of their own discoveries they are more likely to employ these generalizations in other situations.

Another approach would be to use Overing's "orienting problem" technique which, as was previously noted, may serve to induce an appropriate set to discriminate relevant from irrelevant aspects of the situation to which the learned principle is to be applied.

Importance of Cognitive Structure Variables

While lateral transfer of concepts and generalizations seems to require something beyond the meaningful learning of these ideas, it should be remembered that such transfer cannot take place unless the prior meaningful learning has occurred. Certainly, notions which are fuzzy, inaccurate, or confused have very little transfer potential. Consequently the teacher should keep in mind that his first obligation is to insure that the requisite *initial* learning has taken place.

VERTICAL TRANSFER

According to our definition vertical transfer occurs when prior learning at one level in a hierarchy or taxonomy of behaviors influences present learning at a higher level. To return to our original example, the student who has learned to add and subtract integers may subsequently use this information in attempting to solve verbally formulated problems. Similarly, a student might use the *concept* of acceleration in discovering or comprehending the *generalization:*

$$\text{Force} = \text{Mass} \times \text{Acceleration.}$$

Undoubtedly the most sought-after kind of transfer is that in which the learner uses previously acquired concepts and generalizations in the process of problem solving. Since the notion of vertical transfer is thus integrally related to problem solving in most classroom learning, we will encounter this topic again in Chapter 17 when we attempt to summarize what is known about producing or guiding problem-solving behavior.

It seems appropriate, however, to introduce at this time the notion of *task analysis,* a technique which is currently gaining wide attention in conjunction with the problem of vertical transfer and the learning of complex tasks. Simply put, if we expect the student to be able to perform at a high level of behavior, *we must make certain that he possesses the underlying skills upon which this behavior depends.* In other words, it is clear that if some higher-order behavior depends upon lower-order behaviors then it will be impossible to attain this higher behavior unless the preceding links are already in the learner's repertoire.

It may be argued that teachers already perform a kind of task analysis, though perhaps on an informal basis. Actually what has happened in the past few years is that there has been an attempt to make a more detailed analysis of learning tasks than the teacher is typically able to do, an analysis which will frequently reveal "hidden steps" which, although they may seem obvious to the adult who has already mastered the terminal behavior, present real obstacles to the child's learning.

The work of Gagné in this field has been particularly influential.[10] Gagné's approach has been to describe in behavioral terms the terminal behavior or task which the student is to perform. For example, in Figure 6.3, the task selected has been that of finding formulas for N terms in a number series. Gagné begins his analysis by asking the question: "What kind of capability would an individual have to possess if he were able to perform this task successfully, were we to give him only instructions?" (Gagné, 1962a). The instructions serve the purpose of identifying the required terminal performance, recalling relevant information, or "guiding thinking"; their intent is to suggest to the learner "how to approach the solution of a new task" without, however, "telling him the answer."

By answering this initial question, on the basis of logical or psychological analysis or both, a set of prerequisite or subordinate skills (Gagné calls them "learning sets") are defined. For each of these subordinate skills the original question is repeated, and thus a tree structure is gradually developed, the lowest levels of which define the most elementary skills required if the learner is to perform the terminal task. Gagné describes this structure as a "knowledge[11] hierarchy" rather than a behavioral hierarchy (the latter represented, for example, by the successive tasks in our geometry sequence). However, while the technique can be as easily applied to sequential as to vertical transfer situations, the final task typically requires a higher-order behavior (in the taxonomic sense) than the lowest level of skill represented in the structure.

---

[10]Relevant references include: Gagné and Brown, 1961; Gagné and Paradise, 1961; Gagné and others, 1962; Gagné, 1965; Gagné, 1967.
[11]Gagné restricts "knowledge" to problem-solving capabilities. In our view, "knowledge" more typically consists of substantive understandings.

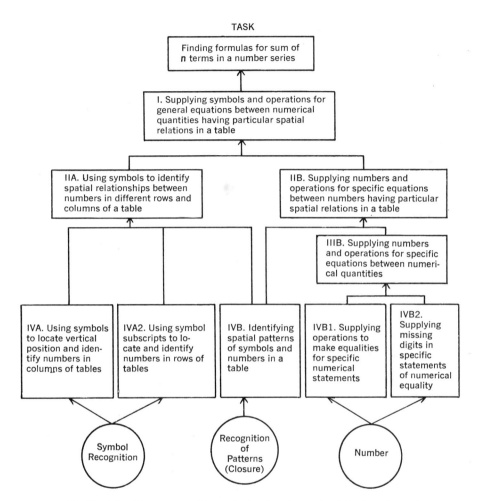

FIGURE 6.3 *Hierarchy of knowledge for the task of finding formulas for the sum of N terms in a number series. From R. M. Gagné, "The acquisition of knowledge," Psychol. Rev., 69, 1962, 355–365. Copyright 1962 by the American Psychological Association, and reproduced by permission.*

If the task analysis is correctly executed, the student should be able to perform at any given level in the structure only if he is able to perform all the behaviors involved in the levels below this. The extent to which the analysis in the example cited meets this criterion is shown in Table 6.8,

TABLE 6.8

Pattern of Success on Learning Set Tasks
Related to the Final Number Series Task
for Seven Ninth-Grade Boys

	TASK								
SUBJECT	*Final*	*I*	*IIA*	*IIB*	*IIIB*	*IVA1*	*IVA2*	*IVAB*	*IVB1*	*IVB2*
WW	−	+	+	+	+	+	+	+	+	+
WG	−	+	+	+	+	+	+	+	+	+
PM	−	−	−	+	+	+	+	+	+	+
GR	−	−	−	+	+	+	+	+	+	+
DJ	−	−	−	−	+	+	+	+	+	+
JR	−	−	−	−	−	+	+	+	+	+
RH	−	−	−	−	−	+	+	+	+	+

Note: + = Pass; − = Fail.
Source: R. M. Gagné, "The acquisition of knowledge," *Psych. Rev., 69,* 1962, 355–365.
Copyright 1962 by the American Psychological Association, and reproduced by permission.

where it is quite clear that a student failing at a given level fails at all
superordinate levels, consistent with the assumptions of the analysis.

Pendulum Example

It will be instructive to consider an additional example to determine how
well the approach applies when we are looking for a more pronounced
vertical transfer effect. We have chosen the pendulum problem since it will
provide a useful illustration in the later discussion of developmental readiness in Chapter 7. In this particular problem the child is presented with a
pendulum with an adjustable length and bobs of various weights. In the
Piaget version of the problem (Inhelder and Piaget, 1958), the child is
shown how to change the length of the pendulum and to exchange the bobs
and is then asked ("given instructions," in the Gagné sense) to determine
which factors influence the time required for the pendulum to make a
complete swing (Figure 6.4).

    For a student in the intermediate elementary school grades the task or
final behavior sought would be a verbal generalization of the form: "The
time required for one complete swing of the pendulum depends only upon
the length of the pendulum; the longer the length, the longer the time for a

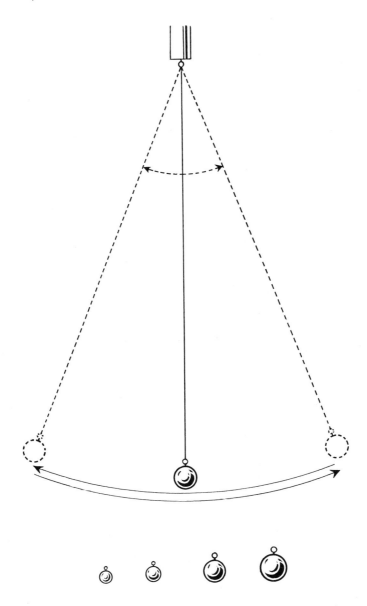

FIGURE 6.4 *Apparatus used in the pendulum experiment. The pendulum problem employs a piece of string which can be lengthened or shortened, and a set of weights of various sizes. Other variables which might initially be thought to be related to the period include the angle of initial displacement and the magnitude of the push.*

swing." A rather gross analysis[12] of subordinate abilities and knowledge required to reach the terminal behavior would yield a list something like the following (working "downward" from the terminal behavior):

> (a) Ability to relate mentally changes in an independent variable to changes in a dependent variable, that is, a (subverbal) awareness of the existing relationship derived from examining, for example, a table of corresponding values;
> (b) In order to generate the information required in (a), an understanding that one independent variable must be manipulated at one time and the effect of this manipulation on the dependent variable observed;
> (c) An understanding of the means of manipulating and recording the values of both independent and dependent variables;
> (d) A knowledge of the variables whose manipulation might influence the dependent variable; knowledge of the dependent variable.

Clearly when a child of the age in question (7–10) encounters a problem of this kind for the first time he will need considerable "instruction" if he is to make any progress at all. In addition to an explanation of the mechanical arrangements (for example, how to change the bob), he will also need help in identifying the independent and dependent variables and in measuring (presumably with a stop-watch) the time required for a complete swing.[13]

However, the crux of the problem for a young child lies beyond acquiring these elementary skills. For, as Piaget has shown, children in this age group will typically vary two independent variables at once (for example, length of pendulum and the weight of the bob) and become quite confused as to which of them is influencing the time of swing. What the child

---

[12]In this example the interdependence of the subtasks is somewhat different from their interdependence in the Gagné analysis. In the latter case, the relationship is one of a more *complex* behavior (higher level) being dependent upon a *less complex* behavior (lower level). In our example, the components are sequentially related in *time* in that a lower order behavior (for example, *identification* of independent variables) must be performed—in a context of any given problem—*before* the higher order behavior (that is, *manipulating* the independent variables). Consequently we could not claim that the higher-order behavior is *necessarily* the more complex one. Moreover, the Gagné criterion for successful task analysis would apply in our example in a special sense, namely, that in any *particular* problem the student who could not, for example, identify the independent variables could not manipulate these variables. This would not preclude, however, the student "knowing how to manipulate independent variables" in some general sense without "knowing how to identify independent variables."

[13]The latter difficulty can be avoided by using two pendulums instead of one and comparing the times of swing. In this case, however, some training is required in starting the pendulums at the same time.

needs to know is that he must manipulate one independent variable at a time and observe its effect on the dependent variable. There is no reason to believe, however, that this central proposition cannot be made meaningful to children of the age under consideration.

Step 1: Name the dependent variable (the "thing" you are trying to change).

Step 2: List the independent variables (the things which might influence the thing you are trying to change).

Step 3: Concentrate on the first independent variable. Make it take different values ("sizes") while changing nothing else. Each time it is changed record its value and the value of the dependent variable.

Step 4: Summarize the results of Step 3 in the form of a verbal statement:
(a) "Changing A does (does not) change B."
(b) "Making A bigger (smaller) makes B bigger (smaller)."

Step 5: Take the next independent variable and repeat Steps 3 and 4. Proceed through all the independent variables.

Step 6: Summarize the overall results in the statement:
"To make B bigger (smaller) I could make _____ bigger (smaller), or make_____, and so forth."

FIGURE 6.5 *Elementary strategy for determining causal relationships in physical phenomena.*

Of course, it is not our intent merely to lead the child to a solution of this particular problem, but rather to provide him with an approach that will apply across a whole class of related problems. With a slight change in the wording shown in Figure 6.5, the previously outlined steps become an elementary "strategy" (set of verbal rules) which the child could apply to the extremely large class of problems which are amenable to treatment by classical experimental methods. Included in this class would be such problems as the inclined plane, laws of acceleration ($F = ma$), gas laws, and so on. It should be noted that what we are asking the child to do is determine which variables are causally related to the dependent variable, and to identify the direction of this covariation. In respect to practical value, it could certainly be argued that as a result of the ability to analyze natural phenomena in this way, the child will possess a means of investigating the lawfulness of his physical environment, and that applying this analysis would allow him to make "directional predictions" (for example, that if we want to have a pendulum with a very long period it will have to have a long arm).[14]

At the same time, the child's knowledge of these phenomena is not complete, for, when he pursues these same topics at a more advanced level, a *new* task will be defined in which these verbal statements of relationship are to be cast into precise mathematical laws. For example, the advanced student of physics will learn that an exact formula for the motion of a pendulum ($t = 2\pi\sqrt{l/g}$) can be derived from a knowledge of Newtonian mechanics. Needless to say, the transition from the child's verbally formulated generalization to the precise mathematical formulation involves a number of steps which again can be determined by a task analysis.

In using a task analysis approach, and after having delineated the component skills required, the teacher will *still* have to determine the level in the hierarchy at which the instruction of *each* child should begin. Certainly the most efficient use of teacher and pupil time requires that the student be placed in the hierarchy, and begin his learning, at the lowest level for which his present knowledge is inadequate. Gagné has suggested that, because individual differences in initial starting points and rate of learning argue against mass instruction, many of the component skills in such a hierarchy should be taught by means of programmed instruction (see Instructional Aids, Chapter 11).

It should be remarked that the approach advocated here seems to be consistent with the emphasis of the new science programs currently being proposed for the elementary school (A.A.A.S., 1967a, 1967b; Burkman, 1967). In the "process approach,"[15] for example, a knowledge of the experimental method is postulated as the apex of a set of processes—observing, classifying, measuring, tabulating, making inferences, and so on—appropriate to the conduct of inquiry within a scientific discipline. Up to the present time, however, the emphasis of the new programs, so far as the elementary school has been concerned, seems to be on these subordinate skills—which we have merely assumed to be teachable to children in the grade level under consideration—without reaching the ultimate behavior intended (that is, the ability to perform simple experiments). In view of our previous remarks on the utility of this strategy, it seems a pity to stop short of it. There is, of course, the question of teachability. We have only a

---

[14]In other words, the "strategy" would seem to make available to the child a large (potentially unlimited) number of "guided discovery" experiences involving physical phenomena. Until the child has some experience along these lines, the teacher would have to provide "instructions" in the form of showing how to adjust equipment, explaining the nature of the dependent variable, and so on.

[15]Our endorsement of the teachability of scientific method does *not* imply endorsement of the view, expressed by the more extreme proponents of the "process approach," that the school should emphasize the *method* rather than the *content* of science.

logical analysis and the experience of working with children on similar problems to support our contention of its feasibility. Clearly, therefore, more definitive and comprehensive research is needed on this point.

PEDAGOGIC FACILITATION
OF SEQUENTIAL TRANSFER

In this section we deal at greater length with the pedagogic implications of the psychological structure of knowledge insofar as it relates to the enhancement of *sequential* transfer. The major implication for teaching perhaps is that inasmuch as existing cognitive structure reflects the outcome of *all* previous meaningful learning, control over the accuracy, clarity, longevity in memory, and transferability of a given body of knowledge can be most effectively exercised by attempting to influence the crucial variables of cognitive structure.

In principle, deliberate manipulation of the relevant aspects of cognitive structure for pedagogic purposes should not meet with undue difficulty. It can be accomplished: (1) *substantively,* by using for purposes of organization and integration those unifying concepts and propositions in a given discipline that have the widest explanatory power, and (2) *programatically,* by employing suitable principles in ordering the sequence of subject matter, in constructing its internal logic and organization, and in arranging practice trials.

The Use of Organizers

The principal strategy advocated in this book for deliberately manipulating cognitive structure so as to enhance sequential transfer involves the use of appropriately relevant and inclusive introductory materials (organizers) that are maximally clear and stable. As pointed out earlier, these organizers are introduced in advance of the learning material itself and also are presented at a higher level of abstraction, generality, and inclusiveness. We can contrast them with the summaries and overviews which are ordinarily presented at the same level of abstraction, generality, and inclusiveness as the learning material itself. These latter devices simply emphasize the salient points of the material by omitting less important information, and largely achieve their effect by repetition and simplification.

The advantage of deliberately constructing a special organizer for each new unit of material is that only in this way can the learner enjoy the advantages of a subsumer which both: (1) gives him a general overview of the more detailed material in *advance* of his actual confrontation with it, and (2) provides organizing elements that are inclusive of and take into account most relevantly and efficiently the *particular* content contained in this material. Any existing subsumer in the learner's cognitive structure which he could independently employ for this purpose typically lacks particularized relevance and inclusiveness for the new material and would hardly be available in advance of initial contact with it. Although students might possibly be able to improvise a suitable subsumer for future learning efforts *after* they become familiar with the material, it is unlikely that they would be able to do so as efficiently as a person sophisticated in both subject matter content and pedagogy.

The effectiveness of organizers would seem to depend upon the particular qualities of the material to be learned. In the first place, they probably facilitate the learning of factual material more than they do the learning of abstract material since abstractions, in a sense, contain their own built-in organizers—both for themselves and for related detailed items. It would, therefore, seem advisable to restrict their use to the learning of material that embraces a substantial body of differentiated or factual content, and hence offers adequate scope for the ideational scaffolding provided by abstract organizers.

Moreover the pedagogic value of organizers would depend upon how well organized the learning material itself is. If it already contains built-in organizers and proceeds from regions of lesser to greater differentiation (higher to lower inclusiveness), rather than in the manner of the typical textbook or lecture presentation, much of the potential benefit derivable from advance organizers will not be actualized. Regardless of how well organized learning material is, however, it seems reasonable to expect that learning and retention can still be facilitated by the use of organizers at an appropriate level of inclusiveness. Such organizers are available from the very beginning of the learning task, and their integrative properties are also much more salient than when introduced concurrently with the learning material. To be useful, however, organizers themselves must, obviously, be learnable and must be stated in familiar terms.

Substantive Factors Influencing Cognitive Structure

The major initial task of any curriculum project is to identify the particular organizing and explanatory principles in the particular discipline under study that manifest the widest generality and integrative properties. While this is obviously a formidable and long-range problem, recent experience with curriculum reform movements indicates that it yields to sustained and resourceful inquiry.

To elaborate somewhat, the essential problem is:

> . . . how to construct curricula that can be taught by ordinary teachers to ordinary students and at the same time reflect clearly the basic or underlying principles of various fields of inquiry. The problem is two-fold: first, how

to have the basic subjects rewritten and their teaching materials revamped in such a way that the pervading and powerful ideas and attitudes relating to them are given a central role; second, how to match the levels of these materials to the capacities of students of different abilities at different grades in school (Bruner, 1950, p. 18).

The "powerful ideas" are those constituting the "structure of the discipline." According to Bruner (1964b):

. . . optimal structure refers to the set of propositions from which a larger body of knowledge can be generated, and it is characteristic that the formulation of such structure depends upon the state of advance in a particular field of knowledge. . . . Since the goodness of a structure depends upon its power for simplifying information, for generating new propositions, and for increasing the manipulability of a body of knowledge, structure must always be related to the status and gifts of the learner. Viewed in this way, the optimal structure of a body of knowledge is not absolute but relative. The major requirement is that no two sets of generating structures for the same field of knowledge be in contradiction (pp. 308–309).

As indicated above, appropriate structure takes into account the developmental level of the student's cognitive functioning and his degree of subject-matter sophistication. Structure that is too elaborate in these terms constitutes more of a handicap than a facilitating device (S. E. Newman, 1957; Munro, 1959; Binter, 1963). Similarly, structure that is appropriate for the teacher is not always appropriate for the pupil. And premature acquisition of inappropriate structures may result in "closure" that inhibits the acquisition of more appropriate structures (Smedslund, 1961).

Once the substantive organizational problem (that is, identifying the basic organizing concepts in a given discipline) is solved, attention can be directed to the *programmatic* organizational problems involved in the presentation and sequential arrangement of component units. Here, it is hypothesized, the various principles concerned with the efficient programming of content are applicable, irrespective of the subject-matter field. These principles naturally include and reflect the influence of the previously listed cognitive structure variables, that is, the availability of a relevant anchoring idea, its stability and clarity, and its discriminability from the learning material.

Progressive Differentiation

When subject matter is programmed in accordance with the principles of progressive differentiation, the most general and inclusive ideas of the discipline are presented first and are then progressively differentiated in terms of detail and specificity. This order of presentation presumably corresponds to the natural sequence of acquiring cognitive awareness and sophistication when human beings are spontaneously exposed either to an entirely unfamiliar field of knowledge or to an unfamiliar branch of a familiar body of knowledge. It also corresponds to the postulated way in which this knowledge is represented, organized, and stored in the human cognitive system. The two assumptions we are making here are, in other words, (1) that it is less difficult for human beings to grasp the differentiated aspects of a previously-learned more inclusive whole than to formulate the inclusive whole from its previously-learned differentiated parts,[16] and (2) that an individual's organization of the content of a particular subject-matter discipline in his own mind consists of a hierarchical structure in which the most inclusive ideas occupy a position at the apex of the structure and subsume progressively less inclusive and more highly differentiated propositions, concepts, and factual data.

It follows that new ideas and information will be learned and retained most efficiently when more inclusive and specifically relevant ideas are already available in cognitive structure to serve a subsuming role or to furnish ideational anchorage. Organizers, of course, exemplify the principle of progressive differentiation and serve this function in relation to any given topic or subtopic where they are used. In addition, however, it is desirable that both the arrangement of the learning material itself, within each topic or subtopic, and the sequencing of the various subtopics and topics in a given course of study also generally conform to the same principle.

This almost self-evident principle is rarely followed in actual teaching procedures or in the organization of most textbooks. The more typical practice is to segregate materials by topics into separate chapters and subchapters, and to order the arrangement of topics and subtopics (and the material within each) solely on the basis of topical relatedness without regard to their relative level of abstraction, generality, and inclusiveness. Thus, in most instances, students are required to learn the details of new and unfamiliar disciplines before they have acquired an adequate body of relevant subsumers at an appropriate level of inclusiveness (Ausubel, 1960). Consequently they typically accomplish this by treating potentially meaningful material as if it were rote in character and experience unnecessary difficulty and little success in both learning and retention.

Progressive differentiation in the programming of subject matter is accomplished by using a hierarchical series of organizers (in descending order of inclusiveness), each organizer preceding its corresponding unit of detailed, differentiated material, and by sequencing the material within each

---

[16]It is appreciated, however, that the learning of certain propositions requires the synthesis of previously-acquired subordinate concepts or propositions (that is, superordinate learning) (Gagné, 1962). The need for periodic superordinate learnings, however, does not negate the propositions that both the psychological organization of knowledge and the optimal organization of subject matter *generally* exemplify the principle of progressive differentiation.

unit in descending order of inclusiveness. In this way not only is an appropriately relevant and inclusive subsumer made available to provide ideational scaffolding for each component unit of differentiated subject matter, but both the ideas within each unit and the various units in relation to each other are also progressively differentiated, that is, organized in descending order of inclusiveness. The initial organizers, therefore, furnish anchorage at a global level before the learner is confronted with *any* of the new material. For example, a generalized model of class relationships is first provided as a general subsumer for *all* new classes, subclasses, and species before more limited subsumers are provided for the particular subclasses or species they encompass.

Integrative Reconciliation

The principle of integrative reconciliation refers to the explicit attempt to point out significant similarities and differences and to reconcile real or apparent inconsistencies between successive ideas presented in a sequential arrangement. This principle is antithetical in spirit and approach to the ubiquitous practice among textbook-writers of compartmentalizing and segregating particular ideas or topics within their respective chapters or subchapters, so that each topic is presented in only one of the several possible places where treatment is relevant and warranted. The assumption made here is that all necessary cross-referencing of related ideas can be performed, and customarily is, by students.

When integrative reconciliation does not take place, it will frequently happen that multiple terms are used to represent concepts that are intrinsically equivalent except for contextual reference, thereby generating considerable cognitive strain and confusion. Moreover, artificial barriers are erected between related topics, obscuring important common features and thus rendering impossible the acquisition of insights dependent upon the recognition of these commonalities. Further, adequate use is not made of relevant, previously learned ideas as a basis for subsuming and incorporating related, new information. Finally, since significant differences between apparently similar concepts are not made clear and explicit, these concepts are often perceived and retained as identical.

The principle of integrative reconciliation also applies when subject matter is organized along parallel lines, that is, when related materials are presented in serial fashion but there is no *intrinsic* sequential dependence from one topic to the next. In this case the understanding of Part II material does not presuppose understanding of Part I, and the order of presentation is therefore immaterial. This situation, for example, prevails in presenting alternative theoretical positions in ethics, religion, and epistemology, opposing theories of biological evolution, and different systems of learning and personality theory.

Nevertheless, earlier-learned elements of a parallel sequence *do* serve an orienting and subsuming role in relation to later-presented elements. The latter are comprehended and interpreted in terms of existing understandings and paradigms provided by analogous, familiar, and already established ideas in cognitive structure. Hence, for learning of the unfamiliar new ideas to take place, they must be adequately discriminable from the established familiar ideas. If, for example, the learner cannot discriminate between the new idea A' and old idea A, A' does not really exist for him; it is phenomenologically the same as A. Furthermore, even if the learner can discriminate between A and A' at the moment of learning, unless the discrimination is sharp and free from ambiguity and confusion, there will be a tendency over time for A' to be reduced to A (as the two ideas interact during the retention interval) more rapidly than is usually the case.

In some instances of meaningful learning and retention, the principal difficulty is not one of discriminability but of apparent *contradiction* between established ideas in cognitive structure and new propositions in the learning material. Under these conditions the learner may either try to compartmentalize the new propositions as isolated entities apart from previously learned knowledge, or he may attempt integrative reconciliation under a more inclusive subsumer. Compartmentalization may usually be considered a special case of rote learning. Through much overlearning, relatively stable incorporation may be achieved, at least for examination purposes, but the fabric of knowledge learned in this fashion remains unintegrated and full of contradictions, and is therefore not viable on a long-term basis.

Ward and Davis (1939) reported a study of meaningful retention in which general science was taught to junior high-school pupils by means of a textbook that made a special point of reconciling and integrating new ideas with previously learned content. Periodic examinations were also given which tested knowledge of earlier as well as of recently presented material. They found that under these arrangements students retained material as well after sixteen weeks as on tests of immediate retention.

Sequential Organization

The availability of relevant anchoring ideas for use in meaningful learning and retention may obviously be maximized by taking advantage of natural sequential dependencies among the component divisions of a discipline, that is, of the fact that the understanding of a given topic often logically presupposes the prior understanding of some related topic. Typically the necessary antecedent knowledge is more inclusive and general than the sequentially dependent material, but this is not always true (for example, superordinate learning). In any case, by arranging the order of topics in a given subject-matter field as far as possible in accordance with these sequential dependencies, the learning of each unit, in turn, not only becomes an achievement in its own right but also constitutes specifically relevant ideational scaffolding for the next item in the sequence.

Sequential arrangement of learning tasks relies on the *general* facilitating effect of the availability of relevant anchoring ideas in cognitive structure on meaningful learning and retention. For any given topic, however, there is the problem of ascertaining what the *particular* most effective sequence is. This involves considerations of logical task analysis, progressive differentiation, developmental level of cognitive functioning, integrative reconciliation, and learning hierarchies. In sequential school learning, knowledge of earlier-appearing material in the sequence plays much the same role as an organizer in relation to later-appearing material in the sequence, in that it constitutes a relevant ideational foundation for this material.

Consolidation

By insisting on consolidation or mastery of ongoing lessons before new material is introduced, we make sure of continued subject-matter readiness and success in sequentially organized learning. This kind of learning presupposes, of course, that the preceding step is always clear, stable, and well organized. If it is not, the learning of all subsequent steps is jeopardized. Thus, new material in the sequence should never be introduced until all previous steps are thoroughly mastered. This principle also applies to those kinds of learning within a larger task in which each component task tends to be compound in content and to manifest an internal organization of its own. Consolidation, of course, is achieved through confirmation, correction, clarification, differential practice, and review in the course of repeated exposure, with feedback, to learning material.

Abundant experimental research (for example, C. P. Duncan, 1959; Morrisett and Hovland, 1959) has confirmed the proposition that prior learnings are not transferable to new learning tasks until they are first overlearned. Overlearning, in turn, requires an adequate number of adequately-spaced repetitions and reviews, sufficient intra-task repetitiveness prior to intra- and inter-task diversification, and opportunity for differential practice of the more difficult components of a task. Frequent testing and provision of feedback, especially with test items demanding fine discrimination among alternatives varying in degree of correctness, also enhance consolidation by confirming, clarifying and correcting previous learnings.[17]

---

[17]Consolidation (through correction and review) of each successive part of a hierarchically organized task does *not* facilitate the *learning* of later segments of the task when a summary and correction-review of the *entire* task are made part of the terminal test on the material (M. D. Merrill, 1965). The results of this experiment are therefore consistent with those of Ausubel and Youssef's (1966) study, in which a summary of Part I was presented as an introduction to Part II, thereby making Part II no longer sequentially dependent upon Part I.

Much additional research is needed to establish both the most economical degree of consolidation and ways of effecting it (for example, through repetition, distribution of practice, feedback, use of organizers, internal logic of the material) that will optimally facilitate the learning and retention of sequentially and parallelly organized subject matter. Such knowledge will obviously have greater pedagogic utility if the effects of these latter variables are differentiated with respect to pupils' level of cognitive maturity, academic ability, and degree of subject-matter sophistication.

TOPICS FOR DISCUSSION AND FURTHER STUDY

1. Cite examples of transfer which the school *assumes* will take place. Classify these in terms of the three-dimensional categorization system proposed in this chapter.

2. Make a complete list of the transfer objectives for the subject-matter field and grade level which you will be teaching.

3. For examples cited in (1) and (2), give observational or other evidence as to whether such transfer takes place. Discuss, where a failure to transfer is apparent, what steps might be undertaken by the classroom teacher or the school generally to enhance this effect.

4. Employers frequently criticize the school on grounds that its graduates are below an acceptable standard in communication and computational skills and in their ability to think independently. Teachers at higher-grade levels make similar criticisms of pupils who come into their classes. To what extent, or in what ways, is failure to transfer implicated and what other causes might be postulated for these shortcomings?

5. What skills or knowledge acquired by the student outside the school transfer to school-learning situations?

6.* Write an organizer to introduce some topic or related group of topics which you will be teaching in the school. Make clear your assumptions concerning the anchoring ideas already possessed by the student and the relationship of superordinate ideas in the organizer to both these anchoring ideas and the central new concepts in the material to be learned.

7.* Examine a textbook that you will use in your classroom teaching. To what extent is the effective use of organizers in evidence? Indicate where organizers could be introduced with advantage.

8. Evidence has been presented that the time spent learning an effective organizer leads to greater subsequent learning and retention than an equal amount of time spent on a purely historical introduction. Despite this fact, can any argument be advanced in favor of a historical introduction?

9. Locate examples of integrative reconciliation employed in this text.

10. As indicated earlier, the function of an organizer is to insure that relevant anchoring ideas are available for the learning of new material. In a field in which there is some controversy, the organizer approach would attempt to resolve the

controversy in advance, possibly by postulating a general idea of which the apparent contradictions are special cases. On the other hand, many teachers would think it advisable to mention the controversy at the beginning, but to leave it unresolved so that it will act as a motivating device for subsequent learning. To what extent are these approaches reconcilable?

11.* Attempt to teach a child (youth, adult) some task which is generally considered very difficult or impossible to learn at his age or level of development (ability). Proceed in the following manner:

    (a) make a task analysis of the problem showing the component skills required;

    (b) determine if, and by what means, these skills may be taught (and teach them);

    (c) test for *limited* transfer (for example, from "pendulum" to "swing");

    (d) test for *general* transfer (for example, from "pendulum" to "inclined plane");

    (e) report your results and conclusions concerning the feasibility of initial learning of the task and concerning limited and general transfer for the age group you are working with.

SUGGESTIONS FOR ADDITIONAL READING

Ausubel, D. P., and D. Fitzgerald. Organizer, general background, and antecedent learning variables in sequential verbal learning. *J. educ. Psychol.,* 1962, *53,* 243–249.

Ellis, H. E. The *transfer of learning.* New York: Crowell-Collier and Macmillan, Inc., 1965.

Frase, L. T. Some data concerning the mathemagenic hypothesis. *Amer. educ. Res. J.,* 1968, *5*(2), 181–190.

Gagné, R. M. The *conditions of learning.* New York: Holt, Rinehart and Winston, Inc., 1965.

Grose, R. F., and R. C. Birney. *Transfer of learning.* Princeton, N. J.: D. Van Nostrand, 1963.

CHAPTER 7

COGNITIVE DEVELOPMENT AND READINESS

In the previous chapter we discussed ways of presenting new material to insure maximum anchorage and retention. We also described the larger curriculum problem to be that of organizing and presenting whole subject-matter fields embracing the content to be offered from the earliest school years through graduate school. In the latter connection we indicated that in many of the "new" curricula, subject-matter specialists have tried to ferret out the central ideas in the disciplines concerned and, with the help of educational psychologists, have tried to determine an appropriate *order* for presenting these new concepts.

Once this work is accomplished there remains the problem of the overall *pacing* of the curriculum. At what age or grade level should the notion of mathematical "sets" be introduced? Can a child profitably be introduced to algebra in the primary grades, or should the ideas in this field be reserved for later study in high school? And is the traditional starting point for formal instruction (that is, grade 1) consistent with what is presently known about the child's ability to profit from instruction?

All of these questions have to do with the notion of *readiness,* another time-honored matter of educational concern. We would be less than candid if we did not point out in advance that the problems in this area are so complex, and the information available so limited, that the number of controversies and unanswered questions vastly exceeds the points of agreement. In addition some of the issues relate to the overall pacing of content within a field, a matter which is rather beyond the classroom teacher's realm of decision making.

The previous acknowledgements notwithstanding, excellent reasons can be advanced for bringing the matter of readiness to the teacher's attention. In the first place, the classroom teacher will have some control over the material to be presented to students, and will therefore have to make decisions concerning the most appropriate time to introduce a new concept. Second, even when the material to be covered by the teacher is prescribed, it is still the teacher's responsibility to determine which *method of presentation* is most likely to be successful, given the child's prevailing state of cognitive development. Third, since the rate of transition from one stage of development to the next is evidently dependent upon the child's particular experience, the teacher must be aware of—and deliberately introduce into his teaching—factors which *facilitate* such growth. Finally, as professionals, teachers should be informed about such controversies as when children should begin formal instruction, whether or not the schools are presently moving too slowly in the presentation of material, and whether children below the normal age of school entry can profit from special programs of readiness training—controversies which are eliciting much attention today among professional writers and the general public.

The Nature of Readiness

Cognitive readiness refers to the adequacy of the student's existing cognitive equipment for coping with the demands of a specified new learning task. In practice, readiness is indicated by the ability to profit from practice or learning experience. An individual manifests readiness when the outcomes of his learning activity, in terms of increased knowledge or academic achievement, are *reasonably commensurate* with the amount of effort and practice involved.

An examination of any specific instance reveals that general readiness has two components. In the first place, the student will possess a readiness to learn algebra only after he has acquired a sufficient mastery of the symbolism and operations of arithmetic. This aspect of readiness, which reflects possession of particular *subject-matter knowledge* (or adequate subject-matter sophistication) for a particular learning task, was dealt with in the preceding chapter when we were considering factors that facilitate *sequential transfer*. The second, or *developmental* aspect of readiness, our major concern here, is a function of general cognitive maturity. Developmental readiness thus constitutes a necessary but not sufficient condition for the learning of any particular item of subject matter (specific antecedent knowledge would be required as well). It reflects the individual's general cognitive maturity or stage of intellectual development. In our algebra example, developmental readiness would be manifested when the student had reached the stage where he was capable of performing the kind of logical operations required in that field and was sufficiently mature to comprehend and remember the new ideas which it presents.

What factors determine developmental readiness itself? One of the major factors is what is termed *maturation,* that is, those increments in ability to perform a task which are not facilitated by special training. Such increments must then be attributed to genic influences or incidental experience, or both. The maturational factor in the learning of a particular task would be demonstrated empirically if an experimental group, having received specific training on the task, did *not* significantly out-perform a control group which was not subjected to this training. Such experiments have been common in the sensory-motor domain. Gesell and Thompson (1929), for example, found that a six-week period of specific training in stair climbing gave an initial advantage to one member of a pair of twins, but that the other member rapidly caught up when a much shorter period of training was given later when the child was "ready" for this kind of performance. The conclusion here, and in similar studies (Strayer, 1930; Hilgard, 1932; Dennis and Dennis, 1935), was that the task involved depended heavily upon genic factors coupled with the incidental experience which the child would obtain in his normal play

When we come to cognitive learning tasks, however, it is quite clear that maturational effects in themselves are insufficient to explain readiness, so that we must also take into account *prior learning.* Prior learning, as for example of a particular kind of subject matter, has two main effects. On the one hand, it determines the child's specific readiness for other *particular* kinds of subject-matter learning, that is, contributes to his *subject-matter* readiness. On the other hand, it also contributes to *general* changes in cognitive readiness that are, at least in part, independent of the kind of subject matter studied. For example, the study of elementary-school science prepares a pupil for high-school science, and the study of elementary-school grammar prepares the pupil for high-school grammar. In addition, however, experience with each subject contributes to the individual's general cognitive functioning. In other words, prior learning of specific subject matter influences both specific subject matter learning and *developmental* readiness. The interrelationship of these variables is illustrated in Figure 7.1.

Controversies Concerning Relative Influence
of Readiness Factors

We could summarize the previous discussion by means of the formula $R_D = f(G + I + L)$, which states that developmental readiness is a function of genic potential, incidental experience, and the effect of prior learning. While this formulation seems noncontroversial enough, there are enormously wide variations in the relative importance which different individuals attach to each factor.

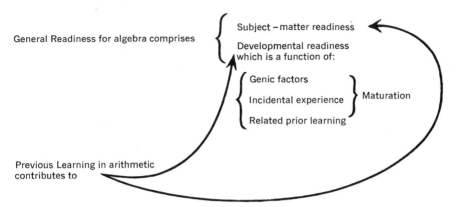

FIGURE 7.1 *Interrelationship of readiness variables.*

At one end of the scale we may place views which hold that the primary determining factor, if not the exclusive factor, is genic potential. The conception of developmental readiness as a process of "internal ripening" essentially independent of all environmental influences—that is, of incidental experience as well as learning—is frequently traced back to Rousseau.[1] In this view readiness becomes a matter of simple genic regulation, unfolding in accordance with a predetermined and immutable time-table; consequently, the school, by definition, becomes powerless to influence developmental readiness. Rousseau's views influenced Froebel, the founder of the kindergarten movement, which perhaps helps to explain why the nursery school, kindergarten, and primary grades have long been a stronghold for this extreme position.

In recent times Gesell (1945) advanced a similar theory which we can characterize as an "embryological" model of development. We may observe that the "internal ripening" thesis fits quite well the sensory-motor and neuro-muscular sequences taking place during the prenatal period and early infancy. Thus in the acquisition of simple behavioral functions (locomotion, prehension) that more or less uniformly characterize all members of the human species irrespective of cultural or other environmental differences, the evidence indicates that for all practical purposes genic factors largely determine the direction and rate of development. Environmental factors influence developmental outcomes only if they are extremely deviant, and then serve more to disrupt or arrest the ongoing course of development than to initiate developmental progressions of their own.

While there can be no objection to the embryological model when it is

---

[1]A link with Darwinian theory can also be argued (see Hunt, 1964).

used in conjunction with the data from which it was derived, one can certainly object to its extrapolation, unwarranted in our opinion, to those more complex and variable components of later cognitive and behavioral development where environmental factors *do* make important conrtibutions to the direction, patterning, and sequential order of all developmental changes.

At the other end of the continuum we find those who give very strong emphasis to the influence of specific training in developing readiness. Actually it is impossible to define an end-point here, since no one believes that genic factors can be ruled out entirely. Nevertheless, as we pointed out earlier, there has been much experimentation during the past few years on the "acceleration of learning," and many experimenters now believe that the traditional school program has vastly underrated the child's capacity for learning at a young age.

It might be fairly said that something of a pitched battle has developed between extremists during the past decade. For some time prior to that, proponents of the "internal ripening" theory, backed by the authority of Gesell and earlier writers, had established a "time-table" setting out appropriate ages for the learning of various school tasks. For example, until a very few years ago it was a byword among teachers that a child must have attained a mental age of six and one-half years before he is ready to begin formal instruction in reading (Morphett and Washburne, 1931). This was no mere theoretical position but a belief which actually governed the admission of children into reading programs. In recent years experimenters opposed to this idea have demonstrated that children can learn to read at a much younger age. O. K. Moore (Pines, 1963) has successfully introduced three- and four-year-old children to formal instruction in reading, and one experimenter (Fowler, 1962b) successfully taught reading skills to a two-year-old.[2]

Faced with such evidence, "internal ripening" exponents have had to admit that children *can* learn at younger ages than the embryological time-clock notion had postulated, but they maintain that acceleration implies a tampering with an internal timing mechanism and must inevitably produce "harmful" results. When proponents of earlier learning have countered by challenging "internal ripening" exponents to produce evidence of such harm, the latter have frequently argued that the negative effects of acceleration might not become *evident* for many years (for example, an early exposure to reading could adversely affect the individual's attitudes toward his own children's reading). Of course, when one postulates the possibility of effects which cannot be readily measured, the controversy is largely removed from the possibility of settlement by experiment or measurement. As we will point out later, the classroom teacher will usually have to rely on his own good judgment as to whether "harm" is likely to be done in any particular

---

[2]See also Chapter 6 and additional references in the last section of this chapter.

acceleration project in which he is engaged.[3] Such harm, if it occurs, will more likely reflect the negative effects of "premature learning," that is, of learning undertaken before adequate readiness is established (for example, the expenditure of undue time or effort or the increased probability of failure).

Curriculum-Pacing Strategy

Irrespective of the position taken on the readiness question, experimenters and curriculum designers have long sought a rational basis for determining the grade or age placement of curriculum content. It was hoped that such a strategy would replace present practice in which the placing of any specific item of content has been determined largely by tradition, intuitive hunches, and trial and error. With the renewal of interest in Piaget's work in North America since 1950, there arose a belief that a "stage" theory of cognitive development would provide a strategy for determining the optimum point for introducing curriculum content, a strategy which was to replace Gesell's already discredited progress charts based on the embryological model. In brief, three phases were seen in executing the curriculum pacing strategy:

(a) The critical characteristics of each cognitive stage would be determined; in other words, each stage would be defined in terms of the kind of cognitive tasks that could be performed at that stage but not before.

(b) The critical attributes would serve as "psychological benchmarks"; further, the extent to which the emergence of the benchmarks could be "accelerated" was to be determined. (Initially it was felt that the point of appearance of benchmarks was dependent upon general environmental and cultural experience, but only to a limited degree upon specific training. Consequently it was believed that a "modal" age of appearance could be determined for each culture or subcultural group.)

(c) Specific items of curriculum content were to be related to the benchmarks. Thus, having determined that "conservation of number" occurs roughly at age seven in North American children, and having also determined that an understanding of "fractions" depends upon the child's having acquired this stage of cognitive development, one would then be able to deduce that the earliest point at which fractions could be successfully introduced would be when the child had reached seven years of age. Or, having shown that the understanding of the experimental method requires the attainment of Piaget's stage of "formal

---

[3]More recently, the controversy has been intensified by the growing awareness in North America of the work of Piaget, a Swiss psychologist who has investigated the thought processes of children for over forty years. Piaget's theory of mental development, which will be referred to later, has been invoked by "internal ripening" exponents as supporting their position. However this conclusion has been attacked by those giving greater weight to environmental influences (see Sullivan, 1967b).

operations," an event which normally occurs during the early high-school years, clear justification would exist for postponing any serious program of science education to the secondary school. (For a review of one attempted application of this approach, see Robinson, 1967.)

In a later section we will return to examine the present prospects for such a curriculum-pacing strategy. However, it will be necessary first to discuss the central task implied in it—that of delineating *general stages of cognitive development*.

STAGES OF COGNITIVE DEVELOPMENT

Further to the foregoing discussion, we are concerned here with the particular developmental changes in *cognitive structure* which affect the learning and retention of meaningful material. Even within this some-what limited emphasis,[4] different experimenters have investigated an enormous range of cognitive capacities which change with age. For convenience, these are summarized in Table 7.1.

As far as educational practice is concerned, the most important of these changes in intellectual development is the gradual shift *from concrete to abstract cognitive functioning*. It defines the principal differences between the respective learning and thinking processes of elementary- and secondary-school pupils as well as the corresponding differences in pedagogical strategy which they imply. This dimension of cognitive development will be considered in detail in a subsequent section and will be related to Piaget's designated stages of intellectual functioning. At this point it will be profitable to consider in general terms both what is meant by a stage of cognitive development and whether the very concept of "stage" is tenable and useful in understanding age-level changes in cognitive ability.

The Meaning of Stages

The term "developmental stages" indicates a sequence of identifiable phases in an orderly progression of development that are *qualitatively* discriminable from adjacent phases and generally characteristic of most members of a broadly defined age group.[5] As long as a given stage occupies the same

---

[4]General theories of intellectual development, such as those advanced by Piaget and his collaborators (Inhelder and Piaget, 1958; Piaget, 1950, 1954a) include age-level changes in at least four major areas of cognitive functioning, namely, perception, objectivity-subjectivity, structure of ideas and knowledge, and the nature of thinking or problem solving.
[5]The stage concept attempts to partition developmental readiness into a number of qualitatively different phases. As we shall see later, most theorists postulate three major stages covering the period of formal schooling.

TABLE 7.1

SOME ASPECTS OF COGNITIVE GROWTH

ASPECTS OF COGNITIVE CHANGE AS CHILD AGES	EXPERIMENTERS INVESTIGATING THIS ASPECT
1. Tendency to perceive the stimulus world more in general, abstract, and categorical terms and less in tangible, time-bound, and particularized contexts.	Gollin (1958) Piaget (1950, 1954a) Serra (1953)
2. Increasing ability to comprehend and manipulate abstract verbal symbols and relationships, and to employ abstract classificatory schemata.	Inhelder and Piaget (1958) Piaget (1950, 1954a) Wallon (1952)
3. Increasing ability to understand ideational relationships without the benefit of direct, tangible experience, of concrete imagery, and of empirical exposure to numerous particular instances of a given concept or proposition.	Goldman and Levine (1963) Inhelder and Piaget (1958) Szuman (1951) Werner (1948)
4. Tendency to infer the properties of objects more from their class membership rather than from direct experience of proximate, sensory data.	Gollin (1958) Reichard, and others (1944) Sigel (1953) Wallon (1952) Wohlwill (1960b)
5. More disposed to use remote and abstract rather than immediate and concrete criterial attributes in classifying phenomena, and to use abstract symbols rather than concrete imagery to represent emerging concepts.	M. Annet (1959) Inhelder and Piaget (1958) Piaget (1950, 1954a) Werner (1948)
6. Acquisition of an ever-increasing repertoire of more inclusive and higher-order abstractions.	Inhelder and Piaget (1958) Serra (1953) Welch (1940) Werner (1948)
7. Cognitive field tends to widen both spatially and temporally.	H. V. Baker (1942) D. S. Hill (1930) Probst (1931)
8. Becoming more capable of making both broader and more subtle inferences from empirical data.	Bruner (1964a) Gollin (1958) Kendler and Kendler (1956)
9. Cognitive products tend to become both selectively more schematic and less subjective and egocentric in nature.	Gibson (1953) H. V. Baker (1942) Piaget (1928, 1929)
10. More capable of viewing situations from a hypothetical ("as if") basis or from the standpoint of others.	H. V. Baker (1942) Piaget (1928, 1929)
11. Attention span increases markedly.	Gutteridge (1935) Van Alstyne (1932)

sequential position in all individuals or cultures, it is perfectly compatible with the existence of variations between cultures, or between individuals within a culture, with respect to the age at which the stage will occur. Moreover, it is equally compatible with the existence of variations within the individual himself as to when the next stage will occur for one school subject as opposed to another.

It is necessary to specify what this definition does *not* imply since many critics attack the notion of "stage" simply because it does not live up to their extreme criteria. For example, although stages of development are qualitatively discontinuous in *process* from one to another, there is no reason why their *manner of achievement* must necessarily be abrupt. This is particularly true when the factors which bring them into being are operative over many years and are cumulative in their impact. Unlike the situation in physical, emotional, and personality development, cognitive development is not marked by the sudden, dramatic appearance of discontinuously new determinants.

It is also unreasonable to expect that a given stage must always occur at the same age in every culture. Since rate of development is, at least in part, a function of general environmental stimulation, the age range in which a stage occurs tends to vary from one culture to another. Thus, considering the marked differences between the Swiss and American cultures, it would be remarkable indeed if comparable stages of development took place at the same ages. Similarly, within a given culture a given stage cannot be expected to occur at the same age for all individuals. When a particular age level is designated for a given stage, it must refer to a *mean* value, and therefore implies that a normal range of variability prevails around the mean. This variability reflects differences in intellectual endowment, experiential background, education, and personality.

Thus a certain amount of overlapping among age groups is inevitable. A particular stage may be generally characteristic of five- and six-year-olds, but also typically includes some four- and seven-year-olds and even some three- and eight-year-olds. Piaget's age levels, like Gesell's, are nothing more than an *average* approximation set for purposes of convenience. Hence to attack the concept of developmental stages on the grounds that a given stage includes children of varying ages, instead of taking place at the precise ages designated by Piaget, is simply to demolish a straw man.

One also cannot expect *complete* consistency and generality of stage behavior within an individual from one week or month to another, and from one subject-matter area or level of difficulty to another. Some overlapping and specificity are inevitable whenever development is determined by multiple, variable factors. A particular twelve-year-old may use formal logical operations in his science course in October, but may revert for no apparent reason to a concrete level of cognitive functioning in November or even several years later, when confronted with an extremely difficult and unfamiliar problem in the same field.

Furthermore, he may characteristically continue to function at a concrete level for another year or two in social studies and literature. Since transitions to new stages do not occur instantaneously but over a period of time, fluctuations between stages are common until the newly emerging stage is consolidated. In addition, because of intrinsic differences in levels of subject-matter difficulty and because of differences in ability and experiential background, both between persons and within any one person (over different subject areas), it is hardly surprising that transitions from one stage to another do not occur *simultaneously* in *all* subject-matter areas and sub-areas. Abstract thinking, for example, generally emerges earlier in science than in social studies because children have more experience manipulating ideas about mass, time, and space than about government, social institutions, and historical events. However, in some children—depending upon their special abilities and experience—the reverse may be true.

The Concrete/Abstract Dimension of Cognitive Development[6]

The concrete/abstract dimension of intellectual development may be divided into three qualitatively distinct developmental stages—the pre-operational stage, the stage of concrete logical operations, and the stage of abstract logical operations. Subject to later discussion, we may for the moment consider these stages to cover respectively the preschool, elementary-school, and adolescent-adult periods of development.

Pre-operational Stage   The pre-operational stage is best understood in terms of the child's capacity to acquire and utilize *primary abstractions* (that is, concepts). Primary concepts are those concepts whose meanings a given individual originally learns in relation to concrete empirical experience. In Chapter 3, we saw how the child might come to acquire the concept "cube." In that example the child was exposed to a series of exemplars of the concept. As a result of this experience he was able to abstract its criterial attributes and to form a representative image (comprising these attributes) which constitutes the meaning of the concept. Of course, the criterial at-

---

[6]Most contemporary stage theories of cognitive development, including the present one, have taken as their starting point the theory advanced by Piaget and Inhelder (Inhelder and Piaget, 1958; Piaget, 1950, 1954b, 1957b). At the same time, the account presented here has been revised to be consistent with the concepts and classroom-teaching emphasis of previous chapters, and so differs from Piaget's theory in certain major respects. We do not present a summary of the Piaget theory itself, but refer the reader to the following sources: Berlyne, 1957; Flavell, 1963; Hunt, 1961; Ripple and Rockcastle, 1964; Sullivan, 1967b; Tuddenham, 1966.

tributes of the concept could be pointed out by a parent or instructor, and such instructions would serve to focus the child's attention upon them (and thus indirectly facilitate the abstracting process). But even here the child would still be required to perceive these attributes in each exemplar and to construct a composite image embodying them (and constituting the meaning of the concept). The essential condition for the learning of primary concepts, then, is that a series of concrete exemplars be available, and that the child recognize that each of these exemplars contains the set of criterial attributes defining the concept.

Once the child has acquired a primary concept, he will be capable of understanding a proposition in which such a concept is embedded. For example, we discussed earlier the process by which the child uses his intuitive understanding of syntactical rules to grasp the meaning of the proposition "cats climb trees," where both "cats" and "trees" have been acquired as primary concepts. Moreover, in certain necessarily restricted and concrete situations, the child will be able to use such propositions in very elementary kinds of problem solving.

The acquisition of the pre-operational stage can be understood in terms of the generation and manipulation of *images,* mental constructs which we previously found to underlie the learning of certain kinds of concepts and generalizations. Piaget has pointed out (Flavell, 1963) that in early infancy the child acts as if he ceases to believe that an object exists after it has passed out of his visual field. In other words, it would seem that during the first part of the so-called "sensory-motor" stage the child can only form images by direct perception, and cannot spontaneously revive some replica of these images for purposes of recalling an object. However, the child at the pre-operational stage (according to Piaget, from the ages of two to seven) is certainly able to revive images of individual objects and has acquired, in addition, the capacity to generate the representative images which constitute the meaning of his earliest concepts. However, his increasing facility in image generation and manipulation is apparently limited, as can be seen in his lack of ability to "conserve." For example, in the conservation of number problem (see Chapter 4) the child apparently cannot spontaneously envisage an inverse physical translation of the circles which would convey them back to their initial position, at which point their one-to-one relationship with the first set of circles would be perceptually obvious.

In other words, it would appear that while the pre-operational child can manipulate images when presented with a proposition in verbal form which, in effect, provides him with cues as to how this manipulation is to be performed (for example, "cats climb trees"), he cannot spontaneously envisage such a transformation when its end-point (the final arrangement which it produces) conflicts with his direct perception of the physically present situation. Thus as Piaget and others have observed, the child's cognitive processes tend to be dominated by his perceptions; he is "stimulus bound," so to speak.[7]

Concrete Operational Stage   The stage of concrete operations, distinguished in the Piagetian system by the emergence of the conservation of mass, weight, number, and volume in that order (Piaget, 1950; Uzgaris, 1964) seems to imply, as we have indicated, an increasing facility to manipulate images. This facility is also reflected in the chief characteristic of this stage: the child's ability to comprehend concepts without proceeding through the abstracting phase characteristic of the learning of primary concepts. Concepts acquired without this abstracting phase are referred to as *secondary abstractions* (concepts). Thus in the concrete operational stage the child may be given a verbal definition containing the criterial attributes of a concept; then, in order to acquire the meaning of the concept, he need only be provided with concrete exemplars of one or more of these criterial attributes. For example, the child at this stage would be able to comprehend the meaning of the term "rhombus" defined as "a quadrilateral with two parallel sides" provided that he was given a concrete example of the notions of "parallel" and "quadrilateral." In this case it would appear, then, that given only the stimulus support provided by concrete images of *exemplars* of the criterial attributes, the child would be able mentally to construct a representative image embodying the meaning of the concept.

The distinguishing characteristic (the ability to comprehend secondary abstractions) of the concrete operational stage may be defined without reference to the very specific and particularized images found in mathematics and science. In the most general terms, we may say that the learner in the second stage does not abstract criterial attributes from a series of exemplars of the concept, but utilizes in his comprehension of the concept specific exemplars of its criterial attributes. Thus, while the concept of "work" is being learned as a primary concept, the *pre-operational* child will eventually hypothesize such attributes as "activity," "necessary," and "useful" as criterial, by abstracting them from "farming," "fixing cars," "keeping house," "nursing," and so on. In this case, however, he tests each of the attributes against each of the exemplars before relating them to his cognitive structure. If the concrete operational child learns the concept of "work" as a secondary concept in elementary school, he is given its attributes in the form of a definition, and may use an exemplar for one or more of the attributes (for example, "necessary") in relating them to his cognitive structure. These

---

[7]Piaget's considerably more sophisticated views on the child's mental images—and their relationship to conservation phenomena—can be found in Piaget and Inhelder (1966), and Piaget (1964). For additional comments see Wohlwill (1967), Piaget (1967), and Carey (1967).

exemplars of the attributes serve as *props* in facilitating the learning of concepts at this stage.[8]

The use of such props in concept acquisition implies a more abstract process of learning than the actual use of "genuine" concrete empirical experience itself for the following reasons:

(a) the exemplars of *attributes* are examples of the *abstracted* properties of concepts—not particular instances of the concept;

(b) a single example of an attribute suffices as a prop as opposed to the multiple exemplars of the concept that are given in concrete empirical experience;

(c) the prop serves mainly as a "crutch" in relating the criterial attribute to cognitive structure rather than as a concrete empirical matrix from which either the criterial attribute itself is derived or in relation to which it derives its potential meaningfulness.

Once secondary concepts are acquired, the concrete operational child is no longer dependent upon props in understanding or using their meanings. However, he cannot yet understand *propositions* involving secondary concepts, or manipulate such propositions in problem solving, *unless* he is provided with a particular exemplar for each of the abstractions involved. For example, if the child has learned the meaning of "trapezium" as a secondary abstraction he would not be able to understand the statement: "a parallelogram is a trapezium in which both pairs of opposite sides are parallel," unless we provided him with a specific instance of a parallelogram and trapezium to use as concrete props for the proposition.[9]

It is clear, then, that during the concrete operational stage, which we have tentatively taken to parallel the elementary-school years, there are definite limitations on the child's ability to comprehend and manipulate abstract verbal propositions (that is, propositions consisting of relationships between secondary abstractions). In effect, these tend to be too remotely removed from concrete empirical experience to be relatable to cognitive structure. This does not mean, however, that autonomous discovery is required before these propositions can be meaningfully learned; as long as concrete empirical props are made an integral part of the learning situation, they (the propositions) are eminently learnable. Concrete empirical props also need not necessarily be nonverbal or tangible (for example, objects,

---

[8]The reader who requires an additional concrete prop to comprehend these ideas should study the "tangent" example at the end of the chapter.

[9]It can also be argued (see Ausubel, 1968) that the ability to understand and manipulate (with the aid of props) relationships between secondary abstractions is central to the "logical operations" which characterize the concrete operational child in Piaget's system. One such operation is "reversibility," which figures predominantly in the child's ability to conserve (Sullivan, 1967b).

pictures). Frequently, words that represent particular exemplars or attributes of a concept are very adequate concrete empirical props in learning abstract propositions and secondary concepts respectively.

Abstract Logical Stage Somewhere near the beginning of the junior high-school period, the student typically reaches the final stage in his decreasing dependence upon concrete empirical props in meaningfully relating abstract relationships to cognitive structure. As a first step in that direction, he becomes able to understand the meaning of secondary abstractions presented verbally to him without having to make even the limited use of props characteristic of concept learning in the second stage. In other words, he is able to relate the criterial attributes of the concept directly to his cognitive structure *without props*, and if he does not know the meaning of a given attribute, it too need only be defined. For example, we pointed out earlier that the adult is quite capable of comprehending the meaning of the concept "surface of genus one" defined as "a surface with exactly one hole in it" without reference to any concrete model whatever. In this case he is able to draw upon images already available in his cognitive structure and to recombine these to form a representative image constituting the meaning of the concept. Similarly, in the "work" example (where concrete images are not as much in evidence), the individual is able to understand the dictionary definition of this term without the aid of props.

The freedom from reliance on props is reflected as well in the adolescent's ability to understand and manipulate the meanings of propositions involving secondary abstractions without having to refer to particular exemplars of the secondary abstractions involved. It is evident that the emerging ability to manipulate abstractions without any reference to present or immediately prior concrete-empirical experience opens up new learning possibilities to the adolescent. Not only is he not bound to the "here and now," but he is able to envisage relationships between concepts which need have no counterpart in physical reality; thus he becomes able to theorize and deal with hypothetical relationships between ideas.

Relationship between Abstract Logical Stage and Piaget's Formal Stage

In previous paragraphs we have described the attributes of what we called the "abstract logical stage." As indicated earlier, it was intended that this stage should parallel what Piaget has termed the stage of "formal operations." Nevertheless certain descriptive terms are frequently used in popular accounts of Piaget's third stage which are not included in the present theory and which, in our opinion, do not describe cognitive processes whose appearance is confined to the most abstract stage of logical thinking.

To begin with, it is sometimes said that it is only at the formal stage that the child is able to engage in "hypothetical-deductive," or "if/then" thinking. However it seems clear that children in the concrete operational stage, and even in the pre-operational stage, *are* quite capable of undertaking a certain kind of "if then" thinking. For example, the pre-operational child's ability to understand the proposition: "if it rains this afternoon we will not be able to go on a picnic," can be inferred from his later deduction: "since it is raining this afternoon, therefore we cannot go on a picnic." For the very young child, the concepts involved in the original "if/then" proposition in our example, and in the manipulation of the original proposition represented by the deduction, are all primary concepts derived from concrete-empirical experience. It is somewhat misleading, then, to suggest that "if/then" thinking is peculiar to the stage of formal operations. Actually, what distinguishes the various stages is not so much *the kind of logical process* involved as the *degree of abstraction* involved in the data upon which this process rests.

It is equally fallacious to conclude that the child cannot engage in "syllogistic reasoning" (for example, drawing conclusions of the form "*A* is greater than *C*" from the premises "*A* is greater than *B*" and "*B* is greater than *C*") before he has attained the formal stage. In a study by S. A. Hill (1961), for example, it was found that most children at the age of six to eight could easily draw correct inferences from hypothetical premises involving abstract relationships provided that they had an opportunity to utilize concrete models or exemplars in the process of such reasoning.

On the other hand," certain of the characteristics of Piaget's formal stage involve an extension of the abilities described in our abstract logical stage. One of the most frequently cited examples is so-called "combinatorial thinking,"[10] or "the ability to envisage all possible relationships between the ideas or variables in a problem situation." Since it is difficult to understand the meaning of this term without reference to the type of situation in which it is exhibited, we will re-examine here the pendulum problem, previously discussed in connection with the technique of task analysis. In the Piaget experiment involving this problem (Inhelder and Piaget, 1958), the subject is presented with a pendulum of adjustable length and with bobs of various size, and he is shown both how to adjust the pendulum and how to attach bobs. He is then asked to see if he can find out what makes the pendulum take longer to make a complete swing.

In Piaget's analysis a special kind of symbolism is employed in which

---

[10]The reader should distinguish this particular meaning of the term "combinatorial" from its earlier use to signify a particular type of relationship between new and existing ideas in cognitive structure.

individual letters stand for statements (representing a change in one of the variables involved in the problems), thus:

> *L* stands for the statement (i.e., is to be read) "a change in the variable: 'length of pendulum.'"
>
> *W* stands for the statement "a change in the variable: 'weight of the bob.'"
>
> *P* stands for the statement "a change in the variable: 'the strength of the initial push.'"
>
> *T* stands for the statement "a change in the variable: 'the period of the pendulum.'"[11]

The negative of each of the propositions is indicated by placing a bar over the letter. Thus, $\bar{L}$ stands for the statement *"no* change in the variable: 'length of pendulum.'"

With this symbolism at hand we can now look at the way in which children of various stages approached the solution of the problem. To begin with, the pre-operational child is unable, according to Piaget, to order elements in serial fashion; that is, he cannot consistently lay out a series of objects in order of increasing size. Consequently he is unable to systematically vary one of the independent variables (for example, the length) and observe its effect upon the dependent variable (for example, the period). Thus there is no possibility of solution, and the children at this stage studied by Piaget show no real progress with the problem.

In the concrete stage the child is able to order objects serially and thus is able to systematically vary the independent variables and observe their effects upon the dependent variables. However, since he is confined essentially to reasoning by simple correlations, he does not effectively *separate* variables and tends to vary them all simultaneously rather than one at a time (we saw earlier that the solution will follow if each independent variable is manipulated while holding the others constant). Because he manipulates all the variables at once as it were, the child erroneously concludes (according to Piaget) that each of them is causally related to the period of the pendulum. In terms of Piaget's symbolism, the child's reasoning is of this form: "Since *L* and *W* and *P* together produce *T,* therefore *L* produces *T, W* produces *T,* and *P* produces *T.*"

It is only in the formal stage, according to Piaget, that the child effectively separates the variables and envisages "all possible relationships"

---

[11]*L, W,* and *P* refer to variables which children (and unsophisticated adults) tend to single out as being potentially related to *T*. In the Piaget analysis, a fourth independent variable— height of bob (or amplitude of swing)—is considered as well, but its exclusion here does not change the form of the analysis.

among the causal factors. In Piaget's symbolism this can be written (where " $\wedge$ " means "and" and " $\vee$ " means "or"):

$$(L \wedge W \wedge P \wedge T) \vee (\bar{L} \wedge W \wedge P \wedge T)$$

$$\vee (L \wedge W \wedge P \wedge \bar{T}) \vee (\bar{L} \wedge W \wedge P \wedge \bar{T}) \vee$$

$$(L \wedge \bar{W} \wedge P \wedge T) \vee (L \wedge \bar{W} \wedge P \wedge \bar{T})$$

$$\vee (L \wedge W \wedge \bar{P} \wedge T) \vee (L \wedge W \wedge \bar{P} \wedge \bar{T}) \vee$$

$$(\bar{L} \wedge \bar{W} \wedge P \wedge T) \vee (\bar{L} \wedge \bar{W} \wedge P \wedge \bar{T})$$

$$\vee (L \wedge \bar{W} \wedge \bar{P} \wedge T) \vee (L \wedge \bar{W} \wedge \bar{P} \wedge \bar{T}) \vee$$

$$(\bar{L} \wedge W \wedge \bar{P} \wedge T) \vee (\bar{L} \wedge W \wedge \bar{P} \wedge \bar{T})$$

$$\vee (\bar{L} \wedge \bar{W} \wedge \bar{P} \wedge T) \vee (\bar{L} \wedge \bar{W} \wedge \bar{P} \wedge \bar{T})$$

In verbal terms this can be roughly expressed by saying "the possible combinations of independent (causal) variables and dependent (effect) variables are L and W and P and T, *or* not L and W and P and T, and so on." At this stage, then, the child is now "hypothesizing" that various combinations of the independent variables will be related to a change in the period of the pendulum and that various other combinations will not be related to such a change. With these possible combinations now laid out, the child can systematically test his hypothesis against reality by actually manipulating variables to determine which ones are in fact true. These true propositions are recombined—utilizing logical properties which characterize the organization (structure) of operations at that stage—and the correct implications emerge, namely that L causes T, W does *not* cause T, and P does *not* cause T. (Or that L causes T independently of W and P.) This example illustrates the sense in which Piaget's theory employs the expression that the "adolescent sees all possible relationships between the variables," and also indicates what is involved in his notion of hypothesizing.

In respect to discrepancies between Piaget's theory and the one offered in this text, it is clear that Piaget's notion of formal thinking is derived from a *problem-solving* task rather than in the context of *acquiring the meaning* of concepts or propositions. And, as usual, there is a considerable gap between the ability to understand abstract concepts and the ability to solve problems. Another way of putting this is to say that the stage of abstract thinking (as we have defined it) constitutes a *necessary* but by no means *sufficient* condition for the *most abstract kind* of combinatorial thinking involved in the Piaget formulation. Further comment on the pedagogical implications of this difference is deferred to a later section.

Determinants of Change

It is hypothesized that the combined influence of three concomitant and mutually supporting developmental trends accounts for the individual's ability to relate increasingly more abstract materials to his cognitive structure as he progresses from stage to stage. In the first place, the developing individual gradually acquires a working vocabulary of "transactional" or mediating terms (for example, conditional conjunctions, qualifying adjectives) that makes possible the more efficient combination of different relatable abstractions into potentially meaningful propositions and their subsequent relationship to established ideas in cognitive structure. Second, he can relate these latter propositions more readily to cognitive structure, and hence render them more meaningful, because of his growing fund of stable, high-order concepts and principles encompassed by, and made available within, that structure. Obviously, a sufficient body of clear and stable abstract concepts is necessary before one can hope to manipulate such concepts to generate meaningful general propositions.

Finally, it seems reasonable to propose that after many years of practice in understanding meaningfully and manipulating relationships between abstractions *with* the aid of concrete empirical props, the older child gradually develops greater facility in performing these operations. Eventually, after acquiring the necessary transactional and higher-order concepts, he can perform the same operations just as effectively *without* relying on these props.

One could, of course, describe the same determinants in terms of images in those types of learning in which such images are strongly in evidence. Thus the individual's growing stock of high order, clearly established ideas is represented, in such areas as mathematics and science at least, by a growing stock of clear, stable, and *retrievable* images. In like manner, the fact that the individual acquires an increasing number of transactional terms means, as we saw earlier, that he acquires the vehicle whereby images can be manipulated or modified to produce new meanings. Finally, it is reasonable to hypothesize that after the individual has had much experience in manipulating images—initially with the stimulus support provided by concrete empirical props—he would eventually arrive at a stage where such manipulations can be performed without stimulus support.

General and Specific Aspects of Stage Transition

In the previous sections we have postulated that an individual's overall developmental status may be described as pre-operational, concrete operational, or abstract operational on the basis of an estimate of his characteristic or *predominant* mode of cognitive functioning. Nevertheless, too much unevenness exists in any individual's experiential background and pattern of abilities for the transition from concrete to abstract functioning to occur *simultaneously* in all areas. Moreover, a stage of development is always referable to a typical range of difficulty and familiarity of the problem at hand. Beyond this stage, regression to an earlier stage of development may occur.

Consequently, even after the individual reaches the abstract stage of development on an overall basis, he necessarily continues to undergo the same transition from concrete to abstract functioning in *each new* subject matter area he encounters. Nevertheless, once he attains the abstract stage *generally,* the transition to abstract cognitive functioning in unfamiliar new subject-matter areas takes place much more readily than is the case at earlier phases of the transition. For example, a cognitively mature adult who has never studied astronomy is not in precisely the same developmental position as an eleven- or twelve-year-old with respect to the concrete/abstract dimension when both begin a course in astronomy. The former is able to draw on various transferable elements of his more general ability to function abstractly, and therefore he passes through the concrete stage of functioning in this subject-matter area much more rapidly than would be the case were he first emerging from the stage of concrete logical operations.

These facilitating transferable elements presumably include transactional terms, higher-order concepts, and the ability to directly understand and manipulate relationships between abstractions. These acquisitions represent in large measure the contribution to *general* developmental readiness resulting from the individual's study of *specific* subject-matter fields.

RECENT "STAGE" RESEARCH AS A SCIENTIFIC GUIDE TO THE PLACEMENT OF CURRICULUM CONTENT

We may now return to the question which precipitated our discussion of "stages" in cognitive development. In brief, it has frequently been held that if one could predict the modal age at which a given stage would emerge in a culture, and if one knew the limitations imposed by this stage upon the treatment of specific items of subject matter, one would then have a timing device which would suggest the minimum ages at which certain kinds of content could be introduced. For example, if it could be demonstrated that successful pedagogical instruction in any subject-matter area depended upon the appearance of the concrete operational stage, and if this stage does not typically occur before seven years of age, then the school would be justified in its present practice of postponing formal instruction until grade 1. How feasible does this plan now appear in the light of the "stage" research which has been undertaken in the past few years?

Replication Studies Involving the Pre-Operational and Concrete Operational Stages

The work of Piaget, and particularly the stages which he proposed, has been the focal point of an enormous amount of recent research. The earliest studies were mainly of a replicatory nature and were designed to assess the validity of Piaget's assertion that the stages existed and that they possessed the characteristics which he postulated. For a variety of reasons these studies concentrated on the pre-operational and concrete operational stages, and the transition between these stages became the most frequent object of study. On the whole, such investigations have been in agreement with Piaget's more recent formulations concerning these age groups.[12]

However, as might be expected, it was soon found that the absolute ages postulated by Piaget (on the basis of his research with children in Geneva) as demarking the boundaries of the stages were subject to considerable variation, depending upon the intellectual endowment, experimential background, education, and personality structures of the group studied. For example, one experimenter found that about half the population of African bush children *never* acquired conservation of volume (Greenfield, 1966). Similarly it has been found that *mental age* is a better indicator of stage than *chronological age* (Goldman, 1965). Further, it has been found that characteristic sex differences (for example, in mathematical thinking) reflecting differences in cultural expectations and experiential background, are found in degree of cognitive development in different subject-matter areas (Elkind, 1962).

None of these observations destroys the validity of the stage concept nor precludes the use of stages as a curriculum-pacing device. All it would mean in the latter case is that expectations concerning the acquisition of subject matter would have to be related not so much to the subject's chronological age as to his intelligence, culture, and experiential background, and that it would vary between subject-matter areas.

---

[12]See, for example: Braine, 1959; Case and Collinson, 1962; Dodwell, 1960; Elkind, 1961; Ervin, 1960; Fleischmann and others, 1966; R. J. Goldman, 1965; Hood, 1962; S. Jackson, 1965; Lindenbaum and Blum, 1967; Lovell, 1959a, 1959b; Lovell and Ogilvie, 1960; Lunzer, 1960; Mannix, 1960; Neimark and Lewis, 1967; Peel, 1959; Shantz and Smock, 1966; Smedslund, 1960, 1961; Wohlwill, 1960.

Studies in the Acceleration of Conservation

Somewhat more distressing to those who have sought a "master plan" for the pacing of curriculum content have been the results of recent research on the possibility of accelerating the appearance of stages. Initially it was believed that little acceleration was possible and Piaget-oriented theorists continue to assert that the appearance of stages is largely determined by genic and incidental learning factors and cannot be substantially facilitated by specific instruction.[13] However the preponderance of recent studies has, in our view, resulted in a somewhat more positive assessment of the possibilities of acceleration.

Research on the Conservation of Substance

For illustrative purposes we might consider recent research on the conservation of substance. In such experiments the child is presented with two equal quantities of a malleable substance—typically, two balls of clay or two quantities of water contained in beakers (Figure 7.2). Initially the pre-operational child maintains that the two balls have the same amount of clay, but when one is transformed in shape he now declares that one ball (usually the long one) has more clay than the other. Similarly when the water in one beaker is poured into a vessel of different shape the child indicates that he believes that the amounts of water are no longer equal. According to Piaget the child does not typically attain a stable notion of conservation (and concomitant freedom from domination by his perception of the situation) until he is approximately seven years of age, on the average.

The objective of recent conservation research has been to see whether, by means of special instruction, an obviously nonconserving child can be brought to achieve conservation at an earlier age than control subjects who are not exposed to instruction, and who ultimately attain conservation spontaneously. Typically, kindergarten children (a conveniently available group) have been used in these experiments, thus providing children one to two years younger than the age postulated for "spontaneous" conservation.

By no means have all such attempts been unequivocally successful. For example, Smedslund (1961) presented a group of nonconserving children (ages five to seven) with equal balls of clay in the manner described above,

---

[13]As late as 1964, Piaget himself expressed considerable scepticism about the prospects for genuine acceleration through specific instruction (Piaget, 1964). In a recent paper, however, one of the chief exponents of the Piaget school (Inhelder and others, 1967) seems to be admitting the possibility that directed learning *can* accelerate conservation, at least to a limited extent, provided that it is based upon the child's existing structure of operations.

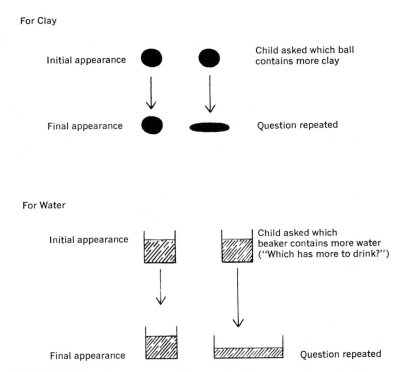

For Clay

Initial appearance — Child asked which ball contains more clay

Final appearance — Question repeated

For Water

Initial appearance — Child asked which beaker contains more water ("Which has more to drink?")

Final appearance — Question repeated

FIGURE 7.2 *Arrangements for standard conservation of substance experiments. The advanced student of conservation phenomena would classify the above instances as conservation of* equivalence *in that it is the equivalence of the two quantities of liquid that is maintained over the transformation. A simpler test, for what is denoted the "conservation of identity," occurs when the child is presented with liquid in a single beaker; here the liquid is poured into a second beaker of a different shape and the child is asked to indicate whether the amount has changed. For analysis of the relationship of these two tasks see Elkind, 1967.*

and divided these children into two groups depending on whether they maintained that the *weight* of the two balls was the same (natural conservers) or not the same (nonconservers) after one ball had been elongated. The nonconservers were provided with special training in which they made predictions (prior to changing the shape of the ball) concerning the equality of weight and subjected these predictions to test on a balance. As a result, a group of students were identified who had apparently acquired conservation and who could provide a rational explanation (for example, "nothing was added or taken away so the weight must be the same"). Then, in order to test the *stability* of the acquired conservation, Smedslund surreptitiously removed a small piece of clay from one of the balls after it had been changed in shape. When the "induced" conservers now discovered that the balls were not of equal weight and were asked why, all eleven of them reverted to pre-operational explanations (that is, to such explanations referring to the perceptual appearance of objects as: "this ball weighs more because it is rounder and fatter"). Only seven of the thirteen natural conservers showed a similar reversion and the subjects who resisted offered such explanations as "you must have taken away some of the clay." In this and other studies Smedslund demonstrated that conservation could be induced by external reinforcement, but he cast doubt upon its permanence in the face of apparent perceptual contradictions.

Experiments which have gone beyond the simple feedback principle used by Smedslund, and have employed instructional techniques involving the verbalization of principles or generalizations, have generally obtained better results. For example, Sullivan (1967a) subjected one group of nonconserving children (ages 6-8) to a film in which an adult model in a conservation of substance experiment verbalized principles supporting his conservation responses (for example, "nothing has been added or taken away, so there is still the same amount"). A second matched group of nonconserving children watched another (filmed) adult model give correct answers, but without verbalizing the principle being employed. As shown in Table 7.2, the great majority of initially nonconserving children were able to conserve after training even when different materials from those used in the training experience were employed. It was also found (Table 7.3) that the students who had (presumably) assimilated the verbal principles were as resistant to extinction (of the Smedslund type) as natural conservers, a result which was consistent with an earlier study by the same experimenter (Sullivan, 1966).

Brison (1966) conducted an experiment with kindergarten children (average age five years, seven months) which utilized both the verbalization of explanations by successful performers *and* enhanced motivation for the task. Groups of children, consisting of two conservers and four nonconservers, were shown identical cylindrical containers with unequal amounts of juice. The experimenter then poured the larger amount of juice into a wider container and the smaller amount into a narrow container and asked the pupil to point to the glass which had the most juice to drink. After each child had made his selection, the juice was returned to the original glasses, and the children were given the amounts they had chosen to drink. A child who made a correct prediction (initially one of the conservers) was asked to explain *why* he had obtained more juice. After five trials of this kind (spread over two days) half of the 24 experimental subjects showed some evidence of having acquired conservation, and considerable transfer of conservation responses to substances not used in the training was also obtained. In

TABLE 7.2

NUMBER OF CONSERVERS AND NONCONSERVERS WHEN NEW MATERIALS WERE USED

GROUP	CONSERVERS	NONCONSERVERS	TOTAL
Verbal principle	17	4	21
No principle	13	6	19
Total	30	10	40

Source: Sullivan, 1967a.

TABLE 7.3

NUMBER OF SUBJECTS SHOWING EXTINCTION
IN CONSERVATION OF SUBSTANCE POSTTEST

GROUP	RESISTED EXTINCTION	EXTINGUISHED	TOTAL
Verbal principle	8	10	18
No principle	5	9	14
Natural conservers	8	14	22
Total	21	33	54

Source: Sullivan, 1967a.

addition, even after this brief training period, five of the experimental subjects showed as much resistance to extinction as a group of "natural" conservers. The explanation offered for the success of the experiment was that the nature of the task motivated the subjects to mentally reverse the transformed shapes to their original states, a task facilitated during the training session by the presence of an empirical referent (prop), and that this practice assisted the child when he had to perform a similar task in the absence of the prop.

In another study Engelmann (1967) taught nonconserving kindergarten and first-grade children verbal rules underlying the conservation of such properties as area, volume, substance and weight—each of which may be conceptualized in terms of a fixed number of elementary units. One such rule has to do with the "compensation of dimensions." For example, the child is shown and required to verbalize a rule indicating that when a rectangle composed of a given number of fixed units is transformed, an increase in height is compensated by a decrease in length (Figure 7.3). After a mean

training time of 54 minutes, ten of the fifteen original nonconservers in the
experimental group met the criterion for conservation of liquid (substance),
while none of the matched control subjects (no training) could conserve.
While Engelmann did not measure stability by attempting to extinguish
conservation responses, he did set relatively comprehensive criteria for the
achievement of conservation.

An experiment by Frank (described in Bruner, 1966) may be regarded as demonstrating the combined effect of verbalization and (initially)
shielding the learner from the perceptual domination which is evident in
nonconserving responses.[14] In this study groups of four-, five-, six-, and
seven-year-olds were first subjected to the standard conservation of substance
(water in beakers) experiment, yielding the proportion of conservation
responses shown in Table 7.4. In a second phase the experimenter began by
showing the child two beakers of different shapes, only one of which contained liquid (the "conservation of identity" arrangement). A screen was
then placed before these two beakers, so that only their tops—but not the
water levels—could be seen, and the liquid was poured from one beaker to
the other. The child was then asked to indicate whether there was the same
amount of liquid as before. As Table 7.4 shows, screening produced a
substantial increase in conservation-like responses across all age groups. The
experiment was then repeated, but this time the screen was removed after
the subject had made his prediction, revealing that the height of the liquid
had changed somewhat as a result of pouring. At this point most of the
four-year-olds reversed their judgments about conservation—overwhelmed
apparently by the change in water level—while the majority of five-, six-, and
seven-year-olds continued to maintain that the amount of liquid was the
same. A short while later the standard conservation test (that is, conservation of equivalence) was repeated, and it is apparent that the five-, six-, and
seven-year-olds profited considerably from their intervening experience.

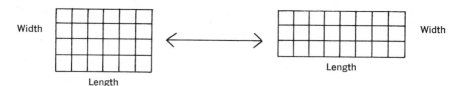

FIGURE 7.3 *Compensation of dimensions rule in conservation training: "If the length increases, the width decreases"; or, "If it gets longer
this way (length), it has to get shorter this way (width)."*

---

[14]The account which follows is considerably abbreviated; for full details the reader should
consult Bruner, 1966.

TABLE 7.4

EFFECT OF PERCEPTUAL SCREENING ON CONSERVATION RESPONSES*

Age	PRETEST: STANDARD CONSERVATION OF SUBSTANCE TEST	LEVELS HIDDEN BY SCREEN	SCREEN REMOVED	POSTTEST: STANDARD CONSERVATION OF SUBSTANCE TEST
4	0	50	10	0
5	20	90	80	79
6	50	80	100	90
7	50	100	100	90

*Percentage of Conservation Responses.
Source: Adapted from Bruner, 1966.

One possible explanation of the results of the screening technique is that it required the enunciation of a verbal form of the conservation response (that is, "they are the same") prior to the introduction of a perceptual contradiction. Moreover, the reconciliation of this conflict apparently causes the child to distinguish between differences in appearance and actual identity, an ability which carries over to their later retesting on the standard conservation test.[15] The results of studies showing conservation as a result of direct or inferred verbal rules are consistent with the explanation offered earlier for the transition between stages in that the use of language, either spontaneously or by instruction, allows the child to generate the kind of image manipulations which are characteristic of the stage of concrete operations.

In summary, the evidence of these and other studies (Brison, 1966; Floch, 1967; Gruen, 1965; Kohnstamm, 1966; Lee, 1966; Murray, 1967; Ojemann and Pritchett, 1963; Ojemann and others, 1966; Sigel and others, 1966; Sonstroem, 1966; Wallach and Sprott, 1964; Wallach and others, 1967) of the acceleration of conservation indicates that a more optimistic view than that which Piaget takes seems to be warranted. Since most of the studies have involved short-term training programs and have produced rather modest results, it is really quite impossible to say what might be expected with concentrated programs of specific training extending over a period of years.

Research on Formal Operations

Considerably less research has been done on the stage of formal operations. However Inhelder and Piaget (1958) presented considerable evidence indi-

---

[15]This study has generated much theoretical heat; for a sampling of the spirited discussion, see: Bruner, 1966; Carey, 1967; Elkind, 1967; Piaget, 1967; Wohlwill, 1967.

cating that "formal" operations appear slightly before the onset of adolescence and, on the whole, their findings have been corroborated by other investigators (R. J. Goldman, 1965; S. Jackson, 1965; Lovell, 1961a; Yudin, 1966; Yudin and Kates, 1963). Lovell's subjects attained this stage of development somewhat later than Inhelder and Piaget's, and Case and Collinson's (1962), somewhat earlier.

There seems to have been very little research attempting to accelerate the appearance of the stage of formal operations. However, experimenters have found that children *are* able to solve problems involving such purportedly formal stage attributes as "hypothetical deductive thinking" and "ideas about ideas" at much earlier ages than Piaget proposes (Case and Collinson, 1962; Englemann, 1967; S. A. Hill, 1961; Suppes, 1965). In part, as we have noted previously, children's earlier-than-expected success on these problems reflects the capacity to undertake such reasoning, provided that judicious use is made of empirical props.

Moreover, as we saw in the pendulum example, it would appear that the child can arrive at a useful and generalizable solution to the type of problem posed by Piaget *without* invoking the detailed combinatorial reasoning which Piaget posits as underlying the thinking processes in the formal stage. While Piaget would probably classify the child who utilizes the previously described method as being in the "concrete operational" stage, the critical concern of the educator is whether the child can actually *solve* the problem, rather than the label which Piaget-oriented theorists would attach to the reasoning processes which the child exhibits.[16] From the point of view of the curriculum-pacing strategy, there seems to be a danger that a literal interpretation of the terms used to describe Piaget's stage of formal operations may be causing some educators to put an unnecessarily low ceiling on the complexity of intellectual tasks to which young children are subjected.

The Curriculum-Pacing Strategy Revisited

Up to this point the chief obstacles posed to the implementation of the curriculum-pacing strategy have been that the appearance of the conservations (one kind of proposed "benchmark") seems to be influenceable—to an unknown degree—by direct training, and that the criteria cited for entry into the formal stage (another proposed benchmark) appear to be more severe than the mastery of the intellectual tasks from which they are allegedly derived seems to require. However the greatest source of pessimism concern-

---

[16]The child (or adult, for that matter) who solved the pendulum problem in the manner described in the previous chapter would not fully exhibit Piaget's "combinatorial reasoning" and therefore would not be considered to have attained the stage of formal operations. However it seems at least a reasonable possibility that Piaget has superimposed upon this problem a conception of thinking which vastly exceeds in complexity that actually employed by mature problem-solvers.

ing the viability of the curriculum-pacing strategy has arisen in conjunction with the third phase, at which it was hoped that one could deduce that the understanding of certain ideas depended upon the attainment of a particular stage. The validity of this proposition now appears to be considerably in doubt. For while experimental results are scanty, Sullivan's (1967b, 1969) analysis of relevant theoretical issues and available data call into question the argument that the existence of a *particular* Piaget stage is a prerequisite for a *specific* kind of school learning; in fact, he contends that it may be just as reasonable to argue that the acquisition of addition and subtraction skills provides readiness for conservation of number, as to assert that the acquisition of number conservation constitutes readiness for addition and subtraction. Moreover, and as will be discussed later, many of the ideas presented in school can be expressed in a manner appropriate to understanding at *each* stage of development if due attention is given to the proper use of concrete aids at the earlier stages.

When all these considerations are put together, the prospect for a grand plan for curriculum pacing seems rather dim indeed, and many curriculum-developers have abandoned it completely. Some go even further and maintain that it is erroneous to conclude that a child cannot understand a particular concept or cope with a particular intellectual task until all possible means of teaching him this task have been exhausted (Bereiter, 1968).

PEDAGOGICAL IMPLICATIONS OF THE READINESS CONCEPT

While the curriculum-pacing strategy hoped for by curriculum developers may not be feasible, this somewhat distressing fact by no means rules out the relevance of readiness considerations for individual teachers. Actually, since the material to be taught at a given grade level will likely be prescribed by a school district or individual school, the major problem facing the teacher may be put as follows: "In what manner should this (given) material be presented to the learner so that it will best be understood, keeping in mind his present stage of development?" Here both the stage theory itself and the broader concept of readiness can provide some assistance.

Gearing Instruction to Present Level of Cognitive Development

To begin with, it seems reasonable that the teacher should attempt to assess the general readiness (that is, both the general stage of cognitive maturity and the particular subject-matter readiness) of each child under his direction and for each area in which instruction is being offered. Although an apparently formidable task, this can be done both indirectly from a knowledge of the student's background and general educational experience as well as directly from observation of the student in the classroom setting. Knowledge of the criterial attributes of each stage is essential here, and will allow the teacher to make incisive and time-saving observations in this task. For example, the teacher can readily ascertain the extent of the child's dependence upon empirical props in comprehending second-order abstractions, and thus make appropriate choices concerning the kind of instructional approach to be used. Many elementary-school children may be identified in this way who are quite capable of understanding propositions involving secondary abstractions without the aid of props. Such children are, therefore, capable of doing a great deal of independent reading and learning on their own.

Of course, once the teacher has a firm impression of each child's stage of cognitive development he will naturally gear his instruction differentially to the different stages of cognitive maturity represented in his class. Previous illustrations have indicated the general outline of the approach which might be taken. Consider, for example, how the teacher would take into account the child's stage of intellectual development in teaching the notion of a tangent (defined for our purposes as "a straight line which touches a curved line at one point but does not cross it"). It is our contention that a pre-operational child could be taught this concept provided that a sequence of exemplars was provided, each exhibiting the criterial attributes (that is, "straight line," "touching at one point," "not crossing") as shown in Figure 7.4. In this case the teacher would define the characteristics of the tangent by identifying the criterial attributes in the first exemplar and would proceed through the series of exemplars by saying (in connection with the second exemplar), "See, this is a tangent because it is a straight line (running finger along the line), it touches this curved line at one point (pointing) but does not cross it," or (with respect to the third exemplar), "See, this is not a tangent because . . . and so on." The concrete operational child, on the other hand, *could* understand the verbal definition if the teacher merely provided a concrete exemplar for each of the criterial attributes assumed to be relatively unfamiliar to the student. In many instances, however, including the present one, the teacher would find it more convenient to illustrate all the criterial attributes in a single exemplar. Finally, the meaning of a tangent could be adequately conveyed to the abstract-stage child through a purely verbal definition.[17]

---

[17]In each case a test of the child's adequate understanding of the concept would take one of the following forms:

    (a) the child is asked to draw a tangent; (b) the child is asked to indicate which of a sequence of drawings (some tangents, some nontangents) actually represent tangents; (c) the child is asked to pick out the correct definition from a set of plausible possibilities.

    Theoretically, the notion of tangent can be conveyed to the pre-operational child by using a sequence of exemplars *only* (that is, no nontangents). It can be argued, however, that mixing of exemplars and nonexemplars renders the learning process more efficient.

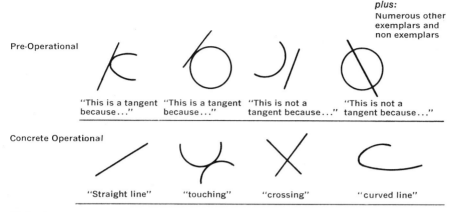

FIGURE 7.4 *Exemplars used in teaching concept of "tangent" to children in pre-operational, concrete operational, and abstract stages of development.*

The existence of wide differences in cognitive maturity within the classroom suggests that it will frequently be wise to use small-group instruction or self-instructional devices in introducing new concepts, rather than directing one's instructional strategy to the whole class. Some children will depend heavily upon concrete props during their entire elementary-school experience, and for slow learners in particular the introduction of new ideas will frequently be limited to concept formation from multiple exemplars of concepts. Cognitively more mature students will not need such stimulus support, and it seems unfair not to allow them to proceed at the more rapid pace of which they are capable, when such time-consuming procedures are not relied upon.

Although the *preschool* child's comprehension is restricted to relatively nonabstract (primary) concepts in the learning of most relational propositions, it is not necessary that *all* relational learning during this period take place on a nonverbal, problem-solving, or completely autonomous self-discovery basis in order to be meaningful. Simple derivative propositions involving primary concepts can certainly be directly apprehended without the use of particular exemplars, and simple, correlative, superordinate, and combinatorial propositions can also be learned on a reception basis—particularly if the teacher provides specific exemplars of the concepts involved, or an opportunity for manipulation of objects or concrete images. Autonomous self-discovery of the proposition to be learned might conceivably enhance current learning and provide additional motivation for future learning, but it is certainly not indispensable for meaningful reception learning.

Neither does the elementary-school child's dependence on concrete empirical props for the understanding of more abstract propositions require that all, or even most, teaching be conducted on an inductive, problem-solving (discovery) and nonverbal basis. The only essential condition during this period for the learning of secondary propositions embodying secondary concepts is the availability of specific exemplars of the concepts in question, and such exemplars may be purely verbal in nature. Didactic exposition with such verbal props can easily be combined with other concrete empirical props in the form of demonstrations, and usually suffices for the presentation of most subject matter that is neither excessively complex nor excessively unfamiliar. In the latter instances, it may be desirable to enhance the understanding achieved through verbal exposition by subjecting the pupil to Socratic questioning or by providing him with a semi-autonomous type of problem solving (guided discovery) in which the discovery itself is accelerated by the arrangement of materials, hints, and Socratic questioning.

Facilitating Growth to Successive Levels

While recognizing the need for designing instructional procedures that are consistent with the child's present level of cognitive maturity, it should be remembered that the teacher is also interested in utilizing present instruction to promote progress to more abstract levels. After a certain degree of consolidation of the pre-operational stage occurs, one can accelerate the attainment of the next stage (concrete operational) by training the child under the learning conditions that apply at the latter stage (that is, by requiring him to relate secondary abstractions and abstract propositions to cognitive structure *with* the aid of concrete empirical props) or by systematically developing his stock of abstract concepts and his ability to manipulate them mentally. In a similar way the transition from concrete to abstract logical operations can be facilitated by gradually withdrawing concrete empirical props as the prior stage becomes consolidated—that is, by withdrawing the props well in advance of the actual attainment of abstract cognitive functioning. Thus it seems appropriate that teachers design experiences which anticipate or point toward the conditions of cognitive functioning of the stage just beyond that which the child is now in.

As an example of the preceding remarks, the elementary-school arithmetic teacher frequently uses specific embodiments of the number line as an empirical prop for explaining the meaning of addition, subtraction, and multiplication to young children. At the earliest possible stage the teacher should have the child internalize (mentally) the number line and practice *envisaging* operations performed on it. In terms of our earlier discussion, both the internalization of the number line (as a now relatively abstract concept), and the practice in performing operations upon it (relating process notions to it), will facilitate developmental readiness. Thus, when the child is later introduced to negative numbers and their operations, he will be able to comprehend these second-order concepts by relating them directly to this internalized set of ideas with little need for further concrete experience.

Use of Concrete Models

The course of cognitive development has been described here in terms of a sequence of stages of increasing independence of concrete empirical data in comprehending the meaning of concepts and propositions and in manipulating these propositions mentally. At the most advanced stage the child is usually capable of understanding secondary abstractions and propositions containing such abstractions without direct reference to concrete models.

This does not mean, however, that instruction at the high-school level and beyond should proceed with *no* recourse to concrete models and exemplars. In the first place, as we saw earlier, when the adolescent or adult approaches a new area of study, or a particularly difficult concept, he will usually revert to a lower stage of cognitive functioning and will therefore require appropriate models and exemplars as an aid to his comprehension. It seems quite clear that this fact is frequently overlooked by high-school and university instructors who blithely assume that a purely symbolic exposition is adequate under all circumstances, and that the adult should be able to understand without the benefit of any sort of example or concrete illustration.

It is also clear that adults frequently become confused, and exhibit a generally low order of reasoning power, when they attempt to debate in purely verbal terms issues which can be conveniently represented by pictorial or graphical methods. For example, many readers of this text would find difficulty in attaining sufficient grasp of the interrelationships between the elements in the following verbal propositions to answer the question posed:

> C is less than M
> D is less than P
> C is greater than T
> D is greater than M
> Which is the greatest?

However, when recourse is had to a pencil, and the elements in these propositions are represented as points on a line, the interrelationships of the propositions are readily made visible and the solution of this example of an important class of "ordering" tasks becomes quite within the capabilities of children at the concrete operational stage.

Generally speaking, the solution of almost any problem in mathematics or the natural sciences, and in many other areas as well, can be facilitated by an appropriate use of models and representational diagrams. The setting and requirements of the geometry problem considered earlier *could* be understood from a purely verbal description, yet obtaining a solution would be a difficult task for most of us without the aid of a diagram. In effect, what the diagram representing the problem situation does is to make all the data relating to the problem *perceptually available at one time*, thus relieving the memory load. Moreover, in the example cited and in similar problems, the pictorial representation of the problem provides stimulus support throughout the essential process of manipulating propositions to find a solution.

In devising an instructional strategy, then, the teacher's thinking must be governed by two considerations. On the one hand, for purposes of efficiency, the presentation of concepts and generalizations should be at the highest level of abstraction of which the student is capable. At the same time, however, the teacher should systematically instruct the student in methods of constructing (or otherwise drawing upon) concrete models to aid him in his applications and problem solving.

Cyclic Treatment of Topics

In many of the new curricula there is a tendency to introduce topics in a preliminary way at much younger ages than that at which they were formerly introduced, and with the clear understanding that these topics will be returned to at a later stage. Some curriculum-builders advocate this so-called "spiral curriculum" approach as a general principle in curriculum construction (Bruner, 1960). It is clear, for example, that the pendulum might be studied at various stages in the student's schooling. The approach suggested by our task analysis might be employed with concrete operational children, who would probably be able to formulate and comprehend the proposition that the period of the pendulum varies with its length, and could use this proposition to make directional predictions (that is, if we want the pendulum to have a shorter period we should make the arm shorter). In high school, once the student has been introduced to Newtonian mechanics the topic could be re-introduced and the precise formula for the period of the pendulum derived. At higher levels the student would encounter compound pendulums (that is, two pendulums hooked together) in an even more abstract treatment of the principles of mechanics (Lanczos, 1949).

The spiral curriculum notion is consistent with what has been said here, in that the developmental characteristics of the elementary-school child's cognitive functioning do not require that we restrict the pedagogic use of these years to teach the "fundamental skills." His cognitive equipment is certainly adequate for acquiring a mature grasp of many concepts of the basic disciplines. Moreover, psychological arguments for introducing in the elementary school some aspects of the disciplines traditionally first encountered in the secondary school are extremely convincing. Considering the broad field of the natural sciences, for example, it is well known that young children spontaneously acquire many animistic and subjectivistic conceptions about the physical and biological universe (Piaget, 1932). These notions also tend to persist and often compete with more mature conceptions, especially when not countered by scientific training. Second, without early and satisfactory instruction in science, it is difficult for children both to assimilate positive attitudes toward the scientific enterprise, and to avoid being negatively conditioned to scientific subject matter. Third, since elementary-school pupils can easily acquire an intuitive grasp of many scientific concepts, failure to provide suitable opportunities for them to do so not only wastes available readiness for such learning, but also wastes valuable time in junior and senior high school that could be used for more advanced instruction in science. Finally, as pointed out above, these intuitive ideas can constitute a foundation for the later assimilation of more abstract, general, and precise treatments of the same content, thereby increasing their potential meaningfulness and preventing rote learning.

In the spiral curriculum approach the teacher's task is that of translating ideas into language that is compatible with the elementary-school child's capacities and level of functioning. For a number of reasons this is a difficult task. First, the teacher's natural tendency is to adopt the same level of discourse in teaching others that he characteristically uses in *learning* new ideas. Again, once he has acquired difficult concepts, he tends to regard them as self-evident and to forget both the limiting developmental factors involved in the learning process and, as well, the numerous misconceptions and ambiguities he had to overcome in the course of learning. After he has mastered a particular discipline, he tends to think of its structure only in terms of the logical relationships between the component ideas, forgetting the psychological process of progressive differentiation involved in acquiring any new body of knowledge. Lastly, because of his more sophisticated and highly differentiated cognitive structure, he is very much aware of the various subtleties, connotations, ramifications, and qualifications connected with even simple ideas, and often fails to realize that the introduction of such complications only confuses his pupils.

It is necessary, however, to have realistic expectations concerning the possibilities of introducing concepts in the elementary grades. It seems quite clear that Bruner's (1960) statement that " . . . any subject can be taught effectively in some intellectually honest form to any child at any stage of development," intended probably to overdramatize the possibilities of early learning, cannot possibly be true in any literal sense. It is, for example, difficult to imagine what "intellectually honest" form of the general theory of relativity could be presented to three-year-olds. Obviously, very careful attention is necessary in selecting such concepts, both from the point of view of their explanatory power in the discipline in question (that is, their value as anchorage for later ideas) and in terms of the possibility of failure and the time and effort required to teach the concept. Unfortunately there are few concrete guidelines available to teachers for selecting such concepts in any given discipline. However, the accumulating experience of new curriculum projects should rapidly help to fill in this gap in our knowledge.

General Acceleration of Learning

In addition to favoring the "spiral curriculum" concept, many new curriculum projects and experimental programs advocate a general acceleration in school learning, that is, advocate that there should be a general downward shift in the placement of curriculum content. It was pointed out earlier that perhaps the most ambitious proposal of this kind to date has been that the entire content of the undergraduate university mathematics course should be taught by the end of high school.

Many experimental projects have demonstrated the feasibility of such acceleration, provided that sufficient resources are devoted to it. Previously we mentioned the work of O. K. Moore (Pines, 1963) and Fowler (1962b) in advancing considerably the age at which children learn to read. Other experimenters have found that with appropriate attention to concrete aids it is possible successfully to teach the elementary-school child many ideas in science and mathematics (Arnsdorf, 1961; Bodanskii, 1967; Brownell, 1960; Bruner, 1960; O. L. Davis, 1958; Dienes, 1964; Englemann, 1967; Ojemann and others, 1966) that were previously thought much too difficult.

It should be clear to the reader by this point that everyone does not favor acceleration and that a variety of arguments will be put forward against it. Some argue that Piaget's stages are inflexible and that they dictate what the child can learn at any particular time; the rather questionable nature of this proposition has already been discussed in detail and need not be repeated here.

Other opponents point out that research has shown that there is no advantage in early learning, since students who start later may learn more quickly and soon catch up. In one progressive school, for example, children who learned no formal arithmetic until the fifth grade equalled matched controls in computation in the seventh grade, and surpassed them in arithmetical reasoning (Sax and Ottina, 1958). Actually it is difficult to find proof in such experiments that the schools fully capitalized on the early learning. Clearly if this is not done it is easy to believe that children with an early advantage will merely "mark time" until their later-starting peers catch up. Certainly if a child learns to read at four rather than the customary age of seven, and if this ability is recognized by the school and the child allowed to proceed with independent reading, then a definite advantage would seem to be inevitable. Again, if the child can be taught how to analyze natural physical phenomena (for example, the pendulum) in terms of cause and effect relationships and if he is encouraged to put this knowledge to use in exploring his environment, he would seem to have a considerable advantage over the student in the traditional program who does not acquire this ability until the high-school years. Consequently, insofar as certain critical skills (reading, reasoning processes, and so on) are concerned, it is difficult to understand how earlier acquisition could not help but benefit the student by increasing his total learning over the span of school years.

Another argument generally voiced against acceleration of learning is that, violating an internal timing mechanism, acceleration will inevitably cause some kind of "harm." We have already considered this matter and have shown that it poses a problem which is not amenable to decision by empirical methods. A more convincing argument that can be made against pronounced acceleration of learning is not that it is undesirable, but rather that it will involve an increase in educational costs which exceeds the taxpayer's tolerance. As a rough guide, we might say that the success of early learning experiments has been roughly proportional to the cost per pupil involved, and that these costs have often exceeded by several times the per-pupil costs of instruction in public schools. However, as the new projects move beyond the trial stage, attempts are being made to obtain comparable results with increasingly larger groups of students, and a point may eventually be reached when the additional cost will be outweighed considerably by the educational gain.

Finally we must return to our original definition of readiness which imposes a criterion of "reasonable economy of time and effort" in assessing whether a child is ready for a given learning task. By this criterion many subject-matter areas that *can* be learned at an earlier age level require undue time and effort and hence could be more profitably postponed until the learner is more mature. In addition, "premature learning" increases the probability of failure and the consequent development of negative attitudes toward a given field of study.

Teacher Involvement in Experimental Programs

Even though the question of acceleration of learning is a controversial one, it would seem beneficial for teachers to have at least limited experience in this direction. What we would propose is that a teacher take an individual child or a small group of children, set some learning goal which is relatively dramatic in terms of the school's present expectations, clearly define the behavioral outcomes desired, design appropriate teaching procedures, and evaluate the outcome. The potential benefits to be derived are considerable. In the first place, the study of an individual child, guided by theoretical concepts, would enable a teacher to acquire a better insight into the child's thinking processes than he could obtain through months or even years of operating as a director of a large group of learners. In other words, it is difficult to conceive of a more stimulating exercise in professional growth than to actually study in depth, plan, and execute a change in the pupil's cognitive behavior which is considerably in excess of that demanded by the school. The benefits of such exercise accrue not only to the individual teacher, however, for a succession of such experiences should give professional educators collectively some idea of the discrepancy between what is possible, given optimum conditions, and what for want of these conditions is actually done in the schools at the present time. In short, experience in accelerating learning would permanently cure the notion, too predominant among educators in our opinion, that the present limitations in student learning in schools may be safely attributed to the operation of some kind of natural law.

TOPICS FOR DISCUSSION AND FURTHER STUDY

1. Select three or four words at random from the dictionary; indicate how you would teach their meanings to children in the pre-operational, concrete operational, and abstract stages, respectively.

2. What concepts typically taught in the high school would, in your opinion, be beyond the comprehension of children in the primary grades (1 through 3) even though suitable use was made of concrete empirical props?

3. Investigate the subject matter that you will be teaching to determine the extent to which the "spiral curriculum" notion is in evidence. Select particular concepts and indicate how treatment of them differs at each successive level.

4.* It has been argued that the apparent limitations in evidence in children's reasoning may reflect, rather, the experimenter's inability to understand the child's real meaning (Braine, 1959; Braine and Shanks, 1965), or the child's inability to use relationed terms (Griffiths and others, 1967). For example, it has been suggested that when the "nonconserving" child in standard conservation of substance experiments says (after pouring) that one beaker has more water than the other, he merely means that the water level is higher in one beaker. To acquire some personal experience, perform the following experiment with a pre-operational child:

(a) Begin with two identical beakers containing visibly *unequal* amounts of pop or juice.

(b) Ascertain that the child knows which beaker contains the most fluid.

(c) Pour the liquid from the beaker containing the least amount into a tall, thin beaker.

(d) Ask the child which beaker now has the most fluid. (Most children will say that the tall, thin beaker has the most.)

(e) Tell the child that he may drink the fluid in *one* of the beakers and ask him which one he wants.

In the authors' experience, most young children will claim that the tall, thin beaker has the most fluid and yet some children, when given a choice, select the other. How does this result bear on the question posed in the first paragraph?

5.* Attempt to induce conservation in a nonconserving child by one of the methods described in this chapter, or in the references alluded to. Test its stability. What educational tasks, if any, might now be performed by the child by virtue of his acquisition of conservation?

6. The norms of many intelligence tests show that one aspect of a child's cognitive capacity which shows a gradual growth, maturing in mid-adolescence, is the ability to remember numerical or verbal symbols (for example, digits). On the other hand, children frequently exhibit an almost uncanny ability to remember complicated verbal expressions (for example, "supercalifragilisticexpialidotious.") What explanation might be offered for this apparent discrepancy? What pedagogical implications, if any, would follow?

7. Discuss some general rules that the teacher might provide to enable students to utilize concrete models to their advantage.

8. The Smedslund test for the stability of conservation judges a student a non-conserver if he is not able to maintain a conservation response in the face of a visual contradiction. What similarity is there between this kind of reversion and the adult's propensity to believe in feats of magic which apparently contradict scientific laws which he has purportedly internalized? Should it be concluded that such adults are operating at a pre-operational stage in their thinking? Is the Smedslund test too severe?

9. For the grade level and subject-matter area which you will be teaching, in what developmental stage would you expect to find most children? How would you rapidly ascertain the accuracy of this judgment?

10. Cite concrete examples of ways in which teachers may facilitate the growth from one developmental stage toward the next. Use illustrative examples from your own area of specialization.

SUGGESTIONS FOR ADDITIONAL READING

Bereiter, C. Psychology and early education. In *Psychology and early childhood education* (D. W. Brison and Jane Hill, Eds). Monograph Series No. 4. Toronto: The Ontario Institute for Studies in Education, 1968.

Brison, D. W. Can and should learning be accelerated? In *Accelerated learning and fostering creativity* (D. W. Brison, Ed.). Toronto: Department of Applied Psychology, The Ontario Institute for Studies in Education, 1968.

Brison, D. W., and E. V. Sullivan. *Recent research on the conservation of substance* Education Research Series No. 2. Toronto: The Ontario Institute for Studies in Education, May 1967.

Bruner, J. S., and others. *Studies in cognitive growth.* New York: John Wiley & Sons, Inc., 1966.

Flavell, J. H. *The developmental psychology of Jean Piaget.* New York: D. Van Nostrand Company, Inc., 1963.

Hunt, J. McV. The psychological basis for using pre-school enrichment as an antidote for cultural deprivation. *Merril-Palmer Quart.,* 1964, *10*(3), 209–248.

Ripple, R. E., and V. N. Rockcastle (Eds.). *Piaget rediscovered: A report of the Conference on Cognitive Studies and Curriculum Development.* Ithaca, N.Y.: School of Education, Cornell University, March 1964.

Sullivan, E. V. *Piaget and the school curriculum: A critical appraisal.* Toronto, Ont.: The Ontario Institute for Studies in Education, 1967.

Tuddenham, R. D. Jean Piaget and the world of the child. *Amer. Psychol.,* 1966, *21*(3), 207–217.

CHAPTER 8

INTELLECTUAL ABILITY

AMONG THE GENERAL PUBLIC THE TERM "IQ" IS PROBABLY
the most widely used of all the concepts that have emerged from psychology.
Indeed, some psychologists believe that this general test of intellectual ability
constitutes "the most important single contribution of psychology to the
practical guidance of human affairs" (Cronbach, 1960). Unfortunately,
widespread usage has not always been accompanied by the understanding of
the intent or nature of such tests; so periodically (and with increasing
frequency in the past few years) they have come under strong criticism
advanced on philosophical, political, social, and measurement grounds. As
the reader may know, at least one large school system has formally banned
group intelligence testing (Loretan, 1965; Gilbert, 1966), and we may safely
assume that informal restrictions on the use of these tests are in effect in
many other systems.

THE NATURE AND INTENT OF IQ TESTS

Despite recent setbacks, we think it likely that tests both of
general and special intellectual abilities will continue to be given for some
time to come. Consequently, the classroom teacher should have an understanding of the nature and intent of these tests and of how they may
legitimately be used to further the goals of instruction.

The Meaning of Mental Age and IQ

The discussion in subsequent sections will be clearer if we follow the various
steps involved in the preparation of a test of intellectual ability. To begin

213

with, the test-developer must possess some conception of the entity he is trying to measure; that is, he must have a *working definition* of "intelligence." And while there are a large number of conflicting formal definitions, most test-constructors would agree that the term "intelligence" refers to a general level of cognitive functioning, as reflected in the ability to understand ideas and to utilize abstract symbols (verbal, mathematical, or spatial) in the solution of intellectual problems.

The test-developer's working definition of intelligence has the effect of defining the domain of intellectual activity which he will sample. His next problem becomes that of devising items which fairly represent this domain. Figure 8.1 shows seven items selected from a group intelligence test which is widely used in Canada at the present time and which is generally representative of most intelligence tests used in North American schools today. The reader will note that the items include: finding opposites (1); picking out a word similar in meaning to a given word (2); solving verbal analogies (3); solving simple "problems" in arithmetic (4); determining missing terms in a number sequence (5); solving spatial analogies (6); and making deductions from simple syllogisms (7).

---

1. What word means the opposite of *hasten?*
   (1) tarry (2) quit (3) return (4) hurry (5) late
2. *Gaudy* means the same as
   (1) worthless (2) expensive (3) showy (4) noisy (5) clumsy
3. *Room* is to *door* as *field* is to
   (1) gate (2) farm (3) wheat (4) fence (5) plough
4. What number is 2 more than the number which 3 is one half of?
5. What number comes next in this list?
   92, 97, 72, 77, 52, 57,

6. ⌐ is to ∟ as F is to
   (1) ⊔ (2) ⊓ (3) ⊢ (4) ⊤ (5) ⊔

7. Bill is taller than Joe and Joe is shorter than Harvey. Therefore, of the three boys:
   (1) It is certain that Bill is the tallest.
   (2) It is certain that Joe is the tallest.
   (3) It is certain that Harvey is the tallest.
   (4) It is impossible to tell just who is the tallest.

FIGURE 8.1 *Sample items from a group test of mental ability. From: The Dominion Group Test of Learning Capacity, Intermediate, Form A, Cat. No. 187. Toronto: The Ontario Institute for Studies in Education, 1962.*

The test must, of course, utilize language and items appropriate to the population for which it is intended (in the example under consideration, children in grades 7 to 11). Moreover, the test-constructor will attempt to choose items which do not deliberately or obviously favor any subgroup within his general target population; he does this partly by choosing items which are "novel" and which therefore could not have been specifically learned, and partly by using other items (for example, simple arithmetic problems) that require for their solution information to which all prospective subjects have been equally exposed. However, it is obvious that tests of intelligence depend heavily upon verbal abilities and, as we shall see later, they actually do favor (in a certain sense) some groups over others.

The test-constructor's next task is to try out the items and to revise the test until it reaches satisfactory levels on such statistical criteria as reliability, validity, and efficiency. He then administers the test to a large representative sample of the population (in our example, all children in grades 7 to 11 in Ontario) to develop test *norms*. In this process he might find the mean score, and the distribution of scores, for the 49 groups whose ages are 12 years, 0 months; 12 years, 1 month; 12 years, 2 months; . . . 16 years, 0 months. These norms indicate the average scores actually earned by individuals of different ages in the target population.

Let us now suppose that James Royal, whose chronological age (CA) is 12, takes the test and earns a score equal to the average score of fourteen-year-olds in the target population. In some tests of intelligence the fact that his intellectual performance equals the average score of children whose chronological age is 14 is interpreted to mean that the child has a mental age (MA) of 14. From this, the IQ, or index of relative intellectual ability, is computed by the following formula: $IQ = MA/CA \times 100$ or, in our example, $IQ = 14/12 \times 100 = 117$. Typically the calculations shown above are made by the test-constructor, who provides a table for converting raw scores into IQ. Not all tests use the Mental Age concept but in those which do not, IQ still represents an index of achieved intellectual status relative to chronological age.[1]

It is evident then that MA, CA, and IQ are related concepts. It is also clear that MA is a better indicator of the student's present level of intellectual development than IQ; for example, a ten-year-old student with a mental age of 11 years, 8 months, would have approximately the same IQ as James Royal but would obviously not have attained the same level of intellectual development.

---

[1] In many individual tests of intellectual ability the computations are considerably more complicated; for further information the student should consult the references at the end of the chapter.

Distribution of IQ Scores in the General Population

IQ scores for any unrestricted (random) sample of children of a given age typically show the kind of "bell shaped" curve illustrated in Figure 8.2, which is plotted from data on the Stanford-Binet, one of the better-known individual intelligence tests. This so-called "normal" distribution, frequently found with psychological and educational data, is consistent with the inter- pretation that intelligence (like many human traits) is *polygenically* deter- mined, that is, determined in large part by the cumulative and additive effects of a large number of genes, each of which exerts a small positive or negative effect upon the development of a trait. As can be seen in Table 8.1, approximately 50 percent of all IQ scores fall within the range 90 and 110. We may also note that very extreme scores (for example, above 140 or below 60) occur in a small fraction of the total number of cases.

TABLE 8.1

PERCENTAGE DISTRIBUTION OF IQ'S
IN TERMAN-MERRILL STANDARDIZATION GROUP

IQ	PERCENT OF CASES	PERCENT OF CASES FALLING IN AND ABOVE EACH INTERVAL
150+	0.2	0.2
140–149	1.1	1.3
130–139	3.1	4.4
120–129	8.2	12.6
110–119	18.1	30.7
100–109	23.5	54.3
90–99	23.0	77.3
80–89	14.5	91.8
70–79	5.6	97.4
60–69	2.0	99.4
50–59	0.4	99.8
Below 50	0.2	100.0

Source: Adapted from Maud A. Merrill, "Significance of IQ's on the revised Stanford-Binet scales," *J. educ. Psychol., 29,* 1938, 641–651.

IQ Differences between Subgroups

A considerable amount of data has been gathered on mental ability scores of members of various occupations, ethnic groups, socioeconomic classes, and

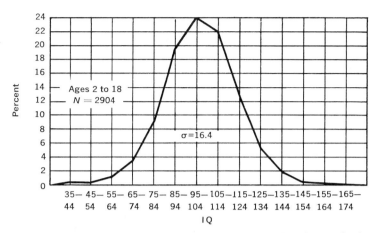

FIGURE 8.2 *Distribution of IQ's in the Terman-Merrill Standardization Group. Scores approximate a normal distribution with a mean IQ of about 100 (actually 101.8). Departures of a given amount from the mean IQ are about equally common in both directions. From: Terman and Merrill,* Measuring intelligence. *Boston: Houghton Mifflin Co., 1937.*

other natural population groupings. One consistent finding is that the mean IQ of rural children is lower than that of urban children and that it also tends to diminish with increasing age (Asher, 1935; Chapanis and Williams, 1945; Wheeler, 1942). The relatively poor performance of rural children tends to be most marked on verbal and speed items, and may be attributable in part to the fact that test-constructors are typically urban dwellers who tend to exhibit some bias in the selection of their items and validation of their tests (H. E. Jones, 1954).

There also appears to be an inverse relationship between the number of children in the family and their average IQ (Anastasi, 1956). Since there is no evidence of any intrinsic relationship between IQ and procreative ability, two other explanantions seem warranted. First, the presence of a large number of children in the family may reduce the amount of cognitive stimulation available to each child, since the number of games, toys, books, pictures, and so on is ordinarily lower when there are a large number of siblings in the family. Even more important in terms of language development is the restricted extent of individual parent-child contact (Nisbet, 1953) in large families. Second, IQ and size of family are indirectly related by virtue of their common relationship to social class status, that is, persons in the upper economic stratas tend to have a higher IQ and to raise relatively small families.

The relationship between IQ and social class has itself been the subject of many investigations. The evidence indicates that significant correlations between IQ and socioeconomic factors do not become evident prior to eighteen months of age (Bayley and Jones, 1937). From this point on, the magnitude of correlational indices increases rapidly, and at school age varies between .3 and .5 for educational, occupational, and economic criteria of social class status (Bayley and Jones, 1937). Probably the early absence of relationship simply indicates that intelligence tests do not measure the same cognitive abilities during infancy as in later years.

Beginning with the preschool period, a range of about 20 points in average IQ separates children of the highest and lowest socioeconomic groups (Terman and Merrill, 1937). The relationship between a child's relative intellectual status and his father's position in the occupational hierarchy varies between .20 and .43 for different tests of intelligence (Eells and others, 1951). Upper socioeconomic groups also contribute a disproportionately large number of intellectually gifted and a disproportionately small number of mentally retarded children to the total population (McGeehee and Lewis, 1942). All of these relationships refer to group averages, since differences within any occupational group are actually much larger than differences between the means of various groups. The differences between social class groups can probably be attributed to three factors: (1) some test-bias in favor of middle-class children; (2) the tendency for fathers in the upper occupational groups to be more intelligent on a genic basis and to choose mates who are also more intelligent; (3) the superior intellectual environment found in middle-class homes.[2]

Variety of Tests of Intellectual Ability

Tests of general mental ability may be either *group* tests, suitable for simultaneous administration (usually requiring half an hour) to all the students in one class, or *individual* tests, requiring that the tester work with one child at a time for a period of about an hour. Since the score for an individual test is based upon a longer testing period and uses the more subtle probes appropriate to single administration, it can be expected to be a more trustworthy and generally a more informative measure than the score derived from a group test. The administration of an individual test requires special training, and even the group test should be administered only by those teachers who are aware of the testing conditions specified for correct use.

The number and variety of tests of general mental ability is so large that we could not begin to do justice to any individual test in this limited treatment. Actually, within any individual school or school system the selec-

---

[2]For a more complete discussion of the relative weight of these three factors, see Ausubel (1968).

tion of tests will be made by guidance personnel or others who have been specially trained for this work. However, if the reader wishes to pursue this topic he should consult any of the references cited at the end of this chapter. *The Mental Measurements Yearbook* (Buros, 1965) is particularly valuable in providing evaluative comment on all major mental tests currently in use.

SOME PERENNIAL QUESTIONS CONCERNING INTELLIGENCE TEST SCORES

With the previous, admittedly sketchy background, we may now profitably turn to some of the perennial misunderstandings and controversies in the field of intelligence testing. These issues are by no means independent, since common themes run through them.

Does IQ Measure Capacity?

As used in this book, the term *capacity* refers to a (hypothetical) "natural" or "innate" potential for acquiring some kind of behavior.[3] When psychologists speak of mental or intellectual capacity they usually have in mind some genetically determined factor which sets a limit on the level of intellectual performance that could be attained, given "ideal" training. One such view is that the number of elementary cells (neurons) in the brain provides a general limiting factor for mental performance (Hebb, 1958).

Obviously capacity *cannot* be measured, and the only information we can obtain about it is indirect and has to do with its relative rather than absolute magnitude. For example, if we wanted to obtain a rough estimate of an individual's capacity (aptitude) for mathematics learning, we might subject him from birth onward to the most highly concentrated and ingeniously taught program of mathematics education presently known. Even after such a program, however, we could not be certain that his natural endowment in this area had been fully utilized, since our teaching methods might have been even more ingenious.

It is clear that intelligence tests cannot measure intellectual capacity

---

[3]Unfortunately there is considerable variation among writers in their use of the terms "ability," "capacity," and "aptitude," and one can only proceed in any particular instance by trying to discern what the writer has in mind. Generally speaking, however, the term "ability" is used to describe something actually measured by *present performance*, while "capacity" and "aptitude" are inferred or hypothetical constructs related to "natural endowment." Of the two latter terms, aptitude tends to be the more specialized, referring to capacity for achievement in a particular field; we speak of general intellectual capacity, for example, but of mathematical or musical aptitude.

and do not pretend to do so. An intelligence test measures *present ability,* that is, the ability to perform the kinds of behavior required *by* the test and *at* the time the test is given. An individual's "intelligence," then, as derived from a general test of mental ability, must be regarded as a measurement construct—that is, as a quantity derived from a particular measuring instrument. Despite this important distinction between capacity and ability, a test of present ability *could* allow one to make *relative* estimates of capacity. If two children from similar family backgrounds and with equal exposures to formal education exhibit markedly different IQ's, one might deduce that one child has a higher capacity for the kind of symbolic tasks represented in intelligence tests than the other. Of course if the children's backgrounds are different, then the different test scores will to some extent have to be attributed to environmental factors rather than to capacity.

Unless appropriate circumstances prevail in the construction of the test and during test administration, the score earned by any individual may not even provide a fair estimate of present ability, let alone capacity. For example, it is possible that through careless test construction the resulting test may unduly emphasize one aspect of cognitive performance over another and may thereby create a bias for or against individuals with particular intellectual abilities. More likely, some students may not be positively oriented toward test-taking and may therefore attain a lower score than other students of equal ability who possess more appropriate test motivation.

The previous remarks concerning the relation between capacity and ability, and the possibility of obtaining scores that do not even represent present ability, may seem so obvious to the reader that he will wonder why we bother devoting space to them. But we think it is necessary because of the many flagrant abuses of intelligence test scores, based apparently upon a misunderstanding of these matters. Quantitative test scores—both of achievement and of ability—have a peculiar fascination for unsophisticated teachers and laymen (and even professional researchers, it must be admitted). In our enthusiasm for supposedly "objective" measures we too often forget all the precautions which we know should be applied, and we read into these measures qualities of accuracy and permanence which they simply do not possess.

Such an abuse of IQ scores occurs, for example, when a school employs a single-group intelligence test score as the sole basis of selecting students for various academic streams. While the educator's increasing sophistication in psychological measurement is tending to eliminate such school-wide misapplications of IQ tests, it will probably be a long time before the last teacher who presently holds the view that an intelligence test measures capacity is convinced otherwise. Often a teacher will observe that a certain student has an IQ of only 88 and immediately concludes that this student simply "lacks the capacity to learn," and the teacher cannot be held responsible if the student fails to learn. Such a teacher provides potent ammunition for the antitesting movement.

The Nature/Nurture Controversy

The nature/nurture controversy arises when, having subjected a group of students to a test of intellectual ability, we ask to what extent the resulting variability in test scores can be attributed to nature (that is, heredity or genic influences) and to what extent to nurture (that is, environmental factors including special training). This controversy is, of course, quite similar to that encountered previously in connection with developmental readiness (Chapter 7). Actually, the major difference is that the nature/nurture dispute originated in the field of intelligence testing and the arguments there have been more statistically (and perhaps less philosophically) oriented than those advanced in the case of readiness.

As one might expect, no definitive answer can be given to the inquiry concerning the relative contributions of heredity and environment to mental ability test scores. However, for some years it has been widely agreed that the bulk of evidence indicates that the influence of heredity is greater. The most convincing support for this position comes from comparisons of the degree of resemblance in IQ between identical twins, fraternal twins or non-twin siblings, and unrelated children. One can interpret this sequence of relationships as defining a dimension of decreasing similarity in heredity (nature, as it were, has conveniently manipulated the heredity variable for us). Experimenters have then sought out instances in which the members of each hereditary group (for example, fraternal twins) have been reared in the same family setting, and instances in which they have been separated and reared in different family settings. The "reared together-reared apart" distinction can be regarded then as a manipulation of the environment variable.

A compilation of such findings (Burt, 1966) is reported in Table 8.2. By comparing the first and third items, we note that by holding environment relatively constant[1]—while manipulating heredity—the IQ correlation changes from .925 for identical twins to .534 for nonidentical twins. At the same time the comparison of items 1 and 2 shows that holding heredity constant while manipulating environment produces a much smaller change. The other correlations reported in Table 8.2 allow similar interpretations. These and comparable data have provided the statistical basis for several qualitative estimates of the relative influence of heredity and environment, as for

---

[1]Actually identical twins also have a more similar environment than fraternal twins, in addition to being genically more similar. The difference in genic similarity, however, outweighs by far the difference in environmental similarity.

TABLE 8.2

RELATIVE CONTRIBUTIONS OF HEREDITY AND ENVIRONMENT TO IQ VARIATIONS*

	CORRELATION
Identical twins reared together	.925
Identical twins reared apart	.874
Nonidentical twins reared together	.534
Siblings reared together	.531
Siblings reared apart	.438
Unrelated children reared together	.267

*Assessments based on scores in individual and group intelligence tests, checked after consultation with teachers.
Source: Burt, 1966.

example Burt's conclusion that at least 75 percent of the variation in intelligence test scores can be attributed to heredity (Burt and Howard, 1957; Burt, 1958).[5]

Within the past decade or so, however, these conclusions have been challenged by a number of people who argue for the possibility of a more dramatic influence of environment, at least on members of atypical populations. Some environmentalists have challenged the traditional summary on the grounds that the actual manipulation of environmental variables in such studies may have been relatively small. It has been argued, for example, that the fact that two children were raised in the same family does not necessarily mean that they were subjected to the "same" environment; similarly—and more important in the present argument—two children may be reared "apart" but exposed, in fact, to essentially similar environments. In other words, it may be that the environmental variations represented in standard calculations are relatively trivial compared to those obtained by contrasting an extremely impoverished environment (Skeels, 1966) with the powerful kinds of educational intervention now envisaged for programs of preschool education and infant stimulation. In this case, it is argued, the data on the contribution of heredity in the *existing* population may cause us to seriously underestimate the potential contributions of early and sustained educational intervention. And, as we indicated earlier, the tendency to assume that a present low level of ability (IQ) reflects genic (and therefore unchangeable)

[5]Burt's data was derived from a sample of London school children. In like manner Nichols (1965), working with a large sample of high-school juniors who took the National Merit Scholarship Qualifying Test in 1962, concluded that about 70 percent of the variance in general ability (as measured by the NMSQT) is attritutable to heredity.

factors has probably been too readily seized upon by some teachers as a rationalization for their own inability to devise effective instructional programs.

On the other hand, it may be that the current emphasis on the importance of environmental factors has gone too far. For example, Jensen (1968) argues that high-level policy-makers are currently in danger of succumbing to the dogmatic assertion that all educationally or socially important differences can be attributed to cultural or environmental factors, a position which does not augur well for a realistic plan to cope with genuine (biologically determined) individual differences. The problem of finding a defensible middle ground will not be an easy one for the teacher; as a step in this direction, the reader might wish to investigate in more detail a number of viewpoints, including those of Jensen (1968), Caspari (1968), Hunt (1964), Nichols (1965), Burt (1958), and Hebb (1958).

Can IQ Be Changed?

Let us suppose that a particular student is found, on the basis of the average of a number of test scores, to have an IQ in the vicinity of 90. What prospect is there for producing a dramatic improvement in this student's index of intellectual ability? The reader will recall that this question was touched upon earlier in connection with the problem of massive transfer. It was noted that Thorndike used IQ gains as the measure of massive transfer and that he found that little such transfer took place when students had already been subjected to the normal educational program.

Further evidence supporting a negative view comes from studies of IQ gains following exposure of typical children to standard preschool or kindergarten programs. These studies have shown that the very small increases in IQ (as compared to control groups) may be attributed to superiority of parental IQ, errors of measurement, and the advantage of superior test rapport (Wellman, 1945). It has also been found that kindergarten children who receive an intensive program of training in activities related to a particular kind of mental ability test make larger gains than control children on these latter tests—but not on a different and more general test of intelligence (Holloway, 1954). This suggests that the improvement in mental test scores following such training is largely a specific practice effect rather than a genuine gain in intellectual status.

Still dealing with normal populations there is evidence, however, that *continued schooling* does produce higher mental ability scores than those earned by nonschooled groups of the same age. For example, follow-up studies of children matched for IQ in the eighth grade indicated that even twenty years later reliable differences in intelligence test scores appeared in favor of those who completed more grades in school (Lorge, 1945). In particular, continued schooling appears to enhance differentiation of general intellectual ability along those abstract verbal lines making for high scores on intelligence tests. In a number of subtests involving reasoning and abstract ability, improvement continues until the end of the college period (Hartson, 1936; Rogers, 1930; Shuey, 1948; R. L. Thorndike, 1948). Furthermore, the particular areas in which greatest improvement occurs (for example, verbal or numerical ability) seems to depend upon the area of specialization in college (Hartson, 1936). It is, therefore, difficult to avoid the implication that schooling differentially influences the growth of the more complex components of verbal intelligence. Nevertheless, when all the evidence is considered, it would seem that these gains tend on the whole to be rather modest.

As pointed out earlier, more spectacular gains can be expected through well-designed educational experiences for children who have been raised in, or long exposed to, environments which, from an educational point of view, might be described as "impoverished." Actually, part of the evidence supporting optimism comes from studies which have shown a progressive *decline* in IQ as a result of immersion in a *nonstimulating* environment. For example, it is found that the longer children remain in orphanages (Skeels and Fillmore, 1937; Skeels and others, 1938; Skeels, 1966) or with mentally retarded mothers (Speer, 1940), the progressively lower their IQ's become in comparison with the IQ's of comparable children reared in a more favorable environment. Similar evidence is found in reports of a progressive decline in intelligence test scores of isolated mountain and canalboat children who may also be considered to be immersed in an intellectually nonstimulating and unchallenging environment (Asher, 1935; H. Gordon, 1923; Sherman and Key, 1932; Wheeler, 1942). Wheeler's study, for example, indicates an average decline of two points in IQ between successive age groups of mountain children over an eight-year period. On the reverse side of the coin, Skeels (1966) found that the removal of children from an extremely impoverished environment (orphanage) led to progressive IQ gains which, at adulthood, meant the difference between economic self-sufficiency and institutional dependence. Equally impressive positive evidence resides in the studies of programs devised to meet the problem of cultural deprivation.

Recently Bloom (1964) has attempted to put various strands of data together to estimate the long-term effects both of extremely deprived and enriched learning environments (Table 8.3). He concludes (and his argument, although empirically based, must be regarded as somewhat speculative) that extremes in environment may make a difference of as much as 20 percent in the mental ability scores earned at maturity (the age of 17 in Bloom's analysis). This would mean, for example, that two individuals with the same innate intellectual potential (capacity) might, because of differ-

TABLE 8.3

Hypothetical Effects of Different Environments
on the Development of Intelligence
in Three Selected Age Periods

AGE PERIOD	PERCENT OF MATURE INTELLIGENCE	VARIATION FROM NORMAL GROWTH IN IQ UNITS			
		Deprived	*Normal*	*Abundant*	*Abundant-Deprived*
Birth–4	50	−5	0	+5	10
4–8	30	−3	0	+3	6
8–17	20	−2	0	+2	4
Total	100	−10	0	+10	20

Source: B. S. Bloom, *Stability and change in human characteristics.* New York: John Wiley & Sons, Inc., 1964.

ences in environmental stimulation, earn scores of 100 and 120 respectively on IQ tests administered at age 17. We can realize the practical significance of this difference if we consider that most universities would consider the latter individual a reasonably good prospect for admittance, whereas they would be inclined to reject the individual with the lower IQ.

Table 8.3 also reflects the widely-held belief that the influence of an atypical environment decreases with increasing age. The suggested substantial effects at early ages are consistent with research reported earlier on the effect of special programs for culturally deprived children. If anything, the latter studies suggest the possibility of even larger IQ gains for these particular atypical children than Bloom's data indicate. In addition, there remains the possibility that a sustained program of stimulation beginning at a very early age could produce substantially higher-than-expected IQ's in children from (what are now considered) "favored" environments.

How Stable Are IQ Scores?

In this section we will not be concerned with changes in IQ produced by placing students in special programs. Rather, we will consider the stability of the IQ of a student who is reared, and remains, in the "typical" educational environment. This problem acquires practical significance when a teacher or school administrator wants to ascertain the student's mental ability, possibly to use it as one criterion for selection into a particular stream or program, or perhaps only as a check as to whether the student's present achievement is comparable to his ability. In such a case the teacher or administrator would consult the school files—and, since intelligence tests are hardly given continuously—would find that the student in question had received, let us say, a score of 105 on an individual test given eighteen months before. The question would then arise as to how accurately the earlier test score reflects his present ability. This is equivalent to asking, in the more general case, how stable a typical individual's IQ will remain over short- and long-term periods of time.

In addition to extreme changes in environment (which we are excluding from our present discussion), many factors can influence the stability of an individual's IQ. Let us recall that the IQ score is derived from a sample of the student's intellectual output at a given time, and therefore it is not surprising that the student's score will vary as we choose different samples and tests at different points in time. On analysis it is revealed that these fluctuations can be attributed to *measurement, genic,* and *environmental* factors. Included under the first heading are:

(a) the *selection* of test items which are not equally representative of generally available experiences—thereby leading to variable amounts of test disadvantage at different points in the life cycle of any particular child;

(b) *errors* of test administration and scoring, especially during infancy and early childhood when communication difficulties are extreme;

(c) *situational variability* in such factors affecting performance as the personality of the test administrator, rapport between the administrator and the student (Pasamanick and Knobloch, 1955), fatigue, physical well-being, general attitude, motivation (Haggard, 1954), attention span, frustration tolerance, self-confidence, level of aspiration, emotional stability, level of anxiety, reaction to failure, venturesomeness, and negativism (Rust, 1931);

(d) *variable exposure* to practice and coaching on intelligence tests (Wiseman, 1954) and to test experience generally.

Perhaps the most important measurement factor making for long-term instability of IQ is the change between age levels in the composition of intelligence tests (J. E. Anderson, 1939; Bayley, 1955). For example, because infant intelligence scales largely measure a type of sensori-motor ability only moderately related at best to the cognitive ability tested at a later age level, a child with high genic ability for abstract performance tends to score much closer to the mean on earlier tests than on later ones; the reverse holds true for the child deficient in abstract intelligence (J. E. Anderson, 1939).

With regard to the second (genic) causes of IQ fluctuation, simply because the hereditary factors underlying intelligence scores remain constant, we cannot assume that their effects on development will necessarily lead to a constant rate of growth for any individual. Longitudinal analysis of individual growth curves by Bayley (1940) and Cornell and Armstrong (1955) are consistent with this interpretation (Figure 8.3). The latter investigators were able to classify most growth curves, under three main patterns—a continuous growth curve from age five to age eighteen, a step-like curve consisting of

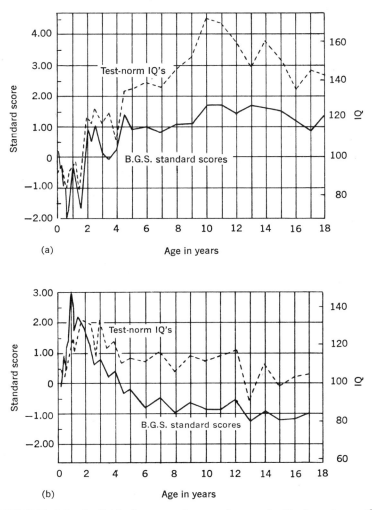

FIGURE 8.3 *Individual rates of mental growth. Each unit on the standard score scale represents about 16 points above or below the average IQ of 100. From: Nancy Bayley, "On the growth of intelligence," Amer. Psychol., 10, 1955, 805–818. Copyright 1955 by the American Psychological Association, and reproduced by permission.*

alternate spurts and pauses, and a discontinuous curve breaking at puberty and showing either a steeper or a more gradual slope thereafter.

Leaving aside long-term immersion in either deprived or enriched learning environments, environmental factors will still constitute a third category of factors contributing to fluctuation in IQ. For example, physical and emotional vicissitudes of a transitory nature (for example, illness and emotional trauma, separation from parents, rejection by peers) may temporarily impair a child's intelligence test performance. Moreover, personality traits associated with parental attitudes influence the constancy of the IQ. For example, it has been found that democratic homes encouraging the development of children's independence tend to be associated with a rising IQ (Baldwin and others, 1945; E. L. Grant, 1939). Gains in IQ have also been correlated with independence (Sontag and others, 1955) and high achievement motivation (Kagan and others, 1958), whereas losses in IQ, especially in girls, have been correlated with dependence (Sontag and others, 1955).

To summarize, a whole host of factors can influence the stability of IQ scores of children in essentially "normal" environments over the long or short term. Since the probability of one or more of the causal factors changing necessarily increases with time, we would naturally expect that the most consistent estimates will be those obtained from tests given in close proximity. The degree of consistency one might expect in this situation is indicated in Figure 8.4, which shows a scattergram of test scores obtained on two forms of the Stanford-Binet, one of the most reliable of all intelligence tests, administered a few days apart. While the correlation between these scores is approximately .91, it will be noticed that there is considerable variation between tests, both for entire IQ groups and (in even more pronounced fashion) for individual students. For example, the average IQ change between forms for students scoring 100 on the first form is approximately 5 points; again, several students show a shift of 15 points and one a difference of 25 points.[6]

Of course, as the time interval between successive tests increases, the reliability coefficients decline. For example, Figure 8.5 shows correlations between IQ scores at differing ages and those attained at intellectual maturity. While stability is a matter of degree, it would seem that it is not until the age of school entrance that scores on intelligence tests are sufficient-

---

[6]If the discrepancies between the scores individual students received on the two tests were plotted, these diffrences would themselves form a normal distribution, clustering around an average discrepancy of zero. From a knowledge of the consistency or *reliability* of the test (.91) in our example), one can compute the proportion of discrepancies which would exceed any given amount. For example, we can determine that for most standard IQ tests about one discrepancy in three will exceed 7.5 IQ units, or about two in three discrepancies will be less than 7.5 IQ units. This measure of the stability of test scores is usually referred to as the *standard error of estimate*.

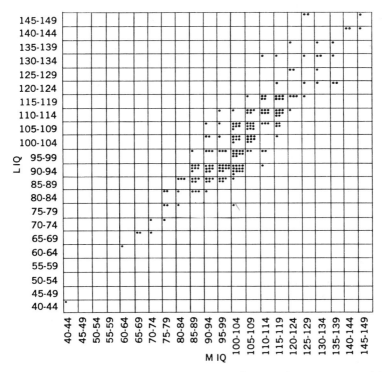

FIGURE 8.4 *Consistency between IQ's obtained by seven-year-olds on two forms of the Stanford-Binet. From: Terman and Merrill,* Measuring intelligence. *Boston: Houghton Mifflin Co., 1937.*

ly well correlated with terminal intellectual status to be used as estimates for that final stage. In particular, it is evident that intelligence test scores obtained below the age of six are not very useful for making predictions. Some of the reasons for this, already advanced in previous sections, are that infant tests measure perceptual-motor abilities which differ qualitatively from the abstract verbal tasks found on later tests, and that measurement problems are particularly pronounced at an age when it is difficult to communicate effectively with the child. We have also noted that early tests probably underestimate the intelligence of children with high potential for abstract reasoning, and vice versa.

The implications of stability studies for the educator vary from the very simple to the enormously complex. To begin with, it is obvious that important decisions utilizing IQ data should be based on current estimates of mental ability, and whether current or past scores are being utilized, the

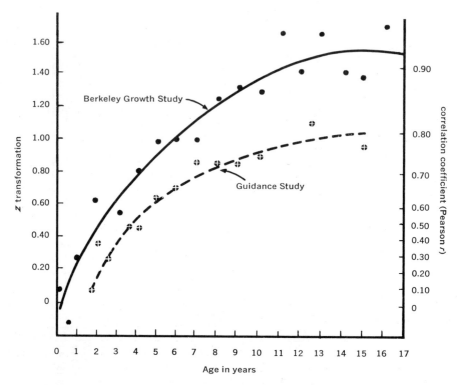

FIGURE 8.5 *Correlation of intelligence scores at 18 years with scores at successive earlier ages. From Jones, 1954.*

educator should make some realistic assessment of the potential amount of intertest variation, possibly by computing a standard error of estimate or some related statistic.

A much more difficult problem arises when the school must decide, again using IQ data as one major criterion, to enroll students into one long-term program or another. Examples here would be selecting students for various acceleration programs in the elementary school or assigning students to different academic streams at the secondary-school level. This is an enormously tricky business, and it would be dishonest to claim that educational science has yet come up with an adequate solution (Finney, 1962). Here again we need only note that since the IQ of one student in 10 can be expected to change by more than 15 points over a five-year period, the group chosen from the general student population as representing the "brightest quarter" at the beginning of that period would hardly contain precisely the same individuals as a similar group chosen on the basis of tests administered at the end of the period.

Pattern of Growth in Intellectual Development

Most investigators agree that the growth of intellectual ability is most rapid in infancy and early childhood and that it tends to increase thereafter at a progressively decreasing rate. A linear growth curve in *mental age* is simply an artifact of the way in which mental-age scores are determined. Thus, in our example, if an MA of 12 corresponds to the average score earned on a test by twelve-year-olds and an MA of 13 to the average score earned by thirteen-year-olds, it follows that on the average one year of mental age will be attained in one year of chronological age. Some time ago E. L. Thorndike and others (1926) postulated a parabolic growth curve for mental growth according to which about half of mature intellectual status is attained by the age of three. More recently, as we have seen, Bloom (1964) reached a similar conclusion, placing the midpoint of attainment of mature intelligence at approximately age four (Table 8.3). Growth begins to taper off in middle adolescence and continues very slowly until ultimate ability is achieved (Bayley, 1949; Freeman and Flory, 1940; Garrett and others, 1935).

Since the tapering-off process is so gradual, it is very difficult to tell when growth actually ceases. The widely accepted finding of Terman and Merrill (1937) that mental age does not increase after the age of fifteen is now attributed to the limited ceiling of the 1937 revision of the Stanford-Binet test. The best estimates, based on testing a wide age sample of a relatively homogeneous population (Jones and Conrad, 1944; Wechsler, 1944) or on retesting the same population at suitable intervals (Bayley, 1955; Freeman and Flory, 1937; Jones and Conrad, 1944; E. L. Thorndike, 1926, 1928) places the age of terminal growth at eighteen or twenty, or even beyond. Gains in intelligence test scores have been reported at twenty-five on the Wechsler-Bellevue test (Bayley, 1955) and at age fifty on the Army Alpha (Owens, 1953) and concept maturity tests (Bayley and Oden, 1955). The age of terminal growth obviously varies for different individuals and for different kinds of cognitive processes (Jones and Conrad, 1944).

What happens beyond the age of terminal growth is not entirely clear. When the first test norms were developed, it was found that test scores declined in representative samples of older subjects. As Figure 8.6 shows, the occurrence of the point of maximum performance and the rate of fall-off thereafter is earlier and steeper respectively for performance tests (that is, tests involving some measure of perceptual or motor skill) than for tasks requiring only verbal performance. However evidence cited earlier would

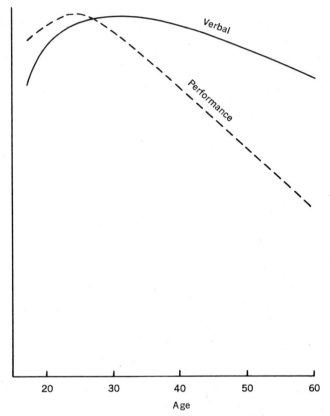

FIGURE 8.6   *Decline in raw verbal and nonverbal IQ test scores on the Wechsler Adult Intelligence Scale. Raw scores on one scale cannot be compared with raw scores on the other, therefore an arbitrary common scale has been employed. Adapted from Wechsler, 1958.*

suggest that the decline in verbal performance could be offset by continued education or participation in an occupation requiring a high level of conceptualization.[7]

It may come as something of a shock to the prospective high-school teacher to learn that many sixteen-year-old students of his own innate capacity will be able to out-perform him on certain kinds of mental tasks. The teacher who doubts this should match his wits against some of his more

---

[7]For a related though somewhat more sophisticated account—based on the notion of "crystallized" and "fluid" intelligence—see Horn (1967). In that treatment the "crystallized" (influenced by learning) components of intelligence are able to compensate for decline in the "fluid" (determined by primitive brain function) components of intelligence until middle age, when a global decline of intelligence begins to appear.

capable students on such tasks as adding numbers, remembering lists of symbols presented on a single occasion, or undertaking coding exercises. In the event that the teacher may feel somewhat despondent about this, we would point out that although an intelligence test does measure a certain kind of "raw" mental ability, the intellectual problems which it poses do not begin to match in complexity the kinds of problems dealt with by the mature adult in his intellectual life. The latter problems require, in addition to raw mental ability, such intellectual possessions as organized bodies of knowledge, problem-solving strategies, and inventiveness. On the first two of these the advantage definitely lies with the adult because of his greater maturity, experience, and (presumably) greater learning. Finally, inventiveness per se is not very highly related to IQ, at least beyond a minimal level of IQ. It is these extenuating circumstances, no doubt, which explain why most of the great contributions to human thinking are made by individuals who belong to an age group which has fallen off a bit (or a lot, depending upon the test) from its "peak" performance in certain elementary mental skills.

Sex Differences

Expressions of male chauvinism to the contrary, sex differences in average intelligence tend to be negligible in magnitude and inconsistent in direction (Terman and Tyler, 1954). The most widely used tests of intelligence—the Revised Stanford-Binet and the Wechsler Intelligence Scale for Children—have, in fact, been so constructed as to eliminate sex differences. Most obtained differences can be attributed to the fact that the particular tests used were differentially weighted with respect to the various component aspects of intelligence in which boys and girls differ in opposite directions—that is, in vocabulary, verbal fluency, rote memory, spatial and numerical abilities (Terman and Tyler, 1954).

While differences between the sexes in average IQ scores are small, proportionately more males are found in the extreme categories. For example, the incidence of intellectual eminence is indisputably higher among males than among females. However we must remember that differential factors of cultural expectation, motivation, and opportunity are certainly operative and may constitute the primary causal factors. Lending support to this interpretation are Terman's findings that in a population of intellectually gifted children, boys more frequently than girls retain their high status as they advance in age (Terman and Oden, 1949). Males also exhibit IQ gain more frequently from adolescence to adulthood than do females (Bradway and Thompson, 1962).

Other complicating factors raise similar questions of interpretation regarding the preponderance of boys in classes for mentally retarded children and in institutions for the feeble-minded. Not only does paranatal brain injury occur more frequently among male infants (Lillienfeld and Pasamanick, 1956), but mental deficiency is also a socially more conspicuous and disabling handicap in the case of boys. Furthermore, parents are less reluctant to commit sons than daughters to institutions. We must conclude, therefore, that until more definitive evidence is available it is impossible to decide to what extent obtained sex differences in variability are attributable to such genuine determinants as genic and relevant environmental factors on the one hand, and to purely extraneous considerations on the other.

Are Intelligence Tests Unfair to Culturally Disadvantaged Children?

We have left to the last the issue on which there is strongest feeling and which undoubtedly lies at the heart of the sharpest recent condemnations of intelligence testing. For our purposes, a "culturally disadvantaged child" will be considered one who, by virtue of the values held and the experiences provided by his cultural group, is at a disadvantage in comparison to the culturally dominant group with respect to the performance of a defined class of tasks. The particular disadvantage we are interested in is the child's inability to cope with cognitive tasks posed by the school. The statement that such disadvantages exist hardly needs statistical documentaion; it is obvious, for example, that an Eskimo child reared in a culture which values hunting and fishing skills, which places little value upon "book learning," and which speaks a language different from that employed in the public school, will be at a considerable disadvantage in learning to read English. We could pick out many such subcultures to which the term "disadvantaged" would apply in varying degrees. However, the most general sociological group which might be said to be disadvantaged with respect to the school—and which cuts across many ethnic, cultural, and geographical classifications—is that of the so-called "lower socioeconomic class."[8]

The criticism that intelligence tests are "unfair" to the culturally disadvantaged child usually rests on two arguments. First, it is claimed that the

---

[8]Socioeconomic class is usually defined either in terms of economic criteria or more broadly in terms of "life style." Cultural deprivation cannot be equated to lower-class status if the narrow (that is economic) definition of the latter term is used, since attitudes and values figure more prominently in "cultural deprivation" than economic impoverishment per se. But in employing the broader definition of social class, it is true, generally speaking, that youth from lower-class homes do not possess—to the same extent as middle-class youth—the needs, motivations, and supportive personality traits which contribute to school achievement. As a possible causal factor, it is well known that lower-class parents do not place the same value on education, on financial independence, on social recognition, and on vocational success, as do middle-class parents.

traditional tests emphasize verbal ability rather than the mechanical and social kinds of abilities in which the lower-class child excels. Second, it is argued that the middle-class environment is more propitious than that of the lower class for the development of verbal intelligence and, therefore, disadvantaged children will show up poorly on such tests regardless of their innate verbal potential.

Although these arguments are factually correct, they do not justify any criticism of unfairness. On the first count, intelligence tests purport to sample the cognitive domain and deliberately exclude ability or performance in the mechanical or social areas. Consequently, it would not seem intrinsically "unfair" to administer a standard intelligence test to our Eskimo child in an attempt to predict how well he would do in school work, even though the test was comprised of tasks which are deemed unimportant in his particular culture and completely ignored other tasks which *are* considered important and which, in fact, constitute intelligence in his culture.

On the second count, it was previously pointed out that an intelligence test attempts to measure operating ability at a given point of development rather than innate potential per se. There can be no quarrel with the proposition that a deprived environment has adverse effects on the student's present performance, but it is the function of the intelligence test to measure this performance (ability) rather than to estimate natural endowment. The error inheres in using IQ scores as estimates of capacity without allowing for the influence of important environmental factors.

The previous remarks notwithstanding, the standard intelligence tests *are* "unfair" in certain respects. It must be remembered that the original Binet scale, and the majority of intelligence tests devised subsequently, have been intended to predict how well students will cope with the kinds of intellectual tasks found in the school. Consequently, there is probably a tendency to equate "intellectual ability" rather too closely with "the ability to perform intellectual tasks posed by the school," even though most formal definitions of intelligence do not expressly require this limitation. In practice it is very easy not only to select items with this bias in view but to employ a specific vocabulary which is commonly used by the middle-class professionals who operate the educational enterprise—and by children reared in this strata of society—but is less well known to children from lower-class homes.

Relevant to this point, Davis (1950) studied the change in difficulty in syllogistic reasoning—a common intelligence test item—caused by substituting words in, but without changing the structure of, the logical problem. The following syllogisms illustrate the approach used.[9]

---

[9]Allison Davis, "Education for the Conservation of Human Resources," *Progressive Education,* 1950, 27, 221–224.

Syllogism A: Higher socioeconomic group out-performed lower group.

> *A* is shorter than *B*.
> *B* is shorter than *C*.
> Therefore,
> (   )   *B* is taller than *C*.
> (   )   *A* is as tall as *B* or *C*.
> (   )   *A* is shorter than *C*.

Syllogism B: Performance of high and low socioeconomic groups equal.

> Jim can hit harder than Bill.
> Bill can hit harder than Ted.
> So which is true?
> (   )   Ted can hit harder than Bill.
> (   )   Bill can hit as hard as Jim and Ted.
> (   )   Jim can hit harder than Ted.

Syllogism A, intended to parallel the wording used in popular intelligence tests, was solved by 67 percent of the children from a high socioeconomic group and by only 45 percent of the children from a lower socioeconomic group. On the other hand, there was no difference between the groups in their ability to solve Syllogism B.

This and similar evidence (Haggard, 1954; Riessman, 1962) suggests that the standard intelligence test *is* biased insofar as it purports to represent general levels of cognitive functioning. Nevertheless, one may still argue that although the syllogisms in our example are identical in logical structure, Syllogism A more closely represents the kind of intellectual functioning required in the school, where words like "shorter" are used more frequently than words like "hit." However, if we adopt this argument we should probably drop phrases such as "intelligence test" and "test of intellectual ability," and use the more appropriate term, "test of general *scholastic* ability." According to Cronbach (1960) trends in this direction were in evidence as early as 1960.

One attempted solution to the cultural bias problem is found in the development of so-called "culture-free" tests of intellectual ability (for example, Eells and others, 1951). Typically, such tests tend to de-emphasize the role of language, to use language more simplified than that found in school settings, and to increase drastically the emphasis on spatial, numerical, or perceptual-motor abilities. As desirable as such tests would appear to be in principle, and despite the fact that they frequently *do* lower the IQ differential between advantaged and disadvantaged groups,[10] school tasks

---

[10]See Jensen's (1968) comments on this point.

themselves tend to be so culturally biased that any increment in "culture-freeness" in a test is usually offset by a proportionate decrement in its predictive value (Millman and Glock, 1965). Moreover, most culture-free tests share with standard intelligence tests such biases against culturally deprived children as reside in the fact that, in comparison with their middle-class age-mates, the former have fewer test-taking skills, are less responsive to speed pressure, are less highly motivated in taking tests, and have less rapport with the examiner (Haggard, 1954; Riessman, 1962). While similar factors operate equally in school achievement—and so do not destroy the predictive power of the test in this respect—their existence does not give the lower-class child a fair opportunity to demonstrate his true attained level of cognitive ability.

SPECIAL INTELLECTUAL ABILITIES

As was pointed out in our initial example, a general test of intelligence is intended to sample the whole domain of cognitive performance. Nevertheless, as an individual matures, and particularly as he moves into the specialized subject-matter areas of the high school, some of his mental abilities become more highly developed than others; this differential growth in abilities is no doubt intensified in his later professional work. Thus a professional writer manifests an outstanding command of language, while the geometer has developed his spatial and analytic abilities to an extraordinarily high level. The question which concerns us here is how early such special intellectual abilities become discernible, and their nature, number, and importance to the educator.

Developmental Changes in Mental Organization

What criteria might be set up for deciding whether the operation of a special mental ability, as distinct from *general* intelligence, can be discerned in the behavior of a group of individuals? The usual *statistical* criterion is that a *factor* (for example, spatial ability) is said to exist when the scores on a group of tests purporting to measure this factor intercorrelate more highly among themselves than each test correlates separately with a test of general mental ability.[11]

Until the last few years there was wide agreement that the weight of evidence indicated three well-defined stages in the organization of

---

[11]Factors are extracted by a process of correlational analysis which, in simplest terms, indicates how many independent dimensions (factors) are required to account for the intercorrelations observed. However, determining that a factor exists statistically does not necessarily guarantee that it reflects an underlying psychological process.

intellectual ability. According to this view the abilities measured by intelligence tests during infancy and the early preschool period are predominantly perceptual and sensorimotor in nature and highly unrelated both to each other and to later manifestations of abstract intelligence. Later, in an intermediate stage from approximately late preschool to preadolescence, abstract intelligence is highly general in nature (that is, cognitive abilities are highly intercorrelated). Finally, in the terminal stage—at preadolescence and beyond— there occurs an increasing differentiation of intellectual abilities.

As for present viewpoints, the existence of the first stage is made apparent either by observing very young children or by examining the content of tests normally used to measure their intelligence. Similarly, there is little quarrel about the existence of well-defined factors in mature intelligence (Garrett, 1946; Garrett and others, 1935; Green and Berkowitz, 1964; Guilford, 1966; Heinonen, 1963; Ljung, 1965; W. J. Meyer, 1960) which appear to be stable over a number of testing situations and age levels.

The extent to which factors can be identified in the second stage, however, is not completely settled and much research on this subject is currently being undertaken. In one approach, a number of "factor" studies of general intelligence at the late preschool level have been able to disassociate verbal ability from other forms of intelligence (Hofstaetter, 1954; Hurst, 1960; Richards and Nelson, 1939; Scott and Ball, 1965). In some instances verbal ability itself has been further analyzed into such factors as word fluency (Gewirtz, 1948). In addition, Osborne (1965) located six factors at the preschool level which remained stable after the first grade. The general conclusion emerging from this research seems to be that even though mental abilities tend to be highly interrelated in the second stage, there is enough differentiation between them to make the concept of separate factors viable (Deal and Wood, 1968; Stott and Ball, 1965).

A second line of research has used a specially devised test to try to isolate the kinds of cognitive abilities not prominently featured, or ignored altogether, in the standard intelligence test. For example, much study has recently been undertaken to determine whether a "divergent" production factor exists; such a factor would represent an ability to provide answers in open-ended situations which call for novelty or a variety of responses, and may be contrasted with the "convergent" abilities which require the production of a single conventional solution. Several studies have suggested the existence of divergent production factors as early as four years of age (McCartin and Meyers, 1966; Miezitis, 1968; Meyers and others, 1964; Orphet and Meyers, 1966).

In summary, an increasing body of evidence indicates the emergence, during the preschool years, of mental abilities that satisfy the statistical criterion for separate factors of intelligence. However, if such factors are to be of any interest to the educator, they must in addition show substantial correlations with the kind of behavior that the latter is attempting to produce (for example, the acquisition of knowledge or the ability to solve problems). Very little evidence exists on this question; for example, Miezitis (1968) found that measures of "divergent production" obtained in the late preschool years do not correlate highly with reading readiness or with subsequent progress in language and arithmetic. Moreover, it is debatable whether the facilitation of divergent production abilities can be considered an educational objective in its own right. Consequently, for practical purposes it would still be reasonable for the educator to think in terms of general intelligence rather than specific factors, during the second stage.

Cause of Increasing Differentiation

The increasing differentiation of mental abilities which may be observed (at least) by adolescence reflects the influence of differential factors of interest, of training, of motivation, of success and failure experience, and of cultural expectation. Original aptitude and experience seem to reinforce each other in circular fashion, since children who are gifted in a particular area appear to benefit differentially from instruction in that area (Lesser, 1962).

It should be remembered, however, that inasmuch as considerable interrelatedness among different cognitive functions still remains at later ages (Schulman and Havighurst, 1947), evidence of increasing differentiation at the older age level does not render the concept of general intelligence completely untenable. Furthermore, relatively high correlations between intelligence test scores obtained in primary grades and retest scores obtained during adolescence indicate that there is much overlapping between the factors determining early levels of general cognitive ability and later levels of differentiated cognitive ability.

Sex Differences in Mental Organization

Differences between the sexes in *particular* cognitive abilities tend to be larger than differences in tests of general intelligence, and to increase with increasing age (Terman and Tyler, 1954). When elementary-school boys and girls are compared on "primary mental abilities," clear differences in favor of girls are found in word fluency, rote memory, and reasoning (Carlsmith, 1964; Havighurst and Breese, 1947; Hobson, 1947). In other areas findings are more equivocal. Most investigators (Carlsmith, 1964; Havighurst and Breese, 1947; Lord, 1941) agree that boys are superior in spatial and quantitative ability, even though Koch (1954) failed to find a significant sex difference at the ages of five and six. The situation with respect to vocabulary is even more confusing. Some investigators (Freeman and Flory, 1937; Hobson, 1947; Koch, 1954) report a difference in favor of boys; some (Conrad and others, 1944; Garrett and others, 1935) report a difference in favor of girls; and still others (Havighurst and Breese, 1947) find no difference.

In view of the fact that, with the exception of verbal fluency, most sex differences in cognitive ability are *not* evident at the preschool level (Terman and Tyler, 1954), it seems reasonable to suppose that such differences are, for the most part, *culturally determined.* Girls seem to be superior to boys in categorizing ability in the first grade, but by the sixth grade this difference is no longer evident (Bruner and Olver, 1963). Although girls generally receive higher grades than do boys in elementary school, achievement test differences tend to disappear beginning in junior-high school.

Girls show a slight superiority over boys in general intelligence during early adolescence (Conrad and others, 1944; Freeman and Flory, 1937) which is related to their more precocious sexual maturation. Differences between the sexes at this age level, however, are larger and more significant when the components of abilities and intelligence are compared. Thus girls are consistently superior on such verbal items as vocabulary (Conrad and others, 1944; Garrett and others, 1935; Kuhlen, 1952), language usage (Kuhlen, 1952), and analogies (Jones and Conrad, 1933), and also on memory (Garrett and others, 1935) and clerical ability (Kuhlen, 1952). Boys are superior on subtests involving spatial relations and mechanical abilities (Kuhlen, 1952) and in arithmetic (Garrett and others, 1935; Jones and Conrad, 1933).[11]

Another male advantage—again culturally determined—has to do not with IQ directly but with use of intellectual potential. As is shown later, by late adolescence the typical female has come to believe that problem solving in mathematics, science, and logic is a uniquely masculine skill, and to feel inadequate when faced with problems requiring analysis and reasoning.

Tests of Special Intellectual Ability

As in the case of general mental ability, the number of tests of special abilities is very large, and we repeat that the teacher who wishes to obtain detailed information should consult Buros (1965). One of the better-known tests was produced by Thurstone on the basis of his analyses of the intercorrelations of a large number of performance scores (Thurstone, 1938). He identified the following six so-called "primary mental abilities": verbal (V), number (N), spatial (S), word fluency (W), memory (M), reasoning (R). Figure 8.7 provides sample items used in tests for four of the factors. As influential as Thurstone's work has been (both in research and in

---

[11]A current comprehensive summary of research on individual differences can be found in Maccoby (1966).

VERBAL MEANING (V)   Indicate the word which has the same meaning as the first word in the row.
Moist: Underground   Damp   Fresh   Cool
Research: Project   Investigation   Hiding   Finding
Reluctant: Solitary   Dependent   Risky   Hesitant

NUMBER FACILITY (N) $899 + 89 =$ (a) 988   (b) 989   (c) 998   (d) 1,789   (f) 8,979
Which number is 6 less than 55,555?
  (a) 55,499   (b) 55,449   (c) 55,549   (d) 55,559   (e) 55,561
$98 \times 76 =$ (a) 754   (b) 784   (c) 6,348   (d) 7,448   (e) 7,648

REASONING (R)   Indicate the next letter in the series.
ZFYEXD   (1) B   (2) F   (3) H   (4) J   (5) W
Find the word that does not belong with the other four:
Suffer   Reproach   Scold   Punish   Tease
Find the next number in the series:
5 6 4 6 7 5 7 8 6   (a) 6   (b) 7   (c) 8   (d) 9   (e) 10

SPATIAL RELATIONS (S)   In each row indicate which figures are the same as the first figure, except that they have been turned around (rotated) on the paper.

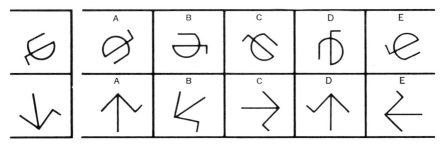

FIGURE 8.7   *Items from the Chicago Test of Primary Mental Abilities. From Thurstone, 1962.*

subsequent test production), the question as to whether the factors represent "real" dimensions of intelligence remains unanswered.

Since Thurstone's early work much research has been done to determine the factorial composition of intelligence. In this process, more and more factors have been identified, to the point where Guilford has advanced a model in which no less than 120 factors are represented (Guilford, 1959, 1966; Guilford and Merrifield, 1960). In this model (Figure 8.8) a specific ability is represented by each cell of the cube and is determined by an *operation,* a *content,* and a *product.* In the first dimension Guilford hypothesizes the following five kinds of mental operations:

Memory—which requires the retention of information

Cognition—which requires the awareness or recognition of information in various forms

Convergent Production—in which one proceeds from given information to a unique or conventionally accepted "best" answer

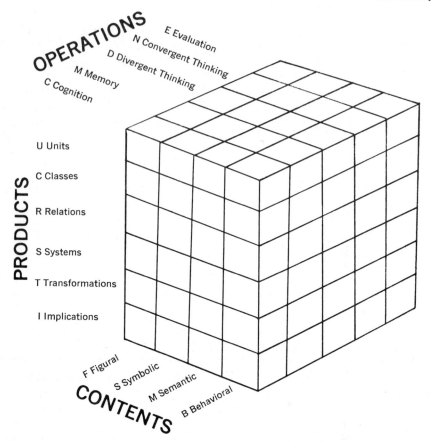

FIGURE 8.8   *Diagram of Guilford's Structure-of-Intellect Model. From: J. P. Guilford, "Three faces of intellect,"* Amer. Psychol., 14, *1959, 469–479. Copyright 1959 by the American Psychological Association, and reproduced by permission.*

Divergent Production—in which one proceeds from given information to a *variety* of adequate solutions (as in thinking of all the possible uses for a brick)

Evaluation—in which one reaches decisions concerning the goodness (correctness, suitability, adequacy, desirability) of information

Each of these mental processes may operate on any one of four kinds of content. *Figural* content refers to concrete spatial relationships and line diagrams; *symbolic* content refers to letters, arithmetical, and algebraic symbols; *semantic* content refers to information given in the form of words; and *behavioral* content refers to the nonverbal behavior (for example, attitudes, intentions) of human beings. The action of an intellectual process upon a particular kind of content can lead to any of the six kinds of *products* shown in Figure 8.8; obviously these vary from the very simple products (units) to the very complex (systems and implications).

Guilford's model will probably remain of more theoretical than practical interest. In the first place, only about two-thirds of the factors have actually been identified in test situations (Guilford, 1966). Moreover, even those that have been identified do not seem to be strongly related to the behavioral outcomes required by the school. Finally, it is inconceivable that testing programs in the school would ever reach the point where the subtle differences inherent in the Guilford model could be recognized and utilized (Carroll, 1968).

The appearance of the Guilford model has had, however, one important implication for education. The distinction between convergent and divergent thinking, and the subsequent tendency to regard divergent production as a form of "creativity," has led to a great deal of research with school children. The nature and implications of this research are discussed in detail in the chapter on creativity.

THE USE OF IQ TESTS

The value of the test of general mental ability lies primarily in the fact that IQ scores (or their near relations) are, of all available ability tests, the most valuable single predictors of school performance. While more specialized tests predict more accurately in more limited areas, the IQ's predictive value extends over the whole range of school activities from likely success in learning to read to expected performance in graduate work. For this reason such tests are the most economical for the school to employ in terms of information obtained per unit of testing time or per dollar invested in tests. Consequently, the test of mental ability should probably be one of the first to be included in the school's battery of psychological measures.

Illustrative Example

An example of the difference between specificity and generality of prediction can be found in the study by Ellis (1965) using a large group of secondary-school students in metropolitan Toronto. The test battery, including mental ability (Scholastic Apitude Test for Ontario),[12] previous general achievement (grade 12 average), and specific previous achievement in history and algebra were used to predict marks in grade 13. Some of the correlations

---

[12]SATO, though called an "aptitude" test, contains items which are similar although more complex than those found in standard group *IQ* tests. The SATO combined score correlates about 0.7 with *IQ* as measured on the Dominion Group Test of Learning Capacity.

obtained are shown in Table 8.4. The conclusions, consistent with those derived from similar studies, can be summarized as follows:

(a) The best single predictor in a single subject which is *sequentially dependent* upon previous learning is a test of achievement in that previous learning. In our example a standardized test of achievement in algebra at the end of grade 12 was the best single predictor of grade 13 performance in algebra and trigonometry, both of which are highly dependent upon previous algebraic acquisitions (see also Sommerfeld and Tracy, 1961).

(b) For subjects which are less sequentially dependent upon previous learning (e.g., history) the best single predictor is general level of academic achievement in the previous grade. Similarly, the grade 12 average provides the best single predictor for total grade 13 performance. Other studies (Endler and Steinberg, 1963) have found that high-school-leaving averages predict academic achievement at the university level better than do scholastic aptitude scores.

(c) A measure of general mental ability, or general academic aptitude, is almost always a good predictor of academic performance, usually correlating about 0.5 with most tests of academic achievement.

(d) Some components of academic aptitude tests (e.g., SATO Verbal Aptitude) are the best single predictors of performance in certain school subjects, as, for example, of English composition in the study cited. (See also: Locke, 1963; J. W. French, 1964.)

TABLE 8.4

THE PREDICTIVE VALUE OF ABILITY, GENERAL PREVIOUS ACHIEVEMENT, AND SPECIFIC PREVIOUS ACHIEVEMENT FOR CURRENT ACHIEVEMENT

	MENTAL ABILITY			PREVIOUS ACHEIVEMENT	
GRADE 13 SUBJECTS	*SATO Verbal*	*SATO Math*	*SATO Total*	*Grade 12 Average*	*Algebra* Achievement Test*	*History* Achievement Test*
Algebra	.38†	.53	.53	.54	.59	.30
Trigonometry	.35	.55	.52	.50	.57	.28
Chemistry	.40	.43	.49	.57	.48	.37
English Composition	.55	.24	.47	.39	.26	.28
History	.32	.20	.31	.48	.27	.38
Grade 13 average	.51	.41	.55	.64	.49	.40

*Standardized tests administered at the end of grade 12.
†Sample size varied from 800–3200 students for the various subjects.
Source: D. Ellis, *Scholastic aptitude scores for some measures of academic achievement.* Metropolitan Toronto Education Research Council, Distributed Report 12, December 1965.

One might ask why the correlation between scholastic aptitude (or general mental ability) and current academic achievement is frequently less than the correlation between the latter variable and previous achievement. One important reason, discussed extensively in Chapter 6, is that current achievement in subjects with a high degree of sequential dependence builds directly upon, and therefore should be closely related to, previous achievement in the same subject. Equally important, however, is the operation of other relevant factors such as motivation, interest, personality traits, and peer-group, social class, and cultural influences—all of which are obviously operative in current learning and which will be reflected in large measure in past achievement. For this reason, previous achievement and current aptitude scores are frequently combined in determining admittance to post-secondary institutions.

The data cited here support the contention that the test of general mental ability is the most economical source of information in terms of the range of predictive information that it allows. Moreover, although its predictive accuracy is frequently bettered by grade-point average, the measure of mental ability can be obtained in as little as one-tenth the testing time required to obtain the grade-point average. However, since grade point (or school leaving) averages are used for promotional and other purposes, it is not a question of *replacing* them by tests of mental ability but of obtaining the optimum *combination* of both (along with other data) to suit the particular purpose at hand.

Mental Ability Tests as Instruments for Guidance and Selection

Because mental ability scores correlate relatively highly with most measures of achievement in school subjects, they are widely used as instruments for the guidance of students and for defining criteria for admittance to different programs. As an example of both practices we may consider the common occurrence of a student trying to decide whether to enter university and, at the same time, of the university trying to decide whether to accept him. Let us assume that University X has maintained a record of the mental ability and achievement scores obtained at the end of the year prior to entry of its students, over a period of years; we may assume further that these two measures have been weighted in some way to form a composite "entrance score," and that a table has been completed similar to our hypothetical example shown in Table 8.5.

It would appear, on the basis of past experience, that the student whose entrance score was in the 40–60th percentile range for the previously established norms would have about one chance in two of successfully completing a Pass Arts (three-year unspecialized) program, and about one

TABLE 8.5

Relationship Between Mental Ability and Success in University
(hypothetical data)

PERCENTILE RANGE OF "ENTRANCE" SCORES	PERCENTAGE OF STUDENTS GRADUATING FROM:	
	Pass Arts 3-*Year Program* (*Percentage*)	*Honors Arts* 4-*Year Program* (*Percentage*)
80–100	87	70
60–80	71	52
40–60	49	32
20–40	29	10
0–20	18	2

chance in three of completing an Honors (four-year specialized) program. If this information were made available to the high-school counselor, he would apprise the student who seems likely to fall in that range, of the odds against which he was working, and draw his attention to the fields of post-secondary education best suited to his talents. If the student did apply to the university, an admissions committee would undoubtedly be strongly influenced by the same expectations, but would perhaps temper these raw statistics with evidence of specific achievement in relevant fields and with his teachers' assessment of his current achievement motivation.

The Achievement Quotient

An under-achiever is usually defined as a student whose achievement is manifestly below his measured mental ability; similarly an over-achiever is a student who achieves at a higher level than that expected on the basis of his measured ability. To identify such individuals, an "achievement quotient" defined as:

$$AQ = \frac{\text{deviation score of achievement}}{\text{deviation score of ability}}$$

is computed[13] and a distribution of such scores is obtained for some group

---

[13]The deviation score is a measure representing the position of an individual score in the total distribution of scores, and is used to allow one to compare scores from different distributions. Essentially, the deviation score is the number of standard deviations of any particular score above or below the mean of the distribution. This method of identification is based on the expectation that an individual who scores one standard deviation above the mean in intelligence should obtain an achievement score which is one standard deviation above the mean achievement score.

under investigation. The individuals whose scores fall in the extreme upper part of the distribution are classified as over-achievers and those whose scores fall in the extreme lower part are declared under-achievers. Consistent with earlier remarks it would seem that the under-achievement syndrome begins as early as the third grade in the case of boys, but not until the ninth grade in the case of girls (Shaw and McCuen, 1960).

While many studies have investigated the correlates of underachievement (Cole and others, 1962; Frankel, 1960; Lesser and others, 1963; Perkins, 1965; Shaw and others, 1960; Todd and others, 1962), it remains one of the great unsolved problems in education and is a frequent target of many lay and professional groups. To some extent under-achievement can be laid to faulty study habits or to conflicts between particular students and teachers, and in these instances it should be at least partly remediable. Again, the chronic under-achievement characteristics of certain cultural subgroups may be in part or wholly remediable provided that special programs are created which cope with the language and motivational deficiencies of these children at an early enough age. Finally, programs which are more directly concerned with students' interests, such as the burgeoning emphasis on technical education in high schools, will no doubt help to engage the interests of many otherwise apathetic and underachieving students.[14]

Mental Ability Scores as Curriculum-Pacing Devices

Together with previous achievement, mental ability scores will frequently be used in determining the pace at which material will be presented to students as the schools move toward nongraded systems. Encouraging evidence comes from studies which show that low intelligence can apparently be compensated for, at least in part, by allowing slow-learning pupils more time to complete learning tasks (Klausmeier and Check, 1962; Klausmeier and Feldhusen, 1959). Moreover, there is considerable evidence that instructional aids, organizational devices, and superior textual materials differentially benefit the duller and initially less knowledgeable as opposed to the brighter and initially more knowledgeable student.

---

[14]Because of the lack of complete reliability of both achievement and intelligence tests, and the less than perfect anticipated correlation between these measures, some educational psychologists have cast doubt on the practical utility of the notions of over-and under-achievement (R. L. Thorndike, 1961, 1963). While it would certainly be questionable to classify a student on the basis of a single set of test results, most teachers have encountered students whose achievement over the years is so consistently below their measured level of intelligence that the matter cannot be dismissed simply as a "statistical fluke." In such instances the "under-achiever" concept in particular would seem to be valuable both as an accurate label for a specific problem and as an incentive to seek solutions.

TOPICS FOR DISCUSSION AND FURTHER STUDY

1. A student is observed to be having some difficulty learning in an "average pace" stream. A check of the school files indicates that the student obtained an IQ of 85 on an intelligence test administered two years previously. A tentative conclusion is reached that the student lacks the general mental ability to cope with this particular stream and that he should be placed in a slower-moving group. Indicate cautions which should be introduced into such a discussion, under the following headings:

(a) Reliability of the IQ score as an estimate of the student's present level of cognitive functioning:
(b) Other factors than intelligence which might account for the student's level of performance and which would not be changed by transfer to a different stream;
(c) Consequences of transfer to a slower-moving stream.

2. Two students, aged six and eight respectively, are found to possess the same mental age. In what other ways may the students differ which would have implications for their school learning?

3. Certain differences between the intelligence of boys and girls have been reported. What implications, if any, would such differences have for educational practice?

4.* It has been suggested (Sullivan, 1967b) that a developmental scale for cognitive tasks should be created, based possibly on Piaget's theory, which would replace the standard IQ test. Cite advantages and disadvantages of such an approach.

5. A teacher constructs a correlation table relating IQ and performance on a midterm examination in a particular school subject. How would he identify students who were "under-achieving" or "over-achieving" in this subject? What purposes might be served by doing this?

6. On an individual intelligence test a student is observed to have a considerably higher "performance" score than "verbal" score. Indicate some possible causes and educational implications of this fact.

7. In at least one European country it has been argued that IQ tests are instruments designed by the bourgeoisie to demonstrate the inferior intelligence of the proletariat and thereby to justify the former's economic exploitation of the latter. On the basis of the discussion in this chapter, or your own convictions concerning intelligence testing, can any logical support be advanced for such a position?

8. Despite their inability to predict academic achievement, what values might "culture-free" intelligence tests have for educators?

9.* Large-scale IQ testing programs have revealed fairly substantial differences between ethnic groups in mean IQ (Jensen, 1968). Moreover, such differences are unequally distributed across verbal, numerical, spatial, and reasoning tests (Stodolsky and Lesser, 1967). Does such evidence justify a conclusion of "genic superiority"? What educational implications would the empirically demonstrated differences hold?

10. It has been indicated in this chapter that IQ is generally a good predictor of academic performance. How would you expect the relationship between IQ and performance to change as one moved to successively higher levels of behavioral outcomes (in the taxonomic sense)? How would you explain any trends which you would postulate?

11.* A long-standing dispute between British and American psychologists has to do with whether mature intellectual performance is best conceived of in terms of an overriding general factor ("g" in British terminology) or a number of specific factors (for example, numerical ability, spatial ability). Read some of the relevant literature (Vernon, 1965, and the references alluded to therein) to ascertain the critical dimensions of the argument. What implications, if any, does this difference in viewpoint hold for educational practice?

12.* What aspects of early child-parent relationships would you expect to correlate with the child's subsequent mental growth? Would these parental factors be different for boys than for girls (Honzik, 1967)?

13.* Investigate Cattell's theory of fluid and crystallized intelligence (Cattell, 1963; Horn and Cattell, 1967; Humphrey, 1967). What new light does this theory cast on the concept of adult intelligence discussed in this chapter?

SUGGESTIONS FOR ADDITIONAL READING

Caspari, E. W. Genetic endowment and environment in the determination of human behavior: Biological viewpoint. *Amer. educ. Res. J.,* 1968, 5, (1), 43–55.

Guilford, J. B. Intelligence: 1965 Model. *Amer. Psychol.,* 1966, *21,* 20–26.

Hebb, D. O. *A textbook of psychology.* Philadelphia: W. B. Saunders Company, 1958.

Honzik, M. P. Environmental correlates of mental growth: Prediction from the family setting at 21 months. *Child Develpm.,* 1967, *38,* 337–364.

Horn, J. L. Intelligence—why it grows, why it declines. *Trans-action,* November 1967, 23–31.

Jensen, A. R. Social class, race and genetics: Implications for education. *Amer. educ. Res. J.,* 1968, *5,* (1), 1–42.

Stodolsky, S., and G. Lesser. Learning patterns in the disadvantaged. *Harvard Educ. Rev.,* 1967, *37,* (4), 546–593.

Vernon, P. E. Ability factors and environmental influences. *Amer. Psychol.,* 1965, *20,* (9), 723–733.

CHAPTER 9

INDIVIDUAL DIFFERENCES IN INTELLECTUAL FUNCTIONING

UNTIL QUITE RECENTLY PUBLIC EDUCATION HAS BEEN "mass" education in the sense that its basic instructional processes were directed at a composite group, comprising from 20 to 35 or more students. In fact, the typical individual "lesson" is still designed and executed in terms of the "class" (or the hypothetical "average student" representing the class) rather than the individual. This central characteristic of public education, forced upon the school by the limitations of finance, has been accompanied by many other procedures which, while facilitating the efficient processing of large numbers of students, give little attention to *differences between students*. To begin with, admittance to formal instruction has been determined mainly by chronological age without acknowledging the enormous differences in readiness among preschool children of the same age. Each starting group was then moved through a "lock-step" system in which it was assumed that every child should cover a fixed amount of material in a given year. If he were not up to an acceptable standard by the end of the year, he was considered to have "failed" and was required to repeat the entire year, including study of the content he had previously learned. It is only now, with public education moving away from most of these practices, that we have come to understand how completely any consideration of *individual* abilities was lost in management of the *group*.

DEALING WITH INDIVIDUAL DIFFERENCES

The full consequences of our past disregard of individual differences may never be fully assessed. It is possible, however, to obtain some idea of the instructional problems posed for teachers by considering

250

what a typical grade 7 class of the pre-1960 period looked like in a school system in which heterogeneous groups of students were moved through the lock-step system. Data based on averages from actual classrooms (Dunlop. 1957) showed a typical IQ range of 50 points, a mental age range of six years, and a range of approximately five grades in grade achievement scores in most of the principal subjects by the end of elementary school.[1] Given these enormous differences between individual students it is understandable that the teacher could do little but gear his instructional strategy toward the "hypothetical average"; the consequences, in terms of the possibility of sustaining interest, or providing a satisfying educational experience for the bright and slow-learning extremes trapped in this system, are rather awesome to contemplate. It is a reasonable inference that the teacher's inability to cater to the remarkably different abilities represented in such a class may have been a large factor in the high failure and dropout rates experienced in the past.

Increasing Emphasis on the Development of Individual Potential

In the past decade there has been rapid movement away from the primitive conditions described above. Among a variety of causal factors one might single out an increasingly painful realization that the almost total neglect of individual differences in our schools stood in stark contrast to the long-avowed aim of educators "to develop the potential of the child to the fullest possible degree." This contrast became a matter of national concern after World War II, when federal planning agencies began to obtain a glimpse of the kind of talent needed for the maintenance and growth of a technological society, and when it became widely realized that the partially educated constitute an economic liability. Moreover, concurrent international developments in science and technology argued for the fullest possible development of high-level ability, particularly in mathematics and the sciences.

Whether these or other factors were primarily responsible, there have certainly been many recent developments in the school giving greater attention to individual differences in cognitive ability. Among these developments are: a rapid increase in the number of special classes for slow learners, gifted students, and children with special learning difficulties; consolidation of elementary-school areas into units sufficiently large to allow specialization of function and ability grouping of pupils; the increasing impact of potential-ly individualized educational aids such as language labs and programmed instruction; an increase in the number of secondary- and post-secondary-school streams, thus allowing more grouping on the basis of ability or interest; and sustained effort by educators to find ways of effectively using

---

[1]Data provided by Goodlad and Anderson (1959) indicate a comparable range in ability in classrooms in the United States.

streaming, acceleration, nongraded plans, self-teaching, and other practices consistent with greater attention to individual differences. At the present time interest in the problem of individual differences has reached an all-time high, and many large-scale research and development projects are currently underway.

Despite these promising signs, however, it is clear that much remains to be done. One bit of data supporting this assertion comes from a recent survey by the National Education Association (1965), which found that only about one-third of even the largest school districts (student population exceeding 12,000) operated one or more nongraded schools. Moreover, even in those systems with some form of nongraded plan, the practice did not appear to be widespread and was concentrated in the primary grades; very few nongraded secondary schools were found. (See also: N.E.A. Research Division, 1967b.) Since the teacher now entering the profession may need to play a stimulating as well as a participating role in producing needed changes, he will profit from understanding some of the current issues and such theoretical considerations as may be brought to bear upon them.

STEPS TOWARD INDIVIDUALIZING INSTRUCTION

Although indicating a desirable direction or intent, the goal of "developing each child's potential to the fullest possible degree" makes sense only as an idealized statement, for even if funds were available without limit such a goal would be impractical. It is surely more realistic to hope that the school might provide a program for each child which is challenging, which results in continuous growth, which taps his unique abilities, and which contains sufficient success experiences to keep motivation at a high level. This is a tall order for, to cite an old educational cliché, each child is indeed unique in his pattern of abilities, interests, and natural endowments.

Table 9.1 examines factors whose specific values in any school system determine the degree to which these practical goals concerning individual differences will be realized. As in the case of curriculum development, many of the most important factors lie beyond the individual classroom teacher's jurisdiction. For example, if the school board in a small town provides just enough funds to hire a minimally qualified teacher for a group of 35 students spanning four grade levels, then any pretense to individualization of instruction (beyond the student's own independent study) becomes a kind of joke. Similarly, although a teacher may try to move his students ahead at their individual rates of ability, such an approach will be of little benefit to the student unless the school is sufficiently flexible to allow something other than the rigid grade system of promotion. In brief then, what the teacher can actually do toward providing for individual differences in large measure

TABLE 9.1

Some Factors Determining Degree to which School Can Provide Programs Suited to Abilities and Interests of Individual Child

LEVEL AT WHICH FACTOR DETERMINED	FACTOR OR VARIABLE	COMMENT
Extra-school (state, provincial, or local government)	Amount of money spent per child	Determines pupil-teacher ratio, extent of opportunities for homogeneous grouping, and availability of teaching aids which could facilitate individualization of instruction
Between levels of school authority	Provision for advanced standing; early entry	Coordination necessary if acceleration is to be feasible
Within school or school system	Provision of: (a) "ability streams" (b) teaching aids facilitating individualized instruction (c) suitable policies concerning acceleration, nongrading, and team teaching (d) nonrestrictive promotion policies (e) special classes or programs for gifted, slow learners, and other special groups (f) adequate library resources for individual study (g) professional and nonprofessional teacher "aides"	Decision usually made by superintendent or principal in conjunction with teachers
Individual classroom	Provision of: (a) within-class achievement or ability-level groupings (b) individual programs (for example, via programmed instruction) (c) opportunities for independent learning (d) training of independent study skills (e) enrichment materials	Depends upon the initiative of the individual classroom teacher

depends upon the outcome of decisions made at higher administrative levels.[2]

Differentiated Ability Grouping

Taken at face value, ability grouping seems to have certain merits in taking account of individual differences. By bringing together children of similar ability, it permits the teacher to gear the level and method of instruction to the *particular* level of ability prevailing in the group. The teacher no longer has to accommodate to the hypothetical ability level of the *average* child as the fairest approximation of the group's ability. Thus he can avoid a pace and level of instruction that is too difficult for the dull pupil and too easy for the bright.

In practice, the amount of homogeneity produced is not as great as one might expect. The reason for this is that no perfect correlation exists between any psychological measure (such as IQ), which might be used as a selection device, and achievement scores; thus grouping on IQ would leave considerable variability on the achievement measures obtained in any given class. For example, the Dunlop study cited earlier indicates what might happen in a school system sufficiently large to operate four grade 7 classes. Table 9.2 shows the degree of variability on achievement scores one might expect (given traditional teaching practices) in the group consisting of the "brightest quarter" (in terms of highest IQ) of the students. By comparison with the heterogeneous grouping data, we can see that while the expected IQ range has been drastically reduced (from 52 to 18 points) by selecting on this variable, the decrease in the expected range of scores in reading, spelling, and language is much smaller. The third column in Table 9.2 shows the expected range in IQ, language, and spelling scores when the upper quarter are selected on the basis of their reading achievement. It is obvious, then, that selection on any particular variable will not result in a group which is homogeneous with respect to other variables, although some reduction in the range of scores will normally result.

What can be done in any particular situation will depend largely upon the number of students available. Obviously if a school system pooled its ten grade 7 classes by creating a junior-high school, then much narrower ranges in IQ could be used to define the groups, and further reduction in variability on other scores could be expected. Moreover, the teacher of the high IQ group in the example cited above might create special learning groups within his classroom, thereby reducing variability further. Clearly no general rule or formula can be provided, and any school or school system must work out the possibilities which exist for it.

---

[2]If favorable conditions *do not* prevail, teachers, as professionals, have a responsibility to argue for working arrangements which *are* compatible with the outcome expected for education. Recently, such concerns have been strongly voiced by teachers' organizations both in the United States and in Canada.

TABLE 9.2

MEAN RANGE IN ABILITY AND ACHIEVEMENT MEASURES
IN UNSTREAMED CLASSES, STREAMED CLASSES,
AND RANDOM GRADE 7 SAMPLE

		GRADE 7 DATA		
VARIABILITY IN:	*Average Range in Unstreamed Classes*	*Range in Class Selected by* IQ *(Upper 25%)*	*Range in Class Selected by Reading Achievement (Upper 25%)*	*Range in Total Grade 7 Sample (N = 140)*
IQ	52*	18	33	71
Reading	5.0†	3.4	1.9	6.0
Spelling Grade	6.0†	3.3	3.3	6.7
Language Achievement	4.6†	1.9	1.9	5.9
Arithmetic Scores	5.0*			

*grade 8
†grade 7
Source: Adapted from Dunlop, 1957.

A second purported advantage of ability grouping is that it allows pupils of comparable ability to interact in the learning process, and it is postulated that a kind of "social facilitation" of learning will occur when bright children are stimulated by their intellectual peers. This latter advantage, however, has not been unequivocally demonstrated. Gurnee (1962), for example, found group learning to be superior to individual learning not because of social facilitation per se but because it provides an opportunity for less successful group members to imitate their more successful classmates. In this and other studies of the relative effectiveness of homogeneous versus heterogeneous grouping, one would hardly expect to find *marked* advantages in favor of the former *unless* the school allows more capable students to move at their own pace and utilizes teaching methods appropriate to their level of development. If, in our hypothetical example, the school operated with a lock-step grade system, then one of the potential advantages of ability grouping—allowing more capable students to move on more quickly—would be lost; under such circumstances, it would not be surprising to find relatively little difference between heterogeneous and homogeneous grouping.[3]

Also, a student's personality may be an important factor in determining the effect of a particular kind of grouping. For example, Atkinson (1965)

[3]For recent summaries of research on the effectiveness of grouping see: Passow (1966); Yates (1966).

advanced a theory predicting that a student with a relatively high need for achievement and a relatively low test anxiety would respond better to homogeneous grouping, whereas a student who had relatively high test anxiety and relatively low need for achievement would do better in heterogeneous classes. Atkinson's experimental data did not completely bear out his predictions, but certainly suggested that these variables are relevant to the question of the kind of group into which a student should be placed.

Ability grouping, moreover, is also not without disadvantages. The most frequently heard argument on the negative side is that ability groupings tend to stigmatize the dull and to generate arrogance and conceit in the bright. But this disadvantage has undoubtedly been overemphasized, since children who do not measure up to their contemporaries almost inevitably appreciate their inferiorities and suffer self-depreciation with or without ability grouping. Moreover, with respect to this objection, it can be argued that grouping promotes the more explicit realization by a child of his relative profile of abilities and thereby facilitates a more realistic self-concept and level of aspiration.

Finally, it should also be remembered that heterogeneity itself has positive values. For example, it enables the child to better adjust to the wide variety of ability levels he will meet outside the school environment. It also provides intellectual stimulation and models for imitation for the dull child, and gives the brighter pupil an opportunity to clarify and consolidate his understanding of concepts by explaining them to his less precocious classmates.

What is the teacher to draw from this discussion? When all factors are weighed it would seem that in the *elementary* grades, when the students are unable to take much responsibility for their own learning and need intensive teacher guidance and confirmation (that is, feedback), some kind of contrived grouping seems desirable, probably on the basis of language development or general intellectual ability. This does not necessarily mean, however, separation into grades labeled "bright," "average," and "dull"—or the more euphemistic "robins," "orioles," and "bluejays"—and learning groups of different levels of ability *within* a single classroom would probably be the best solution. With flexibility, a teacher could provide one kind of grouping for language instruction, another for arithmetical instruction, and enable all ability levels to interact in less skill-oriented subjects. In the *secondary-*school grades many groups will be formed on the basis of interest and post-secondary destination; in both instances a kind of spontaneous ability grouping tends to take place. Moreover, attending to individual differences at this level is probably less of a burden for the teacher, since students of this age are much better able to engage in independent study and problem solving, and to subject themselves to the self-discipline required for programmed instruction and other auto-instructional devices.

Those educators who are responsible for the overall planning of instruction in a school system will undoubtedly profit from reading accounts of the many "methods" of dealing with individual differences currently in effect. For example, in the Dual Progress Plan (Stoddard, 1961) all students are placed for half of each day in a homeroom, with their age-mates and homeroom teacher, for instruction in "cultural imperatives." The rest of the day is devoted to special subjects in which students are taught by specialist teachers in separate classes which are grouped to insure relative homogeneity of ability. The Trump Plan (Trump and Baynham, 1961) involves greater flexibility of administrative arrangements in that the high-school class of 30 is replaced by some large demonstration and lecture classes (utilizing, where advisable, either educational television or specialist "master teachers"), some small discussion groups, and considerable self-instruction and use of programmed learning devices.

Nongraded Classes

As previously indicated, the potential advantage of ability grouping may to a large extent be lost if student progress is hampered by a rigid grade structure. Consequently a useful complement to grouping is the "nongraded school" (Goodlad and Anderson, 1959), a concept which is currently attracting a good deal of attention. As presently applied in Canada (Ritchie and Worth, 1960; Bergstrom, 1965), the nongraded approach typically divides the first six years of schooling into a number of units of work (usually centered around language achievement). In theory, the student progresses through these units more or less at his own rate.

How such a program works out in practice can only be determined by close examination of an on-going instance, and one would expect that the ideal of "continuous progress" may not be attained in all cases (Swartz, undated). For example, in current Canadian programs at least one limitation is inherent in the fact that even in the most flexible systems the student must move through the traditional six grades in somewhere between four and eight years (in less flexible systems the range is considerably narrower). Moreover, if a "small-group" approach is being used, then any individual student would probably stay with that group for one year or more, and would be constrained somewhat by its progress.[4] There also appears to be a problem of coordination in that many of the advantages of a combined

---

[4] One might also wonder how the nongraded approach handles intra-individual differences. For example, a student with pronounced arithmetical aptitudes might be able to cover the first "six years' work" in that subject in four years, while maintaining only average progress in reading. How this student would be placed at the end of six years is not at all clear in most of the descriptions of current programs.

small-group and nongraded program can be lost when it is followed by a graded approach in the junior or senior high-school levels, an unfortunately widespread practice in Canada and the United States. Nevertheless, it is certainly clear that these innovations represent a marked improvement over the "lock-step" approach and that they could go a long way toward meeting individual differences.

Individualized Instruction

The end-point in the continuum of programs catering to individual differences is the provision of individualized instruction (differential assignments) within each group. Under such an arrangement a student would spend the greater part of the school day working independently at his own optimal pace, possibly utilizing sequentially organized programmed materials. Present evidence indicates (Chapter 11) that such self-instruction appears to be at least as efficient for most aspects of subject-matter learning as is regular teacher instruction. The many advantages of programmed instruction include: the opportunity to provide organizing and unifying explanatory ideas; unusual lucidity of presentation; early confirmation, clarification, and correction of newly acquired concepts and principles; consolidation or necessary overlearning of existing knowledge before new learning material is presented; and sequential organization of subject matter.

As will be pointed out later, programmed instruction, as it presently exists, by no means constitutes an educational panacea. For example, certain aspects of instruction in which knowledge is less well defined, and in which the acquisition of independent and critical thinking ability is a major goal, obviously require more class discussion and direct teacher participation. But it can reasonably be argued that teachers would have more time to devote to these latter objectives, to cultivate a questioning attitude toward established knowledge on the part of the pupil, and to focus on the discovery aspects of acquiring new knowledge, if the more stable and substantive aspects of a discipline were learned individually by means of programmed instruction.

Nonpromotion

Nonpromotion constitutes an attempt at homogeneous grouping by withholding progression to the next higher grade from the extremely low achiever. Theoretically, it provides a necessary and desirable second opportunity for mastering the material that the student was not able to learn the first time it was presented. In practice, however, the repeater makes less academic progress than a promoted child of comparable academic ability and achievement (Goodlad, 1952). Although some low achievers do profit from repetition, more actually do worse on achievement tests a year later than immediately after failing the grade in question. It is not repetition per se that has these damaging effects but rather the stigma of nonpromotion, the impairment of morale, and the exposure to the same ineffective methods that had previously led to failure.

Despite advantages of promotion over nonpromotion—in terms of student achievement, self-confidence, and acceptance by peers (Goodlad, 1952; Segel, 1951), it has to be recognized that the "socially promoted" student still tends to be maladjusted and has difficulty keeping up with the class to which he has been promoted. There is a real possibility that unearned promotions tend to generate unrealistic attitudes toward, and expectations about, the general relationship between achievement and reward found in adult life. In the final analysis, it seems better to avoid "failure" in the first place by involving the student in a program, pace, and teaching method which is appropriate to his present state of readiness.

DEALING WITH SPECIAL ABILITY GROUPS

The preceding sections of this chapter have dealt with questions which each school must face when it attempts to cope with the problem of the individual differences inherent in any heterogeneous group of students. Having worked out some general plan, it is still necessary to deal with special groups who have particular learning disabilities or who present special learning problems. As Table 9.3 indicates, such groups include various kinds of "slow learners," emotionally disturbed children, children with speech, hearing, and visual problems, and children with other health problems. In most larger educational systems all of these groups are given some kind of special treatment under the supervision of an appropriately trained teacher. Since the typical classroom teacher's responsibility will be limited to identifying children who may need special help, and who have slipped through the various "screens" provided by the school's psychological testing department, we will not discuss the educational problems which are unique to each group here.[5] The two exceptions to the previous statement are the "gifted" child and the "culturally deprived" child, both of whom are frequently found in regular classrooms.

---

[5]Many readable books and references are available for classroom teachers who wish to pursue these matters. See, for example, Gallagher,1964; Garrison and Force,1965; Johnson, 1963.

TABLE 9.3

PREVALENCE ESTIMATES OF THE SCHOOL-AGE POPULATION
CLASSIFIED AS EXCEPTIONAL FOR SPECIAL EDUCATION PURPOSES

AREA OF EXCEPTIONALITY	PERCENTAGE U.S. ESTIMATE	PERCENTAGE CANADIAN ESTIMATE
Intellectually limited	2.3	2.0
Educable mentally retarded	(2.0)	
Trainable mentally retarded	(0.3)	
Intellectually superior (gifted)	2.0	2.0
Disturbed and maladjusted	2.0	2.0
Emotionally disturbed		
Socially maladjusted		
Speech impaired	3.5	2.10
Hearing impaired	0.6	0.54
Hard-of-hearing	(0.5)	
Deaf	(0.1)	
Visually impaired	0.09	0.13
Partially seeing	(0.06)	
Blind	(0.03)	
Nonsensory physically impaired	2.0	0.47
Crippled	(1.0)	(0.1)
Chronic health problems	(1.0)	(0.37)

Source: EXCEPTIONAL CHILDREN IN THE SCHOOLS edited by Lloyd M. Dunn. Copyright © 1963 by Holt, Rinehart and Winston, Inc. Reprinted by permission of Holt, Rinehart and Winston, Inc.

The Academically Gifted

Definitions of the "gifted" child are varied and numerous (Laycock and Munro, 1966). For present purposes we will use the term to refer to the upper 2 percent in intelligence or academic aptitude. It is clear that, because of the relatively small number of gifted children, a school system would have to be fairly large before it could create a special class for such students. For example, a group of 20 gifted students would be found in a general population of 1000 students and, given present birthrates, an annual number of births of this magnitude would be found only in cities of 60,000 or more population. Presumably, a large proportion of teachers will then be faced with the necessity of coping with a "gifted" child within the context of the typical classroom situation.

Irrespective of whether the gifted are treated in separate classes or within regular classrooms, two approaches are generally advocated. Proponents of *enrichment* suggest that once the gifted child has covered the "normal" work associated with a given age or grade level he should then be subjected to "in depth" expansions, elaborations, and new applications of the ideas he has learned. While this seems to have some merit in theory, what too often happens in practice is that the teacher is much too busy to give sufficient time to locating and organizing such "enrichment" experiences. In sheer desperation—and in fact, as a way of filling time—many teachers choose one of two equally undesirable alternatives. In the first place, it would be unfortunate merely to select topics which the student will eventually study at a higher-grade level, since this practice will insure boredom when the material is encountered later, and since the student should probably get academic "credit" for what he has learned. The second undesirable alternative is to select admittedly difficult but somewhat preposterous applications of standard skills. The teacher who sets the gifted child the problem of computing the product of 987,654 and 123,456 is really not "enriching" the student's educational experience at all, and is probably merely teaching him that it does not pay to move ahead too quickly.

The alternative to enrichment is *acceleration,* that is, allowing the student to cover the content prescribed for a certain grade sequence in less than the normal or usual time. Acceleration can be implemented in many ways: by early admission to kindergarten and college; by double promotions; by admission to college with advanced standing; and by such means of concentrating instruction as lengthening the school year, completing two years' work in one, and more rapid self-pacing in ungraded classes. The latter procedures avoid the hazards of possibly missing important learnings that are essential in sequentially organized curricula.

Arguments against acceleration usually suggest that it may "harm" a gifted child either socially, emotionally, or in terms of his academic accomplishment. However, reviews of acceleration studies (Shannon, 1957) do not support any of these contentions. Children who are admitted to kindergarten at an early age (Worcester, 1956) or who are accelerated from grade 2 to grade 4 after a five-week summer session (Klausmeier, 1963) do as well, or better, academically in the higher grades as other pupils. They are just as well-adjusted emotionally and socially, are just as readily accepted by their classmates, and are more likely to go on to college (Pressey, 1965). Generally, students who enter college at an early age tend to make better grades, are more likely to graduate and go on to advanced studies, manifest fewer disciplinary problems, and tend to be more successful in their careers (Fund for the Advancement of Education, 1957; Pressey, 1962c; Terman and Oden, 1949). In retrospect, the vast majority of such accelerates believe that early admission had a beneficial effect upon them (Pressey, 1967a).

Probably the best argument for the acceleration of academically gifted pupils is the long period of academic training required today for all professions. Acceleration helps avoid the abnormal prolongation of economic dependence and sub-adulthood, as well as undesirable postponement of marriage, that often accompany such training. Early entrance into professional careers is also important from the standpoint of self-actualization and the advancement of knowledge. It has been shown that because of such factors as health, stamina, motivation, interest, and freshness of outlook, research and scholarly productivity are higher in some fields during the early adult years than at any other time of life (Lehman, 1964; Pressey, 1962c).

In summary, it would seem that the teacher should favor enrichment over acceleration only when certain conditions prevail. First, the teacher must be free to plan suitable topics; second, the pupil must have attained a sufficiently high level of cognitive development to work in a semi-independent fashion; finally, the school should have available sufficient library and other resources for realistic enrichment programs. Generally speaking, none of these conditions prevail in the contemporary elementary school. It is true, on the other hand, that in the junior or senior high-school years the student acquires the ability to read critically on his own, to locate information, and to organize to some extent his own learning, so that enrichment may be more realistic at this level. It seems desirable that a major emphasis of enrichment should not be the mere acquisition of *more knowledge,* but an attempt to have the student reach "higher" levels of behavior (as defined by the taxonomy). Enrichment programs which develop the student's powers of analysis, synthesis, problem solving, and original thinking can obviously have a significant impact on his subsequent intellectual performance. In this connection, great advantage can be taken of special-interest clubs, competitions, and contests, such as are now found (for example) in the fields of mathematics and science.

Encouraging the Student To Assume Responsibility for His Own Learning   All of the procedures which have been mentioned to this point can contribute to the problem of meeting individual differences by providing programs commensurate with the student's abilities and interests. Consistent with all of them is the notion that a child should be encouraged to take a large measure of responsibility for his own learning at as early an age as possible. It may be that this will contribute more than anything else to the individualization of instruction.

There is probably justification for criticizing the limited movement in this direction which many classroom teachers have made to date. When asked why teachers do not do more in the way of individual instruction, one has first to face the fact that many teachers find it more satisfying to teach large groups of students. It is certainly "tidier" for the teacher (as classroom manager) to have everyone at the same point at the same time, no matter how over-extended the slower-learning pupil may be, or how colossally bored the gifted child. Another contributing factor, in our opinion, is that the school *vastly underestimates* what children and adolescents are able to do on their own.

Consider, for example, the typical high-school algebra lesson in which the teacher wishes to demonstrate the factorization of $X^2 - Y^2$. It would not be unusual for the teacher to spend as much as 30 minutes developing this theme, during which time he works from very easy to very complex examples, elicits answers from the class, and attempts to insure that the vast majority of his students have grasped the ideas involved. However, the fact is that many of the more able students will already have understood these ideas from principles which have preceded them, or could comprehend them easily by studying the textbook themselves for a period of five minutes. Consequently, it would be difficult to say what such pupils have actually gained from the other 25 minutes, except perhaps some realization of the limited capacities of many of their fellow students.

To take an example from the elementary school, many teachers set out a week's spelling assignment and have all their students spend from 10 to 15 minutes a day practicing the spelling of the new words. Nevertheless, probably as many as 20 percent of the students can adequately spell all of these words before the exercise begins, and they would be much better off spending time investigating new word meanings in a dictionary or undertaking some other form of self-instruction. We find here, as we have in other areas, that there is a great deal of room for teacher ingenuity and experimentation. It would be illuminating for teachers to allow some of their more capable students to obtain limited experiences in self-instruction (through programmed learning materials or regular written texts), and to compare the results with those obtained under the present classroom lesson plans.

Some schools are currently working out independent study programs which center around the notions of "mastery learning" (Bloom, 1968) or "proficiency goals" (Swartz, undated). The basic idea in such plans is that the learning tasks in a given subject-matter field are divided into a number of well-defined subtasks, and that the student works through each task independently (employing self-instructional devices) until he has attained an acceptable level of mastery or proficiency. At this point he earns credit for the unit and, with the teacher's guidance, moves on to the next task. In addition to allowing for large individual differences in ability and eliminating the need for "failing a grade," such plans also give the student an early start in accepting responsibility in managing his own learning experiences (see further comments in Chapter 14).

The Culturally Disadvantaged

In view of recent public attention given to this problem, the reader will be aware that the problem of providing an appropriate education for the culturally disadvantaged has assumed considerable importance in the past few years.[6] It is difficult to determine precisely how many such children are to be found in the public elementary and secondary schools. Data derived in the period 1940–1950 estimated that the so-called "lower-lower class" constituted from 12 percent (Warner and others, 1949) to 25 percent (Warner and Lunt, 1941) of the total population. However, the number of children from this group actually in school would depend on the community and grade level. In one community Warner and others (1949) found that 90 percent of school-age children in the lowest socioeconomic group were not attending school, and that about three-quarters of the dropouts had left school before they reached sixteen years of age. Nevertheless it is clear that in the elementary-school grades culturally deprived children will more frequently be found than either slow learners or gifted children. Thus an awareness of their particular learning problems is important to every prospective classroom teacher.

The Central Problem: Language Retardation   It is in the area of language development, and particularly in the abstract dimension of verbal functioning, that the culturally deprived child manifests the greatest degree of intellectual retardation. Many factors contribute to this unfortunate developmental outcome. The culturally deprived home, to begin with, lacks the variety of objects, utensils, toys, and pictures that require labeling and serve as referents in the middle-class home. The culturally deprived child is also not spoken to or read to very much by adults. For this reason, and because of the high noise level of his home, his auditory discrimination tends to be poor. Unlike the middle-class child, he receives little corrective feedback regarding his enunciation, pronunciation, and grammar (Deutsch, 1963; John and Goldstein, 1964), and the vocabulary and syntactical model provided him by his parents is typically impoverished and faulty.

As a result of these influences, the culturally deprived child's entire orientation to language is different from that of the middle-class child. He responds more to the concrete, tangible, immediate, and particularized properties of objects and situations rather than to their abstract, categorical, and relational properties (Bernstein, 1958; 1960; Siller, 1957). His speech is instigated more by the objects and actions he sees than by abstract ideas emanating from within, and he makes more ancillary use of such nonverbal forms of communication as gestures and facial expressions (Bernstein, 1958; Riessman, 1962). In short, the language of the culturally deprived child is more concrete, expressive, and informal than that of the middle-class child,

---

[6]The meaning which we attach to the term "culturally disadvantaged child" has previously been discussed (Chapter 8), and the reader should review it before proceeding with this section.

showing signs of impoverishment in its formal, abstract, and syntactical aspects (Bernstein, 1960; Deutsch, 1963), and is heavily interlaced with slang and clichés. His sentences are rarely compound or complex in structure (Bernstein, 1960; Deutsch, 1963), and he uses fewer conjunctions, adjectives, adverbs, or qualifying phrases or clauses.

An illustration—and suggestion of the consequences—of some of the latter problems may be found in the Bereiter and Engelmann (1966) analysis of the language problem of the culturally disadvantaged Negro child:

> The culturally deprived child does with sentences what the culturally privileged child does when he is trying to say a big word—he approximates the whole sequence of noises. But the culturally privileged child seems to acquire very early the notion that sentences are made up of words, so that he imitates the noises that occur *within* words but not the noises that occur *between* familiar words. Thus, the culturally privileged child builds up his sentences by adding words to them as he masters them: from "Mommy read" to "Mommy read book" to "Mommy read me book" and eventually to "Mommy, I want you to read me this book." The culturally deprived child grappling with such a sentence would probably start off with some amalgam like "re-ih-bu," with which he would then be stuck. The words "me" and "this" would be lost in noise, as they would be in any other sentences where they occurred, and thus it would be difficult for them ever to emerge as distinct, usable words (p. 36).

Bereiter and Engelmann label this language deficiency "the giant word syndrome" and suggest that it is not merely a manifestation of immature language comprehension, because such children

> have a strong tendency to revert to it even after they have been taught to handle certain patterns of discrete words. This shows up most clearly in arithmetic, where the entire vocabulary is new and the children cannot be accused of lapsing back into imitation of the way they hear the same thing said at home. Children in the Bereiter-Engelmann preschool had learned to handle equations of the form "Two plus one equals three," making substitutions to create other equations, e.g., "Two plus zero equals two." Even here, some children would continually lapse into amalgamations: "Two pluh wunic'k three." Having done this, they were no longer able to substitute other numbers for the "one," it having become fused with the beginning sounds of "equals" (pp. 36–37).

At an older age the most important consequence of the culturally deprived child's language retardation is the slower and less complete transition from concrete to abstract modes of thought and understanding. This transition takes place more slowly and less completely for two reasons. First, the culturally deprived child lacks the necessary repertoire of clear and stable abstractions and "transactional" terms (for example, conditional conjunctives, qualifying adjectives) that is obviously prerequisite for the direct manipulation and understanding of *relationships* between abstractions. Second, for lack of adequate practice, he has not acquired sufficient facility in relating abstractions to each other *with* the benefit of concrete empirical props so that he can later dispense with their assistance at the same age as his environmentally more favored contemporaries. And because concrete thought operations are necessarily more time-consuming than their abstract-verbal counterparts, and also because of his distractability, unfamiliarity with formal language, impaired self-confidence, and unresponsiveness to time pressure, the culturally deprived child typically works more slowly than the middle-class child in academic settings (Chapanis and Williams, 1945).

Can These Deficits Be Overcome by Training? The question which the administrator or teacher must ask himself is whether these obvious developmental deficits are permanent or whether they can be reversed by appropriate training. Consistent with earlier discussions of related problems, it seems realistic to believe that early deficits *can* be reversed if programs specifically devised to remedy them are introduced at the preschool level. We still lack firm evidence, however, concerning the influence of an optimal learning environment on the intellectual development of culturally deprived adolescent children who have been subjected for many years to the frustration and demoralization of inappropriate school experience.

There is reason to believe that such long-term effects may not be *completely* reversible. One view advanced in favor of this position, commonly called the "critical periods" hypothesis, argues that later reversibility of behavioral development is a function of extreme susceptibility to particular types of stimulation during brief periods in individual development when certain types of behavior are shaped and molded for life. By the same token, if the individual is deprived of the necessary stimulation during the critical period, when he is maximally susceptible to it in terms of actualizing particular potential capacities or developing in new directions, some degree of permanent retardation is inevitable (that is, that he will never, or can only partly, attain the capacities in question).

Numerous examples of the existence of the critical periods can be found in the perceptual, motor, and social development of infrahuman mammals. For example, infant chimpanzees isolated from normal tactual stimulation exhibit defective kinesthetic and cutaneous localization (Nissen and others, 1951), and if reared in darkness, they fail to fixate or recognize familiar objects, or to blink in response to a threatening object (Riesen, 1947). However, serious difficulties lie in the path of extrapolating the critical periods hypothesis to human cognitive development (Ausubel, 1965d). In human individuals, especially beyond the prenatal period and first year of life, environmental determinants of behavior are more important, and the rate of maturation is significantly slower. Second, it has never been empirically demonstrated that *optimal* readiness exists at *particular* age periods for specified kinds of *intellectual* activities, and that if adequate conditions for growth are not present during these periods no future period is ever as advantageous, thereby causing irreparable developmental deficits. Hence, if specific intellectual skills or subject-matter content are not acquired at the earliest appearance of readiness, this does *not* necessarily mean that they cannot be acquired later just as well or even better. The same degree of cognitive capacity that establishes readiness at an earlier age would *still* be present at least in *equal* degree at some future date.

There is, however, a more plausible explanation of possible irreversibility in cognitive development resulting from prolonged cultural deprivation (Ausubel, 1965d). We refer to the tendency for existing developmental deficits to become *cumulative* in nature, since current and future rates of intellectual growth are always conditioned or limited by the attained level of development. The child who has an existing deficit in growth incurred from past deprivation is less able to profit developmentally from new and more advanced levels of environmental stimulation. Thus, irrespective of the adequacy of all other factors—both internal and external—this deficit tends to increase cumulatively and to lead to permanent retardation.

Another factor which must be taken into account is the tendency for the *plasticity* of intelligence to decrease with increasing age. At first, intelligence is a relatively undifferentiated capacity that can develop in several different directions. As children grow older, particularly during preadolescence and adolescence, it becomes increasingly more differentiated, as shown by the decreasing intercorrelation among the subtests of a given intelligence scale (Garrett and others, 1935). Hence, by the time an individual reaches adolescence, differential factors of interest, training, motivation, success and failure experience, and cultural expectation operate collectively to develop certain potential abilities and to leave others relatively undeveloped. Children with particular intellectual disabilities also tend to avoid activities involving these disabilities, thus increasing the original deficit (Kirk, 1958). Once intelligence undergoes definite relative commitment in the various aforementioned channels, the individual therefore manifests less potential for growing in areas of minimal development than was the case in the original undifferentiated state. This is not to say, of course, that later enrichment is entirely to no avail, but it may be that some of this failure in developmental actualization is irreversible and cannot be compensated for later, regardless of the amount of hyperstimulation that is applied.

Helping the Culturally Disadvantaged Child

In the present section we shall consider only the cognitive aspects of an appropriate teaching strategy for culturally deprived children. The basic principles underlying this strategy are little different from those applying to the instruction of any pupil except that they take into account the particular deficits of this group. In a later chapter we shall discuss motivational, social, and interpersonal considerations applicable to the culturally disadvantaged.

General Characteristics of Programs   In view of the preceding discussion, it would seem that an optimal cognitive environment for culturally deprived students will focus on the two complementary aspects of cognitive readiness for learning—readiness in terms of general level of intellectual functioning and readiness in terms of specific subject-matter background. Spelling this out in more detail, we would say that an optimal program would give attention to these four considerations:

(a) *prevention* during the preschool years of the intellectual and language retardation characteristic of children growing up under culturally disadvantaged circumstances;

(b) the selection of learning tasks at all stages of the curriculum that are consonant with the learner's *existing state of readiness;*

(c) *mastery* and *consolidation* of all on-going learning tasks before new tasks are introduced so as to provide the necessary foundation for successful sequential learning and to prevent unreadiness for future learning tasks;

(d) the use of structured and *self-pacing learning materials* optimally organized to facilitate sequential learning.

Attention to these four factors could go a long way toward insuring effective learning (for the first time for many students) and toward restoring the culturally deprived child's educational morale and confidence in his ability to learn. Later possible consequences are restoration of both extrinsic motivation for academic achievement, diminution of anti-intellectualism, and decreased alienation from the school to the point where its programs make sense and the student sees some purpose in learning.

Are Conventional Preschool Programs Adequate?   In view of the central symptom of cultural deprivation, it would seem that preschool programs for the culturally disadvantaged should emphasize language acquisition. As Bereiter and Engelmann point out, culturally disadvantaged children at this level are already considerably behind those from more favored environments with regard to language development. Consequently, if the educator intends to enroll culturally disadvantaged children in the regular school program, he has an obligation to help them make up sufficient ground so that they can profit from such a program. Obviously this can only be done if the preschool program to which they are subjected provides an intensified experience, concentrating on the particular language deficits which these children exhibit.

Bereiter and Engelmann's contention, which is valid in our opinion, is that many well-intentioned but misguided preschool programs for culturally disadvantaged children are merely attempting to duplicate the kind of preschool experiences provided for culturally *advantaged* children. Such programs concentrate on play activities, child-child interaction, the physical manipulation of objects, and the encouragement of fantasy and dramatic play (Bereiter and Engelmann, 1966). While for the culturally advantaged child these may be useful complements to his *home* experiences, it is precisely these latter experiences—for example, verbal training, adult-child interaction, the setting of high levels of achievement—which the culturally deprived child needs but does not obtain in such a program. In the Bereiter-Engelmann program the concentrated language experience stresses the learning of transactional terms and syntactical rules through the use of concrete models which exemplify their meaning. For example, if/then relationships are taught to children by using the "five-square model" shown in Figure 9.1, which offers concrete exemplification of such statements as:

> "If a square is big, then it is white."
> "If a square is black, then it is little."
> "If a square is little, then it is white *or* it is black."

The preliminary results of experimental studies using this program seem very promising (see Table 9.4). For example, after being subjected to a two-year program of this kind, severely disadvantaged children (for whom the prognosis based on sibling experience was for early and continuing failure in school) made substantial gains in IQ and were at or above the norms for their age group in language and arithmetical skills.

FIGURE 9.1   *Five-square model for teaching "if-then" relationships.*
From: C. Bereiter and S. Engelmann, Teaching disadvantaged children in
in the preschool. *Englewood Cliffs, N. J.: Prentice-Hall, Inc.,* © *1966.*

TABLE 9.4

Results with Three Groups of Children in the Bereiter-Engelmann Program,
University of Illinois

	STANFORD-BINET IQ	WIDE RANGE ACHIEVEMENT (GRADE LEVEL)		
GROUPS		*Reading*	*Arithmetic*	*Spelling*
I ($N = 14$)				
Fall 1964	95			
Summer 1965 (after preschool)	102	1.0	1.9	.5
Spring 1966 (after kindergarten)	105	1.7	2.6	1.8
II ($N = 11$)				
Fall 1965	96			
Spring 1966 (after preschool)	112	1.2	1.1	1.2
Spring 1967 (after kindergarten)	121	2.6	2.6	1.8
III ($N = 14$)				
Fall 1966	91			
Spring 1967	103	1.3	1.0	1.1

Source: Rusk, 1968.   See also Bereiter and Engelmann, 1966, 1968.

From what has been said earlier concerning differing philosophies of child development, it will come as no surprise to learn that some educators are sceptical regarding the Bereiter-Engelmann program, arguing that it is authoritarian (teacher-dominated), that it emphasizes rote learning,[7] and that it is (on general principles) a "bad thing" to subject preschool children to formal instruction. Nevertheless, results of this kind—particularly if they are replicated in studies using groups of children sufficiently large to make the program economically feasible for the public school—can hardly be ignored by those who profess to be interested in facilitating the assimilation of the culturally disadvantaged into the public school system.

Further Considerations   Much could be said on the other points listed as major concerns in designing a preschool program for the culturally disadvantaged, but a good deal of it will be obvious to the reader. For example, it is essential that the initial selection of learning materials must take into account the student's existing state of knowledge and sophistication in the

[7]The charge of "rote learning" is largely unfounded, since potentially meaningful propositions are presented to children with familiar concrete exemplars.

various subject-matter areas, irrespective of how primitive this knowledge happens to be. Realistic recognition of the culturally deprived child's lack of readiness is not undemocratic, or evidence of social class bias or of a belief in the inherent ineducability of lower-class children. Neither is it indicative of a desire to surrender to the culturally deprived child's current intellectual level. It is merely a necessary first step in preparing him to cope with more advanced subject matter, and hence to eventually reduce social-class differentials in academic achievement. To set the same initial standards and expectations for the academically retarded, culturally deprived child as for the nonretarded middle- or lower-class child is automatically to insure the former's failure and to widen prevailing discrepancies between social-class groups.

On a related matter, culturally disadvantaged children in the preschool and kindergarten stage—like all children at this pre-operational stage of development—are highly dependent upon concrete empirical experiences and on the manipulation of objects or images in relational learning, concept formation, and problem solving; they are unable to relate abstract relationships to cognitive structure in correlative, superordinate, or combinatorial fashion. Because they must also achieve a certain critical level of proficiency in this stage of concrete logical operations before they can advance to the stage of abstract logical operations—and since existing language retardation delays this proficiency—they are dependent for a longer period than are their nondeprived peers on concrete empirical props in various forms of relational learning before attaining the abstract stage of cognitive development.

TOPICS FOR DISCUSSION AND FURTHER STUDY

1. Assuming that the most adverse circumstances prevail in respect to factors influencing individualization of instruction (see Table 9.1), what might the teacher realistically hope to accomplish on his own?

2.* Consult current literature on gifted underachievers and postulate steps which classroom teachers might undertake to cope with this phenomenon (Gallagher, 1964; Dunn, 1964; Goldberg, 1965).

3. The school's attempt to stream, or to otherwise organize learning groups on the basis of ability, frequently meets the charge that it is undemocratic. What arguments can be brought against this criticism?

4. List some legitimate "enrichment" experiences which the elementary-school teacher could provide which would escape the criticisms of current practices advanced in this chapter.

5. Under what circumstances would acceleration be inadvisable for even a very bright child?

6.* Investigate the situation which prevails in some school which is operating under a "nongraded" program. To what extent is the ideal of continuous progress being realized? What problems does the nongraded approach pose to teachers who are accustomed to operating in the traditional lock-step system?

7. In some parts of the world sex constitutes one basis of streaming students. To what extent can this approach be justified in terms of sex differences in cognitive ability? What other factors argue for or against this approach?

8.* Construct two forms of a question representing an intellectual task, one form of which would favor a particular social class. What conclusions can be drawn concerning the utilization of illustrative examples in the classroom?

9.* Many parents "instruct" their children at home, presumably advancing the child's learning beyond that anticipated in the "lock-step" system. How does and should a school react to such parental contributions, and how can these contributions be accommodated to the school's and to the child's advantage?

10. The argument is frequently advanced that the problem of individual differences is most critical at the elementary-school level, that effective work with the young child requires a very small student-teacher ratio, and that the prospects for public support for such a heavy concentration of professionals at this level is very dim. The deduction is made that any realistic attempt to cope with the problem of individual differences must utilize "teacher aides," that is, persons with professional and nonprofessional training who could take on a number of the more peripheral roles, thus freeing the teacher to concentrate his energies where they will be most effective. Discuss the merits of the various components of this argument.

11.* What relationship would you expect to hold between academic performance and such nonacademic performance as is represented by participation in the school's extracurricular program? Do selection procedures (to higher education) eliminate students with other kinds of creativity or talent (Werts, 1967; Holland and Richards, 1967)?

12.* Look up some of the current research on "cognitive style." What implications would the existence of such differences in modes of perceiving and thinking have for the problem of coping with individual differences? (Kagan and others, 1966; Fiebert, 1967; Holtzman, 1966)?

13.* Although we have offered logical and psychological support for the concepts of nongrading and ability grouping, the research concerning these practices tends to be inconclusive. After consulting studies which specify how these practices were used, hypothesize limiting or determining factors which must prevail before such practices will be successful. (References: Nongraded schools—Hopkins, Oldridge and Williamson, 1965; Williams, 1966. Ability grouping—Borg, 1966; Passow, 1966; Yates, 1966).

14.* Consult the literature on independent study and prepare a paper on how it might be utilized at the grade level at which you will be teaching (Bloom, 1968; Swartz, undated; Davis, 1966; Beggs and Buffie, 1965).

SUGGESTIONS FOR ADDITIONAL READING

Beggs, D. W., and E. G. Buffie (Eds.). *Independent study.* Bold New Venture Series. Bloomington, Ind.: Indiana University Press, 1965.

Bloom, B. S. Learning for mastery. *Evaluation comment.* Center for the Study of Education and Instructional Programs, University of California at Los Angeles, 1968, *1*(2).

Borg, W. R. *Ability grouping in the public schools.* Madison, Wisc.: Dembar Educational Research Services, 1966.

Gallagher, J. J. *Teaching the gifted child.* Boston: Allyn and Bacon, Inc., 1964.

Goodlad, J. I., and R. H. Anderson. *The nongraded elementary school.* New York: Harcourt, Brace and World, Inc., 1959.

Johnson, G. O. *Education for slow learners.* Englewood Cliffs, N.J.: Prentice-Hall, Inc., 1963.

Nystrand, R. O., and F. Bertolaet. Strategies for allocating human and material resources. *Rev. of Educ. Res.,* 1967, *37*(4), 448–468.

Swartz, C. A school for human children. State University of New York at Stony Brook (Physics Department), undated (mimeographed).

CHAPTER 10

PRACTICE

THE TOPIC OF THIS CHAPTER IS USUALLY NOT GIVEN MUCH attention in educational-psychology textbooks; typically we find a few pages of discussion dealing mainly with the role of practice in the acquisition of motor skills. And yet, if we consider what the elementary-school teacher actually *does* in the classroom, it would probably be no exaggeration to say that as much as 75 percent of his time is spent, not in the *initial* presentation of new ideas, but in arranging, conducting, and evaluating *practice* sessions. And even in the high school and university, practice remains an important activity.

THE IMPORTANCE OF PRACTICE

School subjects such as arithmetic and spelling provide good examples of an overwhelming emphasis upon practice rather than upon initial presentation. One has only to reflect that in the first four years of arithmetic instruction, comprising some 400 hours or more of work, the student learns at most a few hundred number combinations, or about one new fact per hour of instruction. Thus, most of the student's time is spent in rehearsing these facts in various settings, committing them to memory, and applying them in simple problem situations.

It is true that, to a large extent, practice schedules are *built into* the instructional material which the teacher uses. For example, all the widely used series of readers utilize the notion of a "controlled vocabulary"; that is, the number of new words introduced per page or "story" is controlled, and these new words are repeated again and again in various contexts until the student can rapidly perceive their meaning. The same can be said for arithmetic texts, spelling texts, and almost any structured material authorized by the provincial or state educational agencies. Even in high school the study guide issued by the educational authority is likely to contain specific recommendations concerning the rate of introduction of new ideas and the rehearsal of ideas and skills previously acquired.

From the foregoing remarks it might be argued that it is primarily the educational publishers who will profit from a detailed discussion of practice. While there is some merit in this point of view, there remain good reasons why the teacher as well must be concerned with this topic. We argued earlier that it is a part of the teacher's responsibility as a professional to understand the theoretical principles involved in an educational program, regardless of whether or not he entirely controls this program. In any case, the teacher will invariably exercise some choice as to timing, frequency, and method of practice. Even the arithmetic teacher who follows a prescribed text must make an independent assessment of his class's particular needs and, insofar as is possible, tailor practice sessions to the individual child's particular difficulties. Moreover, the first and perhaps most important practice session frequently occurs in the context of the lesson which originally presents a new idea, and the teacher—whatever his grade level—will usually design this lesson himself.

Why Has Interest in Practice Declined?

The present lack of concern with practice among educational psychologists stands in opposition both to philosophical and lay speculation about its importance in learning. Certainly, throughout educational history, "drill"—a highly structured kind of practice—has been the educator's favorite method for dealing with recalcitrant memories.

A large factor in the declining interest among educational psychologists can be attributed to the work of Thorndike. Originally, Thorndike postulated a kind of "learning by doing" law ("Law of Exercise") which stated that S-R connections are strengthened by use. This law was applied extensively to algebra and arithmetic (E. L. Thorndike, 1922, 1923). In arithmetic, for example, it was argued that the frequent coupling of a response (e.g., "5") with a stimulus (e.g., "3 + 2") would lead to the gradual strengthening of their connecting "bond," so that ultimately the stimulus would acquire the power of eliciting the response.

As the result of his own research, however, Thorndike later revoked his Law of Exercise. For example, he found no improvement in the performance of blindfolded subjects who repeatedly attempted to draw a line three inches long; however, performance did improve if subjects were told (after each trial) the magnitude of their error, or whether they were getting closer to or further away from the desired response. Thorndike concluded that the frequency of pairing the stimulus and the response had in itself little or no impact upon the learning process, and that its supposed influence must be attributed to reward or knowledge of results (1931, 1932). Thorndike's antifrequency position was subsequently bolstered by other theorists; Guthrie (1952), for example, advocated "single trial" learning, and Skinner's theory stressed the prepotence of reinforcement. It would appear that by extrapolating from these theories many educational theorists have arrived at both a denunciation of drill (the most highly structured and repetitive kind of practice) and a tendency to denigrate the importance of practice generally.

The opinions of classroom teachers on this question are probably too diverse to allow a viable generalization. Some teachers, no doubt as a result of their teacher-training courses, reflect an antidrill emphasis and a tendency to be somewhat apologetic for any organized approach to practice forced upon them by the realities of the classroom. On the other hand, many of our older teachers espouse a rather crude form of the "learning by doing" theory and place great emphasis on drill of the most mechanical and unimaginative sort. Where the truth lies in this matter should to some extent be ascertainable from the discussion which follows.

RELEVANT VARIABLES AND THEORETICAL CONSIDERATIONS

While the notion of practice is one of the most commonplace in education, it is by no means easy to come to grips with it conceptually. In the first place, our knowledge of the effects of manipulating practice variables is derived largely from studies of rote or simple kinds of learning. Moreover, as the reader will soon discover, one can identify an enormous number of potentially manipulable and intervening variables, and it becomes extremely difficult to put the various results together in a coherent structure of ideas.

Illustrative Examples

It will facilitate later discussion to have before us some concrete examples. To begin with, let us suppose that a high-school history teacher spends a one-hour class period discussing the causes of the American Revolution; we assume that these ideas are essentially new to the student, so the latter's task during this period will be to comprehend the material by relating it to cognitive structure in a nonarbitrary and substantive fashion. This initial presentation is followed by various practice sessions. First, as a homework assignment the teacher requires his students to read the relevant section of the text and to answer questions testing comprehension of the material. The next day the teacher "takes up" the assigned questions, further rehearsing the material and clarifying misconceptions; later still the teacher conducts a midterm review covering a whole section of the book; at the end of the term an examination is given in preparation for which the student reviews the material; finally, at the end of the school year the teacher undertakes a comprehensive review of the course and administers a final examination (which again requires independent student review). Such a distribution of practice sessions is very common in high-school subjects.

As our second illustration, consider a grade 4 teacher who organizes the original presentation and practice of a week's spelling assignment consisting of 24 "new" words. On the first day of the cycle the teacher presents the list of words, explains the meaning of any that are beyond the students' experience, and points out the extent to which each word fits within the general system of grapheme-phoneme correspondences of which the student already possesses an intuitive or formal knowledge. For each of the next three days the students employ one-third of the new words in composing written sentences, attempt to recall the spelling of these words from memory, and "write out" words which have an unusual spelling. Finally, on the last day, the teacher dictates the words and apprises the student of his errors. As in the previous example, the teacher would later initiate midterm and final reviews. This practice schedule is typical of those one would find in the skill areas of the elementary school.

Relevant Variables To Be Considered in Designing an Optimum Practice Schedule

To come to grips with this topic one must ask what it is that a teacher is trying to do when he deliberately structures a set of practice experiences. Some would answer that the teacher is attempting to arrange an initial-presentation/practice schedule which will bring the student to some prescribed *adequate level of performance in the shortest time possible*. However, given the fact that the teacher must usually cover a fixed amount of material (irrespective of how much students actually learn), it is probably more realistic to say that most teachers currently attempt to arrange a schedule which will produce the *greatest amount of learning* in a *given fixed time*. The first approach seems more desirable but, for a good number of students at least, highly unlikely in a rigid grade system. Such a goal might be feasible given the continuous progress plan described in the previous chapter.

With some idea of what the teacher is attempting to optimize, we may now look at the variables which are relevant to this task. The first class of variables (dependent) considered is the *kind of student behavior* to be maximized. For example, by having the student learn a new idea or skill the teacher may wish to emphasize *short-term retention,* or *long-term retention,* or he may be primarily interested in the *transfer* of this skill to some new learning. Certainly it does not follow that a method which produces maximum performance on one criterion will necessarily do so on another.

We next consider the independent variables, that is, those variables whose manipulation lies within the teacher's control. One such set of factors has to do with the *distribution of time,* as for example between the practice sessions themselves (that is, massed or distributed). Other variables which could be included under this heading are the timing of the occurrence of the *first* practice session, and the extent to which the original presentation of the entire learning task should be broken up by practice sessions inserted between its parts (that is, "whole" versus "part" learning).

TABLE 10-1

MAJOR VARIABLES TO BE CONSIDERED
IN DESIGNING AN OPTIMUM PRACTICE SCHEDULE

NDEPENDENT VA RIABLES	A.	Distribution of Available Time whole versus part learning timing of first practice session massed versus distributed practice
	B.	Kind of Practice recitation versus recapitulation overt versus covert responses amount of guidance and prompting homogeneity versus heterogeneity degree of structure (drill) amount and kind of feedback
QUALIFYING VARIABLES	A.	Subject Matter meaningful versus rote difficulty of material amount to be learned (task size) degree of sequential relatedness
	B.	Learner age intelligence stage of development subject-matter sophistication
DEPENDENT VARIABLES		short-term (initial) learning long-term retention transfer

A second class of independent variables has to do with the *kind of practice* and includes such factors as: relative emphasis on recitation as opposed to repetition of the initial presentation (recapitulation); whether the practice responses made by the student should be overt or covert; the amount of guidance and prompting to be provided in the practice sessions; the relative amounts of structured practice (drill) as opposed to unstructured practice; and the amount and kind of "feedback" to be presented to the student.

Given these sets of independent and dependent variables, one might make generalizations on their interrelationships. However, it is necessary to temper or qualify any generalization in terms of a third group of qualifying variables. Such generalizations would thus take different forms depending upon such *subject-matter* variables as the degree of meaningfulness or rote-ness of the material to be learned, the difficulty of this material, the size of the learning task, and the degree to which the material is sequential or nonsequential in nature. By the same token, such *learner* variables as age, degree of brightness, and ability to undertake unsupervised practice sessions will certainly enter into the picture.

Any teacher therefore who sets out to produce an "optimizing" schedule of practice will be faced with a bewildering complexity of interrelated variables (Table 10.1). However, by knowing the demonstrated relationships between these variables, the teacher is in a better position to take the next and necessary step of trying to incorporate into these generalizations the specific values which the variables take in his own classroom.

SOME THEORETICAL IDEAS RELATED TO PRACTICE

What concepts are useful in organizing and illuminating the various practice effects that have been observed in empirical studies? It is hardly necessary to say that our starting point will again be the notion of cognitive structure and that the effects of practice upon subsequent learning and retention are brought about mainly by influencing existing cognitive structure.

For purposes of clarification let us reconsider our history example. On the first presentation (the initial learning) some of the ideas, probably the most general ones, may be learned in a relatively permanent fashion. The chief effect of a subsequent practice session upon these initially established ideas will be to increase their stability and clarity and, therefore, their dissociability strength. Of course, when a number of ideas are grasped firmly enough on the first presentation to remain above the threshold of availability at the time of the second presentation (or initial review), they provide additional (and highly relevant) anchorage for as yet unlearned ideas.

In the case of other ideas (probably those at a lower level of abstractness), the dissociability strength established on the first presentation will, by the time the second presentation occurs, have fallen below the threshold of availability for recall. Speaking somewhat loosely, we could say that on the second presentation these ideas will be somewhat "more familiar" to the learner than they were on the first. More technically, we might say that since the meanings of these ideas were already grasped on the first presentation, these meanings can be *perceived* immediately on the second presentation of the ideas, so that the learner may now devote his attention solely to attempting to remember them. In a sense, the acquisition on the first presentation, although at relatively low dissociability strength, "sensitizes" the learner to the meanings of these ideas and facilitates his learning of them on later trials.[1]

For this same group of ideas (that is, those learned initially but with dissociability strength below the threshold of availability on the second presentation) we can postulate another phenomenon which helps explain the benefits of practice. If between the first presentation and the first practice trial the learner attempts to recall the meaning of these ideas but is unable to do so, he will differentially concentrate on such meanings in the next presentation. A similar effect will be observed for ideas which the learner failed to comprehend in the first presentation but which he is asked (perhaps by a question in the homework assignment) to recall in the interim; moreover, the same argument may be advanced with respect to the relationships between ideas of both groups.

Consequently, taking the learning task as a whole (that is, considering not only individual ideas but their relationships), we might say that prior forgetting has a facilitating effect on subsequent relearning and retention because, in attempting but failing to remember such ideas (or their interrelationships), the learner tends to become aware of negative factors in the learning situation that promote forgetting, that is, instability, ambiguity, confusion, and lack of discriminability (Ausubel and Youssef, 1965). Thus forewarned, he can take the necessary steps during the relearning session to strengthen particularly weak components of the learning task, to resolve the existing confusion and ambiguity, and to increase discriminability between previously learned ideas and related new propositions. Another way of saying this would be that prior forgetting "immunizes" the learner against the detrimental effects of the above-mentioned factors which cause forgetting.

---

[1]On a first presentation the learner may also be "sensitized" to the meaning of a concept, for example, by perceiving the meanings of the individual words defining the concept. On the second presentation the learner may then rearrange these individual meanings to apprehend the meaning of the total concept.

These explanatory principles are most clearly applicable when; as in the case of our history example, the material to be learned lies relatively near the meaningful end of the rote/meaningful continuum. We might ask how the principles of immunization and sensitization apply in the spelling example, where the principal learning task (recognizing and remembering grapheme-phoneme irregularities and variations) is only marginally meaningful. First, it is true that learning how to spell a word such as "Fahrenheit" does exhibit both of the aforementioned processes. Thus an initial study of the word would allow the student to identify (comprehend) which variant of a particular grapheme-phoneme correspondence is used and to comprehend the syllabification of a word, so that the meaning inherent in these preliminary tasks may become perceptually available on the second encounter (sensitization). Similarly, a form of immunization might occur in that if a student cannot remember the spelling of a particular part of the word he will concentrate on this in the first practice trial.

However, since we have a learning task which is largely of a rote nature, we may also explain the effect of practice in terms of the demonstrated laws applying to such phenomena. Thus, repeated encounters with the same array of stimuli (word, in our example) presumably enhance the learning and retention of the spelling by increasing the strength of discrete, arbitrary, and verbatim *associative linkages*. As many of the previous discussions in this book would suggest, we can expect a considerable difference in the relative importance of practice variables (for example, frequency, feedback, and so on) depending upon the degree of meaningfulness or nonmeaningfulness of the material.

The Significance of Frequency

The role and importance of frequency (number of trials and presentations) in learning and retention have received varying emphases over the years in psychology and education. As we noted earlier, Thorndike's apparent refutation of the Law of Exercise carried with it the implication that frequency (that is, number of presentations) provides merely an *occasion* for the more potent elements in learning, such as feedback, reward, or confirmation. Certain objections can be made to this conclusion, which was based on a widely cited series of experiments in which Thorndike showed that mere frequency in repeating certain tasks (attempting to draw a line of specified length, estimating the length of paper strips) bears no relationship to learning (improvement) (Thorndike, 1931, 1932). For example, in the line-drawing experiment one can argue that the subjects were not in fact practicing the task on which improvement was sought (that is, drawing a line exactly three inches long); they were merely *attempting* to draw lines of this length. In such a situation it comes as no surprise that some knowledge of results (for example, telling the student whether his lines are closer or further away from the desired endpoint) is essential for learning. However, externally provided feedback may not be indispensible for learning in a situation in which the learner's task is simply to reproduce the material that is presented to him, as for example if a three-inch line were provided and the student asked to reproduce it.

Our position on frequency can be deduced from the earlier theoretical discussion. It is clear that frequency is neither a necessary nor sufficient condition for meaningful learning to occur since the substance of much relatively easy, potentially meaningful material can be grasped after one reading. Typically, however, several readings are required for more difficult material, particularly when it is important to produce overlearning, delayed retention, or transfer. Frequency, in other words, usually makes a difference in meaningful learning and retention. On the other hand, no amount of frequency per se can eventuate in substantial amounts of meaningful learning in the absence of meaningful learning set, or of potential meaningfulness, of sufficient effort and attention, of active attempts to understand, of intention to integrate knowledge and to reformulate it in idiosyncratic terms.

In addition, it can be argued that the first presentation of the material, partly through the process of sensitization, changes the nature of the task to be learned on the second presentation; that is, whereas in the first presentation all the ideas were only potentially meaningful and their meaning had to be grasped, in the second presentation some of these ideas have already been incorporated into cognitive stucture and their meanings can be perceived directly by the learner. It can be argued further that this change in the *learning task itself* represents a frequency effect that operates in addition to, and cannot simply be reduced to, the opportunity which subsequent trials provide for other effective variables (for example, feedback) to influence the process and outcome of learning and retention. In other words, we propose that frequency does more than merely make possible a summation of the repeated effects of these other variables.[2]

Frequency per se is obviously insufficient for learning under conditions that lead either to lack of reinforcement or to motivation *not* to learn (for example, punishment). The same holds true for conditions which either presuppose prior knowledge which is absent in a particular learner, or call for discovery or difficult reception learning that may or may not take place. Some learners, for example, may never acquire the necessary insight for certain kinds of problem solving. In other instances, frequency may gradual-

---

[2]Actually, the question of whether frequency per se has an effect over and above the other reinforcing variables has more theoretical than practical significance, since frequency sufficient in itself to produce learning. For a discussion of these and related theoretical points the reader should consult Ausubel, 1968, chapter 8.

ly engender the necessary understanding and insight. Although this insight may appear to arise very abruptly, it may actually reflect the testing of many prior hypotheses and their reformulation following negative results.

RELATIONSHIPS BETWEEN PRACTICE VARIABLES AND LEARNING OUTCOMES

With this preamble we are now able to proceed systematically through the practice variables initially postulated as potentially influential in affecting learning outcomes. Although no logical order of presentation suggests itself, we shall assume that the teacher asks four general questions concerning practice, and in the following order:

1. Should the learning task be presented as a whole or broken into parts?
2. How early should the first practice session occur?
3. Should practice sessions be massed or distributed?
4. What method of practice should be utilized (a question which itself embraces a large number of questions, as we saw in Table 10.1)?

Whole versus Part Learning[3]

Whether it is more effective to practice a given learning task as a whole or to practice its various component parts separately depends on the interaction between a large number of complex variables. Each method possesses certain inherent advantages and disadvantages. Hence neither method can be said to be *invariably* superior to the other. Their relative efficacy varies with the amount, difficulty, and organization of the learning material; with the age, intelligence, motivation, and subject-matter sophistication of the learner; and with the stage and distribution of practice.

The basic advantages of the whole method are both that the learner can better grasp the relationship of each part to every other part as well as to the learning task in its entirety, and that he does not have to forge connecting links between separately learned parts. The part method, in turn, has both motivational and logistical advantages. First, it enables the learner to enjoy early, tangible experience of successful progress toward his goal, thereby rewarding his current learning efforts, enhancing his self-confidence, and encouraging him to persevere. Second, subdivision of a long task into several parts reduces its over-all difficulty, inasmuch as the number of trials neces-

---

[3]Because of the voluminous and somewhat antiquated nature of the research literature in this area, older studies are not cited. Excellent reviews of the literature can be found in McGeoch and Irion (1952, pp. 499–507) and in Woodworth (1938, pp. 216–223).

sary for learning a task tends to increase disproportionately as the amount of material encompassed increases. For example, it takes considerably fewer trials to learn two short tasks, each consisting of ten units, than to learn one long task of twenty units.

Hence the part method tends to become increasingly superior as the learning task exceeds the size of unit that the learner can conveniently manage in one practice trial. But since the optimal size of the latter unit tends to increase with cognitive maturity, subject-matter sophistication, intelligence, and degree of motivation, the increment in amount of material required to weight the balance in favor of the part method must necessarily be greater in the case of older, more sophisticated, more intelligent, and more highly motivated individuals. Further, the disproportion between increase in amount of material and increase in number of learning trials becomes less marked when practice trials are distributed rather than massed, and when learning material is potentially meaningful rather than rote.

The organization of the learning task and its evenness of difficulty also affect the relative superiority of whole or part methods. The "whole" approach is superior only if there is continuity in meaning from one part to the next, that is, if the component units blend into a more inclusive and better integrated whole (Naylor and Briggs, 1963). If its separate parts, on the other hand, constitute natural, logically self-contained subdivisions with little relationship to one another, the "part" method is more effective. The factor of integration is more important than that of task complexity. An increase in task complexity does not reverse the superiority of the whole over the part method when the learning task is highly integrated, but does do so when the task is relatively unorganized (Naylor and Briggs, 1963). The feasibility of the whole method similarly depends on the existence of a relatively uniform level of difficulty throughout the task. If this is not the case, the learner will devote too little time to difficult portions of the material and too much time to easy portions.

Lastly, the importance of immediate rewards for learning varies with the learner's drive and level of maturity. Highly motivated individuals are less discouraged by deferred reward for learning effort, and older, more mature individuals manifest greater frustration tolerance and capacity for delayed gratification. The motivational advantages of the part over the whole method also tend to decrease during the latter stages of practice as the cumulative learning effects of the whole method begin to become manifest, and hence to bolster the learner's confidence in this approach.

To summarize, the whole method is superior to the part method when the amount of learning material does not exceed the size of the practice unit that the learner can conveniently handle, and when continuity of meaning and uniformity of difficulty level are maintained throughout the task. The whole method also becomes more feasible when learners are older, brighter, more highly motivated, and intellectually more mature, when they possess considerable background experience in the learning task, and when learning material is potentially meaningful. Finally, the whole method is more likely to succeed in the latter stages of practice and when practice trials are distributed rather than massed. When the opposite set of conditions prevail, the advantage naturally tends to lie with the part method. Depending upon the prevailing conditions of learning, various combinations of the two methods may be successfully employed (for example, beginning with several "whole" trials, then concentrating selectively on the more difficult parts, and concluding with a review of the material as a whole).

Timing of the Initial Practice Session

For purposes of meaningful learning and retention, should review be introduced shortly after original learning—while the material is still fresh in mind and relatively little has been forgotten—or would it be more useful to introduce review after an appreciable amount of material has presumably been forgotten? This issue has significant implications for the student's study practices and for the programming of potentially meaningful instructional materials. It also has important theoretical implications for the psychology of meaningful learning and retention. Credible arguments can be adduced in support of each alternative, but the issue obviously can be decided only by empirical test.

The theoretical advantages of *delayed* review are perhaps more self-evident than those of early review. In the first place, after a long retention interval, when more material is likely to be forgotten, the learner is more highly motivated to profit from the opportunity for review. He is less likely to regard this opportunity as unnecessary and superfluous, and is therefore more disposed to take advantage of it in terms of effort and attention. Second, and even more important, prior forgetting has the immunizing effect previously discussed in which the student becomes aware of difficulties in the first presentation and takes steps to overcome these difficulties in subsequent presentations. Furthermore, it would seem that greater potential benefit could presumably be anticipated from repetition when a large proportion of the learning task is forgotten, inasmuch as more remains to be relearned under these conditions.

In what ways can *early* review conceivably counter-balance the evident advantages of delayed review? The most likely possibility is that repetition (review) has an *especially* potent consolidating effect on *recently* learned material while it is still appreciably above the threshold of availability—and that this consolidating effect decreases as the material becomes progressively less available. Obviously, another trial provides additional opportunity for the learner to interact cognitively with the learning material and to relate the potential meanings it embodies to his existing structure of knowledge, thereby enabling actual or experienced meaning to eventuate and/or be consolidated. He has, in other words, a second opportunity to acquire meanings potential in the material that he partially or completely missed on the first trial, as well as to consolidate meanings initially established at that time. To be optimally effective, however, the opportunity for such consolidation may very well presuppose a certain minimal level of residual availability.

Another study trial also provides the learner with informational feedback, in the form of textual reference, for testing the correctness of the knowledge he retained from the first trial. This testing confirms correct meanings, clarifies ambiguities, corrects misconceptions, and indicates areas of weakness requiring differential concentrated study. The net effect is consolidation of learning. When the learning task is largely forgotten, however, as in delayed review, the "feedback" role of repetition is minimal. A further advantage in early review derives from the process of sensitization in which ideas, whose meanings are grasped but not retained until the second presentation, serve nevertheless to reduce the difficulties of the learning task on that presentation. It seems reasonable to suggest that the sensitizing effect of repetition is greater earlier, rather than later, during the retention interval, when more of the learned meanings are still available to exert sensitizing effects.

In summary, the principal hypothesized advantages of early review would appear to be a superior consolidation, "feedback," and sensitizing effects in relation to more highly available material, whereas the principal advantage of delayed review probably inheres in the superior relearning of forgotten material, both on motivational and cognitive grounds, Thus, since each kind of review has its distinctive functions and advantages, the two variables are presumably complementary rather than redundant or mutually exclusive, and can therefore be profitably combined.

Experimental data relevant to this problem is not very abundant. Peterson and others (1935) reported no difference between the effects of rereading reviews introduced one or nine days after the original learning period. Sones and Stroud (1940) found there was a slight but nonsignificant tendency for a delayed rereading review to be more effective than an early rereading review. In both instances, however, the findings are somewhat equivocal because the criterion retention test was given an equal number of days after the original learning period; hence the time interval between the early review and the retention test was greater than that between the delayed review and the retention test, thereby tending to bias the results in favor of the latter condition.

Ausubel's (1966a) study was designed to eliminate this methodological difficulty. In this investigation two groups studied and reviewed a passage dealing with Buddhist concepts of God, immortality, soul, faith, salvation, morality, and responsibility. The experiment was so designed (Figure 10.1) that both the delayed review and the early review were given six days before the retention test. Although the results showed a small advantage in favor of early review, the difference in mean scores did not reach statistical significance. It would appear that with this particular material and experimental arrangement the respective advantages of early and delayed review counterbalanced each other.

Delayed Review Group	*Early Review Group*
Initial study of Buddhism passage	Study of unrelated material
Six-day interval	Six-day interval
Study of unrelated material	Initial study of Buddhism passage
One-day interval	One-day interval
Review of Buddhism passage	Review of Buddhism passage
Six-day interval	Six-day interval
Test on Buddhism	Test on Buddhism
$M = 17.87$	$M = 19.14$

FIGURE 10.1 *Experimental design to determine the effects of early versus delayed review.*

General Distribution of Practice

The distribution of practice has long been a favorite topic of research and theoretical inquiry in the psychology of learning. In fact, more empirical evidence is available regarding the effects of massed and distributed practice on learning and retention than there is regarding the comparable effects of simple frequency of practice. Generally speaking, the evidence supports the conclusion that *distributed practice is more effective than massed practice for both learning and retention.* The relative efficacy of distributed practice, however, depends on such factors as the age and the ability of the learner, and the nature (meaningful or rote), quantity, and difficulty of the learning task.

How may we explain the general superiority of distributed practice as well as the major differential effects indicated above? Although many theoretical explanations are offered,[4] the principles advanced in this book argue for a *forgetting* theory which specifies the following ways in which intertrial *rests* can facilitate later learning and/or retention trials:

---

[4]See Ausubel, 1968, chapter 8.

(a) The forgetting of previously learned components that occurs between trials in distributed practice schedules makes it possible for these latter components, as well as for the unlearned components, to profit from the strengthening effect of later trials.

(b) Rest provides an opportunity both for the dissipation of initial confusion and resistance characteristic of initial learning shock and for the forgetting of interfering (wrong, alternative, competing) responses or meanings (Underwood, 1961). The dissipation of initial learning shock here is comparable to that underlying the reminiscence effect in retention, except that it occurs in relation to numerous rest intervals rather than to a single rest interval; the dissipation of the inhibition caused by incorrect or competing alternatives reflects the differentially faster rate of forgetting of these latter relatively weak elements than for their stronger correct counterparts (H. Easley, 1937).

(c) The forgetting that takes place during the intertrial rest enhances the facilitating influence of later trials because, as a result of experiencing and becoming aware of the interfering processes that underlie the loss of associative or dissociability strength and bring about forgetting, the learner is better able to cope with and resist the detrimental effects of these processes when he encounters them again during and after subsequent trials. Previous obliterative experience with interfering processes, in other words, appears to confer some degree of immunity to the recurrence of their detrimental effects on learning and hence to promote a higher residual level of associative or dissociability strength.

The forgetting theory of the mechanism underlying distributed practice effects is not quite as applicable to retention as it is to learning. While the immunizing effect applies to delayed as well as immediate dissociability strength, the other two effects operate mainly to facilitate *immediate learning*.[5] Hence, the superiority of delayed retention following distributed, as against massed, practice must be attributed either to the *direct* immunizing effect of prior forgetting on the retention process per se, or to the *indirect* enhancement of retention that necessarily takes place when learning itself is enhanced (that is, to the fact that if more material is learned under conditions of distributed rather than of massed practice, more will also be retained).

What difference might we expect in the efficacy of distributed as opposed to massed practice for meaningful and rote learning respectively? Experimental results (Ash, 1950; Bumstead, 1940, 1943) indicate that the facilitating effects of distributed practice are less striking for meaningful than for rotely learned material. One reason for this result, presumably, is that

---

[5]These factors—outlined in (a) and (b) above— apply to the *intertrial rest interval* (part of the initial learning sequence) rather than to the retention period.

less intertrial forgetting will occur when the material is meaningfully learned. Fatigue, boredom, and motivational factors are also presumably less relevant for meaningful than for rote learning.

In addition to the previously mentioned results, massed practice has been found more effective for the *immediate* retention of meaningfully learned material (probably because of reminiscence), but distributed practice is superior when *delayed* tests of retention are administered (K. Gordon, 1925). An outstanding practical implication of this fact is the efficacy of cramming for immediate examination purposes but not for long-term retention.

Other research studies have found that the review of meaningfully learned material by *rereading* facilitates retention equally well when it is delayed for about two weeks or when it is given soon after original learning (Peterson and others, 1935; Skaggs and others, 1930; Sones and Stroud, 1940). When the review is conducted by *testing,* however, it is most advantageously given shortly after original learning (Sones and Stroud, 1940; Spitzer, 1939; Tiedeman, 1948). The reason for this latter difference is self-evident: If the material to be reviewed must be supplied from the learner's memory, he must be able to recall enough of it to make review profitable. Hence, review by testing must be undertaken soon after learning, before very much is forgotten. But if the learner is not dependent on memory for his review material, he can wait for the most advantageous moment which, as we have seen, occurs either shortly after original learning or after the original learning has been appreciably but not completely forgotten.

In conclusion, the research evidence taken as a whole indicates the superiority of distributed practice for both learning and retention. These advantages, however, are greater for younger and less able learners—and for long, rote, and difficult tasks—than they are for older and more able learners or for short, meaningful, and easy tasks. With respect to most students and learning tasks found in our schools, it appears that short and widely spaced practice (or review) sessions that are introduced progressively further apart will be better for meaningful learning and long-term retention. One must be careful, however, not to space these sessions so far apart that total practice time is excessively reduced, that too much forgetting occurs, that a long warm-up period is required, or that the learning task is fragmented.

METHOD OF PRACTICE

As previously indicated, the teacher who asks himself what method of practice is optimal is, in effect, inquiring about the single and multiple effects of a large number of variables. These include:

(a) the relative merits of recitation and recapitulation;
(b) the proper balance between overt and covert responses;
(c) how much guidance and prompting should be given;
(d) the optimum level of variety in practice sessions;
(e) the use of structured as opposed to natural settings;
(f) the extent to which knowledge of results should be provided.

A brief account of the theory and relevant research on each of these subquestions is provided in the following paragraphs.

Recitation versus Recapitulation

In reception learning, where the learning task is to internalize presented learning material (facts, propositions, arbitrary associations) so that it is available for later reproduction, the learner may either be presented with numerous study trials or repetitions of the task (recapitulation), or he may elect or be required to spend varying proportions of the total practice time in attempting to recall the material in test trials (recitation), with or without the benefit of prompting. The relevant research findings support the conclusion that whereas increasing proportions of recitation tend to facilitate *rote* learning and retention—and retention more than learning (Forlano, 1936; Gates, 1917; Hovland and others, 1949)—the facilitating effect of recitation on *meaningful* learning and retention is both less striking and more equivocal (Gates, 1917; Michael and Maccoby, 1953; H. A. Peterson, 1944).

In the series of experiments conducted by Forlano (cited in Gates and others, 1948), children in the fifth and sixth grades, working under normal classroom conditions, learned a variety of tasks—including nonsense syllables, spelling of words, and arithmetical facts. The children were to read the material for a given proportion of the available time (from 100 percent to 20 percent depending upon the group to which they were assigned) and then to attempt to recall what they had learned, looking up answers when they were unable to remember them. For these relatively rote learning tasks—the results for spelling are shown in Table 10.2—devoting some of the available time to recitation invariably produced better immediate and delayed (four-hour) retention.

The effectiveness of recitation, particularly for rote material, may be attributed to several factors. First, since the attempt to recall presented material actually tests whether and to what extent internalization (learning) has taken place, the "feedback" that is provided in the next trial is, therefore, a much more significant factor after recitation than after recapitulation: it indicates explicitly and systematically what the correct associations or meanings are, in relation to the internalized learning that has already taken

TABLE 10.2

EFFECT OF INCREASING PROPORTION OF TIME DEVOTED TO RECITATION
ON IMMEDIATE AND DELAYED RETENTION SCORES IN SPELLING

METHOD	IMMEDIATE RETENTION TEST (MEAN SCORE)	DELAYED RETENTION TEST (MEAN SCORE)
1. Reading	7.17	7.30
2. 1/5 of time devoted to recitation	7.34	7.79
3. 2/5 of time devoted to recitation	7.20	7.73
4. 3/5 of time devoted to recitation	8.49	8.54
5. 4/5 of time devoted to recitation	8.53	9.02

Source: Forlano, 1936.

place. Under these circumstances, all of the effects of feedback—as an incentive condition; as cognitive confirmation, correction, clarification, and evaluation of the adequacy of learning; and as reinforcement following reduction of cognitive and ego-enhancing drives—are considerably intensified. A closely related immediate consequence of feedback in this context is that as a result of discovering which parts of the learning task have not yet been sufficiently mastered, the subject is better able to focus his attention and effort selectively on these latter aspects.

Second, the more *active* kind of participation involved in recitation than in rereading implies greater learning effort which, in addition to exerting a general facilitating influence on learning, differentially salvages items at or near threshold strength, and leads to a more active and meaningful organization of the learned material (for example, use of rhythm, mnemonic devices, and conceptual organizers). Lastly, the conditions of recitation more nearly resemble the conditions under which the learning will eventually be exercised than do those of recapitulation.

For rote learning, where prompting is used, recitation is most effective if it is introduced after only a few study trials (Skaggs and others, 1930). Without the benefits of prompting, however, recitation is more advantageously introduced at a later stage of practice (L. O. Krueger, 1930; W. C. F. Krueger, 1930). Recitation apparently cannot prove helpful until enough material is learned so that a test trial can provide almost as much practice as a study trial; but if prompts are furnished to fill in gaps of knowledge, recitation obviously becomes feasible at an earlier point in a series of practice trials. Thus the principle governing the optimal temporal position for introducing recitation is similar to the principle determining the optimal spacing of reviews: if, on any given trial, the *learner himself* has to provide, from what he has previously learned, the stimulus material to be used for that trial (that is, if he is given a *test* trial), the temporal arrangements must be such as to insure the existence of sufficient learning or retention, respectively, to make practice or review profitable. If, on the other hand, the learning task is *presented* to the learner, in whole or in part, sufficiency of learning or retention is a less important consideration.

The markedly reduced effectiveness of recitation with respect to *meaningful* learning and retention is not difficult to understand. To begin with, the logical sequential structure of connected meaningful discourse makes *implicit* recitation possible during the *same* trial; that is, in the course of rereading, subjects typically tend to anticipate the remembered facts and propositions that follow logically from the material they are currently perusing. In the case of meaningful material, also, where the achievement of understanding is both a reward and an incentive in its own right, less effort is required for learning, and the incentive and ego-enhancement values of feedback are less important. Explicit testing is similarly less necessary for the confirmation, correction, clarification, and evaluation effects of feedback in view of the fact that the *internal logic* of the material partly provides its own feedback, that is, enables subjects to appreciate whether they have grasped meanings correctly and, in any case, to test their understandings implicitly against the next presentation of the material. Finally, meaningful learning tasks benefit less from the organizing effects of recitation since they possess an inherent organization of their own. Nevertheless, recitation can still facilitate meaningful learning—even when conducted early in the course of learning and without the use of prompts.

Covertness or Overtness of Response

Closely related to, but not completely coextensive with the recitation-recapitulation issue, is the problem of whether the subject's mode of response during practice should be covert or overt. Overtness of response does not necessarily imply recall or construction, as does recitation, but merely some measure of activity and externality (observability). Hence, while reading, listening to, or "mentally composing" answers to questions can be regarded as "covert" response, both the construction of an appropriate answer and the selection of a suitable multiple-choice alternative must be categorized as "overt." Admittedly, however, constructed responses rank higher on the scale of overtness than do selected responses.

When we examine the reasons why overt responding might be more efficient than covert responding, we discover that most of these conditions apply only to *rote* learning. For example, it seems self-evident that overtness of response will facilitate perceptual-motor learning in instances in which the overtly practiced response itself is one of the objects of learning (that is, part of the learning response).[6] But where the overt response (for example, writing, pressing a lever) is already a well-established component of the learner's response repertoire and constitutes merely a means of responding to test questions, it is obvious that the response acquisition advantage of overtness is irrelevant, and that overt responses are more time-consuming and less efficient than their covert counterparts (Gagné, 1962b; Walker and Stolurow, 1962).

Second, overtness of response plainly makes a more explicit testing of knowledge possible which, in turn, enhances the cognitive, drive-reducing, and motivational effects of feedback. This consideration is very important for rote learning, and undoubtedly accounts for much of the value of recitation when rote materials are used; but, for reasons already specified, it has little applicability to meaningful learning. Meaningfulness of material also negates a third possible reason for the effectiveness of overt responses, that is, the fact that the latter imply greater activity and hence greater effort and more efficient organization of learning.

Lastly, overt response during practice could conceivably facilitate learning by resembling more closely than covert response the response mode that is typically required in the criterial situation. In an empirical test of this hypothesis, however, response mode had no more effect on learning outcomes when the overt response was directly relevant to the behavior sampled on the posttest (Wittrock, 1963), than when such relevance was lacking (Keislar and McNeil, 1962).

Insofar as research is concerned, the overt-covert dimension has been explored principally in relation to a limited variety of automated instruction contexts, that is, those involving meaningful learning, using programs of short duration, and—for the most part—requiring short-term retention. The facilitating effect of overtness is further reduced in such a context, inasmuch as the provision of feedback (a major advantage following from overt responding) tends to make relatively little difference when the error rate is low (Evans and others, 1960a). If because of small-step size (that is, slow rate of introducing new material) the subject's responses are almost invariably correct in any case, he obviously does not stand to profit very much from the potentially facilitating cognitive effects of feedback.

Consistent with these remarks, research findings indicate that subjects

---

[6]Even here, however, covert responding is sometimes more effective than one would imagine. For example, Vandell and others (1943) undertook a study to determine the effect of covert responding on a variety of skilled behaviors including basketball "free throws." In this experiment two groups had practice on the first and twentieth days, the first group undertaking covert practice in the interval and the second group having no practice during that time. A third group practiced on each of the twenty days. Although the effect of covert practice during the intervening period was not quite as strong as the effect of overt practice, it was nevertheless of considerable magnitude and greatly exceeded the effect of no practice.

who respond covertly not only learn and retain verbal material as well as or better than subjects who construct their responses, but also do so more efficiently in terms of learning time (Della-Piana, 1961; Evans and others, 1960c; Goldbeck and Briggs, 1960; Krumboltz, 1961; Lambert and others, 1962; Pressey, 1962a; Roe, 1960; Silberman, 1962; Silverman and Alter, 1960; Stolurow and Walker, 1962; Wittrock, 1963; Yarmey, 1964). Overt selection of multiple-choice answers, for example, by pushing a button, is similarly no more effective than listening to or reading the correct underlined answers (Kaess and Zeaman, 1960; Keislar and McNeil, 1961; McNeil and Keislar, 1961).

Constructed versus Selected (Multiple-Choice) Responses

The rationale advanced for constructing rather than selecting answers during practice trials is precisely the same as that already specified for overtness of response, plus the fact that exposing subjects to wrong answers (in the multiple-choice format) presumably engenders and strengthens undesired competing responses (Skinner, 1958). All of these considerations except the last have been considered previously and shown to apply primarily to the learning of *rote* materials; that a similar assessment can be made in that instance can be judged from the fact that in arbitrary, verbatim learning, the increased availability of competing responses is self-evidently harmful inasmuch as the desired arbitrary response is correct by definition, and only has to be discriminated from similar rote responses that *actually* occur in recent proximity (rather than from all other logically plausible alternatives). In these circumstances, furthermore, one response is inherently just as plausible as another.

In the case of *meaningful* learning, on the other hand, where the new learning task largely consists of discriminating the correct meaning from other relevant alternatives, and where built-in criteria exist in cognitive structure and in the learning material itself for assessing relative degrees of plausibility, identification of the relevant alternatives constitutes the first step in enhancing the discriminability of the newly presented ideas. The clarification of meaningful new ideas, in other words, is primarily a process of differentiating the propositions in question from other related established propositions in cognitive structure and from other plausible alternatives in the learning material (Pressey, 1962a, 1962b).

Thus the results of research on the relative efficacy of constructed and selected responses is not hard to anticipate. Generally it indicates (Briggs, 1958; Coulson and Silberman, 1960; Evans and others, 1960b; Roe, 1960) that the two response modes are not significantly different in terms of learning and retention outcomes, but that the constructed mode is less efficient (requires more time). In the one study reporting a significant difference in favor of constructed responses (Fry, 1960), it is notable that the learning task (Spanish vocabulary) was both more rote-like and relatively difficult (high error rate).

Prompting and Guidance

The learner's response during the course of practice may be completely unaided, on the one hand, or, on the other, receive the benefit of varying degrees of external assistance. The nature and the significance of such assistance obviously differ greatly depending on whether reception or discovery learning is involved. In discovery-learning situations, assistance takes the form of *guidance,* that is, providing cues which detract from the learner's opportunity for autonomous discovery. The provision of complete guidance is tantamount to presenting the learner with the essential content of the learning task (reception learning), whereas the absence of any guidance whatever requires completely autonomous discovery. The degree of guidance furnished in most instances of discovery learning typically falls between these two extremes.

The results of studies employing discovery methods will be discussed in Chapter 16. For the present, we may say that methods involving some measure of guidance have been found to be more effective than either completely autonomous discovery or pure reception learning (provision of complete guidance) in those instances where the object of learning is not merely acquisition of knowledge, but also the development of skill in formulating general principles and applying them to particular problem situations. However, since there are many radical exponents of the proposition that discovery learning is the *only* appropriate method under *any* circumstances, it should be remarked that verbally presented principles—which we have seen to be important in both lateral and vertical transfer—need not be all self-discovered, although actual guided practice in problem solving seems indispensable if the student is to go on to do independent problem solving. When all factors are considered, including the much greater time required for most kinds of discovery learning, it seems that a judicious mixture of the didactic teaching of principles coupled with selective practice in guided discovery will be optimal when we are attempting to help a student master an approach (strategy) that can be applied to a whole class of problems (for example, the pendulum problem). However, when the objective is the acquisition of knowledge, then economy suggests that reception learning should predominate.

In a reception learning situation, external assistance takes the form of *prompting* during the test trials. This assistance does not affect the autonomy of discovery, since the content of the learning task is fully presented in any case, but does influence the economy of reproduction.[7] Prompting is more necessary and effective in the early stages of reception learning because at this time the learner has not yet internalized sufficient material to receive much practice benefit from unaided recitation (Briggs, 1961; Della-Piana, 1961). Furthermore, the provision of prompts at this early point in practice can prevent guesswork and the learning of errors (incorrect competing responses), thus obviating the necessity for costly unlearning. For such reasons, prompting is more efficacious than confirmation (feedback) for relatively short periods of practice in reception learning (Briggs, 1958, 1961; Cook and Spitzer, 1960; Hovland and others, 1949; Kaess and Zeaman, 1960; Silberman and others, 1961a, 1961b; L. M. Smith, 1962). During the later stages of practice these considerations are obviously less relevant. In addition, it is important that the conditions of practice gradually begin to approximate the desired (unprompted) endpoint of the learning product. Hence, as the amount of correct learning increases, both reduction in the completeness and explicitness of the prompts (J. G. Holland, 1960; Israel, 1960; Lumsdaine, 1961; Popp and Porter, 1960) and their replacement by confirmation (Angell and Lumsdaine, 1960; Lumsdaine, 1961; Stolurow, 1961b) are advantageous for further learning. On theoretical grounds it also seems plausible that prompting could be dispensed with earlier in the case of meaningful than of rote reception learning because of the more rapid rate of acquisition and the different role played by competing responses.

Verbatim Recall versus Reformulated Response

In measuring the learner's comprehension and retention of meaningful verbal content, test items can be appropriately constructed either to encourage verbatim recall of the presented material or to lead him to reformulate his understanding of the material in terms of his own vocabulary and ideational background. Although explicit empirical evidence is lacking on this issue, the reformulation approach has at least three theoretical arguments in its favor: (1) it not only constitutes a more valid measure of genuine understanding, but (2) also requires the more active participation of the learner in the testing situation, and (3) tends to discourage the adoption of a rote learning set in future learning efforts. Other ways of accomplishing the same purposes in a formal testing context include the use of a multiple-choice format, employing application or problem-solving items, or measuring ability to learn a new set of propositions presupposing mastery of the content being tested.

---

[7]The learner is assisted, in whole or in part, to reproduce previously presented material which as yet has not been internalized above the threshold of availability. If the entire and explicit substance of the information demanded by the test item is furnished, the stimulus support can be regarded as a *prompt;* if the stimulus support is less complete and explicit during the test trial, it can be considered a *cue.*

In a less formal testing context, the substitution of appropriate recitation trials for study trials tends to encourage reformulation rather than verbatim reproduction.

Natural versus Structured Settings (Drill)

As pointed out earlier, the post-Thorndikian attacks against practice were directed particularly at drill. As a result, educational theorists often tend to minimize the value of drill; in fact, the term still evokes unsavory connotations in some educational circles. Actually, drill is a necessary and indispensable part of classroom teaching. Stroud (1942) puts the matter very well in the following statement:

> In our anxiety over the abuses, alleged and real, we have had a tendency to forget the fact that there are intelligent, constructive uses of drill. . . . Drill is currently purported, and by some who have been identified with education long enough to know better, to be the handiwork of stimulus-response psychology.
>
> In appraising drill as a teaching procedure, it is well to remember that it is not mere repetition but repetition of the conditions of learning that is effective. Drill can be effective, ineffective, or positively detrimental; spirited or spiritless. Pupils do not necessarily learn just because they engage in drill. . . . In the best educational practice, pupils are engaged in drill after the need for it has been demonstrated (pp. 362–364).

Of the various arguments against drill, perhaps the most frequent one—advanced by enthusiastic supporters of project and activity methods— is that practice should take place in natural (real life, uncontrived) settings. Such persons take a rather extreme position on this issue, rejecting all kinds of highly structured practice and advocating, in effect, an incidental type of learning.

It is true, of course (providing that all other factors are equal), that transfer is enhanced when the conditions of practice closely resemble the conditions under which the skill or knowledge in question will eventually be used. Such learning is also less likely to be monotonous, and enjoys the benefit of a higher level of interest and motivation. Wholly natural settings, however, rarely provide the practice conditions which are necessary or optimal for efficient learning. Generally, it is only during the latter stage of learning, *after* component aspects of the learning task have already been identified and mastered in structured practice sessions, that naturalistic "dress rehearsals" become feasible. In the first place, uncontrived learning experiences typically fail to include a sufficient number of properly spaced practice trials as well as opportunity for differential repetition of particularly difficult components. Second, unstructured practice does not receive the benefit of skilled pedagogic selection, presentation, and organization of materials, of careful sequencing, pacing, and gradation of difficulty, and of optimal balancing of intratask repetition, intratask variability, and intertask variability. Lastly, simple considerations of practical expediency rule out the possibility that any sizeable proportion of practice experiences could be conducted in "natural" settings.

Task Homogeneity

The relative degree of task homogeneity is often an important practical consideration in the learning of skills and inductively acquired concepts and principles. The issue here is whether such learnings can be acquired most efficiently as a result of intensive practice with just a few exemplars, or as a result of less intensive practice with a large variety of exemplars. It can be deduced from the theoretical arguments advanced earlier that, other factors being equal, the defining attributes of a given concept are learned most readily when the concept is encountered in many diverse contexts. Such experience obviously lessens the particularity and enhances the generality of abstract knowledge and transferable skills.

It is important to qualify this conclusion, however, by pointing out that if this multicontextual experience is acquired at the expense of attaining adequate mastery of the particular component tasks which comprise it, its overall effect on learning is detrimental. In learning general concepts, principles, and skills inductively, experience with a particular exemplar has a positive transfer effect on other exemplars only if it is adequately consolidated. Similarly, it is only by mastering several examplars in the same fashion that the total experience can be successfully utilized in formulating a transferable generalization.

It seems, therefore, that efficient learning of transferable skills and knowledge demands a proper balance between the overlearning of particular intratask instances, on the one hand, and adequate exposure to intra- and intertask diversity on the other. These two conditions of practice are complementary and mutually supporting rather than antithetical or mutually preclusive, although it is quite probable that their optimal proportions vary in different learning tasks. Many cases of disability in particular academic skills can undoubtedly be attributed to over-emphasis on the importance of diversified experience and unstructured learning situations, with consequent insufficiency of practice and failure to attain mastery of the components from which the skill in question is derived. Hence, we should not lose sight of the fact that the acquisition of general skills is dependent upon the prior consolidation of more particular components, and that these skills are therefore not efficiently or satisfactorily established unless learners practice the underlying exemplars sufficiently to master them thoroughly.

Generally speaking, it would seem that educators have tended to stress the importance of extensity as opposed to intensity in learning. Actually, if a choice must be made, it is preferable to know a few things well rather than to have a passing acquaintance with many. A small quantity of consolidated knowledge is both useful and transferable; a large quantity of diffuse and unstable knowledge is relatively useless.

Another obvious advantage of multicontextual learning—providing it does not interfere with intratask mastery—is that it prevents boredom and enhances the exploratory drive. This is particularly true in the case of the more intelligent learner; less intertask variability is required to sustain the interest of duller students (Armistead, 1961).

Knowledge of Results

It would seem a matter almost of common sense that a knowledge of results (that is, "feedback") would facilitate learning. For example, the child who is practicing the spelling of a particular word, or the student of history who recalls his understanding of the causes of the War of 1812, would certainly stand to profit from some explicit knowledge of the adequacy of his responses.

Depending upon one's theoretical orientation, the benefits of knowledge of results can be argued on reinforcement, motivational, or purely cognitive grounds. While these positions are discussed in greater detail in Chapter 12, it may be said here that behavioristically oriented theorists (J. G. Holland, 1960; Hull, 1943; McGeoch and Irion, 1952; Skinner, 1938, 1958; E. L. Thorndike, 1931; Trowbridge and Cason, 1932) tend to attribute the effects of feedback largely to "reinforcement" or to the direct strengthening effect of drive-reduction on the responses that are instrumental in obtaining a reward and gratifying a drive. Informing the learner that a given response is correct presumably gratifies cognitive, affiliative, and ego-enchancing drives motivating the response and hence, according to such theorists, increases the probability of its recurrence (that is, "reinforces" the response). And, as will be argued later, such gratification also retroactively increases these same motivations for further learning. Moreover, explicit awareness that the results of learning will be made available also constitutes an incentive condition, thereby enhancing the strength of the underlying drive.

However, the facilitating effects of feedback are not exhausted by these reinforcement and motivational mechanisms. Knowledge of results has, as well, purely cognitive effects on learning in that it confirms appropriate meanings and associations, corrects errors, clarifies misconceptions, and indicates the relative adequacy with which different portions of the learning task have been mastered. Thus, as the result of the feedback he receives, the subject's confidence in the validity of his learning products is increased, his learnings are consolidated, and he is better able to selectively focus his efforts and attention on those aspects of a task requiring further refinement.

Type of Learning Task Some theorists (for example, Skinner), generalizing from animal studies, assume that efficient learning requires some *explicit* reinforcing or feedback-providing action on the part of the teacher or program (in programmed instruction). In fact, Skinner's widely cited attack on instruction in the school (Skinner, 1954) was based to a large extent on the proposition that teachers were not providing immediate knowledge of results and that they could not do so without the aid of such mechanical aids as teaching machines.

This argument has surface plausibility perhaps in those instances of school learning which are of a low level of meaningfulness and in which large amounts of reinforced practice seem necessary (for example, learning number combinations, spelling words, learning foreign-language vocabulary). Certainly, and in support of Skinner's condemnations, one can find many contemporary classes where the child completes an arithmetic exercise today and the feedback (via the teacher's marking) occurs, if at all, tomorrow. Both research evidence and common sense suggest that the learning of low-order skills is likely to be very inefficient under these conditions.

Even in such cases of near-rote learning, however, there seems no reason why an eight-year-old, for example, could not be trained to immediately check his attempted spellings against the list in the text, or why an arithmetic student of the same age could not compare his answer with that in the back of the text. It seems, then, that the view that an *external* agent (for example, teacher) must provide an *explicit* act of feedback for every student response gives scant attention to the possibilities for student-generated feedback. Moreover, most of the learning tasks faced by the child have, in varying degrees, *built-in* checks which act as confirming devices. Hence, it is fairly obvious to the algebra student whether or not he has correctly reduced an identity, or to the geometry student whether or not he has proved the desired conclusion. Similarly, the accuracy of subtraction is easily checked by addition, division by multiplication, and the solution of an equation by direct substitution of answers.

Finally, in highly meaningful tasks the student incorporates a new idea into cognitive structure, and the highly integrated organization of that structure provides many internal checks on the adequacy of his understanding. Thus the student who already possesses a highly developed set of geometrical ideas can check the newly acquired meaning of the "rhombus" against related concepts, so that if he is grossly in error the concept simply will not "fit in" with these established meanings. In view of these factors, it is not surprising that explicit, externally applied feedback has not been found to be the crucial variable which Skinner and other early teaching-machine enthusiasts postulated. Indeed, some studies in programmed instruction have found that varying the proportion of feedback (from zero to 100 percent of the total frames used) was not significantly related to the success in immediate (Krumboltz and Weisman, 1962b; Lambert and others, 1962) or delayed (Lambert, 1962) criterion tests of learning.

The reduced importance of feedback in meaningful learning tasks can be argued in motivational terms as well. Since the achievement of understanding is a reward in its own right, and requires less brute effort than rote learning, it is less necessary in meaningful learning to invoke the energizing assistance of extrinsic motives and incentives. Selective reinforcement of successful responses through drive reduction (gratification) is similarly less necessary for learning, even if it were possible, when logical considerations are applicable to the learning tasks than when a purely arbitrary and verbatim connection must be established.

Completeness, Frequency, and Immediacy of Feedback

Questions concerning the immediacy and frequency of feedback are similar to those raised in the previous discussion. In respect to frequency, some investigators have reported (Bourne and Haygood, 1960; Bourne and Pendleton, 1958; Chansky, 1960) that continuously, as opposed to intermittently, administered feedback is more effective in concept learning. In more sequential types of programmed instruction, however, relative frequency of feedback does not appear to influence learning outcomes (Krumboltz and Weisman, 1962b; Lambert, 1962). Chansky (1964) obtained best results with an intermittent type of information feedback and with continuous grading procedures.

With regard to immediacy, some investigators have reported that immediately given feedback has a significantly greater facilitating effect on learning than does delayed feedback (Angell, 1949; S. R. Meyer, 1960b, Sax, 1960). Other investigators (Evans and others, 1960a; Sax, 1960) found no significant difference between the two kinds of feedback on learning and retention. However, the evidence that errors made initially tend to persist despite repeated correction (Kaess and Zeaman, 1960) and that prompting is superior to confirmation (at least in the early stages of practice) suggest that, if at all possible, it is preferable to avoid errors in the first place rather than to correct them immediately.

The research both on frequency and immediacy cited above was concerned with the influence of external feedback, provided usually by the program. Where these results are negative it is difficult to rule out the possibility that student- or task-generated feedback had not compensated for the absence or infrequency of externally provided information. Consistent with this interpretation, for example, is the fact that external feedback is less important in sequential learning, since opportunity for task-generated feedback is very high in this instance. It would appear that the teacher should assume that both frequency and recency of feedback are important, and the learning experience should be so structured that opportunities are available for such feedback—whether it is externally applied or provided by the task or student.

Present evidence also suggests that the efficacy of feedback varies in proportion to its completeness. For example, provision of the entire correct answer facilitates concept learning more than simply indicating "right" or "wrong" (Bourne and Pendleton, 1958; Chansky, 1960), since it enables the learner who does not adequately know the answer to clarify and consolidate his knowledge. In addition, Trowbridge and Cason (1932) found that furnishing the subject with precise information about the magnitude and direction of his error is more effective than telling him "right" or "wrong" when he is learning to draw a line of specified length. Explanation of the logic of the correct answer is another dimension of the completeness of feedback that enhances its influence on learning. Subjects who are told *why* their answers are right or wrong learn more effectively than subjects who merely continue responding and receiving feedback until they obtain the correct answer (Bryan and Rigney, 1956). Finally, Sassenrath and Gaverick (1965) found that discussion of midsemester examination questions has a more beneficial effect on final examination results than does either checking wrong answers from a list of correct answers placed on the blackboard or looking up in a textbook the correct answers to incorrectly answered questions.

TOPICS FOR DISCUSSION AND FURTHER STUDY

1.* Examine a textbook—a reader, spelling, or arithmetic text, for example— and determine the implicit or explicit practice schedule which it contains. To what extent is this schedule consistent with the ideas presented in this chapter?

2.* Design a practice schedule for some particular topic in your subject-matter area which explicitly acknowledges the previously discussed principles.

3. Analyze the practice schedule which you would normally utilize in mastering the content of the present book. In what details is your habitual practice scheduling in agreement, or at odds, with theoretical suggestions?

4. Adult learners frequently use a practice, which they call "scanning," either at the first presentation of the material or as a review. How is scanning related to the notion of "sensitization" presented in this chapter? Indicate the purposes for which, and conditions under which, scanning might be an effective technique as opposed to the thorough digesting of the complete text.

5. To what extent would the principles of practice advocated for the cognitive domain be applied to the practice of motor skills?

6. It is advocated in this chapter, with respect to the homogeneity-heterogeneity issue, that a high level of mastery on limited exemplars should precede practice in

a variety of settings. How may the classroom teacher in any particular instance decide when a specific mastery of the narrow set is adequate?

7. For the particular subject you teach, discuss the extent to which the practice schedule is determined by the text and the amount and kind of freedom remaining to the teacher to vary practice procedures.

8. Discuss ways in which the students at the grade level at which you teach can be encouraged to undertake independently their own practice scheduling.

9. To what extent does the subject matter which you teach contain "built-in" feedback? Cite specific examples. What means can be employed to provide nearly immediate feedback when the material itself does not provide it?

SUGGESTIONS FOR ADDITIONAL READING

Ausubel, D. P. *Educational psychology: A cognitive view.* New York: Holt, Rinehart and Winston, Inc., 1968, Chapter 8.

Stroud, J. B. The role of practice in learning. In *The psychology of learning: 41st Yearbook Nat. Soc. for Stud. Educ.,* Part II. Chicago: University of Chicago Press, 1942, pp. 353–376.

Symonds, P. M. *What education has to learn from psychology.* New York: Teachers College Press, Columbia University, 1958, Chapter 5.

CHAPTER 11

USE OF INSTRUCTIONAL MATERIALS IN OPTIMAL PROGRAMMING

IN PREVIOUS CHAPTERS WE HAVE OUTLINED A THEORY IN-
dicating how the subject matter studied in school is initially related to cognitive
structure, retained, and transferred to new learning tasks. Further, we have
considered how the method of presentation should vary with the stage of
developmental readiness, and how the frequency and distribution of practice
trials influences learning and retention. Finally, we have identified intellectual and cognitive factors which lead to differences between individual students
in the ability to learn.

In designing instructional programs for school children, the educator
will take into account as many of these factors—as well as motivational,
group, and social factors (considered in Part Four)—as he is conversant
with and which seem to apply to the task at hand. Every real program
provided for a child or a group of children will, because of the personal
limitations of the designers of the program, fall short in varying degrees of
the best possible program for achieving a specific set of goals which could be
designed on the basis of present knowledge. The attempted construction of
such a best possible program can profitably be referred to as "optimal
programming," a term which will be found useful in the present and future
chapters.

In our search for variables that must enter into optimal programming,
we have discussed (in the preceding chapter) task variables associated with
the amount and nature of practice. The present chapter extends the study of
relevant programming variables in three directions. First, we complete the
analysis of task variables by considering the nature and difficulty of the
material to be learned, the rate at which new ideas are presented, and the
magnitude of the transition between successive tasks; second, we consider

effective ways of presenting large bodies of material, drawing upon and extending ideas discussed earlier; finally we discuss the use of such instructional aids and media as textbooks, educational television, programmed instruction, and laboratory methods.

THE SIZE, DIFFICULTY, AND PACING OF TASKS

In the classroom the teacher, text, or program presents a series of learning tasks to the students. The demands which such tasks— whether or not they are sequentially dependent—place upon the students may be better understood by analysis of their component ideas or skills.

For illustrative purposes we may consider a grade 4 teacher who is planning the steps by which he will teach the learning task: "dividing a three-digit number by a one-digit divisor." The teacher would probably proceed by analyzing this task to reveal the end-behavior desired, and might arrive at a list of sequentially related subtasks, similar to that shown in Figure 11.1, by which the student could be brought to understand the procedures involved in the standard method of long division.[1] Within such a context the following kinds of task variables can be identified:

(a) *Task size*: The size of a learning task refers to the total number of ideas to be learned or steps to be mastered. The complete task in the example under consideration (comprehending and using efficiently the standard method of long division) is a fairly lengthy one, obviously not suited—at the age level in question—to a single exposition (lesson); perhaps five or six instructional sessions (each elaborating a major idea) would be employed, each followed by sufficient practice to insure the long-term stability of the learning. As an illustration of a difference in subtask length, we might note that the third subtask contains more new steps than the fourth. When the material to be learned consists of a body of interrelated ideas—rather than process steps—we may speak of "amount of material" in referring to task size.

(b) *Task difficulty*: Task difficulty can be measured by the time required to learn a task to some stipulated degree of proficiency; obviously difficulty and length would normally be related, although they may be considered independent variables. Illustrative of these points we

---

[1] It has been pointed out to us that some "modern" approaches to arithmetic stop at subtask 4. While agreeing that the essential ideas of division are contained in these first stages, it would still appear that the algorithm represented by the final step is useful as a labor-saving device. Moreover, we would contend that it can have meaning (or can be meaningfully learned by the pupil) provided that the previous steps are comprehended. (See Chapter 4.)

Subtask 1:   Comprehending division as the inverse of multiplication, that is, a process of partitioning a given set into equal subsets:

Since in *multiplication:*[2] $3 \times 2 = 6$ means $\left\{ \begin{smallmatrix} \cdot \\ \cdot \\ \cdot \end{smallmatrix} \right\} + \left\{ \begin{smallmatrix} \cdot \\ \cdot \\ \cdot \end{smallmatrix} \right\} \rightarrow \left\{ \begin{smallmatrix} \cdot & \cdot \\ \cdot & \cdot \\ \cdot & \cdot \end{smallmatrix} \right\}$

thus in *division:*

$\quad 6 \div 2 = 3$ means $\left\{ \begin{smallmatrix} \cdot & \cdot \\ \cdot & \cdot \\ \cdot & \cdot \end{smallmatrix} \right\} \rightarrow \left\{ \begin{smallmatrix} \cdot \\ \cdot \\ \cdot \end{smallmatrix} \right\} + \left\{ \begin{smallmatrix} \cdot \\ \cdot \\ \cdot \end{smallmatrix} \right\}$

$\quad 6 \div 3 = 2$ means $\left\{ \begin{smallmatrix} \cdot & \cdot \\ \cdot & \cdot \\ \cdot & \cdot \end{smallmatrix} \right\} \rightarrow \{ \cdot \quad \cdot \} + \{ \cdot \quad \cdot \} + \{ \cdot \quad \cdot \}$

Subtask 2:   Understanding the meaning of remainder

$7 \div 2 = 3$ and 1 remainder means $\left\{ \begin{smallmatrix} \cdot & \cdot & \cdot \\ \cdot & & \cdot \\ \cdot & & \cdot \end{smallmatrix} \right\} = \left\{ \begin{smallmatrix} \cdot \\ \cdot \\ \cdot \end{smallmatrix} \right\} + \left\{ \begin{smallmatrix} \cdot \\ \cdot \\ \cdot \end{smallmatrix} \right\} + \{ \cdot \}$

Subtask 3:   Division of three-digit number by repeated subtraction of multiple of 10

```
8 |190          190 ÷ 8 = {10 + 10 + 3} and 6R
   80    10
  110
   80    10
   30
   24     3
    6
```

Subtask 4:   Division by subtracting largest possible multiple of 10

```
8 |190          190 − 8 = (20 + 3) and 6R
  160    20
   30     3
   24
    6
```

Subtask 5:   Moving quotients to "top"

```
     20 + 3      190 ÷ 8 = (20 + 3) and 6R
8 |190
  160
   30
   24
    6
```

---

[2]In some interpretations, the arithmetical expression "3×2" should be read "3 sets of 2" rather than "3 taken twice" (as in our example). Although a purely arbitrary convention, it would appear that the latter form corresponds most closely to the child's visualization of the process (that is, he imagines initially a set of three elements which is subsequently duplicated). In any case, the commutative law ($3 \times 2 = 2 \times 3$) should be introduced at the earliest possible stage, at which point the terminology distinction becomes superfluous.

Subtask 6: Contraction to standard form

$$190 \div 8 = 23 \text{ and } 6R$$

```
        23
   8 | 190
       16
     ------
       30
       24
     ------
        6
```

FIGURE 11.1 *Some subtasks within the learning task "dividing a three-digit number by a one-digit divisor."*

might observe that the third subtask is probably more difficult than the fourth because the former contains more new steps, but that the sixth subtask seems intrinsically more difficult than the third, although containing fewer new component steps.[3]

(c) *Step size:* This variable is concerned with the relative gradualness or abruptness of transition between the component tasks of a sequentially organized program. In our illustrative example the transition between subtasks four and five is very gradual, while the transition between five and six seems rather abrupt.

(d) *Pacing:* The pacing variable refers to the length of time allowed between the presentation of component tasks. In our present example the total task is embedded in a learning experience which also includes the simultaneous development of multiplication skills and the appearance of fractions. How closely the presentation of the various subtasks of the major task should follow each other, as opposed to interspersing related ideas, is clearly a question of considerable concern to the teacher.

In the following section we proceed to examine further each of these task variables. Since we do not wish to limit the discussion unduly, it is pitched at a level of generality sufficient to embrace the learning of a number of different kinds of material. At one end of the scale we could conceive of a large number of subtasks explicitly presented to the learner;

---

[3]Another way of separating length and difficulty is to conceive each task in a sequentially related chain as requiring transformations of ideas in the preceding task. Starting with any given idea, one can make various transformations of it of varying degrees of intrinsic intellectual difficulty, and one can also make a single transformation or a succession of related transformations. Thus two subtasks may possess the same objective difficulty— that is, require the same learning time—although the first task consists of a single intrinsically difficult transformation, while the second contains a number of intrinsically easy transformations and is longer.

such, for example, are the individual frames of programmed instruction which are more finely graded than those indicated in our analysis.[4]

At the other end of the scale the university student may be presented with (or informed of), and required to learn, the ideas contained in a lengthy manuscript on "motivation in school learning." Here the task presented is a large one with no subtasks explicitly indicated. In this case, however, the learner would probably superimpose his own (implicit) system of subtasks, if only by dividing the material by any subheadings provided, by pages of text, or by common themes. Of course it is a major responsibility of classroom teachers to divide tasks into subtasks which lend themselves to the time available in a given learning session, to the structure of the material, and to the age and background of the learner.

Task Size

The amount of material contained in a given learning task, that is, the relative size of the task, is clearly an important consideration in programming subject matter and in arranging practice schedules. In the case of *rote* learning, the paramount consideration in deciding upon task size is the disproportionate increase in learning time that occurs as length of task (for example, memorizing an increasing number of nonsense syllables) increases beyond immediate memory span (Carroll and Burke, 1965; Lyon, 1914, 1917; Robinson and Heron, 1922). This disproportionality shows itself in progressively increasing *learning time per unit of material*. It tends to be more marked when practice is massed rather than distributed (Hovland, 1940; Lyon, 1917) and in slow, as opposed to fast, learners (L. J. Carter, 1959; Reed, 1924). For the most part, the disproportionality seems to reflect the greater opportunity for intraserial interference as the number of units in the task increases (L. J. Carter, 1959; McGeoch and Irion, 1952). To some extent also it reflects the subject's initial discouragement as he contemplates the magnitude of the task confronting him, as well as unnecessary repetition of already learned items while yet-unlearned items in the longer list are being acquired (McGeoch and Irion, 1952). Length of rotely learned tasks, however, apparently has no effect on *retention* per se, that is, apart from its effect on learning. Thus when lists of varying lengths are learned to the *same* criterion of mastery, and are similarly reinforced, they are equally well retained (L. J. Carter, 1959).

---

[4]Indeed in that example we could subdivide each of the tasks by considering: (a) the division of two-digit numbers with no remainder; (b) the division of two-digit numbers with a remainder; (c) the division of three-digit numbers with no remainder; (d) the division of three-digit numbers with a remainder. In this way we could increase the number of steps by a factor of three while decreasing both the average size of the subtasks and the average magnitude of the intersubtask interval (step).

In the case of *meaningful* learning, the same simple disproportionality between increase in learning time and increase in task size presumably does not prevail. The disproportionate increase in intraserial interference accompanying increase in task size, which is evident in rote learning, has little relevance for the kind of learning involved in the incorporation of potentially meaningful material within cognitive structure. Hence, although increasing the length of a meaningful-learning task undoubtedly increases the time required to learn it—all other factors being equal—one might anticipate on theoretical grounds that the increase in learning time would not be disproportionate to the increased task size. Much more important for difficulty of meaningful learning and retention than length of task per se would be the logical structure, the lucidity, and the sequentiality of the material. The optimal size of task that the learner could conveniently manage in a given trial would also depend upon such considerations as age, cognitive maturity, subject-matter sophistication, intelligence, and motivation.

Research evidence on the length/time-of-learning relationship in meaningful learning is sparse and equivocal. Available data clearly suggest that learning time increases much less rapidly with increasing length of tasks when prose passages are learned meaningfully than when they are learned rotely (Cofer, 1941), but the precise relationship between length and difficulty in the former instance is, unfortunately, less clearly indicated. Although Lyon (1914, 1917) found a disproportionate increase in learning time with increase in length of meaningful prose passages (except for lengths of between ten thousand and fifteen thousand words), only verbatim learning was required in his study. Increasing the length of an instructional motion picture by adding more facts, while holding constant *density* (number of facts per minute), but not logical structure and continuity, does not result in a proportionate increase in the amount of information learned, but apparently has no detrimental effect on retention (Vincent and others, 1949). Much more definitive research studies are therefore needed before empirically warranted conclusions can be drawn regarding optimal task length in meaningful learning.

Difficulty of the Material

The difficulty of the learning task obviously affects the amount of material that can be learned and retained in a given period of time. If the material is too difficult, the learner accomplishes disproportionately little for the degree of effort he expends; if it is too easy, his accomplishments are disappointingly meager in terms of what he could have achieved were greater effort demanded of him. In addition, excessively difficult material makes for an undesirably large number of initial errors and misconceptions that have to be unlearned; interferes with necessary intratask mastery and consolidation in sequential learning programs; and depresses the learner's self-confidence, lowers his motivation, increases his anxiety, and promotes task avoidance. In meaningful problem-solving situations, it typically induces perseveration, rigidity, blind trial and error, and disorganization of behavior (Klausmeier and Check, 1962). Inappropriately easy material, on the other hand, fails to stimulate and challenge the learner adequately, thus fostering disinterest.

Since the appropriate level of difficulty of a given task is always relative to the learner's age, cognitive maturity, subject-matter sophistication, intelligence, and motivation, it is best determined on an individual basis. When learning tasks are suitably adjusted in difficulty level to pupils' current achievement level, there are no significant differences between low, middle and high IQ groups in the retention and transfer of the material each group learns (Klausmeier and Check, 1962; Klausmeier and others, 1959; Klausmeier and Feldhusen, 1959).

Step Size

Step size, that is, the relative magnitude of transition between task units, is also an important issue in programming meaningful subject matter. It can be reduced by increasing redundancy or overlapping of content, by making explicit reference to or comparisons with prior task content (integrative reconciliation), and by couching new material in terms of familiar concepts or experience. When large task units are used, it is also meaningful to speak of step size between successive components of the task unit.

The step-size variable is partly coextensive with the previously considered variable of task homogeneity or intertask variability. Unlike task homogeneity, however, it is more concerned with the relative gradualness or abruptness of transition between the component tasks of a sequentially organized program than with relative degree of homogeneity or heterogeneity of the exemplars used to develop a given concept or proposition. The relative effectiveness of different step sizes in a given learning program, therefore, is dependent, in part, upon achieving an appropriate balance between such considerations as conceptual generality, intratask mastery, learning to learn, warm-up effect, perseveration, rigidity, and boredom, which are associated with both of these variables.

Hence the choice of appropriate step size is likely to be quite specific to the particular learning task, the conditions of learning, and the characteristics of the learner. Small steps minimize the possibility of error (Evans and others, 1960c; Klaus, 1964; Skinner, 1958), but are more time consuming (Coulson and Silberman, 1960; W. Smith and Moore, 1962); they are also less necessary when potentially meaningful material and a branching type of feedback are used. Furthermore, as Pressey (1962a) points out, they fragment the learning task without necessarily guaranteeing understanding of the task as a whole or of the relationships among its component parts, despite yielding a low-error rate. It is perhaps because of these counter-balancing forces that research on step size within the context of programmed instruction, confined to small task-unit formats, has been generally inconclusive. On the basis of their research, Maccoby and Sheffield (1961) recommend small step size for initial learning, with progressive lengthening of steps as subjects acquire facility in performing the learning task.

Pacing

Pacing generally refers to the rate of introducing new subject matter material as determined by the length of the time interval between component task units. Other subsidiary ways of influencing rate of coverage include: (1) manipulation of step size (degree of overlap in content between successive task units); (2) increasing or decreasing the density (informational content) of task units; and (3) regulating the number of initial repetitions and subsequent reviews given each task unit. All of these latter manipulations, of course, eventually affect the number of task units covered in a given interval of time, and hence the rate of covering new subject matter. Pacing, in other words, deals with the massing or distribution of *different* task units as opposed to the massing or distribution of trials of a particular task. Considering the potential importance of this variable for the programming of school material, it has been the subject of surprisingly little research.

Theoretically, it would seem plausible that an optimal average intertask interval exists for every kind of subject matter, given learners of specified cognitive maturity and subject-matter sophistication. Thus it probably makes a difference, on the average, if 75 hours are to be spent in learning a particular segment of material, whether this learning time is distributed over two weeks, one month, two months, or a semester. First, sufficient time is necessary to recover from initial learning shock before proceeding to new tasks. Second, the learner requires adequate time to contemplate the material in retrospect, to effect integrative reconciliation, and to conduct adequately spaced reviews. Third, it is important to avoid excessive cognitive strain and a feeling of harassment, on the one hand, as well as unnecessary redundancy, lack of challenge, and boredom, on the other. Lastly, it is necessary to provide sufficient time for practice, particularly for slow learners, so that intratask mastery or consolidation can be assured before new tasks are presented.

In any case, it is apparent that most individuals can be trained to comprehend meaningfully a much more rapid rate of printed or orally presented discourse than that to which they are habitually accustomed. This is the principle underlying current methods of accelerating rate of reading and listening (Orr and others, 1965). Whether material assimilated in this fashion is *retained* as well as material presented at other more conventional rates still remains to be demonstrated.

On logical grounds, because of individual differences in cognitive maturity, intelligence, subject-matter sophistication, and motivation, it would be reasonable to expect that individualized pacing would be more effective for learning than the imposition of a uniform rate of coverage for all learners. Using the quality of past performance as a guide, such individualization could then be regulated by either teacher or pupils, the former having the advantage of greater objectivity and pedagogic sophistication, and the latter possessing more direct information about cognitive strain and degree of challenge, although this information is admittedly contaminated, in part, by such considerations as self-indulgence. Apart from the results of one study (Follettie, 1961), the limited experimental evidence available on the relative efficacy of self-regulated pacing (Mitzel, 1962; Silberman, 1962) does not indicate any superiority over teacher- or program-regulated pacing. This does not mean, however, that differential or individualized pacing is not superior to uniform pacing.

Illustrative Example: Failure To Comprehend

To the classroom teacher the previous discussion may seem a somewhat labored treatment of the obvious. "Surely," it will be argued, "one can trust the innate good sense of educators to realize that tasks must be broken into subtasks and care taken to insure that task size, task difficulty, step size, and pacing schedule are appropriate to the abilities of the learner." The fact is, however, that these variables are by no means universally recognized by educators; in fact, their total disregard in some areas of high school and university teaching results in one of the more disastrous aspects of our traditional educational programs.

Probably the greatest damage can be done through neglect in those highly structured subject areas—such as the physical sciences and mathematics—in which long chains of related ideas or arguments are developed sequentially, each chain in the sequence being dependent upon (often a correlative of) its immediate predecessor. Such material may be represented symbolically as in Figure 11.2. As pointed out earlier, comprehension fails in such a chain when, for one reason or another, one of the links is not adequately grasped and consolidated. One major reason for the student's failure to consolidate—and therefore to comprehend—derives from a naive confusion (by many instructors) of the "logic" of the material and the psychology of learning.

	1st		2nd	
Initial →	Trans-	→ Product →	Trans-	→ Product → ⋯
Idea	formation		formation	
S_0 →	T_1	→ P_1 →	T_2	→ P_2 → ⋯

$$\begin{pmatrix} A \\ B \\ C \\ D \\ E \end{pmatrix} \rightarrow I_{AB} \rightarrow \begin{pmatrix} B \\ A \\ C \\ D \\ E \end{pmatrix} \rightarrow I_{EA} \rightarrow \begin{pmatrix} B \\ E \\ C \\ D \\ A \end{pmatrix} \rightarrow \cdots$$

FIGURE 11.2 *Successive transformations characteristic of sequentially dependent chains of thought.*

To illustrate this point we will consider a somewhat abstract logical example which characterizes in a rather uncontaminated form the sequence indicated in Figure 11.2. In this example, the "given" or "initial axiom" is a sequence of elements arranged in a particular order. The operation designated I_{AB} means "exchange the elements A and B." The student, following an exposition by the instructor of a sequence of such operations, comprehends the argument by mentally performing each of the operations, retaining the results in memory, performing the next operation, and so on, and then checking the results of his mental operations against those provided by the instructor (or text). This is, of course, precisely how the student "follows" any sustained argument presented to him in any subject-matter field, the only difference in the latter case being that both the initial givens and the permissible transformations are much larger in number.

A significant fact about such highly sequential learning, as the reader can easily verify, is that the performance of two operations in sequence, without writing down or otherwise representing visually the intervening product, takes much more time than the performance of two single operations; this is true mainly because in the former case the result of the first operation must be rehearsed until its dissociability strength is adequate to permit recall (that is, the second operation acts on the *recalled product* of the first operation). However, when the first product is represented visually (so that the student does not have to recall it) there would appear to be little difference in comprehension time between a "double" operation and two single operations.

In many, if not most, university lectures and textbooks the instructor expounds his material at a constant rate (that is, in terms of a certain number of ideas per unit of time or paragraph). Moreover, because of his familiarity with the material, the instructor is inclined to telescope or omit steps which seem "obvious" to him, or to rely on a verbal exposition without symbolic or visual representation of the results of each "transformation." Whenever an instructor fails to represent the results of an operation in his exposition and yet proceeds with a constant rate of presenting ideas, the learner is faced with the difficulty that his comprehension time is considerably increased—quite possibly to the point where it exceeds the presentation time. Figure 11.3 exhibits the results of such a presentation. Here we have the common phenomenon of the student comprehending the first few ideas presented in a lecture, but rapidly losing his grip on the logic of the presentation, because he does not have time to mentally consolidate the "unrepresented" results of a logically sequential set of operations.

Of course, if the instructor omits steps altogether the comprehension task is much greater because the student must imagine (that is, deduce, determine by trial and error, or guess) which of the large number of potential transformations was actually used to go from the *given* (S_0) to the "obvious" *result* (P_1). One would expect the comprehension-time curve in this case to be much steeper and the probability of the student's "staying with it" to the end of the lecture much smaller.[5] Unfortunately this practice of ultraterse exposition, coupled with liberal use of the phrase "it is obvious," is considered a mark of cleverness in some mathematical and scientific circles. Under these circumstances students can do little more than copy down (without comprehension) the utterances of the instructor and, with luck, digest them outside the lecture hall.

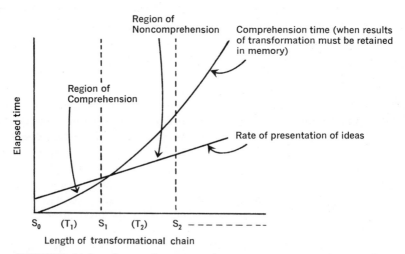

FIGURE 11.3 *Comprehension and presentation time when results of transformation must be retained in memory.*

---

[5] For a different analysis of the relationship between needed learning time, time spent on learning, and amount learned see Sjogren (1967).

ORGANIZATION OF MATERIAL

In addition to paying attention to immediate task variables, the grade 4 arithmetic teacher will also—in the course of optimal programming—give attention to the overall organization of the material (for example, concepts, generalizations, and so on, which are presented to the student). In the following pages we discuss several aspects of this concern. Since the discussion ranges broadly, not all of the considerations raised apply to any specific example, and the reader should think of concrete applications to subject areas known to himself. Some of the remarks apply particularly to material in which a higher order of complexity than that exhibited in our arithmetic example is in evidence. Such instances are found in the teaching of a sequence of interrelated events or concepts in such substantive fields as history, science, English literature, chemistry, or geography.

Emphasis on Cognitive Structure Variables

Throughout this volume it has been repeatedly stressed that the conditions of learning primarily influence the meaningful acquisition and retention of ideas and information by modifying existing cognitive structure. Thus, in school learning, conditions influencing and altering cognitive structure are typically crucial for the acquisition of a particular task as well as for transfer purposes (the learning of related new tasks). Of all the possible conditions of learning that affect cognitive structure, it is self-evident that none can be more significant than organization of the material. In previous chapters we have already considered in great detail how learning material can be most effectively written and organized so as deliberately to induce those changes in cognitive structure that are most advantageous for the learning and retention of meaningful school material. Hence, in the present context, it will be necessary only to summarize briefly the more salient of these considerations.

Organizers versus Overviews

The principles of progressive differentiation and integrative reconciliation have been represented throughout as being of central importance in the programming of meaningful subject matter. Optimal utilization of these principles presupposes not only their consistent use in the sequential presentation of subject-matter material, but also the supplementary availability of a hierarchical series of advance "organizers." These latter organizers provide relevant ideational scaffolding, enhance the discriminability of the new learning material from previously learned related ideas, and otherwise effect integrative reconciliation at a level of abstraction, generality, and inclusiveness which is much higher than that of the learning material itself. To be maximally effective they must be formulated in terms of language and concepts already familiar to the learner, and use appropriate illustrations and analogies if developmentally necessary.

True organizers, thus defined, should not be confused with ordinary introductory overviews. The latter are typically written at the *same* level of abstraction, generality, and inclusiveness as the learning material, and achieve their effect largely through repetition, condensation, selective emphasis on central concepts, and prefamiliarization of the learner with certain key words. Summaries are comparable to overviews in construction, but are probably less effective because their influence on cognitive structure is retroactive rather than proactive relative to the learning task. They are probably more useful, in place of the material itself, for purposes of rapid review than for original learning. However, insofar as they may imply to some learners that the material they do *not* include is relatively superfluous, they may promote neglect of and failure to study or review much significant subject matter. Lathrop and Norford (1949), for example, found that neither overviews nor summaries appreciably improve the learning of instructional films.

Organizers versus Intramaterial Organization

Organizers also have certain inherent advantages both over various kinds of intramaterial organization (organizing aids within the body of the material), and over any existing subsumers within cognitive structure that could be used for organizational purposes. Unlike intramaterial organization that successively provides necessary anchorage for, and differentiation of, new ideas at a *particularized* level *just before each* new idea is encountered, organizers perform the same functions *in advance* at a much more *global* level before the learner is confronted with *any* of the new material. For example, a generalized model of class relationships is first provided as a general subsumer for *all* new classes, subclasses, and species before more limited subsumers (classes or subclasses) are provided for the particular subclasses or species they encompass. The various kinds of forests are first distinguished from each other before the component subforests and trees are similarly differentiated. Spontaneously existing subsumers in cognitive structure, on the other hand, lack both particularized relevance for the new material (since the learner cannot possibly anticipate its precise nature) as well as the benefit of the sophisticated knowledge of subject matter and pedagogy available to expert programmers.

Perceptual Organizers

Perceptual organizers, in contrast to the integrative organizational devices just described, merely provide built-in mechanical aids that make the material perceptually more salient and apprehensible, or otherwise facilitate practice. These include rhythmic aids, vocal emphasis, the isolation[6] and familiarization effects of underlining, and the "fractionation" effect (breaking of wholes into parts) of providing headings and subheadings. Under certain circumstances, however, some perceptual organizers can be said to have true integrative effects (for example, underlining that helps make ideational distinctions or emphasizes central concepts; headings that reveal the organizational structure of the material more clearly).

Perceptual or mechanical organizers generally facilitate meaningful learning—more so in the case of factual than of abstract material. The learning of meaningful material, for example, is enhanced by appropriate vocal emphasis (Dearborn and others, 1949), by underlining (Klare and others, 1955), and by breaking instructional film content into parts by means of inserted questions (Kurtz and others, 1950). Typographical highlighting of the more important material to be learned reduces the amount of learning of less important content but does not facilitate the learning of the more important core content (Hershberger, 1964). The relative effectiveness of such techniques vis-a-vis advance organizers is not known, although a suggestion resides in May's (1965) finding that pre-film *verbal* instructions are more effective for focusing and sustaining attention than built-in *visual* devices.

Northrop (1952) found that the use of headings facilitates the learning of factual films, but either has no significant effect on or inhibits the learning of more abstract films. The abstract material in this study was evidently more highly organized than the factual, simply because the abstract concepts themselves served an organizing function; the learners not only benefited less from the presence of extrinsic mechanical organizers, but also seemed in some instances to be distracted by them. Apparently, integrative organizers are required for material that is more abstract than informational in character. In none of the above studies, however, is it possible to distinguish clearly between the perceptual and the integrative effects of the organizers in question. Conflicting results have also been reported regarding the relative effects of such organizers on bright and dull students.

---

[6]In several adequately controlled laboratory studies, "isolation"—effected by introducing patterned heterogeneity of content or color—has been shown to facilitate rote learning of segregated and immediately adjacent items (Saul and Osgood, 1950; Shay, 1961; M. H. Smith and Stearns, 1949).

Organizers in Textual Material

Generally speaking, therefore, it makes good organizational sense if the presentation of more detailed or specific information is preceded by a more general or inclusive principle to which it can be related or under which it can be subsumed. This not only makes the new information more meaningful—and enables the student to anchor more easily forgotten specifics to more easily remembered generalizations—but it integrates related facts in terms of a common principle under which they can all be subsumed. Thus, in a physics, an engineering, or a biology course, the *general* characteristics of *all* regulatory or cybernetic systems should be presented before considering any *particular* regulatory or cybernetic system. The latter, in turn, should be explicitly related to the more general principles, showing how they exemplify them. This makes for some redundancy; but such redundancy, in turn, greatly reinforces the general principles. Of course, the general principles themselves must be stated in terms and concepts that are already familiar to the learner. Many teachers and many textbooks are guilty of introducing complex and detailed information for which no adequate foundation has been laid in terms of organizing, unifying, or explanatory principles.

Thus a substantive introductory statement of the principal new ideas to be considered in the chapter, stated at a high level of generality and inclusiveness, to which the more detailed information in the chapter can be related, could be very helpful in absorbing the latter information. For example, an organizer consisting of the main ideas underlying Darwin's theory of evolution would be of greater functional utility in learning the more detailed mechanisms through which evolution operates, or the different kinds of evidence for evolution, than a purely historical or anecdotal introduction (which typically provides much folksy biographical information about Darwin or anecdotal material about how he arrived at his theory). The same applies to introductions that merely list the topics to be covered.

It is not only desirable for the material in each chapter to become progressively more differentiated (to proceed from ideas of greater to lesser inclusiveness), but for textbooks as a whole (from one chapter to another) to follow the same organizational plan. The *spiral* kind of organization, in which the *same* topics are treated at progressively higher levels of sophistication in successive sections, is an extension of the same principle. Textbook series in a given field that are intended for use at different instructional levels (elementary-school, high-school, undergraduate, and graduate) can also follow this organizational plan. In this instance there is a progressive increase in scope, depth, complexity, level of abstraction, and level of sophistication at successively higher grade levels, with the earlier acquired knowledge serving as a foundation for the more abstract and complex material introduced later.

In addition, however, some *entirely new* topics are introduced at the higher levels, since many advanced topics are too complex and abstract to be taught successfully on an intuitive basis.

In instances where new concepts are introduced that are similar, or related to but not identical and hence confusable with previously learned concepts, it is advisable to point out *explicitly* the similarities and differences between them and to make this connection in *both* contexts. This practice integrates knowledge by making relationships between concepts explicit; by preventing artificial compartmentalization and the proliferation of separate terms for concepts that are basically the same except for contextual usage; and by differentiating between ostensibly similar but actually different concepts.

Organizers that are intended for elementary-school pupils should be presented at a lower level of abstraction and should also make more extensive use of concrete-empirical props. They should take into account rather than ignore pre-existing organizing principles (preconceptions) in the learner's cognitive structure. Often these preconceptions are based on widely accepted elements of cultural folklore that are very tenacious unless explicitly undermined.

Pervasive Themes

Good organizational advantage can be taken of pervasive or recurrent themes that can integrate or interrelate many different topics or general ideas. In one version (Green) of the *Biological Sciences Curriculum Study* approach to modern biology, for example, the beginning chapters on the "web of life" are used as an integrative device throughout the entire book.[7] None of the three B.S.C.S. versions, however, makes adequate use of Darwinian theory as a pervasive organizing principle. Evolutionary theory can be related to such varied concepts as uniformity and diversity in nature, genetic continuity, the complementarity of organism and environment and of structure and function, the classification of and interrelationships between organisms, population genetics, the role of sexual reproduction in producing diversity, the geography of life, and the need for a self-replicating mechanism as well as the biological significance of mistakes in self-replication. It is obviously necessary for pervasive themes to be introduced early in the book if they are to serve an integrative function.

---

[7] The three textbooks referred to are the Yellow Version (*Biological Science: An Inquiry into Life.* New York: Harcourt, Brace & World, Inc., 1963); Blue Version (*Biological Science: Molecules to Man.* Boston: Houghton Mifflin Company, 1963), and Green Version (*High School Biology.* Skokie, Ill.: Rand McNally & Company, 1963). For a full critique of the approach found in these texts, see D. P. Ausubel, "An evaluation of the B.S.C.S. approach to high school biology," *American Biology Teacher,* 1966, *28,* 176–186.

"Conceptual Schemes" Approach to Science Teaching

The search for pervasive themes is sometimes carried considerably beyond the confines of a single discipline, emerging as a set of *conceptual schemes* intended, in some extreme cases, to integrate the substantive content of *all* scientific disciplines (N.S.T.A. Curriculum Committee, 1964). As admirable as this search may be in intent, certain reservations need to be acknowledged at this point.

First, each separate science has its own, somewhat idiosyncratic, undergirding themes and methods of inquiry. Consequently, an all-encompassing set of schemes is apt to be characterized: (1) by a level of generality that is reminiscent of the philosophy of science, and hence beyond the cognitive maturity and scientific sophistication of elementary- and high-school students; and (2) by far-fetched relevance and applicability to many scientific disciplines. The seven Conceptual Schemes prepared by the N.S.T.A. Curriculum Committee are characterized by both of these features. They are both stated at a high level of generality, and are applicable to the physical sciences but not very applicable to biology, psychology, and the social sciences.

Secondly, even if an epistemologically tenable set of principles comprehensive enough to embrace *all* sciences with equal aptness and relevance *could* be formulated, its very utility (that is, its transferability to the separate sciences, its ability to serve as superordinate subsumers for the less general themes characterizing any single discipline) would obviously be dependent on its being understood and applied at the high level of generality implicit in any such formulation. On developmental grounds, however, elementary-school pupils could, at the very most, hope to understand these themes at an intuitive (semiabstract, semigeneral) level if at all; and high-school and undergraduate students would typically lack sufficient sophistication in a wide-enough variety of sciences genuinely to understand principles at this philosophical level of generalization about science.

The solution to this problem of curriculum development in science does not lie in abandoning the "conceptual schemes" approach. The "conceptual schemes" approach is philosophically, psychologically, and pedagogically sound, provided that it is modified so that a *separate* set of conceptual schemes is made available for each particular discipline or for each group of related disciplines for which an integrating superordinate structure can be established. For example, a report from the Learning Research and Development Center at the University of Pittsburgh (Cohen and Shepler, 1967) describes a project in elementary science which identifies energy, force, mass, equilibrium, and conservation as examples of "permeating" or "unifying" concepts for the fields of physics, chemistry, and biology. It is the intent of this program that "a child completing the elementary school program should have a real awareness of and be able to demonstrate and verbalize the meanings of these permeating concepts."

In addition to developing conceptual schemes—essentially high-level conceptual or propositional organizers—the new science programs are also stressing training in *processes* such as categorizing, measuring, inferring (in distinction to observing), and predicting, which are again assumed to be transferable across scientific disciplines. Indeed, the degree of transferability seems larger here than in the case of concepts. For example, the basic skills of measurement have wide interdisciplinary application, as does the process of categorizing or inferring, or the technique of "experiment by deliberate manipulation of independent variables." In fact, on this last point we shall see in Chapter 18 that the experimental method in educational research, at least in its simple forms, can be understood as a derivative of the classical experimental method encountered in the pendulum problem.

EFFECTIVE COMMUNICATION

Effective communication in the classroom, that is, appropriate translation from the highly sophisticated cognitive structure of the teacher or textbook writer—in terms of cognitive maturity and subject-matter knowledge—to the less highly sophisticated cognitive structure of the student is a complex and delicate art. Sufficient redundancy is necessary both for purposes of ordinary comprehension and retention (Cantril and Allport, 1935) and to take account of unfamiliarity of ideas and occasional wandering of attention. Such redundancy, however, should take the form of paraphrase, example, and applications to other problems rather than of sheer repetition. An effort should be made to arouse interest and to achieve lucidity and incisiveness of expression. One topic should lead naturally and obviously into another. Tangential "asides" and digressions should be avoided. Long quotations from original or archaic sources generally serve no useful purpose.

The writing style should be as simple as is consistent with precise expression, but not so simple as to give the impression of "talking down" to students (as is the case, for example, in most textbooks in education). Teachers and writers should remember that no amount of linguistic simplification can make inherently complex ideas easy to grasp; and whereas initial simplification is always pedagogically defensible, misleading oversimplification is worse than no simplification at all. Since a new subject is most difficult in the beginning, it should be presented simply at first, with level of difficulty increasing progressively as the student's level of sophistication increases. To maintain effective communication, some type of frequent feedback is necessary. This may take the form of quizzes, Socratic questioning, class discussion, and questions from students.

Examples and illustrations should clarify and not serve as superfluous padding or generate a spurious aura of scientific authenticity. If they are permitted to become excessively detailed, complex, or esoteric, they tend to become ends in themselves, thereby obscuring rather than clarifying the ideas they exemplify. It should be borne in mind that intellectually mature students (those who are adolescent or older) do not require examples routinely in understanding concepts and generalizations, but only for atypically difficult or unfamiliar ideas. At the same time, even beyond the elementary-school period, examples are frequently necessary for purposes of illustration or clarification of difficult abstractions.

In presenting instructional material, it is almost always advantageous to proceed from the familiar to the unfamiliar, using previously acquired knowledge and experience both as a foundation for understanding, interpreting, and remembering related new material that is less familiar, and as a means of rendering the latter less threatening. Thus, in elementary biology it is advisable to consider mammals before simpler animals, and flowering plants before simpler plants. Order of presentation should not be determined on the basis of level of biological organization ("from molecule to man") or level of phyletic complexity. The phyletic principle of organization may conform to some abstract canon of scientific logic, but it violates everything we know about the psychology of learning, and it runs counter to the intuitive judgment of anyone who has ever done any classroom teaching. In ascertaining what is more or less familiar, or more or less difficult, psychological principles of learning and of intellectual development are more relevant and reliable guidelines than the questionable assumption that level of phenomenological complexity in science necessarily parallels level of learning difficulty.

Level of Sophistication

In optimal programming considerable effort must be made to discriminate between basic and highly sophisticated content—between what is appropriate and essential for an introductory course and what could be more profitably reserved for more advanced courses. There would appear to be an inappropriately high level of sophistication in the material appearing in many current curriculum reforms (including the Blue and Yellow Versions of the previously mentioned B.S.C.S. project). Undoubtedly this represents a deliberate over-reaction to the outdated content, paucity of explanatory ideas, and the trivial level of difficulty characterizing most traditional textbooks in these areas. But since the unsophisticated student cannot be expected to distinguish between more and less important material, he either throws up his hands in despair, learns nothing thoroughly in the effort to learn everything, or relies on rote memorization and "cramming" to get through examinations.

It is true, of course, that subjects once thought too difficult for high-school students (for example, set theory, analytic geometry, and calculus) can be taught successfully to bright high-school students (and in some instances to bright elementary-school students) with good quantitative ability. But in the latter instances, students are adequately prepared for these advanced subjects by virtue of being exposed to the necessary preliminary, and sequentially antecedent, ideas in mathematics. Moreover, it should be remembered that college-level mathematics is not considered appropriate for *all* pre-university students, but only for those brighter students with better-than-average aptitude in mathematics, who are college-bound and intend to major in such fields as mathematics, science, engineering, and architecture.

An introductory high-school course in any discipline should concentrate more on establishing a general ideational framework than in putting flesh on the skeleton. Generally speaking, only the framework is retained after a considerable retention interval. If more time is spent on overlearning the framework, plus a minimum of detail, than in superficially learning a large mass of oversophisticated and poorly understood material, more of the important ideas are retained in the case of students taking the subject terminally, and a better foundation is laid for students who intend to take more advanced courses later.

Oversophisticated detail is not only unnecessary and inappropriate for a beginning course, but it also hinders learning and generates unfavorable attitudes toward the subject. The student "can't see the forest for the trees." The main conceptual themes get lost or become unidentifiable in a welter of detail. For example, both the average student and the student not particularly interested in science would tend to feel overwhelmed by the vast quantity and complexity of detailed terminology, methodology, and historical material in the Blue and Yellow versions. And a student who feels overwhelmed by a subject tends to develop an aversion toward it, and to resort to rote memorization for examination purposes.

It is not necessary for a beginning student to be given so much sequential historical detail on the development of particular ideas, related experimental evidence from original sources, and pedantic information about all of the various misconceptions and twistings and turnings taken by these ideas before they evolved into their currently accepted form. As a result, the ideas themselves—the really important things to be learned—tend to be obscured and rendered less salient. This practice also places an unnecessary and unwarranted burden on learning and memory effort—effort that could more profitably be expended on learning the ideas themselves and the more significant aspects of their historical development.

For example, to give students the flavor of biology as an evolving empirical science with a complex and often circuitous history, it would suffice to cite several instances of the evolution of particular concepts. It is unnecessary to give the detailed ideational and experimental history of *every* biological concept and controversy. Unsophisticated students also tend to be confused by raw experimental data, and by the actual chronological and experimental history underlying the emergence of a biological law or theory—especially when long quotations are given from original sources using archaic language, referring to obscure controversies, and reporting findings and inferences in an unfamiliar and discursive manner. It is sufficient to review the historical background of biological concepts in a schematic, telescoped, simplified, and reconstructed fashion, deleting most of the detail and disregarding the actual chronological order of the antecedent ideas and their related experiments.

INSTRUCTIONAL AIDS

An important task in optimal programming is to select an appropriate medium for conveying ideas to, and developing skills in, the learner. While teachers 50 years ago were confined to the use of their voice, chalk, and the blackboard, today's schools make available to the teacher a vast array of teaching aids, including texts and reference books, schematic models, laboratory equipment, motion picture projectors, educational television, programmed instruction, and language laboratories. And although it is clear that the use of instructional aids in education is rapidly increasing, a good deal of doubt remains as to how their potential is to be fully utilized.

Some idea of the present usage of the major teaching aids in American schools can be had from Table 11.1. Since teachers normally exercise a good deal of choice in the selection and utilization of such aids, some discussion of the evidence concerning their effectiveness seems warranted.

Programmed Instruction

The terms "programmed instruction," "automated instruction," and "teaching machine" gained prominence in the educational world in the mid-1950s. At that time an American psychologist, B. F. Skinner (1954), leveled scathing criticism at the school on the grounds that the teaching of knowledge and intellectual skills was inefficient and that the pervading motivational drive was the avoidance of aversive stimulation (reprimand and ridicule). Skinner went on to propose remedies which involved an extrapolation of his laboratory research to the design of teaching machines. His early dramatic experiments launched a period of program writing and great optimism concerning the possibility of speeding up learning. Essentially the rationale for programmed instruction was envisaged as follows:

TABLE 11.1

PERCENT OF U.S. TEACHERS USING INSTRUCTIONAL AIDS (SPRING 1967)

	PERCENT OF TEACHERS USING RESOURCES		
	All Teachers	*Elementary*	*Secondary*
Silent filmstrip projector	81.2	89.0	72.2
Phonograph	79.0	92.8	63.3
Charts and maps	77.4	85.0	68.7
16 mm motion picture projector	74.3	74.1	74.6
Overhead projector	61.5	59.3	64.1
Audio tape recorder	53.8	61.2	45.5
Opaque projector	49.4	54.0	44.2
Sound filmstrip projector	43.9	40.8	47.6
Programmed instruction materials	28.6	31.3	25.5
Educational TV broadcasts	26.1	40.1	10.5
8 mm motion picture projector	16.0	15.4	16.6
Commercial TV broadcasts	13.5	16.2	10.4
Closed circuit television	7.0	10.2	3.4
Computer-based teaching terminals	1.4	1.0	1.9

Source: *N.E.A. Research Bulletin,* 1967.

(a) A particular instructional goal (for example, the mastery of multiplication facts) is defined in behavioral terms, that is, in terms of the behavior the child should exhibit when he is judged as having satisfactorily attained the objective.

(b) The total task is broken down into a large number of subtasks, so finely graded that the motivated student has little opportunity to make an error. Thus progress toward, and the final attainment of, the behavioral goal is all but inevitable. In common practice the subtasks are tried out on a number of students and rejected (or reconstructed) if the error rate exceeds 5 percent.

(c) Each subtask (frame) requires the student to make a response, that is, "construct" an acceptable answer.

·(d) The student is told immediately whether his answer is right or wrong. In the teaching machine the student might select a response, and pull a lever; if his answer is correct the "program" (set of frames) will advance by one step; if incorrect, the next frame will not appear until the student has constructed another (correct) answer. In the programmed textbook, the correct answer may appear overleaf.

An example of a "linear" program—so named because each student moves through the same fixed sequence of subtasks—is shown in Figure 11.4.

In the early years of the programmed-instruction movement enthusiasm for such devices was virtually unbounded, and it was predicted that "twice as much (learning) in half the time" would result from their widespread adoption by the schools. The program, with or without the machine (the latter was intended mainly to facilitate the presentation of the program), was seen as a way of allowing each student to move confidently forward at his own pace, and to be subjected to little or no aversive stimulation. It was also predicted that students would find "knowledge of results" sufficiently motivating to keep them them working at the sequence of tasks set.

A second major kind of programmed instruction, associated with Crowder (1960), is sometimes described as "intrinsic" or "branching." Both terms indicate the basic intent, which is to make the next subtask to be presented to the individual depend upon the adequacy of his response to the present task.[8] In the Crowder-type program, an example of which appears in Figure 11.5, the student is first presented with material, ranging from a paragraph to a page in length, which explains some idea or concept. A question is then posed testing the individual's understanding of the concept, and his answer determines where he next proceeds in the program. If his answer is correct he proceeds to the next prose frame; if not, the particular nature of his error is explained to him, and he is required to go back and select the correct answer. In this way it is believed that the program subjects the individual to a form of Socratic questioning.

---

[8]Skinner's small-step programs can also have branching techniques built into them. In the simplest case the student obtaining an incorrect answer is merely asked to re-answer the question. In more complicated cases the program presents critical questions (sometimes referred to as "gates") which determine which of two or more parallel tracks the student will follow.

SENTENCE TO BE COMPLETED	WORD TO BE SUPPLIED
1. The important parts of a flashlight are the battery and the bulb. When we "turn on" a flashlight, we close a switch which connects the battery with the _____.	bulb
2. When we turn on a flashlight, an electric current flows through the fine wire in the _____ and causes it to grow hot.	bulb
3. When the hot wire glows brightly, we say that it gives off or sends out heat and _____.	light
4. The fine wire in the bulb is called a filament. The bulb "lights up" when the filament is heated by the passage of a(n) _____ current.	electric
5. When a weak battery produces little current, the fine wire, or _____, does not get very hot.	filament
6. A filament which is **less** hot sends out or gives off _____ light.	less
7. "Emit" means "send out." The amount of light sent out, or "emitted," by a filament depends on how _____ the filament is.	hot
8. The higher the temperature of the filament the _____ the light emitted by it.	brighter, stronger
9. If a flashlight battery is weak, the _____ in the bulb may still glow, but with only a dull red color.	filament
10. The light from a very hot filament is colored yellow or white. The light from a filament which is not very hot is colored _____.	red
11. A blacksmith or other metal worker sometimes makes sure that a bar of iron is heated to a "cherry red" before hammering it into shape. He uses the _____ of the light emitted by the bar to tell how hot it is.	color
12. Both the color and the amount of light depend on the _____ of the emitting filament or bar.	temperature
13. An object which emits light because it is hot is called "incandescent." A flashlight bulb is an incandescent source of _____.	light
14. A neon tube emits light but remains cool. It is, therefore, not an incandescent _____ of light.	source
15. A candle flame is hot. It is a(n) _____ source of light.	incandescent
16. The hot wick of a candle gives off small pieces or particles of carbon which burn in the flame. Before or while burning, the hot particles send out, or _____, light.	emit

FIGURE 11.4 *Initial section of a linear program in high-school physics. The student is presented with one item at a time. After completing the item, the student uncovers the corresponding correct answer shown at right. From Skinner, 1960.*

Page 101
Now, you recall that we had just defined

$$b^0 = 1$$

for any b except where b = 0. We had reached this definition by noting that our division rule,

$$\frac{b^m}{b^n} = b^{(m - n)}$$

will give b^0 as a result if we apply it to the case of dividing a number by itself. Thus,

$$\frac{b^3}{b^3} = b^{(3 - 3)} = b^0$$

but $\frac{b^3}{b^3}$, or any number (except 0), divided by itself equals 1, so we defined $b^0 = 1$.

We used a division process to find a meaning to attach to the exponent 0. Very well, let's see what other interesting results we can get with this division process. Let's apply our division rule to the case of $\frac{b^2}{b^3}$. What result do we get?

ANSWER	Page
$\dfrac{b^2}{b^3} = b^1$	94
$\dfrac{b^2}{b^3} = b^{(-1)}$	115
The rule won't work in this case	119

The student who elects to turn to Page 94 will find:

Page 94

YOUR ANSWER: $\dfrac{b^2}{b^3} = b^1$

Come, come, now. The rule is $\dfrac{b^m}{b^n} = b^{(m - n)}$.

Now, in the case of $\dfrac{b^2}{b^3}$, we have m = 2 and n = 3, so we are going to get

$$\frac{b^2}{b^3} = b^{(2 - 3)}.$$

So, 2 – 3 isn't 1, is it? It's – 1.

Return to Page 101, now, and quit fighting the problem.

The student who elects Page 119 will find:

YOUR ANSWER: The rule won't work in this case.

Courage! The division rule got us through b^0, where $m = n$, and it will get us through the case where m is smaller than n. In this case we have

$$\frac{b^2}{b^3} = ?$$

and applying the rule

$$\frac{b^m}{b^n} = b^{(m-n)}$$

we get

$$\frac{b^2}{b^3} = b^{(2-3)}.$$

So the exponent of our quotient is $(2 - 3)$ which is -1, isn't it? So just write

$$\frac{b^2}{b^3} = b^{(2-3)} = b^{(-1)}$$

as if you knew what it meant.

Now return to Page 101 and choose the right answer.

And the student who chooses the right answer will find:

Page 115

YOUR ANSWER: $\frac{b^2}{b^3} = b^{(-1)}$

You are correct. Using our rule for division

$$\frac{b^m}{b^n} = b^{(m-n)}$$

in the case of $\frac{b^2}{b^3}$ we get

$$\frac{b^2}{b^3} = b^{(2-3)} = b^{(-1)}.$$

Now, by ordinary arithmetic, we can see that

$$\frac{b^2}{b^3} = \frac{b \times b}{b \times b \times b} = \frac{\cancel{b} \times \cancel{b}}{\cancel{b} \times \cancel{b} \times b} = ?$$

So how shall we define $b^{(-1)}$?

ANSWER	Page
$b^{(-1)} = \frac{0}{b}$	95
$b^{(-1)} = \frac{1}{b}$	104

FIGURE 11.5 *Example of an "intrinsic" program. From Crowder, 1960.*

Research on Programmed Instruction

A considerable amount of research has been conducted with programmed instruction, either to determine its efficiency relative to "traditional" instruction or to determine how programming variables (for example, size of subtask, steps between subtasks, constructed versus multiple-choice reponses) influence learning outcomes. On the first matter the evidence, though by no means unanimous, and seldom involving long-term studies, can perhaps be fairly represented by the following conclusions:

(a) In a majority of studies programmed instruction has produced as much or more learning as traditional instruction (Glaser, 1965; Hughes and McNamara, 1961; Joos, 1961; Ter Keurst, 1965; S. R. Meyer, 1960b; W. F. Oakes, 1960; Poppleton and Austwick, 1964; Schramm, 1964; Whitlock and others, 1963). However, wide variations in effectiveness have been found, depending, as one might expect, upon a whole host of variables, including the quality of the program. Some studies have indeed verified the "twice as much in half the time" prediction, while other attempts to utilize programmed instruction have resulted in near educational catastrophes.

(b) Programmed instruction has not been equally effective over the whole taxonomy of educational behaviors, and its effectiveness seems to decline at the higher levels. Thus while programmed instruction has been effective in tasks involving comprehension (Porter, 1959; S. R. Meyer, 1960b; Joos, 1961), little evidence of success and some evidence of lack of success (Beane, 1962) is available in respect to its efficacy in developing problem-solving abilities. In recent years the programmed-instruction approach to the development of problem-solving skills seems to have given way somewhat to the task-analysis method described earlier. It would appear that the incremental progress through a conventional linear program may not lend itself to the student's obtaining an overview or "strategy," which seems essential to successful problem solving. This may, however, be merely a limitation of existing programs; certainly programmed materials *can* be used to train component skills in a task analysis.

(c) Programmed instruction seems to be more successful with adults than with children. Certainly this technique has been very successful in industry where adults are strongly motivated to learn (thereby enhancing their vocational opportunities). School children, particularly in the early years, seem to require teacher approval as well as informational feedback on the adequacy of their response, and students at all levels tend to become disenchanted with programmed instruction if subjected to it for long intervals (Eigen, 1963; Frey and others, 1967; Porter, 1959; Randolph, 1965; Roth, 1963).

The research on program variables has been exceedingly complex and surprisingly little can be said for any particular format or any combination of task variables; consequently trying to achieve an adequate overall synthesis is virtually impossible. Certain results, however, can be cited for a particular variable, and these results can give some guidance to teachers who will examine characteristics of programs before utilizing them:

(a) *"Branching" versus linear procedures:* On purely theoretical grounds the branching program should be superior to the linear procedure, because it requires both that all learners devote selectively greater learning effort to those items they find more difficult and that less able learners, on the average, take more practice trials than more able learners in mastering a given unit of the material. More complex "branching" also takes into account the particular reasons or misconceptions underlying errors in each individual and endeavors to correct rather than to ignore them.

Although research evidence regarding this issue is far from being definitive, it certainly suggests that branching programs, requiring either simple repetition of incorrectly answered items or more differential corrective exercises, are not only more efficient in terms of learning time (Briggs, 1958; Coulson and Silberman, 1960), but also result in learning outcomes that are either equal to (Beane, 1962; Briggs, 1958; Coulson and Silberman, 1960a; and S. R. Meyer, 1960a; Silberman and others, 1961b) or better than (Coulson and others, 1962; Holland and Porter, 1961; Irion and Briggs, 1957) those of linear programs. The magnitude of the differences obtained, however, has typically not been very large. (See also Briggs, 1968.)

(b) *"Overtness" versus "covertness" of response:* Although it was initially postulated that overt responses (writing answers, marking correct alternatives, pushing appropriate buttons, and so on) would improve the learning performance over covert responses, analysis of the learning mechanisms involved reveals that any benefits accruing to overt responses should be expected in essentially rote learning tasks. Thus, as previously indicated, one should not be surprised that no benefits have been found to follow from overt responding in programmed instruction (which involves meaningful learning for the most part). In fact, the chief effect of overt responding seems to be an increase in learning time.

(c) *Constructed versus multiple-choice answers:* The rationale and research concerning these methods were reported earlier. In brief, while theory suggests that the multiple-choice format should lead to superior learning and retention of meaningful material, empirical studies have found no differences on these criteria between the two response modes when the student has worked through each program an equal number of times. However, the constucted mode does appear to be less efficient, in that a comparable level of learning is achieved with it only by a greater expenditure of time.

(d) *Immediacy of "feedback":* Although a central principle of programmed instruction is that the student should be told immediately by the program whether his answer is correct or incorrect, evidence cited in the previous chapter indicates that the benefits of immediate feedback are hard to demonstrate. It was argued there that one plausible explanation of the apparent lack of benefit from programs or machines providing immediate "external" reinforcement is that in meaningful learning the task itself is frequently so highly structured that immediate feedback is provided automatically.

(e) *Completeness and frequency of feedback:* While most programs provide 100 percent (every trial) "external" feedback, the arguments of the previous section (immediacy of feedback) predict that little difference in effectiveness will be found between such programs, and those providing feedback on a less frequent ratio, when structured or sequential material is involved. Such speculation is corroborated by experimental results (Krumboltz and Weisman, 1962b; Lambert and others, 1962).

(f) *Task size:* The fragmentation of learning into small bits is perhaps the chief characteristic of Skinner-type programs. While such an approach seems natural, if not unavoidable, for unstructured rote-type learning, arguments are advanced below which suggest that it has very little rationale for the highly structured material normally studied in school. Research on task size within the context of programmed instruction has been confined to the small task unit (or step size), format, and thus, because of the existence of counterbalancing factors cited earlier, has been generally inconclusive. Coulson and Silberman (1960) found a small-step program more effective than a large-step program in terms of scores on a criterial learning test, but less effective in terms of learning time. Other investigators either found no significant differences between the two types of programs (Briggs, 1958; Shay, 1961; W. Smith and Moore, 1962) or reported their findings in terms of the more equivocal criterion of error rate (Evans and others, 1960c).

The results of this research, though disappointing in that they discredit almost every thesis upon which the programmed instruction movement was founded, do have the merit of suggesting to the teacher that he should choose programs largely on the basis of evidence of performance (that is, learning outcomes produced with groups comparable to his own classes), rather than any particular philosophy or psychological system indicating what, in theory, should work.

Programmed Instruction as Optimal Programming

To what extent does programmed instruction represent optimal programming in the sense defined earlier? Our position is that some of the better prepared commercial programs may well represent near-optimum programming in limited subject areas comprising material that is relatively simple in logical structure. At the same time, most commercial programs seem to fall considerably short of what might be done when the principles of learning advanced in this text are utilized to full advantage.

Perhaps the crux of the matter lies in the fact that a relatively small task size is one of the characteristic features of the currently flourishing automated-instruction movement. As noted earlier, Skinner (1958) presented a strong case for the prevailing practice of using small task units in programming subject matter. By making learning easy and painless and guaranteeing success, this approach is supposed to enhance the learner's self-confidence and encourage him to persevere in his efforts. Furthermore, by insuring a low-error rate, it avoids the initial occurrence and hence the recurrence of misconceptions and wrong responses, maximizes positive reinforcement, and minimizes negative reinforcement. Lastly, it makes possible immediate confirmation, clarification, and correction, and practically guarantees that consolidation of prior material in the sequence occurs before new material is introduced. When larger task units are used, it is claimed, misconceptions cannot be corrected immediately after they arise, and there is no assurance that the learner will consolidate prior learnings before proceeding to later sections of the material.

Nevertheless, the small task-size approach in programming subject matter has many serious shortcomings. Although concerned with meaningful learning, it adopts a rote-learning strategy in handling the task-size variable; that is, it places major emphasis on the length-difficulty relationship, and ignores the logical structure of the material—both as a criterion of optimal task size and as a determinant of task difficulty in meaningful learning. In terms of both the logical requirements of meaningful-learning material and the actual size of the task that can be conveniently accommodated by the learner, the frame length typically used in Skinner-type programs is artificially and unnecessarily abbreviated. It tends to fragment the ideas presented in the program so that their interrelationships are obscured and their logical structure is destroyed. As Pressey (1962a) observes:

The student is shown this material one bit or frame at a time in the window of a mechanism or space of a programmed textbook. He cannot readily look back at what he has been over or ahead to sense what is to come, or discover any outline or structure in the material. . . . For effective reading, for general understanding of main ideas, and for adequate study and review, this procedure seems to be as clumsy as asking a person to apprehend a picture by letting him see, in a set order, only one square inch at a time. . . .

Study of a complex and structured subject seems better begun by an overview of reading matter to display the structure and order the complexity. A good book will show its structure in the table of contents and catalog its contents in the index; with such aids the learner can easily move about in its numbered pages with only the flick of à finger, using page headings and subheads in the text to guide him. He may turn back and forth from table or graph to rlated text, skip something already known, review selectively for major and difficult points. . . . Only after first contact with a complex structured topic should a student turn to auto-instruction for review and differentiation of major points in material. . . . The auto-instruction will then assure the student when he is right and identify and correct any misconceptions—as a good teacher or tutor might then do. Auto-instruction as an adjunct to the usual materials and methods of instruction would seem both more widely useful and more practicable than current efforts to replace textbooks and methods with radical initial programming (pp. 31–33).

Further, just because task size is small and error rate is low, one cannot warrantedly assume that the learning of sequentially presented ideas is necessarily rendered easy and successful, and that consolidation of existing material is therefore assured before new material is presented. In fact, the very fragmentation of content may serve to insure mastery of the component task units at the expense of understanding the logic of the larger segments of subject matter of which they are a part. Beane (1962), for example, programmed geometric proofs so that:

. . . most of the proofs involved less than seven steps but still required the student to keep in mind a sizable amount of information. . . . The steps of the program were small enough that the student could usually answer the next question regarding a particular step in a proof without difficulty. Evidence supporting this point of view is the relatively low error rate of approximately eight percent for the low ability students on the linear program. However, this does not mean that the student necessarily had a good grasp of the logical sequence or plan of the whole proof. This provides a real challenge to programmers of material concerned with involved, logical arguments. Insuring that the student can take the next step successfully in a program, by sufficiently granulating the material and then arranging it systematically, is no guarantee that he will understand the logical development involved. Also the student will not remember very well the facts he does learn if he fails to comprehend the logical structure and relationships of the concepts presented (p. 85).

That failure to appreciate logical structure and relationships *actually* affects meaningful learning and retention adversely is shown by the fact that criterial *posttests* often reveal relatively little residual learning and retention as a whole despite a very low error rate *while* each fragmented unit itself is being learned.

Finally, many of the advantages attributed to the small task-size format of teaching machines are not really inherent in small task size per se, but reflect small step size and careful sequential organization. Both of these latter procedures, of course, are perfectly compatible with the use of larger task units. While employing the larger task-unit format, one can also help insure consolidation of earlier presented material within the same task by using appropriate organizers, by increasing the lucidity of presentation, and by maximizing sequential organization and reducing step size between component sectors of the task unit.

In view of the preceding remarks, it seems a reasonable conclusion that whatever effectiveness automated instruction has been found to possess can be attributed to such factors as consolidation, lucidity, individualization, prompting, and confirmatory and corrective feedback. The important programming principle of sequentiality has not really been tested yet on a long-term basis. Since most programs (at least insofar as sub-units *within* a given learning task are concerned) do not presuppose a logical sequence of items such that each sub-unit is sequentially dependent on the preceding intratask sub-unit, it apparently makes little difference whether the frames are carefully sequenced or presented in random order (N. R. Hamilton, 1964; Levin and Baker, 1963; Roe and others, 1962). Also, apart from several short-term studies, the effects of both substantive aspects of programming as well as of such programmatic principles as progressive differentiation, integrative reconciliation, the use of organizers, spaced review, and attention to the internal logic of the instructional material, have not been investigated. Pressey's (1962a, 1962b, 1967b) adjunctive use of self-scoring devices makes possible only those beneficial effects on learning that follow from evaluation and feedback, and does not deal with the optimal organization and presentation of subject matter.

Uses of Programmed Instruction

The present inadequacy of programmed instruction must be balanced against the fact that optimal programming has not yet taken place. In some subject areas with simple logical structure current programs can be used for regular instruction with the expectation that they will yield learning at least equal to that of conventional instruction. In fields with more complex material the teacher will probably be better advised to organize the material as best he can under the circumstances.

Existing programs would seem to have many legitimate uses. In some instances a child will be absent from school because of illness and, missing key concepts, he will jeopardize his future progress in some subject area. If such children are unable to benefit from reading the standard large-step textbooks, they may well profit from a program which uses smaller steps and places less premium on sheer verbal comprehension. Similarly, the student who falls progressively behind in a sequentially organized field such as mathematics can be brought to the point where he can profit from current classroom instruction through self-instruction via programmed materials. Aside from their purely remedial uses, programs can be used as part of the normal instructional sequence in the elementary school to rapidly consolidate (by practice) such skills as spelling and arithmetical computation, and in the secondary school to review and clarify ideas presented initially by the teacher or textbook.[9] In such instances the fact that existing programs may deviate from the optimum seems of no great consequence in the light of benefits to be derived.

As an example of a legitimate use of programmed instruction, one Ontario school system customarily provided "remedial instruction" for students who had fallen behind in their acquisition of arithmetical skills to the extent that they could not legitimately be promoted to the secondary school. Teaching remedial arithmetic can be a frustrating and boring task for a teacher, governed as it is by the need for continuous, repetitive drill. In this experiment, the use of a specially prepared (Skinner-type) program *without any teacher assistance whatsover* produced results at least as good as those produced by regular (teacher) remedial instruction (Carbno and others, 1967). Here, then, programmed instruction provides an opportunity to free teachers for more creative and stimulating tasks.

Postscript: The Future of Automated Instruction

The reader should note that our criticisms and statements of caution have been carefully prefaced by the assertion that we were dealing with conventional format (linear) programmed instruction. At the present time much research and development is going forward on the use of computer-assisted instruction. To what extent the earlier criticisms will apply to these much more sophisticated programs cannot be answered until they become more widely available to classroom teachers. On the surface it would seem possible from a technological point of view for computer-assisted instruction to escape some of the obvious shortcomings of earlier programs. For example, there

---

[9]Encouraging results have also been reported for the use of programmed instruction with *retarded* (Stolurow, 1966; Malpass and others, 1965) and *deaf* (Roy and others, 1965; Beckmeyer, 1965) children.

seems no reason why a student could not be presented with a computerized program which utilizes advance organizers, in which the values of the pacing, step size, practice schedule, and feedback variables—determined on the basis of immediate past performance—are adapted to his individual abilities. In such a program the student could call for recapitulations in the form of prose passages, for audio-visual displays, elaboration of ideas at graded levels of abstractness, demonstration of strategies for solving classes of problems, or directions for locating further information or conducting experiments. Clearly such a program is far removed from the conventional small-step linear program.

While all of the positive features listed above—and undoubtedly many more—are technologically possible at the present time, it is not yet known how much is economically feasible or what new problems will arise in implementing such programs. Automated instruction is still in its infancy and the prospective teacher may expect to see it emerge with a new and important role during his teaching career (Gentile, 1967; Carter, 1967; Kristy, 1967).

Other Teaching Aids

Our considerable emphasis upon programmed instruction derives from its recent history, current popularity, and explicit psychological rationale. Other commonly used aids to the teacher in his instructional role include printed materials, laboratory experiments, educational television, and motion pictures. Each is discussed briefly in the following paragraphs.

Printed Materials For the routine transmission of subject-matter content, printed materials are undoubtedly the method of choice. Not only can a much greater quantity of material be presented in a given unit of time, but rate of presentation is also under the control of the learner. Thus, the latter can pace himself in accordance with his intelligence, reading skills, and subject-matter sophistication. He can also take as much time as he wishes to savor the language, to reflect on the material, and to relate it to other relevant ideas. The objective of increasing the speed of reading to the point that precludes these latter activities is educationally unsound. Contrary to general belief among teachers and students, N. E. James (1962) found that the use of a preferred method of learning meaningful material (for example, reading versus lecture) makes no difference whatever in learning outcomes.

The deficiencies frequently ascribed to textbooks are not really inherent in the medium per se, but reflect, rather, deficiencies that are common to all inadequately prepared instructional materials, such as lack of lucidity, ineffective communication, inappropriate level of sophistication, and absence of explanatory and integrative ideas. Relatively few textbooks have ever been written which take into account considerations such as progressive differentiation, integrative reconciliation, sequentiality of subject-matter content, and use of organizers. Although textbooks may contain some built-in adjunctive feedback and evaluative devices and can, to a limited extent, stimulate and guide the student's independent study, thinking, and problem-solving activities, further provisions along these lines must be made by the teacher. The latter is also responsible for such matters as differential practice, review, recitation and prompting, and for coordinating the textbook with lectures, discussion, laboratory work, other audio-visual aids, supplementary reading, and independent student projects (for example, essays, reports).

Laboratory   This medium of instruction implies more than direct contact with, and observation of, objects and events. As differentiated from demonstration and observation, it also involves discovery experience and concern with such aspects of the process of science as hypothesis-formation and testing, designing and conducting experiments, controlling and manipulating variables, and making inferences from data. The importance attached to such experience in contemporary science education is apparent in the N.S.T.A. Curriculum Committee's statement to the effect that:

> . . . a heavy emphasis should be placed on the nature of science or the *process* by which new knowledge is obtained. Instruction should be planned to develop understanding of the basic ideas of science concomitant with the appreciation of the methods of science; these two aspects should not be treated independently (N.S.T.A. Curriculum Committee, 1964, pp. 17–18).

The trouble with this statment, in our opinion, is that it is not sufficiently explicit. It emphasizes the role of the laboratory in teaching the process of science, and the importance of coordinating laboratory and expository instruction—and certainly they should not be treated independently. But *primary* responsibility for transmitting the content of science should be delegated to teacher and textbook, whereas primary responsibility for transmitting appreciation of scientific method should be delegated to the laboratory. It is understood, of course, that laboratory and classroom should be coordinated, and that related substantive and methodological principles should be considered together whenever relevant.

Yet science courses at all academic levels are traditionally organized so that students waste many valuable hours in the laboratory collecting and manipulating empirical data which, at the very best, help them rediscover or exemplify principles that the instructor could present verbally and demonstrate visually in a matter of minutes. Hence, although laboratory work can be invaluable in giving students some appreciation of the spirit and methods of scientific inquiry, and of promoting problem-solving, analytic, and generalizing ability, it is a very time-consuming and inefficient practice for routine purposes of teaching subject-matter content or illustrating principles when didactic exposition or simple demonstration are perfectly adequate. Knowledge of the methods whereby data and principles in a particular discipline are acquired also need not be gained always through self-discovery in the laboratory. In many instances, this purpose can be accomplished much more efficiently through didactic exposition in conjunction with demonstrations and exercises.

Laboratory work in this context refers to inductive discovery experience and should not be confused with demonstrations and simple exercises. Nevertheless, it involves a contrived type of discovery that is very different from the truly autonomous discovery activities of the research scholar and scientist. The immature or unsophisticated student is only confused by the natural complexities of raw, unselected, and unsystematized data. Before he can discover concepts and generalizations efficiently, the problem must be structured for him, and the available procedures and methods of handling data must be skillfully "arranged" by others (that is, simplified), and sequentially organized in such a way as to make ultimate discovery almost inevitable. Occasional independent design of experiments may have a salutary effect in conveying the actual spirit of scientific inquiry, but should hardly be a routine procedure.

Thus, in dividing the labor of scientific instruction, the laboratory should carry the burden of conveying the method and spirit of science, whereas the textbook and teacher should assume the burden of transmitting subject-matter content. The laboratory, however, should be carefully integrated with the textbook, that is, it should deal with methodology related to the subject matter of the course and not with experiments chosen solely because of their suitability for illustrating various strategies of discovery. It goes without saying, of course, that laboratory methods can be used only where the underlying methodology and substantive principles are thoroughly understood rather than followed mechanically in cookbook fashion (Ausubel, 1963).

Educational Television and Motion Pictures These self-contained instructional media have certain advantages over the conventional lecture. In the first place, the expository aspect of instruction is usually handled by a pedagogically more highly skilled and substantively better informed individual than the average classroom teacher. Second, these media can provide much vicarious experience that would otherwise be either totally unavailable or available only with great expense and difficulty, for example, close-ups of surgical operations, demonstrations of counseling and classroom teaching, descriptions of remote regions and complex events, historical pageants, demonstrations involving expensive equipment and special personnel. Third, through such techniques as animation, schematic diagrams and flow charts can be presented more effectively. Fourth, by means of videotape recordings one can preserve a complete record of student teacher or student physician performance for later feedback, critical analysis, and guidance where otherwise such records would be irretrievably lost. The absence of direct, "live" contact between instructors and students is not necessarily an insurmountable handicap, since at least some of the feedback, guidance, discussion, and evaluative aspects of instruction can be carried out by teachers in small groups preceding and following the audio-visual presentation.

A more serious limitation is the fact that educational television and motion pictures are typically intended for mass presentation. But this deficiency is not necessarily inherent in the media; most of the dimensions of instructional materials that can be geared to individual differences in learners can be suitably manipulated in educational television. This becomes possible by producing multiple versions of the same material and by providing for individual projectors that enable students both to adjust the speed of presentation and to repeat portions of the material.

On balance, therefore, it is hardly surprising that typical studies of the efficacy of these instructional media show that they are approximately as effective as conventional teaching methods in high school and college with respect to such criterial objectives as long-term retention, problem solving, ability to synthesize information, interest, and motivation (Siegel and Macomber, 1957). This is so, even though students generally prefer conventional media of instruction (Torkelson and Driscoll, 1968). As primary, self-contained sources of subject-matter material, however, they are undoubtedly less efficient than appropriately programmed textbooks. They are most useful as adjunctive devices for making available to students vicarious concrete-empirical experience that they could not otherwise obtain.

Resistance to the Use of Teaching Aids

There is good reason to believe that teachers in today's schools are not making as much use of teaching aids as the latter's potential would seem to warrent (Flory and others, 1967). It is still too frequently the case that the teacher's use of aids extends little beyond the blackboard and chalk. And while it has been difficult to prove by conventional tests that children learn substantially less than they would if better use were made of aids, it is reasonable to assume that such children miss the enriched experience which is possible only through the use of certain aids (for example, the immediacy of TV) but which is not measured in such tests. Moreover, there is always the possibility that at least the abler learners in traditional classrooms compensate for a relatively inefficient teaching strategy by greater effort.

To what may we attribute this apparent resistance to the use of teaching aids? In the first place, a certain degree of initial caution *was warranted,* not only because of the exaggerated claims of educational innovators, but because the early products tended to be rather shoddy in quality; certainly a teacher cannot be faulted for hesitating under these circumstances. Another factor which acts against the utilization of aids is a rigid administrative system in the school. It is obvious, for example, that the intelligent use of educational television requires scheduling of unusual flexibility, which some school administrators appear to be either unwilling or incapable of undertaking. Again, programmed instruction, and the individualization of instruction generally, can only be fully utilized in a system which allows something approaching continuous progress.

However, we must also recognize that teachers, like other human beings, develop patterns of behavior which appear to produce satisfactory results and which are not, therefore, readily changed. For example, small-step programs tend to be rather bulky and their handling makes considerable demand upon a teacher's logistical skill. In this connection it should be remembered that Pressey and his associates, after demonstrating many years ago that adjunct programming seemed to provide benefits beyond those obtained by standard teaching methods, did not continue with the development and utilization of this technique simply because its proper use involved too much effort (Pressey, 1960).

Perhaps another form of teacher resistance to innovation stems from the fact that such innovations are frequently heralded as presaging profound changes in the teacher's role. For example, it was argued that both educational television and programmed instruction could displace the teacher from his central role as the presenter of ideas and central source of information in the classroom. Accordingly, the teacher would then be freed to devote time to planning, conducting discussions, attending to individual needs, evaluating achievement, and guiding independent study, thinking, and problem solving. It is maintained, in other words, that the teacher is too valuable a person to spend his time giving routine lectures about relatively stable and fixed areas of knowledge (Ericksen, 1967; Novack, 1965). As admirable as this shift from information-provider to director of learning may be, we have to face the fact that many of our present teachers *like* to explain ideas and feel uncomfortable and threatened in more open-ended roles. It is to be hoped that new teachers, anticipating these developments in advance, will be more flexible in their approach and adjust to these seemingly inevitable new roles from the outset of their professional careers.

TOPICS FOR DISCUSSION AND FURTHER STUDY

1.* Investigate the research on the language laboratory. On what criteria has it been shown to be effective? What issues remain in doubt? (For current references see: Torkelson and Driscoll, 1968).

2.* Read Levonian's (1963) survey of studies attempting to produce attitude change through motion pictures. What particular techniques have been found successful? (See also: Winick, 1964; Auster, 1966.)

3.* A common argument advanced against the use of television for direct instruction is that it does not allow for immediate feedback to students. By consulting the research literature, investigate the validity of this assumption. (See: Johnson, 1962; Woodward, 1965; Gropper, 1967.)

4.* Investigate other viewpoints on the obstacles to widespread use of audiovisual aids. What power does the teacher have in facilitating their wider use? (See: Godfrey, 1965; Green, 1965; Miller, 1965.)

5.* It is commonly assumed that more learning will result if the instructor can engage more than one sensory channel simultaneously (that is, that a combined visual and sound presentation is better than a separate presentation of either, or that pictures added to complex verbal textual material enhance meaning). By consulting appropriate references, determine conditions under which such use of two or more channels is likely to be effective. (See: Conway, 1967; Severin, 1967; Travers and others, 1966.)

6.* While self-paced learning seems, on logical grounds, to have many benefits in dealing with individual differences, research has not always borne out this expectation (Gropper and Kress, 1965). What other factors might enter to affect the anticipated benefits?

7.* The question of the relative value of auditory as opposed to visual media for presenting information to the learner has long been a matter of speculation. By consulting research findings determine the age group, difficulty of material, and other circumstances for which each mode has shown to advantage. (See: Cooper and Gaeth, 1967; Rohwer and others, 1967.)

8.* A recent emphasis in the research literature on programmed instruction has been to investigate the interaction of student characteristics and learning outcomes under programmed instruction. Hypothesize the outcomes you would expect between:

    (a) IQ and performance
    (b) need for achievement and performance
    (c) anxiety and performance

(See references in Briggs, 1968.)

SUGGESTIONS FOR ADDITIONAL READING

Briggs, L. J. Learner variables and educational media. *Rev. educ. Res.,* 1968, *38* (2), 160–176.

Glaser, R. (Ed.) *Teaching machines and programmed learning II: Data and directions.* Washington, D.C. National Education Association, Department of Audio-Visual Instruction, 1965.

Lumsdaine, A. A. Instructions and media of instruction. *In Handbook of research on teaching* (N. L. Gage, Ed.). Skokie, Ill.: Rand McNally & Company, 1963, pp. 583–682.

Reid, J. C., and D. W. MacLennan. Research in instructional television and film. U.S. Office of Education Identification No. OE–34041. Washington, D.C.: Government Printing Office, 1967.

Torkelson, G. M., and J. P. Driscoll. Utilization and management of learning resources. *Rev. educ. Res.,* 1968, *38* (2), 129–159.

PART FOUR

AFFECTIVE AND SOCIAL VARIABLES IN LEARNING

We have now advanced a theory of learning which emphasizes the crucial role of existing ideas in the learner's cognitive structure. We have considered the important variables associated with such anchoring ideas (for example, their hierarchical organization, clarity, discriminability from new ideas) and examined how they operate in retention, transfer, and practice. Several applications were made, as for example the utilization of advance organizers to insure that potential anchoring ideas are activated in the learner's cognitive structure if they already exist, or are introduced into cognitive structure if they do not exist. We have also seen how the individual's capacity to comprehend ideas changes over a sequence of developmental stages in which he becomes progressively less dependent upon concrete props. Finally, we have considered how the material to be learned should be organized, presented, and practiced to take into account the previously mentioned cognitive structure and developmental variables.

The present section deals with two shortcomings of the theory as it has been developed thus far. In the first place, we have to acknowledge that the learner is not merely a *cognitive* entity; on the contrary, he exhibits *affective* or emotional states in his motivations, attitudes, personality, anxieties, intentions, and beliefs—all of which influence his learning in both direct and indirect ways. Thus, a first task of this section is to indicate basic differences in the mechanisms by which cognitive and affective variables, respectively, influence learning. In our treatment, affective variables are postulated to act primarily during the *initial learning* phase, at which point they serve a diffuse or non-specific *energizing* function which (under conditions to be specified) may facilitate the initial anchorage of a new idea and, therefore, strengthen its initial dissociability strength. Unlike cognitive variables then, affective variables do not continue to exert a direct influence during the *retention* phase itself, since they lack a mechanism for doing so. It is also hypothesized that if the affective state is too intense it may interfere with, rather than facilitate, initial learning, at least when complex or novel—as opposed to simple or routine—learning tasks are involved. Finally, while cognitive and affective variables have been separated for convenience of presentation, in practice these variables operate concurrently. A good example can be found in attitudes which, though usually thought to be largely affective in nature, seem more adequately conceptualized as a cluster of ideas coupled with attendant affective states. Such a conceptualization predicts that the cognitive component of attitudes (ideas in cognitive structure that can anchor new information about a subject) will be a potent, though hitherto ignored, factor determining in large measure what the individual actually learns about the subject.

The second limitation of the theory presented in previous sections is that it focuses on the *individual* cognitive structure, or considers the learner in isolation as it were. Yet we know that man is a social being and that his behavior is influenced by others, not only by those who are immediately present (for example, group learning influences) but more subtly—and perhaps more pervasively—by the norms, traditions, and attitudes of the social, ethnic, religious, and other groups to which he belongs. While group and social factors affect both the learner's cognitive and affective variables, their influence is most visible in the latter domain. Thus the student's overriding motivations toward school achievement, his attitudes, and his tendency to respond to novelty with flexibility or with stereotyped thinking—essentially affective behaviors which reflect prior social experience—may assume critical importance in the learning which actually takes place.

Many explanations have been advanced by personality theorists as to how social factors—particularly the early interaction between the parent and the child—eventuate in the particular affective states which an individual exhibits in later life. The theory advanced here postulates a critical point in early childhood (between the ages of two and three) at which the child's relationship with his parents exhibits one of two basic forms. The *satellizing* child is intrinsically valued (that is, valued for his own sake) by the parent, so that this child comes to acquire an essentially indestructible feeling of self-esteem which is independent of what he can accomplish on his own. The *nonsatellizing* child, on the other hand, is either rejected by his parents or valued extrinsically (that is, because of his potential to augment the parent's own ego) so that, not acquiring a feeling of intrinsic self-worth, he must *earn* self-esteem by his own accomplishments.

The subsequent influence of these early forms of identification can be traced through several contexts, and these links provide a thread of continuity through the chapters which follow. For example, in relating the satellizer/nonsatellizer distinction to school motivation, we can understand why the satellizer—whose basic self-esteem is *not* tied to independent accomplishment—is dominated in his early school years by the *affiliative* drive (that is, the need to please parents, teachers, and other individuals with whom the child identifies). The nonsatellizer, on the other hand, whose feelings of value *are* tied to independent accomplishment, is dominated by *ego-enhancement* drive (the striving to *earn* status through superior achievement). Because of his need for achievement the nonsatellizer typically exhibits relatively high levels of aspiration. Often these goals are unrealistically high, and thus lead to subjective feelings of failure. When this happens, the nonsatellizer has no intrinsic feeling of self-worth to fall back upon, and his self-esteem may be permanently damaged. The satellizer, even though he sets lower goals, may fail as well, of course; but although he may feel failure acutely, it will not impair the intrinsic feeling of self-worth which he acquired as a child.

We may next relate the satellizer/nonsatellizer distinction to anxiety, a fear-like state of considerable significance in education. The nonsatellizer who has suffered an impairment of self-esteem tends to be seized with acute fear whenever he is placed in a situation (for example, coping with difficult learning tasks) where further damage to his self-esteem could result. Such "neurotic" anxiety is always excessive in terms of the objective threat to self-esteem which is actually present, and flares up whenever the individual faces a complex or novel (potentially threatening) task in which routine or habitual responses will not lead to satisfactory performance. Satellizers, who are not as likely to have developed neurotic anxiety, may also exhibit a form of anxiety; however, this normal (or situational) anxiety *is* commensurate in magnitude with the threat to self-esteem which is actually present and is, moreover, less intense and less destructive to adequate performance.

The satellizer/nonsatellizer distinction, together with its previously mentioned correlates, allows further explanation and prediction. We would predict, for example, that different teacher personalities will be required to get the best from these two different types of personality structure. Thus, satellizing children, dominated in the early school years by affiliate drive, should respond best to a warm, sympathetic teacher (parent surrogate) with whom they can identify. Nonsatellizers, with strong ego-enchantment drives and a higher incidence of neurotic anxiety, would seem to require teachers who are nonthreatening and sufficiently orderly in their approach so that the channels to achievement, and therefore to status, are always clear to the child. Differential predictions can similarly be made for the behavior of satellizers and nonsatellizers in group-learning situations.

Finally, the satellizer/nonsatellizer distinction has an important developmental dimension. The primary motivations which we have described earlier relate to the first years of schooling. As the child approaches adolescence, however, greater cultural stress on earned status serves to weaken the affiliative drive in satellizers, and provides additional opportunities for self-enhancement for the nonsatellizer. Nevertheless, some residue of the early pattern of identification remains and helps to predict how well the individual will orient himself to the new situations and the conflict which will emerge at this crucial developmental juncture.

The following four chapters add ideational substance to the logical skeleton indicated in the previous paragraphs. To begin with, Chapter 12 (Motivation) examines the *motivational sequence* in which: (1) drives are activated, (2) drive-satisfying goals are sought, (3) goals are achieved, and (4) subsequent behavior is modified in some way. It then examines in detail the mechanisms underlying the operation of motivational (affective) variables, and identifies the principal drives inherent in school achievement. In addition to the "affective" and "ego-enhancement" drives previously encountered, "cognitive" drive—the desire to know or understand for the sake of knowing—is postulated as a potentially valuable (but presently underdeveloped) source of school motivation. The important phenomena of reward and punishment are discussed, and it is seen that their effects may either be *motivational* (in which the drives in operation when they are brought to bear may be either strengthened or weakened) or *cognitive* (in which they provide the learner with knowledge concerning the adequacy (correctness-incorrectness) of his response.

Chapter 13 deals with *personality* factors which are like motivational variables in that they involve primarily the affective domain (and so serve mainly a nonspecific energizing function in learning), and are *unlike* the latter variables in that they define *enduring* and *self-consistent* individual differences in learners. In probing the origins of long-term affective-social dispositions which are important in school learning, Chapter 13 describes the early *identification* process in some detail, and traces the chain of evidence linking this process to *level of aspiration* (that is, relative ambitiousness of goals), and to *normal* and *neurotic anxiety*. Since anxiety acts as a drive state, it can have beneficial effects—for example, when a normal individual anticipates failure and is thus activated to do something positive about it—or interfering effects—for example, when the high-anxiety student, facing a complex problem, reacts with nonadaptive or "face-saving" behavior.

Chapter 14 (Group and Social Factors) is not easily described since it deals with a variety of group and social factors impinging upon classroom performance and general motivation toward schooling. The important role which the adolescent peer group serves in providing a source of status, an agency for training, and a vehicle for desatellization is discussed at some length. The restrictive, anti-adult, and in some instances anti-school norms of this group, and its ability to coerce uniformity to these norms (through its ability to confer or remove status) poses problems both for educators and parents. This chapter also deals with group learning and with the use of competition—both of which have clearly describable advantages and disadvantages. Finally, racial factors in education and the problems of motivating culturally deprived children are discussed, and the somewhat paradoxical suggestion is made that the latter problem may be best tackled through the enhancement of cognitive drive.

This section closes (Chapter 15 — Teacher Variables)

with a discussion of the vast and mainly inconclusive literature on teacher variables which have been found to relate to student achievement. As anticipated, both "warmth" and "a businesslike manner" correlate positively with such criteria as high ratings by superiors and with student learning. In addition, a "stimulating" approach has been found to be effective, probably because it utilizes and enhances cognitive drive. Finally, one would hypothesize that the quality of orderliness also characterizes teachers who have few discipline problems.

The reader should keep in mind that in discussing such affective-laden content as intent, personality, and motivational states we must cope with concepts and theories which (generally) lack the precision possible in the cognitive domain. Moreover, since the possibilities for genuine experimentation in the affective domain are rather limited, one must rely more heavily upon correlational studies and clinical observations for the validation of one's hypotheses (typically, one cannot, for example, manipulate personality variables). It would be somewhat misleading, therefore, to present the theory introduced in these chapters as though it had the stamp of incontrovertible scientific truth upon it. Such "truth" is not possible in even the most tangible parts of social science theory; and in the affective-social domain reasoned plausibility is perhaps all that we can claim at the present time. We strongly believe, however, that the hypothetical links outlined below form a coherent and consistent set of ideas which will be useful to the teacher and which, while by no means completely documented, are supported by empirical data at many critical points.

CHAPTER 12

MOTIVATIONAL FACTORS
IN LEARNING

THE TERM "MOTIVATION" IS USUALLY FELT TO DESCRIBE the "second primary factor" in school achievement, its influence on learning rivaling that of ability. In the most general terms, the question posed by motivation is: what prompts human beings to behave in certain ways, or to pursue the goals they do? Such a question requires that we speculate on the mainsprings of human action, and thoughts on this subject are frequently fraught with romantic conceptions of what man is or what he should be. For example, one extreme view is that school learning should be motivated entirely by the desire to know, and that we should therefore not force children to learn anything they do not want to learn. A corollary is that all forms of negative motivational stimuli (for example, threat of failure) are to be avoided. While it is not our intent to incite controversy, nevertheless some of the commonly held views will be explicitly challenged in this chapter.

As it turns out, the majority of children present no serious motivational problem for the teacher: they want to learn, initially to please the teacher or their parents, and later to earn status, to ward off the threat of failure, or simply for the love of learning. The generally high level of motivation for school learning in evidence at the present time probably indicates that the economic and social values of education have become evident to parents and children in all strata of society. On the other hand, the teacher will most certainly encounter a minority of children who do not seem to exhibit the needs inherent in school motivation, and it is in understanding and attempting to cope with such children that a knowledge of motivational theory will be particularly useful. Our task in this chapter, therefore, will be to attempt to conceptualize motivation in terms of the theory previously offered, to discuss the variety and relative importance of different kinds of achievement

351

motivation, to indicate ways in which such related variables as intention, ego-involvement, and attitude influence learning, to discuss the role of reward and punishment, and to indicate ways in which motivation may be enhanced by the teacher.

THEORIES OF MOTIVATION

The Motivational Sequence

Discussions of motivation theory are hampered by a considerable difficulty in conceptualizing and describing the processes involved, and by wide variations in word usage and explanatory arguments. All motivation theories, however, postulate a temporally related sequence of events similar to that shown in Figure 12.1. The components in the sequence, as well as the varying emphases encountered in different theories, may be better understood by considering the parallel examples which follow:

(a) *Drive determinants* comprise needs and noxious or other stimuli which, in the early life of the organism, are related to its physical survival. A need is activated, for example, when an organism is temporarily deprived of food; the result of this particular deprivation would be represented by a change in blood chemistry and hormonal secretion. At a later stage, and more germane to school learning, a need to know and understand may be activated in the algebra student; what physiological mechanism (if any) is involved here will not be of great concern to the theory presented in later sections.

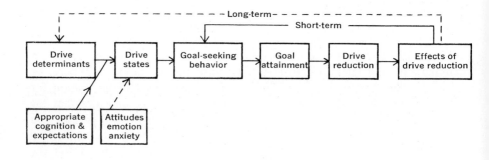

" ⟶ " means "leads to"
" – – → " means "enhances" or "augments"

FIGURE 12.1   *Time-related events in the motivational sequence.*

(b) *Drive states* result from the operation of a <u>drive determinant</u> <u>(need)</u>. The activation of this altered behavioral condition (drive state) enhances (energizes) learning activities that potentially satisfy the need in question. Thus food deprivation normally leads (unless the organism is otherwise distracted or asleep) to the subjective awareness which we term "hunger" and to the enhancement of hunger-satisfying behavior. Similarly, <u>the activation of "cognitive drive" (that is, a postulated need</u> <u>to know and understand)</u> will, under appropriate conditions, carry over into its corresponding drive state. Such <u>drive states</u> are considered to possess an intensity or strength which, in physiologically-oriented theories, is commonly referred to as <u>"drive level"</u> (or, currently, as <u>"arousal</u> level") and is either measured directly through physiological indices (for example, heart rate) or inferred from the intensity of a relevant drive determinant (for example, hours of food deprivation). The present theory also uses the term drive level for the strength of the drive state, but does not postulate a necessary link with any individual physiological process or group of processes (that is, it regards the drive state as a purely psychological phenomenon).

(c) *Goal-seeking behavior* follows the activation of a drive state; it involves the pursuit of goals or incentives[1] which are capable of satisfying or removing the original drive determinant. In our example the food-deprived organism seeks food, which is capable of satisfying the original need and reducing the intensity of the hunger state. Alternately, the student of algebra attempts to expand his present knowledge of that discipline or to solve some specific problem which it poses.

(d) *Goal attainment* is self-explanatory. The hungry infant locates his bottle, and the algebra student learns a new theorem or solves the problem.

(e) *Drive reduction* results from attainment of the goal. For example, eating the food or solving the problem tends to satisfy the underlying need and reduce (temporarily) the intensity of the drive.

(f) *Effects of drive reduction* are variously explained. Most forms of stimulus-response theory, derived from a consideration of cases similar to our hunger example, have emphasized the "reinforcement" value of drive reduction, that is, the increase in the probability of the occurrence of the response which led to such reduction. Thus if a hungry animal finds food at the end of a particular path in a maze, the satisfaction of his hunger will increase the probability that he will select this par-

---

[1] A distinction is usually made between the terms "goal" and "incentive," the former being defined from the learner's point of view as that thing, object, or state which he wishes to acquire (for example, to become proficient in algebra), while the latter refers to specific tangible need-satisfiers, usually applied or controlled by an external agent (for example, the marks, "stars," and praise of the teacher).

ticular path over alternate routes when he next finds himself hungry and in the maze.[2] The theory advanced here to deal with meaningful school learning, however, stresses the ability of drive reduction (that is, reward) to strengthen (on a long-term basis) the drive that is operative in instigating the behavior in question. Thus the student of algebra, having experienced success with a problem in that field will both experience an increase in his underlying cognitive drive and manifest an increased tendency to seek out algebra as a means of satisfying that drive.

We may now introduce some further terminological distinctions which will facilitate the discussion to follow. To begin with, the complete chain of events described above might be referred to as the *motivational sequence*. Second, when we say that an individual is motivated we mean simply that he exhibits goal-directed behavior. Third, for the sake of brevity, the term *drive* will refer either to drive determinants, drive states, or both. However, the precise meaning intended will be obvious from the context or will be otherwise noted. Finally, the term *motivational variable* will refer either to specific drive determinants (for example, postulated needs), or to such variables as attitudes, anxiety, or emotions, which are postulated to enhance drive states.

Some stages in the sequence are clearly observable, while others are based upon inference. Thus one can *observe* goal-seeking behavior, but one can only *infer* or postulate the existence of drive states. Again, while primary needs (for food, water, and so on) can be empirically demonstrated, many higher-level needs are inferred from observed human behavior.

Systems of Needs

In order for the motivational model to be of much benefit in the prediction and control of behavior it is necessary that we have some conception of the number and kind of "needs" which figure so prominently among drive determinants. Many such lists have been proposed, including those of Murray (1938) and Maslow (1948). Murray's list, although quite detailed, postulates no hierarchical order among the organisms needs. Maslow's system (Figure 12.2), on the other hand, assumes an order of primacy in that the individual will act to satisfy his physiological needs before his safety needs, his safety needs before his love and belonging needs, and so on, so

---

[2]As pointed out later, increased probability of response occurrence following drive reduction may be explained by a differential lowering of corresponding response and perceptual thresholds when the drive state is reactivated, and is found only in actual behavioral responses, perceptions, and rote learning. In more complex cognitive learning, no mechanism exists for reinforcement or lowering of the threshold of availability.

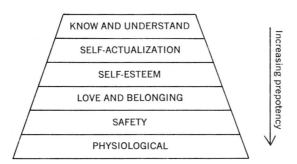

FIGURE 12.2 *Maslow's hierarchical need system. Adapted from: A. H. Maslow, "A theory of human motivation," Psychol. Rev., 50, 1943, 370–396. Copyright 1943 by the American Psychological Association, and reproduced by permission.*

that the "desire to know and understand" comes into play only after lower categories of needs have been satisfied. The plausibility of this hierarchy becomes apparent when one reflects that even highly task-oriented university professors tend to become somewhat crochety—and to be distracted from their more scholarly pursuits—when the lunch hour has passed and their need for food remains unsatisfied.

Since teachers are constantly exhorted to attend to the child's "needs, interests, and abilities," it is no doubt useful for teachers to be acquainted with these general need systems. If the hierarchy concept has any validity, such knowledge is important because a child in the classroom may be attempting to satisfy some prepotent need when the teacher is attempting to activate the desire to know and understand. Frequently a none too perceptive teacher will facilely designate such a child a "trouble-maker," the very label indicating a lack of understanding of motivational dynamics. At other times a frustrated teacher may lash out at a student who is not giving sufficient attention to the purposes of the lesson, and thereby unwittingly satisfy the student's stronger craving for the teacher's attention. In this case the student's strategy, having led to a tangible reward, may be expected to recur.

Although a case is made for the teacher possessing some conception of the overall domain of needs, it must be remembered that a variety of agencies exist to cater to most of them. In fact, now that most large school systems have specialists catering to the child's mental and physical health needs, the typical classroom teacher can probably feel justified in focusing his attention on needs related to *school achievement*. It is these particular needs, rather than the whole substructure of human motivation, which concern us in the remainder of this chapter.

Are Needs Learned?

It is clear that some needs are inborn and tend to appear in all societies and among various strata within the society. Various physiological needs constitute one such example. On the other hand, a child is not born with the need to achieve in school, so it is clear that he must learn this need in some way. Similar evidence on this point appears in the fact that there are large differences between the primary social motivations (for example, ego-enhancement drive) visible in different societies, and that even within a given society the discernible needs of individuals vary considerably, depending upon their experience.

To what extent, and by what process is an infant's initial set of essentially physiological needs converted into the complex and hierarchically organized needs system of the teenager? It has seemed reasonable to many psychologists to suppose that if the child's initial set of limited needs are the primary energizers of his behavior, then the learning of secondary needs must somehow be related to the satisfaction of these primary needs.

A common explanation of how the need for parental approval (associated with the affiliative drive) is developed in the child will provide some idea of the flavor of these arguments. A reinforcement theorist would probably argue that from the earliest ages the mother's approval and affection are associated with the satisfaction of primary needs, as when the mother fondles and beams at the child in the process of feeding him. According to this theory, the mother's approval comes, through its association with the primary reinforcement (food), to acquire the power of a *secondary* reinforcer. More than this, however, the same kind of motherly affection is associated with the process of elimination, the relief of gastric pain, and the act of sleeping. Through its association with a variety of primary reinforcements, the mother's affection and approval are said to acquire the status of *generalized* reinforcers.

Both secondary and generalized reinforcers possess the capability of reinforcing behavior not associated with primary needs although, as we might expect, the potency of the generalized reinforcer is considerably greater in this respect. Thus, the mother's approval can be subsequently used to reinforce the child's first attempt to walk, to imitate the speech of his parents, to engage in constructive play, and to become increasingly self-reliant. On the negative side, the real or threatened withdrawal of the mother's approval can be used to inhibit or eliminate unwanted forms of behavior, including overly strong dependence upon the mother and insufficient effort to achieve on one's own. In time, then, the child behaves as though he were actively seeking, or had a "need" for, his mother's approval, and the latter inferred need exhibits the same kind of drive-determining power as a primary need.

While such arguments may plausibly explain some of the derived needs, their extension to all inferred or observed human needs becomes cumbersome and tenuous. For example, a simple explanation of the origin of the affiliative drive can be advanced on the basis of identification. The latter view is consistent with the theory that new needs emerge frequently, and with little visible connection with the organism's initial physiological need structure, in the course of new experience and the development of personality. Thus it is argued that as the child's perceptual, motor, cognitive, and social abilities expand, he simultaneously develops needs to put these new abilities to work in such ways as explaining the environment and giving and receiving affection. It is assumed that these goals and activities arc pursued simply because they are usually found satisfying.

MOTIVATION IN SCHOOL SETTINGS

What is generally regarded as *achievement motivation* in school settings possesses at least three component drives. The first—centering around the need to know and understand, to master knowledge, and to formulate and solve problems—gives rise to what we will call *cognitive drive*.[3] Cognitive drive is completely *task-oriented* in the sense that the need for becoming involved in the task in question (as, for example, acquiring a particular segment of knowledge) is intrinsic to the task itself, that is, is simply the need to know. Hence the reward (the actual attainment of this knowledge) also inheres completely in the task itself and is capable of wholly satisfying the underlying need.

A second component of achievement motivation, however, is not task-oriented at all. The underlying need is for *ego-enhancement,* and school achievement may satisfy this need because such achievement leads to *primary* or earned status, which generates in the student feelings of adequacy and self-esteem. The ego-enhancement component of motivation is therefore directed both toward the attainment of current scholastic achievement or prestige and toward the future academic and career goals that depend upon the former. We shall see later that one of the principal ingredients of such motivation is *anxiety*—fear resulting from the anticipated loss of primary status (and self-esteem) that would follow from academic failure. Approval

---

[3]The cognitive, affiliative, and ego-enhancement "drives" discussed in this section (and throughout the chapter) are more precisely described as drive *determinants* than as drive *states.*

from teachers satisfies the ego-enhancement component of achievement motivation by constituting confirmation of achievement or by acting as a source of primary status.

The third component of achievement motivation is based upon the need for *affiliation* and is neither task-oriented nor primarily ego-enhancing. It is not oriented toward academic achievement as a source of primary status, but rather toward such achievement insofar as it assures the individual of the approval of a superordinate person or group with whom he identifies in a dependent sense, and from whose acceptance he acquires vicarious or *derived* status. The latter kind of status is not determined directly by the individual's own achievement level, but by the continuing intrinsic acceptance of him by the person with whom he identifies. And the person who enjoys derived status is motivated to obtain and retain the approval of the superordinate person—by meeting the latter's standards and expectations (including those for academic achievement)—since such approval tends to confirm his derived status.[4]

Relative Influence of Components of Achievement Motivation

At any point in time any or all of the three components of achievement motivation may be in play in a particular student's behavior. Obviously we would expect the relative strength of the components to vary from child to child at any time, and within a particular learner over an extended period of time. Generally speaking, affiliative drive is most prominent during childhood when children largely seek and enjoy a derived status based on dependent identification with, and intrinsic acceptance by, their parents. During this period they strive for academic achievement as one way of meeting their parents' expectations and, hence, of retaining the approval they desire. Actual or threatened withdrawal of approval for poor performance, therefore, motivates them to work harder to retain or regain this approval. Since teachers are partly regarded as parental surrogates, they are related to in similar fashion.

During late childhood and early adolescence, affiliative drive both diminishes in intensity and is redirected from parents toward age-mates. At this age, academic competition against the opposite sex or other age-grade classes can, under certain circumstances, constitute a powerful motivating factor (Maller, 1929; Sims, 1928). Desire for peer approval, however, may *depress* academic achievement when such achievement is negatively valued

---

[4]The relationship of the three postulated components of achievement motivation to Maslow's list of needs will be clear to the reader. Thus the cognitive drive component is related to the "desire to know and understand," ego-enhancement needs correspond roughly to "esteem needs," and the affiliative needs correspond to the "love and belonging needs."

by the peer group. This is a more common occurrence among lower-class and certain culturally deprived minority groups (Ausubel, 1965e). Middle-class peer groups, as pointed out later, generally place a high value on academic achievement and expect it from their members.

In most cultures, and particularly in western civilization, ego-enhancement drive is the dominant component of achievement motivation in adolescence and later life.[5] Traditionally, this has been especially true among males and middle-class groups in our culture. However, for a period after World War II, the drive for competence and earned status gave ground somewhat, in the United States and other countries, to the affiliative drive as epitomized by the character structure of the "organization man." At this point affability, social poise, and the ability to "get along," "play it safe," equivocate, conform, and "swim with the tide" tended somewhat to displace initiative, competence, individualism, and forthrightness as the dominant values in American society. Then, partly in response to the challenge emanating from spectacular Soviet achievements in science and technology, traditional American values staged a remarkable comeback during the 1960s. Indeed, some would argue that a new and emergent feature of this latter shift in cultural values has been an almost cult-like veneration of intellectual achievement and creativity.

The Advantages and Disadvantages of Ego-Enhancement Motivation

On the average, ego-enhancement motivation seems clearly the strongest motivation available during the active portion of an individual's academic and vocational career. More than any other factor, it accounts for the persistence of high levels of aspiration (Ausubel and Schiff, 1955; Ausubel and others, 1953a; P. S. Sears, 1940) and task attractiveness (Schpoont, 1955) both in laboratory and "real life" settings, despite exposure to repeated failure experience. Consistent with this, individual rivalry seems to stimulate academic performance more than does group rivalry (Maller, 1929; Sims, 1928); Ausubel (1951) found that gifted elementary-school children work much harder at an academic task in response to a prestige incentive than when they are merely "trying their best" and believe their work products are anonymous.

Thus, despite the tendency on the part of many educators to denigrate ego-enhancement motivation, the research evidence indicates that it is a

---

[5]With increasing age, material rewards are sought less as ends in themselves than as symbols of earned status, prestige, and ego-enhancement. Remote goals also become more salient as long-term ambitions displace the needs for immediate gratification, as the temporal dimensions of the child's psychological world expand, and as his frustration-tolerance increases.

potent factor in school learning. Certainly the need for ego-enhancement, status, and prestige through achievement, and the internalization of long-term vocational aspirations are traditional hallmarks of personality maturation in our culture. Educational aspirations and achievement are both necessary prerequisites for, and stepping stones to, their vocational counterparts. Consequently, in addition to encouraging intrinsic motivation for learning, it is also necessary, from the standpoint of personality maturation, to foster ego-enhancement and career-advancement motivations for academic achievement. Furthermore, since few individuals ever develop enough cognitive drive to master large bodies of subject matter as an end in itself, long-term ego-enhancement motivation is also necessary.

Common sense would indicate, however, that this type of motivation may be carried to excess with undesirable consequences. It has been shown, for example, that extreme ego-enhancement motivation may generate sufficient anxiety to disrupt learning (Ausubel and others, 1953a). It may also lead to highly unrealistic academic and vocational aspirations that are later followed either by catastrophic failure and collapse of self-esteem (Ausubel, 1956) or by disinvolvement from academic tasks as manifested by unrealistically low levels of aspiration (P. S. Sears, 1940). A related possibility is that excessively high needs for academic achievement may impair the student's capacity for perceiving his limitations, may predispose him to rationalize his failures, and may discourage him from acknowledging that his views are logically or empirically untenable.

Another disadvantage of exaggerated ego-enhancement motivation is that its utilitarian orientation limits its longevity. Thus a student whose academic motivation is primarily extrinsic tends to perceive little value in a subject after he passes a course—or in continuing to learn after he receives his degree—if such knowledge is unrelated either to future course work or to vocational success. In other words, he no longer evinces a desire to learn when he does not have to.

Cognitive Drive as a Component of School Achievement Motivation

Educators like to believe that cognitive drive is, or could become, the most potent kind of motivation in school learning. And certainly, because meaningful learning provides its own reward, cognitive drive plays a more important role in it than in rote or incidental learning. In fact, it is probably not too much to say that cognitive drive is *potentially* the *most important* kind of motivation in meaningful learning. However this potential importance is mitigated to a great extent in our utilitarian, competitive, and achievement-oriented culture in which such extrinsic considerations as ego-enhancement, anxiety reduction, and career advancement become—with increasing age—progressively more significant sources of motivation for school learning.

If a desire to learn and understand is almost invariably exercised in a context of competing for grades, obtaining degrees, preparing for a vocation, striving for advancement, and reducing the fear of academic and occupational failure, there is little warrant for believing that much of it survives as a goal in its own right. This trend is reflected in the progressive decline in school interests and intellectual enthusiasm as children move up the academic ladder (Jersild and Tasch, 1949). It is true, however, that some cognitive drive may be developed retroactively as a functionally autonomous by-product of successful learning, even though the intellectual activity in question was originally motivated by extrinsic considerations.

Hence, if we wish to develop cognitive drive so that it remains alive during the school years and adult life, it will be necessary to move still further away from the educational doctrine of gearing the curriculum to the current concerns and life-adjustment problems of pupils. Although it is undoubtedly unrealistic and even undesirable in our culture to eschew entirely the utilitarian, ego-enhancement, and anxiety-reduction motivations for learning, we must place increasingly greater emphasis on the value and pleasure of knowing and understanding as goals in their own right, quite apart from any practical benefits they may confer. Instead of denigrating subject-matter knowledge, as has been done so often in the past fifty years, we must discover more efficient methods of fostering the long-term acquisition of meaningful and useful bodies of knowledge, and of exploiting the potential inherent in such material for engaging the student's interest and intellectual abilities.

Enhancing Cognitive Drive through Cognitive Conflict The extent to which individual differences in cognitive drive are innate—based perhaps on genically determined brain properties (see next section)—or are acquired and shaped by experience, cannot be resolved with any greater finality than any other aspect of the nature-nurture controversy. In all such questions, the most appropriate stance for the teacher would seem to be that of respecting genic differences, and yet believing that an appropriate educational environment can produce change which is quite startling in terms of conventional standards and expectations.

An instructional strategy for enhancing cognitive drive (at least in the short run) can be derived from the theory presented in earlier chapters. There it was argued that in the normal process of meaningful learning new concepts and generalizations are introduced into cognitive structure and subsumed (as derivatives or correlatives) under more inclusive ideas. However, when a new idea can (ostensibly) be anchored under two conflicting propositions, or when an idea already anchored to proposition A appears to be anchorable to a converse proposition (not A), the learner finds himself in a state of conflict, doubt, or uncertainty. Generally speaking, the learner will find such "cognitive conflict" annoying, and so will be motivated to seek some way of resolving the conflict;[6] this might be done, for example, by locating a higher-level idea than presently exists in cognitive structure (of which A and not-A may be seen to be special cases, valid under specified circumstances), or by obtaining further evidence to indicate that the ostensibly correlative relationship of the new or existing idea to one of the opposed alternative anchors is not valid.

---

1. It is known by prior learning, or by perception of collections of objects, that 2 and 3 are *not equal*, yet reason indicates that:

$$2 - 2 = 3 - 3,$$
$$\text{so that } 2(1 - 1) = 3(1 - 1),$$
$$\text{so that } \qquad 2 = 3$$

2. It is obvious either perceptually or on the basis of simple matching operations that *the number of elements in a set of objects must be greater than the number of elements in any of its subsets.*

Yet: Consider the set I of integers (1, 2, 3, 4, . . .) and the subset S consisting of the squares of integers (1, 4, 9, 16 . . .)

Every element in I can be paired with an element of S as follows

I: 1. 2, 3, 4, 5, ...
S: 1, 4, 9, 16, 25, ...

Therefore *the number of elements in the subset equals the number of elements in the set.*

FIGURE 12.3 *Examples of conceptual conflict. In both instances there is a conflict between what one believes on the basis of prior learning and the conclusion to which one is apparently led by reasoning. This conflict engenders a tendency to find additional information or a plausible explanation. In the first case the explanation is that the conclusion is erroneously arrived at by cancelling a factor of 0 from both sides of the equation; in the second case the conflict is resolved by appreciating that the inequality between whole and part does not always possess meaning when applied to sets which have an infinite number of elements. (Examples provided by S. M. Avital.)*

---

[6]Other ideas which closely parallel the notion of cognitive conflict include Festinger's (1958) cognitive *dissonance,* Piaget's (1950) *accommodation* of existing schemata, and Berlyne's (1960) conceptual conflict. In addition, a number of drives related to intrinsic motivation have been postulated during the past fifteen years including *curiosity* (Berlyne, 1960), *exploration* (Montgomery, 1954), *activity* (W. F. Hill, 1956), *manipulation* (Harlow, 1950; Terrell, 1959), mastery or *competence* (White, 1959), and the *need for stimulation* (Butler, 1954).

In Figure 12.3, we show examples illustrating how the teacher might *deliberately* introduce conceptual conflict to motivate the student to expand his ideational structure. Thus, in the first example, the student already comprehends the proposition that $n + 1 > n$. However, proceeding by rules which are also comprehended (for example, subtraction, division, cancelling a common factor) a conclusion is reached which is both a correlative of the initial correct statement (that is, $3 - 3 = 2 - 2$) and a contradiction of the general proposition ($n + 1 > n$). The resolution of the conflict comes by comprehending the proposition that "division by zero is not permissible," which can be understood as a superordinate proposition dealing with the concept of division, the concept of zero, or both.

As indicated above, the use of cognitive conflict may be a promising device for inducing *short-term* cognitive drive, particularly where such drive (or other school-achievement drives) are lacking. When the student is already motivated, however, the use of expository teaching—which utilizes *conflict-reducing* organizers—would generally seem to be more efficient in terms of learning per unit of instructional time. Here, as elsewhere, the teacher must find a balance appropriate to his particular class and to individual students within the class. It should be remembered that, in the long term, cognitive drives come to reflect more clearly the influence of prior successful learning. While the mature mathematician thus exhibits a strong desire to know, understand, and solve problems in his own field, other intellectual activities may not satisfy his cognitive drive. As indicated later, such specialization and intensification of drives seems most plausibly accounted for by prior learning successes.

Does Cognitive Drive Have an Innate Physiological Basis? In recent years there has been an attempt to link cognitive drive to innate curiosity tendencies and to relate the latter to basic physiological processes in the brain. In Berlyne's theory (1960), for example,[7] it is assumed that there is an optimum level of "arousal"—a measure of brain excitation and a concomitant of drive states—and that the human organism will act in such a way as to maintain this optimal level. Thus, if the arousal level is too low the organism will attempt to raise it, perhaps by seeking raw stimulation (as in the apparently "unmotivated" exploration or manipulation of the environment). If the arousal level is too high, however, the organism will attempt to reduce it. One important class of arousal-generating situations are those in which the individual is faced by a conflict.[8] Such conflicts may exist either

---

[7] Related viewpoints can be found in the following sources: Dembar and Earl (1957); Fiske and Maddi (1961); Glanzer (1958); Hebb (1955).

[8] The "conflict" in question is between competing tendencies to respond to a stimulus situation in a particular way. In Berlyne's theory, the competing responses are usually "symbolic," that is, they are implicit rather than overt, and frequently represent some fractional part of an overt response (such as adjusting the sense receptors or performing an ordering operation on a collection of physical objects).

at the perceptual or the conceptual level, or there may be a conflict between a perception and what one knows (or expects) on the basis of one's previous knowledge. An instance of the latter would occur when the process of logical reasoning leads to a conclusion which contradicts an immediately available (perceptual) datum.

The previously discussed examples (shown in Figure 12.3) may be reinterpreted from a conceptual conflict viewpoint. Thus it is hypothesized that the learner, faced with such an arousal-generating stimulus situation, will exhibit "curiosity," which will in turn generate a tendency to obtain more information about the situation so that the conflict can be resolved and the arousal-level reduced to its optimum level. As indicated earlier, it seems clear that the master teacher relies more or less intuitively on a variety of conflict-generating situations to catch the attention and interest of his students when appropriate drive states are not already in evidence.[9]

Although some primitive physiological process may underlie the intrinsic motivation aroused by a particular learning task, such processes would seem to be specific in content and direction and do not, therefore, readily explain why some individuals are motivated to solve one kind of intellectual problem, other individuals a different kind of problem, and still other individuals manifest little cognitive drive at all. We might, of course, assume that there exist different innate predispositions in respect to optimum levels of arousal, or preferences for a certain type of arousal-generating stimulus situation. Even so, it would seem that one can only account for the highly specific yet stable cognitive drives among mature adults on the basis of previous experience. In sum, then, while physiologically oriented theories of conceptual conflict have a natural appeal, and may in time explain aspects of motivation which are now poorly understood, at present their pedagogical implications seem less specific and comprehensive than those derived more parsimoniously from a theory of meaningful learning.

HOW MOTIVATIONAL VARIABLES INFLUENCE LEARNING AND RETENTION

We have previously described motivational variables as constituting either drive determinants or factors such as emotion, anxiety, or attitude which enhance drive states. We now ask how motivational variables actually influence meaningful learning and retention and how this influence differs from that of the cognitive variables considered in previous chapters.

---

[9]While the detailed application of this theory to educational practice remains to be worked out, some interesting suggestions can be found in the following references: Berlyne, 1954b, 1965a, 1966; Caron, 1963.

For illustrative purposes we refer again the student who is learning a history passage on the causes of the American Revolution. Previously we saw that the important factors in the learning and retention of the new ideas in this passage were such cognitive variables as the clarity, stability, and discriminability of existing ideas in cognitive structure. We argued further that these variables not only determined the dissociability strength immediately after learning but that they continued to act during the retention phase to maintain this dissociability strength above the threshold of recall, thus making the new idea retrievable from memory. In brief then, cognitive variables influenced directly the very conditions determining the interaction between new learning material and existing cognitive structure during both the learning and retention phases. As we shall see, motivational variables are unlike these critical cognitive variables in that they act primarily during the initial learning phase, during which they serve a nonspecific energizing function.

Effect on Initial Learning

Motivational variables are not *directly* involved in the interaction process which characterizes the initial learning phase. Rather, they *energize* and expedite this process by enhancing effort, attention, persistence and immediate readiness, without affecting any of the basic cognitive variables (for example, the availability of relevant appropriate subsumers; the latter's stability, clarity, and discriminability from the learning task). In other words, when our history student relates the ideas in the learning passage to his cognitive structure, the drive states involved in his motivation to learn do not strengthen the dissociability strength of any *particular* idea in the passage, but act more like a catalyst on the learning of the whole passage, resulting in an indirect, nonspecific, overall increase in the dissociability strength for *all* the ideas contained in it.

At a finer level of analysis one can discern the separate effects of motivational variables in the enhancement of effort, attention, persistence, and immediate readiness for learning. For example, through such motivational effects as mobilization of effort and persistence, more repetitions of the material can be completed within a stipulated learning time, and each repetition will be conducted more efficiently. Again, the enhancement of attention will result in a larger acquisition of information per unit of learning time. Finally, in mobilizing the individual's immediate readiness for learning, motivation lowers the thresholds of those general kinds of perceptions and responses that are customarily implicated in the learning process. Exemplifying this latter mechanism is the lowering of reaction times that occurs in response to instructions to "work faster" (Owens, 1959), as opposed to task-oriented instructions or instructions to relax.

A good deal of evidence is available concerning the general energizing effect of motivation on learning. For example, Feather (1961) found that subjects who have high needs for achievement are more persistent, and Kight and Sassenrath (1966) found that such students learn more effectively. Persistence in task performance has also been found to be related to strength of cognitive drive (Kohn, 1965) and to the relative incentive value of the task (Nakamura and Boroczi, 1965). On a long-term basis, high-achievement motivation tends to be associated with greater academic achievement (Krug, 1959; Uhlinger and Stephens, 1960) and measures of such motivation, when used in conjunction with measures of academic aptitude, are excellent predictors of college performance (Weiss and others, 1959).

An investigation by French and Thomas (1958) indicates the kind of results frequently obtained. In this study a selected group of highly intelligent subjects was divided into two groups on the basis of their "need for achievement" scores.[10] When presented with a difficult intellectual problem, the members of the high *n*-achievement group worked about twice as long at it before giving up, and a much larger proportion of them were successful in arriving at a solution. The experimenters also found that the motivational factor was a better predictor of success than was an ability measure.

Influence of Motivation on Retention and Reproduction

Once new ideas have been presented to cognitive structure and the interactional products formed, no channel exists for the further influence of motivational variables on dissociability strength itself. Whatever *direct* influence motivational factors have on the *retention* and *reproductive* phases must result, therefore, from their effect in either raising or lowering particular thresholds of recognition and recall. Both theoretical considerations (Ausubel, 1968) and the weight of the available evidence suggest that

---

[10]The "need for achievement" (or *n*-achievement) score purports to measure a generalized trait of achievement motivation and is derived from an unstructured test in which the subject invents a story to describe what he thinks is about to happen in various pictures representing human interaction. While *n*-achievement has been found to correlate significantly with school performance (Caron, 1963; Feather, 1961; French and Thomas, 1958; Kight and Sassenrath, 1966; Todd and others, 1962; Uhlinger and Stephens, 1960; Weiss and others, 1959), this measure apparently lacks long-term stability (Birney, 1959). Moreover, there is the problem that fantasy measures of achievement motivation may not necessarily reflect accurately "real life" levels of achievement motivation (Scanzoni, 1967). While research with this measure continues (for example, Caplehorn and Sutton, 1965; Schmiedler and others, 1965; Weiner, 1965, 1966a), a recent review (Shaw, 1967) indicates growing dissatisfaction and a tendency to search for complex measures of motivation, for example, the "motivation-hygiene" concept (Haywood and Wachs, 1966).

motivational factors influence meaningful retention selectively by inhibiting (*raising*) rather than facilitating (*lowering*) both of these thresholds. Thus positive ego involvement and favorable attitudinal bias do *not* increase retention by *lowering* thresholds of availability, but strong motivation to forget and certain kinds of attitudinal bias (e.g., in ego-threatening or anxiety-producing situations) may selectively promote forgetting by *raising* thresholds of availability (repression). Therefore, unlike the situation in learning, not only is the direct selective influence of motivational variables on meaningful retention inhibitory rather than facilitating (catalytic), but the influence of these variables is also mediated solely through a change in thresholds of elicitation, without any change whatsoever in dissociability strength itself. Consequently, since the recall of ego-threatening or anxiety-producing information would be relatively infrequent in typical classroom situations involving meaningful learning, it would appear that the effect of motivation on the retention phase would not be a predominant consideration in school learning.[11]

Motivational factors can have two other effects during the retention and reproduction phases. In the first place, it is theoretically conceivable that motivation (for example, strong incentive to recall) could *indirectly* lower thresholds of availability by counteracting or disinhibiting certain inhibitory factors (for example, distraction, inattention, inertia, disinclination toward effort) that temporarily raise such thresholds. Relevant to this point, we have already observed how various inhibitory conditions such as initial learning shock and the competition of alternative memories tend to dissipate spontaneously, and how hypnosis can reduce the inhibitory effect both of competing memories and of motives and attitudes promoting repression, as in the case of anxiety-producing material. Second, as Bartlett (1932) points out, motivational variables are probably also involved in the reconstructive aspects of the reproductive phase of memory, that is, in making a selection from among the available remembered items and in organizing them into a coherent, verbal response to meet the demands of the current situation.[12]

---

[11]The situation with respect to rote learning seems much more complex. As in meaningful learning, negative motivational factors could certainly raise the threshold of elicitation for particular stimulus-response units, so that when such factors are operating a higher associative strength would be required for recall. On the other hand, it can be argued (Ausubel, 1968) that motivational factors can also *enhance retention* in rote learning, not by lowering thresholds directly, but by sensitizing them to later reduction by particular drives. Thus, it is postulated that if a particular response (e.g., seeking food in a particular location) has been instrumental in procuring an incentive which satisfies the underlying need (for food), the threshold for the elicitation of this response will be differentially lowered when the drive next becomes operative.

[12]A recent compilation of research on the effects of motivation on retention can be found in B. Weiner, 1966b.

Effect of Intention on Learning and Retention

Intention to learn can be regarded as a manifestation of a motivational state; it indicates a striving toward a particular goal, where such striving is either self-directed or results from explicit instructions. As in the case of motivation generally, one may learn something without a specific intention to do so. The reader of this chapter probably intends to find out as much as possible about motivation for school learning (possibly as a result of the explicit direction of his instructor), but he may also learn something incidentally about the authors' writing style.

As might be expected, however, many experiments have shown that deliberate learning in response to explicit instruction is both more effective (Bromer, 1942; Huang, 1944; G. C. Myers, 1913; H. B. Reed, 1946) and is more precise and specific (Postman and Senders, 1946) than is unintentional or implicitly instructed learning. These results are not difficult to understand in view of the previously discussed energizing and expediting effects of motivational states on learning.

A more interesting question is whether intention facilitates retention itself (as well as learning) or whether the observed effects on later retention can be explained by assuming that intention to learn leads to greater initial learning, and that it is this greater initial learning which explains enhanced recall. Most of the experiments showing greater recall when the subject is given an expectation that he will be asked to recall the material (Biel and Force, 1943; Geyer, 1930; Thisted and Remmers, 1932; Lester, 1932) have provided the expectation in advance of the initial learning. Consequently all of the superior retention in these studies could be plausibly attributed to the energizing effects of the intention on learning, without assuming that it had any independent influence on retention.

To test this latter interpretation, Ausubel and others (1957b) conducted an experiment in which undergraduate students learned an extended historical passage, and were then tested on it immediately afterward. *After* this test, an explicit intention to remember was induced by announcing that an equivalent form of the test would be given two weeks later. A similar procedure was followed with a control group except that an unannounced retest was administered. The two groups were not significantly different in mean learning scores or in the percentage of material retained from test to retest. It was concluded, therefore, that intention to remember in the previously reported studies primarily facilitated retention by enhancing learning rather than by virtue of an effect on the retention process itself. These results are, of course, consistent with the general thesis that motivational variables act primarily on the initial learning of meaningful material.

Effect of Attitudes on Learning and Retention

An attitude might be defined as a predisposition to make positive or negative evaluations about people, events, and objects. The structure of an attitude is characterized by a complex of ideas together with various affective or feeling components. As a result of these affective states, individuals possessing the attitude will be disposed (motivated) either to seek out or to avoid the object of the attitude.[13] Thus a child in school may have a negative attitude toward arithmetic, in which case we may think of him as either not motivated to learn it (the affective component may be fear, dislike or boredom) or motivated to escape from this particular learning situation.

The educator has two concerns in connection with attitudes. In the first place, schools have an obligation to assist in transmitting to pupils the major attitudes and values of our society, including those (such as the social equality of persons irrespective of race, religion, and ethnic origin) that are honored more in theory than in practice. The educator's second concern, and the focus of the present section, is the effect of attitudes on the learning of the substantive bodies of knowledge which the school is expected to transmit. Fortunately the student initially brings either neutral or positive attitudes to the learning of most school subjects, and such negative attitudes as may develop probably result from his subsequent experiences.

However there does occur the case in which the student brings negative or inhibiting attitudes into the learning situation. Such instances occur most frequently in the teaching of controversial material, as for example, different accounts of the causes of important historical developments, or examination of data on interracial differences in intellectual capacity, or the treatment of most topics touching upon religious or political beliefs. In these instances the teacher must take attitudinal bias into account in attempting to have new ideas understood and retained.

Effect on Initial Learning Little doubt exists that the learner's attitudinal structure differentially enhances or inhibits the *learning* of controversial materials that are congruent and incongruent, respective, with it. For example, A. L. Edwards (1941), Levine and Murphy (1943), and Zillig (1928) demonstrated that controversial materials are learned most readily when they are consistent rather than inconsistent with the subject's evaluative framework.

Since attitudes have both cognitive and affective components, we would expect both to be operative in new learning. When the affective components

---

[13]Since the affective component of attitude contributes to drive states, the former may be thought of as belonging to the class of drive determinants.

of attitudes toward controversial material are positive, subjects are highly motivated to learn. They thus put forth much more intense and concentrated effort, and relevant perceptual, cognitive, and response thresholds are generally lowered. In addition, a strong need to reduce conflict between ideas—operating either as a generalized personality trait or as an aspect of cognitive style, or more specifically in relation to a particular set of strongly-held beliefs—may lead to a closed-minded attitude that obviously impairs ability to learn new ideas contrary to existing beliefs. A person who summarily dismisses new ideas on this basis fails to learn them adequately because he may not even be willing to read or listen to them, because he makes little or no effort to reconcile them with existing beliefs, or because he selectively misunderstands, distorts, discounts, or reverses their implications in accordance with his own bias. It is clear, then that the affective component of attitude leads to particular positive or negative motivations with respect to learning and that these motivational effects influence initial learning either positively or negatively.

While these motivational factors have long been known and postulated to be the primary variables in the influence of attitudes on learning, the relative potency of the *cognitive* component of attitude has been recognized only more recently (Peak, 1955). According to this view, the person who is favorably disposed (that is, has a positive attitude) toward a new idea is more likely to have a well-established cognitive component of this attitude possessing clear, stable, and relevant anchoring ideas for incorporating the new idea. On the other hand, for the person learning "other side" arguments, the conceptual schema constituting the cognitive dimension of attitudes is usually devoid of relevant anchoring ideas to which the new material can be functionally related. In this case, the new material cannot be readily anchored to cognitive structure, competes with existing meanings, and is consequently ambiguous and subject to rapid forgetting.

In the studies mentioned previously (A. L. Edwards, 1941; Levine and Murphy, 1943; Zillig, 1928), despite the fact that selective learning was attributed solely to affective mechanisms, no attempt was made to differentiate between the respective effects of the cognitive and affective components of attitude structure. However, Fitzgerald and Ausubel (1963) conducted a classroom experiment involving the ability of central Illinois high-school students to learn the Southern point of view about the Civil War, in which the effect of cognitive factors (knowledge about the Civil War period) was statistically eliminated. The learning difference attributable to *affective* factors or to attitudinal bias per se under these conditions (Table 12.1, first column) was in the predicted direction (that is, in favor of the relatively pro-Southern or positively biased group) but was not statistically significant. In the same study, two additional findings pointed to the influence of *cognitive variables* on learning outcomes. Not only did cognitive organizers

TABLE 12.1

Effects of Attitudinal Bias on Learning and Retention

ATTITUDE GROUP	GROUP A TESTED FOR INITIAL LEARNING (MEAN SCORES)*	GROUP B TESTED FOR RECALL (MEAN SCORES)*	DIFFERENCE BETWEEN GROUP MEANS
Pro-Southern	27.1	19.8	7.3
Neutral	25.9	17.6	8.3
Pro-Northern	25.1	16.4	8.7

*Means corrected for prior relevant knowledge.
Source: D. Fitzgerald and D. P. Ausubel, "Cognitive versus affective factors in the learning and retention of controversial material," *J. educ. Psychol., 54,* 1963, 73–84. Copyright 1963 by the American Psychological Association, and reproduced by permission.

facilitate the learning of the controversial material, but the more knowledgeable subjects—irrespective of attitudinal bias—were also better able to learn the material, presumably because they found it more discriminable from previously learned related ideas than did the less knowledgeable subjects.

Further evidence concerning the role of cognitive factors and the effect of attitude structure on learning comes from Jones and Kohler's (1958) studies of the interaction between attitudinal bias and plausibility in their effects on learning. These investigators found that prosegregation subjects learned plausible prosegregation and implausible antisegregation statements better than they learned implausible prosegregation and plausible antisegregation statements. The reverse was true of antisegregation subjects. Evidently, plausibility enhanced the learning of the position favored by a particular subject and inhibited the learning of the position he opposed. These latter results must be viewed with some caution, however, since a number of replication studies (Waly and Cook, 1966) failed to confirm the earlier findings.

Effect on Retention As we have seen, attitudes have both cognitive and affective (and derived motivational) components. In line with previous discussions we would expect both the cognitive and motivational components to affect initial learning, but only the cognitive component to have a direct impact on the retention phase. And as in the case of previously cited studies on the effect of intention on retention, investigations of attitude which merely measure recall (Alper and Korchin, 1952; Clark, 1940; Watson and Hartmann, 1939) would not distinguish effects upon initial learning from effects on the retention process itself. However some studies (A. L. Edwards, 1941; Levine and Murphy, 1943; Taft, 1954) in which retention was measured

TABLE 12.2

EFFECTS OF THE COMBINED INFLUENCE OF ATTITUDINAL BIAS
AND PRIOR RELEVANT KNOWLEDGE
ON LEARNING AND RETENTION

ATTITUDE GROUP	GROUP A TESTED FOR INITIAL LEARNING (MEAN SCORES)*	GROUP B TESTED FOR RECALL (MEAN SCORES)*	DIFFERENCE BETWEEN GROUP MEANS
Pro-Southern	27.5	20.9	6.6
Neutral	25.8	16.8	9.0
Pro-Northern	26.6	14.5	12.1

*Means corrected for verbal ability.
Source: D. Fitzgerald and D. P. Ausubel, "Cognitive versus affective factors in the learn-ing and retention of controversial material," *J. educ. Psychol., 54,* 1963, 73–84. Copy-right 1963 by the American Psychological Association, and reproduced by permission.

both immediately after learning and at subsequent intervals thereafter found that the original differences in learning tended to widen progressively during the course of the retention interval.

Although such studies suggest that attitude structure exerts a facilitating effect on retention, independent of its effect on initial learning, they do not separate or provide any estimate of the relative contributions of the cognitive and motivational components in the retention phase. The hypothesis that the effects of attitudinal bias on the retention phase can be attributed largely to the *cognitive* component of attitude was tested in the previously cited experi-ment by Fitzgerald and Ausubel. The relative effects of the affective and cognitive components may be seen by comparing Tables 12.1 and 12.2. In Table 12.1, when the cognitive variable (relevant background information) is controlled, differential rates of forgetting—which can be attributed to the affective component of attitude—are small, though in the anticipated direc-tion. On the other hand, when the cognitive component is not controlled (Table 12.2), differential rates of forgetting—now attributable mainly to the cognitive component—are very noticeable. The interpretation of the result, then, is that it is the possession of suitable anchoring ideas during the retention phase rather than attitudinal bias per se (that is, the affective component of attitude) which is the significant factor in retention.

Drive Level and Performance

Since drive states act upon initial learning by energizing the process of incorporating new ideas into cognitive structure, one may ask what level (strength) of drive best facilitates this process. The answer is reasonably complex since it depends upon the complexity of the task to be learned.

To begin with, it seems clear that learning can take place in the absence of any identifiable drive state relative to the learning task at hand. For example, in the course of taking the subway to the university campus, the reader—specifically motivated to attend a lecture—will learn a good deal incidentally about the dress and manners of early morning travellers, the operation of trains, and the general geography of the city. In other words, there is some sense in the assertion that learning can take place in the absence of task-specific motivation, although one can never be sure whether or not other drive determinants (for example, the "need for stimulation" component of cognitive drive) are in play.

It is obvious, of course, that the operation of specific drive states will provide more efficient learning[14] because of the enhancement of such previously discussed factors as attention, persistence, and immediate readiness, and that the classroom teacher will attempt to utilize such drive states wherever possible. Nevertheless the fact that learning can take place incidentally has the important pedagogical implication that the teacher need not always wait for appropriate interest and motivations to develop. When other methods fail, the only way of teaching an unmotivated student may be to ignore his motivational state for the time being and to concentrate on teaching him as effectively as possible. Some degree of learning will probably ensue in any case, and from the initial satisfaction of learning the student will *develop* the motivation to learn more. This last assertion reflects the general thesis that the causal relationship between motivation and learning is typically more reciprocal than is generally realized. Thus not only do drive states energize learning, but successful learning enhances the underlying drive determinants.

At the other end of the scale, it would appear that very intense drive states (like very low drive levels) are not conducive to learning, at least when complex tasks are involved. Evidence on the apparent interfering effect of intense drive upon complex performance comes from many studies in which drive states were raised to a high level by the inducement of strong emotion or by anxiety, specific fear, or the application of such physiological annoyances as electrical shock (for example, Ausubel and others, 1953a; Bruner, 1957; Cowan, 1952; Diethelm and Jones, 1947; Gaier, 1952; Lefford, 1946; Patrick, 1934). What has emerged from these studies is the hypothesis that the relationship between drive level and performance in complex tasks resembles the "inverted U" shown in Figure 12.4; after an initial gain from increased drive, an optimum drive level is reached, beyond which further increases in drive level impair performance. At the same time,

---

[14]Moreover, as Paradowski (1967) recently demonstrated, the elicitation of task-specific motivation may increase *incidental* learning of material associated with the task as well as the learning of the task itself.

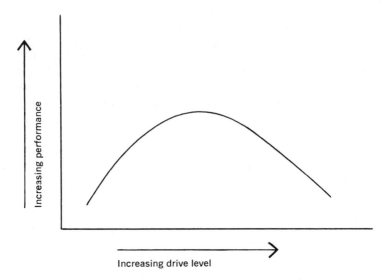

FIGURE 12.4 *Postulated relationship of drive level to performance in complex learning tasks.*

the postulated relationship between drive level and performance on *simple* tasks is thought to be more linear—increases in drive level uniformly improving performance—within wide drive limits (but stopping short of actual feelings of pain).

How are these differential effects to be explained? The clue lies in the fact that "simple" tasks refer to learning situations in which there is only one correct response (for example, moving one's hand away from a hot object) or where, if alternate responses exist, one is clearly prepotent (for example, $2 + 2 = 4$). In "complex" tasks, on the other hand, there exists a choice between what appear, at the time of learning, to be reasonable alternatives (for example, different paths in a maze, or the choice between alternate propositions in the geometry problem cited earlier). High drive may facilitate "simple" learning by speeding up, or intensifying, the tendency to utilize the one correct response. However in complex learning, although some drive is necessary to energize learning, high drive may cause the learner to emit the most predominant response without due regard for the legitimate alternatives (which, in a true problem situation, may very well be the correct ones). In other words, high drive is inimical to the suspended judgment and critical evaluation of alternatives which is crucial in problem solving.[15]

---

[15]It should be remembered too that "problems," which typically involve competing alternatives may, according to Berlyne's theory, generate drive states via conflict (leading to physiological arousal). Such task-induced drive would, one may assume, be added to the drive states which the learner brings to the problem situation.

It is clear that the classroom teacher will have to take drive level into account in fashioning an appropriate motivational strategy. Such attempts must take into consideration not only the type of task, but also the individual's normal level of anxiety. An additional factor, if the matter should not yet be thought sufficiently complicated, is that the optimum level of drive for tasks involving rote learning or comprehension of uncomplicated meaningful material depends upon whether the "performance" one is striving for involves immediate recall (as in remembering an address or other information of short-term value) or more permanent retention. A number of studies indicating that a relatively high drive level impedes initial recall but facilitates later retention (in comparison with relatively lower levels of drive) are reported in Berlyne (1967) and Levonian (1967). Levonian's 1967 study is particularly relevant since it utilized continuously presented classroom material.

REWARD AND PUNISHMENT IN SCHOOL SETTINGS

Extreme views on the legitimate place of reward and punishment are one of the legacies of contemporary education from the thinking of earlier periods. In one early view, previously described as the "faculty theory of mental discipline," it was assumed that man (*ergo* the child) is bad by nature and that forced labor at difficult intellectual tasks was a useful exercise to strengthen the faculty of will. Under such a conception, the child's failure to learn was assumed to result from obstinacy or laziness and, constituting thus an immoral act, called for harsh punishment. Readers of educational history or biography will know of the whippings, the dunce's cap, the kneeling on peas, and the variety of other ingenious punishments devised in earlier periods for the general improvement of the child's motivation.

Of course such views are no longer accepted, except perhaps in certain private schools. It is now assumed that since the child spends a good proportion of his life in or concerned with school, the latter ought to provide as pleasant an experience as is consistent with reasonably efficient learning. It would appear however that this desirable objective is sometimes taken too far, for in some circles it is assumed that "aversive stimulation" (that is, stimulation which the child would avoid if given a choice) should *never* be used, and that the learning child should be at all times anxiety-free and exclusively happy.

The extreme reaction against aversive stimulation is frequently based on a number of misconceptions. In the first place, there has been a tendency to think in terms of a punishment-reward *dichotomy* without realizing that there are many recognizable steps on the path from the most positive kind of reward to the most severe kind of punishment. For example, both criticism of shoddy work and physical punishment for serious misdemeanors constitute forms of "aversive stimulation," although one might expect considerable difference in their effects under normal circumstances.

A second source of confusion is more semantic, emanating from a failure to distinguish between the more restricted meaning of "punishment" in psychology, as the opposite of reward (that is, as non-reward or as the threatening consequences of failure to learn or perform successfully), and its more general meaning as a penalty for *moral* infractions (blame, rebuke, chastisement, censure, reprimand). Thus the suggestion that punishment, in the more restricted sense of the term, be used for motivational purposes tends to arouse a storm of protest simply because of the confusion with its more general meaning as retribution for moral wrongdoing. Actually, moral censure is never seriously advocated today for honest mistakes or failure to learn, but only for irresponsibility, laziness, culpable neglect, or inexcusable failure to display reasonable effort.

Finally, critics of aversive stimulation in the school environment apparently fail to appreciate that its objective is the facilitation of learning through the *threat* of failure (thereby overcoming inattention, procrastination, laziness, and lack of effort), rather than through the application of the punishment itself. Its aim, in other words, is to make the student avoid punishment by learning, rather than to experience punishment by failing to learn. Thus, in the vast majority of instances, serious punishment is never experienced because it is circumvented by the learning that is motivated by the fear of the threatened consequences.

The Reward-Punishment Dimension in the Classroom

While reward and punishment are treated as a dichotomy in educational controversies, analysis suggests that this is far too simple a view to take of classroom learning. Let us consider, for example, the grade 6 student of spelling, and examine the variety of distinguishable events which might impinge upon him and which could be placed on a reward-punishment dimension. Without straining the imagination we might produce a list such as the following:

(a) *Reward:* This would be represented by the provision of some tangible thing (incentive) which satisfies one of the student's drive determinants. Thus if Johnny is producing good work (in the teacher's opinion), he may receive stars, written comments on his spelling assignment, or the teacher's verbal praise.

(b) *Removal of aversive stimulation:* This might occur if our student had been working at a set of spelling tasks too difficult for his level of readiness and had consequently been receiving considerable correction and indications of error (aversive stimulation); if the teacher now chose tasks more commensurate with his capabilities, the incidence of aversive stimulation could be reduced or completely eliminated.

(c) *Confirming feedback:* In this case the student may attempt to recall the spelling of a word, and then look up its correct spelling in the text or dictionary (or be provided with it in a teaching machine). If correct, he would probably obtain some satisfaction in confirming his correct response, but this satisfaction is not likely to have the same strength as the teacher's personal commendation.

(d) *Corrective feedback:* In this case checking in the text would reveal that the word was incorrectly spelled. No doubt this would be mildly irritating to the student and an experience he would avoid if possible; consequently, it can probably be regarded as a weak form of aversive stimulation.

(e) *Removal of regular award:* In this case our hypothetical student, after a series of rewarded experiences, might exhibit carelessness or otherwise make errors which will not earn him the teacher's approval or positive comment.

(f) *Explicit expression of disapproval by the teacher:* If Johnny's work falls below a standard expected by the teacher to a degree that cannot be attributed to mere chance, the teacher would probably express some disapproval: "You can do better work than this, Johnny." Presumably this would be moderately discomfiting to a child with high affiliative or ego-enhancement drive.

(g) *Hint of failure:* If because of willful neglect Johnny's work continues at a poor standard, a point would be reached at which the teacher would inform him that the work is not passable. Here the anticipation of failure enters his mind (perhaps for the first time) and will probably generate anxiety, hopefully leading to increased effort.

(h) *Actual failure:* If poor performance is sustained the teacher may be obliged to have the unlearned work repeated or not allow the student to pass into the next unit or stage with the group in which he has been working. Thus a real experience of failure occurs.

(i) *Physical punishment:* Most contemporary schools have abolished physical punishment completely. However in some schools Johnny might receive such treatment if his non-task-oriented behavior went so far as shredding the speller, or persistently obstructing the progress of the class.

In the above examples, probably the first three events could be interpreted as "reward" and the last six as instances of "aversive stimulation." Since the effect of each may well be different, our understanding is not likely to be greatly increased by controversies that are stated in terms of forced dichotomies.

The Effects of Reward and Punishment

The previous section indicates that a discussion of the effects of reward and punishment is likely to be somewhat general in nature since it must cover a broad continuum of distinguishable events. Nevertheless, certain generalizations may be made if we allow for the fact that the intensity of the effects may vary from situation to situation. In the following paragraphs it will be convenient to discuss reward and punishment under their "affective" and "informational" effects.

Affective Effects Rewards and punishments generate feeling states, reward usually producing satisfaction or pleasure, and punishment usually producing frustration, anxiety, or displeasure. On the positive side, a reward may augment on a long-term basis whatever drive determinants are originally operative in energizing and directing behavior toward them. Thus if cognitive drive is usually rewarded in the school context we may expect a continuing increase in its overall strength. At the same time differential success (and reward) in various subject-matter fields within the school would lead to some specialization in cognitive drive; thus one child develops a strong drive toward arithmetic, another toward spelling. Punishment, as one might expect, has diametrically opposite effects. On a long-term basis it weakens drive determinants that lead to punishment, and differentially causes such drives to be weakened in different areas of endeavor.

The effects just described are *long-term,* operating at least over a group of tasks if not over longer periods of time. The short-term, or within-task effects can be inferred from the fact that the affective aftermath of reward and punishment influences drive states and, therefore, produces the previously discussed effects of motivational variables in general. Thus in *rote* learning, rewards may increase the relative probability of response recurrence by selectively "sensitizing" to later lowering the thresholds of elicitation of the particular responses that lead to the reward (and thus temporarily satisfied or reduced the drive). Similarly, punishment may decrease the selective probability of a response recurrence by failing to sensitize its threshold of elicitation. As previously observed, however, in *meaningful* learning the threshold-lowering effect of reward does not seem to apply.

One can also single out other short-term effects of reward and punishment. Awareness of successful learning (satisfying cognitive, affiliative or ego-enhancing drives for acquiring new knowledge) energizes *subsequent* learning efforts by enhancing the learner's self-confidence, by encouraging him to persevere, and by increasing the subjective attraction of the learning task. At the same time it motivates the learner to make use of what he has already learned. The experience of failure (a form of punishment), on the other hand, generates considerable aversive (that is, avoidance) motivation. The learner is thus generally motivated to avoid subsequent learning failure by paying attention, by displaying suitable effort and perseverance, and so on. In addition, when informed that a particular, previously learned, understanding is incorrect, the threatening implication of this report motivates him, to some extent, to avoid it—presumably raising thereby its threshold of elicitation. The facilitating effects of infrequent aversive stimulation[16] undoubtedly more than counter-balance the negative impact of such failure itself on the long-term strength of the underlying motivation and on long-term task attractiveness. However, when experience of failure predominates, or when aversive motivation is unsuccessful in avoiding failure, this is obviously not the case.

Cognitive Effects   When the student receives reward or punishment he is, in effect, informed about (or provided with "feedback" on) the adequacy of his responses or understandings. These effects have been discussed earlier and need only brief mention here. Both reward and punishment successively help to clarify the nature of the task; when told he is "right," the student has reconfirmed for him the accuracy of his understanding of a particular meaning, thereby enhancing its clarity, stability, and discriminability. Similarly, being told he is "wrong" eliminates at least one alternative meaning for the learner. In most instances reward is superior to punishment on the feedback dimension simply because it provides more "information," that is, leaves the learner less doubtful about the most appropriate response or meaning.

Level of Aspiration

Additional considerations concerning the effect of reward and punishment are raised in studies of *level of aspiration*. This term refers to the short-term goal an individual sets for himself in a learning task, that is, what he expects to do in an immediately-following learning task. Most of the studies in this area have been concerned with the effect of previous success or failure—two specific points within the reward-punishment continuum—on subsequent goal-setting.

In perhaps the most widely cited study of this kind (Sears, 1940), groups of fourth-, fifth-, and sixth-grade children were judged "successful" or "unsuccessful" in terms of their previous performance in all school subjects

---

[16]These facilitating effects can be long-term as well. When the individual is informed of, or otherwise anticipates, the possibility of failure, threat to the satisfaction of his ego-enhancing or affiliative drives generates anxiety which, if not too intense, enhances an appropriate drive state facilitating the learning necessary to avoid long-term failure.

(including arithmetic and reading) and their subjective feelings about this experience. A third group (designated the "differential" group) had been successful in reading but had done poorly in arithmetic. These children were now given series of familiar learning tasks in reading and arithmetic, of the type and under the circumstances to which they had become accustomed in school. After each task the child was asked to estimate how long he would take to perform the next in the series, and this latter estimate was taken as his level of aspiration. Taking the actual and estimated times for the whole series, one obtains an idea of the relation between past success and failure and the degree of realistic thinking represented in the child's present level of aspiration (large discrepancies between actual time and level of aspiration representing unrealistic short-term goal-setting). The results (Figure 12.5) showed that children who had a previous history of success tended to set realistic goals, while many of those with a record of failure tended to set unrealistic levels of aspiration, either greatly underestimating or overestimating their actual performance time. The third (differential) group tended to

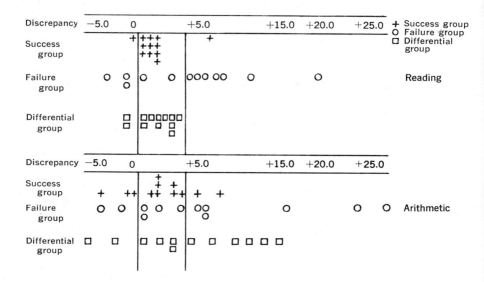

FIGURE 12.5 *Effect of long-term success and failure on setting of short-term goals. From: Pauline S. Sears, "Levels of aspiration in academically successful and unsuccessful children," J. abnorm. soc. Psychol., 35, 1940, 498–536. Copyright 1940 by the American Psychological Association, and reproduced by permission.*

set realistic goals in the area (reading) in which they had previously experienced success.

After this initial experience, short-term feelings of success and failure were induced by telling half the students in each group that they had done very well in the previous set of exercises, and telling the other half that they had done very poorly. The assessment in each case was decided by chance and had nothing to do with the actual performance. The experimental subjects were then set to work on similar tasks and again asked to provide estimates of the time they would require on each task (that is, of their level of aspiration), thus yielding a discrepancy score (actual time less estimated time) under induced short-term feelings of success and failure. The results (Figure 12.6) are generally in agreement with the long-term effects, in that short-term success tended to induce more realistic goal setting than occurred (for corresponding groups) in the neutral condition. Short-term failure, however, seemed to have less pronounced effects overall and almost negligible effects on the long-term success group.

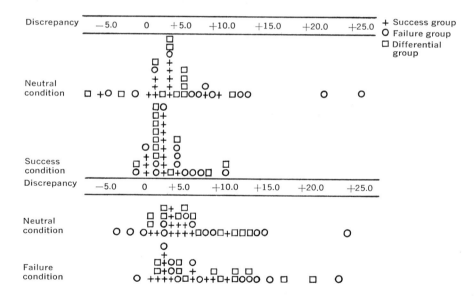

FIGURE 12.6 *Effect of short-term success and failure on setting of short-term goals. From: Pauline S. Sears, "Levels of aspiration in academically successful and unsuccessful children," J. abnorm. soc. Psychol., 35, 1940, 498–536. Copyright 1940 by the American Psychological Association, and reproduced by permission.*

Further explanation of the cause of unrealistic goal-setting by the students who had experienced failure can be found in a later discussion of anxiety. For the present it is sufficient to note that failure—a form of "punishment"—seems to have negative effects, generally speaking, on realistic goal-setting. However, in thinking of the general implications of this study for the classroom use of "success" and "failure," it should be remembered that the short-term success and failure experience was contrived in such a way that the anxiety-producing effect of "failure" was undoubtedly artificially raised. Thus, the student who had a previous record of success and who had completed the initial task in a manner consistent with his previous experiences—thereby expecting to be judged successful—would receive quite a shock to be told (arbitrarily) that he had done "very poorly." Even so, the effect of this "failure" did not seriously upset the realistic expectations which the student had developed previously, so that we find here no real condemnation of short-term failure experiences.[17]

Reward and Punishment: Concluding Remarks

Certain conclusions appear warranted from the previous discussion of the effects of reward and punishment. In the first place, the child's experience in school should be one of receiving a preponderance of "rewards" over "punishments." This conclusion is reached whether one considers the informational aspects, affective effects, or influence on level of aspiration of reward and punishment respectively. It seems clear, for example, that instances of major traumatic "failure" should be eliminated by nongraded systems.

Second, the teacher whose reward-punishment repertoire is limited to the punishment end of the scale is probably concocting an educational disaster for many children. The general anxiety, fear, and unpleasant emotions occasioned by punishment easily transfer to objects and persons associated with the punishment, including the subject itself, the teacher, or the school.

However, the occasional use of aversive stimulation, contrary to the romantic notions of some reformers of education, (for example, Skinner, 1954), is a necessity in the proper conduct of education. Among its legitimate and inevitable uses are the following:

---

[17]Related to the latter point, Rotter (1966) reported on a series of experiments indicating that the effects of success and failure may depend upon the individual's belief concerning the extent to which he controls the rewards or punishments administered to him (as opposed to control vested in an external agent). Apparently those subjects who have feelings of self-determinacy are more likely to shift their aspirations upward or downward, after success or failure, respectively. For other (more recent) studies involving level of aspiration see: Feather (1966), Gibby and Gibby (1967), and Murstein (1965). Also see Silvertsen's (1959) critique of level of aspiration studies.

(a) Children who make mistakes need to be corrected by being told that they are wrong. This correction, however, should normally be followed by an opportunity to obtain the correct answer and thereby obtain reward. Such short-term aversive stimulation can hardly be thought of as disrupting behavior—unless the teacher foolishly accompanies his correction with sarcasm, ridicule, or other ego-damaging tactics.

(b) As much as we are loathe to admit it, the threat of possible failure is probably necessary to keep most of us working, and the teacher may occasionally have to remind the student of this possibility when there is reason to believe that the latter could do better with more concentration or effort.

(c) Situations will occur in which a fairly strong form of aversive stimulation (for example, a sharp reprimand) will be necessary to reduce the strength of a response which is completely disruptive of learning. In doing this, of course, it will be the teacher's intention to encourage the student to substitute more acceptable, reward-earning behavior for it.

CONTROLLING MOTIVATION IN THE CLASSROOM

Despite ample theorizing and laboratory research, the classroom management of motivation remains something of an art. Certainly we must admit that there is a large distance between the theoretical principles cited in the previous pages and the skillful moment-by-moment performance which characterizes the effective control of motivation in the classroom. At the same time we feel that, for most beginning teachers at least, the theoretical principles cited earlier will help in illuminating relevant variables, and in generally facilitating the teacher's progress toward an effective motivational strategy. Moreover, advice offered on the basis of such principles may well capture in general terms some of the ideas which good teachers have discovered by intuition or long experience. The following paragraphs contain suggestions which seem to be consistent with the theory.

Developing a Realistic View An important first step is for the teacher to develop a realistic conception of motivation as it actually applies in the classroom. While taking as his goal the maximizing of intrinsic motivation, he must recognize the role of ego-enhancement and affiliative drives and the need for the judicious use of aversive stimulation.

Assessing Learners' Needs When encountering a child who does not respond to the normal motivational devices of the teacher, the latter should ascertain insofar as he is able the needs which seem to be motivating the child's behavior. If an algebra student has little desire for teacher approval and little hope of achieving status through achievement in algebra, aversive stimulation can have little long-term positive effect. In fact, if the teacher loses his equanimity he may well be strengthening illegitimate forms of attention-seeking behavior. Frequently the teacher may be able to find some nondisruptive outlet for drives which are not task-oriented.

Developing Cognitive Drive   Clearly we should make every effort to utilize cognitive drive when it is present and to develop it when it is not. As a beginning, a reduced emphasis on learning for examination purposes should be possible now, in both the elementary and secondary school, with the gradual disappearance of rigid grade systems (and the need for annual "life-or-death" examinations) and with the increasing tendency to determine admittance to university by aptitude tests and teacher assessment of achievement over a broad area.

Second, most teachers could do a great deal to utilize such devices as novelty, surprise, and incongruity to enlist the student's interest when little cognitive drive is in evidence. A student may have no particular drive to learn algebra but may become intrigued by an apparent logical paradox or contradiction. Once having resolved these—and having obtained some satisfaction thereby—he may subsequently be more favorably disposed to look on this subject as a possible vehicle for the satisfaction of cognitive drive. Most school subjects contain paradoxes, or conflicting opinions among experts, or apparent contradictions of common sense, and if these are pointed out to the initially disinterested student they may have strong motivational effects which can carry learning forward until other relevant drives become operative.

Tapping Related Interests   There are many ways in which a teacher can tap related interests and try to make subjects more attractive to students. For example, we might appeal to a student's ego-enhancement drive by indicating how the learning of mathematics opens up prestigious job opportunities in a variety of occupations. Using another tack, we can (in many school subjects) choose as illustrative cases examples that are known to be of interest to particular students. Beyond that, a good teacher can, by sheer force of his enthusiasm, make a subject seem important; such teachers are able to relate their subject to broader human goals and aspirations.

Use of Competition   As indicated in a later chapter, evidence seems to justify a judicious use of competition between individual students (for prizes, awards, and so on) which clearly relies on ego-enhancement drive. However the student can also be brought to compete with his own past performance or with certain idealized standards of excellence. Much good use can be made of interschool competitions such as those now employed in the fields of mathematics and creative writing, which make a powerful appeal to ego-enhancement drive, yet which remove the kind of obvious "failure" that is present in the situation in which promotion is dependent upon marks. If such an approach is to work with any sizeable proportion of the students, a variety of competitions—exploiting talents in many areas—must be used.

Teaching in the Absence of Motivation   As a last resort, the teacher may be well advised simply to begin teaching a subject in the absence of any specific motivation on the part of the student to learn it. As indicated earlier, meaningful tasks can frequently be learned with little effort (and low drive levels) so that the "unmotivated" algebra student may learn despite his lack of specific intent to do so. Having had an initial success, however, we can expect that cognitive drive will be sufficiently increased to spur the student on to further learning.

Use of Appropriate Drive Level   While enhancing motivation in the ways mentioned previously, the teacher should keep in mind that very high drive levels may inhibit the learning of complex tasks. This means that simply "putting pressure" on the student who is having difficulty with a problem will likely do more harm than good. As the next chapter shows, the likelihood of "overarousal" is greater with children whose behavior is characterized by a high level of anxiety.

Analyzing and Refashioning the Learner's Reward and Punishment Schedule   Some children, particularly if they fall behind in a sequentially organized subject such as mathematics or science, or a foreign language, have traditionally been subjected to long periods of almost uninterrupted aversive stimulation, relieved at last only by withdrawal from school. With existing opportunities for streaming and the availability of self-instructional devices for remedial work, there is little excuse for this to happen in today's classroom.

TOPICS FOR DISCUSSION AND FURTHER STUDY

1. Some schools use a "barrier approach" in which the disinterested student of Latin, for example, is required to make an effort in that subject to earn the "privilege" of participating in the school's extracurricular program. It is hoped, of course, that initial successes in learning Latin will strengthen cognitive drive in that subject so that, in time, the extrinsic goal will no longer be necessary. Discuss the merits and possible dangers of this approach.

2. Compose examples from your own area of specialization to indicate how the principle of conceptual conflict could be used to advantage.

3. According to the theory advanced in this text, one should deliberately forestall possible conceptual conflict by introducing advance organizers which show clearly and unambiguously the relation of ideas to be learned to existing ideas in cognitive structure. How can the approaches advocated by these two notions (that is, "organizers and "conceptual conflict") be reconciled in planning instructional sequences?

4. Analyze the motivational techniques employed by a teacher whom you observe during your practice teaching. What assumptions seem to be implicit in his approach? What specific techniques does he employ which are not treated in this chapter?

5.* It has been suggested that teachers can enhance student motivation, and through it student achievement, by putting "personal" remarks on assignments or tests (for example, "good work—keep it up" or "I believe that you can do better than this") in addition to the grade or mark assigned. Research evidence seems somewhat divided since Page (1950) found the result anticipated while Waterman, Northrop and Olson (1967) did not. What hypotheses might be advanced—involving the kind of student motivation, kind of subject matter involved, grade level, and other variables—as to when this "personalized marking" technique will be effective?

6.* In what way would perseverance be related to the types of drives postulated as underlying school achievement motivation? What other characteristics would you expect to find in a child who perseveres at school learning tasks (Wyer and Bednar, 1967)?

7. It has been found (Bryan and Locke, 1967) that the setting of specific goals (rather than merely exhorting students to "do their best") can be used to motivate subjects who bring a low degree of motivation to the task situation. Cite instances where this finding might be applied in the context of regular classroom instruction.

8. It is frequently assumed that the student will come to enjoy performing a particular kind of task in proportion to the success which he has had with it, an assertion which empirical studies bear out (Locke; 1966, 1967). How would you explain this phenomenon in terms of the concepts employed in the present chapter? Can you envisage any circumstances under which this effect might not hold?

9.* A recent line of interest lies in the development of tests of "curiosity" (Penney and McCann, 1964; Smock and Holt, 1962; Day, 1966; Maw and Maw, 1962), a trait presumably implicated in cognitive drive. What degree of correlation would you expect between curiosity and general intelligence? To what extent would you expect children to exhibit a "generalized curiosity," as opposed to a number of specific curiosities? To what extent could the educator rely on innate curiosity tendencies in planning the instructional program? (See: Acker and McReynolds, 1967; Friedlander, 1965.)

10.* It has been observed (Atkinson, 1958; Brody, 1963) that students with lower achievement scores take *extreme* risks, that is, risks in which the chance of success is either virtually assured or practically impossible. It has occurred to various experimenters (for example, Kolb 1965; Klein and others, 1967) that if students were trained to take more reasonable risks, their achievement motivation, and actual school achievement, might be influenced positively. Investigate the techniques employed in these studies, and indicate how such procedures might be adapted for use by school personnel.

SUGGESTIONS FOR ADDITIONAL READING

Archambault, R. D. The concept of need and its relation to certain aspects of of educational theory. *Harvard educ. Rev.*, 1957, *27,* 38–62.

Berlyne, D. E. Curiosity in education. In *Learning and the educational process* (J. D. Krumboltz, Ed.). Skokie, Ill.: Rand McNally & Company, 1965.

Madsen, K. B. *Theories of motivation.* Cleveland, Ohio: Howard Allen, Inc., 1961.

Sears, P. S., and E. R. Hilgard. The teacher's role in the motivation of the learner. In *Theories of learning and instruction: 63rd Yearbook Nat. Soc. Stud. Educ.* Part 1. Chicago: University of Chicago Press, 1964.

Shaw, M. C. Motivation in human learning. *Rev. educ. Res.*, 1967, *37*(5), 563–578.

Symonds, P. M. *What education has to learn from psychology.* New York: Teachers College Press, Columbia University, 1958. Chapters 1 (Motivation), 2 (Reward), 3 (Punishment), and 6 (Emotion and Learning).

CHAPTER 13

PERSONALITY FACTORS
IN LEARNING

THE TERM "PERSONALITY," AS USED BY LAYMEN AND EDU-
cators, usually takes one of two meanings. The first meaning equates personality to social skill in the sense of eliciting positive responses from other
individuals. Thus when the teacher writes on a report card that the child has
a "well-rounded" personality, he probably is referring to the fact that the
child is able to relate well to other pupils and to the teacher in the particular
contexts found in the school. Another tendency is to single out and use as a
description of personality the salient impression which the individual creates
in others. In this way arise the major personality dichotomies, as when the
teacher speaks of the child as being "shy" as opposed to "outgoing," "aggressive" as opposed to "submissive," or "open-minded" as opposed to "prejudiced."

THE STUDY OF PERSONALITY

Popular and "Scientific" Views of Personality

It would probably be pretentious to assert that the study of personality has
been elevated to an exact science or that it is even amenable to such
treatment. Some would say, in fact, that the most penetrating analyses of the
depths and workings of personality are still to be found in purely literary
productions—the novel or the play. Some psychologists have, for example,
attempted to analyze and attach labels to the personalities of such literary
figures as Hamlet. These descriptions seem to fall short somehow of capturing the full complexity of the human being as portrayed by a sensitive writer.

388

As for the scientific approach to personality definition and measurement, it must be remembered that the early personality theorists worked outside the mainstream of academic psychology. For example, Freud, Jung, and McDougall were clinically rather than experimentally oriented, and their speculations on personality organization and development arose in the context of dealing with patients who were suffering from severe forms of maladjustment. Such theorists gave free scope to their imaginations and, actively antagonistic to quantitative and experimental methods, they produced systems which are rich in imagery, complex, frequently vague, and for the most part untested by empirical investigation. Most readers will be at least vaguely familiar with the influential writings of Freud, which explain many kinds of personality malfunctions (neuroses and psychoses) in terms of the arresting or inhibition of natural developmental relationships between a metaphorical triumvirate comprising the "id" (the reservoir of primitive impulses and organic energy), the "ego" (the conscious agent of personality which deals with objective reality), and the "superego" (the internalized, cultural, and familial values which place limits upon the individual's behavior).

According to Hall and Lindzey (1957), the multiplicity of systems and approaches precludes the possibility of a "substantive definition of personality [which] can be applied with any generality." According to these authors, some theorists employ a biosocial or *social stimulus* value notion similar to the first of the two lay views described above. Others employ an "omnibus" definition which speaks in terms of the sum total of the individual's propensities to behave in various ways in different situations. Further approaches include emphasis on: the *integration* of various behavior patterns to give coherence to the individual's total behavior; the *total adjustment* of the individual to his physical and social environment; the *unique aspects of behavior* which set an individual apart from his fellows; and the "essence of man" or "what a man really is" notion.

There are perhaps two characteristics of the scientific approach to personality theory which set it apart from the speculations of the layman or the nontechnical writer. In the first place, the personality theorist invariably emerges with a wide-ranging theory whose systematically organized explanatory concepts are applied to diverse phases of human functioning. Such theories usually possess a developmental component which explains structural changes in personality from birth to maturity. Personality theories, then, are invariably more complex in their conceptualization and comprehensive in their applications than lay speculation. Second, some personality theorists have either derived or verified their theories from the analysis of large bodies of behavioral data, data derived from individuals' reactions to stressful situations, from their answers to questions probing specific attitudes and feelings, or from their responses to relatively vague stimuli upon which the subject must project some meaning. As a result a large number of personality tests, inventories, and scales have been available in recent years which provide scores for various hypothesized "dimensions" of personality.

Emphasis on Affective Factors

Most definitions of personality would refer at least indirectly to cognitive attributes of the individual; for example, we have previously seen that a stable attitude—commonly considered to be a component of total personality structure—comprises both cognitive structure and affective variables. Nevertheless, personality theories have traditionally assigned the central role to affective states (Hall and Lindzey, 1957), and the major personality dimensions we will discuss in the ensuing paragraphs are best understood in terms of these latter variables. Personality variables may therefore be thought of primarily as defining stable and self-consistent individual differences in learners in the affective-social (rather than the cognitive) domain. They differ from motivational variables in that they define *self-consistent* and *stable* individual differences, and from cognitive variables in that they affect meaningful learning *catalytically* and *nonspecifically*.

Personality Dimensions and Concepts
Relevant to School Learning

In the following section we select several personality dimensions and related concepts which seem to be particularly relevant to school learning. These dimensions are not all drawn from a single unified theoretical system and they represent, of course, only a limited sampling of the various personality variables which have been postulated at one time or another to have some direct or indirect relationship to performance in school.

SATELLIZATION VERSUS NONSATELLIZATION

Whenever interpersonal and group life is characterized by differences in roles and status, and by dependence of one person on another or on the group as a whole, one of the more basic kinds of human interaction that arises is *identification* of the dependent party with the superordinate party. In considering this type of relationship we must be careful to distinguish two essentially different kinds of identification, each of which involves the reciprocal relationship between a relatively dependent and subordinate individual, on the one hand, and a relatively independent or dominant individual (or group) on the other (Ausubel, 1952).

One type of identification, which is characteristic of the early parent-child relationship in humans, has been called *satellization* (Ausubel, 1952). In a satellizing relationship the subordinate party (child) does not strive for an independent, earned status of his own, but accepts a status dependent upon the status of the superordinate party (parent); the superordinate party, in return, accepts him as an intrinsically valuable entity in his own right. The satellizer thereby acquires a *vicarious* or *derived* status which is wholly a function of the dependent relationship and independent of his own competence, and which is bestowed upon him by the fiat of simple unqualified acceptance by a superordinate individual whose authority and power to do so are regarded as unchallengable.

On the other hand, the parent and child could relate to each other in quite a different way. The subordinate party (child)—in this case a *non-satellizer*—could accept his dependency simply as a temporary, regrettable and much-to-be-remedied fact of life requiring, as a matter of expediency, various acts of conformity and deference, but without really accepting a dependent and subordinate status as a *person* (Ausubel, 1952). In turn, he could either be rejected outright or could be accorded acceptance—not unqualified as an individual for himself—but in terms of his present or potential usefulness to the superordinate party. The act of identification, if it occurs at all, consists only of the child using the parent as an *emulatory model* so that he can learn the latter's skills and methods of operation and thus eventually succeed to his enviable status. Consequently the only type of status the child can hope to enjoy in this type of relationship is a primary (earned) status that reflects his own degree of functional competence or performance ability.[1]

The nonsatellizing type of identification occurs primarily for one (or both) of two reasons. Either the superordinate party does not extend unqualified intrinsic acceptance (that is, the parent either rejects the child or values him basically for extrinsic, ulterior, self-enhancing purposes of his own) or the subordinate party is reluctant to, or incapable of, accepting a dependent role. Illustrating the latter possibility is the typical cat who condescendingly does his "master" a favor by drinking his milk, in contrast to the typical dog who simply oozes devotion, slavishness, and self-effacement. It would also be reasonable to expect that children who are temperamentally more assertive, self-sufficient, independent, and "thick skinned" would be less disposed to satellize than children with the opposite set of characteristics. Differences related to culturally determined social sex role might also be anticipated. For example, when an experimental popula-

---

[1]Satellization and nonsatellization should be thought of as representing opposite ends of a continuum rather than a true dichotomy. Most satillizers exhibit some nonsatellizing traits, and vice versa.

tion of ten-year-olds in Champaign, Illinois, (Ausubel and others, 1954a) rated 36 items of parent attitude and behavior reflecting acceptance-rejection and intrinsic-extrinsic evaluation,[2] girls were found to be (or perceive themselves to be) more highly accepted and intrinsically valued than boys.

Effects on Achievement Motivation

From the standpoint of school learning, the wider significance of satellization versus nonsatellization on personality development is that each of these outcomes is associated both with a distinctive pattern of achievement motivation and with a distinctive mode of assimilating norms and values. As indicated above, the satellizer enjoys both an assured derived status and accompanying feelings of intrinsic adequacy or self-esteem that are relatively immune to the vicissitudes of achievement or competitive position. Thus he has relatively little need to seek the kind of status that he would have to earn through his own competence—the kind of status that would generate feelings of extrinsic adequacy commensurate with his degree of achievement. He does not, in other words, seek academic achievement as the basis of his status or as the measure of his worth as a person; it is merely a means of meeting the expectations of his parents and of retaining, thereby, the approval that confirms for him his good standing in their eyes. Nevertheless, if parents set high standards of performance in school as a condition of approval, the child with a strong affiliative drive will expend considerable effort in meeting these standards.

The nonsatellizer, on the other hand, is either rejected or accepted on an extrinsic basis by his parents. Enjoying no derived status or intrinsic self-esteem, he has no choice but to aspire to a status that he earns through his own accomplishments. Since his feelings of adequacy are almost entirely a reflection of the degree of achievement he can attain, he necessarily exhibits a high level of aspiration for academic achievement and prestige—a level that is relatively higher and more tenacious in the face of failure experience than that of satellizers. This is obviously a compensatory reaction on his part which reflects his lack of derived status and intrinsic self-esteem. Consistent with his higher aspirations for independent achievement he also

---

[2]These scores were obtained from the *Parent Attitude Rating Scale* (Ausubel and others, 1954a), in which the following kinds of parental behavior and attitudes are regarded as reflecting *rejection:* neglect, physical separation, disavowal of responsibility; denial of legitimate needs and wishes of the child; imposition of unjust punishment; criticism or humiliation; lack of patience, consideration, and affection; unwillingness to accept inconvenience for the sake of the child; and inability to inspire his confidence.

Criteria of *extrinsic valuation* by the parent include: excessive concern with the child's school accomplishment as a vehicle for enhancing his own status; evidence of overmotivating the child and planning for his career in grandiose terms; and excessive public display of his school and other accomplishments.

manifests more disagreement with perceived parental opinions than the satellizer (Ausubel and others, 1954a).[3]

In summary, the nonsatellizer exhibits a higher level of achievement motivation in which the ego-enhancement component is predominant, whereas the satellizer exhibits both a lower level of achievement motivation and one in which the affiliative component tends to predominate prior to adolescence. Of course, significant changes (as well as individual differences) in the balance between primary and derived status occur during the course of ego development. But initial ways of relating to others tend to persist, especially if they occur at critical periods of socialization. Thus, although it is true that as the satellizing child grows older he increasingly strives for primary status, he will, even as an adult, continue to enjoy the residual sense of intrinsic worth which his parents earlier conferred on him and will continue to satellize in some respects of his ongoing interpersonal relationships.

Effects on Value Assimilation

The satellizing and nonsatellizing modes of identification also have important implications for the mechanisms by which norms and values are assimilated from elders and from membership and reference groups. The essential motivation directing the satellizer's organization of his value system is the need to retain the acceptance and approval of the person or persons who provide his derived status. Hence he develops a generalized set to perceive the world in the light of the values and expectations he attributes to these latter individuals. Value assimilation is thus an act of *personal loyalty* in which the actual content of what is internalized is largely irrelevant from a motivational standpoint. When ideas are accepted on a satellizing basis, resistance to new learning stems largely from conflicting ideational trends in the new set of values, which can be accepted only at the cost of repudiating prior loyalties and assuming the associated burden of guilt.

The nonsatellizer, on the other hand, is primarily motivated in his acceptance or rejection of values by considerations of expediency and the

---

[3]Other aspects of the parent-child relationship have been implicated in the development of achievement motivation. Achievement motivation tends to be higher in those children whose parents have high intellectual achievement aspirations both for themselves (Katkovsky and others, 1964a, 1964b) and for their offspring (Rosen and D'Andrade, 1959); whose parents stress independence training and high standards of excellence (McClelland and others, 1953; Winterbottom, 1958); and whose parents, when present in problem-solving situations with their offspring, exhibit greater participation, instigation, encouragement, and disapproval (Katkovsky and others, 1964b; Rosen and D'Andrade, 1959). It is also apparently stronger in instances where an achievement-oriented mother is dominant in the home. A dominant, demanding, and successful father, on the other hand, is perceived by his sons as providing a competitive standard that is too overwhelmingly superlative to be challenged successfully (Strodtbeck, 1958). All such generalizations should undoubtedly be accepted very tentatively, however, since they are probably as hazardous as those pertaining to the relationship of child-rearing practices to the child's cognitive development (on the latter point see: Freeberg and Payne, 1967).

attainment of primary status. Hence his motivational set is not to accept values blindly and uncritically but in accordance with these general aims. The prestige of authority figures, in this instance, is not derived from the learner's need to agree with them, but from his acknowledgment of their suitability as emulatory models and stepping stones to power and prestige. In confirmation of this it has been found that nonsatellizing elementary-school children are more disposed than satellizing children to disagree with the perceived opinions of their parents (Ausubel and others, 1954a).

For the nonsatellizing child, new ideas are resisted because they constitute a potential threat to his self-esteem by challenging his existing system of values, which has been organized on an ego-prestige basis. Because he lacks intrinsic feelings of worth and is therefore more vulnerable to the ego-deflating implications of failure, he is more reluctant than the satellizer to venture into new areas of learning where his capability still remains to be demonstrated (for example, where problem solving or adaptability are required). Resistance to new learning, however, as well as to new values, is usually overcome when he is able to perceive their usefulness for future ego-enhancement.

Effect on School Achievement

It is evident that the excess of ego-enhancement drive derived from a nonsatellizing relationship can have long-term effects on the child's school achievement only if it is a highly stable and somewhat generalized personality trait. Research data clearly indicate that both of these conditions prevail. Moss and Kagan (1961) for example, have produced impressive evidence of stability characterizing achievement motivation from age six to adult life, and it would seem that such motivation reflects, in large measure, the strongly enduring properties of ego-enhancement drive derived from the parent-child relationship; that it is also a reasonably generalized trait can be inferred from the moderately high intercorrelations both among levels of aspiration and goal tenacity scores over a variety of laboratory tasks and "real life" achievement situations, and among goal tenacity scores over a range of hypothetical vocational situations (Ausubel and Schiff, 1955; Ausubel and others, 1953b).[4]

---

[4]The concept of level of aspiration has already been encountered in a previous context. Goal tenacity, a related measure, represents the relative tendency of an individual to *maintain* a high level of aspiration *in relation to his past performance*. The laboratory tasks referred to above involved materials commonly used in level of aspiration studies: simple arithmetic exercises; reading exercises (marked for speed); substitution of symbols for numbers; and a blindfolded stylus maze test. "Real life" achievement situations involved performance in school. Vocational tenacity was measured by asking the student to imagine that he is preparing for careers in a number of occupations and that he encounters certain (defined) obstacles. The high tenacity student is one who would pursue the original goal at all costs; the low tenacity student would abandon it completely.

Despite the foregoing remarks, the actual effect of extreme ego-enhancement motivation on school achievement depends on many factors—age, sex, anxiety level, and other personality traits. Thus, although it is empirically demonstrable that high ego-enhancement drive (reflecting parental rejection or extrinsic acceptance) generally leads to higher levels of aspiration (Ausubel and others, 1954a), the school performance of these individuals is not necessarily superior to that of intrinsically accepted pupils of comparable academic ability. In some individuals the corollary need for avoiding failure is so much stronger than the need for success that the level of striving is grossly lowered to prevent even the remotest possibility of failure. Other individuals with high ego-enhancement motivation lack the personality traits (persistence, self-denial, high-frustration tolerance, ability to defer hedonistic gratification) necessary for implementing high aspirations; merely possessing high aspirations, without ever intending to implement them may yield a certain compensatory measure of ego-enhancement.

A third factor interfering with the facilitating effect of high ego-enhancement drive on academic achievement is a correlated disabling high level of anxiety, particularly the kind that leads to withdrawal from competitive situations or to paralysis of adaptive behavior. Moreover, cultural influences mediated through age and sex role expectations are important determining factors. Thus, low nurturant and unaffectionate mothers tend to have daughters (but not sons) with superior school achievement in the elementary school (Crandall and others, 1964), since such ahievement constitutes a culturally sanctioned form of compensatory ego-enhancement for girls at this age level. At the late adolescent and young adult level, on the other hand, the much greater stress on male vocational achievement is apparently responsible for the association of parental rejection with high anxiety and academic achievement in male but not female prospective teachers (Gnagey, 1966).[5]

ANXIETY AND SCHOOL LEARNING

Anxiety differs from ordinary fear and from insecurity in that both of these latter emotional states result from threats to one's physical well-being, fear resulting from a present threat and insecurity from an anticipated threat. Anxiety, on the other hand, results from a threat to one's *self-esteem,* either current or anticipated. Thus, whereas one is fearful when

---

[5]The reader should compare the present section with earlier remarks on the influence of ego-enhancement motivation. It should be noted that the earlier section was concerned primarily with the ego-enhancement component of the *typical* student's motivational structure, while the present treatment deals with the intense ego-enhancement motivation associated with nonsatellization.

confronted by a mad dog and made insecure by the prospect of automation rendering one's job obsolete, threatened or actual failure in school would tend to generate anxiety. Despite these logical distinctions it is clear that many present or anticipated events can pose threats to both physical well-being and self-esteem.

Since anxiety enhances drive states, it represents a potential source of motivation for energizing school learning. Our concern in this section is with the circumstances under which this facilitating potential is realized and, conversely, the circumstances under which anxiety is debilitating. As it turns out, the widespread generalization that anxiety is a thing to be avoided by the school at all costs does not do justice to the available facts.

Kinds of Anxiety

It is apparent that at least two different "kinds" of anxiety can fit within the definition cited above. First, it is clear that all human beings are prone to what might be called *normal* anxiety. Most new ventures in school, business, sports, or family life carry with them varying degrees of threat of failure and concomitant damage to one's self-esteem, and tend therefore to engender at least some degree of anxiety in most people. Similarly, feelings of guilt associated with anticipated wrong-doing can generate anxiety by exposing the individual to a sullied, reprehensible image of himself, at odds with the moral values he has internalized. And anxiety is commonly aroused during transitional periods of personality development, such as adolescence, when individuals have to achieve a new biosocial status and are kept in a prolonged state of uncertainty regarding the outcome.

These different instances of normal anxiety have one property in common which distinguishes them from what might be termed *neurotic* anxiety. In each situation described above, anxiety is instigated by an *objective* threat to self-esteem. In some instances, this threat may be external in origin, as for example when one pits one's skills and reputation as a sprinter against a competent rival. In other instances, the source of the threat is within the person—it may come from aggressive impulses or from the individual's awareness that he has violated certain of his moral scruples. The important thing in all these cases—regardless of whether the source of threat is internal or external—is that the threat is objectively capable of impairing self-esteem in normal persons. In other words, the threat comes from a source distinct from the entity (that is, self-esteem) which is being threatened, and the response to the threat is appropriate and proportionate to the objective degree of jeopardy confronting the individual's self-esteem.

In neurotic anxiety, on the other hand, the essential threat to self-esteem does not lie outside self-esteem but is to be found in severe impairment of self-esteem itself. Hence, a person suffering from neurotic anxiety apparently *over-reacts* with fear to a perceived threat. But this response is an over-reaction only when considered in relation to the ostensible or objective source of the threat to self-esteem; it is not an over-reaction when considered in relation to the major source of threat to self-esteem which lies *within* self-esteem itself. Moreover, since most new ventures contain potential threats to self-esteem, the neurotically anxious person exhibits a kind of generalized fearfulness in many of the major transactions of his life.

The distinction between normal and neurotic anxiety can be highlighted with an analogy from heart physiology. When a person has a normal, undamaged heart, he can develop heart failure only by being subjected to tremendous exertion without rest, prolonged exposure to heat, severe pulmonary disease, and so forth. The threat to cardiac adequacy when one has a normal heart, therefore, lies in an objectively punishing situation. Less rigorous threats to cardiac adequacy are easily compensated for because of the great reserve power of the heart. If the heart shows signs of beginning to fail when the external pressure increases, the outcome is hardly disproportionate to the degree of strain involved.

But a person with a damaged heart has already exhausted all of his power to compensate for increased external demands. Require him to run up a flight of stairs quickly, and he will be thrown into heart failure. In his case, the source of the threat to cardiac adequacy lies in his own damaged heart muscle, just as the source of the threat to self-esteem in a person with neurotic anxiety lies in his own damaged self-esteem. Certainly he is over-reacting with signs of cardiac insufficiency to a flight of stairs, just as the anxiety neurotic is over-reacting to a new adjustive situation with signs of fear and further impairment of self-esteem. But in neither case is the reaction disproportionate to the *actual* degree of jeopardy confronting the heart or self-esteem.

A common form of anxiety may involve either normal anxiety or a limited form of neurotic anxiety. This is seen most clearly perhaps in the phenomenon of "number anxiety," the tendency to exhibit fearfulness in situations calling for the production or comprehension of arguments couched in mathematical language. The interesting thing about this affliction as it is found in adults is that if there is any impairment of the self-esteem of the sufferer it is not a general impairment, but occurs only in this particular area. Many capable adults who literally cringe at the appearance of a mathematical symbol have otherwise a realistic and generally positive view of their abilities and approach novel tasks in nonmathematical areas with no more than the mild normal (or situational) anxiety which characterizes any learner's approach to novelty.

The Origin of Neurotic Anxiety

No definitive answer can be given to the question of how neurotic anxiety develops. However, one plausible explanation of both an initial impairment and susceptibility to further impairment can be traced to the satellizer/nonsatellizer distinction made earlier. The satellizing child acquires feelings of self-esteem, a deep inner conviction that he is important and worthwhile for himself, through identification with his parents. As long as he possesses this feeling of intrinsic value, failure to achieve superior competence may be intense and deeply felt—but is always peripheral to basic self-esteem and hence never catastrophic. Thus the satellizing child not only acquires an initially high self-esteem, but retains this almost as a buffer against potentially self-esteem-destroying events later in life. It is, of course, true that as he becomes older he will increasingly strive for more primary status based on his own accomplishments and will develop feelings of self-esteem related to them. But there will always remain a residual sense of worth which his parents conferred on him by fiat—when as a child he perceived this to lie within their power.

The nonsatellizer is, unfortunately, in a much less favorable position. First, he does not acquire any vicarious status or intrinsic feelings of self-esteem from identification with his parents. Hence, from the very beginning his self-esteem becomes a function of what he is able to do and accomplish. Such a child is, therefore, likely to be motivated to aspire to higher goals and ambitions than the general run of mankind and frequently these goals are not only unrealistic in terms of the child's ability but extremely resistant to lowering in the face of realistic evidence for doing so. Such children, being no more than normally gifted, face a good chance of failure and large-scale collapse of their grandiose and unrealistic aspirations. Since they have no intrinsic self-esteem to fall back upon, such a defeat is centrally traumatic to self-esteem and commonly precipitates acute anxiety. Furthermore, if they should recover from this temporary setback, there is nevertheless a tendency to retain a permanently damaged self-esteem or chronic anxiety neurosis which may flare up at any time and become acute when the environment becomes too threatening.

The cause of "number anxiety" probably yields to a similar explanation. The child with intrinsic self-esteem approaches the learning of mathematics with a typical nonneurotic type of mild anxiety associated with any new learning. A series of failures would intensify the anxiety associated with any subsequent new learning in that area. However, such anxiety—although now intense—is normal in that it is reasonably and objectively related to the potential external threat to self-esteem inherent in the new learning and does not permanently impair the individual's overall feeling of worth. For the nonsatellizer, however, early experiences of failure could damage his self-esteem, although the resulting neurotic anxiety is associated only with his performance in this particular area.

Effect of Anxiety on Learning

Generally speaking the results of research on the relationship between anxiety and performance parallel the conclusions reached earlier in respect to the relationship between level of motivation and learning. This is not surprising since both anxiety (an emotional state) and motivation involve drive states which tend to energize the learning process. Thus, consistent with previously mentioned studies, it is generally found that both induced normal anxiety or neurotic anxiety facilitate rote and less difficult kinds of meaningful reception learning, but have an inhibitory effect on complex learning tasks that are more dependent upon improvising skill than upon persistence (Ausubel and others, 1953a; Caron, 1963; Casteneda and others, 1956; Lantz, 1945; McGuigan and others, 1959; Marks and Vestre, 1961; Palermo and others, 1956; Pickrel, 1958; Russell and Sarason, 1965; Sarason and others, 1960; Scharf, 1964; Stevenson and Odom, 1965; Tomkins, 1943; Zander, 1944).

We might explain these results by again postulating the "inverted U" curve as a plausible statement of the relationship between drive level and level of performance, with maximum performance occurring at some intermediate drive level (Teece, 1965). A novel learning task is in itself arousal-inducing irrespective of whether the student is neurotically anxious or not. For the normal child, however, the problem[6] posed (plus whatever mild anxiety he might bring into the situation) would not produce a drive level above the critical value, and the resulting state of arousal would under most circumstances be facilitating. However, the neurotically anxious child brings a surplus of anxiety into the learning situation, particularly when it is truly novel and, therefore, potentially threatening to his self-esteem. For such a child the combined effect of the problem-induced arousal and the neurotic anxiety-induced arousal results in a drive level which is much too high for the improvisation necessary in the problem concerned.

The reactions of the "overaroused" student at this point are interesting and can be commonly observed in many classrooms or verified from personal experience. Initially the student's anxiety may cause his attention to be deflected from the problem to the cause of his anxiety, that is, his feelings of

---

[6]Novel learning tasks (that is, those requiring some measure of improvisation) would be classified at the level of problem solving or creativity in the standard taxonomy. The present discussion is concerned with behavior at these levels, rather than with straightforward comprehension or application of algorithms in familiar situations.

inadequacy. As Gaier (1952) puts it: "Thoughts about the self increase as the individual's oppositional tendencies increase, and these thoughts tend to grow more self-critical as negativism grows more intense . . . . The thinking is mostly about the individual's personal and intellectual adequacy (or inadequacy) related to the other class members." However, the individual remains under duress to solve the problem and he may effect a "face-saving" solution either by searching his repertoire for some plausible solution, often a memorized answer to a similar problem, or by reducing the complexity of the problem by ignoring relevant information (in effect, solving a simpler problem). In case of extreme arousal the student may mentally "freeze" and respond in a repetitive and nonadaptive way.

For example, in one experimental study of the effects of anxiety on learning (Ausubel and others, 1953a), university undergraduates who showed either low or high levels of endogenous anxiety were required to solve a stylus maze blindfolded. This situation constituted a mild form of threat to self-esteem, for if the subject was not able to solve the problem he demonstrated to the experimenter and to himself that he was not very good at a certain type of learning (even rats are reputed to learn to solve mazes). For all the subjects in the study, maze-learning represented a novel learning task for which past experience was not only of no help but was actually a hindrance. Successful solution of the problem could not be accomplished without improvisation.

The low-anxiety subjects with normal self-esteem tended to assume they could learn to improvise successfully with a little practice. And if they failed, so what? So they weren't good at solving mazes blindfolded. The high-anxiety subjects had a different orientation. Lacking normal self-esteem, they lacked confidence in their ability to cope with new adjustive situations. They were frightened when their habitual visual learning cues were removed, when they had to improvise. And lacking any intrinsic feelings of adequacy, they were naturally very dependent on the self-esteem they could achieve through successful performance. Thus they could less afford to say, "So what?" to failure.

What were the results? The high-anxiety subjects apparently overreacted to the threat to self-esteem emanating from the maze situation. On the first trial of the maze they became panicky and flustered, making a significantly greater number of errors than the low-anxiety subjects (see also: Scharf, 1964). But after the first trial the maze was no longer a new learning task requiring improvisation. It became more and more familiar and "old hat." By the end of ten trials, there was no longer a significant difference between the two anxiety groups.

This study suggests then that the debilitating effects of high anxiety will occur in genuinely novel learning situations, and that with experience with a given kind or class of problems the anxious learner may become "desensitized" to the point where he exhibits marked improvement. This result is consistent with studies which have shown that anxiety may enhance the learning of complex tasks when they do not seriously threaten self-esteem, that is, when they are not inordinately novel or significant (Van Buskirk, 1961; Wittrock and Husek, 1962); when the anxiety is only moderate in degree; or when the learner possesses effective anxiety-coping mechanisms (Suinn, 1965).

There remains for the teacher the difficult question as to which school-learning situations actually induce debilitating anxiety—in the short and long term—in both normal and neurotically anxious children. The learning of complex verbal materials in a typical classroom setting, for example, would seem to be a relatively familiar and nonthreatening task. On the other hand, genuine problem solving in science or mathematics or the demand for original or novel performance in any school subject might well be highly threatening for some students, depending upon their ability. Obviously a final answer for any particular student and kind of task can only be determined by close observation.

Effect of Anxiety on School Achievement

As could be reasonably anticipated, the effects of anxiety on school achievement are comparable to its effects on learning, except that on a long-term basis their destructive influence on most children is much less intense. No doubt this can be related to the fact that some school achievement tasks tend to lose their threatening implications as students gain experience in coping with them. Thus, at the elementary-school level anxiety generally depresses scholastic achievement (Cowen and others, 1965; Feldhusen and Klausmeier, 1962; Lunneborg, 1964; Reese, 1961; Sarason and others, 1964; Hill and Sarason, 1966). In high school, as the motivational effects of anxiety become stronger relative to its disruptive effects, the negative correlation between anxiety and academic achievement decreases, especially in boys; it is either weaker or entirely absent when grades are used as an index of achievement (Sarason, 1961, 1963; Walter and others, 1964). This weak, negative, or zero correlation also prevails at the college level (Alpert and Haber, 1960; Grooms and Endler, 1960; Spielberger and Katzenmeyer, 1959) or is replaced by a positive relationship between anxiety and academic achievement (Lundin and Sawyer, 1965), especially among academically superior students (Spielberger, 1962). In highly structured learning tasks such as programmed instruction, a positive relationship has been reported between anxiety and achievement (Kight and Sassenrath, 1966; Traweek, 1964). This finding is consistent with the fact that anxious pupils, particularly when compulsive, do much better in highly structured learning situations where novelty and the need for improvisation are minimal.[7]

OTHER RELEVANT DIMENSIONS OF PERSONALITY

Dogmatism and Authoritarianism

The term "dogmatism" is used to refer to a personality trait defined by the following kinds of behavior (Rokeach, 1960):

(a) closed-mindedness—unwillingness to examine new evidence after an opinion is formed; a tendency summarily to dismiss evidence or logic in conflict with one's position;

(b) a tendency to view controversial issues in terms of blacks and whites;

(c) opinionation—a tendency to form strong beliefs, highly resistant to change, on the basis of equivocal evidence;

(d) a tendency to reject other persons because of their beliefs;

(e) a tendency to isolate contradictory beliefs in logic-tight compartments;

(f) intolerance for ambiguity—a need for early closure in reaching conclusions about complex issues.

Not too unexpectedly, high close-minded scores are correlated negatively with verbal ability, school achievement, initial adaptation to concept learning tasks, and ability to form remote verbal associations (S. R. Baker, 1964; Ladd, 1967; Zagona and Zurcher, 1965; J. McV. Hunt, 1961). Dogmatism, the more general term in Rockeach's formulation, has been found to be inversely related to problem-solving ability and synthetic thinking and positively correlated with anxiety (Fillenbaum and Jackman, 1961; Rokeach, 1960). Apparently the relationship of dogmatism to the comprehension of classroom material is not clear since, in a number of studies with university sociology and psychology courses (Christensen, 1963; Costin, 1965; Ehrlich, 1961a, b; White and Alter, 1967; Zagona and Zurcher, 1965) correlations, though generally negative, varied from $-.54$ to $+.16$.

---

[7]Other recent studies indicating a positive relationship between school achievement and anxiety are: Degnan, 1967; Roy and Sinha, 1966; Robinson, 1966; Denny, 1966; and Katahn, 1966. The latter two studies indicate that high ability and high anxiety combine potently to facilitate achievement. Presumably students possessing these qualities, because of their superior ability, are able to attack novel learning situations with learned strategies, thereby reducing uncertainty and putting their high drive to work to their advantage.

The term "authoritarianism" is used to describe a related personality trait that is characterized by orthodoxy, veneration of traditional beliefs, and a tendency to overconform uncritically to the views of authority figures (Adorno and others, 1950). The authoritarian personality tends to be ethnocentric, prejudiced against minority groups, and intolerant of ambiguity (Adorno and others, 1950), and is found more commonly in lower-class and low-occupation groups (Adorno and others, 1950; Livson and Nichols, 1957). Students making high scores on scales of authoritarianism are more likely to structure novel stimuli in rigid fashion, to reach closure more quickly, and to change their attitudes in response to prestige suggestion (Duncan and others, 1964; Harvey, 1963; Wright and Harvey, 1965; Vaughan and White, 1966).

It seems clear that the traits of dogmatism and authoritarianism comprise a cluster of affective-social and cognitive variables such that both would influence those kinds of school learning in which attitudes, beliefs, and value judgments are brought into play. Moreover the highly dogmatic or authoritarian person seems predestined to do poorly in problem-solving and thinking tasks which require, in fact, that he possess the opposite of many of the attributes listed. Both traits probably reflect a need to maintain congruence or internal consistency among one's ideas and beliefs—a need which apparently varies considerably from individual to individual. Although this latter point suggests some innate predisposition toward authoritarianism and dogmatism, wide differences between cultures and socioeconomic, political, and religious groups on these measures suggest that a form of learning—probably through early identification with authoritarian and dogmatic parents—is an important factor.

Introversion and Extroversion

The introversion-extroversion dimension of personality is widely alluded to in popular and professional discussions of personality types. The term "introvert" refers to a person who tends to withdraw from social interaction and to be interested in his own thoughts and feelings rather than in on-going events in the world around him. The term "extrovert" describes an outgoing person whose interests are directed toward people and things in the outer environment. The educator's interest in this particular dimension stems from the fact that the introvert seems to be more easily "conditioned," that is, his behavior is more readily brought under the control of social and self-generated stimuli (Eysenck and others, 1960). If this is a viable generalization, it would suggest that the two personality types would react differently to a given program of reward, punishment, or reinforcement generally.

Support for this latter hypothesis comes from a study by Thompson and Hunnicutt (1944) in which both praise and blame treatments were employed with both introverted and extroverted fifth-grade pupils, yielding the following groups: (1) extrovert — praised (EP); (2) extrovert — blamed (EB); (3) introvert — praised (IP); (4) introvert — blamed (IB). Despite the fact that the "praise" and "blame" treatments were rather weak (that is, making the notation "good" or "poor" on the child's test paper), significant differential effects became evident over a series of tests (Figure 13.1). In brief, repeated praise was more effective with introverts than repeated "blame," while the opposite was true for extroverts. Although not shown on this diagram, all four groups out-performed a matched control group which received no praise or blame whatever.[8]

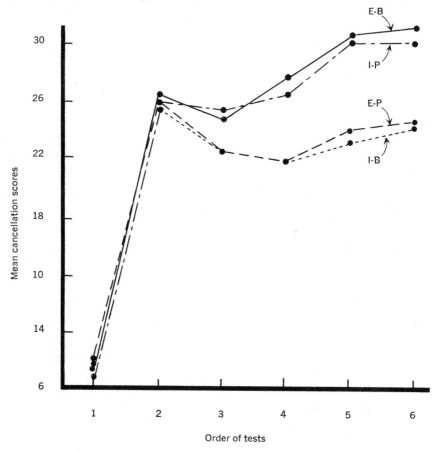

FIGURE 13.1   *The effects of praise and blame on introverts and extroverts. From: G. G. Thompson and C. W. Hunnicutt, "The effect of repeated praise and blame," J. educ. Psychol., 35, 1944, 264.*

Self-Concept and Defense Mechanisms

In previous sections we spoke of an individual's "self-esteem" to refer either to the intrinsic feeling of value acquired by identification with his parents or to the feeling of worth acquired by accomplishment (earned status). The term *self-concept*, although clearly related to self-esteem, is usually somewhat broader in intent. An individual's self-concept is the set of cognitive and affective states which define his attitudes toward himself; that is, it is a more or less consistent and integrated view of himself which the individual carries from one situation to another. The self-concept is obviously a very complex entity embracing mental, physical, emotional, moral, and social attributes.

Presumably it is important for a normal individual to have a stable, essentially favorable view of himself, and he will therefore frequently distort or reject interpretations of reality which would conflict with this positive assessment.[9] For illustrative purposes, we may consider the student who is facing the prospect of an important examination. If the impending event is perceived in advance to be threatening to his self-esteem, anxiety will be generated and the individual may be activated either to avoid the threatening situation or to prepare to cope with it through study. Suppose, however, that the examination has occurred and the student has done poorly. How is he then to protect his self-concept from this (objectively) damaging evidence of failure?

As suggested above, he will tend to interpret the event in a way which, while protecting his self-esteem, would not be considered an objective assessment of the facts by an unbiased observer. Such biased and self-esteem-protecting interpretations are usually designated "defense mechanisms." For example, the individual might *rationalize* the event by saying that he did not study enough for the examination, or that obtaining a high grade is not important to him, or that the marking was unfair; in this case he has offered a causal explanation of his poor performance which does not conflict with his

---

[8]Studies probing the effects of the teacher's praise and reproof on children with other personality characteristics have been conducted by White (1967) and Feshbach (1967). White found that praise was generally more effective (irrespective of personality type) and Feshbach found that advantaged children imitated a (positive) reinforcing teacher more often than a negative teacher; disadvantaged children imitated teachers of either kind less.

[9]There will, of course, exist large differences in the degree of positiveness inherent in the self-concepts of different individuals. Such differences have been shown to relate to school achievement (Quimby, 1967; Bhatnager, 1966) with the more adequate self-concept (that is, more closely related to the individual's "ideal self"—what he would like to be like) being associated with higher achievement.

concept of himself as a capable individual. Another mechanism, called *repression,* occurs when the individual suppresses threatening information about himself. In our example this might happen years later when the individual, still thinking of himself as a person possessing considerable intellectual acumen, "forgets" about the particular negative instance.

Another so-called "defense mechanism" is termed *projection,* and refers to the attempted justification of our actions by attributing our own motives to other persons. For example, if the student resorts to cheating on the examination he may convince himself that he is only doing what others do, or that he is merely defending himself against a biased or punitive teacher (Knowlton and Hamerlynck, 1967).

Such attempts by the student to retain a positive view of himself are frequently in evidence in the on-going drama of the classroom. Forewarned, the teacher will at least be able to understand these behaviors for what they are. Moreover, since both withdrawl and the defense mechanisms are generally detrimental to further learning, the teacher ought to be concerned that prevailing conditions will elicit a minimum number of instances of these responses.

IMPLICATIONS FOR THE SCHOOL

Having dealt with a limited portion of the vast literature on personality variables, we must now ask what the teacher is to do with this information. Although the advice which can be offered is not as unequivocal as one might wish, some suggestions may be advanced on the utilization of personality variables to facilitate learning and on the school's responsibility for promoting personal adjustment and growth.

Personality Adjustment and School Achievement

Certainly it is not surprising that poor personality adjustment is negatively related to school achievement, inasmuch as all of the symptoms of such maladjustment interfere in one way or another with cognitive and motivational factors promoting effective long-term learning. Evidence on this point comes from many sources. We previously saw that anxiety is correlated negatively with achievement in the elementary school, and that both high anxiety and the dogmatism-authoritarianism syndrome inhibit learning which requires flexibility in novel situations. In addition, it has been found that both teachers' rating of adjustment (Ausubel and others, 1954b; Ullman, 1957) and scores on the California Psychological Inventory (Gough, 1964) are moderately correlated with such criteria of success in school as grade-point average, completion of high school, and graduation with honors.

Many other studies have demonstrated a relationship between specific aspects of personality adjustment and school performance (Brookover and others, 1964; Byers, 1962; d'Heurle and others, 1959; Frankel, 1960; Todd and others, 1962; Wattenberg and Clifford, 1964). To some extent a "halo effect" may be operating[10] in some of these studies, since teachers tend both to downgrade the academic achievement of poorly adjusted children (particularly if they are aggressive, inattentive, or hyperactive) and to give poor adjustment ratings to nonachieving students. Despite this tendency to create artificial correlations between achievement and adjustment scores, it is clear that some real relationship remains.

Increasing Knowledge of Individual Differences in Personality

In view of the foregoing, one would think it generally advisable for the teacher to be sensitive to the personality characteristics of each child. There is, however, reason to believe that classroom teachers are not very skilled in such assessment. For example, it has been found that they cannot predict very accurately student response to questions on their hobbies, interests, problems, and personality characteristics (Amos and Washington, 1960; H. L. Baker, 1938); their motivations and their academic strivings (Ausubel, 1951; Ausubel and others, 1954b); their scores on objective and projective tests of adjustment (Ausubel and others, 1954b); their satisfaction with school (Jackson and Lahaderne, 1967); and the extent to which they are accepted by their classmates (Ausubel and others, 1952; Bonney, 1947; Gronlund, 1950). These perceptions become more inaccurate as students progress through the grades (Ausubel and others, 1952; Moreno, 1934).

It is not difficult to find explanations for these findings. Teachers are simply not aware of the distinctive standards and values that operate in the lives of their students. By the age of adolescence the estrangement between children and their elders has made considerable progress and is often compounded by the outright hostility and anti-adult attitudes manifested by youth. Channels of communication break down, and teachers are obliged to interpret their students' behavior at face value or by their own standards and frames of reference. Consequently they fall back upon interpretive biases from recollections of their own adolescence and from norms of behavior that pertain exclusively to their own middle-class background. Teachers also tend to over-value the popularity of children with whom they have satisfactory relationships (Bonney, 1947; Gronlund, 1950).

---

[10]A "halo effect" is a tendency to be biased in rating an individual on characteristic B because of a known previous rating (good or bad) on some irrelevant characteristic A.

There is some evidence, however, to support the contention that teachers who are better informed about students' personality structures, and who are aided in designing specific plans to utilize this information, will produce more effective learning. In a study by Ojemann and Wilkinson (1939) the teachers of an experimental group were given detailed analyses of their students' personality as well as specific suggestions for planning learning experiences based upon these data. The investigators not only interviewed the teachers individually but made periodic visits to their classrooms to discuss student progress and emerging problems. At the end of one year of this intensified program significant gains in achievement, attitude, and personal adjustment had been made by students in the experimental group— gains not evident in the matched control group which had been taught with the usual amount of attention paid to personality variables. Another study (Hoyt, 1955), however, found no relationship between teacher knowledge of student characteristics and achievement, although attitudes toward the teacher became more favorable in the group taught by more knowledgeable teachers. Taking these results together, it would appear that knowledge is insufficient in itself and that the teacher needs guidance in utilizing this knowledge to cope with learning problems posed by individual students.

Differential Treatment of Students

The previous remarks beg the question of *how* the teacher is to modify his teaching strategy to accommodate individual personality traits. Clearly an explicit answer would have to be given for each of the numerous dimensions of personality. However, as a specific example we might consider the satellizer/nonsatellizer distinction mentioned earlier. On theoretical grounds, satellizers should learn best in a warm and supportive interpersonal environment in which they can relate to teachers as parent surrogates. In this connection it has been shown that they achieve best when teaching methods are "indirect" rather than "direct" (Amidon and Flanders, 1961). At the same time teachers must always guard against the tendency of satellizers to overconform to their directions and expectations (Kagan and Mussen, 1956; Livson and Mussen, 1957), since both their resistance to and acceptance of new values stem largely from considerations of personal identification and loyalty.

Nonsatellizers, on the other hand, require teacher approval as objective evidence of achievement rather than as confirmation of personal acceptance. In the most general terms, such students would seem to do best in learning situations which are sufficiently structured so that the route to achievement (and hence to self-esteem enhancement) is well-defined and unobstructed by acute anxiety-inducing elements. For example, novel learning tasks and methods of instruction should be presented to them gradually (that is, with as much prefamiliarization as possible). Moreover, over-critical, deprecatory, demanding, and authoritarian teacher behavior should be avoided, since it would seem likely to raise the anxiety level of anxious nonsatellizers, precipitating hostility, aggressiveness, and withdrawal.

The teacher can also attempt to influence specific attitudes which are antagonistic to particular ideas or viewpoints. This situation will arise, for example, when the material to be learned evokes affective or value-laden responses (controversial material) so that the student's negative bias may actually interfere with the learning of the cognitive content of the material. When such material is to constitute a complete course or a lengthy instructional sequence, the teacher might find it profitable to attempt to modify unfavorable attitudes before commencing, or during the course of teaching, the unit.

Although it is admittedly difficult through mere presentation of facts to change attitudes that are firmly established both on a cognitive and an emotional basis, this can be accomplished if it is attempted systematically and if the implications of the facts for the attitudes in question are drawn explicitly. Bond (1940) demonstrated this to be the case in modifying racially prejudiced ideas through a special instructional unit on genetics. Greater lasting change in attitudes can be effected if a two-sided presentation of the issues is made (Lumsdaine and Janis, 1953). This approach not only discounts the counter-arguments in advance, but it is also less likely to give the impression of constituting biased propaganda. The evidence is equivocal whether discussion leads to more lasting changes of attitudes than does mere presentation of the controversial position in lecture form, or whether the presentation of a point of view by a prestigious figure has any long-term effect (Kelman and Hovland, 1953), but it does appear that a greater change in opinion occurs if the individual plays the role of a sincere advocate of a given point of view (Janis and King, 1954).

The School's Responsibility for Promoting Personality Growth

What has been said above refers to the utilization of personality variables in an attempt to produce behavioral changes in the cognitive domain. At the same time, most reasonable people would agree that the school also has some responsibility with respect to mental health and personality development itself, if for no other reason than that it is the place where children spend a good part of their waking hours, perform much of their purposeful activity, obtain a large share of their status, and interact significantly with adults, age-mates, and the demands of society.

Particularly during adolescence, problems of adjustment—vocational choice, emancipation from parents, somatic deviations, relationships with peers, adults, and members of the opposite sex—are very real and important to students. Psychologically, these developmental tasks are too urgent to be ignored, and if young people perceive the school as uninterested in them, they will react either by losing interest in the academic areas the school values or by feeling guilty for being preoccupied with these supposedly "trivial" matters. As long as the organizational, administrative, disciplinary, and interpersonal aspects of the school environment inevitably affect the mental health and personality development of its future citizens, it obviously behooves society to arrange these matters as appropriately and constructively as possible. Nevertheless, because the mental-health role of the school has been oversold and misrepresented frequently by educational theorists, it will be worth our while to consider some of the more serious misconceptions about the mental-health functions of the school.

The Primary Responsibility of the School It must be restated that the primary and distinctive function of the school in our society is not to promote mental health and personality development but to foster intellectual growth and the assimilation of knowledge. Moreover, the school's role in personality development can only be supplementary to those of other socializing agencies such as the home, the church, and the neighborhood. And, as indicated above, much of the school's legitimate concern with interpersonal relations in the classroom does not stem merely from an interest in enhancing healthful personality development as an end in itself, no matter how important this objective may be, but reflects appreciation of the negative effects which an unfavorable social and emotional school climate has on academic achievement, on motivation to learn, and on desirable attitudes toward intellectual inquiry.

The Limits of Normality Some educators tend to exaggerate the seriousness and permanence of the effects on mental health of minor deviations from the norm of desirable hygienic practice. There is every reason to believe, however, that a wide margin of safety is the rule in mental as well as in physical health. Within fairly broad limits, many different kinds of teacher personality structures and ways of relating to children are compatible with normal mental health and personality development in students. In general, children are not nearly as fragile as we profess to believe, and do not develop permanent personality disabilities from temporary exposure to interpersonal practices that fall short of what the experts currently regard as appropriate. Furthermore, many students who manifest signs of behavioral disturbance in school either do so temporarily (D. B. Harris, 1960; MacFarlane and others, 1954) or fail to show any signs of maladjustment at home or in the peer group.

The Cult of Extroversion Several studies, all undertaken more than a decade ago (Wickman, 1928; Stouffer, 1952; Schrupp and Gjerde, 1953), suggested that when teachers and clinical psychologists are asked to select personality traits indicating poor adjustment, teachers tend to stress behavior which disrupts classroom learning routines while clinicians stress behavior indicating withdrawal from a conflict situation, shyness, and fearfulness (Table 13.1). It may be that these findings have had an influence on teacher training programs; in any case, more recent informal evidence, including notes which teachers append to report cards, suggests that many current graduates of teachers' colleges (and particularly those destined for work in the elementary grades) have moved far beyond the position taken by the clinicians in regarding a shy, withdrawing personality as a sign of potential maladjustment.[11]

According to some of the more extreme present viewpoints—which are consistent with the "go-go" emphasis of the "mod" set—the well-balanced or healthy personality is warm, outgoing, amiable, and extroverted; on the other hand, the child who is reserved, contemplative, and unconcerned about the opinion of his peers tends to arouse the clinical concern of the child guidance specialist. Similarly while many excellent teachers who happen to be shy and introverted are viewed with alarm by their psychologically-oriented superi-

TABLE 13.1

Traits on Which Greatest Disagreement Appears When Rated by 1951 Teachers and Clinicians

TRAITS RATED MORE SERIOUS BY TEACHERS	RANK DIFFERENCE	TRAITS RATED MORE SERIOUS BY CLINICIANS	RANK DIFFERENCE
1. Impertinence, defiance	26.5	1. Shyness	31
2. Impudence, rudeness	26	2. Suspiciousness	27.5
3. Obscene notes, pictures, and so forth	24	3. Dreaminess	25.5
4. Disobedience	24	4. Fearfulness	22
5. Disorderliness	24	5. Sensitiveness	20.5
6. Heterosexual activity	23	6. Overcritical of others	19
7. Masturbation	20	7. Imaginative lying	16
8. Untruthfulness	16	8. Nervousness	16

Source: M. H. Schrupp and C. M. Gjerde, "Teacher growth in attitudes toward behavior problems of children," *J. educ. Psychol., 44,* 1953, 203–214.

---

[11]Consistent with this, Tolor and others (1967) found that beginning teachers rated a much higher proportion of the items on a behavioral checklist as indicative of "abnormal behavior" than either experienced teachers or clinical psychologists. However, the areas of greatest concern to teachers in this particular study—regressive behavior (for example, "carries a blanket"); aggressive behavior (for example, "hits or attacks other children"); and affect expression (for example, "shows inappropriate feeling")—do not entirely support our contention of a swing toward concern for introversion and shyness.

ors, there is absolutely no evidence that they impair their students' mental health, even though they may conceivably be less popular as individuals than their extroverted colleagues.

As far as student popularity is concerned, it has been convincingly established that this characteristic may be a grossly misleading index of social adjustment. An ostensibly popular student may be little more than a "stranger in his group" in terms of the depths of his attachments, or may be popular simply because he is docile, conforming, and willing to be directed and "used" by others (Wittenberg and Berg, 1952). Contrariwise, the student who is unpopular because of temperamental shyness or strong intellectual interests is not necessarily socially maladjusted or inevitably fated to become so (Morris and others, 1954).

The Teacher's Responsibility
in Handling Personality Maladjustment

In view of the foregoing discussion it seems reasonable to conclude that the teacher's actual role in handling the behavior disorders lies in recognizing signs of serious maladjustments and in referring disturbed students to counselors, school psychologists, and psychiatrists. It is important, however, that they view realistically what such referrals can typically hope to accomplish. First, it would seem that counseling and psychotherapy have been somewhat oversold. The analogy of mental disease to physical disease is still quite optimistic, since incomparably less is known about the causes, nature, and treatment of the former than about corresponding aspects of the latter. Second, many of the persons pressed into service as counselors or school psychologists have had little more clinical training and supervised clinical experience than teachers. However, despite existing shortcomings, the school's psychological service will frequently be able to provide invaluable assistance to the student and to the teacher.

TOPICS FOR DISCUSSION AND FURTHER STUDY

1. It has frequently been suggested that male teachers should be encouraged to take positions in the primary grades. In what respects would this be an advantage (or disadvantage) for elementary-school children? As far as possible, support your assertions by reference to the concepts advanced in this chapter.

2.* Assess the opinions of teachers observed in your practice teaching on the characteristics of the child for which one should have concern from a mental health point of view. What general emphasis may be observed? Compare this emphasis with the viewpoint reported in the text.

3. The child who does not identify with his parents in a positive, dependent sense (that is, the nonsatellizer) may set high levels of aspiration with respect to school achievement. In what other, essentially negative, ways may he seek ego-en-

hancement? What factors will determine whether his ego-enhancement drive is directed toward positive or negative social goals?

4. What means exist for the teacher to determine whether the child is dominated by affiliative or ego-enhancement drive? Assuming that this has been determined, describe the differential treatments that one might employ in dealing with such children in the context of a particular classroom lesson.

5. What means exist for the teacher to determine whether the child is introverted or extroverted? Assuming that this has been determined, describe the differential treatments that one might employ in dealing with such children in the context of a particular classroom lesson.

6.* Investigate methods of attitude change. Propose how the school staff might utilize such methods in counteracting prejudice.

7. Evidence has been cited to the effect that teachers are unable to assess student personality variables, their liking for school, their popularity, and so on. How can the teacher's insights become more incisive? To what extent, and under what circumstances, would greater perception of the student's affective and social characteristics (on the part of the teacher) lead to improved student learning?

8. Assume that a nonsatellizing child has grown up and become a parent. What hypotheses might be advanced concerning the identification patterns of his own children?

9.* Investigate the origin of aggressive behavior in your children (Bandura and Walters, 1963; Wodke and Brown, 1967). What implications would current theoretical viewpoints have for the school's treatment of aggressive behavior?

10. What methods might be proposed for insuring that the child's anxiety level does not reach the point where complex performance is inhibited? What merit would there be in using isolation techniques for individual problem solving?

SUGGESTIONS FOR ADDITIONAL READING

Ausubel, D. P. *Ego development and the personality disorders.* New York: Grune and Stratton, Inc., 1952.

Ausubel, D. P. and others. Perceived parent attitudes as determinants of children's ego structure. *Child Development,* 1954, *25,* 173–183.

Bandura, A. and R. H. Walters. *Social learning and personality development.* New York: Holt, Rinehart and Winston, Inc., 1963.

Hall, C. S. and G. Lindzey. *Theories of personality.* New York: John Wiley and Sons, Inc., 1957.

Hill, K. T. and S. B. Sarason. The relation of test anxiety and defensiveness to test and school performance over the elementary school years. *Monogr. Soc. Res. Child Developm.,* 1966, *31* (2), (Serial No. 104).

McDonald, F. J. *Educational psychology* (2d edition). Belmont, Calif.: Wadsworth Publishing Co., Inc., 1965. Chapter 8 (The Learning of Attitudes), Chapter 9 (The Learning of Attitudes: Communication Processes), and Chapter 11 (Personality and the Self-Concept).

Wodtke, K. H. and B. R. Brown. Social learning and imitation. *Rev. Educ. Res.,* 1967, *37* (5), 514–538.

CHAPTER 14

GROUP AND SOCIAL FACTORS
IN LEARNING

IN THE TWO PRECEDING CHAPTERS WE HAVE SEEN HOW PERsonality and long-term motivational variables influence the child's learning. To some extent both of these factors may be thought of as the result or residue of the child's interaction with a group outside the student-teacher dyad. In our treatment to date, the essential outside "group" has been the family, and particularly the parents. Developing further the educational implications of group and social forces, this chapter begins with the individual student, progressively widens its focus to envisage this student in a succession of group memberships, and attempts to assess the influence of each membership on classroom performance.

Part of the significant interaction in the classroom lies outside the student-teacher (or student-learning material) dyad. Usually the individual student is working in the presence of other members of his *classroom group*. Sometimes he is specifically engaged in competition with such members; at other times he is working in cooperation with them (as in sharing ideas in discussion) or in working toward a group product. As will be pointed out below, all of these relationships influence the individual's learning to some extent.

Moving outside the immediate confines of the classroom, we first encounter the *peer group*, a phenomenon closely associated in contemporary North American society with school attendance (in one sense the school's extracurricular program provides the central locus of peer group activities). Since the peer group does not always cherish, and may systematically oppose, the values inherent in school achievement, this phenomenon is one of central importance to the educator. Our particular emphasis will be on the *adolescent peer group,* an entity of much interest and some consternation in contemporary educational thought.

Expanding our view beyond the peer group to incorporate the earliest influence of the home setting, we must recognize that the child's *social sex group* provides one of his most fundamental class memberships. The fact is that from an early age it is made clear to the child that differential cultural expectations exist with regard to the school achievement of male and female students. Moreover, although the evidence is somewhat debatable on this point, it is frequently suggested that the school itself reflects these cultural expectations, and that teachers treat boys and girls differently as *learners,* at first to the disadvantage of the boys, but ultimately to the disadvantage of girls.

With respect to other group memberships which have implications for classroom learning, it has been known for some time that children of certain *socioeconomic* and *ethnic* groups suffer from sizeable educational disadvantages, such disadvantages resulting from an impoverished preschool learning environment and continued exposure to strong anti-school attitudes. The failure of the traditional school to make much impact on these children has acquired considerable significance in the past decade, during which this failure has been increasingly linked to the problem of minorities. And with the recognition of failure has come a plethora of suggestions for a more potent (usually earlier) form of educational intervention. Clearly the prospective teacher must be provided with viewpoints on these important social issues, including that provided by educational psychology.

INTERACTION OF LEARNERS IN THE SCHOOL SETTING

If one were to observe the kinds of interaction which take place during the course of the typical lesson in today's classroom, three basic patterns would emerge. First, one would observe *teacher-pupil* interaction as, for example, when the teacher instructs and the pupil listens or when either party asks questions and the other clarifies. Second, one would find *student-instructional material* interaction when the student works on a problem in a text, reads a passage, or looks up a definition, Finally, one would find *pupil-pupil* interaction when students react to each other's opinions and attitudes during discussions of controversial material, or when teams are formed to work cooperatively on problems.

In the traditional classroom, the first two patterns of interaction predominated and the third tended to be discouraged. However, several recent emphases in education—including discovery learning, group problem-solving approaches, and the increased value placed on discussion skills—have resulted in greater acceptance of the legitimacy of pupil-pupil interaction and an increased interest in determining the conditions under which such interaction promotes learning. There is no single answer to this question since it depends greatly upon the nature of the task, on the extent to which task solutions require information residing outside the learning situation (Roby and others, 1963), on the size and composition of the group (Tuckman, 1967; Glanzer and Glanzer, 1961), on the cohesiveness of the group (Lott and Lott, 1961, 1966), on the effectiveness of leadership (Maier, 1967; Roby and others, 1963), and on whether our criterion of superiority is a group product or the individual products of the component group members. Nevertheless, some useful observations can be made by a judicious combination of common sense and research findings.

Advantages of Student Interaction

In performing simple or routine tasks requiring little or no thinking, the concomitant activity of other similar individuals seems to serve as a stimulus, generating contagious behavior and competitive striving—either when people work by themselves in the presence of others (Mukerji, 1940) or when they work in pairs (Myers and others, 1965). This effect is comparable to the heightened rate of activity stimulated by a pace-setter, and it is by no means confined to children, since the reader of this text may well find that he works more assiduously when there are others about him working than he does on Sundays or holidays when others are at their leisure.

A second advantage of group learning occurs in complex problem-solving tasks where obtaining a correct solution is facilitated by generating a multiplicity of alternative hypotheses (that is, divergent thinking). In this situation group effort is apparently superior to individual effort (M. Goldman, 1965; Klausmeier and others, 1963; Lorge, 1955; Marquart, 1955; Shaw, 1932; G. B. Watson, 1928). Closer analysis reveals that group effort is more effective under these circumstances, largely because it increases the probability of having at least one person who can arrive independently at the correct solution. Also, if the task requires evaluation or decision making, cooperative deliberation and the reaching of consensus is usually superior, because it avoids the pitfalls of idiosyncratic or extreme judgment (Barnlund, 1959). Classroom illustrations of these particular advantages are not hard to find. For example, if a mathematics problem or puzzle requires some extremely innovative approach, a solution is more likely to occur to a group of students than to any one of its individual members. Again, a group discussion of the "merits and demerits of the present system of taxation" is more likely to bring a balanced view and curb the excesses inherent in the individual judgments.

If the learning product of each group member is used as the criterion of success, it is evident that the less able members of a group can accomplish more than they would individually, if they are stimulated by working with—and being able to adopt the ideas and strategies of—the more able students (Gurnee, 1962). In effect, such students would to some extent enjoy the benefit of student tutors. Thus studies of gains in skill in cooperative learning sessions have tended to show that it is the low-ability pupil who profits most (M. Goldman, 1965).

A final advantage of pupil interaction occurs in discussion, which is the most effective and perhaps the only feasible method of promoting intellectual growth with respect to the less established and more controversial aspects of subject matter. In such areas discussion provides the best means of broadening the pupil's intellectual horizons, of stimulating his thinking through cross-fertilization, of clarifying his views, and of measuring their cogency against the viewpoints of others. Interaction with peers, furthermore, helps the pupil overcome both his egocentricity and his childhood perception of adults as the absolute source of truth and wisdom with regard to all value judgments. He learns the extent to which both his ideas and those of the teacher represent idiosyncratic positions along a broad spectrum of opinions whose validity is indeterminable.

Disadvantages of Student Interaction

A first disadvantage can be inferred from the observation that if the slower-learning child is helped by the bright child acting as tutor, then the pace of learning for the bright child in that situation may be slowed to some extent. This would commonly be the case if pairs or small groups of children were set to work on almost any kind of "linear-convergent" learning task, that is, one which—like an arithmetical calculation but unlike a jigsaw puzzle—can be solved by performing a sequentially dependent set of calculations with conventional techniques (Klugman, 1944; Husband, 1940). How the teacher would assess the slow learner's gain against the fast learner's loss seems a rather moot point.

Another disadvantage will occur in the situation in which an aggressive student dominates one who is more reticent. Generally speaking, one would think that in a small group—given proper directions by the teacher—each individual could make a contribution and thereby increase his problem-solving skills. In a large group, on the other hand, the individual's opportunity for participation is not only limited by the number of participants but also by the fact that the most aggressive members tend to take over and monopolize the problem-solving activity (Carter and others, 1951). Even when the aggressive student does not monopolize, the advantages of group discussion and problem solving will be vitiated if the group is so congenial (Back, 1951;

Shaw and Shaw, 1962) or if its leadership is so personal (Fiedler, 1958) that considerable time and effort is diverted into purely social activity.

Another potential disadvantage of student interaction in classroom learning is that certain students will not freely enter into the interaction, but will feel anxious, and their performance will deteriorate accordingly. Some children work better on their own, producing solutions to problems which they check against the answers in the book or submit to the teacher for his assessment. Many such children, while feeling comfortable and adequate in their private speculations, would be hesitant about, and even fearful of, exposing these thoughts to the scrutiny of their peers.

Finally we must consider that many intellectual problems are best solved in isolation. It is clear, for example, that while a group of students or adults may work together to compile information for a report, it is usually more economical for one individual to write the report. As another specific example, one might observe that even though a group of individuals is more likely than any individual member to produce a solution to a problem involving a higher degree of novelty, it remains an open question as to whether group experiences of this kind provide the best training for the novel but solitary thinking which the individual must do in his later school or adult life (Hudgins, 1966). Relative to the latter point, productive adult intellectual behavior still remains primarily an individual rather than a group activity.

Individual Orientations to Group Experience

A brief word might be said at this point about students' differential personality orientations toward experience. The child's idiosyncratic manner of relating to significant persons in the family setting has ample opportunity to become solidified long before he is ever permitted to venture unmonitored from the home. It is hardly surprising, therefore, that his approach to interpersonal experience with his earliest socializers should be generalized to other kinds of social situations. To the satellizing child, the peer group provides derived status in much the same way as the parent, except that the status-giving authority resides in a group of which he himself is part. By relating to it he obtains the same supportive "we-feeling" that he experiences in the family group.

The nonsatellizer, on the other hand, cannot assume an internalized position of self-subserviency in relation to the group. The field of intragroup relations, like the home, is no place for "we-feeling"; it is just another arena in which he contends for primary status, prestige, power, and self-aggrandizement. He does not subordinate himself to group interests or experience spontaneous satisfaction in gregarious activity. Social moves are carefully deliberated for possible advantages that may follow from them; and, not by nature gregarious, he may synthetically manufacture the attitudes, remarks, and behavior that can be construed as conventionally appropriate for the specifications of a given situation. He is quite capable, of course, of harvesting vicarious status from identification with prestigious membership or reference groups; but since no subservience of self is required, it bears little resemblance to the derived status of satellizers. The prestige of family, club, college, and nationality is incorporated merely as a gratuitous form of ego-enhancement or as a springboard for the realization of personal ambitions. As already pointed out, the nonsatellizing orientation to group experience tends, on a normative basis, increasingly to characterize the maturing individual as he approaches adulthood. Nevertheless, the ex-satellizer continues to display satellizing-like attitudes in many group situations, particularly those which are informal and hence not directly related to his functional competence.

Educational Implications

Given advantages on both sides, the balance to be obtained in group as opposed to individual learning experiences constitutes a problem which cannot be solved by formula. Perhaps as a rough guide we might reasonably conclude that, other things being equal, the incidence of the two kinds of learning experiences should be roughly proportioned to their incidence in real life. Certainly, at some point in the future, today's school child will be called upon to work on a committee, to act as a member of a research team, or as one half of a husband-wife dyad. In all instances some prior experience in working cooperatively in groups would probably be to his advantage; on the other hand, the mature individual, either as a student of some field of knowledge, or simply as a thinking adult, will frequently, if not typically, find himself in the position where he has to solve problems on his own.

COMPETITION AND COOPERATION

Competition ordinarily is a form of ego-enhancement motivation involving self-aggrandizing activity in which the individual vies with others for status or preeminence. Cooperation, on the other hand, is a group-oriented activity in which the individual collaborates with others to attain some common goal. Nevertheless these two activities are by no means antithetical to each other: both imply at least some degree of interaction within the group as opposed to individual behavior that is carried on with little reference to the activities of others. Furthermore, much competition *between* groups occurs in the context of intense cooperation and affiliative drive *within* groups.

The relative prominence of cooperation and competition varies greatly with the cultural environment (Mead, 1937). Our own culture values both kinds of behavior, often inconsistently, and hence fosters a great deal of ambivalence. Generally speaking, ego-enhancement motivation has a self-aggrandizing and competitive flavor in our culture which varies from one social class to another. Although lower-class preschool children tend to be more competitive than middle-class children in play situations (McKee and Leader, 1955), the latter eventually internalize higher aspirations for academic and vocational prestige. Boys in our culture are consistently more competitive than girls during both early and later childhood (McKee and Leader, 1955).

Many activities in the peer group evoke cooperative and competitive behavior either simultaneously or alternately. Team games are competitive contests between two cooperatively organized groups. However, members of the same team may compete against each other while striving jointly for a distinctive team goal, or several teams may compete against each other in furthering a cause common to all. Some children are competitive under neutral or cooperative conditions (Ausubel, 1951), others are cooperative under competitive conditions (Stendler and others, 1951), and still others are task-oriented under any conditions (Ausubel, 1951). Thus, despite the purportedly cooperative or competitive conditions characterizing a particular enterprise, the extent to which a given child is ego-oriented, task-oriented, or group-oriented can be ascertained only by individual motivational analysis.

Competition has both desirable and undesirable effects on personality development. On the credit side it stimulates individual effort and productivity, promotes higher standards and aspirations, and narrows the gap between capacity and performance. Children of elementary-school age work harder under competitive conditions than when working anonymously (Ausubel, 1951). They also work harder for individual rewards than for group prizes (Maller, 1929; Sims, 1928), but, even so, are highly responsive to such natural competitive situations as contests between boys and girls, teams, and classrooms (Maller, 1929). By enabling the individual to obtain a more realistic estimate of his own capacities in relation to those of others, competition also exerts a salutary effect on self-critical ability. Under the stimulus of competition the child is better able to discover both his own limitations as well as hitherto unrealized capacities, and is motivated to overcome objectionable personality traits. Competition makes group games more interesting and everyday tasks less monotonous, and properly used, it can contribute to group morale (Fiedler, 1967). Children in competitive situations have also been found to be more sensitive to the performance of their classmates, with the result that their behavior is shaped more easily by indirect reinforcement (Sugimura, 1966).

On the debit side, competition may inhibit learning by arousing undue anxiety (Shaw, 1958). When carried to unwholesome extremes, it fosters feelings of inadequacy in less able children, encourages them to withdraw from activities in which they do not excel, and unduly depresses their status in the group (under less extreme conditions, however, it helps them to adjust to the competitive organization of our culture in which individuals must still continue striving even though they realize that preeminence is beyond their reach). It may lead to a tense, hostile, vindictive, and negative group climate (Sherif and Sherif, 1953) in which ruthlessness, unfairness, and dishonesty are condoned in the interests of emerging victorious. In such an atmosphere, the demonstration of superiority and the pleasing of authority figures become the primary goals, whereas the intrinsic value of the activity, self-expression, and creativity are de-emphasized. Finally, when excessive value is placed on superior achievement, children became obsessed with the notion of self-aggrandizement and lose sight of human values. Prestigeful attainment becomes the sole criterion of human worth and source of self-esteem.

The adverse consequences of competition have undoubtedly been exaggerated, however, because of a tendency to view the matter in all-or-none terms. Competitive and noncompetitive activities are by no means mutually exclusive. A program of interscholastic athletics, for example, does not preclude in any way adequate attention to the physical education needs of the athletically less talented. Neither is it necessary to carry competition to extremes. Under experimental conditions moderate forms of competition do not lead to more negative interactions among pupils (Stendler and others, 1951), decrease group cohesiveness (Phillips and D'Amico, 1956), or increase cheating on a self-scoring test (M. M. Gross, 1946).

Educational Implications

From the foregoing remarks it would appear that a limited amount of interpersonal competition in the classroom seems warranted. Many time-honored practices—spelling bees; posted progress charts; competition between the "rows," sex groups, or other natural classroom groupings; and display of outstanding work on the bulletin board—probably work in conjunction with ego-enhancement motivation to produce greater effort and achievement. Naturally the sensitive teacher will be alert to circumstances in which individual children or whole groups will be adversely affected, and will eschew attaching such importance to the outcome of the competition that the mere desire to win at any cost provides the child's sole motivation.

The theoretical and practical cogency of traditional modes of interper sonal competiton does not mean, however, that the school should not experiment with different emphases and approaches. For example, on the general premise that cognitive drive underlies the most desirable kind of achievement motivation, it would seem worthwhile to make greater efforts to engage the student in competition with *himself,* in the sense that he would continually try to improve his present understanding of, or skill in, a given subject. In an experiment in elementary-school arithmetic (N.S.S.E., 1930), children were taught to keep records of their cumulative progress by means of charts and graphs. The knowledge that progress was being made led to significant improvement in performance over that shown by a control group. Such information probably serves a variety of motivations, including those based on ego-enhancement and affiliative needs; but it seems likely that the child's knowledge that he is making progress—a fact not always evident in the repetitive practice and incremental growth which occurs in typical classrooms —enhances cognitive drive as well.

Extending the previous idea, Bloom (1968) advocates that the child's progress be measured against *absolute standards* constituting "mastery" of a subject area, rather than against the performance of other children in the group. The latter practice, according to Bloom, coupled with the teacher's tendency to distribute marks on the so-called normal curve, means that the performance of many students will be judged inadequate because of their position in the distributions of marks and irrespective of the average score of the distribution. Moreover, since fixed allotments of time are given to particular learning tasks, the slower-learning child has no opportunity to compensate for this slowness and therefore cannot escape the lower end of the distribution ("failure").

Bloom's contention is that the vast majority of children can be brought to master the subject content areas provided that individual pacing is employed, a variety of materials and techniques are available, and the student can obtain advice on how he should proceed to use these materials. In the program envisaged, the standard which will constitute "mastery" of a subject area is clearly defined and the student works toward this expected level, guided by frequent diagnostic tests. The evidence so far is promising; a comparison of the mastery approach with conventional methods in a number of schools revealed an increase from 20 percent to 80 percent in the proportion of students receiving "A" grades on the same examination.

The self-competition and mastery approaches, which are clearly quite compatible, seem particularly well suited to a school program that attempts to cope with individual differences in cognitive abilities. In advocating them, however, the teacher should not succumb to the romantic notion that individual competition is thereby eliminated, for it is a safe bet that students—and their parents—will compare mastery units earned in a given year or by a given age. Nevertheless, these approaches seem capable of de-emphasizing the more unfortunate aspects of traditional classroom competition (failure and inappropriate pacing for many students) while allowing each student some taste of genuine mastery, which results in an almost certain impetus to cognitive drive.

THE ADOLESCENT LEARNER AND THE PEER GROUP[1]

It is impossible for anyone to teach in a secondary school or college for any length of time without becoming aware of the fact that the values of the adolescent culture are apparently at variance with those of the school. This conflict is a source of concern for the school because it extends beyond such peripheral matters as dress and language and tends to be focused on the value of academic achievement. Most adolescents accept scholastic achievement as necessary for college entrance and for the middle-class rewards of managerial and professional status, but they do not typically regard it as a legitimate basis for high status in the peer group or as a value worth striving for in its own right (Coleman, 1961; J. B. Marks, 1954). What are some of the origins of this adult-youth value conflict?

Adolescents in our culture naturally have the same needs for greater earned status and (volitional) independence that adolescents have in more primitive and traditional cultures. But the greater complexity of our techno-logical society necessitates an extended period of education and economic dependence on parents, prolonged vocational training, and the postponement of marriage well beyond the age of sexual maturity. Under these circum-stances, the adolescent cannot experience any *real* independence in the adult sense of the term, and can obviously acquire only a token earned status outside the mainstream of adult culture. He not only resents his exclusion from adult spheres of independence and status-giving activities, but also tends to resent such adult-controlled training institutions as the home, the school, and various organizations, because they conduct their training func-tions entirely apart from any opportunity for him to exercise independence, or to acquire earned status within the context of the adult culture. He is thus alienated from adult status-giving activities and from adult training institu-tions and, accordingly, from adult standards as well.

The Role of the Peer Group in Adult-Youth Alienation

Since the modern urban community does not provide teenagers with the kind of earned status, volitional independence, and training in social skills that

---

[1]Peer group influences on the learner exist both before and after adolescence. However, we confine our attention to the adolescent peer group, which clearly presents the greatest challenge to the educator.

they desire, the adolescent peer group is constituted to gratify, in part, these crucial needs. It is the only cultural institution in which their position is not marginal, in which they are offered earned status, independence, and social identity among a group of equals, and in which their own activities and concerns reign supreme. The peer group is also the major training institution for adolescents in our society; in the peer group the adolescent, by *doing,* learns something about the social processes of our culture, clarifies to some extent his sex role by acting and being responded to, and experiences cooperation, competition, social skills, values, and purposes (Tryon, 1944).

By virtue of performing these essential functions, the peer group also displaces parents as the major source of attributed status during adolescence. By identifying with and acquiring acceptance in the group, the adolescent gains a measure of intrinsic self-esteem that is independent of his achievement or relative status in the group. This "we-feeling" furnishes security and belongingness, and is a powerful ego-support and the basis of loyalty to group norms.

How does all of this increase adult-youth alienation? In the first place, the adolescent's very membership in a distinctive peer group, with its own status-giving activities, standards, and training functions, puts him in a *separate* subculture apart from adult society. Second, since he is largely dependent on the peer group for his volitional independence, for his earned and attributed status, for his sense of belongingness, and for his opportunities to acquire social skills and to practice his sex role, he accordingly tends to assimilate its standards, and he becomes increasingly more indifferent to adult norms and values. Lastly, the peer group's exaggerated needs for rigid conformity to its norms, as well as its power to exact conformity from its members, further accentuate the adolescent's alienation from adult society.

Limitations of Adult-Youth Alienation

With respect to the preceding section it must be remembered that adult-youth alienation is hardly an all-or-none matter. That is, operating simultaneously with the various factors causing adult-youth alienation there are also two general factors within each adolescent that maintain or increase his *identification* with adult society. In the first place adolescents, particularly those from middle-class backgrounds, are intensely concerned with educational and other pursuits that serve as stepping stones to genuine adult status. Their *ultimate* goals are *not* high status in the peer group—that is, the distinction of being the best dancer, the most prestigious athlete, the most popular and most frequently dated girl, the most daring drag racer—but rather, well-paid professional or managerial jobs, a comfortable home in the suburbs, marriage, and a family. They realize that attainment of these goals requires long-term striving, self-denial, the approval of persons in authority, restraint of aggressive impulses, and avoidance of an unsavory or delinquent reputation. Furthermore, the assimilation of new peer group values does not by any means imply *complete* repudiation of adult values assimilated in an early stage of intense identification with the parent.

Thus, it greatly overstates the case to claim that adolescents are *entirely* oblivious of adult approval, that they completely reject adult values and standards. This much is clearly evident when we pause to consider that one of the principal functions of the peer group is to transmit from one generation to the next the appropriate social-class values, aspirations, motivational patterns, and character traits that adolescents are often unwilling to accept from parents and teachers, but *are* willing to accept from their age-mates.

It must be admitted, however, that developments characterizing our culture since World War II have tended to undermine the counter-balancing effect of aspirations for genuine adult status and previously assimilated adult values on adult-youth alienation. Since the adolescent now perceives adults as being able to "get ahead" without fully exemplifying the traditional middle-class virtues, he is naturally led to believe that he too can achieve the adult status and independence he craves without thoroughly acquiring these same virtues himself, and that adults are not really concerned whether or not he acquires these virtues. Thus, he is not as highly motivated as were prewar adolescents either to develop such traits as self-restraint, willingness to work hard, a sense of responsibility, impulse control, self-denial, personal integrity, and respect for the rights and property of others, or to seek adult approval for so doing. Moreover, the adolescent's awareness of the grievous lack of moral courage in the adult world and of the premium that adults place on conformity and expediency furnishes him with a very poor model for holding fast to his moral convictions in the face of group pressure. Both of these factors are conspicuous in the repudiation of middle-class respectability as hypocrisy, characterizing the current student revolt and "New Left" movements.

Conformity in the Adolescent Peer Culture

The exaggerated patterns of conformity within the adolescent peer group constitute perhaps its most unique structural characteristic in comparison with groupings of children and adults. As adolescents become more and more resistive to adult suggestion and increasingly indifferent to adult approval and disapproval, "the approval or disapproval of peers becomes progressively the most influential force motivating adolescent conduct. For the adolescent there can be no stronger argument for having or doing a thing than the fact that all the others are doing it. Nothing is likely to awaken so great an emotional disturbance or cause so much worry as the feeling that he is in some way different from the others" (Blos, 1941).

It is necessary for two important reasons that the peer group demand considerable conformity from its members. First, in its efforts to establish a new and distinctive subculture and to evolve a unique set of criteria for the determination of status and prestige, the peer group must do everything in its power to set itself off as recognizably distinct and separate from the adult society which refuses it membership. And if this distinctiveness is to be actually attained, widespread nonconformity obviously cannot be tolerated, Second, conformity is also essential to maintain the group solidarity that is necessary to offer effective and organized resistance to the encroachments of adult authority (Tryon, 1944). If an appeal to precedent or to a prevailing standard of adolescent behavior is to be the basis for exacting privileges and concessions from adults, a solid and united front with a minimum of deviancy must be presented to the world.

Because of the adolescent's marginal status, the peer group is in an excellent position to demand conformity from him as the price of its acceptance. Much more than the child or adult, he is desperately dependent upon the peer group for whatever social status and security he is able to achieve during these hectic years of transition. The group implicitly and explicitly makes clear to him that it expects conformity to its standards, interests, activities, and value systems in return for moral support, the feeling of belongingness, the attributed status, and the opportunities for earned status that it extends to him. To allay the anxiety from the threat of disapproval, he tends to conform more than is objectively necessary to retain group acceptance or to avoid censure and reprisal (Ausubel, 1955; Newstetter and others, 1938).

After he wins an assured place for himself in the group, other factors continue to reinforce conforming tendencies. He learns that group approval brings a welcome reprieve from anxiety and uncertainty, for if the group approves he can feel absolutely certain of the correctness of his position. Feelings of loyalty also influence him to render conformity automatically as a voluntarily assumed obligation. Finally, if these implicit group pressures and internalized restraints and dispositions of the individual are insufficient to keep him in line, explicit sanctions are imposed. Depending on the seriousness of the offence and the functions and nature of the group, the punishment may vary from ridicule to physical chastisement and complete ostracism.

Qualifications and Positive Aspects   Lest we tend to take too dim a view of these seemingly negative features of adolescent conformity, it is important that we now consider some of the more positive aspects of this phenomenon. First, the transfer of allegiances from parental to peer group standards constitutes more than an exchange of one type of slavish conformity for another. By providing a new source of values and standards, as well as experience in behaving as a sovereign person, the peer group plays an important role in devaluing parents and promoting desatellization. In switching his basic loyalties to the peer group, the adolescent takes great strides toward emancipation. He finds a new source of basic security to supplant the emotional anchorage to parents that had hitherto kept him confined within the dependent walls of childhood. By vesting in his peers the authority to set standards, he affirms his own right to self-determination, since he is patently no different from them. No longer need he implicitly subscribe to the belief that only parents and adults can determine what is right and wrong.

The peer group's desatellizing influence also carries over into the sphere of ideas and moral values. Its norms provide the adolescent with a new and stable frame of reference for moral judgment and conduct. It furnishes relief from uncertainty and anxiety about proper ways of thinking, feeling, and behaving. Because the peer group is never dignified by the same halo of sanctity surrounding parents, the adolescent can experiment more freely with functional concepts of moral law and with a more impersonal and logical approach to value judgments. To be sure, full exploitation of this new active, independent, and critical approach to moral values is limited by his need to conform to peer group norms. The difference, however, is that now he conforms to external standards because he consciously recognizes the expediency of so doing rather than because he implicitly accepts their validity.

Finally, the dreary picture of adolescent conformity must be qualified by certain limiting factors. In the first place, its existence tends to be restricted to the particular developmental requirements of the adolescent period that induces it.[2] One of the surest signs of approaching adulthood is a resurgence in the legitimacy of deviancy. Secondly, along with their conforming tendencies adolescents display a "concomitant urge to be unique, to achieve individuality and 'separateness.' After the young adolescent has submerged himself in the group to the point where he cannot be criticized for nonconformity, he . . . then proceeds to gain recognition for himself as an individual" (Tryon, 1944). Lastly, as we know from the history of innumerable youth movements, there is among many adolescents a vigorous strain of exuberant idealism and impatient dissatisfaction with many outmoded traditions and features of contemporary life. This aspect of adolescent personali-

---

[2]Costanzo and Shaw (1966) studied conformity in a laboratory setting in which subjects were forced to agree or disagree with "rigged" group assessment of perceptual inequalities (that is, the subject was given false information to the effect that the group had judged two unequal lines to be equal). Maximum conformity to these erroneous judgments occurred in the 11–13 age group for both boys and girls. In a similar type of experiment, Iscoe and others (1963), found maximum conformity at age twelve for females and age fifteen for males, although the difference between the twelve- and fifteen-year-old groups was small.

ty, when channeled intelligently, constitutes a most strategic means for effecting social change.

DEALING WITH ADOLESCENTS: SOME PRESCRIPTIONS FOR EDUCATORS

Conformity and Nonconformity

Where do these developmental and cultural considerations regarding conformity and individuality leave us in proposing a feasible and morally defensible prescription for adolescents? The crucial role of the peer group as a socializing agency and as a source of earned and attributed status counsels a certain degree of deference to its standards during the limited period when such an exaggerated premium is placed on the value of conformity. During adolescence deviants are not in an enviable position. In varying degrees they all face social ridicule, abuse, and isolation. The fortunate ones achieve some measure of status and security by forming warm attachments to age-mates of their own kind. Sometimes a sympathetic adult friend or teacher will offer them affection, direction, and encouragement. Often, however, they are left to flounder uncertainly, to drift further and further away from group living, to develop feelings of anxiety and inferiority, to withdraw deeper and deeper into themselves or into a compensatory world of unreality.

As far as the wider community is concerned, the adolescent should be encouraged to adjust satisfactorily to the kind of world that currently exists, "not the kind adults wish existed but as yet have been unable to create . . . . Even while endeavoring to change them it is necessary to recognize established laws and customs, irrational or otherwise" (Partridge, 1947). This does not imply that the status quo must be implicitly accepted for what it is, but rather that a mature attitude toward social change be adopted, an attitude that does not "encourage the adolescent to batter his head against the wall of custom simply because these customs are inconsistent."

At the same time, those who counsel adolescents would be remiss in their responsibility if they failed to appreciate the importance of nonconformity for self-realization, and for the development of moral courage and the ability to stand alone without group support. Moreover there are undoubtedly large individual differences in the need to conform. The highly self-assertive teenager, for example, can only restrain his individuality to a point, and the introvert inevitably draws a line beyond which he refuses to participate in socially exhibitionistic activities. Other individuals may have all-absorbing interests that are regarded with scorn by their age-mates. Finally, the mental hygiene dangers of nonconformity and social unpopularity during this period have been vastly exaggerated. It has been found, for example, that the peer group tolerates much more deviancy than the adolescent's anxiety and marginality of status lead him to believe (Ausubel, 1955; Newstetter and others, 1938).

Classroom Climate

Although the weight of the evidence indicates that the choice between authoritarian and democratic classroom climates in the United States has little effect on subject-matter achievement (G. G. Stern, 1963), there is good reason to believe that it has profound effects on attitudes toward school, on general social behavior in the school, and on the learning of adult values (Ausubel, 1965c; G. G. Stern, 1963). It seems reasonable to suppose that as children in a democratic society become older, particularly at adolescence and beyond, authoritarian controls should be progressively liberalized to meet increasing needs for self-determination and growing capacities for self-direction and self-discipline. This is generally the case in most American and Canadian secondary schools, but prevailing practice in many schools still falls far behind desirable standards of democratic classroom practice.

In general, overt compliance is the most common response that pre-adolescents and adolescents make to excessive authoritarianism in the classroom, especially if they are girls, and if they come from middle-class homes that place a great premium upon success in school. Adolescents from other backgrounds, however, may react with open aggression and hostility to teachers, with negativism, or with passive sabotage. Still others may drop out of school as soon as it is legal to do so. Yet even those adolescents who apparently become overtly reconciled to a continuation of an incongruously submissive childhood role probably do not really accept the authoritarianism to which they outwardly defer, but respond with suppressed resentment and variously negatively-toned emotional reactions.

Older children and adolescents also do not satisfactorily internalize values that are indoctrinated in an authoritarian fashion if the adult culture itself is organized along democratic and egalitarian lines. Under these circumstances they feel unjustly treated and discriminated against. Not only do they tend to resent the authoritarian discipline that is imposed upon them, but also to conform to adult standards only under threat of external compulsion. This is particularly true if they perceive that many adults do not honor these standards but, nevertheless, presume to punish them whenever they are guilty of lapses. Hence, when adults preach the virtue of hard work, ambition, responsibility, and self-denial, but do not practice these virtues themselves in occupational life, children tend to emulate their example rather than their precepts. They become habituated to striving and working hard under external pressure but fail adequately to internalize these values. Thus when they finally enter the adult vocational world and the customary authoritarian demands for conscientious effort are lifted, the tenuous structure of their disciplined work habits tends to collapse in the absence of genuinely internalized needs for vocational achievement.

Children *are* able to internalize satisfactorily adult personality traits and mature attitudes toward authority, even in an authoritarian home and school environment, providing that personal, social, and working relationships among adults are similarly authoritarian, and that adults generally make as stringent demands on themselves as they do on young people. In countries such as Germany and Switzerland these latter conditions prevail, and therefore authoritariansim in the home and school has few adverse effects on mental health and personality development. In New Zealand and the United States, on the other hand, authoritariansim in the home and secondary school has more serious effects because it contrasts sharply with the egalitarian and generally relaxed character of vocational and social life in the adult world (Ausubel, 1965b).

In all cultures, however, even those which are generally authoritarian, there are credible grounds for supposing that a punitively authoritarian classroom climate would have negative effects on creativity and problem solving, and lead to less effective group planning, teamwork, and self-direction. Spaulding (1963), for example, found that punitive teachers, emphasizing shame as a technique of control, tend to inhibit student creativity. It also seems likely that an authoritarian and punitive classroom climate would increase the anxiety level of less able and anxious pupils and make them more defensive about exposing their inadequacies.

SOCIAL SEX ROLE IN THE SCHOOL

The quite different social sex roles of boys and girls at all age levels have important effects on their respective adaptations to the school environment. By virtue of their differential training in the home, girls find it much easier than boys to adjust to the demands of the elementary school. We have already observed that they are more intrinsically accepted by parents; satellize more; identify more strongly with authority figures; have less insistent needs for independence, earned status, and emancipation from the home; and are more habituated from the very beginning to docility, sedateness, conformity to social expectations, and restraint of overt physical aggression. It is hardly surprising, therefore, that boys find it correspondingly more difficult to identify with the school, with the teacher, and with classroom activities. Girls play "school" as readily as they play "house," whereas most normally robust boys would not be caught dead playing either game.

The young boy's problem is not merely that most elementary-school teachers are women, but also that feminine values prevail in the school with respect to what is taught and the kind of behavior that is expected and approved: propriety, obedience, decorum, cleanliness, tidiness, submissiveness, modesty, paying attention to what one is told, remembering, facility in handling verbal symbols, and the control of fidgetiness, curiosity, and aggressiveness. As might be expected, then, girls tend to receive much more approval and considerably less scolding and reproval from teachers (Meyer and Thompson, 1956).

In terms of cultural expectations and peer group norms, success in school is much more appropriate to the female than the male sex role in elementary and junior-high school. At this age level the higher achievement motivation of girls is largely a reflection of their greater desire for approval from authority figures and for the vicarious status that this confers. In sum, it is not at all surprising that boys furnish a disproportionate share of the nonreaders, the underachievers, the truants, the behavior problems, and the dropouts in the elementary and beginning high-school years (Durrell, 1956; Tyler, 1947; Bentzen, 1963).

A perennial question is whether female teachers show "favoritism" toward female students or discriminate against males, thus to some degree "causing" the relatively poor male performance (Ayres, 1909; St. John, 1932; McNeil, 1964). Data gathered by McNeil (1964), based upon teacher and student perceptions of their interaction, gave support to this suggestion. A recent study by Davis and Slobodian (1967), however, conducted in first-grade reading classes, again indicated that children *perceived* teachers to be discriminating against boys, but showed that an actual analysis of teacher-student interaction did not bear out this perception. In other words, teachers gave boys equal opportunity to read or respond during reading class, and did not treat boys' responses differently than girls'; the fact that boys were reprimanded or corrected more often than girls was determined by their *behavior* rather than by teacher bias. Nevertheless, the fact remains that the kind of interaction between female teachers and male students seems to have something to do with the latter's low achievement. McNeil did find, for example, that while girls outperformed boys in regular reading classes, boys outperformed girls when programmed instruction was the principal vehicle of instruction.

Beginning in middle adolescence cultural expectations change radically. Academic achievement becomes a more acceptable male virtue and, accordingly, the achievement gap between boys and girls begins to close. Boys with low intrinsic self-esteem and high anxiety seek more than do their female counterparts to find compensatory ego-enhancement and anxiety-reduction in school achievement, and gifted boys tend to maintain their high IQ's better in late adolescence and adulthood.

While males collectively thus seem to "come through" in the end, there are substantial grounds for believing that a similar statement is much less applicable to females. It is not so much that a smaller proportion of females go on to higher education (Werts, 1966a)—a tendency which may be compatible with ultimate occupational goals—but that they may adopt socially shaped attitudes which lead to a serious underdevelopment of their intellectual potential. Kagan (1964), for example, suggests that the female student soon comes to believe that the ability to solve problems in mathematics, science, or logic is a uniquely masculine skill, and that her motivation to attack such problems is low. As early as eight or nine years of age, a sex difference in analytic attitude, independence of thought, and persistence in problem solving begins to appear. This difference, according to Kagan, ". . . increases with time, and by late adolescence and adulthood the typical female feels inadequate when faced with most problems requiring analysis and reasoning."

Coleman (1961) evinced an equal concern for the apparently negative influence of the adolescent subculture on the performance of female high-school students. According to Coleman's data, the high-ability female who wants approval from the peer group, and realizes that very high scholastic performance is not likely to enhance her popularity, adopts a level of aspiration beneath her real potential (although sufficiently high for university entrance standards). Coleman found, for example, that the girls earning the highest marks were not those with the highest ability and, consistent with the above analysis, clever and status conscious girls learn quickly that they should not compete with males in the latter's traditional intellectual sanctuaries of mathematics and science.[3]

It seems clear that concern for the underdevelopment of female intellectual potential is on the upswing because of the intensive search for talent at all levels of society. The greater participation of women in the traditionally "male" occupations (medicine, engineering, scientific work) in many European countries has suggested that at least partial solutions are not impossible to find.

SOCIAL CLASS STRATIFICATION AND EDUCATION

The social class membership of a pupil has important implications for his school achievement, his aspirations for academic success, his achievement motivation, and his attitudes toward school. A good deal of evidence collected in the period 1940–1960 indicated a moderately high relationship between socioeconomic status and school achievement (Hav-

---

[3]There is some suggestion that these results, based on data from the late 1950's, may now need some qualification. Wetherford and Horrocks (1967) for example, employing students from grades 9 and 12, found evidence that popularity with one's peers is related, up to a point, to achievement comparable to the level of one's potential.

ighurst and Breese, 1947; Havighurst and Janke, 1944; Janke and Havighurst, 1945; Pierce-Jones, 1959b). One experimenter found this relationship to be greater at the junior high-school age than that between IQ and achievement (Kahl, 1957).

Some necessary qualifications of these findings seem worth noting. In the first place, social class differences in motivation and academic success are understandably becoming less distinct now as college education becomes more prevalent among lower-class groups—although a majority of intellectually able lower-class youth, for financial or other reasons, still do not proceed beyond high-school graduation (Havighurst and Neugarten, 1962; Armstrong, 1967). Moreover, in particular studies it has been found that the characteristic impact of social class membership on school achievement does not seem to prevail among high-ability sixth graders (R. L. Curry, 1962), after students enter college (Washburne, 1959), or in upwardly mobile populations (Udry, 1960). Apparently the limiting effects of social class conditioning cease to operate as fully beyond certain critical ability and achievement levels. Once students exceed these levels, they seem to be influenced more by the new student subculture with which they identify than by their social class origins. Nevertheless, even at the college level lower-class males have been found to be high in interpersonal anxiety and more threatened in situations where their status is being judged by middle-class standards (Endler and Bain, 1966).

Lack of Supporting Traits   Recent research (Ausubel, 1965e; Hanson, 1965; Sherif and Sherif, 1964) has made it clear that the vast majority of youth of all socioeconomic ranks have assimilated the scholastic and vocational aspirations associated with material affluence in modern Western society. It is not the appropriate aspirations that are lacking, therefore, but rather those factors that are necessary for their implementation, namely, underlying needs and motivations for achievement, supportive personality traits, and perceived pressures and opportunities for academic and occupational success (Ausubel, 1965e; Rosen, 1964).

In the first place, lower-class parents do not place the same value that middle-class parents do on education, financial independence, social recognition, and vocational success. Hence they do not encourage, to the same extent, implementation of these aspirations by voicing appropriate expectations, making unequivocal demands, dispensing suitable rewards and punishments, and insisting on the development of the necessary supportive traits (Ausubel, 1965e).

Second, since lower-class adolescents are understandably dubious about the attainability of the promised rewards of striving and self-denial for persons of their status, they do not develop the same internalized needs for vocational achievement and prestige, and thus see less point in developing to the same degree as their middle-class contemporaries the supportive middle-class personality traits necessary for the achievement of academic and vocational success (A. Davis, 1943). These supportive traits include habits of initiative and responsibility and the "deferred gratification pattern" of hard work, long-range striving, thrift, orderliness, punctuality, restraint of sexual and aggressive urges, and willingness to undergo prolonged vocational preparation (A. Davis, 1943; Havighurst and Taba, 1949; Schneider and Lysgaard, 1953).

It is hardly surprising, therefore, that lower-class children are less interested in reading than are middle-class children, take their school work less seriously, and are less willing to spend the years of their youth in school in order to gain higher prestige and social rewards as adults. Lacking the strong ego-involvement which middle-class pupils bring to school work and which preserves the attractiveness of academic tasks despite failure experience, they more quickly lose interest in school if they are unsuccessful.

Attitudes toward Authority   The working-class mother's desire for unquestioned domination of her offspring, her preference for harsh, punitive and suppressive forms of control, and her tendency to maintain considerable social and emotional distance between herself and her children are probably responsible, in part, for the greater prevalence of the authoritarian personality syndrome in lower- than in middle-class children (Dickens and Hobart, 1959; I. Hart, 1957; Lipset, 1959). Lower-class children tend to develop ambivalent attitudes toward authority figures and to cope with this ambivalence by making an exaggerated show of overt, implicit compliance, by maintaining formally appropriate social distance, and by interacting with these figures on the basis of formalized role attributes rather than as persons. Their underlying hostility and resentment toward this arbitrary and often unfair authority is later expressed in such displaced forms as scapegoating, prejudice, extremist political and religious behavior, ethnocentrism, and delinquency (Dickens and Hobart, 1959; I. Hart, 1957; Lipset, 1959). They are coerced in school by the norms of their peer group against accepting the teacher's authority, seeking her approval, or entering into a satellizing relationship with her.

Social Class Bias of the Schools

While the available research gives a somewhat mixed picture, studies both of the existing teaching body (N.E.A., 1963) and those proposing to enter it (J. A. Davis, 1966; Pavalko, 1965; Werts, 1966b) indicate that the majority of teachers either have middle-class backgrounds or are upwardly mobile from lower socioeconomic groups. But even if teachers originate from other than middle-class environments, they still tend to identify with the school's implicit mission of encouraging the development of middle-class values. Thus, quite apart from the issue of whether this mission is appropriate and desirable for our culture, teachers find it difficult to understand the goals, values, and behavior of students from other social class backgrounds. Normal ethnocentric bias predisposes them to believe that their own class values are true and proper, and that deviations from them necessarily reflect waywardness. On the other hand, since middle-class boys and girls behave in accordance with their expectations and accept the standards of the school, teachers are usually as prejudiced in their favor as they are prejudiced against children from other social strata.

In addition to their natural inclination to reward conformity to middle-class ideology, teachers are influenced by other pressures in giving preferential treatment to students whose families enjoy high social status. Middle- and upper-class parents are active in civic and school affairs, members of school boards, and leaders in parent-teacher associations. Even if no implicit pressures are exerted, teachers and school administrators, knowing on which side their bread is buttered, are disposed to see things their way. Teachers are also intimidated somewhat from taking action against refractory but popular members of leading student cliques who, when supported by their clique-mates, may be surprisingly rebellious (Hollingshead, 1949). Under such circumstances, many teachers are reluctant to force a showdown that would provoke the enmity of students who are influential in their own right as well as through the position of their parents.

The organization of the high school also tends to favor the retention of middle-class students and the earlier dropping out of lower-class students. A disproportionate number of the latter are placed in slow-learning sections— not only on the basis of low ability and motivation, but also because of their social background (Hollingshead, 1949; Havighurst and Neugarten, 1962). Similarly, a disproportionate percentage of lower-class students are found in the vocational, commercial, and general high-school curriculums, rather than in the college preparatory curriculum. Thus, as a result of being typed and stigmatized as members of these low-prestige groups, and of enjoying relatively low scholastic morale, lower-class students are more disposed to drop out of school.

The values of the dominant peer group in high school are based upon middle-class norms and standards and, as in adult society generally, there exist subtle and intangible barriers to participation in the more intimate crowds and cliques; very little crossing of social lines occurs in school clique organization (Hollingshead, 1949). Boys and girls from lower social class strata bitterly resent the patronizing and condescending attitudes of their more fortunate middle-class contemporaries, and the fact that the latter occupy the choice elective and activity positions (Havighurst and Taba, 1949; Hollingshead, 1949; H. P. Smith, 1945). They feel snubbed, unwanted, and left out of things. When this situation becomes intolerable it undoubtedly influences their decision to leave school (Havighurst and Taba, 1949; Hollingshead, 1949; Johnson and Legg, 1944).

RACIAL FACTORS IN EDUCATION

In contemporary North America, membership in an ethnic group is correlated with socioeconomic status. Nevertheless, within any ethnic group one will find a range of socioeconomic levels represented; similarly not all members of any socioeconomic class are drawn from a single racial group. In addition, ethnic group membership carries with it distinctive cultural patterns not intrinsic to socioeconomic classifications (for example, language, religious beliefs, traditions, and so on).

A complete treatment of ethnic factors in education would have to deal with a considerable number of groups, each possessing a unique set of problems. It is apparent, for example, that a set of prescriptions for dealing with the problems of the American Negro would hardly suffice for the Canadian Eskimo, given the differences in their aspirations and relationships with the majority groups in their respective societies. Since a choice of treatment had to be made, we have selected the particular ethnic group, the American Negro, which not only constitutes the largest minority, but which is also undoubtedly the greatest focus of current research on educational intervention.

All of the earlier listed properties of the lower-class environment also apply to the segregated Negro community. Most authorities on Negro family life agree that well over 50 percent of Negro families live at the very lowest level of the lower-class standard (M. C. Hill, 1957). In addition, however, Negro families are characterized by a disproportionate number of illegal and loosely connected unions (M. C. Hill, 1957). Illegitimacy is a very common phenomenon and is associated with relatively little social stigma in the Negro community (Cavan, 1959).

Negro families are much more unstable than comparable lower-class white families. Homes are likely to be broken, fathers are more frequently absent, and a matriarchal and negative family atmosphere more commonly prevails (Dai, 1949; Deutsch and others, 1956; M. C. Hill, 1957). Thus, the lower-class Negro child is frequently denied the benefits of biparental affection and upbringing; he is often raised by his grandmother or his older sister while his mother works to support the family deserted by the father (Deutsch and others, 1956). One consequence of the matriarchal family climate is an open preference for girls. Boys frequently attempt to adjust to this situation by adopting feminine traits and mannerisms (Dai, 1949).

Negro family life is even more authoritarian in nature than is that of the lower social class generally. "Children are expected to be obedient and submissive" (M. C. Hill, 1957), and insubordination is suppressed by harsh and often brutal physical punishment (Dai, 1949; M. C. Hill, 1957). "Southern Negro culture teaches obedience and respect for authority as a mainspring of survival" (Greenberg and Fane, 1959). Surveys of high-school and college students show that authoritarian attitudes are more prevalent among Negroes at all grade leveis (Greenberg and others, 1957; Greenberg and Fane, 1959; Smith and Prothro, 1957).

Being a Negro also has many other implications for the ego-development of young children that are not inherent in lower-class membership. The Negro child inherits an inferior caste status and almost inevitably acquires the negative self-esteem that is a realistic ego reflection of such status. Through personal slights, blocked opportunities, and unpleasant contacts with white persons and with institutionalized symbols of race inferiority (for example, segregated schools, neighborhoods, amusement areas)—and more indirectly through the mass media and the reactions of his own family— he gradually becomes aware of the social significance of racial membership (Goff, 1949). The Negro child perceives himself as an object of derision and disparagement, as socially rejected by the prestigeful elements of society, and as unworthy of succorance and affection (Deutsch and others, 1956; Lefevre, 1966). Having no compelling reasons for rejecting this officially sanctioned negative evaluation of himself, he develops a deeply ingrained negative self-image (Bernard, 1958; Wertham, 1952; Gibby and Gabler, 1967).

In addition to suffering ego-deflation through awareness of his inferior status in society, the Negro child finds it more difficult to satellize and is denied much of the self-esteem advantages of satellization. The derived status that is the principal source of children's self-esteem in all cultures is largely discounted in his case, since he can satellize only in relation to superordinate individuals or groups who themselves possess an inferior and degraded status. Satellization under such conditions not only confers a very limited amount of derived status but also has deflationary implications for self-esteem. We can understand, therefore, why young Negro children resist identifying with their own racial group,[1] why they seek to shed their identities (Deutsch and others, 1956), why they more frequently choose white than Negro playmates (Stevenson and Stewart, 1958), why they prefer the skin color of the culturally dominant caste (Clark and Clark, 1947; Goodman, 1952), and why they tend to assign negative roles to children of their own race (Stevenson and Stewart, 1958). Such tendencies persist at least into late adolescence and early adult life, insofar as one can

---

[1]See also Gregor (1965) on this point.

judge from the attitudes of Negro college students. These students tend to reject ethnocentric and anti-white ideologies and to accept authoritarian and anti-Negro propositions (Steckler, 1957).[5]

Educational Achievement of Negro Children

Partly as a result of unequal educational opportunities, Negro children show serious academic retardation. They attend school for fewer years, and on the average, learn much less than white children do (Ashmore, 1954; Bullock, 1950; Cooper, 1964; Osborne, 1960), this latter discrepancy increasing with successive years of education (Coleman and others, 1966). One of the chief reasons for this discrepancy is the inferior education and training of Negro teachers, who themselves are usually products of segregated education. The inequality of educational facilities exists not only in the South, but also in the urban North as well, where, for the most part, de facto segregation prevails (Smuts, 1957). Eighty-four percent of the top 10 percent of Negro graduates in one Southern high school scored below the national mean on the Scholastic Aptitude Test (Bullock, 1950). Thus the incentive of reaching the average level of proficiency in the group is not very stimulating for Negro children, since the mean and even the somewhat superior child in this group are still below grade level. Teachers in segregated schools also tend to be overly permissive and to emphasize play skills over academic achievement; they are seen by their students as evaluating them negatively, and as more concerned with behavior than with school work (Deutsch and others, 1956).

Even more important perhaps, as a cause of Negro educational retardation, is the situation prevailing in the Negro home. Many Negro parents have had little schooling themselves and hence are unable to appreciate its value. Thus they do not provide active, wholehearted support for high-level academic performance by demanding conscientious study and regular attendance from their children. Furthermore, because of their large families and their own meager schooling they are less able to provide help with lessons. Keeping a large family of children in secondary school constitutes a heavy economic burden on Negro parents in view of their low per capita income and the substantial hidden costs of "free" education. The greater frequency of broken homes, unemployment, and negative family atmosphere, as well as the high rate of student turnover (Conant, 1961; Sexton, 1959), are also not conducive to academic achievement.

Negro students are undoubtedly handicapped in academic attainment by a lower average level of intellectual functioning than is characteristic of

---

[5]In recent years, with rising Negro militancy and counter-chauvinism (Black Power movement), this finding is obviously less descriptive of the actual attitude of present-day Negro students.

comparable white students. In both Northern and Southern areas, particularly the latter, Negro pupils have significantly lower IQ's (Carson and Rabin, 1960; Dreger and Miller, 1960; Osborne, 1960), and are retarded in arithmetic, reading, language usage, and ability to handle abstract concepts (Bullock, 1950; Osborne, 1960). The extreme intellectual impoverishment of the Negro home *over and above* its lower social class status reflects the poor standard of English spoken in the home and the general lack of books, magazines, and stimulating conversation.

Educational and Vocational Aspirations

All of the factors inhibiting the development of achievement motivation and its supportive personality traits in lower-class children are intensified in the segregated Negro child. His overall prospects for vertical social mobility, although more restricted, are not completely hopeless. But the stigma of his caste membership is inescapable and insurmountable. It is inherent in his skin color, permanently ingrained in his body image, and enforced by the extralegal power of a society whose moral, legal, and religious codes formally proclaim his equality.

Rosen (1959) compared the educational and vocational aspirations of Negro boys (age 8–14) and their mothers to those of white Protestant Americans, French-Canadians, American Jews, Greek-Americans, and Italian-Americans. The mean vocational aspiration score of his Negro group was significantly lower than the mean scores of all other groups except the French-Canadian. Rosen concluded that although Negroes have been exposed to the liberal economic ethic longer than most of the other groups:

> . . . their culture, it seems, is least likely to accent achievement values. The Negro's history as a slave and depressed farm worker, and the sharp discrepancy between his experience and the American Creed, would appear to work against the achievement values of the dominant white group. Typically, the Negro life-situation does not encourage the belief that one can manipulate his environment, or the conviction that one can improve his condition very much by planning and hard work (p. 55).
> . . . Negroes who might be expected to share the prevalent American emphasis upon education, face the painfully apparent fact that positions open to educated Negroes are scarce. This fact means that most Negroes, in all likelihood, do not consider high educational aspirations realistic, and the heavy dropout in high school suggests that the curtailment of educational aspirations begins very early (p. 58).

Ethnicity was found to be more highly related to vocational aspirations than was social class; sizable ethnic and racial differences prevailed even when the influence of social class was controlled. These results are consistent with the finding that white students tend to prefer "very interesting jobs," whereas Negro students are more concerned with job security (Singer and Stefflre, 1956).

Sex Differences

Girls in the segregated Negro community show much greater superiority over boys in academic, personal, and social adjustment than is found in the culture generally (Deutsch and others, 1956). They not only outperform boys academically by a greater margin, but also do so in all subjects rather than only in language skills (Deutsch and others, 1956). They have higher achievement needs (Gaier and Wambath, 1960; Grossack, 1957), have a greater span of attention, are more popular with classmates, show more mature and realistic aspirations, assume more responsible roles, and feel less depressed in comparing themselves with other children (Deutsch and others, 1956). Substantially more Negro girls than Negro boys complete every level of education in the United States (Smuts, 1957).

Adequate reasons for these differences are not difficult to find. Negro children in this subculture live in a matriarchal family atmosphere where girls are openly preferred by mothers and grandmothers, and where the male sex role is generally deprecated. The father frequently deserts the family and, in any case, tends to be an unreliable source of economic and emotional security (Dai, 1949; Deutsch and others, 1956). Hence the mother, assisted perhaps by her mother or by a daughter, shoulders most of the burdens and responsibilities of child-rearing and is the only dependable adult with whom the child can identify. In this environment male chauvinism can obtain little foothold. The preferential treatment accorded girls is even extended to opportunities for acquiring ultimate primary status. If the family pins all of its hopes on and makes desperate sacrifices for one child, it will often be a daughter in preference to a son. Over and above his handicaps at home, the Negro boy also faces more obstacles in the wider culture in realizing his vocational ambitions, whatever they are, than the Negro girl in fulfilling her adult role expectations of housewife, mother, nurse, teacher, or clerical worker (Deutsch and others, 1956).

Implications for Education

Before Negroes can assume their rightful place in a desegregated American culture, important changes in the ego-structure of Negro children must first take place. They must shed feelings of inferiority and self-derogation, acquire feelings of self-confidence and racial pride, develop realistic aspirations for occupations requiring greater education and training, and develop the personality traits necessary for implementing these aspirations. Such changes in ego-structure can be accomplished in two different but complementary ways. First, all manifestations of the Negro's inferior and segregated caste status must be swept away—in education, housing, employment, religion, travel, and exercise of civil rights. This in itself will enhance the Negro's self-esteem and open new opportunities for self-fulfillment. Second, through various measures instituted in the family, school, and community, character structure, levels of aspiration, and actual standards of achievement can be altered in ways that will further enhance his self-esteem and make it possible for him to take advantage of new opportunities.

Desegregation Desegregation, of course, is no panacea for the Negro child's personality difficulties. In the first place, it tends to create new problems of adjustment, particularly when it follows in the wake of serious community conflict. Second, it cannot quickly overcome various long-standing handicaps which Negro children bring with them to school "such as their cultural impoverishment, their helplessness or apathy toward learning, and their distrust of the majority group and their middle-class teachers;" nor can it compensate for "oversized classes, inappropriate curriculums, inadequate counseling services, or poorly trained or demoralized teachers" (V. W. Bernard, 1958).[6] Yet it is an important and indispensable first step in the reconstitution of Negro personality, since the school is the most strategically placed social institution for effecting rapid change both in ego-structure and in social status. A desegregated school offers the Negro child his first taste of social equality and his first experience of first-class citizenship. He can profit from the stimulating effect of competition with white children and can use them as realistic yardsticks in measuring his own worth and chances for academic and vocational success. Under these circumstances, educational achievement no longer seems so pointless, and aspirations for higher occupational status in the wider culture acquire more substance.

Consistent with this, Coleman and others (1966) found that for minority groups from relatively nonsupportive backgrounds, attendance in a school with others from supportive backgrounds and higher aspirations was likely to have a positive influence on achievement. Similarly, another group of investigators (Robbins and others, 1966) found support for the hypothesis that the more children having social characteristics associated with good school performance, the better will be the performance of the remainder of the student

---

[6]A study by Herriott and St. John (1966) casts some doubt on the "demoralized teacher" contention. These investigators found that while slum teachers would welcome transfer to a school in a better neighborhood, they did not evince significantly less career satisfaction than their more favored colleagues. But teachers in high-status schools were older, on the average, more likely to be white, and of higher socioeconomic status. Another investigator (Wayson, 1966) found that teachers who stayed on at inner-city teaching positions reduced their academic expectations and increased their acceptance of non-middle-class behavior.

body. For reasons indicated above, however, desegregation will not always bring about immediate benefits. For example, in one study (Beker and others, 1967) it was found that over the course of a year the educational aspirations of a group of junior high-school Negroes attending a white school *fell* from a level equal to that of the predominant white group to a position somewhat below it.

It is also reasonable to anticipate that white children will be prejudiced and continue to discriminate against their Negro classmates long after desegregation accords them equal legal status in the educational system. Attitudes toward Negroes in the South, for example, are remarkably stable, even in periods of rapid social change involving desegregation (Young and others, 1960), and are not highly correlated with anti-Semitic or other ethnocentric trends (Greenberg and others, 1957; Kelly and others, 1958; Prothro, 1952). Prejudice against Negroes is deeply rooted in the American culture (Raab and Lipset, 1959) and is continually reinforced both by the socioeconomic gain and by the vicarious ego-enhancement it brings to those who manifest it (V. W. Bernard, 1958; O. M. Herr, 1959; Rosen, 1959). It is hardly surprising, therefore, that racial prejudice is most pronounced in lower social class groups (Westie, 1952), and that these groups constitute the hard core of resistance to desegregation (Killian and Haer, 1958; Tumin, 1958). Increased physical contact per se between white and Negro children does little to reduce prejudice (Neprash, 1958; Webster, 1961), but more intimate personal interaction under favorable circumstances significantly reduces social distance between the two groups (Kelly and others, 1958; Mann, 1959; Yarrow and others, 1958).

Community Action   The support of parents and of the Negro community at large must be enlisted if we hope to make permanent progress in the education of Negro children.

> One needs only to visit . . . a [slum] school to be convinced that the nature of the community largely determines what goes on in the school. Therefore, to attempt to divorce the school from the community is to engage in unrealistic thinking, which might lead to politics that could wreak havoc with the school and the lives of children (Conant, 1961, p. 20).

> Whatever can be done to strengthen family life and to give the fathers a more important role in it will make a significant contribution to the development of Negro potential (Smuts, 1957, p. 462).

Present research evidence (Coleman, 1966; Mackie and others, 1967), as well as logical analysis of the existing situation, suggest that the influence of the home may be even more important to sustained achievement than that of the school. Thus, working with mothers and getting them to adopt a more positive attitude toward school is an important first step in improving the educational achievement of urban Negro children. Typically only 10 percent of Negro parents are high-school graduates and only 33 percent complete elementary school (Conant, 1961). It would seem that enrollment of parents in adult education programs would significantly raise the cultural level of the Negro home and "stimulate an interest in magazines, newspapers, and possibly even books. One of the troubles . . . is that when the children leave the school they never see anyone reading anything—not even newspapers" (Conant, 1961). The "Higher Horizons" project in New York City is a good example of a recent attempt to discover academically talented children in slum areas and encourage them to aspire to college education. This program embodies cultural enrichment, improved counseling and instruction, and the sympathetic involvement of parents.

Counseling Because of current grave inadequacies in the structure of the lower-class urban Negro family, the school must be prepared to compensate, at least in part, for the deficiencies of the home, that is, to act, so to speak, *in loco parentis*. Teachers in predominantly Negro schools actually perform much of this role at the present time. As one Negro teacher said to Conant (1961):

> . . . We do quite well with these children in the lower grades. Each of us is, for the few hours of the school day, an acceptable substitute for the mother. But when they reach about 10, 11, or 12 years of age, we lose them. At that time the "street" takes over. In terms of schoolwork, progress ceases; indeed, many pupils begin to go backward in their studies (p. 21).

It is apparent therefore that trained counselors must assume the role of parent substitute during preadolescence and adolescence. They are needed to offer appropriate educational and vocational guidance, to encourage worthwhile and realistic aspirations, and to stimulate the development of mature personality traits. In view of the serious unemployment situation among Negro youth, they should also assist in job placement and in cushioning the transition between school and work. This will naturally require much expansion of existing guidance services in the school.

Research has shown that Negro children's distrust of white counselors and authority figures in general makes it

> . . . difficult for a white counselor to create an atmosphere wherein a Negro could gain insight . . . The fundamental principle of counseling—to view the social or personal field as the counselee does—is difficult to attain in such a situation. The white person only imagines, but never knows, how a Negro thinks and feels, or how he views a social or personal situation. The cultural lenses which are formulated from unique milieus are not as freely transferable as it is assumed, or as we are led to believe (W. B. Phillips, 1959, p. 188).

The American Negro: Postscript

At the time this is written (May 1968) the transition in the role of the Negro in the United States, which for a long time proceeded slowly, has reached a point of acceleration if not discontinuity. The combined effects of many social and economic reforms, coupled with growing dissatisfaction of the Negro himself, have created a situation in which predictions concerning the course of future events are hazardous. And while our description of the problem and prescribed course of action appears to us to be valid in the light of conditions which have prevailed for many years, some current movements, not treated here, may well have a profound influence on events in the future. For example, our account dwells heavily upon the lower-class status of the Negro without adequately recognizing the existence of a growing Negro middle class. Considerable evidence exists, however, that the discrepancy between Negro middle- and lower-class attitudes and aspirations is large and tends toward the same direction as the discrepancy between the corresponding classes in the white culture.

One study (John, 1963), for example, found consistent class differences in language skills between groups of Negro children of different socioeconomic levels. Another investigation (Radin and Kamii, 1965) found that middle-class Negro mothers set definite limits on behavior, and valued self-expression and independence in their children, in contrast to the behavior of lower-class mothers who (consistent with earlier remarks) tended to be over-protective and controlling, and to repress sexual expression. Further, Hess and others (1965) found that middle-class Negro mothers used more verbal cues and showed less anxiety in teaching their young children simple tasks than did lower-class Negro mothers.

In other words, it seems clear that Negro middle-class parents exhibit somewhat the same child-rearing practices as do white parents from the same socioeconomic level. One might argue that significant differences remain between children from these two middle-class groups; that one should not assume that these differences will necessarily favor whites is demonstrated by one study (Brown, 1965) which, in comparing vocational aspirations of Negro and white sixth graders, found that the Negro group aspired to occupations of higher status than did the white group. What significance the Negro middle class will have in the future development of that race is not clear at the present time. It does appear, however, that generalizations based upon the characteristics of the Negro *lower-class* population will become increasingly unrepresentative as time passes.

Undoubtedly a more profound and significant contemporary event resides in what appears to be an incipient change in the basic sense of identity, self-concept, and level of aspiration of the American Negro. Although little tangible research evidence exists to document this change, it is nonetheless manifest in the social and political philosophies which are emerging from within the group.

MOTIVATING THE CULTURALLY DEPRIVED PUPIL

We have already considered the cognitive characteristics of culturally deprived pupils as well as various instructional measures that can be taken to prevent and ameliorate their educational retardation. This section will examine some *motivational* considerations that apply to culturally deprived pupils. The problem of reversibility is particularly salient here, inasmuch as the environment of cultural deprivation typically stunts not only intellectual development but also the development of appropriate motivations for academic achievement.

Extrinsic Motivation

It is clear that the school must give special attention to the motivation of the culturally deprived child, exploiting to best advantage all the potential drives which are inherent in achievement motivation. In the early elementary years some use can be made of affiliative drive, even though it may not be as strong or persistent as in the case of children from more favored environments.[7] Thus wise utilization of the affiliative drive in those critical early years—by providing tasks with which the culturally deprived child can cope—can establish a motivational beachhead for the crucial preadolescent period when alienation from school would normally reach sizable proportions. Such early school successes will strengthen the ego-enhancement drive as well and direct it toward school tasks.

As the culturally deprived child nears the end of the elementary-school grades, he will need intensive counseling to compensate for the absence of the appropriate home, community, and peer group support and expectations necessary for the development and implementation of long-term vocational ambitions. By identifying at this stage with a mature, stable, striving, and successful male adult figure also, the derprived boy can be encouraged to internalize long-term and realistic aspirations, as well as to develop the mature personality traits necessary for their implementation.

---

[7]Greenberg and others (1965), for example, found that attitudes of young Negro children from even severely deprived environments toward school and learning are not necessarily negative.

Later encouragement to strive for more ambitious academic and vocational goals can be provided by making available abundant scholarship aid to universities, community colleges, and technical institutes; by acquainting culturally deprived youth with examples of successful professional persons originating from their own racial, ethnic, and social class backgrounds; and by involving parents sympathetically in the newly-fostered ambitions of their children. The success of the Higher Horizons Project in New York City indicates that an energetic program organized along these lines can do much to reverse the negative effects of cultural deprivation on the development of extrinsic motivations for academic and vocational achievement.

Intrinsic Motivation

The previous paragraph suggests that, as in the case of cognitive development, there is hope for motivating the culturally deprived child toward school achievement provided that educational intervention takes place at an early stage. But what can be done when the teacher encounters a culturally deprived youth with a record of failure in the school, a maturing set of anti-teacher, anti-school attitudes, and minimal academic and vocational aspirations? In view of the- anti-intellectualism and pragmatic attitudes toward education that is characteristic of lower-class ideology, a superficial case could be made for the strategy of appealing to the job-acquisition, job-retention and job-advancement incentives that now apply so saliently to continued education because of the rapid rate of technological change. However, as we know from the high dropout rate of culturally deprived high-school youth, appeals to such motivation are frequently not very effective because of the prevailing lower social class ideology. Among other reasons, this ideology reflects: a limited time perspective focused primarily on the present; a character structure that is oriented toward immediate rather than delayed gratification of needs; and the lack of personality traits necessary to implement high vocational aspirations—due to the absence of necessary family, peer group, and community pressures and expectations. It also reflects the seeming unreality and impossibility of obtaining the rewards of prolonged striving and self-denial in view of current living conditions and family circumstances, previous lack of school success, and the discriminatory attitudes of middle-class society.

Somewhat paradoxically then, the most promising strategy for such youth appears to lie in the development of *cognitive* drive, that is, of the desire to acquire knowledge as an end in itself. It must be conceded, however, that culturally deprived children manifest little intrinsic motivation to learn. They come from family and cultural environments in which the veneration of learning for its own sake is not a conspicuous value, and in which there is little or no tradition of scholarship. Moreover, they have not been notably successful in their previous learning efforts in school. Nevertheless we need not necessarily despair of motivating them to learn for intrinsic reasons. Psychologists have been emphasizing the motivation-learning and interest-activity sequences of cause and effect for so long that they tend to overlook their reciprocal aspects. Since intent to learn is not an indispensable condition for short-term and limited-quantity learning, it is not necessary to postpone learning activities until students develop appropriate interests and motivations. Often, as we stated before, the best way of motivating an unmotivated pupil is temporarily to by-pass the problem of motivation and to focus on the cognitive aspects of teaching. Much to his own surprise and to his teacher's, he will learn despite his lack of initial intent; and from the satisfaction of learning, thus satisfying the latent cognitive drive, he will characteristically develop the motivation to learn more on the same basis.

We may discover that the most effective method of developing intrinsic motivation to learn in a culturally deprived student is to concentrate on teaching him as effectively as possible in the absence of motivation, and to rely on the cognitive motivation that is developed retroactively from successful educational achievement. This is particularly true when the teacher is able to generate contagious excitement and enthusiasm about the subject he teaches, and when he is the kind of person with whom culturally deprived children can identify. Masculinizing the school and dramatizing the lives and exploits of cultural, intellectual, and scientific heroes can also enhance the process of identification. At the same time, of course, we can attempt to combat the anti-intellectualism and lack of cultural tradition in the home through programs of adult education and cultural enrichment.

Use of Aversive Motivation

With regard to the use of aversive motivation, it is evident that failure and fear of failure cannot motivate academic strivings when students have never experienced any success in school, have given up hope of succeeding, and have internalized no aspirations for academic success. But the remedy does not lie in removing the threat of failure from the category of respectable motivations. Nor does it lie in the self-defeating practice of "social promotion" which fools nobody, least of all the child who is ostensibly rewarded for failing to learn. To be sure, his ultimate academic achievement might be slightly higher if he moves ahead to the next grade instead of repeating the same one; and he may be better adjusted socially by not being stigmatized as an oversized dullard by his younger classmates. Nevertheless, he is still acutely aware of his actual failure in school, acquires unrealistic perceptions about the competence-reward relationship in the real world, and enters high school as a rebellious semi-literate. The more constructive remedy is to change the preschool, classroom, and social environment of the culturally deprived child so that academic success not only becomes a realistic possibility for him, but also becomes internalized as a realistic aspiration. When this happens, he too will be positively motivated, as other students are, by desire for knowledge as an end in itself, by ego-enhancing rewards, and by aversive motivations as well.

TOPICS FOR DISCUSSION AND FURTHER STUDY

1. Describe some instance in which small-group learning might be utilized effectively in your subject-matter area. How would you decide the composition of the learning group? What advantages would you expect to follow from this experience? What disadvantages? How could these be determined?

2.* Observe a school group-learning situation in which members are (purportedly) working together to produce a given product. Note the involvement and contribution of each child. What do you think these children are receiving from the experience which they could not receive in individual study or through a demonstration by a teacher?

3.* In observing an ongoing classroom, determine what form of competition is being used explicitly by the teacher. Are there implicit forms of competition which are not in evidence? Is there evidence of over- or under-use of competition?

4. What opportunities exist in your subject area to engage the student in competition with himself or in competition against an absolute standard? What benefits should follow? How could these benefits be assessed?

5. What advice can be offered to the school in relation to coping with student "fads" (for example, long hair, idiosyncratic dress)?

6.* Coleman (1961) suggested that the school might enlist the energy and support of the adolescent subculture for its educational goals if it were able to make school achievement reflect credit on the group, thus contributing to a "we" feeling, rather than being a purely personal and individual accomplishment. In this connection he suggested that interschool academic competition might be employed to parallel interschool athletic contests. Determine whether such an approach has been tried in your vicinity and what the results have been. What other methods might be employed to obtain more explicit peer approval of academic achievement?

7. How important is peer group influence on school learning in the preadolescent stage? At what age does it make itself felt, and what useful social function does it serve? To what extent is it counter-balanced by school achievement drives?

8.* In this chapter our discussion of adult-youth alienation has centered on the temporary importance of peer acceptability (based essentially upon nonacademic criteria) to the adolescent; however, in this alienation the peer group implicitly *accepts* the values and goals of adult society (for example, material comfort, prestige, security, and so on) and its members will make sufficient academic progress to insure that these goals are not jeopardized. In a more recent form of alienation, the youth *rejects* outright the values and set goals of adult society and the means (standard educational achievement) of attaining them. To what extent is the phenomenon in evidence in the school system to which you will be attached? What, if anything, can the school do about it?

9. To what do you attribute the present tendency to deride all forms of conformity as an evil? In respect to specific examples, discuss the proposition that the nonconformist often conforms more closely to the norms of his deviant group than so-called "conforming" individuals do to general societal norms?

10. Some sociological studies have shown that the adolescent conforms to the peer group more than is necessary to assure his acceptance, that is, that he underestimates the divergence tolerated by the group (Ausubel, 1955; Newstetter and others, 1938). Cite instances of "safe" nonconformity to peer group standards for the adolescent.

11. What prescriptions might be offered to the teacher for the greater development of mathematical and scientific ability among girls? At what age would one have to begin, to insure that the ability of boys and girls is equally developed?

12. How realistic in your view is the assertion that when motivation is lacking one should merely begin teaching, counting on the learning which will ensue to enhance the cognitive drive? When would such an approach fail?

SUGGESTIONS FOR ADDITIONAL READING

Ausubel, D. P. *Theory and problems of adolescent development.* New York: Grune & Stratton, Inc., 1954.

Bard, B. Why dropout campaigns fail, *Sat. Rev.,* September 17, 1966.

Bloom, B. S. Learning for mastery. *Evaluation comment.* Center for the Study of Education and Instructional Programs, University of California at Los Angeles, 1968, *1*(2).

Bronfenbrenner, U. The split-level American family. *Sat. Rev.,* October 7, 1967.

Coleman, J. S. *The adolescent subculture.* Glencoe, Ill.: The Free Press, 1961.

Conant, J. B. *Slums and suburbs.* New York: McGraw-Hill, Inc., 1961.

Goodman, P. *Growing up absurd.* New York: Vintage Books, 1956.

Harvard educ. Rev., Winter 1968, *38*(1). Special issue on equal educational opportunity (contains articles by James Coleman and others).

Kagan, J. Acquisition and significance of sex typing and sex role identity. In *Review of child development research,* Part 1 (H. L. Hoffman and L. W. Hoffman, Eds.). New York: Russell Sage Foundation, 1964.

CHAPTER 15

TEACHER CHARACTERISTICS

THE CLOSE COUPLING OF THE WORDS "TEACHING" AND "learning" in our culture attests to the strength of our belief that teacher characteristics constitute the most important variables influencing learning outcomes. Certainly parents, the general public, and other educators are quite ready to judge teachers as "good" or "poor," and such judgments presumably purport to reflect the teacher's impact upon student learning. It is somewhat paradoxical therefore that the empirical evidence as to which teacher variables relate to "good teaching" is—although voluminous—mostly inconclusive (Barr and others, 1953). However some of the findings do seem to be sufficiently suggestive to warrant inclusion in a text of this kind.

CHARACTERISTICS OF EFFECTIVE TEACHERS

Logical Considerations

To a certain extent, the theory advanced in previous chapters helps us to formulate hypotheses as to which teacher variables will be related to pupil learning. In the cognitive domain, since meaningful school learning typically involves the incorporation of the organized body of ideas constituting a school discipline into a developing cognitive structure, one would predict that the presence of certain kinds of knowledge should be a factor in teacher effectiveness. Thus one would expect that knowledge of the subject matter itself should be an important variable—not so much the total quantity of knowledge possessed but appreciation of the structure or organizing ideas of a discipline. Similarly, one would suppose that the ability to assess the state of the learner's cognitive structure and motivational drives, on the basis of observation and theory-based interpretation, should be a prerequisite to the effective planning of lessons. And certainly knowledge of how to present ideas in a way most suited to the student's existing state of cognitive development and subject-matter readiness should be relevant to teacher competence.

The effects of the teacher's personality are, no doubt, somewhat more complex. Nevertheless, one would think that teacher personality ought to be linked with student motivation, for it is evident that some teachers are able to motivate particular students while other teachers, with the same apparent cognitive knowledge and abilities, cannot do so. Pressing this motivational link further, it might reasonably be hypothesized that the important teacher personality variables will be those related to the principal motivational drives which are in evidence in school learning (that is, affiliative, ego-enhancement, and cognitive drives).

What sort of teacher behaviors would we expect to most effectively utilize or enhance these particular drives? To begin with the affiliative drive, if the child is to identify with his teacher in much the same way as he did initially with his parent—and through this identification learn in order to please the teacher—then the teacher must obviously be the same kind of warm, supportive individual the parent was. The utilization of ego-enhancement drive, on the other hand, requires that the learning outcomes by which status is earned be clearly defined, that procedures for working toward these outcomes be well organized, and that unequivocal recognition of levels of performance be made; it would seem that the teacher who would create such conditions will be task-oriented and possess a high degree of personal organization. Finally, the student with high cognitive drive would respond best, one would think, to teachers who are able to convey some sense of the importance, excitement, and possibilities for intellectual conquest which are present in their subject fields.

In other words, it would seem reasonable to predict—other things being equal—that clusters of teacher variables characterized by "warmth," "orderliness," and "intellectual excitement" would serve to obtain the best results from children with strong affiliative, ego-enhancement, and cognitive drive respectively. Of course we are not suggesting that teachers can be neatly or exclusively located in a single category, for one would expect that they will possess such characteristics in varying proportions, in the same way that the motivational patterns of children contain varying proportions of each of the basic achievement drives.

Difficulty in Obtaining Definitive Evidence

The present dearth of conclusions as to which variables are crucial to teaching effectiveness cannot be said to result from a lack of effort to find out. The problem lies, rather, in the complexity of the phenomena we are trying to measure. In effect, an empirical investigation in this area will attempt to relate definable teacher characteristics (independent variables), either experimentally or statistically, to variables comprising "teaching effectiveness." The heart of the problem of course, is to define and measure the entity represented by the dependent variables.

In practice, two general methods have been employed to provide measures of teacher effectiveness. The most common has been to obtain the ratings of supervisors. It may be somewhat distressing to the teacher in training (who will be subjected to such ratings) to learn that they tend to have little inter-rater consistency; that is, a group of administrators may be able to agree fairly well on who are the outstanding and who the inept teachers, but their ratings of individual teachers in the vast middle group are likely to vary considerably (Barr and others, 1961; Biddle, 1964), presumably because rating criteria tend to be very subjective.[1]

One might think that an obvious way to bypass subjectivity would be to equate "effectiveness of teaching" to the amount that students learn in a particular year. While this procedure undoubtedly yields the most objective and valid results, it is not without difficulty. Perhaps the most serious problem is that classroom achievement tests are notoriously unreliable and tend to favor abilities at the lower levels of the taxonomy, and that standardized achievement tests—while performing better statistically—are not particularly valid when applied to courses for which they were not specifically designed. Another difficulty in using "student achievement gains" as a criterion is that one cannot entirely rule out either concurrent or prior influences of some factor other than the teacher in question. For example, while the fact that Albert learned a good deal of algebra in grade 11 may be largely attributable to his teacher, some part of his proficiency may stem from a particularly good grounding in arithmetic, or from the fact that he is currently taking a physics course in which algebraic principles are recalled and applied in solving problems.

A third, recently initiated, line of inquiry should ultimately bear on teacher effectiveness. Aimed immediately at conceptualizing instructional strategies, this research undertakes detailed analyses of the interaction between pupils and teachers; thus a complete record is kept as to how the teacher distributes her time between giving directions, asking questions, clarifying ideas, responding to students' questions, praising students, presenting new ideas, and so on. Sequences of interaction are conceptualized in such units as "episodes" (Smith and others, 1964), "incidents" (Nuthall and Lawrence, 1966), and "teaching cycles" (Bellack and others, 1965). While this is an interesting and potentially productive field, the interaction indices

---

[1]Brown (1966a, 1966b) found that the "system centered" principal employed different criteria in rating teachers than the "individual centered" principal and that both bases of judgment differed sharply from that of teachers. Over the total group of principals, however, ability to maintain classroom discipline was the most salient criterion of effective teaching, "stimulatingness" was second, and a positive attitude toward the job was third.

do not themselves provide a measure of effective teaching but must be related to some more fundamental dependent variable such as student achievement. To date, the relationship between the interaction variables and true dependent variables is far from completely understood.

Another difficulty in obtaining striking empirical generalizations in this field is that the intrinsic correlations between variables in unrestricted populations are frequently distorted or obscured by a *restricted* sample. For example, if one took a random sample of individuals from the general public (average IQ of 100), one would probably find a fairly high correlation between intelligence and teaching effectiveness. However, since teachers are drawn mainly from the upper 25 percent of the intelligence distribution, the resulting correlation between intelligence and teaching effectiveness is greatly curtailed. Thus the empirical finding that there is a low correlation between these two variables would not mean that dull people can become good teachers, but rather that *above a certain critical* (and perhaps fairly high) *level* intelligence bears little relationship to effectiveness.

Finally, it is extremely difficult to determine the extent to which the student, particularly if he is mature and capable of undertaking independent reading, will *compensate* for poor teaching, thereby destroying any inherent relationship between quality of teaching and learning outcomes. For example, a mature learner in high school or college will readily attain a reliable impression of the "expectations" which the institution has with respect to learning—as represented, for example, in school-leaving examinations and the traditional "hurdles" which are so familiar in North American education. Moreover, the individual will tend to set a level of aspiration with respect to these standards; that is, he may wish to have "first class" standing, may be satisfied with earning sufficiently high marks to get by, or may be reconciled to inevitable failure. Consequently, the student may well maintain his desired position relative to the institutional standard by varying his effort in inverse ratio to the effectiveness of the instructor. In brief, the existence of well-defined expectations, combined with a stable level of aspiration relative to these expectations and compensatory increased effort, can lead to nonsignificant relationships between instructional variables (including the characteristics of the teacher) and measured learning outcomes.

THE ROLES OF TEACHERS

One approach to evaluating teachers' characteristics in terms of their relevance for teaching effectiveness is to consider both the different roles that teachers play in our culture and the relative importance of these various roles. In recent times, the scope of the teacher's role vis-à-vis pupils has been vastly expanded beyond its original instructional core to include such functions as parent surrogate, friend and confidante, counselor, adviser, representative of the adult culture, transmitter of approved cultural values, and facilitator of personality development. Without in any sense disparaging the reality or significance of these other subsidiary roles, it is nevertheless undeniable that the teacher's most important and distinctive role in the modern classroom is still that of *director of learning activities.*

Retrospective reports from former students are somewhat inconsistent as to how well the teachers perform in their various roles. One sample of college students, for example, reported that only 8.5 percent of their teachers had an important influence on their intellectual or personal development; no appreciable influence in this regard was attributed to over three-quarters of the teachers in question (Allport, 1964). On the other hand, Hall (1965) found that one-fifth of another sample of college students credited their former teachers with decisively influencing their choice of career. And Wright and Tuska (1966), in a study of teachers-in-training, concluded that both female secondary-school teachers and male teachers at both elementary and secondary levels had closely identified with and strongly admired their former teachers, probably as a result of failing to identify with their own parents. (Elementary-school female teachers had identified strongly with their mothers, and it was suggested that teaching might offer a kind of "mothering" experience for them).

One interesting study of adolescent students' perceptions of teachers indicates that teachers are seen as playing three major kinds of roles—friends, opponents, and manipulators of status in learning situations (R. Cunningham, 1951). As friends, they are "older and wiser" persons, helpful counselors, heroes, givers of security, confidantes and occasionally "pals." As opponents, they are cast as "kill-joys" who arbitrarily interfere with legitimate pleasures, as "enemies" to be "fought" and "outwitted," and as demons of power to be feared, respected, and placated. Much of this latter role obviously represents a displacement of hostile feelings from original parent targets. Teachers also share much of the brunt of adolescents' general anti-adult orientation. In the learning aspects of the school situation they are perceived as "efficient organizers in the direction of work projects," as "necessary evils" in the acquisition of knowledge, as "stepping stones" to future status rewards, as dispensers of approval and disapproval, and as moral arbiters who can absolve from guilt or point the accusing finger.

COGNITIVE ABILITIES

Intellectual Abilities

It would appear at first glance that the general intelligence of teachers should be highly related to success in teaching (Gage, 1967). Nevertheless, teacher effectiveness, as measured by pupil gains in achievement and by principals' and supervisors' ratings, is only slightly related to teachers' intelligence (Barr and others, 1958; Morsh and Wilder, 1954). As suggested earlier, it would appear that intelligence operates as a limiting factor in its influence on teacher success, and that beyond some critical point other more important cognitive and personality variables account for most of the difference in effectiveness between successful and unsuccessful teachers.

More pronounced effects have been attributed in empirical studies to special aspects of intelligence. For example, the learning of facts by pupils has been found to be significantly related to clarity and expressiveness in the teacher (Solomon and others, 1964), presumably because the initial presentation of ideas as well as the provision of effective feedback depends on the clarity and fluency of teacher expression. Consistent with this finding is the fact that ideational fluency correlates significantly with ratings of teacher effectiveness (Knoell, 1953).

Subject-Matter Knowledge

It seems evident that a teacher cannot furnish adequate feedback to students or clarify ambiguities and misconceptions unless he has a meaningful and adequately organized grasp of the subject he teaches. However, there is, at present, no adequate measure of a teacher's grasp of his subject-matter field in terms of such crucial dimensions as: comprehensiveness; cogency; stability; lucidity and precision of concepts; integration of relationships between the component aspects of the field; awareness of significant theoretical issues and underlying philosophical assumptions; and the appreciation of methodological and epistemological problems. Although such factors presumably influence many significant aspects of the students' mastery of subject matter and affect his general level of interest and intellectual excitement about a given discipline, we still know little that is definite about these important relationships. Obviously, the same difficulties that stand in the way of measuring these significant cognitive variables in teachers create obstacles in measuring corresponding learning outcomes in students. Actual investigation along these lines has therefore been restricted to the study of relationships between relatively formal and superficial aspects of teachers' and students' mastery of subject matter (see also: Gage, 1968).

Training in Subject

In general, degree and quality of teachers' academic preparation, as indicated by grade-point average, amount of work taken in the major field, and achievement test scores, bear only a low positive relationship to student learning outcomes and supervisors' ratings of success in teaching (Barr and others, 1958). On theoretical grounds, however, it seems somewhat unlikely that these aspects of academic preparation are not more highly related to success in teaching than they appear to be. The empirically demonstrated low relationship may conceivably reflect in part the superficiality and low intrinsic validity of both the pupil and teacher measures of subject-matter mastery. It is also possible, of course, that academic preparation, like intelligence, may influence teaching effectiveness only when it is below a critical value. And it may be that, in some subject-matter fields in which the demand for qualified personnel is great (for example, science, mathematics) those who have come into teaching with an impressive list of courses taken may not have been the strongest candidates in other respects.

Other Cognitive Knowledge

Knowledge of the principles of development, learning, and motivation should be of help in the overall planning and adaptation of instruction to individual differences and should be related, therefore, to learning outcomes. We saw earlier, for example, that the teacher's knowledge of student personality characteristics can produce improved achievement if the teacher is assisted in using this information in a specific way. It has also been found (Schunert, 1951) that the teacher's knowledge of child development and learning related significantly, but at a low level, to achievement both in algebra and geometry. And Fattu (1963) found that teachers who are adept at diagnosing learning difficulties and in appreciating the relevance of particular instructional materials for the acquisition of particular learnings are more successful than less adept teachers in terms of student achievement. Unfortunately, no evidence is currently available about the relationship between the teacher's effectiveness and his ability to adapt the communication of ideas to the student's level of intellectual maturity and subject-matter sophistication. Particularly at the elementary school and less advanced levels of instruction, this ability should be significantly related to the acquisition of clear, stable, and unambiguous meanings.

PERSONALITY CHARACTERISTICS

While teacher personality characteristics have not been found to be highly correlated with effectiveness in teaching, research does support the earlier speculation that clusters of traits associated with effective teaching are relatable to the overall motivational patterns visible in students. For example, in one of the largest studies to date of the characteristics of teachers (Ryans, 1960), the following three behavioral patterns emerged as possessing special significance:

Pattern A: characterized by warm, understanding, and friendly (as opposed to aloof, egocentric, and restricted) teacher behavior;
Pattern B: characterized by responsible, businesslike and systematic (as opposed to unplanned, evasive, and slipshod) teacher behavior; ·
Pattern C: characterized by stimulating, imaginative, and enthusiastic (as opposed to dull or routine) teacher behavior.

It must be pointed out, however, that this study was concerned primarily with teacher *characteristics* rather than teacher effectiveness per se, and did not take into consideration specific pupil motivational states; consequently the data do not provide a direct test of our earlier hypotheses. Moreover, the relationship between teacher personality variables, student motivational states, and learning outcomes is undoubtedly complex, not only because any individual teacher may possess each of the characteristics to some degree (and each student will be motivated to some extent by each kind of drive), but also because of the operation of interacting group, cultural, and economic factors.

Nevertheless, the evidence from the Ryans studies (1958, 1960, 1961) and those cited below, does argue for the kind of link between teacher personality variables and pupil motivation postulated earlier. Evidence therefore *does* suggest that teacher warmth is related to student achievement. Teachers with warm personalities tend to be rated more favorably by principals, supervisors, pupils, and other observers (Cook and others, 1951; McGee, 1955; Ryans, 1960; Solomon and others, 1964). And while the evidence concerning actual achievement is not entirely unequivocal (Flanders, 1960; Medley and Mitzel, 1959), teacher warmth has been found to be significantly related to the amount of work performed by students (Cogan, 1958), with their interest in science in general science classes (H. B. Reed, 1961), and with "productiveness" of student behavior in the elementary school (Ryans, 1961). In addition P. S. Sears (1963) has presented some evidence which suggests that student achievement is more "creative" when teachers are warm and encouraging.

The "warm" teacher described in these studies is one who provides emotional support for pupils, is sympathetically disposed toward them, and accepts them as persons. Characteristically, he distributes much praise and encouragement and tends to interpret student behavior as charitably as possible. He is relatively unauthoritarian and is sensitive to students' feelings and affective responses. For all of these reasons he tends to score high on the Minnesota Teacher Attitude Inventory, which is keyed in this direction, and to promote more wholesome self-concepts in elementary-school students (Spaulding, 1963).

Although the studies did not identify the motivational states of students involved, it seems reasonable to assume that the apparent effectiveness of teacher "warmth" can be traced to the fact that such persons act as parent surrogates for many elementary-school children. The child, identifying with this source of acceptance and approval, is disposed to assimilate the teacher's values and is thus more highly motivated to learn and to attain a higher level of academic achievement in school. Consistent with these speculations, it is known that at all grade levels, including elementary school, teacher warmth is less important for students whose motivational orientation to learning is largely ego-enhancing rather than affiliative. For such pupils, liking a teacher is not related to the latter's degree of warmth or to his score on the Minnesota Teacher Attitude Inventory (Della-Piana and Gage, 1955); it is this group of students that we might expect to respond particularly well to a teacher's orderliness and sense of direction.

Although (and we must say this again) the existing studies do not allow us to determine the interaction of particular student motivational states with teacher personality characteristics, it is known that orderliness facilitates learning. For example, Spaulding (1963) found a positive relationship between teacher orderliness and reading achievement. Moreover, students within a given classroom who judge the teacher as orderly and systematic in his classroom management and arrangement of learning activities report greater accomplishment of work than those of their classmates who make less favorable judgments of the teacher in this regard (Cogan, 1958); their classroom behavior is also more productive at the elementary-school level (Ryans, 1961). And teachers rated as "superior" by their principals tend to be characterized more than are teachers rated as "inferior" by a pattern of orderly, systematic, responsible, and businesslike behavior in their classroom procedures (Ryans, 1960).

Finally, ability to generate intellectual excitement and intrinsic motivation for learning does appear to have significant implications for the instructional effectiveness of teachers. Teachers who are lively, stimulating, imaginative, and enthusiastic about their subject are judged to be more successful by their principals and other experienced observers (Ryans, 1960). Under this kind of stimulation student behavior is also more productive, both in primary and secondary school (Ryans, 1961), and greater gains in student comprehension are made (Solomon and others, 1964). As suggested above, this result may plausibly be attributed to the dynamic teacher's ability to generate and utilize cognitive drive.

Related Studies

Although their studies are not entirely interpretable within the motivational framework we have adopted, other experimenters have investigated the effects of specific personality variables on teaching outcomes. For example, Heil and others (1960) were able to relate three teacher "types" to learning outcomes. The first type was characterized by turbulence, impulsiveness, and spontaneity. The second or well-integrated type was characterized by self-control, orderliness, and goal orientation. A third group was characterized by fearfulness, anxiety, and tendency to over-adhere to rules. The turbulent teachers were effective only with "strivers" and "conformers," and the fearful teachers (least effective of all groups) were effective only with "strivers." The well-integrated teachers were superior to those falling into the other categories over all groups of students (combined) but seemed to do particularly well with anxious and hostile children.

Two recent lines of research on the teacher's "conceptual systems," based upon the Conceptual Systems Theory (Harvey and others, 1961) show considerable promise for the future.[2] In one approach it is postulated that individual belief systems can be ordered on a concreteness-abstractness dimension. The TIB ("This I Believe") test developed specifically as a measure of such systems (Harvey, 1964), requires subjects to indicate their beliefs on a number of socially and personally relevant concepts by completing the phrase "this I believe about_____." System 1 responses, representing the most concrete level of conceptualization, are characterized by platitudes, absolutism, and positive attitudes toward American moral values. System 2 responses are also highly evaluative and absolutist, except that negative attitudes are shown toward such referents as marriage, religion, and the American way of life. System 3 responses are characterized by increased relativism and by strong positive beliefs about interpersonal relationships. In System 4, the highest level of abstraction, the subjects' responses show novelty, use of multidimensional interpretative schemata, and independence without negativism.

It has been shown (Harvey and others, 1968) that teachers who are high in abstractness tend to be more resourceful (for example, ingenious in improvising teaching materials), less dictatorial, and less punitive. Hunt and Joyce (1967), working with a different measure of abstractness (the Conceptual Level test) found that abstract teachers tend to be more "reflective," that is, more capable of utilizing the learner's frame of reference to encourage questioning and hypothesizing. It is postulated further that the capacity to radiate a reflective educational environment indicates a general ability to create a wider variety of educational environments (Hunt and Joyce, 1967), thus (presumably) making the teacher more effective as an instructional agent.[3]

To date it would appear that no long-term assessment has been made of

---

[2]Although originating in a developmental theory of personality, the conceptual systems approach might as plausibly have been included under the heading, "cognitive abilities."
[3]Since reflective teachers would seem to be, by definition, extremely flexible, the results cited are consistent with the findings of Sprinthall and others (1966) that a teacher's cognitive flexibility is highly related to his teaching effectiveness.

the effectiveness of "abstract" teachers in bringing about classroom learning. In the Harvey and others study (1968), the students of abstract teachers were rated as being more involved, more active, more cooperative, and higher in achievement than students of concrete teachers. However, the assessments of achievement were based on ratings obtained in a two-hour observation of the teachers' classrooms, rather than on achievement test scores. Although these approaches look promising, the long, arduous and (to this point) essentially futile search for the characteristics of the effective teacher argues for reservation until evaluation of long-term learning can be undertaken.

The Effect of Punitive Teachers

In an earlier chapter we indicated that aversive stimuli not only have a legitimate place in classroom instruction, but that long-term learning is probably impossible without them. Nevertheless, it is almost self-evident that the use of aversive stimulation can be carried too far. Several research studies have explored the effect on learning and other student behaviors of teachers who use a preponderance of aversive stimulation, or a degree of severity in its use out of all reasonable proportion to its legitimate function. For the present discussion we will refer to such teachers as being "punitive."

In a study of "desist" techniques with eighth- and ninth-grade children, Kounin, Gump, and Ryan (1961) found that an intensive punitive reaction to student misbehavior (involving the threat of extremely unpleasant consequences if the behavior recurred) produced more interference with attention to the task and more negative ratings of teacher fairness, in the class as a whole, than a matter-of-fact statement by the teacher that the behavior should be terminated. In another study (Kounin and Gump, 1961), three pairs of teachers—each consisting of a punitive and a nonpunitive teacher— were selected from the elementary schools, and their students were asked to indicate what they considered to be "the worst thing to do in school." The experimenters found that children in the punitive teachers' classes were more concerned with actual acts of aggression, while children with nonpunitive teachers were more concerned with failure to achieve and violation of school values and rules. The data supported the hypothesis that children under punitive teachers develop a distinct distrust of school.

In another area, it has been suggested by some theorists (Kris, 1952; Kubie, 1952) that creative thought requires freedom in the impulsive, unconscious, or preconscious mental processes. A deduction would be that the fostering of creativity calls for the tolerance and encouragement of atypical behaviors, a practice hardly consistent with general punitiveness. It is not surprising then that Spaulding (1963) found strong negative correlations between the expression of creativity in elementary-school children and teacher behavior which combined formal group instruction with shame as a punishment technique. On the other side of the coin, Sears (1963) has shown that creativity is more in evidence in teaching situations in which "the child can permit himself more leeway in the expression of unconventional ideas without [the] threat of devastating criticism."

Finally, although we know of no direct evidence on the relationship between punitiveness and problem-solving performance, one would expect the results to be similar to those cited above for creativity. The classroom of the punitive teacher is probably characterized by high levels of anxiety which, as we have seen, are not conducive to effective problem solving. It should not be inferred, of course, that all forms of punishment or criticism impair student performance. Rosenfeld and Zander (1961), for example, found that teacher disapproval has a deleterious effect on students' performance and level of aspiration only if the student feels that he has done as well as he can; when the performance is clearly inadequate, teacher criticism is accepted by the student.

Taking the results as a whole, however, there is strong evidence of undesirable outcomes following the indiscriminate or generalized use of punitive techniques. Although the evidence is far from complete, and while effects will depend somewhat upon the child's personality structure, it seems clear that the teacher who discovers that he is not able to enter into a relationship with children which, if not warm, is at least neutrally toned and businesslike, should seriously consider other lines of endeavor. Moreover, school authorities would seem to have a responsibility for insuring that classes are not staffed by teachers for whom increasing age or decreasing patience has made day-by-day association with young (and frequently irritating) children a hazardous undertaking at best.

TEACHING STYLE

The term "teaching style" is so varied in meaning that it almost defies clear definition. By way of explanation let us suppose that a number of high-school history teachers approach their classes with an identical set of behavioral goals. If we observe these teachers at any length we will undoubtedly find consistent idiosyncratic differences in the way they operate in the classroom. To begin with, we would find wide differences between them on the warmth-coldness, orderliness-disorderliness, and stimulating-dull dimensions we have discussed earlier. Careful observation would also reveal that teachers differ in their reward-punishment schedules, in the extent to which they take responsibility for setting goals and for deciding how these goals should be achieved, in their tendencies to provide all the information themselves as opposed to having the students contribute from their researches conducted in the course of assignments, and so on.

There is perhaps no limit to the number of ways of conceptualizing the individual differences exhibited in our hypothetical group of teachers. But we might use the term "teaching style" either in a limited sense, to denote some particular dimension on which differences may be noted, or in a more general way to refer to a *number of related isiosyncratic features* of the teachers' behavior.

Lecture versus Discussion

One rather limited aspect of the teaching style discussion centers around the relative efficacy of "lecture" as opposed to "discussion" approaches. Neither term is well defined and what is meant by them varies considerably from study to study. If a logical distinction can be made, one would say that it is the intent of the lecturer to offer what he regards as an adequate exposition of a subject without recourse to feedback about the reaction or understanding of the audience; thus, a celebrated chemist expounding contemporary chemical theory on Continental Classroom would provide a pure example of a "lecture."[4] The "discussion" method, on the other hand, implies that at least some elements of the learning (ideas, concepts, or attitudes) are derived from the group itself rather than from the instructor. The students in a particular class might compare impressions of places visited or argue the merits of a particular political decision, thereby adding content or influencing each other's attitudes.

Most of the studies concerned with this problem report little difference between the "lecture" and "discussion" methods in terms of student mastery of subject matter (Asch, 1951; Bills, 1952; Eglash, 1954; Maloney, 1956; Stern, 1963). Where differences do appear they are usually (Remmers, 1933; Ruja, 1954) in favor of the lecture method. Some studies have indicated advantages for the discussion method in developing positive attitudes toward material learned (McKeachie, 1963), in changing student behavior (Rasmussen, 1956), and in reducing student stress in a followup testing situation (Faw, 1957).

As the reader might have guessed, these studies have been conducted at the college level and in conjunction with courses which students were taking for credit. Under the circumstances, any differences in the intrinsic effectiveness of the two methods is probably masked by the fact that mature students will adapt themselves to the standards set, and to that extent will

---

[4] In this context "teaching" differs from lecturing in that the teacher gears the pace and difficulty level of his presentation to the students' ability to comprehend, the latter being determined by questioning or other forms of "feedback."

compensate for relatively ineffective methods. For example, every reader has probably had the experience of being subjected to an abominable lecturer in whose course one was, however, able to make an acceptable grade by undertaking intensive outside reading and by spending long hours disentangling lecture notes.

It is obvious that no pure "lecture" method will be used in the elementary or secondary school, except perhaps by very unsophisticated novices. For even when great reliance is put on lecturing (as would seem justifiable in the secondary school, given the evidence), it is clear that some discussion is necessary if students are to receive adequate feedback, and if the teacher is to ascertain whether his listeners are following him. In the final analysis the choice between methods centering around "information transmission" as opposed to "discussion" will depend upon the personality of the teacher and on whether the topic in question is more or less factual or controversial. Some teachers are more capable than textbook writers of drawing together scattered materials from diverse sources, of presenting alternative viewpoints in a highly organized and incisive fashion, or of presenting materials in a manner likely to be understood by students. Yet the same teachers may be relatively incapable of, and feel very uncomfortable about, directing discussion. Others are masterful in guiding discussion along fruitful lines or in using a Socratic type of questioning. The unique advantages of discussion, particularly in controversial or in poorly established areas of knowledge, have been described in another context. It cannot be too strongly emphasized that discussion techniques cannot be expected to enhance learning outcomes unless students possess the background knowledge which is prerequisite to intelligent and informed discussion. When this prerequisite condition is lacking, discussion inevitably amounts to little more than a sharing of ignorance, prejudice, platitudes, preconceptions, and vague generalities.

Group-Centered versus Teacher-Dominated Approaches

A number of studies have investigated the relative effects of what might be termed "teacher-dominated" as opposed to "group-centered" approaches. In general terms, the group-centered approaches place greater emphasis on student activity, on student participation, initiative, and responsibility in setting course objectives, determining course content, and evaluating learning outcomes, and on the teacher's role as a nondirective group leader.

Undoubtedly the most widely cited investigations in this area are those of Lewin, Lippett, and White concerning the effects of "authoritarian," "democratic," and "laissez-faire" leadership upon the behavior of boys in a club setting. The actual conduct of each type of leader cannot be simply described (an instructive point for the reader of brief research summaries) and so is outlined in some detail in Lippitt and White (1958):

Plan for authoritarian leadership role. Practically all policies as regards club activities and procedures should be determined by the leader. The techniques and activity steps should be communicated by the authority, one unit at a time, so that future steps are in the dark to a large degree. The adult should take considerable responsibility for assigning the activity tasks and companions of each group member. The dominator should keep his standards of praise and criticism to himself in evaluating individual and group activities. He should also remain fairly aloof from active group participation except in demonstrating.

Plan for the democratic leadership role. Wherever possible, policies should be a matter of group decision and discussion with active encouragement and assistance by the adult leader. The leader should attempt to see that activity perspective emerges during the discussion period with the general steps to the group goal becoming clarified. Wherever technical advice is needed, the leader should try to suggest two or more alternative procedures from which choice can be made by the group members. Everyone should be free to work with whomever he chooses, and the divisions of responsibility should be left up to the group. The leader should attempt to communicate in an objective, fact-minded way the bases for his praise and criticism of individual and group activities. He should try to be a regular group member in spirit but not do much of the work (so that comparisons of group productivity can be made between the groups).

Plan for laissez-faire leadership role. In this situation, the adult should play a rather passive role in social participation and leave complete freedom for group or individual decisions in relation to activity and group procedure. The leader should make clear the various materials which are available and be sure it is understood that he will supply information and help when asked. He should do a minimum of taking the initiative in making suggestions. He should make no attempt to evaluate negatively or positively the behavior or productions of the individuals or the group as a group, although he should be friendly rather than "stand-offish" at all times.[5]

Among the findings of several studies of this type were that:

1. There was much more aggressive behavior in the group with the authoritarian leadership when the leader left the room or when the students moved to another setting.
2. The authoritarian leader was disliked while the democratic and laissez-faire leaders were both liked.
3. When the authoritarian leader left the room the proportion of time spent by the group in actually working on tasks fell off dramatically, although it did not do so in the other groups (Figure 15.1).

[5]From "An Experimental Study of Leadership and Group Life" by Ronald Lippitt and Ralph K. White, from READINGS IN SOCIAL PSYCHOLOGY, 3rd edition, edited by E. E. Maccoby, T. M. Newcomb, and E. L. Hartley. Copyright 1947, 1952, © 1958 by Holt, Rinehart and Winston, Inc. Reprinted by permission of Holt, Rinehart and Winston, Inc.

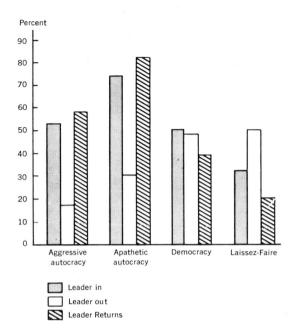

Percent

Leader in
Leader out
Leader Returns

FIGURE 15.1 *Percent of time spent in task involvement under different types of leadership. From "An Experimental Study of Leadership and Group Life" by Ronald Lippitt and Ralph K. White, from READINGS IN SOCIAL PSYCHOLOGY, 3rd edition, edited by E. E. Maccoby, T. M. Newcomb, and E. L. Hartley. Copyright 1947, 1952, © 1958 by Holt, Rinehart and Winston, Inc. Adapted and reprinted by permission of Holt, Rinehart and Winston, Inc.*

This experiment is frequently cited as proving that "democratic leadership" is superior because it produces more socially acceptable behavior and a greater tendency to stick to the learning task. It has been a launching pad for several ferocious attacks on the "authoritarian" structure of the school.

However, it should be noted that similar results have not been consistently obtained even when the settings were relatively similar (R. Anderson, 1959), so that one would not be surprised to find considerably different results in *school* settings. On the latter point, Spaulding (1963) in a study involving 21 elementary-school teachers, found that neither students' self-concepts, achievement, nor creativity were related to the presence or absence of democratic patterns of teaching. Extrapolations of the Lewin, Lippitt, and White results to school settings may be hazardous for a variety of reasons, primary among them being that the school is quite dissimilar to a club attended voluntarily and on the expectation of "having fun." In the school, where learning goals have been defined *prior* to the students' arrival, and where the achievement of these goals may be prerequisite for ego-enhancement and the approval of those with whom he identifies, the child may be much more willing to accept strong teacher direction, which can help him achieve such goals; indeed, it is known that students who have a need for direction and organization react favorably to a directive approach and with anxiety to a more permissive one (Wispé, 1951). And further to the question of teacher direction, Horwitz, Goldman, and Lee (1956) found that students resented being "outvoted" by their teacher in decision-making matters only when they had been led to expect that they had more power than they, in fact, did. Given the normal set of school expectations children need not show resentment to teacher-directed learning.

Although a summary of findings in this area is hazardous, it seems that teacher-dominated and group-centered teaching methods apparently do not differ significantly with respect to their effects on student achievement or on liking for subject matter (R. C. Anderson, 1959; Spaulding, 1963; G. G. Stern, 1963). Group-centered methods seem to be somewhat superior however with respect to such outcomes as increased group cohesion (Benne and Levit, 1953; Lippitt, 1940; Tizard, 1953), less dependence on the teacher (Asch, 1951; Lippitt, 1940), and improvement in group and adjustment skills (Asch, 1951; Lippitt, 1940). But because of the vagueness of the terminology, the teacher would be well advised to take such generalizations with a grain of salt until he has investigated the exact treatments employed and the outcomes obtained in these studies.

If a group-centered approach is to be used, care must be taken to neither confound democratic discipline with a laissez-faire approach nor to abdicate the school's primary responsibility for organizing the curriculum. Students should not be given a great deal of responsibility for structuring courses or for evaluating learning outcomes unless their background in the field is adequate and unless they have prior experience in independent study and group-centered techniques. On the whole, students who prefer nondirective approaches tend to be more secure and independent (Patton, 1955; Wispé, 1951), to be more flexible, to have more self-insight, and to be better able to cope with ambiguity (McKeachie, 1963). It is also unwise for teachers to adopt a nondirective teaching style either when they feel temperamentally uncomfortable with it or when students are generally insecure, compulsive, or of lower-class origin.

SCHOOL DISCIPLINE

The Definition and Functions of Discipline

The term "discipline" means the imposition of *external* standards and controls on individual conduct. Permissiveness, on the other hand, refers to the absence of such standards and controls. To be permissive is to "let alone," to adopt a laissez-faire policy. Authoritarianism is an excessive, arbitrary, and autocratic type of control which is diametrically opposite to permissiveness. Between the extremes of laissez-faire permissiveness and authoritarianism are many varieties and degrees of control. One of these, to be described in greater detail below, is democratic discipline. When external controls are internalized we can speak of self-discipline; it is clear, nonetheless, that the original source of the controls, as well as much of their later reinforcement, are extrinsic to the individual.

Discipline is a universal cultural phenomenon which generally serves four important functions in the training of the young. First, it is necessary for socialization—for learning the standards of conduct that are approved and tolerated in any culture. Second, it is necessary for normal personality maturation—for acquiring such adult personality traits as dependability, self-reliance, self-control, persistence, and ability to tolerate frustration. These aspects of maturation do not occur spontaneously, but only in response to sustained social demands and expectations. Third, it is necessary for the internalization of moral standards and obligations or, in other words, for the development of conscience. Standards obviously cannot be internalized unless they also exist in external form; and even after they are effectively internalized, universal cultural experience suggests that external sanctions are still required to insure the stability of the social order. Lastly, discipline is necessary for children's emotional security. Without the guidance provided by unambiguous external controls they tend to feel bewildered and apprehensive—too great a burden is placed on their own limited capacity for self-control.

Discipline in the School Setting

Since a certain minimal level of order and decorum is necessary for efficient school learning, discipline is a real and prevalent problem in the classroom. It is a serious concern of most teachers and especially of those who are beginning their teaching careers (Eaton and others, 1957; Ladd, 1958). It is not, as is sometimes maintained, just a problem of the ineffective or maladjusted teacher.

It is unfortunate that the question of discipline is much less a science than a matter of opinion. It not only shifts in response to various social, economic, and ideological factors, but also manifests all the cyclical properties of fads and fashions. Objective scientific evidence about the relative merits of different types of discipline is extremely sparse. Indeed, it is highly questionable to what extent valid empirical data are obtainable and even relevant in matters of discipline. Whether or not particular disciplinary practices are appropriate depends, in the first place, on the particular values, institutions, and kinds of personal relationships prevailing in a given culture; and, second, any definitive empirical test of appropriateness would have to be conducted over such an extended period of time that its conclusions would tend to be rendered obsolete by intervening changes in significant social conditions. For all practical purposes, therefore, the choice of disciplinary policy involves taking a rationally defensible and self-consistent position based on value preferences, on relevant considerations of child development, and on individual experience and judgment.

Although discipline cannot be placed on a largely scientific basis, this does not mean that one position is as good as another or that no public policy whatsoever is warranted. Society is continually obliged to resolve issues of much greater moment with even less objective evidence on which to base a decision. Under the circumstances all we can reasonably expect is greater humility and less dogmatism on the part of those engaged in formulating disciplinary policy.

Democratic Discipline

The proponents of democratic classroom discipline believe in imposing the minimal degree of external control necessary for socialization, personality maturation, conscience development, classroom learning, and the emotional security of the child. Discipline and obedience are regarded only as means to these ends, and not as ends in themselves. They are not striven for deliberately, but are expected to follow naturally in the wake of friendly and realistic teacher-student relationships. Explicit limits are not set routinely or as ways of showing "who is boss," but only as the need arises, that is, when they are *not* implicitly understood or accepted by students.

Democratic discipline is as rational, nonarbitrary, and bilateral as possible. It provides explanations, permits discussion, and invites the participation of children in the setting and enforcement of standards whenever they are qualified to do so. Above all, it implies respect for the dignity of the invididual, makes its primary appeal to self-control, and avoids exaggerated emphasis on status differences and barriers to free communication. Hence it repudiates harsh, abusive, and vindictive forms of punishment, and the use of sarcasm, ridicule, and intimidation.

The aforementioned attributes of democratic classroom discipline are obviously appropriate in cultures such as ours where social relationships tend to be egalitarian. This type of discipline also becomes increasingly more feasible as children become older, more responsible, more capable of self-control and group control, and more capable of understanding and formulating rules of conduct based on concepts of equity and reciprocal obligation. But contrary to what the extreme permissivists would have us believe, democratic school discipline does not imply freedom from *all* external constraints, standards, and direction, nor freedom from discipline as an end in itself. And under no circumstances does it presuppose the eradication of all distinctions between student and teacher roles, or require that teachers abdicate responsibility for making the final decisions in the classroom.

Distortions of Democratic Discipline

Many educational theorists have misinterpreted and distorted the ideal of democratic discipline by equating it with an extreme form of permissiveness. According to one widely held doctrine, only "positive" forms of discipline are constructive and democratic. It is asserted that children must be guided only by reward and approval; that disapproval, reproof, and punishment are authoritarian, repressive, and reactionary expressions of adult hostility which leave permanent emotional scars on children's personalities. Such criticisms ignore the fact that it is impossible for children to learn what is *not* approved and tolerated simply by generalizing in reverse from the approval they receive for behavior that *is* acceptable. Even adults are manifestly incapable of learning and respecting the limits of acceptable conduct unless the distinction between what is proscribed and what is approved is reinforced by punishment as well as by reward. Furthermore, there is good reason to believe that acknowledgment of wrong-doing and acceptance of punishment are part of learning moral accountability. Few, if any, children are so fragile that they cannot take deserved reproof and punishment in stride.

A second widespread distortion of democratic discipline is reflected in the popular notion among educational theorists that there are no culpably misbehaving children in the classroom, but only culpably aggressive, unsympathetic, punitive, or incompetent *teachers*.[6] If children misbehave, according to this point of view, one can assume either that they must have been provoked by repressive classroom discipline or that the teacher does not know how to "handle" children. While some pupil misconduct *is* instigated by harsh and abusive school discipline, it can also be influenced by factors originating in the home, the neighborhood, the peer group, and the mass media. Thus some children are emotionally disturbed, others are brain-damaged, still others are aggressive by temperament; and there are times when even the best behaved children from the nicest homes develop an irresistible impulse—without any provocation whatever—to test the limits of a teacher's forebearance.

---

[6]Relevant to this point, Turner (1965) found that in school systems with predominantly working-class pupils, difficulties with discipline brought the beginning teacher substantial supervisory help but apparently led to a rating of his (the teacher's) performance below that of teachers who had not needed such help. In middle-class districts, however, problems with discipline did not seem to be an important factor in principals' ratings of teachers.

The Initial Steps

It is perhaps presumptuous to offer detailed prescriptions on school discipline. Yet this matter weighs so heavily on the beginning teacher's mind that we cannot resist a few observations which seem consistent with previous remarks and with our general theoretical orientation.

In the first place, it seems important that the teacher moving into a new (perhaps his first) teaching position should establish an understanding at the very outset concerning expected conduct in the classroom. A clear statement by the teacher will help structure the situation for most children and relieve their uncertainty and need to investigate the teacher's intentions by trial and error; such a statement should make it clear that students are in class under the expectation that they will learn and that the teacher cannot allow behavior which disrupts learning and which acts, therefore, contrary to the students' best interests. Some teachers feel disposed to break the ice by "laying down the law," that is, listing punishments to be exacted for various misdemeanors. Such an inventory probably does little good, however, and in all likelihood serves only to generate high anxiety.

Despite these initial precautions there will inevitably arise the "test case" in which some student willfully acts against the rules of appropriate conduct outlined by the teacher. There are a number of reasons why this might happen: the student (and class) may want to find out whether the teacher is serious and what they can actually get away with, irrespective of the teacher's theoretical position; other students may simply be seeking attention, the applause of their peers, or may be motivated by more hostile intentions.

The advice frequently given to teachers is that they should "make an example" of the first offender; what is often implied in such a prescription is that the maximum penalty allowed under the circumstances should be exacted, coupled (by implication) with the use of sarcasm or other ego-deflating techniques. A more useful approach in our opinion would be the clear identification of the behavior in question as a violation of the rules and a firm declaration that such behavior will not be permitted. The latter approach seems more likely to convince students that the teacher is rational and task-oriented rather than merely punitive.

A particularly difficult problem for the beginning teacher is learning how to handle the misdemeanor that carries a clear threat to his self-esteem. The young teacher brings a certain amount of normal anxiety into the teaching situation and, not too sure of his ability to keep students under control and earn their respect, he is "primed" to over-react to such threatening behaviors as willful disobedience (challenge to authority) or other evidence of lack of respect (threats to self-esteem). Since high anxiety never induces clear thinking, the young teacher may grossly misinterpret or over-read such common student tendencies as to attach a none-too-flattering nickname to the teacher, use his first name, or make "humorous" (in the child or adolescent's frequently painful terms) remarks about him. While such behaviors are difficult to reconcile with one's newly acquired "professional" image, none of them is necessarily indicative of disrespect or lack of affection. It will no doubt seem like banal moralizing to suggest that the teacher will gain stature by ignoring such behaviors when they do not interfere with the primary function of the class; yet this is reasonable counsel under the circumstances.

Evidence has been cited earlier to the effect that an orderly, businesslike approach is correlated with teaching success at all levels. We might add that such an approach also minimizes the opportunities for discipline problems to arise. The teacher who allows the distribution of materials, conduct of experiments, or comings and goings to and from the classroom to be the occasion for pandemonium is feeding what appears to be, both in children and adults, an appetite for the occasional spontaneous (tension-reducing) generation of chaos. Most principals have seen the sad spectacle of the class, comprised often of so-called "nice kids," who have the teacher completely on the run and who are enjoying every minute of it. Once the minimal superstructure of order dissipates, even the students motivated by ego-enhancement and cognitive drive can profit little from sticking to the task and will readily join in the bedlam. While the teacher's weaknesses in such cases are probably numerous, there will invariably be little evidence of even the most elementary rules for handling the normal logistical problems of classroom transactions.

All the previous advice notwithstanding, the teacher will inevitably encounter discipline cases for which, and through no fault of his own, no solution can be found in the normal classroom setting. The sequence of events will probably proceed as follows: A student continues to violate the norms of conduct despite the teacher's remonstrations. When this happens the teacher should try to determine what is prompting the student's behavior and if he can do anything constructive about it. For example, if the student is merely an attention-seeker, the teacher may find some alternate way of satisfying this need. When such strategies are exhausted, and if the student continues to constitute an impediment to the class's progress, the teacher has no alternative but to remove him from the situation.

Here, of course, the attitude of the school administrator is crucial (Blumberg and Amidon, 1965), and one could generalize and say that the willingness of the school administration to declare itself firmly on school discipline and to support its teachers unequivocally before parents, school officials, and the general public when the teachers act within agreed rules, is absolutely essential for desirable discipline practices in the school. Unfortunately, for reasons indicated earlier, some officials make teachers feel guilty when they bring their unmanageable students to the principal's attention, the unwarranted assumption being made that the teacher should always be able to cope with such problems himself, or that he has, in fact, *caused* them. The administration's attitude on rules of conduct and their enforcement is a matter which teachers should look into before signing a contract since sometimes, as much as any other factor, it will determine whether classroom teaching is a pleasant occupation or a daily round of personal torment.

Discipline and the Lower-Class Student

The comments in previous sections will apply to the teaching situations of most beginning teachers. However, in inner-city schools generally and in certain classes in other schools where lower-class children predominate, a rather different set of conditions will prevail. The central problem is that such students, as we have seen, tend to exhibit less cognitive, ego-enhancement and affiliative motivation insofar as school achievement is concerned. Thus, for example, lower-class children are less disposed to satellize with the teacher and to conform with his achievement expectations to win the latter's approval. Similarly, such children do not strive to earn status through academic achievement. Another factor which intensifies the teacher's problem is that peer group standards in the lower class often sanction, if not encourage, hostility toward the teacher and the school.

No single prescription can be offered for coping with this problem. However, it seems clear that teachers who are able to survive under such conditions (with apparent job satisfaction) increase their acceptance of non-middle-class patterns of behavior and reduce (at least initially) their academic expectations for these students (Wayson, 1966). It should also be remembered that lower-class children are accustomed to authoritarian discipline in the home and that they react unfavorably to permissiveness and unstructured activities (Riessman, 1962). It would seem to follow from this that the teacher should adopt a firm, structured, and businesslike stance without trying to be "in" with the peer group; this stance can be progressively relaxed after rapport and control have been established and the work pattern has become routine. Hopefully, the gradual relaxation in control will be balanced by an increase in task-directed motivation resulting from early learning successes.

TOPICS FOR DISCUSSION AND FURTHER STUDY

1. In view of the largely frustrated attempts of professional researchers to reliably evaluate teaching effectiveness, how do you propose to satisfy yourself that you are performing an adequate job as a classroom teacher?

2. To what extent do you feel that you have been personally influenced by your previous teachers? What was the nature of this influence, and in what manner was it brought to bear?

3.* List the specific behaviors which you would expect a "warm" teacher to exhibit. Check this against the actual performance of a classroom teacher observed in your practice-teaching experience.

4. Indicate how the concept of an "orderly," "businesslike" approach can be put into practice at the grade level at which you will be teaching. Cite specific instances of orderly and disorderly approaches.

5.* Observe the performance of a teacher who is generally regarded as "stimulating." What specific techniques is he employing?

6.* Discuss the problem of discipline with a teacher who is effective in this area. What hypotheses underlie his approach? What techniques has he worked out? Compare his classroom performance with that of a teacher who has manifest problems maintaining classroom discipline.

7.* How can the postulated effectiveness of Hunt's "reflective" (abstract) teacher be reconciled with the characteristics of effective teaching identified by research? How is reflectiveness related to the facilitation of meaningful learning.

8. If Hunt's "reflective teacher" hypothesis is correct (that is, that this trait is associated with effective teaching), what useful educational roles can be served by teachers who are highly concrete in their thinking? To what extent, if any, would the development of a reflective approach be amenable to specialized training?

9.* To what extent is popularity among students an important consideration for teachers? Are students capable of distinguishing between those teachers whom they "like" and those teachers for whom, whether they like them or not, they have respect? (See: Smith and Lutz, 1964; Wright and Sherman, 1965.)

10.* What sort of image do teachers project among nonteachers? In what ways would the latter group change the teacher's major characteristics? (See: T. E. Smith, 1965.)

11.* Do you feel that a large proportion of teachers become disillusioned with their classroom role? Suggest ways in which the occurrence of such disillusionment may be related to such factors as the teacher's socioeconomic background, sex, and education. (See: Wright and Tuska, 1966.)

12.* Consult Solomon's (1964) analysis of the research on the effects of punishment, and Kennedy and Willicutt's (1964) review of studies of the effectiveness of praise and blame. Are these findings consistent with the assertions of this chapter concerning the consequences of punitive teaching? What differential effects might be predicted for different student personality types?

13.* In a recent article, Rosenthal (1968) describes research in which teachers were led to believe that certain children (who were actually chosen at random by the experimenter) could be expected to show an increase in IQ. As it turned out, such children actually did show gains in IQ relative to students for whom such an expectation was not created in the teacher's mind. How would you explain these results? How do they relate to the observations concerning expectations at the beginning of the chapter?

SUGGESTIONS FOR ADDITIONAL READING

Anderson, R. C., Learning in discussions: Resumé of authoritarian-democratic studies. *Harvard Educ. Rev.,* 1959, *29,* 201–215.

Gage, N. L. (Ed)., *Handbook of research on teaching.* Skokie, Ill.: Rand McNally & Company, 1963.

Gage, N. L., Can science contribute to the art of teaching? *Phi Delta Kappan,* 161.

Gage, N. L., Can science contribute to the art of teaching. *Phi Delta Kappan,* 1968, *49*(7), 399–403.

Harvey, O. J., M. Prather, B. J. White, and J. K. Hoffmeister. Teacher's beliefs, classroom atmosphere and student behavior. *Amer. Educ. Res. J.,* 1968, *5*(2), 151–166.

LeFevre, C., Teacher characteristics and careers. *Rev. educ. Res.,* 1967, *37*(4), 433–447.

Ryans, D. G., Some relationships between pupil behavior and certain teacher characteristics. *J. educ. Psychol.,* 1961, *52,* 82–90.

Sears, P. S., and E. R. Hilgard. The teacher's role in the motivation of the learner. In *Theories of learning and instruction: 63d Yearbook Nat. Soc. Stud. Educ.,* Part I. Chicago: University of Chicago Press, 1964.

PART FIVE

DISCOVERY LEARNING

In Part Two a basic distinction was made between discovery and reception learning. In brief, in reception learning a new proposition (concept or idea) to be learned is presented to the learner (for example, by the teacher directly or by a written passage) in its final form and the student needs only to incorporate it into his cognitive structure. In discovery learning, on the other hand, the learner must rearrange given data to *produce* (himself) the generalization *prior to* its incorporation into cognitive structure. Another relevant point was that the reception/discovery and meaningful/rote dimensions are plausibly regarded as independent so that—contrary to what is frequently asserted—*both* reception and discovery learning can be *either* meaningful or rote, depending essentially on what happens *after* the new idea is presented to cognitive structure. In terms of the behavioral categories described in Chapter 3, discovery learning enters prominently (if not exclusively) in concept formation, formulation of generalizations, problem solving, and creativity.

The present section discusses the latter three behavioral categories in considerable detail. In Chapter 16, which deals mainly with the discovery of generalizations, it is argued through specific examples that many distinct points can be discerned on the discovery/reception dimension, so that the simple assertion that one "method" is superior to the other makes little sense. Both theoretical analysis and common sense reveal that discovery learning (in some form) is indispensible in testing the acquisition of problem-solving skills, and that it possesses advantages—mainly in the enhancement of cognitive drive—in the learning of generalizations.

Unfortunately, these legitimate claims for discovery methods have been magnified and distorted into what may best be called a "mystique" of discovery learning. The latter phenomenon, which is strongly in evidence in many current curriculum movements, is subjected to detailed analysis in Chapter 16. Such analysis reveals that many of the extreme arguments in favor of discovery methods fail to take into account that its positive aspects are offset by the fact that learning time can be expected to *increase* in proportion to the *decrease in guidance* provided by the teacher; this is clearly an important consideration when the efficient acquisition of large bodies of organized knowledge is an acknowledged goal.

Chapter 17 deals with problem solving and creativity, the two highest categories in the behavioral taxonomy presented in Chapter 3. Both behaviors can be profitably discussed within a single paradigm which describes how the "gap" between the learner's knowledge and some given or self-defined *end-point* can be filled by transforming relevant propositions and concepts in the learner's cognitive structure by means of rules of inference. Such transformations may be undertaken on a *random* basis (as in trial-and-error problem solving) or may be guided by a *strategy* (that is, a set of specifiable rules which set priorities among the many admissible operations). Within this paradigm a valid distinction between problem solving and creativity is that, in the latter behavior, the learner draws upon background knowledge not explicity taught (or otherwise commonly thought of) as being relevant to the task at hand, and that his strategy is not explicitly formulated.

From this analysis it can be argued that considerable optimism is in order regarding the improvement of problem-solving skills in the major school subjects. In that connection, the paradigm itself suggests that the most fruitful points of attack will be: (1) attempting to improve the organization of the learner's relevant background knowledge and making such knowledge more readily available (for example, categorizing it in tabular or graphical form); (2) instructing the student in ways of concretely representing (and thereby reducing his errors in the use of) complex inferences; and

(3) teaching strategies which apply to specific *classes* of problems.

Less optimism seems warranted with respect to the development of creative behavior since, in terms of the preceding analysis, it is in at least one important respect unteachable (that is, in that the strategy cannot be explicitly formulated). Chapter 17 cautions that the school should be wary of the prevalent assumption that the so-called "divergent production abilities" (for example, the child's being able to suggest several unusual uses for a brick) is a true manifestation of creativity rather than, as is maintained here, merely a supportive intellectual trait. Although present evidence suggests that divergent production abilities can be strengthened by training (at least in the short term), the school would seem better advised to recognize and encourage genuine creativity in the context of the major subject-matter fields studied in school. In these fields, which possess a highly developed logical structure, the child's "creative" productions are subjected to much more substantial criteria than are found in "content free" tasks, and appropriate restraints are put on mere verbal facility and glibness.

CHAPTER 16

LEARNING BY DISCOVERY

EVEN THE MOST CURSORY EXAMINATION OF NEW CURRICU-
lum proposals indicates that there is presently a strong movement toward
introducing a larger component of "discovery" experiences into the elementary and secondary schools. In many school systems where such ideas are
being tried out, the discovery approach is like a breath of fresh air in what
has been frequently a depressing and restrictive school environment. However, while one's educational convictions should be argued with passion, it
seems a sensible requirement that they should also be informed with reason.
And it was a sensed lack of realism and reasoned argument among the more
extreme discovery enthusiasts which prompted Ausubel (1963) to prepare a
critique of the "mystique" which seems to have grown up around this
approach.

During the preparation of this book, our first inclination was to omit a
detailed discussion of the merits and pitfalls of discovery learning, on the
assumption that the wave of enthusiasm evidenced in the early 1960s had
passed and that more sober viewpoints now prevailed. However, a survey of
current professional literature, after-dinner talks to teachers' conventions, the
pronouncements of many educational psychologists themselves, and the opinions of elementary-school teachers who have come into our courses has
convinced us that our initial opinion is entirely unfounded. For example, in
the province in which one of the authors is located, a prestigious government
commission has recently issued a report containing an unequivocal (and
virtually unqualified) endorsement of discovery learning, without serious
reference to reasoned counter-arguments or potential weaknesses.[1] It is our

---

[1] *Living and Learning: A Report of the Provincial Committee on Aims and Objectives of
Education in the Schools of Ontario.* Toronto: Newton Publishing Company, 1968. One
half of the overriding recommendation of this report is that it is "the responsibility of
every school authority to provide a child-centered learning continuum that invites learning
by individual discovery and inquiry."

firm conviction, therefore, that the issues of half a decade ago are still very much alive; for that reason we present here an abridged version of the 1963 statement, together with further analyses and recommendations.

AN OVERVIEW OF DISCOVERY LEARNING

Historical Background

To what may the present enthusiasm for discovery methods be attributed? To begin with, the progressive education movement undoubtedly furnished a major impetus to its utilization and appeal. One aspect of this movement was a growing dissatisfaction with the empty formalism of much educational content in the latter part of the nineteenth and the early part of the twentieth century; with stultifying drill and catechism-like methods of teaching; with the curriculum's lack of relatedness to the everyday experience of the child, his physical world and social environment; and with pupils' rote verbalization and memorization of ideas for which they had no adequate referents in experience. The progressive educator's overreaction to these faults took the form of an exaggerated emphasis on direct, immediate, and concrete experience as a prerequisite for genuine understanding, on problem solving and inquiry, and on incidental learning and learning in natural uncontrived situations. From this type of emphasis grew activity programs and project methods and the belief in "learning for and by problem solving."

A second aspect of the evolution of the discovery method was the child-centered approach to instruction that originated in the educational philosophies of Rousseau and Froebel. The adherents of this approach emphasized the importance of structuring the curriculum in terms of the nature of the child and of his participation in the educational process, that is, in terms of his current interests, his endogenously derived needs, and his state of intellectual and emotional readiness. According to this point of view, the educational environment facilitates development best by providing a maximally permissive field that does not interfere with the predetermined process of spontaneous maturation. The child himself, it was asserted, is in the most strategic position to know and select those educational ingredients that correspond most closely to his current developmental needs, and hence are most conducive to his optimal growth. Propositions such as these clearly make a fetish of autonomy and self-discovery, and take an extremely dim view of any form of guidance or direction in learning, particularly the communication of insights or generalizations by teacher to students. Herein lies, in part, the origin of the notion that expository teaching is, on developmental grounds, inherently authoritarian, and that self-discovered insights are uniquely and transcendentally endowed with meaning and understanding that can be achieved through no other means.

These two strands—emphasis on the child's direct experience and spontaneous interests, and insistence upon autonomously achieved insight free of all directive manipulation of the learning environment—set the stage for the subsequent adulation of problem solving, laboratory work, and questionable emulation of the scientific method. Many mathematics and science teachers were made self-conscious about systematically presenting and explaining to their students the basic concepts and principles of their fields because it was held that this procedure would promote glib verbalization and rote memorization. Although enthusiasts are reluctant to admit it, the new emphasis on problem solving often meant little more than that the students ceased to memorize *specific* formulas but memorized instead *type* problems, learning how to work exemplars of all the kinds of problems they were responsible for, and memorizing not only the form of each type but the solution as well. This was paralleled in science courses by laboratory experiences in which the student proceeded mechanically through a set of instructions without any real appreciation of the concepts or hypotheses at issue, arriving finally at the predetermined conclusion set out in the manual. The result of these experiences was far from the hoped-for aim of self-discovered generalizations. In the final analysis it produced an approach to problem solving which was frequently just as formalistic, mechanical, passive, and rote as the worst form of verbal exposition.

The previously mentioned factors contributing to the advocacy of the discovery method have been in operation over long periods of time, and do not in themselves explain the intensity of current interest. These attitudes and beliefs, existing both in latent and active forms in many educational circles for several generations, were galvanized into widespread overt expression by at least three recent occurrences. The first was the curriculum "revolution," commencing in the early postwar period and accelerating thereafter, which brought with it a great emphasis on the "heuristics of discovery"; this emphasis was itself premised on the argument that, given the inevitability of change, the student is best prepared for life by "learning how to learn." A concurrent influence was the rediscovery of the writings of Piaget by North American educational psychologists and the questionable assertion that his theoretical speculations and research results argue conclusively for the necessity of a discovery approach to the learning of concepts (Sullivan, 1967b). Finally, it seems that many contemporary high-school and college officials are looking toward greater student activity and initiative with respect to their own learning (for example, through a heavier emphasis on inquiry and discovery methods) as one means of combatting apparent student disenchantment with both the substance and method of instruction at these levels. However, it is not our purpose in this chapter to discuss the reasonableness of the latter arguments, but rather to analyze the discovery method in more detail so that its potential advantages and weakness can be better understood.

Nature of Discovery Learning in School Settings

The essential criterion for discovery learning is that the material to be learned is *not* presented to the learner in final form, but that he must reorganize or transform it in some fashion prior to its incorporation into cognitive structure. As we saw earlier, discovery learning ranges in complexity from concept formation and the formation of generalizations to problem solving and creativity. In these particular kinds of learning *there is no alternative* to discovery learning, so that a discovery-reception controversy makes no sense there.

The real controversy then is not whether discovery learning is desirable or undesirable (since under certain circumstances it is unavoidable), but rather the *relative emphasis* upon these respective modes of learning which is most appropriate at various stages of the learner's development. While the opportunity for discovery learning exists across the whole behavioral hierarchy, the controversy concerning this approach has been centered at the level of generalization learning. The reason for this is that the generalization or principle expresses the ultimate result of most investigations or experiments which the student might undertake.

While we tend, for convenience, to speak of reception and discovery as though we were dealing with a true dichotomy, analysis of teaching methods employed in the classroom indicates that there are a variety of approaches which can be ordered along a dimension of *increasing direction* on the part of the teacher. Consider for example the various ways in which we might attempt to have a child come to understand the proposition that "the sum of the angles in a triangle equals 180 degrees." In a "pure discovery" approach (only very occasionally found in the school), we would provide the child with numerous triangles and such measuring instruments as rulers, compasses, and protractors and simply allow him to "play" with the materials, giving no specific directions whatsoever. While the child might well make some useful discoveries, the probability that he would arrive at the desired generalization entirely on his own seems rather remote.

At a second level of directedness the teacher would attempt at least to steer the child's thinking in the direction of the intended generalization, as for example by asking him to "see if you can find any interesting facts about the angles of triangles." Again the probability of the emergence of the correct generalization seems rather remote but is distinctly higher than in the first case.

At a third level of directedness, the child might be given the instructions: "Measure the angles of a triangle and add the results together. Repeat this for a number of triangles and see if you can state any conclusion which applies to all the triangles." The directions now have become quite specific and would in most cases be sufficient to allow the child to formulate the generalization.

At a fourth level—where we encounter a procedure commonly used in classrooms—the teacher would draw a number of triangles on the board and ask various students to come forward to measure the angles and perform the requisite addition, and would then invite the class to formulate a generalization. Here the teacher exerts even greater control over the learning process (insuring, for example, that the angles are added properly) and most of the children are deprived of the opportunity to measure the angles themselves; but an opportunity still exists for each child to formulate the generalization independently. Consequently, this approach could still qualify as discovery learning.

At the fifth level of directedness, the teacher would probably first enunciate the generalization and then have various children confirm it with examples drawn on the board, or have each child verify it in his workbook. We have now passed into reception learning, since it is no longer the child but the *teacher* who formulates the generalization.

Finally, at the sixth level—which might be appropriate to adolescents and adults—the teacher would merely enunciate the generalization and, without offering corroborative evidence, utilize it as the basis for further learning (for example, the fact that the sum of the angles in a rectangle—comprising two triangles—must equal 360 degrees).

It is clear then that generalizations concerning the relative merits of discovery (as compared with reception) approaches must take into account the degree of direction or guidance involved in the particular discovery method in question. For example, while the most extreme form of reception learning would take considerably less time than most of the discovery approaches, the difference in learning time between the fourth level (discovery) and the fifth level (reception) would seem to be minimal.

In the same vein, we should recognize that the current change in emphasis in schools is not from pure reception to pure discovery learning. Probably it would be far more accurate to say that while most teachers have traditionally chosen methods at the fourth or fifth level, schools are currently introducing a larger proportion of activities at the second and third levels. It is also interesting to note that in teaching which can be classified at the fourth level—where the teacher typically calls upon one child to formulate the generalization—it is difficult to say whether any other particular child is engaged in guided discovery learning (that is, is formulating the generalization himself) or reception learning (that is, relating to his cognitive structure a generalization formulated by *another student*).

Psychological and Educational Rationale of the Discovery Method

What are some of the legitimate claims, the defensible uses, and the palpable advantages of the discovery method? Several can be cited under the headings indicated in the paragraphs below.

Transmission of Subject Matter   In the first place, under certain circumstances some variants of the discovery method may have advantages over reception learning in the transmission of subject matter itself. In particular, occasional use of inductive discovery techniques for teaching subject-matter content is didactically defensible when pupils are in the *concrete operational* stage of congitive development. It is true, of course, that only the availability of some concrete empirical experience is necessary to generate the semi-abstract level of meaningfulness characteristic of this stage of cognitive development. Hence, either simple verbal exposition, using concrete empirical props, or a semi-autonomous type of discovery accelerated by the judicious use of prompts and hints, is adequate for teaching simple and relatively familiar new ideas. But when the learning task is more difficult and unfamiliar, a more autonomous measure of discovery learning probably enhances intuitive meaningfulness by intensifying and personalizing both the concreteness of the experience and the operation of abstracting and generalizing from empirical data. In these circumstances, also, the time/cost disadvantage of discovery learning is not very serious, since the time-consuming concrete empirical aspect of learning must take place anyway.

To a lesser degree this same rationale also applies to adolescents and adults who are relatively unsophisticated 'in the basic concepts and terminology of a given discipline. The older individual, however, has the benefit of greater cognitive sophication and linguistic facility, as well as of past successful experience in meaningfully relating abstractions to each other without the aid of concrete empirical props. He will therefore move through the intuitive, subverbal phase of insightful understanding much more rapidly than the unsophisticated child and, unlike the latter, will soon dispense with this phase entirely.

Testing Meaningfulness of Learning   One obviously *necessary* use of the discovery method is in evaluating the meaningfulness and depth of the learning of a particular concept or generalization. For example, if the child has been taught (via reception learning) the generalization that objects expand when heated, the learner's understanding might be tested by asking him to supply specific examples of this generalization from the environment. Again, if the learner has been taught a formula (that is, a principle) for determining the area of a triangle, an appropriate test of his comprehension would be to have him apply this generalization to a number of exemplars which he had not seen before. In both cases there is a modicum of discovery required. In the first instance the child is not presented with the exemplars, but must select them from a variety of environmental stimuli, and in the second case the child must select various lines as representing the base, height, and so on of the triangle. In both cases, then, there may be said to be some transformation of perceptual data to fit the conditions of the generalization prior to the incorporation of the exemplars into cognitive structure as derivatives of the generalization.

Problem Solving   Discovery learning is of course crucially implicated in problem solving. One can teach strategies (verbal rules) by a reception approach, but one can never tell whether they are comprehended and utilizable until the learner attempts to apply them to novel cases. Moreover, even though the strategy offers guidance to the learner there is still a considerable need for "discovery" within the resulting procedural framework. In the pendulum problem for example, the learner operating under the general strategy provided must identify the independent variables and, after manipulating data, formulate a generalization relating the variables to the period of the pendulum. Similarly, in our geometry problem, the strategy does not determine an invariant order for combining or manipulating relevant propositions, but merely defines choice points at each of which the learner must discover which of a number of relevant propositions might be applied, and what further conditions must hold before this application can be made.

Transfer   One might expect greater transfer, particularly of the lateral type, if the student actually formulates his own generalizations. This would be true because such a learner would tend to have experiences with a greater variety of exemplars and should therefore be able to recognize these more easily when they occur in different contexts. Such facilitation or transfer would compensate, to some extent, for the longer time usually required in discovery approaches.

Motivation   The last advantage of discovery learning which we will cite, and this perhaps its most salient one, has to do with the enhancement of motivation. One would think, for example, that the student whose motivation is based primarily on ego-enhancement drive would obtain a greater feeling of self-esteem from independent discovery than from being told a result or principle. Certainly in our contemporary value system discovery learning is accorded a higher status and would therefore seem to have more potential for ego-enhancement than reception learning. Similar arguments would apply to the efficacy of discovery learning in satisfying affiliative drive, for parents and teachers are more likely to recognize, and therefore show explicit approval of, the child who makes a discovery on his own (frequently a more conspicuous activity than the deceptively passive-appearing reception learning). Where the advantage might lie in respect to cognitive drive is a rather difficult question, for if there exists a "desire to know, to understand, and to acquire knowledge for its own sake" then this drive could equally well be satisfied by both discovery and reception modes of learning. However if, in accordance with our definition, cognitive drive also includes the desire to solve problems, then in this particular respect the discovery approach would provide opportunities for enhancement not available in reception learning.

PSYCHOLOGICAL AND EDUCATIONAL LIMITATIONS OF LEARNING BY DISCOVERY

If proponents of discovery learning confined their assertions to the legitimate claims outlined above there would be no cause for concern. Unfortunately, many present claims go so far beyond that to which one can reasonably subscribe that it seems necessary to analyze and refute some of the arguments advanced in its support. Such arguments can be conveniently considered under the following ten headings.[2]

1. All Real Knowledge Is Self-Discovered

The most general and metaphysical of the ten propositions is the familiar assertion that to *really* possess knowledge or acquire an idea the learner must discover it by himself or through his own insight. It is true that one cannot simply soak up one's culture like a piece of blotting paper and expect it to be meaningful. The very processes of perception and cognition necessarily require that the cultural stimulus world must first be filtered through each individual's personal sensory apparatus and cognitive structure before it can have any meaning. Meaning can never be anything more than a *personal* phenomenal product that emerges when potentially meaningful ideas are integrated within an individually unique cognitive structure. All of this, however, is recognized and accounted for in any program of meaningful expository learning.

In the final analysis the proposition that everyone must discover for himself every bit of knowledge that he *really* wishes to possess is a repudiation of the very concept of culture. For perhaps the most unique attribute of

---

[2]This account is abridged from Ausubel (1963, 1968).

human culture, which distinguishes it from every other kind of social organization in the animal kingdom, is precisely the fact that the accumulated discoveries of millenia can be transmitted to each succeeding generation in the course of childhood and youth, and need not be discovered anew by each generation. This miracle of culture is made possible only because it is so much less time-consuming to communicate and explain an idea meaningfully to others than to have them discover it by themselves.

2. Meaning as an Exclusive Product of Nonverbal Discovery

A related proposition holds that abstract concepts and propositions are forms of empty verbalism unless the learner discovers them directly out of his own concrete, empirical, nonverbal experience. This assertion concerning "empty verbalism" seems to rest on the following three logical errors: (a) a misinterpretation of verbal learning as a passive rote phenomenon; (b) confusion between the reception/discovery and rote/meaningful dimensions of learning; and (c) an unwarranted generalization to adolescents and adults of the child's dependence upon concrete empirical props in comprehending and manipulating abstract ideas. Meaningful knowledge, however, is not an exclusive product of creative nonverbal discovery; for potentially meaningful *presented* material to become meaningful knowledge, the learner need only adopt a set to relate and incorporate its substantive import nonarbitrarily within his cognitive structure.

3. Subverbal Awareness as the Key to Transfer

Hendrix (1961), in attempting to construct a more systematic and sophisticated pedagogic rationale for the discovery method than had been attempted previously, denied that verbal

> generalizing is the primary generator of transfer power. . . . As far as transfer power [is] concerned the whole thing [is] there as soon as the nonverbal awareness [dawns]. . . . The separation of discovery phenomena from the process of composing sentences which express these discoveries is the big new breakthrough in pedagogical theory (pp. 290, 292).

Support for this position was adduced from an experiment (Hendrix, 1947) involving three matched groups of elementary-school children working in arithmetic. Two groups acquired meaningful nonverbal awareness of a principle; the first group immediately attempted to verbalize the principle, the second did not, and both groups subsequently attempted to transfer this understanding to a new problem. The third group had the principle explained to them verbally. Although differences were not large enough to be statistically significant, the group which did *not* attempt to verbalize their subverbal awareness made better transfer scores than the group which did, and both groups out-performed the group which had been taught the principle by verbal exposition.

The generalization formulated from these results (Hendrix, 1947) is that the state of awareness constituting the discovery is generated in an initial nonverbal stage and that it is only when this stage is complete that there exists something which can be transferred. It is asserted, moreover, that verbalization is not only unnecessary for the generation and transfer of ideas and understanding, but is also positively harmful when used for these purposes. Language only enters the picture because of the need to attach a symbol or label to the emerging subverbal insight, so that it can be recorded, verified, classified, and communicated to others; but the entire substance of the idea inheres in the subverbal insight itself. The resulting problem then, according to Hendrix (1961), becomes one of how to plan and execute teaching so that language can be used for these necessary secondary functions *"without* damage to the dynamic quality of the learning itself." Clearly this view is not congenial to the notion of reception learning advocated in this book.

The unqualified generalization that verbalization of an insight prior to its use inhibits transfer lacks both logical cogency and empirical support.[3] Nonverbal understanding of principles undoubtedly exists, especially in children and unsophisticated adults, as a precursor to some verbal understandings (Hull, 1920; Luchins and Luchins, 1947). This, of course, does not mean that *nonverbal* concept meanings and propositions are actually used in the *generation* of new insights. Such a feat would be very difficult because ideas that are not represented by words lack sufficient manipulability to be used in any complex type of thought process. It merely suggests that a preliminary intuitive (subverbal) stage exists in the *product* of thought when the emerging new insight is not clearly and precisely defined. However, when this product is eventually refined through verbalizing, it acquires thereby a much greater transfer power.[4] The verbalization of the insight that takes place at this point is actually a later phase of the thought process itself and is not to be confused with the still later representational process of *naming* verbalized meanings, as a result of which the latter meanings become more manipulable for purposes of thought.

---

[3]For a methodological critique of the Hendrix study, see Ausubel, 1968.
[4]Direct evidence that verbalized insights are more transferable than subverbal insights comes from experiments on the ability to solve transposition and discrimination problems (Spiker and Terrell, 1955; Weir and Stevenson, 1959). Indirect evidence comes from studies in which verbalization during attempts to discover underlying principles (Gagné and Smith, 1962) or the knowledge of underlying verbal principles (Ewert and Lambert, 1932) facilitated problem solving.

In light of the foregoing remarks, what explanation can be offered for Hendrix's (1947) finding that immediate verbalization of newly acquired subverbal insight apparently renders that insight less transferable than when verbalization is not attempted? First, it seems likely that *premature* verbalization of nonverbal insight—before such insight is adequately clear, stable, complete, and consolidated further by extensive use—may well interfere with its more adequate emergence and consolidation at this level, as well as encourage rote memorization of the marginal and ineptly stated verbal proposition. Even more important, however, is the likelihood that a verbally expressed insight—when ambiguous, unstable, unconsolidated, ineptly expressed, and only marginally competent—possesses less functional utility and transferability than the ordinarily more primitive and less transferable subverbal insight that is more adequate in these latter respects. This is particularly true in the case of children, because of their limited linguistic facility and their relative incompetence in formal propositional logic.

Drawing these various strands of argument together, what can we legitimately conclude at this point? First, verbalization does more than just encode subverbal insight into words. The use of manipulable words to represent ideas makes possible, to begin with, the very process of transforming these ideas into new insights. Moreover, the verbalization of emerging subverbal insights into sentences is an integral part of the thought process that greatly enhances the precision and explicitness of its products. It therefore makes possible a qualitatively higher level of understanding with greatly enhanced transfer power. Second, direct acquisition of ideas from verbally presented abstract propositions presupposes both that the learner has attained the stage of formal logical operations and that he possesses minimal sophistication in the particular subject matter in question. The typical elementary-school child, therefore, tends to be limited to an intuitive, semi-abstract awareness of difficult abstractions. The older, cognitively mature individual, however, who is also unsophisticated in a particular subject-matter area, is able to dispense with the semi-abstract phase of awareness rather quickly, that is, as soon as he attains the necessary degree of sophistication. Once he attains it, he probably short-circuits the semi-abstract phase completely. Lastly, premature verbalization of a nonverbal insight, when this latter insight is still incomplete, unclear, and inadequately consolidated, probably decreases its transferability.

4. The Discovery Mehod in Transmitting Subject-Matter Content

Educators who are convinced that abstractions are mere glib verbalisms unless independently discovered by the learner have no logical alternative to advocating the use of discovery techniques—in high school and university as well as in the elementary school—as a principal method of transmitting the substantive content of subject matter. Easley (1958, 1959) for example, argues strenuously for reorganizing, in whole or in part, the curricula of science, mathematics, and other secondary-school and college-level subjects along lines of inductive discovery. He also insists that nonverbal understanding and application of principles should be required of and demonstrated by students before they are permitted to use them in verbal form.

The first argument which must be brought against this claim resides in the time/cost factor. As we saw earlier, a case can be made for some use of the discovery method in the concrete operational period, particularly when the material to be learned is complex or abstract and where one would normally resort to empirical props in any case. However the fact that most discovery approaches are incomparably more time-consuming (and, therefore, more costly) than reception approaches presents a strong argument against more than their limited use (confined mainly to highly directed kinds) for transmitting subject matter at the high-school level and beyond.

Another difficulty in using discovery as a *major* source of acquiring subject matter is that children (even when quite young) usually start with some preconceptions or spontaneous models derived from their own experience or from prevailing folklore. Hence when they are supposedly discovering principles inductively, they may be really attempting to use empirical experience to confirm their existing preconceptions. It is "unpromising to base a teaching program on the expectation that children can invent . . . modern scientific concepts, because their spontaneously invented concepts . . . present too much of a block." A more realistic approach "is for the teacher to *introduce* . . . modern scientific concepts . . . [and] follow the introduction with opportunities for the children to discover that new observations can also be interpreted by the use of the concept" (Atkin and Karplus, 1962).

A further disadvantage in using a discovery approach for the presentation of subject-matter content inheres in the difficulties caused by children's subjectivism and by their exaggerated tendency to jump to conclusions, to overgeneralize on the basis of limited experience, and to consider only one aspect of a problem at a time (Inhelder and Piaget, 1958; Karplus, 1962; Piaget, 1932). It is true that one objective of the elementary-school science curriculum (to enhance appreciation of scientific method) implies an effort to educate them out of these tendencies. But it is one thing to do so as part of a limited and directed laboratory program, and quite another to struggle full-time with this handicap as children are required to self-discover everything they have to learn.

5. Problem-Solving Ability as a Primary Goal of Education

A fifth proposition underlying the learning-by-discovery thesis is a belief that the development of problem-solving ability is the primary goal of education.

The development of problem-solving ability is, of course, a legitimate and significant educational objective in its own right. Hence it is highly defensible to utilize a certain proportion of classroom time in developing appreciation of, and facility in the use of, scientific methods of inquiry and of other empirical, inductive, and deductive problem-solving procedures. But this is a far cry from advocating that the enhancement of problem-solving ability is *the* major function of the school. As the reader will appreciate from earlier sections, it is the consistent thesis of this book that the acquisition of subject-matter knowledge is itself a major goal of the school, and one which should not be subjugated to problem solving—as important as the latter may be. Although these two sets of objectives can be mutually supportive, they are far from being identical. Hence it cannot be argued that methods promoting one objective necessarily promote the other. In particular it cannot be assumed that the learner will acquire all the subject-matter content he needs in the course of learning how to solve problems autonomously.

On a related matter, many current writers (Bruner, 1961b; Easley, 1958; Hibbs, 1961; Suchman, 1961) in the field of science education express the view that the principal objective of science instruction is the acquisition of general inquiry skills, of appropriate attitudes about science, and of training in the "heuristics of discovery." Implicit or explicit in this view is the belief that the particular choice of subject matter chosen to implement these goals is a matter of indifference so long as it is suitable for the operations of inquiry. Thus, Hibbs (1961) states:

> It does not matter whether the student learns any particular set of facts, but it does matter whether he learns how much fun it is to learn—to observe and experiment, to question and analyze the world without any ready-made set of answers and without any premium on the accuracy of his factual results, at least in the field of science.

The significant difficulty with this approach is that its proponents are, in effect, asserting that the goals of the scientist are identical to the goals of the science student and that students can learn science most effectively by playing the role of junior scientist. Yet the scientist is engaged in a full-time search for new general or applied principles in his field, while the student should be primarily engaged in an effort to learn the same basic subject matter in this field which the scientist learned in his student days, and also to learn something of the method and spirit of scientific inquiry. Thus, while it makes perfectly good sense for the scientist to work full-time formulating and testing new principles, it is quite indefensible (in our opinion) for the student to be doing the same thing—either in real discovery, or in the sense of rediscovery. It is the student's business to learn these principles as meaningfully and critically as possible, and then *after* his background is adequate, to try to improve on them if he can. If he is ever to discover, he must first learn. He cannot learn adequately by pretending that he is a junior scientist.

In our opinion, then, any realistic science curriculum must be concerned with the systematic presentation of an organized body of knowledge as an explicit end in itself. Even if it is relatively superficial and organized on an intuitive basis, as it must be in the elementary school, the science curriculum should make a start in this direction and give the student a feeling for science as a selectively and sequentially organized structure. This is no less important than imparting the view that science is a method of inquiry.

6. "Every Child a Creative Thinker"

Discovery methods are often rationalized in terms of the currently fashionable notion that the school's chief responsibility is to make every child (or nearly every child) a creative thinker. This extreme notion is based on the highly questionable assumption that all discovery activity, irrespective of degree of originality, is qualitatively of one piece; on a watered-down, "democratic" definition of creativity broad enough to include any type of independent discovery; on the belief that the very multiplicity of human abilities gives every individual a good chance, genically speaking, of being creative in at least one area; and on naive *tabula rasa* conceptions of human plasticity which maintain that even if a given child has no creative potentialities, good teachers can take the place of missing genes.

The general plausibility of these arguments will be examined in a later chapter. At this point we need only say that they are highly unrealistic, and that while efforts must be made to develop creative potential in those children who possess it, schools should give priority to the as yet unattained task of having each child master the basic intellectual skills as well as a reasonable proportion of the more important subject-matter content of the major disciplines.

7. Expository Teaching as Authoritarianism

Advocates of the discovery method also take advantage of the disfavor attached to authoritarianism in education to discredit didactic exposition. When a teacher stands in front of a classroom and presents facts, concepts, and principles, he is—according to some discovery enthusiasts—behaving in an authoritarian fashion. In his role of expositor the teacher is allegedly coercing pupils, by the prestige of his position and by his power to dispense reward and punishment, into unquestioningly accepting on faith his own version of "the truth" instead of giving them an opportunity to discover it for themselves.

This distressing picture of expository teaching seems a bit overdrawn. We do not deny that schools and colleges abound in such teachers. But this characterization is certainly not true of all didactic exposition, nor is it inherent in the method itself. There is nothing inherently authoritarian in presenting or explaining ideas to others so long as the hearers are not obliged—either explicitly or implicitly—to accept them on faith. The deference to authority implied in accepting already discovered knowledge has been condemned out of all reason, for if students were required to validate independently every proposition presented by their instructors before accepting it, they would never progress beyond the rudiments of any discipline. We can only ask that established knowledge be presented to them as rationally and nonarbitrarily as possible and that they accept it tentatively and critically, as only the best available approximation of the "truth."

8. Discovery Organizes Learning Effectively for Later Use

We turn now to three recently propounded propositions (Bruner, 1961a) which, taken together, may be said to constitute a proposed psychological— rather than philosophical—rationale for the discovery method. First, it is suggested that emphasis upon discovery in learning has the effect upon the learner of leading him to be a constructionist, to organize what he is encountering in a way not only designed to uncover regularity and relatedness, but also to avoid the kind of information drift that fails to keep account of the kind of uses to which information might have to be put.

However, learning by discovery—in our opinion—does not *necessarily* lead to more orderly, integrated, and viable organization, transformation, and use of knowledge. It does so only insofar as the learning situation is highly structured, simplified, and skillfully programmed to include a large number of diversified exemplars of the same principle, carefully graded in order of difficulty. But under these circumstances one must, in all fairness, attribute these latter outcomes to the teacher's or the textbook writer's organization of the data from which the discovery is made, rather than to the act of discovery itself.

Concern with the "structure" of a discipline is certainly not indigenous to the discovery method, since it is also the basis of all modern approaches to expository teaching or reception learning. In fact, concern with presenting the unifying principles of a discipline is the main substantive rationale of expository teaching. The more unstructured discovery methods, on the other hand, tend to ignore the particular substantive content of a discipline as long as this content can be used to further problem-solving or inquiry processes. In Suchman's "Inquiry Training," for example, there is no attempt to present systematically the content of a scientific discipline. Content is largely a matter of indifference, or incidental to the process of discovery. Any kind of content is as good as any other so long as it lends itself to discovery and inquiry. Hence unsystematic and haphazard sampling of scientific concepts is characteristic of his Inquiry Training Program.

9. Discovery as a Unique Generator of Motivation and Self-Confidence

Discovery enthusiasts (Bruner, 1960, 1961a, 1961b; Hendrix, 1961; Suchman, 1961) perceive learning by discovery as a unique and unexcelled generator of self-confidence, of intellectual excitement and of motivation for sustained problem solving and creative thinking. While certain motivational advantages have already been mentioned, including the fact that the successful discovery experience enhances the individual's feeling of confidence, it seems a mistake to believe that positive motivational effects accrue exclusively to this method. For as any student who has been exposed to competent teaching knows, the skillful exposition of ideas can also generate considerable intellectual excitement and motivation for genuine inquiry. Moreover, self-confidence can certainly be bolstered by the act of simply understanding arguments on a reception basis. Most of us, for example, could receive a considerable boost in our self-estimate—as well as a great deal of sheer intellectual pleasure—if we could meaningfully comprehend the lofty speculations of the general theory of relativity.

10. Discovery as a Prime Source for Intrinsic Motivation

A related motivational proposition (Bruner, 1961a) states that "to the degree that one is able to approach learning as a task of discovering something rather than 'learning about it,' to that degree there will be a tendency for the child to carry out his learning activities with the autonomy of self-reward or, more properly, by reward that is discovery itself." Bruner feels that learning by discovery frees the child from the immediate control of such extrinsic motives as high marks, desire for parental and teacher approval, and the need to conform to the expectations of authority figures.

In our opinion, however, there appears to be no *necessary* association between a discovery approach to learning and intrinsic motivation, on the one hand, and the reception approach and extrinsic motivation, on the other. At the same time, one must acknowledge that independent discovery, in our culture, has come to acquire considerable prestige—whose acquisition is, of course, satisfying to the ego-enhancement drive. Consequently it could be argued that rather than being uniquely powered by intrinsic motivation, learning by discovery may appeal relatively more to the extrinsic ego-enhancement drive. Moreover, since high achievement at a prestigious task is essential for children who lack intrinsic self-esteem, we might speculate that it will be the latter child in particular who will aspire to successful discovery performance.[5] To be sure, there are individuals who are driven to discover principally because of a compelling need to express their individuality or creative urges, to find the answers to haunting problems, or to discharge their feelings of moral obligation to the social community. But in our particular culture with its emphasis on status, prestige, ego-aggrandizement and material rewards—especially among individuals who lack intrinsic self-esteem— such motives for discovery tend to be the exception rather than the rule.

RESEARCH EVIDENCE

In this section we will examine a representative sample of the more significant published research bearing on the discovery method. The professional literature on "learning by discovery" regrettably exemplifies, as clearly as any research in education, the all too frequent hollowness of the phrase "research shows." Careful examination of what research supposedly "shows" in this instance yields these three disheartening conclusions: (1) that most of the articles most commonly cited in the literature as reporting results supporting discovery techniques actually report no research findings whatsoever, and consist mainly of theoretical discussion, assertion, and conjecture, of descriptions of existing programs utilizing discovery methods, and of enthusiastic but wholly subjective testimonials regarding the efficacy of discovery approaches; (2) that most of the reasonably well-controlled studies report neutral findings at best; and (3) that most studies reporting positive findings either fail to control other significant variables or employ questionable techniques of statistical analysis. Thus, actual examination of the research literature allegedly supporting learning by discovery reveals that valid evidence of this nature is virtually nonexistent. Moreover it appears that enthusiasts of discovery methods have been supporting each other by citing one another's opinions and assertions as evidence and by generalizing extravagantly from questionable findings.

Long-Term Studies

Despite their frequent espousal of discovery principles, the various curriculum reform projects have failed thus far to yield any research evidence in support of the discovery method. This is not to say that the evidence is negative, but rather that there just is not any evidence one way or the other.

---

[5]Other speculations include that of Cronbach (1967b), who suggests that "pupils who are negativistic may blossom under discovery training, whereas pupils who are anxiously dependent may be paralyzed by demands for self-reliance." In an empirical study, Carlow (1967) found that students who are submissive and have low conceptual level scores (as defined in Chapter 13) do poorly under discovery approaches.

One reason for the lack of evidence is that the sponsors of some of these projects have not been particularly concerned about proving the superior efficacy of their programs, since they have been thoroughly convinced of this from the outset. Hence in many instances they have not even attempted to obtain comparable achievement test data from matched control groups. And only rarely has any effort been expended to prevent the operation of the crucial "Hawthorne Effect," that is, to make sure that evidence of superior achievement outcomes is attributable to the influence of the new pedagogical techniques or materials in question rather than to the fact that the experimental group is the recipient of some form of conspicuous special attention, that something new and interesting is being tried, or that the teachers involved are especially competent, dedicated, and enthusiastic—and receive special training, attend expense-free conventions and summer institutes, and are assigned lighter teaching loads.

A number of long-term curriculum studies in the older literature are frequently cited as providing empirical support for the discovery method. Using basically identical research designs. T. R. McConnell (1934), Thiele (1938), and E. J. Swenson (1949) compared the so-called "drill" and "generalization" methods of teaching number facts to second-grade pupils. The drill approach emphasized rote rules, whereas the generalization method stressed meaningful perception of relationships and derivation of generalizations. Students taught by the generalization method also had the added benefit of concrete props in the McConnell study, and of organized grouping of materials in the Swenson study. A well-known study by G. L. Anderson (1949) was also conducted along very similar lines, but used fourth-grade pupils.

Needless to say, the generalization method was found to be superior in all four studies, except in criterion situations calling for immediate and automatic recall of knowledge relatively unchanged in form from that learned in the training situation. Much more salient than the *discovery* variable in each of these studies, however, is the *rote/meaningful* factor. In two of the studies, the differential availability to the "generalization" group of visual aids or of organized grouping of learning materials, further complicated interpretation of the findings. It should be remembered also that it is precisely in relation to this age group of young learners first entering the stage of concrete logical operations, and still completely unsophisticated in a new, difficult, and abstract subject matter, that the efficacy and feasibility of the discovery method are least disputed.

Short-Term Studies in the Gestalt Tradition

The well-known Gestalt writings on insightful problem solving by Köhler (1925), Wertheimer (1959), Duncker (1945), and Katona (1940) are traditionally cited in the "discovery" literature as supporting the discovery method of teaching. Wertheimer, for example, found that students who have been taught (via relatively rote reception learning) a procedure for finding the area of a parallelogram (dropping lines from the two top corners perpendicular to the base—thus forming a rectangle) and who could do routine examples, became confused when the orientation of the parallelogram was changed (for example, stood on its narrow base). On the other hand, some children who had obtained insight into the structure of the parallelogram—in effect seeing it as a distortion of a rectangle—were able to handle much more difficult cases, such as the one presented in Figure 16.1. Without disputing these results, it should be observed that this and other studies following the Gestalt emphasis on insight (like the early "generalization" studies) deal far more with the rote/meaningful dimension of problem solving than with the relative efficacy of the expository (reception) and discovery approaches. And as pointed out earlier, both reception and discovery learning may each be either rote or meaningful, depending on the conditions under which learning occurs.

Köhler's, Wertheimer's, and Dunckers' monographs also do not really report research findings in the usual sense of that term. They are, rather, sophisticated analyses of the nature and conditions of insightful problem solving from the Gestalt point of view, which use observations, informal experiments, anecdotes, ar.d demonstrations to illustrate the principles under discussion. Katona's studies, on the other hand, are more genuinely experimental but, at the very most, demonstrate that the understanding of a principle, as opposed to rote memorization, leads to superior retention and transfer. One experiment in particular shows that a rotely memorized verbal principle is less transferable to new problems than is mere empirical experience with problems exemplifying the principle in question. But this indicates only that understanding of a principle, even when it is unverbalized, is more

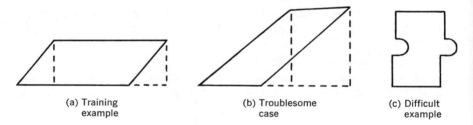

| (a) Training example | (b) Troublesome case | (c) Difficult example |

FIGURE 16.1   *Insight experiments with parallelograms. Based on figures from pp. 14–19 in PRODUCTIVE THINKING, Enlarged Edition, by Max Wertheimer. (Harper & Row, 1959) Reprinted by permission of the publisher.*

transferable than *rote* memorization, not that newly emerging nonverbal awareness is *always* more transferable than verbal understanding.[6]

Studies Involving Varying Amounts of Directedness

We finally come to a series of experimental studies in which varying amounts of guidance were furnished to different groups of subjects in problem-solving situations. Stacey (1949) studied the effects of directed *versus* independent discovery on solving a group of simple meaningful "problems," each of which required subjects to identify the one item in a set of five that did not "belong." He found that active participation and self-discovery were more efficacious for learning than was "passive participation involving only recognition or identification of information" presented to the learner. This finding, of course, was wholly predictable since the fostering of such complete passivity in problem-solving experience as providing the correct answer for each problem, as well as the reason for the answer, seems inadvisable and is seldom if ever practiced today. But even so—and this is rather surprising—significant differences were not found between these extreme treatment groups on a transfer test.

Using similar kinds of material, but with college students rather than sixth-grade pupils, Craig (1956) obtained results even less favorable for the discovery method. His "directed" group, which received a brief verbal explanation of principles during the training period, learned and retained significantly more principles than did his "independent group," which had no help whatsoever in the training situation. As in the Stacey study, however, the two groups were not significantly different with respect to mean score on a transfer test. Kittell's (1957) findings in a similar type of experiment with sixth-grade pupils were, if anything, even more damaging to the discovery cause than were Craig's. The group in his experiment which received an "intermediate" amount of guidance, but nevertheless an amount which was somewhat *greater* than that received by Craig's "directed" group (that is, explanation of principles *plus* organization of materials) was superior in learning, retention, *and* transfer to groups receiving either less or more direction. Pooling the findings of these three studies, therefore, the evidence supports the conclusion that in this type of "problem-solving" exercise, guidance in the form of providing information about underlying principles facilitates learning, retention, and possibly transfer, more than either the provision of less guidance or the furnishing of specific rules for each of the problems.

---

[6]This study is reminiscent of Hendrix's (1947) investigation, whose conclusions were discussed earlier in some detail.

Haselrud and Meyers (1958) conducted a coding study with college students, which was explicitly designed to rebut the Craig and Kittell findings. However, their subjects exhibited significantly better learning on problems where the coding rules were given than where they had to be independently derived. Furthermore, on a delayed transfer test there was *no* difference whatsoever in the number of correct code identifications made for the problems learned originally with the rule given and the problems learned originally by independent derivation of the code.

Other studies in this area by Kersh (1958, 1962) yielded results practically identical to those of Craig, Kittell, and Haselrud and Meyers on the test of original learning, but results opposite to those of Kittell on the delayed retest. By using an ingenious research design, however, Kersh was able to explain this latter finding on the basis of the greater interest and motivation, on the part of the "independent discovery" group, to continue practicing the task during the test-retest interval. Kersh concluded that discovery experience per se does not enhance understanding or meaningfulness.

Larson (1963) found that at least part of the superior retention of Kersh's discovery group was attributable to the Zeigarnik effect, that is, a tendency to remember more incompleted than completed tasks. Craig's (1965) findings suggest that providing continuing tasks and not stating the rule at the conclusion of initial learning, rather than discovery per se, enhance motivation to learn in this context.

In another group of studies on the effects of varying amounts of guidance on problem solving, either no differences were found between treatment groups, or a limited amount of guidance ("guided discovery") was found to be superior both to no guidance whatsoever or to complete guidance. J. Moss (1960), Maltzman and others (1950), Tomlinson (1962), and Forgus and Schwartz (1957) reported no significant differences in delayed retention and transfer between "direct-detailed"[7] and "guided discovery" types of learning groups. W. E. Ray (1957) and Rowlett (1960), on the other hand, found that guided discovery was superior to direct-detailed instruction in remembering and transferring principles of micrometer use and orthographic projection. In a study of programmed learning, Gagné and Brown (1961) reported that a small-step, guided discovery method of programming was superior both to the "ruleg" method (in which generalizations are provided first and then a supporting example) and to a large-step prompted discovery procedure. Corman's findings (1957) were differentiated with respect to the ability level of his subjects; highly explicit instructions were most effective with his more able subjects, whereas his less able subjects benefited equally from more and less explicit instructions. Grote (1960) found that the direct-detailed method was superior for high-ability

---

[7]A relatively complete, explicit, step-by-step type of guidance.

students and that the guided discovery procedure was superior for average-ability students in learning a lever principle.

Concluding Statement

The reader will recognize that there is no simple way of "adding up" the results of the various experiments. The principal difficulty is that these studies vary in many significant details, the most important of which are probably the amount of actual guidance or direction in the "guided discovery" treatment, and the taxonomic level of the task involved (for example, comprehension, application, problem solving). In addition, it is not always clear—even in the published research reports, unfortunately—whether all treatment groups received an equal allotment of learning time or, if they did, how the most "directed" group could have been profitably employed on the task to be learned while the most "undirected" group went through the time-consuming task of formulating the principles themselves.

The foregoing reservations notwithstanding, the research literature does provide us with a range of serious attempts to measure the effect of various degrees of directedness in instruction over a variety of tasks similar to those which are now (or might be) taught in school. Our assessment of the evidence is that, if any conclusion can be drawn, it must be that the traditional emphasis of capable teachers has *not* been shown to be demonstrably in error. That is, there is nothing in the research evidence to suggest that is is inappropriate to use a fairly high level of directedness (perhaps the fourth or even the fifth level in our earlier example) with, of course, a concomitant use of props appropriate to the stage of cognitive development in question—when the intention is adequate comprehension of a principle or concept. When application or genuine problem solving are hoped for, however, there is some warrant for a less directed teaching of the principles to be employed in the criterion task; but even here, a degree of structuring at the third (or fourth) level of our initial example seems clearly preferable to more autonomous discovery. Finally, little evidence of advantage exists for minimally structured or completely unstructured instructional methods. It would seem that they should be used sparingly and on the acknowledged gamble that even their theoretical advantage—that is, a possible enhancement of long-term cognitive drive—has simply not been assessed in the (essentially short-term) studies which comprise the research literature.

SOME CONSIDERATIONS IN ORGANIZING CLASSROOM DISCOVERY EXPERIENCES

In view of the foregoing remarks, considerable caution is necessary in planning discovery learning experiences for school children. The vigorous statements of support for discovery learning in many new curriculum projects, coupled with the equally strong convictions of teachers who are using these new apphoaches, lead us to believe that most of the extreme views discussed earlier are very much in evidence today. The authors have found, for example, that it is extremely difficult to get a teacher who is "sold" on the discovery method even to entertain the proposition that a child might learn as much or more in a learning situation within which reception learning plays a larger part.

Having set out the pros and cons—as is the educational psychologist's customary stance—we must now declare more directly our personal beliefs as to how the educator should proceed. There seems little doubt that a certain amount of planned discovery (of generalizations or principles) is desirable for the child, although experience at the undirected end of the discovery/reception scale should not take up a very large proportion of total instructional time. In our opinion, the benefits of discovery approach to the acquisition of knowledge can be realized in the elementary school if, among the half-dozen or more subject areas in which the student works at any one time, the program in *one* area currently involves a preponderance of minimally directed student discovery experiences (that is, a combination of activities from the first, second, and third levels indicated earlier). Planned discovery-oriented units of several weeks' duration—embedded in a larger program of reception-oriented instruction and rotated among the subject areas—would seem well suited to provide students with scope for independent activity in each area, without jeopardizing the acquisition of a coherent body of content.[8]

At the same time, of course, the elementary-school teacher will use strongly guided approaches as a regular teaching strategy in most subjects. Such methods, while allowing the child to formulate generalizations himself, both provide necessary consolidation of the ideas learned (Carlow, 1967) and move the student along at a steady pace. Moreover, genuine problem-solving experiences, which involve the utilization of learned principles in the "discovery" of solutions, should also constitute a regular part of the child's education from the earliest school years.

Precautions

It seems very important that teachers develop realistic attitudes concerning the advantages and disadvantages of the discovery method, for those who

---

[8]A unit of such duration would seem useful when the teacher is first accommodating himself to less directed classroom activities, and will need time to work out effective classroom arrangements. In addition, a fairly lengthy discovery experience will provide the teacher with some basis for evaluating the learning which takes place.

now harbor fantastic or one-sided views are inviting disillusionment at a later stage. Perhaps the only way for "sold" teachers to acquire such attitudes is to obtain first-hand evidence as to how more directed (even reception) approaches would work in the same circumstances. In respect to making realistic comparisons, teachers are at a disadvantage because the discovery approaches characteristic of the new curricula not only change a *teaching method* (that is, from reception to discovery) but involve as well changes in *content,* degree of *teacher freedom* to set independent goals, incidence of *team approaches* to learning (that is, a group of students cooperating to make discoveries), and in some instances utilization of the teaching staff itself (for example, team teaching). The change in content may in itself be highly significant, since many new programs utilize more careful sequencing and a greater preponderance of organizing themes and concepts than do traditional texts.

Over and above this is the fact that many of the new approaches involve more expensive materials, equipment, and classroom facilities than reception learning methods. Consequently, the teacher is in no position to determine—by casual inspection alone—to which of these many variables any observed improvement in student performance can be attributed, and singling out the discovery method as the causal variable may frequently be erroneous. Under the circumstances the temptation is strong to fall back upon student enthusiasm as the criterion of success. This is extremely hazardous because heightened student enthusiasm tends to appear in most new programs and need not reflect superior achievement.

An illustration of these dangers can be seen in a study on the Cuisenaire method conducted in one Canadian city (Sweeney, 1964). In this particular school system a group of competent and highly interested elementary-school teachers produced achievement in arithmetic with the Cuisenaire rod approach which clearly exceeded that which children had been making in traditional classes. Initially it was widely concluded that this effect could be attributed to the new method itself. However, as a check on this hypothesis, an experiment was conducted in which an equally competent and well-motivated group of teachers was given the same freedom as the Cuisenaire teachers to set higher standards, to meet together to discuss their common instructional problems, and to enjoy the "Hawthorne Effects" which are usually found in experimental ventures. The interesting finding was that this second group, although using essentially *traditional* methods, also produced achievement which was vastly in excess of that typically obtained. In fact, the second group actually out-performed the Cuisenaire group, although not by a statistically significant amount. The conclusion which one must draw is that it was not the method itself that had been effective, as had been postulated, but rather such other factors as increased expectations and greater opportunities to plan and to exchange ideas with colleagues.

Because of the lack of specific research-documented prescriptions on the proper use of discovery learning, it is our conviction that schools which are moving into more widespread use of this technique—particularly of the free inquiry variety—should attempt to set up some internal comparisons which will allow teachers to attain the realistic attitudes which are so badly needed. For example, in a large school with a number of classes at the primary level, it would seem feasible for the teachers involved to agree on a common set of goals (that is, concepts, skills, and generalizations to be learned) and for a number of clearly formulated teaching approaches—which vary in the degree of discovery—to be tried out for a period of time. At the end of this period the approaches should be compared on a broad range of criteria including the mastery of concepts and skills produced, resulting ability to solve problems, attitude effects, time required to attain this mastery, and transfer or side effects accruing outside the particular subject area in question. Very careful attention will have to be given—and appropriate tests devised—to determine whether children who have discovered generalizations themselves have any firmer or deeper appreciation of these generalizations than children who have learned them through more reception-oriented approaches. Such informal "experimental" arrangements, although lacking the rigor of laboratory studies, provide a much better basis for reaching informed conclusions about teaching procedures than mere speculation unaided by any objective comparisons.

QUESTIONS FOR DISCUSSION AND FURTHER STUDY

1. List instances of faulty conceptions which children might attempt to "verify" in unguided discovery experience. Could a similar list be prepared for adolescents or adults?

2.* Analyze a complete lesson taught by a demonstration teacher in terms of emphasis (instances of use) on discovery with varying degrees of teacher-directedness.

3.* Question a teacher involved in a discovery-oriented program or review a popular article on this subject. What merits are argued for this method? To what extent are the untenable positions discussed earlier in evidence in the teacher's (author's) expressed viewpoints?

4. To what extent does the discovery-reception distinction hold up in the field of English composition? What "discovery" could the student be said to make?

5.* Read and prepare a class report on some curriculum project in your subject area which stresses the discovery approach. Offer a critical assessment in terms of empirical evidence concerning outcomes, or on purely theoretical grounds. (See, for example, *The Schools Council, 1965.*)

6.* Investigate and report upon efforts to train students in the general process of inquiry (Suchman, 1959, 1960, 1961, 1962; Karlins and Schroeder, 1967). What appeared to be proven (or hypothesized) benefits of these approaches? What criticisms can be brought against them?

7.* It was reported in this chapter that Hendrix (1961) found that in certain circumstances the verbalization of generalizations inhibited transfer. Other experimenters (for example, Gagné and Smith, 1962) have found that the verbalization of general principles underlying the solution of problems *facilitated* transfer. How would you reconcile or explain these different results?

8.* What cautions concerning the discovery method are urged by Friedlander (1965) that are not indicated in the present chapter?

SUGGESTIONS FOR ADDITIONAL READING

Ausubel, D. P. *Educational psychology: A cognitive view.* New York: Holt, Rinehart and Winston, Inc., 1968, Chapter 14.

Bruner, J. S. The act of discovery. *Harvard Educ. Rev.,* 1961, *31,* 21–32.

Cronbach, L. J. The logic of experiments on discovery. In *Learning by discovery: A critical appraisal* (L. S. Shulman and E. R. Keislar, Eds.). Skokie, Ill.: Rand McNally & Company, 1967.

Friedlander, B. Z. A psychologist's second thoughts on concepts, curiosity and discovery in teaching and learning, *Harvard Educ., Rev.,* 1965, *35*(1), 18–38.

Karlins, M., and H. M. Schroder. Discovery learning, creativity, and the inductive teaching program. *Psychol. Rep.,* 1967, *20*(3), Part I, 867–876.

Shulman, L. S., and E. R. Keislar (Eds.). *Learning by discovery: A critical appraisal.* Skokie, Ill.: Rand McNally & Company, 1967.

CHAPTER 17

PROBLEM SOLVING AND CREATIVITY

OUR OPERATIONAL DEFINITIONS OF PROBLEM SOLVING AND creativity have already been put forward (Chapter 3) and will be adhered to, although elaborated somewhat, in this section. Moreover, in Chapter 6 we encountered task analysis, a pedagogical technique which has shown promise of success in devising ways of promoting these higher-level behaviors. The reader is advised to review the appropriate sections before proceeding with the present chapter.

It will come as no surprise that problem solving and creativity, representing the upper reaches of cognitive performance, are less well understood than concept formation or the learning of generalizations. By the same token they are considerably harder to produce in the classroom, and educational psychology offers fewer clues as to how to go about it. Nevertheless we believe that a careful analysis of these behaviors as they occur in school settings will yield valuable procedural insights; certainly there is reason to believe that with pedagogical ingenuity we could achieve—in problem solving at least—levels of performance superior to those presently attained in our schools.

PROBLEM SOLVING

Earlier we took the view that problem solving was a complex kind of discovery learning, which is properly located on a behavioral hierarchy above (in terms of the sophistication of the processes involved) routine "application" of established propositions, and below (in the same sense) "creativity." Utilizing the geometry problem as a prototype, we indicated that problem solving involves a gap between what the student *currently knows* and what he is *required to find out*. Furthermore, we saw that the gap could be filled by manipulating, or transforming, known propositions under the general guidance of a strategy or set of rules, thus creating a sequence of transformations of known or given data. Finally, we indicated that a true problem would not involve a well-defined or invariable sequence of transformations which had been practiced to the point where they could be run off routinely as a straightforward application or mere recollection of a rehearsed solution. In problem solving there is inevitably a residual element of choice as to which propositions are to be employed or the order in which they are to be employed, Clearly the lower and upper boundaries of problem solving are somewhat blurred, and a judgment as to the proper placement of any particular task would require knowledge of the student's previous experience. Thus what constitutes a problem for one student may, because of the rehearsal of solutions of similar tasks, constitute simple application for another student.

THE PROBLEM-SOLVING PARADIGM

Following is an elaboration of the conception of problem solving outlined above. We begin by examining the problem format as it

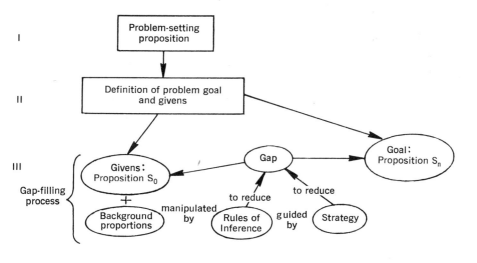

FIGURE 17.1 *Problem-solving paradigm.*

is found in mathematics and the physical sciences, and go on to examine its applicability to "real life" problems and to "problem-like" tasks found in other school subjects.

In mathematics and science settings, then, we are able to distinguish a number of steps or phases which are related as indicated in Figure 17.1, and as discussed in the following paragraphs.

Problem-Setting Propositions

In the subject areas mentioned, the problem-setting proposition is invariably given to the student. Thus the geometry student is provided with a diagram and asked to make a specific deduction; the student of algebra is asked to show that two given algebraic expressions are identical, that is, that one may be reduced to the other; the student of physics is asked to calculate the magnitude and direction of the velocity of a particle after it collides with another particle of specified weight and velocity; and the student of chemistry is required to determine the heat generated in the reaction of given quantities of specified elements.

Definition of Goal and Present Position

The problem-setting proposition is initially only a potentially meaningful statement of the problem. If the student possesses relevant background knowledge (anchoring ideas) he will be able to relate the problem-setting proposition to his cognitive structure and thus understand the nature and conditions of the problem confronting him. The student who is experienced in a given field will be able to perceive the meaning of the proposition directly; the inexperienced student will have to go through the more extended process of identifying the meanings of individual concepts and then grasping the meaning of the proposition as a whole. The comprehension of the problem-setting proposition serves two functions. First, it defines the *goal* or end-point of the problem-solving process. Second, it defines the student's *initial position* with respect to that problem, that is, provides the initial grounds upon which his reasoning may build.

Gap-Filling Process

With the third phase we come to the heart of the problem-solving process. The individual perceives a gap between his "givens" (that is, where he is) and his goal (the point at which he must arrive). Into the gap he brings the following concepts and processes.

Relevant Background Information   The problem-solver in school mathematics and science is systematically accumulating knowledge (facts, generalizations) in those fields; indeed, the problem set him frequently follows the learning of a new proposition, theorem, or law. In these situations there is, then, a more or less clearly defined set of propositions which the student will draw upon in his attempt to find a solution. Our geometry problem provides an example where the relevant background information can be explicitly listed and made available for reference; an equally "tightly" defined system of background propositions can be found, for example, in problems in Newtonian mechanics (based essentially upon four laws), in chemistry, in symbolic logic or in trigonometry. In other cases, however, the field of relevant propositions may be much broader, as for example in algebra where several dozen results (identities, rules, generalizations) may be available to the senior student, or in Euclidian geometry when the advanced problem-solver may draw upon as many as a hundred or more proven propositions.

Rules of Inference Within any reasoned argument—or process of logical thought—there are explicit or implicit rules for reaching conclusions on the basis of arguments presented or data marshalled. Such rules are rarely made explicit, a notable exception occurring in the field of symbolic logic, where formal rules are admitted for handling such tasks as combining the statements *"P implies Q"* and *"P is true"* to reach the conclusion *"Q is true,"* Whether such explicit formulation facilitates problem solving is a rather interesting question to which we will return later.

These two ingredients alone—relevant background propositions and implicit rules of inference—are adequate to allow many problems to be solved by a process of *trial and error.* In this approach the problem-solver draws upon the background propositions more or less at random and examines them—and such extensions as can be wrought by the rules of inference— for relevance to the existing gap. If the first selected proposition does not satisfy the requirements, the individual then examines the second one, and so on. The term "trial and error" is not intended in an opprobrious sense since there is probably an irreducible element of it in any real problem (where there is a residuum of choice). Certainly the trial and error component in many very respectable scientific activities is necessarily very high, particularly when an original product is required.

Strategies In general terms, a problem-solving strategy is a set of rules for selecting, establishing an order of priority among, combining, modifying, or otherwise manipulating background propositions in order to fill a gap inherent in a problem. The function of the strategy is to reduce the randomness in the trial and error approach, thus reducing as well the time required for, and increasing the probability of, a solution. The inefficiency of a purely trial and error approach becomes greater as the amount of relevant background information increases, that is, as a student proceeds through a field of knowledge, or as the problem "gap" increases in length. Most efficient problem-solvers develop their own strategies in time, although they may not be able to state them explicitly. For example, the adept student of Newtonian mechanics develops a way of classifying all the available date pertaining to the problem, thus revealing where data is missing and suggesting the direction for immediate search.

In general, the strategy sets out a series of steps for moving from one end of a gap to the other. In some cases, as in our geometry example, and in task-analysis in general, one begins with the "required" (conclusion or end behavior) and *works backwards* through a process of continual questioning of the form: "What would I need to know (establish) to be able to do (prove) this?" In a *forward moving* strategy, as represented by that derived for the pendulum problem—one begins with the "givens" (variables of the pendulum) and moves toward the "required" (statement as to which variables are causal in its operation). In neither case (nor in general), does the strategy—designed for a *class* of problems—prescribe steps in such detail that choice and doubt are completely removed, that the problem becomes mechanical (that is, an algorithm), or that solution is inevitable. In the geometry problem, for example, the strategy generates a series of choice points at which the student must select a relevant proposition. Thus the strategy does not dictate an invariable sequence of transformation of the propositions or eliminate the student's need for making necessary deductions. Similarly, in the pendulum problem the student must identify the relevant independent variables, make accurate observations, logically eliminate irrelevant variables, and formulate a generalization.

Post-Solution Verification or Communication

Once the solution—or at least what seems to qualify as one—has emerged there would normally follow some form of *verification* (to check for errors in reasoning), *simplification* (assuring that the gap-filling path is the most direct one), *generalization* (in terms of verbally formulated principles), or simply *communication* (in which one records in written form the nature of the solution. As the geometry problem indicates clearly, the sequence of steps by which one fills a gap (backward strategy in that instance) need not correspond to one's formal proof or statement of solution.

SOME COMMON DISTINCTIONS
IN PROBLEM-SOLVING PROCESSES

The literature on problem solving is large and littered with vague terms, some of which once enjoyed popularity but have now fallen into disuse. Other distinctions remain with us but, because of a rather cavalier attitude toward terminology, often elicit more confusion than clear meaning.

Problem Solving and Creative Behavior

While all creative behavior can be said to involve the solution of a problem, some means should be found of distinguishing the two terms. Moreover, the means of distinction should indicate why creative behavior is a rarer and more psychologically complex process than problem solving. Our problem-solving format allows this distinction. Here creative behavior is more difficult (psychologically) in two ways. First, the set of relevant propositions *is not specifically taught* as being related to the class of problems, nor can we expect the student to have formed any firm tendency to regard them in this light. Second, whatever strategy may exist for manipulating the propositions to derive a new product is not available as an explicit set of verbalized rules.[1]

Trial and Error versus Insight

The terms "insight" or "insightful problem solving" have traditionally been set in opposition to the essentially random approach of trial and error methods. Although somewhat vaguely formulated, insightful problem solving implies in its most general sense a "set" that is oriented toward discovery of a meaningful means-end relationship underlying the solution of a problem. It may involve either simple transposition of a previously learned principle to an analogous situation, or more fundamental cognitive restructuring and integration of prior and current experience to fit the demands of a designated goal. Characteristically, insightful solutions appear to emerge suddenly or discontinuously. They are also invariably accompanied by at least some implicit appreciation of the principle underlying the solution of a problem—even if it cannot be successfully verbalized. This understanding is demonstrated functionally both in being immediately reproducible upon subsequent exposure to the same problem, and in being transferable to related problems. Hence, not only is insightful solution frequently a reflection of transfer or application of relevant established principles to new variants of the same problem, but transfer ability itself is perhaps the most important criterion of insight.

A somewhat extreme variant of the insightful problem-solving hypothesis was put forward by Gestalt writers (Kaffka, Köhler, Wertheimer). These theorists argued, in opposition to the prevailing *S-R* emphasis on discrete

---

[1]Some writers regard the ability to *formulate* significant problems (that is, define gaps that are worth filling) as an act of creativity. While this view is not incorporated into the problem-solving ability/creativity distinction made above, it is certainly compatible with it and the paradigm (Figure 17.1) which provides a general framework for this chapter.

associative chaining of responses as the basis of thought, that the learner responds to the problem situation as a structured *whole* (which is not the sum of its parts) and that "insight" emerges when this learner becomes aware of the total structure of the problem situation—and sees how its various parts can be interchanged to form a new "organic" unity.

A classic example of "insight" in a school situation is provided by Wertheimer (1959) in conjunction with the problem of finding the area of a parallelogram, having first been shown how to find the area of a rectangle. As we saw previously, children who had merely memorized rules became confused when the situation was modified slightly (so that the established procedure failed). On the other hand, it was shown that even very young children are *capable* of reacting to the structural properties of the problem, thereby achieving an insight as to how the elements should be reorganized to obtain a solution. One child, for example, after indicating a dissatisfaction with the appearance of the ends of the parallelogram ("this is no good"), took a pair of scissors and cut the parallelogram in two pieces, thus reconstructing it as a rectangle (Figure 17.2), and thereby obtaining a solution.

What has been said so far refers to "insight" as a *process* of problem solving; however, the term is also used frequently to describe the *product* of meaningful problem solving. In this case it possesses characteristics which are both *subjective* (a pleased feeling of apt discovery, of "seeing the light," or "eureka!") and *objective* (immediate reproducibility and transposability). In the first case we are dealing with a largely affective reaction to the learning product; in the second case we are specifying what we can do with the insight once it is achieved. As we have seen, the emergence of insight usually depends on more than just the structure of the problem task; thus it is by no means independent of the learner's prior experience. Moreover, it rarely

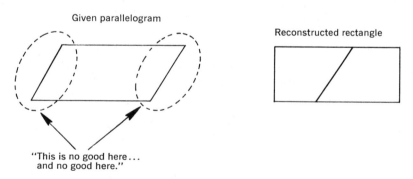

FIGURE 17.2 *Insight into parallelogram problem. Based on figures from pp. 47–48 in PRODUCTIVE THINKING, Enlarged Edition, by Max Wertheimer. (Harper & Row, 1959) Reprinted by permission of the publisher.*

appears abruptly and immediately, despite subjective feelings to the contrary. More commonly it follows a period of fumbling and search, of gradual emergence of a correct approach. Thus the emergence of insight typically reflects a process of clarification of means-end relationships in which the formulation, testing, and rejection of alternative choices plays a crucial and integral role in the appearance of correct solutions.

Types of Thinking

Conventional distinctions—implying a sense of opposition—between *induction* and *deduction* also tend to be somewhat misleading. Inductive thinking refers to the situation—found most frequently in problems amenable to scientific experimentation—in which one jumps mentally from particular instances to a general statement of principle. Deduction is usually considered to be the reverse process of proceeding from the general principle to the specific conclusion ("All A's have property X; this is an A, therefore it possesses property X"). Actually, induction and deduction cannot be so neatly separated in most problem-solving situations. In the pendulum problem, for example, the child may be said to reason inductively from particular instances to the general proposition that the weight of the pendulum bob does not influence its period. Yet these inductive episodes are enmeshed within a general strategy which conspicuously employs deduction; in effect, the formal reasoning might be outlined as follows:

> *hypothesis:* The weight of the bob is a factor influencing the period of the pendulum.
> *deduction:* If the hypothesis is true, changing the weight of the bob should change the period of the pendulum.
> *induction:* Changing the weight of the bob does not change the period of the pendulum.
> *deduction:* Weight (of bob) is not a causal factor.

Similar comments can be made concerning the distinction between *convergent* and *divergent* approaches to problem solving. In most instances the typical sequence of operations involves the generation of multiple hypotheses or courses of action (divergent thinking) followed by the gradual elimination of those hypotheses that are untenable (convergent thinking).

PROBLEM SOLVING IN OTHER SCHOOL SUBJECT AREAS

There is no doubt that the problem-solving model that we have discussed applies most clearly to mathematics and science. That we should begin there is not remarkable, for the vast part of the research literature draws upon examples from these fields. The advantage in using such examples is that the problem situations (givens and goal) can be clearly defined, and the relevant background propositions easily identified; thus one can track more closely the student's gap-filling thinking processes than one could under less neat arrangements.

The close identification of problem solving—both in theory and research —with particular fields leads one to inquire whether in fact "problem solving" as we have defined it can be found in other school subjects. This is hardly a frivolous question since many teachers in nonscientific fields themselves believe that problem solving is "something you do in math or science," and that it invariably involves quantitative procedures.

In examining this question, it would seem initially that some school subjects do not offer the same potential for formal problem solving as do mathematics and science. In defence of this contention, one can argue that knowledge in the nonscientific fields is not organized in as highly sequential a fashion, nor do these fields possess organizing principles to the same degree. Consequently, it is relatively more difficult to create learning tasks which require the manipulation of interrelated principles according to some well defined strategy. And certainly while traditional learning tasks in these fields have called for *knowledge* ("what is the chief product of _____?"), *comprehension* ("explain the principle of _____"), *application* ("apply the principle of _____ to _____"), *synthesis* ("write a short original essay on _____"), *analysis* ("compare and contrast _____"), and *evaluation* ("discuss instances of the effective use of imagery in _____"), the problem format as we have set it out has not been greatly in evidence.

However, the authors' experience with subject-matter specialists in nonscientific fields suggests that it will frequently be of advantage to such teachers to attempt to reanalyze some of the higher-level tasks in terms of the problem-solving paradigm provided here. How plausible would it be and what advantages might accrue, for example, if teachers of English were to think of the writing of a composition as a problem to be solved by the student, rather than as a (somewhat unanalyzed) instance of synthesis? With respect to plausibility, the major components of the problem-solving paradigm do seem to be in evidence here. To begin with, the student possesses relevant background knowledge (concepts and propositions) concerning the subject of the composition. Second, corresponding to rules of inference are a broader class of rules for transforming words into grammatically acceptable sentences and sentences into acceptable paragraphs. Thus—and consistent with his behavior in mathematical problem-solving tasks—the student may more or less randomly apply these rules until he obtains a product (the "solution") which satisfies some minimal criterion of adequacy. Or, he may be formally taught (or somehow acquire on his own) superordinate rules ("style") for the effective manipulation of a given set of ideas.

This parallel can be pressed further in differentiating competence in composition writing (problem solving) from creativity. Consistent with our earlier definitions, a first distinction is that the competent writer is one whose style is analyzable, that is, whose strategy can be verbalized, whereas the truly creative writer possesses a style which may be copied to a point, but never fully replicated. The second distinction is that, given a particular theme (which dictates the endpoint or goal), the competent writer draws upon a circumscribed set of ideas which are normally thought to relate to the subject at hand, whereas the creative writer is able to bring to bear a wider system of ideas which he relates—frequently in remote or metaphorical fashion—to his topic.

As for the advantages of this analysis, one might first argue that there is merit in any conceptualization which reduces the current compartmentalization of our thinking about school learning, and which allows prospective teachers a common ideational framework for viewing both the similarities and differences between the learning tasks for which they will be responsible.[2] But even more important, if the parallel is a valid one, the teacher of English may find in the more elaborately developed thinking about problem solving in scientific fields suggestions concerning both the sources of difficulty in problem solving and ways of improving this skill. In the former category, for example, common observation suggests that there exists something in writing behavior parallel to the "rigidity" obsserved in scientific problem solving, so that one would wonder whether the proposed solution in the latter case (subjecting the student to a sequence of problems which require a variety of different transformations of the basic data) might have any merit in remedying stereotyped expression.[3]

The most promising suggestion, however, would be that writing style, like problem-solving strategies in general, is perhaps more capable of analysis and enhancement by training than has been thought possible in the past. Indeed, a prominent traditional approach to the teaching of style has been based on the assumption that through exposure to good writing something will "rub off" on the student, so to speak. This approach, however, would seem to put the learner in somewhat the same position as the young child who is forced to master syntax (by a process of abstraction) through exposure to spoken language, and it does not seem to do justice to the older

---

[2] Certainly there are important differences between the present example and those studied earlier. For example, the end-point (for example, a composition which meets acceptable grade 9 standards) is by no means so well defined as the end-point in the gometry problem (that is, a demonstration of the fact that $RT = ST$).

[3] Maltzman's originality training, which seems somewhat related to this hypothesis, is discussed in a later section.

learner's capacity to learn generalizations more readily if they are presented explicitly to him. Consequently, current projects which are attempting to analyze and teach style explicitly, beginning in the elementary school, seem defensible in theory and may reasonably be expected to produce a standard of writing which is considerably beyond the school's present expectations. As desirable as this would be, it should not be thought, however, that we will thereby produce *creative* writers. Style is undeniably a component of creative writing, but it serves mainly as the means of expressing the ideational content.

In the preceding paragraphs we have chosen to discuss what might be considered a "far out" or extreme example. Our contention would be, again based on the experience of practicing subject-matter specialists, that the general problem-solving paradigm can be exploited advantageously in those subject fields—for example, history and geography—that stand in an intermediate position with respect to the existence of organized principles and sequentially related content. In fact, as soon as the latter factors are in evidence at all, a *generalized* strategy, exemplified in a particularized form by the three steps of the geometry problem, would seem to be applicable. An appropriate (generalized) wording for the stages in any one cycle of this strategy would be:

(1) What is the nature of the task?
(2) What background knowledge is relevant to the task?
(3) How must the background knowledge be modified or extended to be applicable to the task?

However, to be of any value in a particular field, such a generalized strategy must be elaborated in two respects. First, as can be seen by their embodiment in the geometry strategy, each of the three statements must be particularized to meet the major task classifications (step 1) and propositional format (step 2) which exist in the field. Second, as we shall see later, further analysis of each major step reveals particular difficulties (for example, in maintaining logical distinctions, or in handling perceptual complexity) which are highly *idiosyncratic* to the field in question, and which call for additional sub-strategies.

"REAL LIFE" PROBLEMS: A CASE STUDY

In what important ways do "real life" problems differ from the format described earlier? What implications would such deviations have for the value of problem solving in school as training for problem solving in real contexts? To begin with, some real life problems are virtually *identical* to those studied in school. An adult might, for reasons other than sheer curiosity, want to ascertain the cause-effect relationship in a simple phenomenon; perhaps he might want to remedy the malfunctioning of a mechanical device (the toaster, for reasons to be ascertained, transforms bread into sheets of charcoal) and might proceed in much the same way as one analyzes the pendulum problem. Of course in today's opulent society the availability of specialists removes most of the practical need for such problem-solving skills. There remain, however, all the important, though "messy," problems with which humans must deal.

For example, the reader of this text will soon face the problem of manipulating classroom variables to produce the closest possible approximation to desired student learning. This innocent-sounding formulation masks a problem which in potential complexity vastly exceeds anything encountered in school mathematics or science. For illustrative purposes let us suppose that a new grade 9 general mathematics program has been devised in one of the new curriculum projects. The writing group, then, has in effect determined the *content* to be taught, and the teacher's job is to determine the *method* which will be used to teach it.

Let us suppose further that a group of mathematics teachers in a fairly large high school, who are well acquainted with the generalizations of educational psychology and the findings of educational research, decide that current ideas in the field should be examined for their applicability to the problem of finding the "best" method. These teachers agree on a criterion test—defining the desired behavioral outcomes—thereby setting themselves the specific problem: "what method can we use to maximize student performance on this test?" Casual inspection of the vast array of variables that might be manipulated—in various combinations and to various degrees— suggests that the number of distinguishable treatments is limited only by our imaginative capacities. Consequently, the teachers must select from this infinity of choice a limited number of well defined treatments centered around certain key hypotheses. Let us suppose then that as a result of preliminary reading and reflection, the following treatments are selected as possible courses of action:

> *Method A:* which stresses the teaching of problem-solving strategies;
> *Method B:* which stresses the use of organizers and such related ideas as integrative reconciliation;
> *Method C:* which stresses training in logical thinking (that is, rules of inference).

We have, of course, selected our hypothetical treatments to correspond to the three major components of the gap-filling process. Clearly each treatment would have to be spelled out in considerable detail before it became an operational set of teaching procedures. It would be possible, of course, to combine these approaches in varying degrees so that our abbreviated descriptions merely describe relative emphases.

Each proposed treatment may be regarded as an hypothesis concerning the best method of solving the problem. How then are teachers to choose between these hypotheses? The dimensions of the problem facing the teacher can be presented graphically as in Figure 17.3, which shows the major alternatives and the criteria proposed for desirable outcomes. In constructing the criterion test the teachers will have explicitly or implicitly assigned relative weights (reflecting their assessment of importance) to each outcome category. The next task becomes that of predicting or determining how each method will perform on the criteria. While the generalizations of educational psychology would reduce the teacher's uncertainty here, they would by no means lead to anything like absolute certainty. For example, theory suggests that the use of organizers would result in a higher level of performance in comprehension and application than if standard introductory materials (for example, historical background) were used, but no direct comparison of "organizers" versus "rules of logical inference" has been made, so that predictions regarding their differential effectiveness would be very difficult. Moreover, how the organizer approach would fare in problem solving, in comparison with a heavier emphasis on strategies, is not known.

Thus, although educational psychology offers guidance through its gen-

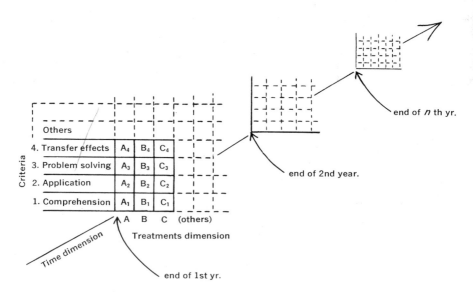

FIGURE 17.3   *Dimensions of decision between three alternative methods of teaching.*

eralizations, much more information is required before one could opt for any particular course of action, especially if—as is usually the case—we might expect a program, once instituted, to be in operation for a period of years. Our teachers, therefore, might attempt to obtain some of this information by evaluating the three programs—through an experimental arrangement—in their local settings. Leaving the technical details as to how this might be done to the next chapter, we will suppose that at the end of the year the students have registered gains in each criterion score shown (by algebraic representation) in Figure 17.3, and that, if the criteria are given equal weight, the strategies treatment shows slight overall advantage.

Can a decision be made at this point (that is, an alternative chosen) which could be said to have solved the problem? Not really, unless one were willing to take the most superficial view of "maximizing the outcome"; for as we well recognize, the aims of mathematics education are seldom expressed in terms of immediate performance at the end of a course. Rather, such aims (for example, "improve the student's ability to solve problems") must be measured in long-range terms. Thus rational decision-making must take into account the time dimension as well, and we must imagine, in effect, that the results of training have been determined at different points on this dimension. For example, at the end of the second year we could determine how knowledge learned during the initial year influenced performance in that latter year, and we could ask how much of the initial learning had been retained. At this point on the time dimension the criteria have become more complex, a process which would continue as one moved to more and more remote points of time.

In theory, determining which of the three initially selected methods is best requires that one take into account long-term projections of outcome. In practice this cannot be done through measurement, and one can only make reasoned speculations, guided again by certain theoretical principles. Might it be reasonable to speculate, for example, that the organizer approach would confer considerable advantage in comprehension and application in subsequent sequentially related courses (since it provides appropriate anchorage) and that it would do this to a greater extent than the strategy approach would influence subsequent problem solving (which may require completely different strategies)? And what speculation can one offer about less direct transfer effects of the initial learning, as for example the influence of any increments in self-confidence in one's ability to solve problems which might be produced by the strategies approach? In selecting one alternative our teachers must somehow put together all these data and reasoned speculations, thereby arriving at some conclusion as to which method actually maximizes the now extremely complicated "desirable outcomes." How such integration takes place is really not known; in practice a point is reached where—if only for the lack of time or to escape mounting cognitive strain—one decides to set a kind of boundary around the considerations that will be taken into account, and having effected this closure, a decision is made.

As tortuous as the preceding problem-solving example may seem, it is typical of the complexity of the considerations involved in any sophisticated approach to "real life" problems. Our example reveals that such problems differ from the model offered earlier in certain fundamental ways.

(a) *The goal is not easily defined:* In the present case we want to maximize output; but even when the criterion test is agreed upon, the "desired output" turns out to be a very complex function of scores based upon this criterion test.

(b) *Uncertainty concerning the "correctness" of the solution:* The two major sources of uncertainty as to whether the best alternative has been chosen reside in (1) the guesswork involved in the initial selection of three alternatives for further study, alternatives which were chosen from a potentially infinite set, and (2) the uncertainty as to which of the three alternatives studied performs best on the complex criterion.[4]

(c) *Unlimited number of relevant considerations:* In our above analysis we have dealt merely with the irreducible logical kernel of the problem. Thus we could proceed considerably beyond what we have done by considering a much larger number of different criteria, adding more evaluation points, taking into account cost-output considerations.[5]

(d) *Decision involves extra-logical processes:* In a geometry deduction or in the analysis of the pendulum problem, one can demonstrate the correctness or adequacy of one's solution through impeccably logical procedures. This is clearly not the case, however, in the example considered above since the final "synthesis and closure" which precedes the choice is not defensible in purely logical terms. Two people given the same objective data might well reach different "solutions". In part this is due to their different estimates of what the future states of the "outcome matrix" will look like. In most real life problems, agreement concerning the weighting of criteria are not easily obtained, so that

---

[4]Realistically, these two sources of uncertainty taken together should cause us to change our goal from finding a teaching procedure that "maximizes output" to finding a procedure that is "better than those presently in effect."

[5]Without wishing to complicate matters further, we should acknowledge that differential costs must usually be taken into account in choosing between alternate school programs. If it happens that the best-performing treatment is the cheapest, then we have no difficulty in making a decision. What is more likely, however, is that the best-performing treatment is also the most expensive, in which case we must weigh performance gains against cost increases.

which alternative any individual would choose depends very much on the *value* he assigns to each outcome category.

Conclusions

The previous paragraphs present what is, in our opinion, an honest account of the (often unrecognized) complexity of real life problem-solving. In pointing out the many dimensions of the task and the essential incompleteness of the solution, however, there is the danger of engendering pessimism concerning the applicability of rational processes and experimentation to genuine problems in general and (because of the example chosen) to curriculum decisions in particular. This is, of course, not our intent nor does it reflect our convictions. In fact, in the latter case we think it possible to demonstrate in purely logical terms (Robinson, 1965) that if a set of criteria for a program are agreed upon—so that a behavioral "output" can be defined—and if decisions concerning the means of realizing these aims are based upon the application of research-based generalizations, or upon an empirical test of designs resulting from these generalizations, then such decisions can be trusted to increase the "output." At the present time, it is true, we must rely to a very large extent upon demonstrations involving a finite set of criteria, and the tacit assumption is always made here that "other (unmeasured or long-range) outcomes are equal." While this assumption may cause us some concern, we may be assured that as the body of educational research findings grows, and particularly as it increasingly comes to reflect the results of long-range studies with comprehensive criteria, much less will be left in doubt concerning these, presently intangible, outcomes.

At the same time, however, the considerable differences between mathematical-logical and real life problems require that we ask whether training on the former (which is the only kind of problem-solving training which the school now provides in a systematic fashion) will transfer substantially, and in a positive sense, to the latter. In other words, does the attainment of a high degree of efficacy in filling the well defined, essentially narrow, gaps of the mathematical problem operate to one's advantage when coping with a problem which is somewhat fuzzy in its conception, possesses the opportunity for infinite and varied gap-filling activity, and requires—at the final stage— that relevant information be ignored on the basis of alogical judgments. Since we know of no evidence on this question, we can only speculate. If the student's problem-solving experience in mathematics and science has given him an intolerance for ambiguity and a passion for logical certainty, then it would not seem to have helped him much with the larger problem-solving experiences. The tendency to "logicize" or "mathematicize" (that is, to force complex social problems into a narrow and inappropriate model), a trait easily recognized in our culture, may derive in part from negative transfer of the kind suggested.[6]

On the positive side, the student who becomes adept at narrow-gap problem solving possesses an idealized model of the intellectual stance appropriate to ideational gap-filling. Thus he will be particular about clear definitions of the problem, conscious of admissible knowledge and logical operations, and sensitive to the logical adequacy of the solution. This stance would seem to be an appropriate one to bring to any problem-solving activity involving intellectual processes, and is manifestly absent from the thinking of many adults. The educational goal, always ambitious, is to produce the best of both worlds, that is, the individual who has the appropriate intellectual stance and who will press intellectual activity as far as it will go, yet who will stop short of forcing a premature solution by insisting that only logical considerations be admitted.

FACTORS INFLUENCING PROBLEM SOLVING

A good deal of general information has been acquired about process factors influencing problem solving by comparing the respective performances of successful and unsuccessful problem-solvers (Bloom and Broder, 1950). To begin with, successful problem-solvers flounder less; they are more decisive in choosing "some point at which to begin their attack." In many instances this simply reflects greater attention to and comprehension of the directions. Second, they focus more on the problem to be solved, rather than on some irrelevant aspect of the problem. Third, they can better bring to bear on the problem the relevant knowledge they possess; they perceive more clearly the implications and applicability of their knowledge to the problem at hand, and are less confused by a change in wording or notation. Fourth, they exhibit a more active and vigorous process of search; their approach is less passive, superficial and impressionistic, and they tend to apply solutions from previous problems less mechanically. Fifth, they are more careful and systematic in their approach (See also Duncan, 1964). Their efforts are less haphazard and less characterized by guesswork. Sixth, they tend more to follow through a line of reasoning to its logical conclusion; they are more persistent and less distractible in their performance. Seventh, their attitudes toward the value of reasoning are more positive and less fatalistic. Eighth, they exhibit greater self-confidence in their ability to solve problems and are less discouraged by complexity. Ninth,

---

[6]It may also derive from a general personality trait (akin to closed-mindedness) for which mathematical and scientific models merely provide a vehicle of expression and an intellectual filter for reducing the complexity of social data.

their approach to problem solving is more objective and impersonal; they are influenced less by affective and subjective considerations (see also Tate and Stanier, 1964). Lastly, they are able to overcome more easily the negative transfer effect of an interfering set (Duncan, 1959; O. W. McNemar, 1955).

Task Factors

Practice with a variety of problems in a given class tends to enhance transfer in problem solving (Duncan, 1958). Heterogeneity of exemplars presumably discourages blind perseveration, forces the subject to remain alert and attentive, and increases the generality and hence the transferability of a solution. For purposes of transfer, even the presence of irrelevant information is sometimes helpful (Overing and Travers, 1966) because it adds variety to the problem task. As pointed out previously however, the transfer effects of heterogeneity are likely to be negative unless mastery *within* each problem type is achieved.

The development of high-level problem-solving ability obviously requires long-term experience in coping with problems. Similarly guidance in the form of hints will clearly tend to facilitate problem solving (Burack and Moos, 1956; Maier, 1930; Maltzman and others, 1956; M. R. Marks, 1951; Reid, 1951), and it is easily believed that hints would be pedagogically effective in developing problem-solving skills, at least in the early stages.

Intrapersonal Factors

Intelligence is one of the most important determinants of problem-solving ability. For one thing, reasoning power is a prominent component of all intelligence tests. For another, many other intellectual abilities measured by the intelligence test (for example, comprehension, memory, information processing, ability to analyze) affect problem solving. IQ is positively related to both trial and error (Munn, 1954; Nelson, 1936) and to insightful problem solving (Gellerman, 1931; Harootunian and Tate, 1960; Munn, 1954). However, for those kinds of problem solving that depend upon cumulative incidental experience, for example, causal thinking (Deutsche, 1937) and applications of the lever principle (G. M. Peterson, 1932), grades in school are a more significant correlate of success than either IQ or socioeconomic status. In addition, in certain classes of problems some particular components of general intellectual ability will correlate more highly with problem solving than IQ itself. Thus Robinson (1959) found that spatial ability was a better predictor of performance in solving geometry problems than either IQ or scores on the Watson-Glaser test of "critical thinking."

Other cognitive traits such as open-mindedness, flexibility, capacity for generating multiple and novel hypotheses, attentiveness, incisiveness, problem sensitivity, intellectual curiosity, and ability to integrate ideas influence problem solving in rather self-evident ways. Cognitive style is obviously a relevant factor, particularly with respect to general strategies of problem solving. Although evidence is lacking, it seems reasonable to suppose that problem-solving ability is not a highly generalized trait within a given individual, varying rather on the basis of interest, experience, and aptitude in different areas of human endeavor.

Motivational traits such as drive, energy level, persistence, and frustration tolerance affect problem-solving outcomes in a positive way (Alpert, 1928; French and Thomas, 1958), but excessive drive or emotionality tends to constrict the cognitive field and to promote rigidity and perseveration (Bahrick and others, 1952; Easterbrook, 1950). Many temperamental and personality traits such as high kinetic level, decisiveness, venturesomeness, self-confidence, and self-critical ability (Alpert, 1928; Kempler, 1962) facilitate problem solving when present in a moderate to high degree; but when venturesomeness or decisiveness approaches impulsiveness (Kagan and others, 1966), when self-confidence borders on dogmatism or complacency, and when self-criticism becomes self-derogation, the opposite effect may be anticipated. Anxiety level, as pointed out earlier, has a negative effect on problem solving, particularly in the case of novel and difficult tasks, because of its relationship to rigidity, constriction of the cognitive field, perseveration, indisposition to improvise, premature closure, and intolerance for ambiguity.

Personality variables undoubtedly interact with such situational factors as success and failure. Success experience enhances self-confidence, venturesomeness, and disposition to improvise, whereas failure experience has the opposite effects (Rhine, 1955). A mild degree of failure, however, may prove salutary by increasing drive, attentiveness, and willingness to consider alternatives (George, 1964).

Developmental Stage

Developmental changes in problem solving reflect all of the age trends described for cognitive functioning as a whole and, more particularly, those occurring in concept acquisition. Especially in the area of thinking and problem solving it is important to distinguish between those developmental changes that are qualitative in nature and those that are merely quantitative. Despite Piaget's (Inhelder and Piaget, 1958) assertions to the contrary, the weight of the evidence points to the conclusion that some kinds of thought processes, logical operations, and problem-solving strategies are employed at all age levels, differing principally in degree or complexity (Burt, 1919; Long and Welch, 1941a, 1941b; Welch and Long, 1943; Werner, 1948). The older child's greater competence in using these operations largely depends on his superior ability to think abstractly and to generalize. Similarly, the use of trial-and-error and insightful approaches to problem solving does not undergo qualitative change from one age level to the next. Neither approach can be said to be characteristic of children at a designated stage of intellectual development; both are found at all age levels. The choice between the two approaches depends, mainly, on the intrinsic difficulty and complexity of the problem, on the individual's prior background of experience and general degree of sophistication in the problem area, and on the susceptibility of the problem to logical analysis and a strategy-oriented mode of attack. It is true that older children, on the whole, tend more to use an insightful approach, but this is so only because their greater capacity for abstract thinking makes such an approach more feasible.

On the other hand, certain qualitative changes in thinking do occur with increasing age. These are gradually occurring changes in kind that emerge after a certain threshold value of change in *degree* has been reached. One such change consists of a gradual transition from subjective to objective thought, that is, of an emergent ability to separate objective reality from subjective needs, wishes, and preferences. A second qualitative change in thought, of course, reflects the transition from concrete to abstract cognitive functioning, and illustrates all of the characteristic features of this transition.

IMPROVING PROBLEM SOLVING IN SCHOOL SETTINGS

In this section we discuss some suggestions for the improvement of problem solving which follow from the model presented earlier. It is our belief that the schools are not presently achieving satisfactory results in this area, and that much could be done to improve the present state of affairs.

Awareness of Problem Solving as a Distinct Intellectual Phenomenon

It is unlikely that problem-solving activity will be encouraged by teachers who are not able to distinguish it from lower orders of behavior, who have no way of conceptualizing what is taking place when the child solves a problem, or who are not able to construct appropriate test items. Various descriptions of the problem-solving process are available. For example, Dewey's (1910) account is still much cited today. His five stages, in the order given are:

(a) a state of doubt, cognitive perplexity, frustration, or awareness of difficulty;

(b) an attempt to identify the problem, including a rather nonspecific designation of the ends that are sought, the gaps to be filled, or the goal to be reached, as defined by the situation that sets the problem;

(c) relating these problems and problem-setting situations to cognitive structure, thereby activating relevant background ideas and previously achieved problem solutions which, in turn, are reorganized (transformed) in the form of problem-solving propositions or hypotheses;

(d) successive testing of the hypotheses and reformulation of the problem if necessary;

(e) incorporating the successful solution into cognitive structure (that is, understanding it) and applying it both to the problem at hand and to other exemplars of the same problem.

Actually, of course, not all instances of problem solving manifest all of these stages or follow the typical sequential order. Much creative thinking, for example, short-circuits or telescopes many of the steps in this sequence. It is clear that this general description runs parallel to our own particular one, the difference lying chiefly in the fact that in school-posed problems (unlike real life problems) the problem-setting propositions are relatively specific and are provided by the instructor.[7]

The Role of Cognitive Structure

That existing cognitive structure plays a key role in problem solving is evident from the fact that the solution of any given problem involves the reorganization of relevant propositional and other knowledge to fit the particular requirements of the problem situation. Since ideas in cognitive structure constitute the *raw material* of problem solving, whatever transfer—positive or negative—occurs, obviously reflects the nature and influence of cognitive structure variables. Moreover, it is those ideas of greatest generality and inclusiveness in the mature cognitive structure, reflecting the central ideas of the discipline in which the problem is engendered, which have the most generic power and problem-solving potential for problems in that discipline.

As one might expect, it is not difficult to show empirically that the possession of relevant background knowledge (concepts, principles, transactional terms, "available functions") in cognitive structure, particularly if stable, clear, and discriminable, facilitates problem solving (Saugstad, 1955; Saugstad and Raaheim, 1960). Without such knowledge, as a matter of fact, no problem solving is possible (aside from purely logical or "content-free" problems) irrespective of the learner's degree of skill in discovery learning. Without it he could not even begin to understand the nature of the problem

---

[7]Other—and essentially similar formulations—have been offered by Thompson (1959), Merrifield and others (1960), and Polya (1945).

confronting him. Still another cognitive structure source of transfer inheres in applicable general elements of strategy, orientation, and set that reflect prior experience with related problems. In other words, once a strategy is learned it becomes a part of the individual's cognitive structure and may be employed within (and in some cases beyond) the class of problems in respect to which it was taught. Finally, cognitive structure is related to problem solving in a repository as well as in the determinative sense; the substantive or methodological product of the problem-solving process is incorporated into cognitive structure in accordance with the same principles that are operative in reception learning.

For all of these reasons, it appears that the teacher's first concern in promoting problem solving will be to insure that the individual has a *meaningful* grasp of the relevant concepts, propositions, and strategies. Limited understanding or rote memorization augurs poorly for problem solving since the individual will lack the flexibility to cope with even the limited manipulation required in application, let alone the complex sequential operations involved in genuine problem solving.

Rigidity Cognitive structure also provides a source of *negative* transfer to problem solving. One type of transfer reflects the perseveration of inapplicable habitual sets (Einstellungen) derived from prior experience with similar problems (Luchins, 1942). The solution of novel problems obviously requires both improvisation and a search for new directions—a requirement that is often interfered with by the tendency to use the same approach that was found successful in previous problem-solving experience (Maier, 1930). The latter experience thus generates both helpful and interfering sets whose relative strength is a function of such factors as primacy, recency, frequency, vividness, flexibility, and level of anxiety.

A brief account of a classical experiment on Einstellungen will give the reader a clearer picture of the nature of this phenomenon. In the well-known "water jar" experiment, Luchins (1942) exposed students to a series of problems involving the utilization of three jars of different capacity to arrive at a stated measure (Table 17.1). For example, the second problem, and most of the succeeding ones, can be solved by the procedure:

(1) Fill the second container (B).

(2) Pour enough out of B to fill the first container (A), leaving (B) − (A).

(3) Fill the third container (C) twice from the residue in container B, leaving (B) − (A) − 2(C) in container B (which is the correct amount).

Luchins found that students who were shown such a procedure used it consistently, even when a simpler solution would suffice. For example,

TABLE 17.1

PROBLEMS EMPLOYED IN THE TEST OF "RIGIDITY"

PROBLEM	GIVEN THE FOLLOWING EMPTY JARS AS MEASURES			OBTAIN THE SPECIFIED AMOUNT OF WATER
1	29	3		20
2	21	127	3	100
3	14	163	25	99
4	18	43	10	5
5	9	42	6	21
6	20	59	4	31
7	23	49	3	20
8	15	39	3	18
9	28	76	3	25
10	18	48	4	22
11	14	36	8	6

Source: Adapted from A. S. Luchins, "Mechanization in problem solving; the effect of Einstellung," *Psychol. Monogr.*, No. 248, 1942. Copyright 1943 by the American Psychological Association, and reproduced by permission.

problem 7 can be solved by the procedure represented by (A) − (C), while the solution to problem 10 can be represented by the operation (A) + (C), In another group, however, students were alerted ("Don't be blind") after the sixth problem. In this case most students apparently reappraised their procedure, for a majority adopted the easier solution to problem 7.

The teacher will not have to look far to find examples of Einstellungen phenomena in the classroom. Simply have adults or children complete a number of examples of the type:

$$(25 \times 18) + (16 \times 14) = (\quad)$$

by multiplying twice and adding, and when they are well accustomed to this procedure, slip in (inconspicuously) the following example:

$$(73 \times 43) + (43 \times 27) = (\quad)$$

Most subjects will determine the answer the long way, although inspection reveals that in the combined product 43 is taken a total of 100 times, yielding the answer 4300 immediately. It is common to inveigh against such rigidity and teachers are rightly encouraged to attempt to counteract it. It is necessary, however, to distinguish "inefficient" rigidity from a truly "dysfunctional" kind. For example, most of us display monumental rigidity as we make our way to the university each morning. Having once determined what seems to be a reasonably efficient route we doggedly stick to it, even though day-by-day variations in traffic and weather periodically make this route less efficient than some others which we could determine if we thought about it. But we knowingly incur this slight inefficency for the luxury of not having to think about it, which is "stupid" behavior only when our inefficiency becomes out of proportion to the extra effort involved in thinking of a new approach. Since the solution of Luchins' seventh problem, and our own arithmetic example, are easily solved by their respective algorithms, one can sympathize with those students who continue to use such thought-eliminating devices.

Rigidity becomes dysfunctional when the learner becomes so habituated to an algorithm that he continues to attempt to use it when it will not work. Here it is not a question of relative efficiency, but of success or failure. Perhaps the best way to forestall such rigidity in the classroom is to avoid long series of exercises which lend themselves to the application of a single algorithm. In other words, as has been mentioned in another context, one should vary tasks—once initial mastery is attained—so that a variety of approaches will be brought into play.

Training in Logical Forms

The tendency to equate logic and thought is a fairly common one today and has no doubt gained strength from Piaget's (1957a) emphasis upon the purely logical aspects of thought, and the fidelity with which the logical operations he identifies in children's thought parallel the formal structure of operations found in logic and mathematics. However, it seems clear that most of the real life problems which confront individuals are not entirely amenable to logical proof or cannot be solved merely by invoking the application of rules of inference to given data. In our classroom decision-making problem, for example, the reach of purely logical devices leaves one a long way from the actual decision. In evidence at this crucial end-point are evaluation, speculation, synthesizing, and weighing processes which lie outside the framework of logical exposition.

At the same time, logical forms and rules of inference should be given their due. In some cases problem solving will be facilitated if such functions are explicitly taught, if only because certain legitimate methods of proof or reasoning never occur to many students. One such example is the method of *indirect proof* whereby one establishes the truth of proposition *A* by demonstrating that the proposition "not *A*" is false. It is quite clear from the behavior of children and adults that they do not always spontaneously think of this particular stratagem. A more complex case can be found in the rules of mathematical induction in which one establishes the truth of the proposition S_n by showing that S_{n-1} implies S_n, and that S_0 is true (thus since S_0 is true, S_1 is true; since S_1 is true, S_2 is true, and so on).

Actually it is not the logical forms themselves (most of which we seem to acquire incidentally) but rather the symbolic or graphical representation of logical forms and arguments which will assist the problem-solver most. Earlier we saw that the representation of ordering relations by diagrams provides a concrete prop which greatly facilitates the production of valid inferences and conclusions. Frequently, too, the condensed symbolism of logic can be applied to fairly detailed verbal arguments in which particular propositions are represented by individual symbols, thus allowing a degree of facility in manipulation which is rarely achieved when the more awkward verbal form is used.[8]

Teach Strategies

The heart of the task of effective problem-solving behavior is to acquire strategies which apply to broad categories of problems; without these most students will flounder and do little more than memorize or run off type solutions. While the determination of precise and powerful strategies will often require considerable ingenuity on the teacher's part, a general approach is to apply task analysis to an exemplar of a class of problems, to ascertain the general steps which close the gap in that instance, and determine whether these steps are generalizable across the entire class of problems. This method has been illustrated in Chapter 5 and will be again in Chapter 18. In the geometry problem, the strategy requires that the student engage in an ongoing recycling (although essentially simple) task analysis (What kind of fact am I to establish? What propositions could I use? What would I need to use this proposition? Recycle.) which continues until the gap is filled. As we saw earlier, this cyclical task analysis may define a generalized strategy appropriate to classes of problems in various fields where solution depends upon a distinguishable class of background propositions. While this general strategy requires particularization in at least two respects before it becomes operational in any particular field, it can provide a profitable starting point for further analysis.

In our view, having ascertained that the student comprehends the background propositions, the most efficacious approach for the teacher to take to problem solving is to teach strategies applying to the significant classes of problems which the student will encounter in substantive fields of knowledge. At the same time we have to concede that some students will

---

[8]An illuminating example of this approach in social science theory can be found in: Coleman, J. S., *Introduction to Mathematical Sociology*. New York: Crowell-Collier and Macmillan, Inc., 1963.

proceed to a point in a field of knowledge where no ready-made strategies are available, so that the learner must work out his own. Moreover all students have to cope with real life problems, for which a strategy yields no precise solution. These latter considerations suggest that the student needs problem-solving experiences beyond applying (taught) sets of procedural rules. Moreover, in view of our earlier remarks concerning tendencies to logicize, all students should have the experience of attempting to apply problem-solving approaches to social and personal issues, and to determine from this where such approaches facilitate thought, and at which point one must proceed beyond them.

Use Concrete Props and Mnemonic Devices

In our opinion, the failure of children to solve problems cannot be laid to any alleged inability to reason but rather to (1) lack of experience as to how to approach the problem (that is, lack of strategy); (2) over-reliance on concrete modes of representation; and (3) limitations in memory, with a concomitant tendency to confuse the "proven" and the "to be proved." The limitation inherent in (2) suggests that teachers must be careful to present the problem at the right level of abstraction, and should instruct students in ways of representing logical forms, complex concepts, and the relationships between variables. To overcome memory limitations (3), the child should be instructed in ways of organizing and recording (for visual availability) the major background propositions which bear on a particular class of problems, the steps in the strategy, and the information generated at each step of the solution. All of these procedures were indicated in the pendulum problem where the independent variables were listed, strategy written down, and the results of each manipulation recorded in a table. And frequently, as in the geometry problem, the use of such aids as color schemes can keep the "facts known to be true" separate from the "facts we need to prove true."

Provide Ample Practice

In problem solving as elsewhere, nothing succeeds like success. Once a students "gets the sense of" a strategy and independently and successfully applies it to some new example, a rather dramatic change can often be observed in his performance. Aside from the enhancement of cognitive drive in the area in question, the essential gain is, of course, in self-confidence. For in problem solving (as contrasted with simple computation) the student typically must proceed on his own for an appreciable period of time before he obtains feedback as to the correctness of his approach. Without a measure of self-confidence, and the persistence it engenders, many students soon give up or resort to guessing. The early stage in confronting a new class of problems is a critical one, and the teacher must on the one hand resist the tendency to jump in and tell the student how to do it, and on the other hand not let the student flounder in increasing confusion and loss of self-confidence. Leading a student rather closely through a few exemplars is a good way to start, withdrawing direction gradually as the student's independent thinking takes over. Beyond that, ample and varied practice is essential if a strategy is to be internalized to the point where it becomes second nature.

Creating the Proper Atmosphere for Problem Solving

The teacher should remember that problem solving and high anxiety tend to be mutually exclusive—particularly when quite novel approaches are required. High pressure approaches utilizing speed criteria, which may be appropriate to the practice of arithmetical skills, are not likely to bring good results when more complex mental processes are involved. Similarly, asking students to solve problems at the board, or to stand at their seats and analyze a problem verbally—common practices in both elementary- and high-school classes—seems likely to depress the performance of all but the most extremely self-confident. Effective individual problem solving requires a measure of privacy, or at least temporary withdrawal from public scrutiny. In fact, most of the student's really effective problem solving will be done in a homework assignment or in the study hall.

An Illustrative Example

Several of the points made in previous paragraphs can be sharpened by reconsideration of the strategy for solving geometry problems which was discussed in general terms in Chapter 2. There it was indicated that a sequence of decision-points could be generated by the student asking himself the following questions:

(a) What sort of fact am I to prove (for example, one line equals another, one angle equals another, or one triangle is congruent to another)?
(b) Which of the results (propositions) which I already know might be utilized to establish this fact?
(c) What additional facts would I need (or what other conditions must hold) before I could use this proposition?

Examination of current secondary-school mathematics texts reveals that this strategy is widely advocated and (presumably) used by teachers. And yet, pessimism regarding the problem-solving abilities of students is apparently so widespread that there seems to have emerged an "unwritten law" among mathematics teachers that examinations should contain sufficient comprehension items and problems solved in class to allow most students to make acceptable grades, and that the solution of "originals" (that is, genuine problems) should be used chiefly to distinguish and challenge the capable minority.

How can we reconcile the alleged potency of a strategies approach with the apparently unimpressive problem-solving abilities obtained even when the strategy is employed? One might, of course, argue that the background propositions have not been learned meaningfully, so that the strategy itself is rendered impotent. While there may be some truth in this assertion, our own experience in working with students on an individual basis indicates that other factors may operate to the disadvantage of the student after he has meaningfully learned the relevant propositions.

In the first place, the second step of the strategy may seem deceptively easy to the adult, given that the entire set of background propositions and concepts had been made available to the problem-solver in tabular form (Chapter 2, Figure 2.1). However, we have found that some students cannot easily make the jump from the *proposition* "If two sides of a triangle are equal, then the opposite angles are equal" to the *operational rule* "If I want to prove two angles are equal, it is sufficient to show that the sides opposite these angles are equal." Moreover, the student's difficulty is compounded here by the fact that several propositions establish sufficiency for this particular class of "facts to be proved" (that is, an angle equals an angle").

Two suggested improvements follow from this observation. First, the student should be specifically trained to recast the original proposition into its operational-rule form. Second, an additional tabulation should be made available which brings together all propositions which establish sufficiency for a given class of facts to be proved.

A third difficulty resides in the fact that in the repeated application of the strategy (that is, in recycling) the student—possibly, in complex problems, because of memory limitations—fails to maintain the distinction between what is given or already proved and what is still required to be proved; more specifically, in the Nth recycling of the strategy, he will *assume* some fact which is itself an unproved sufficiency condition from an earlier cycle. In a simple form this would occur in the example in Chapter 2, (Figure 2.3) if in the second cycle the student assumed that $\triangle PRT$ and $\triangle PST$ are congruent, forgetting that (from cycle 1) he is to *prove* these triangles congruent to establish that $RT = ST$. Clearly, the opportunity for this kind of confusion increases with the number of cycles through which the student has progressed.

Again two concrete suggestions arise for an improvement in strategy. First, some benefit may be derived merely by having the student verbalize at the end of each cycle which facts *cannot be used* as givens in subsequent cycles. In working with younger children (ages seven to ten), however, we have found that the use of a concrete prop—a color scheme—facilitates the child's maintaining the necessary distinctions. In this approach the original fact to be proved $(RT = ST)$, and all sufficiency conditions arising in subsequent cycles, are designated by red markings, and it is clearly understood (the child is required to verbalize the proposition) that "the facts indicated in red cannot be *assumed* to be true."[9]

In conclusion, as we have seen earlier, the geometry problem-solving strategy is a particularized version of a more general form which seems applicable to a number of subject-matter fields. However, continued analysis of the component tasks leads to the conclusion that even within this specific format additional steps may have to be introduced (particularly for young or relatively incapable students) which reflect difficulties that are idiosyncratic to this particular subject-matter field (that is, geometry).[10] With respect to our optimism concerning the enhancement of problem-solving skills, it must be admitted that definitive empirical evidence is lacking—in fact, the "problems" dealt with in the research literature (for example, water jar problems, or concept-learning tasks) are much less complex than our geometry example, and our own experience with the latter is confined to a small group of children on an individual basis. Nevertheless, in our opinion the formulation of detailed strategies does appear to have sufficient plausibility to warrant classroom experimentation by teachers with the expectation of substantial improvement in problem-solving skills.

CREATIVITY

In Chapter 3 a distinction was made between the "creative person" and "creativity" (or "creative behavior"). In this book we reserve the former term to designate the individual who makes a unique contribution to art, science, philosophy, government, or some other area of human endeavor. He is by definition a rare individual, and his contribution is novel or original not merely in terms of his own life experience, but in terms of

---

[9]These illustrations do not exhaust possible refinements of this particular strategy. For example, since (young) children are often confused by the overlap of geometrical figures, they can be trained to separate such figures so that at each stage only the relevant triangle is visually available.

[10]The discussion of strategies at different levels of generality can be summarized briefly as follows. The generalized strategy describes primarily a sequence of *logical* steps (embodying a recycling task analysis) which seem to have applicability in different fields. At the first level of particularization, the *substantive* requirements of a specific field (for example, classes of definable end-points, and form of propositional knowledge) are imposed, yielding, for example, the geometry problem-solving strategy introduced in Chapter 2. At the second level of particularization, the *psychological* problems inherent in the transformation of this particular content are resolved by the addition of further steps.

human knowledge in an absolute sense. Creative behavior, on the other hand, may refer to productions which are novel only in that they lie outside the individual's past experience.[11] Even so, as we use the term an individual's behavior must exhibit a high level of synthesis, originality, and relevance to the problem at hand in order to qualify as "creativity," the highest category in our behavioral hierarchy. From these definitions it follows that creative behavior will be observed more frequently in any given population than creative persons, and one may expect the former behavior to be normally distributed in this population in the same manner as most physical or mental characteristics.

As found in the classroom in the context of learning and utilizing organized bodies of knowledge, creative behavior produces a product in some subject-matter field. A further distinction has to be made, then, between creativity and the *supporting intellectual abilities, personality variables and problem-solving traits* which are measured by many of the subject-matter-free tests of "creativity" which have become available during the past decade. Their cognitive component—that is, the postulated supporting intellectual skills—have been alluded to in previous discussions of intellectual ability and differential aptitude tests. There we noted widespread interest in *divergent production* (that is, the production of novel or varied responses in open-ended situations)—in distinction to *convergent production* (in which one proceeds from given information to produce a unique or conventionally acceptable "best answer"). Convergent production would require, for example, that one produce the answer "25" to the question, "What is the square of 5?" Divergent production would require (to cite one particular test) that one find unusual uses for a brick.

Table 17.2 provides an example of a criterion task for five of the eighteen postulated divergent production factors. Sixteen of these factors have actually been empirically identified in factorial studies (Taylor, 1965b). The particular tests listed are those which have been frequently used in experimental work with school children, or have served as the basis for tests constructed by other experimenters.[2]

The Divergent Production Controversy

The argument concerning divergent production centers around the following major questions: (1) is divergent production sufficiently distinct from gener-

---

[11]The distinction we are making here is analogous to that one normally makes when, while admitting that every human being has some measure of intelligence, we regard only persons who have *unusual* amounts of this quality—that is, above some hypothetical cut-off point—as "intelligent persons."

[12]The reader should compare these items with the *convergent* tasks described earlier as exemplifying standard intelligence tests.

al intelligence to be regarded as a true (that is, separate) factor in intellectual functioning; (2) is divergent production a precursor (and, therefore, a
predictor) of the kind of originality exhibited by the creative person (as for
example the creative scientist who makes a major discovery in his field); (3)
does divergent production possess any value as a predictor of school success;
(4) does divergent production have utility in its own right, that is, is it a kind
of behavior which the school should promote as one of its legitimate goals.

In respect to relevant developments, the proposition that intelligence
(as measured by standard tests) and creativity might not be closely related
has been advanced at least as long as intelligence tests have been generally
available (see, for example: R. M. Simpson, 1922). By 1950 the issue
became somewhat more precisely stated when it was observed (Guilford,
1950) that the divergent production abilities in the structure-of-intellect
model—which one might initially think to be related to creative behavior—
were not typically assessed by IQ tests. Later, Getzels and Jackson (1962)
conducted an influential study comparing high IQ students ("favored convergent modes of thinking") and high creative ("favored divergent modes of
thinking") students. They found that while the high creative group equaled
the other group in school achievement, and out-performed it in tests of
originality and inventiveness, nevertheless teachers showed a preference for
the high IQ student. Many educators have extrapolated from these findings
and moved effortlessly to the conclusion that the schools are actually inhibiting the development of genuine creativity; of course, in the process, they
make a number of assumptions, among them that proficiency on divergent
production tasks is a sign of latent creativity in the mature sense.

Divergent Production and IQ   The question here has to do with whether divergent production can be regarded as a domain of intellectual functioning separate from intelligence as measured by conventional tests. As pointed
out earlier, the argument hinges on whether the intercorrelations between
divergent production measures exceed their individual correlations with intelligence scores. Over a large number of studies (Cline and others, 1962;
Cline and others, 1963; Drevdahl, 1956; Getzels and Jackson, 1962; Guilford, 1950; J. L. Holland, 1961; Klausmeier and Wiersma, 1965; McGuire
and others, 1961; Torrance, 1960a; Torrance and others, 1960; Yamamoto,
1964a,b,c) the correlation obtaining between divergent production and IQ
measures has fallen in the interval $r = .25$ to $r = .30$, although Flescher
(1963), Wallach and Kogan (1965) and Miezitis (1968) found very small
correlations. At the same time, several studies have shown that the intercorrelation of divergent production tests is of the same order of magnitude as
their correlation with IQ (Cline and others, 1962; Cropley, 1966; Getzels
and Jackson, 1962; Ohnmacht, 1966; Piers and others, 1960; R. L. Thorndike, 1963). Nevertheless, to repeat an earlier statement, while divergent

TABLE 17.2

CRITERION TESTS FOR FIVE DIVERGENT PRODUCTION FACTORS IN THE GUILFORD MODEL

CLASSIFICATION IN GUILFORD MODEL	COMMON NAME	SAMPLE TESTS
DSU: Divergent Production of Symbolic Units	Word fluency	(1) Write words containing a specific letter (for example, the letter "s"). (2) Write words ending with a specific suffix (for example, "sion").
DMU: Divergent Production of Semantic Units	Ideational fluency	(1) Write names of things fitting relatively broad categories (for example, "white" and "edible"). (2) Lists uses for a common brick. Score is total number of different responses.
DMC: Divergent Production of Semantic Classes	Semantic spontaneous flexibility	(1) List uses for a common brick. Score is the number of *shifts* in classes in consecutive responses. (2) List as many as six uses for an object, such as a newspaper, other than the common use, which is stated.
DFI: Divergent Production of Figural Implications	Figural elaboration	(1) Given articles of furniture and other objects in outline form, add decorative lines and markings. (2) Given a very simple line or two, build upon the given information to produce a nonmeaningful figure. Score is determined by amount of detail added.
DMT: Divergent Production of Semantic Transformations	Originality	(1) Write titles for a short story, only clever titles being accepted. (2) Give remote (distant in time or in space or in sequence of events) consequences of a specified event.

Source: Adapted from Guilford and Hoepfner, 1963.

production factors can hardly be regarded as completely separable from IQ tests, some informed observers (Thorndike, 1963) do believe that the domains are not entirely coextensive. Also, it is clear that scores on divergent production tests can by no means be accounted for or accurately predicted by IQ scores. In any case, judging from current comments it seems clear that the issue is by no means decided.[13]

Divergent Production as an Index of Creativity   It is perhaps unnecessary to say that insufficient time has elapsed for any long-term studies to have emerged relating divergent production scores earned during the school years to adult creativity (which typically can be measured only after one has been working in a field for a number of years). However some attempts have been made to relate divergent production scores to independent assessments of the child's "creativity." At the preschool level, Lieberman (1965) found a positive correlation between divergent production measures and teacher ratings of "imaginativeness in play situations," and Miezitis (1968) found that the former measures were positively related to teacher ratings of the child's "creative self-expression." With older children both Torrance (1962) and Yamamoto (1964d) found positive relationships between divergent production scores and teacher and peer ratings on several criteria of "creative thinking" (for example, having many or different ideas; using a variety of approaches, and so on). Torrance (1965a), who has been a pioneer in developing such tests, indicates further that at the college level indications of the validity of the divergent production measures have come from "original projects, scores on subject-matter tests requiring creative problem solving, self-initiated learning, and from faculty nominations in a technical college where there are numerous opportunities for creative achievement of various kinds."

By what calculus can we add this evidence? Certainly it is clear that no evidence is available on the value of divergent production measures as indicators of the kind of talent that will later become mature creativity. On this point it is interesting to note that at least some large research projects into the correlates of adult creativity—aimed at early identification—do not employ the standard divergent production tasks. For example, MacKinnon (1965), reporting on research conducted at Berkeley on creative performance in such fields as mathematics, the physical sciences, engineering and the graphic arts, states:

> Our conception of creativity forced us . . . to reject as indicators or
> criteria of creativeness the performance of individuals on so-called tests of

---

[13]For recent comments on the IQ-divergent production question see: Shulman, 1966; Wallach, 1968. It would appear that the clearest separation of IQ and divergent production scores occurs when fluency is stressed and when the divergent production tests are administered in a "play" rather than "conventional test" atmosphere.

creativity. While tests of this sort—that require that the subject think, for example, of unusual uses for common objects and the consequences of unusual events—may indeed measure the infrequency or originality of a subject's ideas in response to specific test items, they fail to reveal the extent to which the subject, faced with real life problems, is likely to come up with solutions that are novel and adaptive and which he will be motivated to apply in all of their ramifications (p. 160).

In like manner, Taylor (1965a) suggested that when the work on creative adults moves downward through the high-school grades and work on creativity in children moves upward into these same grades, the two research groups may find that they are exploring rather different phenomena.

The conclusion warranted concerning divergent production and *creative behavior in subject-matter fields* is perhaps more encouraging, since some of Torrance's studies do suggest, albeit tentatively, that the two measures are related. Divergent production skills could hardly be thought a sufficient condition for creativity, however, since subject-matter knowledge is clearly prerequisite.

Divergent Production and School Achievement[14]   The relationship of divergent production measures to school achievement has been investigated in two principal ways. One approach involves a comparison of students scoring at the extremes of divergent production and intelligence distributions (Getzels and Jackson, 1962; Torrance, 1960a; Yamamoto, 1964a,b,c). For example, Getzels and Jackson (1962) selected gifted students who scored in the top 20 percent on divergent production measures, but not in the top 20 percent on IQ measures (mean IQ = 127), designating this group "highly creative." The second group, designated "highly intelligent," consisted of students who scored in the top 20 percent on IQ measures (mean IQ = 150), but not in the top 20 percent on the divergent production measures. The two groups were found to achieve at a comparable level academically despite their 23-point difference in average intelligence. While these results have been frequently quoted as indicating that divergent production measures are good predictors of school achievement, it would appear that this interpretation may be questioned on statistical grounds (Burt, 1962; De Mille and Merrifield, 1962; R. W. Marsh, 1964). In any case, Edwards and Tyler (1965) obtained contradictory results, finding that a highly intelligent group of ninth graders was superior to a highly creative group on both achievement test scores and grade-point average. Similarly, Hasan and Butcher (1966), in a partial replication of the Getzels and Jackson study in Scotland, found that high IQ children outperformed high creative children in academic achievement.

---

[14]Based on a review by Miezitis (1968).

A second approach involves the computation of correlation coefficients between divergent production and achievement scores. An examination of the results of several studies (Cicirelli, 1965; Cline and others, 1963; Feldhusen and others, 1965; Flescher, 1963; Getzels and Jackson, 1962; Ohnmacht, 1966; Torrance, 1959) indicates that the size of the correlation coefficient varies greatly ($r = -.07$ to $r = .73$) from one study to the next, which is not surprising in view of the fact that investigators have used different divergent production and achievement measures. Despite this considerable variation, the relationship between divergent production and school achievement in most studies employing grade 4 to grade 12 subjects is generally positive and significant, and remains so even when IQ is controlled statistically (Cicirelli, 1965; Cline and others, 1963; Torrance, 1959; Wodtke, 1964). Exceptions to this rule include Feldhusen and others (1965) who reported significant positive correlations for two of their divergent production measures (originality and flexibility) but near zero correlations for ideational fluency, and Flescher (1963) who reported very low correlations ($r = -.07$ to $r = .15$) between a divergent score based on five Guilford-type tests and the Metropolitan Achievement battery.

Can and Should Divergent Production Abilities be Trained? Preliminary studies on the training of abilities represented by divergent tests have produced some, if limited, success (Anderson and Anderson, 1963; Cartledge and Krauser, 1963; Crutchfield and Covington, 1963; Freedman, 1965; Jenks, 1966; Mednick and others, 1964; Ridley and Birney, 1967; Ray, 1966; Simon and others, 1966; Torrance, 1959). Torrance, for example, trained primary-school children (grades 1 to 7) to use principles derived from Osborne's (1957) elaboration of the "brainstorming" technique. The task required that the children provide ideas for improving a common toy (for example, toy dog) so that it would be "more fun . . . to play with." Experimental groups, provided with such strategies as (1) make it bigger or smaller; (2) change it in color or shape; (3) change the position and relationship of its parts, and so on—produced significantly more ideas which were judged to be actual improvements in an eight-minute test period than matched control groups who had not received such training.

Maltzman and his associates have also conducted a number of studies in this area (1958, 1960, 1964). In general the technique has been to provide groups of college students with stimulus words, to invoke or reinforce novel responses to these words (rather than common responses obtained in a "free association," where the subject says the first word that comes into mind), and then to see whether the subjects thus trained give more novel responses on a free association test using new words, or earn higher scores in the unusual uses test. Although a variety of techniques yielded positive results, the most effective training method (of those tried) seemed to consist

TABLE 17.3

THE EFFECT OF TRAINING ON DIVERGENT PRODUCTION SCORES

GROUPS	MEAN ORIGINALITY SCORE ON FREE ASSOCIATION TEST[*]	MEAN SCORE ON UNUSUAL USES TEST (ORIGINALITY)
X	68.77	1.42
C	84.46	1.06
X_2	79.20	1.49
C_2	87.79	1.21

[*]Corrected for initial difference on pretest; lower scores indicate high originality.
Source: Adapted from I. Maltzman, S. Simon, D. Raskin, and L. Licht, "Experimental studies in the training of originality," *Psychol. Monogr.*, No. 493, 1960, 1–23. Copyright 1960 by the American Psychological Association, and reproduced by permission.

of presenting the initial list several times and asking the subject to attempt to give a different response each time the same stimulus word was presented. The magnitude of the results obtained by means of such a procedure are shown in Table 17.3.

In this study (Maltzman and others, 1960) four groups were given a preliminary free association test. Groups X and X_2, the experimental groups, were presented with the same training list on five additional occasions with instructions to give a different response than the ones used before on each re-presentation of the stimulus. Groups C and C_2, the control groups, were given only the initial task. Criterion tests were administered to groups X and C one hour after the initial list was presented (Group C), or training completed (Group X). The comparable delay for Groups X_2 and C_2 was two days. Table 17.3 indicates that the effect of training on scores earned on the unusual uses test persisted over the two-day period. During the same time interval, however, some loss of the effect of training is visible in the originality scores earned in the free association test. Clearly, despite the mild optimism allowed by these results, a great deal needs to be known about the breadth and duration of the experimental effects before any sweeping conclusions are made. (See also Ridley and Birney, 1967.)

Anyone who questions whether "creativity" training is desirable is not likely to win friends, given the sentiments of educators on this subject. Actually, no empirically based argument can be brought *against* it.[15] What concerns the present authors—aside from the fact that no evidence exists that divergent production is a precursor of mature creativity—is that whereas

---

[15]At the same time, Shulman (1966) commenting on Wallach's and Kogan's (1965) proposal that creative thinking be taught, asserts: "I do not believe that we have any empirical evidence, either from this book or any other, that such teaching is justified."

mature creativity requires strong tendencies to reject or inhibit the frivolous, glib, or impulsive first groping toward solutions, many divergent tests seem to veer dangerously close to encouraging the uncritical acceptance by the student of such behaviors. One can put this another way by saying that acceptable divergent production behaviors—as for example, a listing of a number of different uses for a brick—must conform to only the most elementary and loose constraints; yet in truly creative behavior the product is subjected to a variety of complex judgments imposed by the structure of the discipline as well as considerations of parsimony, elegance, and aesthetic appeal. Certainly the bright "divergent" student must learn somewhere along the line that the criteria for mature creative production are vastly more complex and invariably require more inhibition of the essentially trivial than successful performance on divergent tasks would lead him to believe.

CHARACTERISTICS OF CREATIVE INDIVIDUALS

We now turn to a brief discussion of the characteristics of persons who have demonstrated mature creative ability in a particular field (that is, who are, in terms of our earlier definition, creative individuals).

Intelligence

First, with respect to intelligence (as measured on standard IQ tests), the evidence invariably shows that creative individuals in art, literature, and science are *more* intelligent than noncreative individuals (Drevdahl and Cattell, 1958; Hitt and Stock, 1965) and that high IQ persons contribute much more than their share of notable and original discoveries in the various disciplines (Terman and Oden, 1959). This suggests that intelligence, like other supportive cognitive traits, makes possible and implements the expression of substantive creativity (Price and Bell, 1965). In other words, a certain minimal degree of intelligence above the average is usually necessary for the actualization of creative potentialities. But above this critical level the relationship between intelligence and true creativity is approximately zero (Drevdahl, 1956; MacKinnon, 1962; Terman and Oden, 1959). The noncreative high IQ individual who does very well in academic tasks and is vocationally successful, but who never generates an original idea, is a very familiar figure in our culture.

Contrariwise, many highly creative individuals do not sport spectacularly high IQ's. Taylor (1965a), for example, reports the interesting case of a boy with a measured IQ of 86 who produced several creative ideas in a summer research project in science. This is undoubtedly an extreme instance, but it does serve to show that some individuals who would be rejected by the university as "lacking academic ability" may possess the characteristics capable of maturing into pronounced scientific ability. Taylor suggests that self-reported biographical data tapping such attributes as the individual's interest in intellectual things generally, interest in learning on one's own, self-confidence, self-sufficiency, and striving for independence is a better predictor of later scientific creativity than standard batteries of intellectual measures.

Personality Correlates

Considerable research has also been conducted on the personality characteristics of persons who have been rated by competent judges as creative in such areas as art, architecture, literature, and science. In general, these traits are consistent with what one would expect of original and talented individuals who have achieved success and recognition in their chosen fields. On the cognitive side, creative individuals tend to be original, perceptive, insightful, independent in judgment, open to new experience (especially from within), sceptical, and verbally facile. They are flexible, open-minded, and tolerant of ambiguity; have wide-ranging interests; prefer complexity; and are less interested in small details and in the practical and concrete than in theoretical ideas and symbolic transformations (Barron, 1963; Drevdahl, 1956; Drevdahl and Cattell, 1958; MacKinnon, 1960, 1961, 1962). In general they delight in paradoxes and in reconciling opposites.

From a motivational standpoint, highly creative individuals are ambitious, achievement-oriented, dominant, and have a sense of destiny about themselves. They tend to be emotionally mature, venturesome, self-sufficient, and emotionally and aesthetically sensitive. Their self-image abounds in such traits as inventiveness, determination, industry, independence, individualism, and enthusiasm. On the whole, they exhibit higher ego strength and self-acceptance, more introspectiveness, and greater femininity than noncreative individuals. In their relations with others they are unconventional, rebellious, disorderly, self-centered, exhibitionistic, and prone to retreat to the role of observer. They tend to make deviant scores on the Minnesota Multiphasic Personality Inventory, but this is undoubtedly more reflective of complexity of personality, candor, lack of defensiveness, and openness to experience than of genuine personality distortion (Barron, 1963; Cashdan and Welsh, 1966; Drevdahl, 1956; Drevdahl and Cattell, 1958; Hammer, 1961; MacKinnon, 1960, 1961, 1962).

Characteristics of the Creative Process

There is no widely accepted account of the creative process. How it happens that some individuals are able to undertake the high-level syntheses and utilization of remote analogies which characterizes mature creativity is not really known. In a number of studies, scientists and artists have introspected on the sequence of events which transpired during the creation of a new theorem, or the plot for a story, or other original products (Wertheimer, 1945; Poincaré, 1913; Hadamard, 1945; Findlay, 1948; Patrick, 1937). Generally the mental activities reported fall into the four-stage model suggested by Wallas (1921), which embraces "preparation," "incubation," "illumination," and "verification."

In the preparation stage the scientist prepares himself for a creative advance by cognizing the critical requirements of a problem, by activating particularly relevant knowledge, and by studying the interrelationships of various hypotheses and theorems bearing on the problem. In a sense he is creating an informational and theoretical matrix within which the solution of the problem must lie. Sometimes such preliminary ruminations occur over a period of years. It is reported, for example (Wertheimer, 1959) that Einstein became troubled by some difficulties with the speed of light when he was sixteen years of age, that he worked over relevant data for seven years before a solution, the theory of relativity, emerged.

The fact that a solution or creative discovery does not follow immediately or mechanically from the preparation stage has led to the notion of a period of "incubation." Many classical solutions in science and mathematics have been preceded by a period in which the scientist, having apparently reached a dead end, put the problem out of his conscious thoughts and turned his attention to other matters. Some theorists would claim that the dynamic processes instituted consciously in the preparation stage continue on in the incubation stage, but at the level of subconscious thinking; some argue further that it is the lack of conscious controls (which carry with them the constraints of conventional ways of doing things) in unconscious thinking that makes a new synthesis or viewpoint possible.

In any case, at some point a solution may occur—often with dramatic suddenness—and frequently when the scientist is not actually thinking about the problem. Among the solutions occurring in dreams was Descartes' conception of analytic geometry and Kekules' discovery of the benzine ring; the solution of a difficult mathematical problem occured to Poincare as he boarded a train, his mind on mundane matters. Many readers have probably had a similar experience, on a much more modest scale, of "awakening to a solution" of an unsolved problem.

Finally, the validity of the solution must be consciously tested against reality and the requirements of the problem. And of course many ideas which strike us as brilliant solutions in a moment of "inspiration" turn out to have glaring flaws when examined in detail. As indicated above, this proposed sequence of events, though reported by artists as well as scientists, hardly represents a scientific analysis of the processes involved in mature creativity.[16] Nevertheless, the stages are sufficiently suggestive and congruent with common experience that they have become part of the language in which creativity is discussed. For example, we find Taylor (1965a), in the midst of a description of the scientific assessment of personality variables associated with creativity, falling back upon the four-stage model. And as recently as 1967, Gall and Mendelsohn tested the efficacy of the incubation period. (They found, incidentally, that when the problem-solving task was convergent, subjects did better if they continued to work at it.)

FOSTERING CREATIVITY IN THE CLASSROOM

What advice should be given with respect to the fostering of creativity in the classroom? To begin with, the teacher should recognize that while the path to mature creativity is but dimly perceived, it would seem reasonable to believe that the critical elements are a genic potential, some aspect of personality which crystallizes early in the child's life as a result of interaction with parents, intense early stimulation (Fowler, 1967), or some combination of these factors. This means that the romantic notions of some educators—to the effect that every child has creative potential if education can only set it free—should be tempered with realistic thinking concerning the limitations of human plasticity. Our schools will have done a creditable job, and a good deal more than they are now doing, if each child is brought to understand the central ideas which comprise the results of human thinking, and has acquired the ability to cope with intellectual problems with some assurance and effectiveness. To say that the school probably cannot *create* mature creativity does not, however, mean that it cannot *support* its development. For it seems quite likely that while some potential geniuses may thrive under the most adverse circumstances, others will fail to achieve their potential through want of encouragement or active suppression of their creative impulses.

As to specifics, we have already indicated our scepticism concerning the training of divergent production behaviors. On occasion, such exercises may provide short-term stimulation and have some positive effect on the child's intellectual outlook; nevertheless, the earlier remarks concerning lack of response inhibition in such measures should alert the teacher to the possible undesirability of sustained work in this direction. The teacher's major

---

[16]There have, however, been some sophisticated attempts to relate higher creative performance to postulated psychological or physiological mechanisms. For two recent comprehensive efforts in this direction see Anderson (1966, 1968).

effort, in our opinion, should be to foster creativity *within the context of subject-matter disciplines* and the related artistic and cultural activities of the school. Even at a young age most children are capable of going beyond their previous knowledge to make discoveries which are novel for them. Such self-referenced discoveries will rarely (a few child geniuses aside) increase man's total stock of knowledge, or contribute to his cultural treasures, but they can be of immense value to the individual. A major advantage in employing substantive fields of knowledge is that, particularly as children become older and acquire more subject-matter background, the internal constraints of this knowledge eliminate the possibility of solution by trivial or facile verbalization, and will teach the child that genuine discovery involves a considerable measure of reflection and critical appraisal. Moreover, among those who indicate an early bent for original discoveries in substantive fields are likely to be found those who will later make a unique contribution.

TOPICS FOR DISCUSSION AND FURTHER STUDY

1. Discuss, with examples, the applicability of the problem-solving paradigm to subject areas not treated in this chapter (for example, spelling, reading, geography, history, economics). How is such problem solving different from that encountered in mathematics and science? To what extent could a "strategy" be said to be involved? (See Rohman and Wiecke, 1964.)

2.* Analyze a recurring class of problems in your subject-matter speciality and outline a detailed teachable strategy for solving such problems. Indicate problems which are idiosyncratic to your particular field. Can any use be made of memory aids and schematic representations?

3.* Construct a series of tasks to illustrate both "ineffective" and "dysfunctional" rigidity. Try these out on a class or on a teaching colleague. What is the effect of suggestions that the subject should "think"?

4. Describe in your own words the limitations of a logical approach to some "real life" problem. How would you demonstrate that the application of logic and problem-solving strategies is preferable to acting on the basis of intuition, hunch, or "expert" advice?

5. Indicate some kinds of behavior that you would consider "creative" at the grade level at which you will be teaching. What opportunities can be provided to develop or stimulate such behaviors?

6.* What relationships would you hypothesize between divergent production scores and curiosity? What personality characteristics would be associated with high divergent production? (See Lazare, 1967.)

7.* In this chapter we have pointed out that the relationship between divergent production and school achievement is somewhat debatable. What relationship would you expect to hold between more direct measures of creativity at the high school and college levels and achievement at these levels? (See Holland, 1967.)

SUGGESTIONS FOR ADDITIONAL READING

Aschner, M. J., and C. E. Bish (Eds.) *Productive thinking in education.* Washington, D. C.: National Education Association, 1965.

Getzels, J. W., and P. W. Jackson. *Creativity and intelligence: Explorations with gifted students.* New York: John Wiley & Sons, Inc., 1962.

Hudgins, B. B. *Problem solving in the classroom.* New York: Crowell-Collier and Macmillan, Inc., 1966.

Kleinmuntz, B. *Problem solving: Research, method, and theory.* New York: John Wiley & Sons, Inc., 1966.

Torrance, E. P. *Rewarding creative behavior.* Englewood Cliffs, N.J.: Prentice-Hall, Inc., 1965.

Wallach, M. A., and N. Kogan. *Modes of thinking in young children.* New York: Holt, Rinehart and Winston, Inc., 1965.

Wertheimer, M. *Productive thinking.* (Enlarged ed., Michael Wertheimer, Ed.) New York: Harper & Row, Publishers, 1959.

PART SIX

THE TEACHER'S ROLE IN HYPOTHESIS REFINEMENT AND EVALUATION

In this section we develop further ideas raised in the first chapter. There it was observed that the process of change in education is characterized by a sequence of events which include: goal setting, design of new programs to accomplish these goals (employing generalizations derived from basic research), testing, evaluation, and implementation. We also observed that this sequence occurs both at the state, provincial, and local school board level and, in somewhat reduced form at the *individual classroom level*.

The latter case, the subject of Chapter 18, is distinguished by the fact that the teacher *utilizes* (rather than generates) research-based generalizations as *hypotheses* which require elaboration, modification, and extension to fit local conditions. The modification required to make such hypotheses fiit the unique conditions of a given classroom can only be determined by carefully arranged tryouts (or classroom experimentation). Chapter 18 follows the progression in the teacher's thinking as an hypothesis is selected, an experimental tryout is arranged, and the hypothesis refined in light of the data obtained.

Since the hypothesis predicts "better" outcomes, an important first step will be to define criteria for desired behavior. Moreover, the efficacy of the proposed program must be measured against some standard, usually taken as the ongoing or "traditional" practice in the school; thus a fair comparison will require, among other things, that two treatments (experimental and ongoing) be tried with groups which have been "equated" in their essential statistics (usually by randomly assigning students between the treatments). Once the experiment is completed the teacher will have to interpret any difference obtained in terms of both "educational" significance (that is, is this degree of difference worth the cost and effort?) and statistical significance (could this difference be explained by the operation of "chance" factors?).

Chapter 19 deals in more detail with the phase *following* design in the process of change—the *evaluation* phase. The term "evaluate" means to assess the adequacy of a program against the aims which have been set out for it. Evaluation is, then, an integral part of the process of refining hypotheses (or the particular designs to which they lead). But, *in addition,* some form of evaluation is an almost continuous activity of the teacher irrespective of whether specific changes or new programs are under investigation. For in its broadest sense, evaluation has such other functions as providing feedback to students, eliciting attention to (and practice of) material learned in school, providing data for placement decisions and information for reports of progress to parents.

Formal evaluation is almost invariably preceded by some form of *measurement.* In its widest meaning, measurement ranges from purely descriptive or categorizing procedures (such as indicating that a child is "independent" or "dependent") to highly quantitative procedures involving the assignment of numerical scores (which can be treated like arithmetical numbers) to student behaviors. One important consideration is that the assignment of numerical scores to student performance, and the subsequent undertaking of arithmetical calculations (for example, computing means) with these scores, must be approached with caution and with full knowledge of what one is doing. Another consideration is that tests used by teachers—whether they be *standardized* (that is, commercially prepared to meet rigorous technical criteria), *teacher-made* (that is, developed for use in an individual classroom), *objective* (having unequivocally correct answers) or *essay*—should meet certain statistical and practical criteria. The most important of the elementary statistical criteria are that a test should be *reliable* (give consistent measures of a stable entity), and *valid* (measure what it purports to measure). Chapter 19 concludes by suggesting that measurement and evaluation practices in today's classrooms are capable of considerable improvement, and by indicating concrete steps which the individual teacher might undertake toward this goal.

CHAPTER 18

HYPOTHESIS GENERATION AND REFINEMENT IN THE CLASSROOM

FROM THE TEACHER'S POINT OF VIEW THE GENERALIZA-
tions of educational psychology are incomplete. They represent general statements of relationships, derived from theory or research, between variables
which can be manipulated or accommodated in classroom settings and the
behavioral manifestations of the aims of the school. In most cases, the
"generality" of the generalization inheres in the fact that it describes observed *tendencies* across a number of experimental arrangements, subject
areas, teaching styles, and pupil characteristics. In other cases such generalizations represent the results of *reasoned argument* without (as yet) definitive
empirical support. Hence, because of their lack of specificity and/or somewhat tenuous validity, the generalizations of educational psychology should
be regarded more as *hypotheses suggesting appropriate action* than as specific procedural rules; such hypotheses need refinement at the classroom
level to determine their viability and proper application. In some cases they
must be drastically altered to meet the specific conditions which obtain in a
given classroom; in other cases they may be rejected as invalid under the
circumstances.

FROM THEORY TO PRACTICE

Who is to undertake this task of deriving a set of procedural rules from the generalizations of educational psychology? At the state or
provincial level, this work would be undertaken in a research and development institute where subject-matter specialists, educational psychologists, and
practicing teachers design new curriculums for particular subject-matter
fields. In addition, a great deal could be done—and hopefully will be done—

by greater cooperation between the educational-psychology instructor and the "methods" teacher in the teacher-training college. Thus after the teacher-in-training is acquainted in the educational-psychology course with theoretical principles concerning the use of organizers, a cooperating methodologist could provide considerable help in demonstrating the application of these principles in the specific subject-matter field for which he is responsible. Both of these procedures have the effect of particularizing the generalizations of educational psychology to meet the requirements of the substantive content of a given discipline.

The arrangements we have suggested are not yet in effect, and will not happen overnight. And when they do occur there will remain to the teacher the further necessity of refining hypotheses to take into account his particular classroom "givens" and to determine what specific emphases will be best for his students. We cannot assume that mere raw experience via exposure in the classroom will accomplish this, however. Somehow within the ongoing classroom activity the teacher must develop a way of analyzing and refining the hypotheses which guide the selection of the procedures which he utilizes to achieve the aims of education.

Some Preliminary Steps

Hypothesis refinement must, of course, be preceded by specific hypothesis formulation and this, in turn, by a sustained analysis of the learning task. Such an analysis will begin with a clear formulation of the goals to be achieved. It is our belief that education will benefit if the teacher, as far as is possible, attempts to relate these goals—as they are found in course outlines—to specific student behaviors. For example, if problem solving is an expected outcome, then the teacher must have a clear notion of what constitutes a problem and what constitutes performance that is below the level of problem solving.

Once such translation of goals into behavioral outcomes has been completed, the teacher will be in a position to assess the adequacy of present practices and to determine where changes need to be made. Do the students, for example, show an adequate understanding of the concepts taught in a particular course? Do they understand the relationships between these concepts? Is the student's ability to utilize such concepts and generalizations in problem solving up to the level which might reasonably be expected (for example, to the level which has been achieved in current experimental projects)? From such informal assessments the teacher will determine an order of priority among the improvements which might be attempted.

The third stage will be to analyze the variables which the teacher might actually manipulate to produce more acceptable outcomes. Usually this stage is undertaken either implicitly or intuitively, since the teacher soon comes to recognize those factors which lie within his power to change and those factors which can only be changed by action at a higher administrative level. One of the hoped-for benefits of an educational-psychology course is to sensitize the teacher to potentially important variables which might not otherwise occur to him. For example, the conceptualization of learning tasks in terms of step size, step interval, and difficulty reveals variables which can be manipulated independently but which are usually not explicitly conceptualized in the teacher's thinking. Similarly, not all teachers recognize the various gradations of discovery-reception learning or of reward-punishment which exist and which, theoretically at least, may have differential effects on student outcomes. Similar statements could be made, of course, for most of the cognitive structure, practice, motivational, and group factors discussed in previous chapters.

Having identified an area of weakness (that is, a failure to produce satisfactory results on some desired behavioral goals) and possessing a clear conception of the manipulable instructional variables, the next step is to formulate hypotheses which would indicate how the latter should be manipulated to produce more desirable values of the former. There are many possible sources for such hypotheses. It is hoped, of course, that at least some of them will be found in this text, or in such applications of the theoretical ideas presented (to specific subject-matter fields) as may be undertaken by a cooperating methodologist.

However, since both theory and empirical generalizations in educational psychology are increasing in both number and quality, the teacher cannot rely entirely on what was learned during the period of pre-service training. Like any other professional, the teacher must be prepared to undertake at least a minimal amount of reading of current theory and research. Some professional magazines contain readable accounts of studies of interest to teachers; other sources of hypotheses are compilations within a given area (for example, research on creativity in children) and the various editions of the Encyclopedia of Educational Research. Finally, many of the larger school systems have research personnel or staff psychologists whose primary function is to facilitate the teacher's thinking about his own educational problems; such individuals are a potentially useful source of hypotheses or critical assessment of the teacher's hypotheses.

It would be completely unrealistic, of course, to believe that the teacher will be able to adopt a theory and research stance with any appreciable proportion of the hypotheses he must act upon. Some of these latter hypotheses will arise in the barrage of social data with which the teacher is incessantly bombarded. For example, while teaching a particular concept the teacher may notice that Johnny is not paying attention. Theoretically the teacher might postulate a number of possible reasons for this inattention, hypothesize the likely outcomes of each of several possible corrective actions, ruminate over relevant data, and rationally select one particular course of action. Practically, however, the whole episode will pass in a few seconds and a procedural decision must be made "on the fly" so to speak, without, in fact, diverting the class's attention from the task at hand. While it may make sense to assert that *some* hypothesis—for example: "speaking to the student in a terse, firm manner will redirect his attention to the learning task"— underlies the teacher's corrective action, it is doubtful that such an hypothesis would be explicitly formulated in the present instance.

A great deal of the teacher's explicit hypothesizing will be done outside class, in retrospecting upon the day's experience, the result of a recent test, or the behavior of particular students. "The class did not seem to grasp the generalization concerning the weight of a floating body," he will recall. "Perhaps I should review it briefly tomorrow with a wider variety of concrete examples." Or he will reflect that the class did not perform up to expected standards on the current set of problems. Perhaps the underlying propositions are not well-enough understood, or a more detailed strategy is required. Or, "Jay has been a destructive influence in the class again; is his motive mere attention-getting, and if so, what can I do tomorrow to head off another recurrence? Perhaps if I . . . ." And so it proceeds, a constant wash of formal and informal hypotheses across the input-output interface; the aim—to produce student behaviors which approximate the goals of education.

Informal and Formal Procedures for Testing Hypotheses

Whenever a teacher acts on an hypothesis, whether it is generated on the spur of the moment or more deliberately in advance of action, he will tend to evaluate the effectiveness of his action, that is, to determine how well it works against his expectations or purpose for undertaking it. Such evaluations will exhibit as much variability in complexity as the hypothesis-generating process itself. Some evaluations will be as fleeting as the circumstances which prompted the teacher's action: Having noticed Johnny's attention wandering, the teacher asks him to pay attention, and when inspection reveals that this simple instruction has achieved its purpose, the teacher will dismiss the matter from his mind. Again, the teacher who was concerned about the class's understanding of a particular generalization might act on his hypothesis (that is, to use a variety of concrete models) and by careful questioning on the following day determine to his satisfaction that the corrective measures have worked.

This necessity of "decision making within an ongoing process" will characterize much of the teacher's experience. Unlike the laboratory experimenter, the teacher rarely has time to conceptualize emerging problems well in advance, to formulate and subject to critical scrutiny the hypotheses linking manipulable variables and desired outcomes, and to define in unequivocal terms the treatments that he will use. In the vast majority of cases the teacher must make the best analysis, formulate the best action hypotheses, and undertake the most complete evaluation that he can under the circumstances. No one can find fault with this; in fact, with a knowledge of relevant theory—which enters, often imperceptibly, into his thinking, providing a matrix or ideational scaffolding for his decision making—this teacher may make remarkably wise decisions which differ little from what he would do given much more time for reflection.[1]

At the same time the teacher, singly or in cooperation with his colleagues, will *occasionally* make some *substantial* innovation which calls for more sustained advance planning. Herein lies both an opportunity and a responsibility for more *formal* hypothesizing, experimentation, and evaluation of results. The intention of the following section is that of following through a single example to indicate how such hypothesizing and testing might be accomplished in a school setting, and to suggest some of the problems which would be encountered along the way. This account will have the additional benefit of acquainting the prospective teacher with some of the more important methods of reasoning and terminology he will encounter in his later reading of research reports in professional journals.

CASE STUDY: AN EXPERIMENTAL TRY-OUT OF THREE NEW APPROACHES

For illustrative purposes we will continue with the example discussed as a "real life" problem in the preceding chapter. As the reader will recall, the problem there was to choose a method of teaching the content of a new mathematics course which would "maximize" student learning as measured by a well-defined criterion test. For purposes of the present discussion, we will simplify the problem somewhat by dropping one of the proposed treatments.

In Figure 18.1 we have set out what might be considered a task analysis of the process of adapting and refining a hypothesis to suit the conditions of a particular school system. This sequence of activities to be performed begins

---

[1]In other words the fleeting character of much the greater part of teacher decision making in no way diminishes the value of theoretical sophistication on his part. On the contrary, possession of a generalization will frequently act as either a prompt to, or an appropriate restraint upon, the teacher's hurried actions. For example, the teacher who comprehends the relationship between anxiety level and problem-solving performance, when confronted by a student who is doing poorly at such tasks, would be unlikely to subject the student to increased pressure if he (the teacher) senses that the student's anxiety level is already high. Thus, even though the decision is made rapidly and with no opportunity to study the problem at leisure or in detail, the posession of a theoretical concept and generalization does influence, in some positive sense, the teacher's decision.

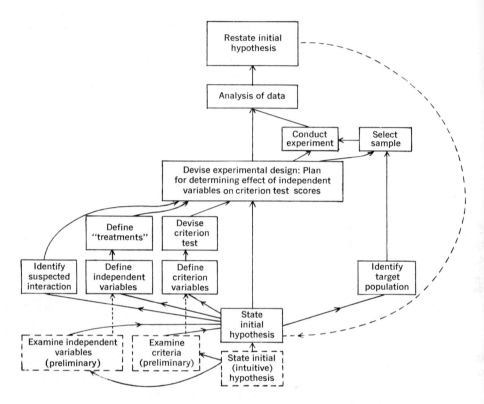

FIGURE 18.1   *Steps involved in hypothesis refinement.*

with some initial hypotheses and moves through various stages, ending with a restatement of the initial hypothesis. In this section we follow the diagram in examining the nature of the activities at each stage.

Evolution of the Hypotheses

At the beginning of the hypothetical project, a group of teachers has available a statement of the content to be included in a new course for grade 9 mathematics. We shall imagine that this course, authorized by the state or provincial educational authority, carries the usual set of objectives which embrace such abilities as the comprehension of mathematical concepts and generalizations, and the ability to utilize these concepts in applications and problem solving. In keeping with current practice, the set of objectives would not indicate how the teachers are to achieve these aims, so that considerable freedom exists for the improvisation of teaching methods.

At this stage the teachers' "hypothesis" may be little more than a vague (intuitive) feeling of the sort: "perhaps there is a way to achieve these objectives more completely than through a continuation of the teaching methods which we have traditionally employed." Following through with this initial exploration, they would conceptualize somewhat more clearly the nature of the outputs to be achieved (for example, what do "comprehension," "problem solving," and so on mean), and would examine independent variables at least to the extent of convincing themselves that sufficient freedom was available with respect to the manipulation of instructional and other variables to warrant the design of a new approach. Concurrently, of course, the teachers in question would seek relevant hypotheses as to how the behavioral outcomes can be improved—through reading, the exchange of ideas and experiences, or consultation with professional research or psychological personnel.

As a result of this preliminary activity, we will assume that the teachers have encountered the literature on the use of organizers, and that they now entertain an hypothesis which might be stated: "the use of organizers will facilitate comprehension and application." These teachers have also become interested in the notion of strategies and are entertaining a second hypothesis which might be put: "training in the use of strategies will lead to improved independent problem-solving performance within the class of problems for which the strategy is designed."

These two hypotheses will be referred to as the "initial hypotheses," and the object of the project will be to assess their validity and to refine them, if necessary, to fit the particular course and unique characteristics of the local situation. We will assume that in the particular city school system in question, six grade 9 teachers are selected from a group who have indicated interest in the project, and that each of these six teachers is drawn from a different school.

Identification of Independent Variables and Design of Treatments The six teachers in our project meet during the summer prior to the implementation of the new program to discuss goals, design criteria, and to develop in detail the procedures and materials they will use. On the latter count, a first step will be a more precise delineation of the independent variables. Thus, for example, the new course material will have to be examined to determine the structure which it exhibits and the opportunities which it provides for utilizing organizers. Similarly, the various classes of problems to be encountered in the material will have to be delineated, to determine if they are sufficiently numerous and varied to warrant a strategies approach.

Having ascertained that the existing situation (that is, curriculum to be taught) contains the possibilities for fruitful manipulation of input variables related to the hypotheses at hand, the teachers must then move on to a more detailed construction of the "treatments". We will assume that special arrangements are made for the project so that each participating teacher, who would normally have two grade 9 classes, is allowed a third class; further it is agreed that each teacher will use *each* of the new methods with *one* of the three assigned classes, while continuing with his "traditional" method (which he is not yet convinced he should give up) with the other class.

We cannot, of course, specify in detail here what each program might be. However, in general terms the organizer approach will introduce the course with a substantial section on the structure of the mathematical system involved, indicating how the central ideas in each of the major topics to be studied during the year can be related to this general structure and, through it, to the arithmetical concepts that have been studied earlier. Further, each new idea will be introduced by a specific organizer which relates the new idea to the initially developed structure and to the ideas that have preceded it in the sequence. Finally, emphasis will be placed on the use of the principle of integrative reconciliation, in this case explicitly pointing out at each stage any significant interrelationships between ideas not already made apparent by the organizer, and checks will be made to insure that adequate comprehension is being attained. Ample time will be allowed for application and independent problem solving, but it will be the primary assumption of this group that the best way of facilitating these latter abilities is through the proper initial organization of the learner's cognitive structure.

The strategies approach, on the other hand, will concentrate on a guided discovery approach to the generation of problem-solving strategies; this approach will involve both small-group instruction and some individual work with each pupil by the teacher. The initial teaching of the underlying concepts and generalizations will not be ignored, of course, although it will be assumed that after a brief initial presentation by the teacher the student will be able to grasp these concepts on his own, so that the teacher's time may be directed more completely toward the facilitation of higher-level performance.[2]

When the teachers' "design" work is complete the intended treatments should be set out (written down) in sufficient detail so that they could be reconstructed by other teachers who might be interested either in utilizing the method (if it is found effective) or merely in replicating the experiment to

---

[2]It is reasonable to argue that two separate experiments are going forward here. In the first, the teachers are hoping eventually to improve comprehension through the use of organizers; they are assuming that advance preparation of materials will bring about this improvement with no loss—over traditionally taught groups—in problem solving. In the second approach the teachers' main interest is in facilitating problem solving through formal instruction in strategies. The tacit assumption here is that the comprehension of the material will not suffer in this approach in comparison with that exhibited by students taught by traditional methods.

determine if the same result would be obtained in their classrooms. The written statement should indicate, for example, the content of the organizers, whether such content is to be taught by the teacher or read by the pupil, the precise nature of the strategy to be employed, and so on. While exact replication is probably a theoretical ideal which is achieved only in laboratory settings, considerable improvement can obviously be made over such global statements as that a "guided discovery approach" was used.

Dependent Variables and Design of Criterion Test

The nature of the dependent variable was already clarified to some extent in the preliminary thinking; thus one might assume that the six teachers in question would reach consensus as to what constitutes problem solving, adequate comprehension, and application. There remains, however, the task of designing the criterion test, a task which should be undertaken *before* the experiment begins. Thus, the teachers would construct in advance a number of items in each of the categories of comprehension, application, and problem solving. Relative weight would have to be assigned to each of these categories; in the present instance it is assumed that each category of outcomes will be given equal weighting in the final assessment of the merit of the methods. The teachers would, of course, have to agree not to teach the specific problems or applications that appear in the criterion test, since in this case correct student answers might reflect little more than rote recall or simple comprehension.

The teachers probably will not be content with the application of the criterion test at the end of the course. They will recognize that—as pointed out at various places in this text—short-term performance does not represent an entirely adequate measure of most educational goals, since the latter typically refer to long-range effects. Consequently it is agreed that an attempt will be made to discern whether the present year's training will have any influence on performance in grade 10. To this end, it is agreed that a similar test will be administered at the end of the grade 10 course (which is taught in the traditional manner) and that student performance on it will be related to the treatment that he received in grade 9. Such a comparison would be exceedingly difficult to make because of many contaminating influences, but it is decided that, despite these risks, the information obtained will be useful in making overall assessment of the two new grade 9 treatments.

Delineation of Potential Interaction Variables

The preliminary hypotheses are stated in terms of expected effects over groups of students, various types of subject matter, various teaching styles, and the like. A central aspect of the refining process is to determine the differential effects of the treatments with respect to these other variables. For example, the literature on the use of organizers suggests that this technique may be differentially more effective (in comparison with traditional methods or a strategies approach) for students of low mental ability (or low levels of related previous knowledge) than for students of high verbal ability (who may be able, in effect, to construct their own organizers).[3] Such results are by no means conclusive and can be taken merely as a suggestion of an effect one might look for in a particular subject area. Similarly, one might postulate that the relative effectiveness of an organizer approach (as compared with a strategies approach) would be dependent upon the teacher's characteristic "style" or on specific teacher personality variables. Any variable for which the treatments may produce such differential effects may be referred to as an "interaction" variable. The selection of a particular variable to be tested for interaction will depend a good deal upon the kinds of subsequent discriminations and special groupings which can be made at the classroom level. For example, an interaction between intelligence and the organizer-strategies treatments could be easily studied, since standard IQ scores are readily available. Moreover, such an observation would have considerable practical utility because the IQ is frequently used as the basis for grouping or streaming students. In other words, if it turned out that one treatment was particularly effective with low IQ groups and another with high IQ groups, it would be possible to use differential treatments with these groups in subsequent years. As we shall see later, there is a practical limit to the number of observed interactions one could reasonably be expected to act upon in the classroom. For this reason the experiment should be concerned with those potential interactions of most local interest.

Definition of Target Population and Selection of Sample

It is important to note that the teachers in our hypothetical experiment are not merely interested in the result which will be obtained with students *actually present in the coming year*. On the contrary, if a particular treatment proves effective and is subsequently introduced on a wide scale, it will likely be used with students in grade 9 classes for a considerable number of years (some practices, as we now well know, are retained for several decades).

The group of students upon whom the treatment which is finally chosen as "best" will be used may be referred to as the "target population." Of

---

[3]Another way of putting it would be to say that the differences in mean scores between high and low IQ groups would be *smaller* for the organizer treatment than the corresponding differences for each of the other two groups.

course, to determine the relative merit of the approaches with respect to this target population, one should try out the methods on a random sample taken from it. Unfortunately this is rarely possible, since it is conceivable that some members of the target population may not be yet born. Consequently, we must resort in practice to using a sample which we believe to be *representative* of the target population in its essential characteristics. Normally, unless the nature of the school population is changing radically, one can assume that the students coming into Grade 9 five years from now will be essentially similar to those presently found there, so that one can infer that what works now will stand a good chance of working at that time. However, if the population should change radically—as it might in rapidly growing suburbs— any conclusion reached at the present time would have to be subjected to further validation when it was felt that the population had changed sufficiently to challenge the earlier results.

In the present instance the three schools included in the sample were selected to represent, as closely as possible, the grade 9 students in the city in question in terms of ability level and socioeconomic background. Further, it is decided that each of the cooperating teachers will select three of the available grade 9 classes in his school, again on the basis of their representativeness of the entire student body at that level. Ideally, the teacher would be allowed to randomly select the 75 students (who will constitute the three classes) from the entire student body at that grade level. However, in many if not in most instances, other requirements of the ongoing school program will make this impossible.

Experimental Design

The question to be answered here is how we will arrange matters so that any differential outcomes between the control and experimental groups can be safely attributed to differences in treatment, rather than to the operation of unplanned, random, or extraneous variables. Comparison with the classical one-variable experimental design in the physical sciences, as represented by the pendulum problem, will indicate the magnitude of the difficulties facing the experimenter in the social sciences. In the pendulum problem the "treatments" were, in effect, the independent variables (for example, length of pendulum arm, weight of bob, and so on) and the dependent variable was the period of the pendulum. In experiments with inanimate objects, it is often possible to take the treatments one at a time, to vary the treatment in intensity (for example, vary the length of the pendulum) and to observe directly and sequentially the effect of these treatments upon the outcome. The facilitating factor is that the treatments can be applied *sequentially* to the same object (pendulum) because the treatment has no permanent effect on the behavior of the object.

560 *Hypothesis Generation and Refinement*

Obviously one usually cannot use such an approach in most educational experimentation, because subjecting a child to method A leads to *permanent* changes in his behavior (in terms of knowledge and skill acquired, and so on). In other words, the child (unlike the pendulum) cannot be "turned back to zero" so that the effects of treatment B may be similarly determined. The strategem resorted to is to create "equal" groups of students and to subject one group to treatment A and the second to treatment B, thus determining the relative efficacy of the treatments on the best available approximation to the "same" group.

While "equality" of groups cannot approach the equality inherent in using the same object (pendulum), one can get a satisfactory approximation by randomly assigning the available students to the various treatment groups. Thus if each of our teachers has 75 students available, he would proceed by randomly assigning (for example, by drawing names from a hat) 25 of the students to each of the experimental groups (that is, organizer and strategies approach) and 25 to the control group (that is, traditional instruction). The effect of the randomization process is to equate the *expected values* of all revelant variables between the three groups; thus, having used this procedure, the mean IQ's, the average age, the average achievement in previous related learning, and the proportion of boys and girls should be nearly equal between the two groups.[4]

If the interaction of "IQ" and "treatment" was designated in advance to be of interest, then the *experimental design* employed in each school could be thought to comprise *six* groups—a "high IQ" and "low IQ" group for each treatment. In this case, in order to insure that the three means for the "high IQ" groups (and, likewise, the three means for the "low IQ" groups) were closely equated, we might use an assignment procedure similar to that indicated in the footnote to the previous paragraph. Alternately, we might

---

[4]More precisely, the expected values of these variables would be the same. Technically this means, in the case of IQ for instance, that if one multiplies the probability that any given student will appear in group A by his IQ score, sums these products over the whole group of students, and divides by the total number of individuals, thus computing the "expected" value of the IQ for group A, this latter statistic will be precisely the same as the "expected value" of the IQ for groups B and C (because each student has exactly one chance in three of being in each group). Practically it means that the group means will be very nearly the same, except for the operation of random factors (for example, by some particularly unlucky shake of the dice, a disproportionately high proportion of high IQ students may appear in group A). When the number of students available for random selection is large, the probability that the obtained means will differ appreciably is very small. However, with small groups chance factors can play a significant role and can be overcome to some extent by a matching procedure. For example, if we wanted to insure that the mean IQ's in the three groups were practically identical, we would list the 75 students available (to one of the teachers) from highest to lowest IQ and, beginning with the first triplet, assign one member randomly to each of the three groups. The result of this procedure, of course, would be to insure that an equal proportion of high and low IQ students appear in each group.

divide the 75 available subjects into "high IQ" and "low IQ" students, randomly assign the "high IQ" students to the three treatments, then do the same for the "low IQ" students. In any case, in each school the participating teacher will use the organizer method with one experimental class, the strategies approach with another, and his conventional method with the control class. It is understood that the same time will be given to experimental and control groups; homework assignments—if not eliminated—will be closely controlled and equated. It is also understood, of course, that the teacher will not deliberately bias his efforts to favor the success of any one approach.

In this connection, one of the most difficult contaminating factors to control in such research is the operation of the so-called "Hawthorne Effect." As mentioned in previous chapters, the Hawthorne Effect refers to an increase in output which results, apparently, from the higher morale and interest on the part of the learners when they recognize that they are part of an experimental program and are, therefore, being given "special treatment." In the present case one of the usual problems is eliminated because the same teachers are in charge of the experimental and control groups. Moreover, the students in all three groups will be exposed to new material and so no differential motivational effect should accrue there. However, the teachers should also attempt to make the control groups feel that they are as much involved in a novel undertaking as the so-called experimental groups; sometimes this can be done by judicious hinting which, though residing possibly on the far side of the truth, may be thought excusable under the circumstances.

Conduct of the Experiment

It is understood that the teachers will not, except by mutual agreement and plan, deviate from the treatments agreed to at the outset of the experiment. If it should happen that one approach appears to be obtaining disastrous results, we would naturally expect some change in the proposed course of action. However, if the exercise has been well planned and thought out, this should not occur.

Analysis of Data

Up to this point we have described the origin of the experiment in terms of a group of teachers attempting to work out effective teaching methods for a new curriculum. While this would perhaps be the typical approach in the schools at the present time—particularly when there is as much advance preparation (with its attendant cost) as is indicated in our example—an individual teacher working in his own school could, of course, have proceeded through all of the steps indicated so far. Because of our consistent focus on the individual teacher, we will proceed to analyze the data from a single classroom and to study its implications for the hypothesis refinement and decision making of the teacher involved (who, for purposes of convenience, will be referred to as Jones). Later we shall return briefly to the original experiment to indicate some of the more complex considerations which must be faced if the results of the multiple-school experiment (six teachers) were to be used as the basis for a system-wide decision (that is, a decision as to which approach should be used in all schools).

Tabulate Results   A first and fairly obvious step would be for Jones merely to compute the mean criterion scores of the three treatment groups and to present them in tabular form (Table 18.1) so they are available for visual inspection. The data are, of course, purely hypothetical and have been concocted for discussion purposes only.

The inspection of means reveals that both the organizer and strategies approaches produced somewhat higher overall results (that is, on the combined test), although the effectiveness of each method was somewhat different for each level of performance. Thus the organizer approach showed advantages at the level of comprehension and application while the strategies approach produced better overall problem-solving scores. It would also appear that there was some loss in comprehension—in comparison with traditional methods—in the use of the strategies approach.

Examination of Interaction Effects   It is sometimes helpful to use graphical means to examine interaction effects. In Figure 18.2, we have plotted the achievement scores obtained by each of the three treatments, for each of the high and low IQ groups respectively, on the comprehension

TABLE 18.1

HYPOTHETICAL TREATMENT MEANS

TREATMENTS	CRITERION TEST (MEANS SCORES)			TOTAL SCORE ON CRITERION TEST
	Comprehension	*Application*	*Problem Solving*	
Organizer N = 25	18.2	15.7	11.4	45.3
Strategies N = 25	14.9	15.5	15.7	46.1
Control N = 25	16.6	13.6	11.2	41.4

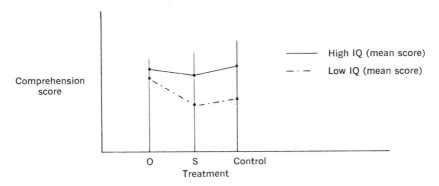

FIGURE 18.2   *Graphical indication of a treatment* × *IQ interaction.*

subtest. A similar analyses would, of course, be made for the application and problem-solving subtests as well.

With respect to Figure 18.2, however, it may be noted that interaction effects are visibly in evidence. For example, the difference in performance between the high and low IQ groups with the organizer approach is much less than the difference between these groups in either of the other approaches; this suggests that the organizers have differentially helped the comprehension of low-ability students in Jones' classes.

Tests of Statistical Significance   If professional help is available or if the teachers have had training in methods of statistical inference, they may with profit proceed to determine whether the differences in means and the interaction effects are "statistically significant" or whether, on the contrary, they may be attributed to "chance." While we cannot adequately discuss this topic here, we may say that it depends on the following line of reasoning.

Let us suppose that we have access to a population of test scores, and that we draw from this population two random samples containing 30 scores each; further, having obtained our sample we will average the scores to obtain two means M_1 and M_2. Now as one can verify either by experiment or by reasoning, one would not expect the two means to be exactly identical. For example M_1 might be found to be 36.2, and M_2 might be 35.8. The differences between these means can be said to have occurred because of the operation of the chance factors associated with sampling or, more briefly, to have occurred by "chance."

When we undertake a test of statistical significance we ask, in effect, whether the observed difference between means (of achievement scores) can be said to have occurred by "chance" in the sense indicated above. The sequence of steps in the thinking typically employed is somewhat indirect and proceeds as follows:

(a) Let us *assume*, for the moment, that *the two samples of scores which we have obtained from the experimental and control groups have been drawn from a common population of achievement scores*. This initial hypothesis, which is usually formulated to be rejected, is referred to as the *null* hypothesis.[5]

(b) If the null hypothesis were true, then the difference in means should be small and within the results which one would expect from the operation of sampling factors. However we know from theoretical and empirical studies what probability there is of obtaining a difference in means of any specified size when the samples are in fact drawn from the same population. Let us suppose that, by consulting an appropriate table, we find that one would obtain differences between the means of the size observed in our study only three times in a hundred if the samples *were* randomly drawn from a common population. Under these circumstances we would conclude that it is highly unreasonable to believe that the samples were drawn from the common population. Consequently, we would *reject* the null hypothesis and conclude that the samples were drawn from populations of achievement scores having *different* means (that is, infer that one treatment was superior to the other).

(c) Traditionally, null hypotheses are rejected when the chance of obtaining differences in means as large as the ones actually observed is less than five in a hundred (5 percent level of significance), or one in a hundred (the 1 percent level of significance). When the null hypothesis is rejected at a given level, say 5 percent, the difference in means is said to be "statistically significant at the 5 percent level." In our example we would say that the difference in means was statistically significant at the .05 level but not significant at the .01 level. In formal experimentation, the experimentor sets out his acceptable level of significance in *advance* of the actual computations.

While this indirect form of argument can be helpful to the teacher, the determination of levels of "statistical significance" may become such a fetish that it stands in the way of valid commonsense reasoning. For example, whether or not one will reject the null hypothesis in any particular instance depends very much on the size of the sample involved. Thus if we drew random samples of ten men and ten women from a general population, a difference in their mean heights of 2.8 inches might well be judged "nonsig-

---

[5]If the two groups were random samples from the target population of students, then the achievement means provide estimates of the effect of the treatments on that population. In this case, the null hypothesis says, in effect, that the two populations of *achievement scores* (obtained by applying each treatment to the target population of students) are the *same* or, in other words, that the treatments do *not* have differential effects on the target population.

nificant," while a difference of the same amount may be "highly significant" if there were a hundred measurements in each sample. Certainly, the fact that one cannot establish statistical significance does not necessarily demonstrate that there is "no difference in the effectiveness of the treatments." In fact, the actual difference obtained between the means of the treatment groups provides the best estimate of the difference between the means of the populations of treatment scores. This line of reasoning indicates—as does common sense—that if a teacher has conducted a well-controlled experiment and determines that one treatment performs in a superior manner, and that other relevant factors (that is, cost, time required to implement, and so on) did not put this alternative at a disadvantage, then the reasonable thing to do is to act on the alternative in question irrespective of the outcome of the test of statistical significance.

As a second example, it is too often forgotten that statistical significance by no means implies educational significance. For example, if one had very large samples (say one thousand students in each) the difference between means of 82.1 and 82.4 might be highly significant statistically and yet be of no *educational* significance whatever.

This is not to say, of course, that statistical significance tests have no value in the interpretation of experimental results or in subsequent educational decision making. If, for example, a treatment which gave superior results also cost a good deal more (for example, the use of language labs as opposed to traditional methods), we would want to be sure that a true null hypothesis (that is, no actual difference in effect) was not wrongly rejected, and we would likely set a very high level of significance in using the appropriate statistical test. In other words, before investing sizable funds we would want to be very sure that the difference in results could not be attributed to "chance" in the sense indicated above.

This type of consideration (involving large differential costs) would seldom enter into the type of decision which lies within the teacher's jurisdiction. In the case of teacher research, the crucial work is done in the experimental stage, that is, in randomly assigning the subjects between treatment groups and in accurately administering the defined treatments. Once the means have been obtained the most important intellectual work lies in determining possible contaminating factors and in assessing the educational value of the differences obtained, both of which depend more upon common sense and logical astuteness than upon statistical expertise. Such expertise can be of value to the teacher, but its absence by no means rules out the use of experimental approaches.

Interpretation of Results and Restatement of Hypothesis   On the basis of the results obtained Jones would now be in a position to reformulate or refine the initial hypotheses. For example, it can be stated that in comparison with the methods which he has used in the past, an emphasis on organizers may reasonably be expected to improve performance in comprehension and application without a commensurate loss in problem-solving ability. A further refinement would be to the effect that the chief improvement in comprehension seems to lie with the low-ability group. Similar refinements of the hension seems to lie with the low-ability group. Refinements of the initial hypotheses could be made with respect to the strategies approach as well.[6]

Recycling These refined hypotheses can, of course, become the initial hypotheses of another cycle in the sequence. For example, it is conceivable that the teachers, after two or three years of experience with the new methods, might wish to explore the effectiveness of the respective treatments with students of different personality structure (for example, introvert versus extrovert). There is no theoretical limit to this refining process, although there are obviously practical limits to implementing the results. For example, if the hypotheses concerning the organizer approach were refined to take into account two levels of ability, three levels of performance (for example, comprehension, application, and problem solving), and two student personality types, one would have (potentially) twelve different treatment groups in the classroom. Clearly, the teacher could not provide this degree of differentiation in his instruction and so would have to ignore some of the possible classifications, even though he might know full well that the particular instruction which he was giving to a specific group (for example, high-achieving extroverts) might not be the best that could be provided for them according to the evidence. In other words, and somewhat paradoxically, it would be possible to refine a generalization to the point where it contains far more information than the teacher could utilize in any real group-instruction approach. In the final analysis, practical considerations must determine where the teacher should terminate the refinement process.

Action Following from the Study

Our example, although hypothetical as far as the data is concerned, represents the kind of decision problem with which the teacher will be faced when he attempts to refine hypotheses and adapt them to local usage. After the empirical data have been obtained, there remains the all-important

---

[6]By implication, such generalizations are intended to apply to the "target population" which, in Jones' case, would be the group of students coming into his grade 9 classes during the period in which the new program is in operation. The validity of this extrapolation depends, of course, on how adequately the sample represents the target population. In the light of the previous discussion on the selection of the sample, the extrapolation would seem to be defensible in this case.

question of bringing professional judgment to bear on the question of whether the current procedures (practices) will be modified and, if so, in what way. While the data obtained is reasonably unequivocal, it by no means prescribes a clear course of action. If Jones believes that comprehension and application are the most important educational objectives, he will no doubt change from a traditional to an organizer-based approach, even though this technique brings only mediocre results in problem solving. On the other hand, if he believes that problem solving is the most important outcome, he would probably favor the strategies approach. Of course, in reaching a decision on a course of action he should follow, Jones would be influenced by the numerous considerations concerning the limitations of the criteria employed, the fact that only a finite number (from the potentially infinite set) of treatments were tested, the problem of cost in effort and time in utilizing or adapting to the particular approach, and the many other factors which have previously been discussed as complicating classroom decision making.

The fact that even research conducted in the classroom setting will not result in definite prescriptions for action should not be entirely discouraging to the classroom teacher who is hoping to profit from scientific intervention in education. What the hypothetical experiment has done is to provide a better estimate than our teacher previously had as to what will happen if certain well-defined treatments were employed in his classroom.[7] Perhaps this concrete information provides only an empirical foundation upon which professional judgment and educational philosophy build in reaching a decision, but it must be a contention of reasonable men that the trustworthiness of the final judgment will be proportionate to the strength of this initial foundation. And it is perhaps a very desirable thing that final prescriptions cannot be made, so that in the last analysis the teacher is left with enormous freedom to choose between alternatives which will have significantly differential effects on student learning.

---

[7]Frequently, however, the teacher who is making a major innovation will be unable to establish any sort of control group and must fall back in his evaluations upon comparisons with the achievement of students in former years. In this case some previous class (or classes) acts as the control group and its achievement is compared with that of the present year (which constitutes the experimental group). Such comparisons can be strengthened by the application of a few common-sense procedures. For example, if the teacher really hopes to compare this year's class with last year's, then it seems clear that a common test should be administered to the two groups. Similarly, such comparisons will make little sense unless the teacher sets out to obtain the same goals and allots the same time and enthusiasm to his work. Finally, such comparisons must take into account the relative ability of the students, and other variables which might have influenced the learning outcomes. While random assignment—the most convenient device—is not possible under these circumstances, it is frequently sensible for teachers to compare (by matching) the performance of students of comparable ability who have been subjected to the different methods.

Experimentation for System-wide Decisions

In the preceding sections we have looked closely at the analysis and interpretation of the data as it bears on the hypothesis refinement and curriculum decision making of a particular teacher. However, our hypothetical project initially involved six teachers, and if typical circumstances prevailed, it might well have been initiated by someone who makes a decision (or who advises decision-makers) across the whole system. The intent of the experiment in this case would be to adapt the initial hypotheses to the system as a whole (or at least to all grade 9 classrooms in the system), and the hoped-for result would be evidence as to which alternative gave the best results, according to the criterion tests, over this population.

Large-scale (multiple classroom) research introduces new problems which we will not dwell upon here, because a school system which contemplates such projects will undoubtedly seek advice on statistical design and analysis. Consideration of our six-teacher experiment, however, does reveal the nature of one of the additional problems encountered at this level. If the results which Jones obtained were paralleled by those of the other teachers in the experiment, there would be warrant for restating the initial hypotheses (in the manner indicated earlier) as applying to the whole system, and, by extrapolation, to the target population (again assuming adequate sampling). From the results on the total criterion test would follow the logical justification, if not the professional justification, for a system-wide decision to the effect that a particular approach should be used.[8]

If, however, some teachers obtained better results in problem solving with an organizer approach, others with a strategy approach, and still others with traditional method, then no clear system-wide generalization could be formulated concerning the adequacy of a strategies approach in problem solving vis-a-vis other methods. Moreover, if the results on the *total* criterion test showed a similar variability among teachers (that is, some got the best overall results with one method, some with another), then there would be little statistical justification, and no professional justification whatsoever, for a system-wide decision as to which method should be used. A visual examination of the degree of the latter variability could be had by constructing a graph of the teacher-treatment interaction. This would resemble Figure 18.2 except that the two lines there would become six (each representing a teacher) and the points on these lines would represent the total criterion

---

[8]It is doubtful that many school systems today would *force* a particular teaching method on a teacher. What is more likely to happen (in the case where one method could be thought to have clear system-wide superiority) is that curriculum consultants would actively promote the method, as for example by writing it up in a set of "suggested procedures" for teachers.

scores made by each treatment. Again, if the lines were reasonably parallel, then no interaction exists; in an experiment of this complexity, however, it would probably be decided to apply a more formal test of the significance of the interaction as well.

TOPICS FOR DISCUSSION AND FURTHER STUDY

1. Discuss methods commonly used by teachers to assess whether instructional innovations represent an "improvement" over procedures which they supersede. In what way might such procedures be strengthened?

2. Discuss the defensibility of the often-heard argument, "Since you cannot measure the really important outcomes of education, there is little point in using experimental design and formal measurement in the classroom; whether a new program is better or worse than that which it replaces can only be judged by the perceptive teacher."

3. Outline hypotheses advanced in this text which would lend themselves to classroom refinement. What interaction effects would you expect? Describe briefly how you would proceed to refine your initial hypothesis.

4. Indicate how the possession of a theoretical generalization would facilitate, and influence positively, the rapid decision making that is characteristic in on-going classroom activity. Cite examples other than those indicated in the text.

SUGGESTIONS FOR ADDITIONAL READING

Campbell, D. T., and J. C. Stanley. *Experimental and quasi-experimental designs for research*. In *Handbook of research on teaching* (N. L. Gage, Ed.). Skokie, Ill.: Rand McNally & Company, 1963.

Garrett, H. E. *Statistics in psychology and education* (5th ed.) New York: David McKay Company, Inc., 1958.

Lindquist, E. F., *Design and analysis of experiments in psychology and education*. Boston: Houghton Mifflin Company, 1953.

CHAPTER 19

PRINCIPLES OF EVALUATION
AND MEASUREMENT

MEASUREMENT AND EVALUATION TECHNIQUES ARE CRUCIAL for the teacher's effective guidance of classroom learning and are, therefore, of interest to the discipline of educational psychology. However, since these topics are dealt with in specialized texts and courses offered to teachers-in-training, our treatment here will be brief and will concern itself with such general issues as: the purpose and limitations of measurement and evaluation; the requirements that an effective measurement instrument must meet; the nature of standardized tests; the interpretation of test scores; and various informal methods of measurement and evaluation.

THE MEANING OF MEASUREMENT
AND EVALUATION

Although "measurement" and "evaluation" are frequently coupled, they may be separated logically in terms of the temporal sequence in which they occur. Evaluation is the end-point in a sequence of events which comprises the following steps:

(a) *Setting of behavioral goals:* The preliminary step is the setting of goals. What is it that the program is intended to do? What behaviors should students exhibit when they have completed the program?
(b) *Design and execution of a program to accomplish goals:* This is, of course, the principal task of curricular and methodological invention. Hopefully it is primarily at this stage that the insights (hypotheses) of educational psychology are brought to bear.

570

(c) *Measurement of outcomes of program:* When the program is completed it is necessary to ask: how well did the student perform? Measurement procedures provide qualitative or quantitative data on this question.

(d) *Evaluation of outcomes:* In the final step, evaluation, one must make a judgment as to the adequacy of the program in achieving or approximating the original goals.

In this context, then, *evaluate* means to make a judgment of worth or merit, to appraise educational outcomes in terms of whether they fulfill a particular set of educational goals.

Measurement is a complex activity which cannot be adequately dealt with in this essentially nontechnical discussion. We should point out, however, that in its broadest sense "measurement" ranges from simple classification through various rank-ordering procedures to such "strong" procedures as the assignment (to pupil behaviors) of numbers possessing the properties of the real numbers of arithmetic.

At the lowest or "weakest" level of measurement the teacher might classify children as "outgoing" or "shy"; this is a purely descriptive classification in that no order (of merit or magnitude) is postulated between the two resultant classes. Most teacher measurements, however, do imply an order of merit, at least between designated classes; thus the reading progress of elementary-school children is frequently classified as "superior," "above average," "average," "below average" or "unsatisfactory." An even stronger form of measurement would be to *rank-order* children in terms of achievement. Thus it has been customary in many schools and universities to determine the student's rank or standing, for example, fifth in a class of thirty-four.

The strongest form of measurement is that in which the intervals or ratios between scores acquire meaning and can be treated arithmetically. Most scales of this type are found in the physical sciences where, for example, if three objects weigh 10, 20, and 30 pounds respectively it is sensible to assert that:

(a) The difference in weight between the second object and the first is *equal to* the difference in weight between the third object and the second.

(b) The ratio of the weight of the second object to the weight of the first object is *greater than* the ratio of the weight of the third object to the weight of the second.

It is highly questionable whether educational measurements reach this level of strength. Clearly, an advance in a classroom achievement test score from 85 to 95 must be considered "a greater amount of achievement" than an advance from 60 to 70, when, as often occurs, 100 is thought to represent a state of perfection approached only in rare cases. Similarly, it would usually be extremely hazardous to claim that an achievement score of 80 represents "twice the achievement" represented by a score of 40.

What implications result from this discussion of measurement? First, educators should be cautious about treating educational measurements as though they possess the properties of arithmetical numbers. For example, although a common practice in our schools, there is little statistical justification for averaging raw scores from different subjects to obtain a composite average which is subsequently used to determine standing.[1] This preliminary discussion will also indicate that educational measurement is sufficiently complex that it contains many traps for the unwary; and since the recommendations following from such measurements are of considerable importance to students, there is warrant for a strong measurement component in the teacher's training program.

Measurement and Evaluation in Practice

The goal-setting/design/measurement/evaluation model is a hypothetical sequence of events which is realized in widely varying degrees of sophistication and completeness in particular instances of classroom practice. For example, it frequently (if not almost invariably) happens that goals are either *not* set out in advance or are described in such global, vague, or diffuse terms that one is left in doubt as to what a behavioral manifestation of their accomplishment might be. Under these circumstances any alleged evaluation is likely to be as fuzzy as the aims, and the temptation will be great to rely entirely on impressions and subjective ratings.

It is true, of course, that "adequate evaluation" faces some sizable obstacles. First, the fact is that the objectives of education are long-term in nature, so that it is not the student's performance at the end of the course (a measurable entity) which is of interest to the educator, but rather his subsequent performance in later courses or in "real life." Thus the school teaches reading not in order that the student shall demonstrate proficiency at the end of eight years of elementary schooling, but that he will use this skill in learning other ideas or in reading for sheer enjoyment as an adult. One might argue that the degree to which these long-term goals are actually achieved could and should be measured, but the practical difficulties seem gargantuan. Consequently, the educator must be content with immediate

---

[1] A more appropriate technique would be to convert the raw scores either to "σ scores" or to "standard scores," which may more legitimately be averaged and otherwise treated as arithmetical quantities.

measures of performance supplemented with reasonable guesses as to how these relate to long-term outcomes. |

A second difficulty inheres in the process of measurement itself. Even the direct measurement of pupil performance is not easily done, particularly when no standardized test exists which is appropriate to the particular classroom in which evaluation is to take place. As we shall soon observe, teacher-made tests tend to be somewhat unreliable. Even worse, however, is that the detection of subtle attitude changes and transfer effects—by no means excluded from the legitimate aims of education—all but defy our present measurement instruments.

Finally, as pointed out in the previous chapter, the teacher is required to make not only year-end evaluations of pupil growth and the effectiveness of courses, but moment-by-moment evaluations of the effectiveness of particular techniques, methods of questioning, effects of specific types of reward on particular students, and the like. These fleeting evaluations cannot be thought entirely rational—in the sense of utilizing a large proportion of the relevant available facts and drawing reasoned inferences from them—but they are inevitable nonetheless.

Opponents of scientific intervention in education—and they are many and vociferous—draw upon these and other arguments to suggest that the notion of measurement and evaluation is farcical and pompous, that it destroys more than it creates, and that we should trust instead the intuitions and sensitivities of teachers. We believe, however, that measurement and evaluation techniques can be an aid to the judgment of the teacher, as for example in assisting him to refine or verify hypotheses which guide his choice of instructional methods. We also believe that the outlawing of measurement and formal evaluation would open the door to chaos and lack of direction as serious as that manifest in the thinking of those who oppose such techniques. For the chief characteristic of most opponents of measurement and evaluation is an utter failure to offer any precise set of prescriptions for the desired behavioral outcomes of educational programs, or to forward any proposal for determining what outcomes have in fact been obtained.

THE PURPOSES OF MEASUREMENT AND EVALUATION

In general, the function of evaluation is to determine the extent to which various significant educational objectives are actually being attained. Within this general function, however, many specialized purposes—both long- and short-term—can be recognized, and some of these are of sufficient interest to warrant further consideration.

To Facilitate Student Learning

A primary purpose of evaluation is to *monitor* the student's learning, that is, to constitute an objective check on both his progress and ultimate achievement so that if either is unsatisfactory, suitable remedial measures may be instituted. Thus, a really adequate evaluation program not only assesses the extent to which student achievement realizes educational objectives, but also attempts to account for unsatisfactory achievement—irrespective of whether this inheres in unsuitable instructional methods or materials, in incompetent teaching, in inadequate student morale or motivation, or in insufficient readiness and aptitude. As a product, student learning is no different than any other significant human endeavor that society takes seriously: Considerations of efficiency and quality control presuppose systematic and rigorous assessment.

Apart from its monitoring function, evaluation facilitates student learning in many ways. In the first place it encourages teachers to formulate and clarify their objectives and to communicate their expectations to students. Nothing indicates more unambiguously what knowledge and skills teachers regard as important than the kinds of examination questions they set. It has been shown that students distribute their study time and apportion their learning efforts in direct proportion to the predicted likelihood of various topics and kinds of information being represented on examinations (Keislar, 1961). It is evident, therefore, that if teachers wish to influence learning outcomes in particular ways by the kinds of evaluative devices they use, they must formulate their objectives clearly, communicate these objectives explicitly to students (instead of trying to "outwit" them), and construct reliable and valid measuring instruments that test the degree to which these objectives are realized. Educational objectives, no matter how praiseworthy, simply go by the board if they do not receive representation in the scheme of evaluation. But if communicated adequately and anticipated on examinations, they can direct the kind of learning that takes place.

Second, the examination itself is a significant learning experience. It forces students to review, consolidate, clarify, and integrate subject matter in advance of being tested, and also performs a comparable review function during the course of the test. Feedback from an examination confirms, clarifies, and directs ideas, and differentially identifies areas requiring further study. This corrective function of feedback is extremely important since students often feel "certain" about incorrect answers (Kooker and Williams, 1959).

Third, as we pointed out earlier, examinations play a significant motivating role in school learning. Within limits, desire for academic success, fear of failure, and avoidance of guilt and anxiety, are legitimate motives in an academic setting. It would be wholly unrealistic to expect students to study regularly, systematically, and conscientiously in the absence of periodic examinations. Frequent quizzing markedly facilitates classroom learning (Fitch and others, 1951; Kirkpatrick, 1939; Ross and Henry, 1939).

Lastly, from the experience of being subjected to external appraisal, students learn how to independently evaluate their own learning outcomes. Such self-evaluation enhances school achievement (Duel, 1958) and is particularly important once students complete their formal schooling. It is also part of the long-range objective of increasing students' capacity for appraising their abilities and achievement validly and realistically.

To Facilitate Teaching

Measurement and evaluation provide teachers with essential feedback regarding the effectiveness of their instructional efforts. They indicate to the teacher how effectively he presents and organizes material, how clearly he explains ideas, how well he communicates with individuals who are less sophisticated than he is, and how efficacious particular instructional techniques or materials are. Feedback from examinations identifies areas requiring further explication, clarification, and review, and is invaluable in the diagnosis of learning difficulties, both individual and group. The objective examination is also a necessary corrective against the subjectivity and impressionism of more informal methods of evaluation which are frequently contaminated by favoritism and reward for docility and neatness (R. S. Carter, 1952).

To Test and Refine Curriculum Hypotheses

As indicated in the previous chapter, measurement and evaluation are essential steps in the testing and refining of hypotheses concerning the curriculum, that is, in assessing the merit of a particular sequence and organization of courses embracing designated subject-matter content, instructional materials, and methods of teaching. The data they furnish are also helpful in making such administrative decisions as the grade placement of subject matter and the optimal sequencing of courses. It goes without saying that more formal research on curriculum and on the learning process itself would also be impossible without reliable and valid measures of learning outcomes.

To Assist in Guidance, Counseling, and the Individualization of Instruction

Systematic measurement and evaluation of aptitude, achievement, motivation, personality, attitudes, and interests is necessary for individualizing instruction and for purposes of individual guidance and counseling. We must know the current ability levels of pupils and the current state of their subject-matter knowledge before we can "prepare curriculum materials appropriate to ability levels (and) adapt teaching methods to the learners and the content to be learned" (Adkins, 1958). In the absence of such information, intelligent decisions cannot be made about grade placement, grouping, the pacing of study, promotion, choice of courses, academic and vocational goals, and remedial work. These data, finally, are essential for reporting pupil progress to parents and for explaining to them the basis on which particular decisions are made.

LIMITATIONS AND ABUSES OF EVALUATION AND MEASUREMENT

In the long history of the measurement movement in education, many objections have been raised both to the goals of educational measurement and to the effects produced by particular techniques of measuring learning outcomes. Some of these objections do, in fact, identify palpable limitations, abuses, and shortcomings. Others are based on sentimental and semimystical conceptions of the educative process. It is important to scrutinize these objections carefully and to distinguish between those which are based either on correctable abuses or on attainable capabilities that are as yet unrealized.

First, it is argued that educational tests tend to evaluate the more tangible, trivial, and easily measurable as opposed to such more significant outcomes of education as genuine understanding, originality, problem-solving ability, ability to think independently, ability to retrieve information, and ability to synthesize knowledge. This criticism, however, is warranted only in relation to the early standardized tests measuring rote retention of factual information. It must be remembered that objective tests are now available which measure both comprehension of general principles and ability to interpret and apply knowledge. Furthermore, many other kinds of measuring devices can be used to evaluate some of the more elusive outcomes of education. These include observation, self-reports, peer judgments, essay tests, oral examinations, work samples, practical examinations, research papers, and so on. It is true that valid measures of such important traits and abilities as cognitive style, creativity, flexibility, and problem sensitivity have yet to be devised. But there is no reason to believe that currently encountered difficulties in devising these measures will not eventually be overcome.

Second, it is frequently alleged that educational measures fail to test the attainment of objectives that are idiosyncratic to a particular school system, curriculum, institution, or teacher. Again this objection mistakenly regards the use of national standardized tests as coextensive with educational measurement. There is no incompatibility between using tests standardized on a broad, representative sample and tests prepared especially for a particular school system, school, curriculum, or classroom. Where advisable both kinds of measures can and should be used.

Third, test scores and school marks often become ends in themselves, displacing in importance and presumed validity the knowledge, competencies, and scholastic achievement they are intended to sample and represent. When this happens cognitive drive atrophies, pupils lose interest in subject matter as soon as their grades are recorded, and society places greater weight on a test score or on a diploma from a prestigious institution than on intrinsically more valid long-term evidence of scholarship and fitness to practice a profession.

However, the tendency to regard test scores as ends in themselves and as more important than the knowledge they represent is much more a *reflection* of undesirable social attitudes about the real value of scholarship than a cause of such attitudes or an inevitable product of measurement and evaluation. Similarly, if teachers are guided in their choice of subject-matter content solely by the desire to prepare students for the standardized test, and even go to the extent of coaching them on type questions, it is more rational to blame the existing values of parents, educators, and school boards than to blame the tests themselves. It makes more sense, in our opinion, to prevent such abuses by increasing the level of public enlightenment about the relevant issues involved in intelligent use than by abolishing or outlawing the practice in question.

Fourth, advocates of child-centered teaching and client-oriented counseling insist that genuine learning, independent thinking, and creativity are possible only in a "non-evaluative" classroom atmosphere. They assert, furthermore, that evaluation induces tension, anxiety, excessive competitiveness, and overemphasis on extrinsic motivation. In our opinion, this position greatly overstates the case. It is true that unintelligent and authoritarian use of evaluative techniques may encourage uncritical acceptance of ideas, suppress originality, and generate undesirable levels of anxiety, competitiveness, and interpersonal tension. Nevertheless, a reasonable degree of evaluation is still absolutely essential, not only for monitoring and motivating learning but also for setting necessary and desirable standards of critical and original thinking. In a completely non-evaluative setting, creative effort is dissipated in amorphous, undirected, and undisciplined output. Freedom from anxiety is also an unrealistic goal since *no* significant or creative achievement is possible without *some* degree of anxiety; the very act of aspiring to master a body of knowledge or to create something original raises the possibility of failure and depression of self-esteem, and hence is anxiety-producing by definition.

Fifth, evaluation has frequently been misused by teachers as a means of rewarding students for conformity and docility and of punishing them for nonconformity and independence of thought. In many schools and universities it is still employed as a weapon for controlling and intimidating students, for frightening and impressing them (as well as colleagues), and for making them feel inadequate, subservient, and deferential. It is these very same teachers who conceive of examinations as a contest in which students are to be outwitted and trapped into error. Needless to say, however, this crude abuse of evaluation hardly constitutes a valid argument for non-evaluative teaching.

Sixth, it can be claimed with some justification that good scores on achievement tests are presently beyond the reach of low-ability students. In a very real sense, then, the current use of grades based on relative standing in the class depresses their self-esteem and discourages them from putting forth their best efforts. Such detrimental effects, however, can be largely mitigated by concomitant evaluation in terms of their ability level or in terms of progress from initial levels of performance.[2] These two different bases of evaluation are by no means mutually exclusive. We need to know how well students are progressing *both* in terms of their own potentialities *and* in terms of group norms. Furthermore, the negative impact of informing students that they are inferior to their peers in ability and achievement has undoubtedly been exaggerated. Realistic awareness of our relative intellectual status among our peers is a fact of life to which all of us must eventually adjust— and the sooner the better for everyone concerned. There is no profit either in sugar-coating the truth or in self-delusion.

Finally, measurement and evaluation often fail to facilitate learning or teaching because they provide no meaningful feedback. This is particularly true when only final examinations are given and when only composite scores are reported to students without comment, explanation, specification of component strengths and weaknesses, or opportunity for identifying and correcting errors. Such examinations encourage cramming, provide an unrepresentative picture of student achievement, and abet "book slamming" as soon as the grades are in. Any defensible program of evaluation therefore relies on periodic and frequent testing—before, during, and at the end of instruction; uses several kinds of measures; reports scores in differential rather than composite terms; and stresses the feedback and diagnostic function of tests.

REQUIREMENTS OF AN EFFECTIVE TEST

Tests used for evaluation purposes are classified in many ways. An *objective* test is one in which the questions have specifiable,

---

[2]An alternate approach utilizing "mastery" units was previously discussed as a promising means of allowing every child to make good grades, while moving forward at a pace commensurate with his abilities.

"correct" answers which can be set down in advance and agreed to by all competent markers. In such a test, in other words, nothing is left to the judgment of the marker. In an *essay* test, on the other hand, some part of the total mark is usually awarded for style, lucidity of presentation, esthetic appeal of the product, and other factors which do depend upon the personal judgment of the marker.

Another distinction is made between *standardized* and *teacher-made* tests. In the former, considerable care is taken in the selection and rejection of items to insure adequate performance on statistical criteria, specific instructions are laid down for administration of the test, and norms for student performance (based upon widespread testing over some defined student population) are provided. Obviously such tests require considerable preparation and will normally apply to broad areas of achievement (for example, American history) rather than to a specific course taught in a particular school. Teacher-made tests, on the other hand, are designed to measure the specific outcomes of a particular course taught in a particular year to a particular class. Whatever the classification of the test, however, it should be valid, reliable, representative, and feasible, and should also discriminate adequately between individuals and groups of individuals tested.

Validity

The validity of a test refers to the extent to which it measures what it purports to measure. The question of validity is always relative to the stated objectives of a test. A test that is valid for one purpose (for example, to "screen out" gross personality deviates) is not necessarily valid for another (for example, to make precise assessments of personality status, to make a specific diagnosis of behavior disorder, or to make predictions of individual outcomes).

The problem of validity arises in the first place because psychological and educational measures tend to be indirect and inferential rather than based on direct behavioral samples of the trait or ability in question. An achievement test, for example, merely *assumes* that ability to answer correctly a particular set of subject-matter items is really reflective of degree of mastery of a designated discipline or subdiscipline; unfortunately, there is no more direct way of measuring knowledge. If, on the other hand, we endeavor to measure the trait of academic honesty by assessing behavior in controlled situations in which cheating on examinations can be detected unbeknown to and unsuspected by the subjects (Canning, 1956; Hartshorne and May, 1928), the question of test validity is irrelevant; the only relevant question in these circumstances is that of reliability, that is, will equivalent degrees of academic honesty be exhibited in a later time sample of the same situation, in different but comparable samples of the same situation, or in related but different situations?

The more indirectly and inferentially a test score is related to the trait or ability it purports to measure, the more important the issue of validity becomes. Thus, although an achievement test score is admittedly not coextensive with degree of mastery of a discipline, it involves much less indirectness and inference, for example, than does an intelligence test score. In the latter situation, the trait itself is much more of a hypothetical and debatable construct, the tests used to measure it are much less homogeneous and much less self-evidently related to the trait, and there is a much greater presumption of the predictive value of the test score (that is, of the constancy of the trait over age).

Several different types of validity have been delineated. A good test is characterized by at least one, and hopefully by more than one, of these types. *Content* validity is a form of face validity that is invoked for many psychological and educational tests. An achievement test, for example, may be claimed as valid "on the face of things" if it contains an adequate and representative sample of items—both in terms of the particular subject-matter knowledge it purports to measure and the kinds of competencies or understandings that purportedly reflect such knowledge.

Concurrent validity is present when test scores correlate reasonably well with some *contemporaneous* criterion of behavior, preferably ratings based on direct observation. Typically the question of concurrent validity arises when some short-cut method of assessment is devised to replace a more exhaustive and time-consuming measure. The difficulty in these instances is one of finding an appropriate criterion that is itself relevant, reliable, and valid. School grades, for example, are a commonly used criterion for determining the validity of academic aptitude tests despite the fact that the former are usually less reliable and less valid than the tests themselves, and are also influenced by such extraneous factors as the motivation, deportment, docility, and conformity of students and the personal social-class biases of teachers. Before any evidence of concurrent validity is applicable, it is also necessary to demonstrate that one's population is comparable in all relevant respects to the sample on which the instrument was originally validated.

When the criterion behavior to which test scores are related is some *future* measure of performance, we deal with *predictive* validity. If scholastic aptitude scores, for example, correlate reasonably well with later school grades or academic achievement scores, the aptitude test may be said to exhibit predictive validity. The problem of finding a suitable criterion still remains. A test measuring aptitude for medicine may yield scores that correlate satisfactorily with grades earned in medical school, but to what extent are these scores related to success in the practice of medicine? Not only is it very difficult to measure professional success in medicine, but there are also many different criteria of success, varying for the most part with the individual's particular career choice (for example, general practice, specialty practice, research, teaching, writing, public health, hospital administration).

A final type of validity that is often invoked when the other three evidences of validity cannot be demonstrated—either "because the universe of content cannot be adequately specified" or because of the absence of a suitable criterion—is known as *construct* validity. This is based on logical or defensible inferences from experimental or other evidence. In the case of an achievement test, the failure of a totally naive student population to obtain better than chance scores on an achievement test would provide one form of such evidence. Other kinds of relevant evidence would include improvement in mean test scores from one grade level to another in such hierarchically ordered competencies as reading and mathematics, and a strong positive relationship between aptitude and achievement at each grade level.

Validity in Achievement Testing From the standpoint of meaningful verbal learning, a truly valid test of subject-matter achievement must measure whether mastery of a designated body of knowledge is sufficiently stable, clear, and well-organized to reflect the structure of ideas in a given discipline, to make long-term retention possible, and to serve as a foundation for further learning in the same discipline. Because a short retention interval cannot adequately test the organizational strength and viability of a body of knowledge, conventional retention tests—covering previously studied materials and administered at the end of a given course of instruction—are not truly reflective of the later availability of this material for new learning. They fail to distinguish adequately between the student who merely understands and retains material well enough at the moment of testing to answer rote and meaningful questions correctly, and the student whose understanding and retention are sufficiently stable on a long-term basis to serve as a springboard for learning new, sequentially related material. Both individuals may make identical scores on immediate tests of retention. Problem-solving or application items provide a partial solution to this difficulty since they are less influenced by rote memory, and also directly test ability to use and apply retained knowledge. But since successful problem solving also depends on many *other* traits (for example, venturesomeness, flexibility, perseverance, problem sensitivity) that are unrelated to the functional availability of knowledge, success or failure on such items is as much a reflection of the influence of these latter traits as of the availability of usable knowledge.

Three other solutions to this problem of achievement test validity are available, none of which is mutually preclusive of the others or of the use of problem-solving items. First, the optimum programming approach, which implies testing, feedback, and consolidation after *each* unit (for example, topic, chapter) of subject-matter material, provides safeguards for the true stability and clarity of knowledge and insures against the dangers of cramming and rote learning. If students are given such weekly tests, quarterly and final examinations serve more of a review function and become truly valid measures of subject-matter mastery. Second, comprehensive tests of achievement that are given six months to several years after the completion of a course also measure the functional retention of genuine knowledge as well as discourage the "book-slamming" phenomenon. Such delayed tests, however, obviously become measures of cramming ability unless they are preceded by weekly, quarterly, and final examinations.

Finally, perhaps the most valid way of testing the organizational strength and viability of knowledge is not to test retention per se, or to use problem-solving items, but to measure retention in the context of sequential learning, that is, in situations where ability to learn new material presupposes the availability of the old. The "transfer retention" test (Ausubel and Fitzgerald, 1962) constitutes a new approach to the problem of measuring functional retention. It attempts to do this by measuring the extent to which retained knowledge of subject matter is sufficiently stable and well-organized to be available as a foundation for new learning of sequentially dependent material that could not be efficiently learned in the absence of such availability. At the same time, of course, it also provides a measure of knowledge available for problem solving, because if retained knowledge is available for new sequential learning, it is reasonable to assume that it is also available for problem solving.

The transfer retention test may be administered in addition to, or independently of, the conventional retention test. When used for routine course examinations, the test procedure requires that students study an unfamiliar new learning passage that is sequentially related to and presupposes knowledge of the previously studied material on which they are being examined. Their scores on a test of this *new* material are "transfer retention scores" and measure the functional availability of the previously learned material for new learning.

Turning to another matter, achievement tests tend to lose validity if they contain items that presuppose knowledge of materials that are not ordinarily included in the scope of the discipline or subdiscipline which they are designed to measure. Many teachers, for example, believe that they can discriminate more adequately between bright and average students if they use such questions. Actually the reverse is true because these items either cannot be answered correctly by any students or else measure knowledge of some other field of study. A good examination should emulate a good detective story: The solution of problems should not depend on information that is unavailable to students or that they are not expected to learn.

The validity of an achievement test depends in part on how well it tests the actual competencies that are demanded of an individual in those real life performances for which he is being trained or educated. This is the issue of concurrent or predictive validity. For example, a multiple-choice examination on "rules of the road" may exhibit good content validity, but obviously has less concurrent and predictive validity in relation to current or ultimate driving performance than an appropriate road test. Similarly, patients do not enter a hospital tagged with alternatives of probable diagnosis, indicated diagnostic procedures, and rational therapeutic measures from which the physician makes the most appropriate choice. He is not only obliged to *spontaneously* generate relevant diagnostic hypotheses, perform relevant tests, eliminate all diagnostic possibilities other than the one he designates as most probable, and prescribe appropriate treatment, but in most instances he must also elicit the pertinent facts of clinical history, obtain significant data from observation and physical examination, and interpret the results of diagnostic tests. It is apparent, therefore, that multiple-choice tests, valuable as they are, cannot possibly serve as complete substitutes for open-ended and practical examinations in the measurement of clinical competence in medicine.

Reliability

Any measuring instrument, if it is to be used with confidence, must exhibit a satisfactory degree of consistency or reliability. That is, it must yield self-consistent scores. If a clinical thermometer on three successive determinations, for example, yielded readings of 97°, 103°, and 99.6° for the same patient, it would not be considered very reliable. Reliability, of course, is a necessary but not a sufficient condition for using a test. A highly reliable test may be totally invalid or may not measure anything that is psychologically or educationally significant. The reliability of a single test score may be expressed quantitatively in terms of the instrument's *standard error of measurement*. If the standard error of measurement, for example, is 2.5, we can say that there are approximately two chances in three (more precisely, 68 in 100) that the "true" score falls between 72.5 and 77.5 when the obtained score is 75.[3] By definition, highly unreliable tests cannot possibly be valid. The necessary degree of reliability, however, depends on the use that is made of test scores. If they are used for purposes of individual assessment and guidance, a much higher degree of reliability is obviously necessary than if they are used for gross screening or research purposes.

Three types of coefficients are used to express the reliability of most psychological and educational tests. The coefficient of *equivalence* is the correlation coefficient that results when scores derived from comparable sets of items are correlated. This can be determined from "equivalent" (parallel)

---

[3]A "true" score for any individual is defined as the mean of a large number of scores earned by that individual on the same test or on parallel forms of the test. In practice it is not actually determined but rather its position is estimated. The reader should note the difference between the *standard error of estimate* and the *standard error of measurement*. While both refer to the reliability of the test, the first measure enables us to determine with what degree of assurance we can predict an individual's score on form B of a test when we know his score on form A, while the second tells us how adequately the score obtained on form A represents the "true" score.

forms of the same test or, if only one form exists, by correlating scores derived from one randomly drawn half of the test (for example, odd items) with scores derived from the other half of the test (even items). The latter coefficient of reliability is known as "split-half reliability"; it also reflects, of course, internal consistency or generality over items, and is, therefore, often referred to as a "coefficient of internal consistency." It represents a measure of reliability in terms of the equivalence between two halves of a homogeneous test. Thus, it is primarily used when a parallel form of the test is not available for determining the degree of equivalence between two different sets of items purportedly measuring the same ability or behavior. Since the split-half coefficient of realibility is obtained by correlating only half of the total number of available items in the instrument against the other half, it furnishes an underestimate of the instrument's actual coefficient of equivalence. Thus to estimate the reliability of the full-length instrument, a correction formula (Spearman-Brown) is frequently applied. Various mathematical formulas (for example, Kuder-Richardson Formulas 20 and 21) have also been devised for arriving at a more generalized estimate of generality over, or intercorrelation among, homogeneous test items.[4]

The coefficient of *stability*, on the other hand, measures consistency over time or short-term constancy of a trait when the same set of items is used. It is determined from successive administrations of the same test. Over short intervals of time the ability or trait being measured can be regarded as not undergoing significant change. Over longer intervals, however, a loss of stability is more reflective of developmental changes in the nature of a trait or of inconstancy in rate of growth than test unreliability.

The coefficient of *generality,* finally, reflects the self-consistency of a test when it is composed of heterogeneous but unrelated measures of the same trait. Tests of intelligence and of creativity, for example, typically consist of a battery of subtests, each of which measures a different facet of the trait in question. When the scores on these subtests are intercorrelated, the average intercorrelation may be taken as the coefficient of generality. Unless this coefficient is reasonably high, it is obviously unwarranted to regard the various subtests as measuring anything in common.

The length of a test is the most important single factor influencing its reliability. Obviously, the shorter a test is the more likely it is that test scores will be influenced by chance sampling or situational factors. Failure to allow sufficient time for most students to complete a test has the same effect on reliability as reducing the number of items. The reliability of a test is also decreased by inaccurate or subjective scoring and by the presence of items that lack discriminating power. Lastly, inadequate or fluctuating motivation

---

[4]See any of the texts on testing, measurement, and evaluation listed at the end of the chapter.

may impair test reliability. The inference that a test score actually measures true ability rather than mere performance on a single occasion presupposes that the subject is trying his best.

Representativeness

Almost all psychological and educational measures are based on the principle of sampling. Since it is virtually impossible, for example, to test a subject for mastery of *all* the facts, concepts, and principles in a given course of study, we typically select a sample of such content as a basis for assessing the universe from which the sample is drawn. For this procedure to be logically defensible, at least two important conditions must be met: (1) the sample must be adequately representative of the universe, and (2) within the constraints imposed by the requirements of representativeness and significance, the sample must be randomly drawn. The reasons for these conditions are rather self-evident: if, for example, all of the examination items test knowledge of only one chapter of an assigned textbook, or if the items on each chapter cover only a restricted segment of its content, the resulting achievement test score can hardly be claimed to measure knowledge of the textbook in question. Not only would such an achievement test lack content validity, but it also would inevitably (and on a purely chance basis) overestimate the knowledge of some students and underestimate the knowlege of others. Nevertheless many achievement tests, particularly those that are teacher-made, do not meet these two conditions, representativeness and randomness.

Two other unfortunate practices commonly result from failure to appreciate the nature of a test as a representative sample. Teachers who give "hints" about examination questions or who repeat the same questions year after year obviously render untenable the inference that scores on such an examination are actually representative of the students' knowledge. An even more serious error is committed by individuals who regard test scores, based on a representative sample of items that are inferentially related to a given trait or ability, as more valid measures of the trait or ability in question than is direct behavioral evidence over a period of years. This situation arises when test scores, degrees, or licenses are regarded as status symbols rather than as fallible sample and inferential measures of competence. The IQ and the M.D. are two such measures that have achieved almost magical or sacred status in our culture.

Total evaluation is feasible for certain aspects of competence or achievement and can be used concurrently with a sampling approach. A teacher, for example, may wish to evaluate all of his students' homework assignments, laboratory reports, histology drawings, woodshop products, or clinical performances. All other factors being equal such measurement not only exhibits a high degree of validity and reliability, but also tends to motivate students consistently to put forth their best efforts and to generate a high degree of responsibility and accountability for performance.

Discriminating Power

An obvious attribute of an effective test is ability to distinguish maximally between individuals who vary with respect to the trait or competence being measured. In large part, of course, this attribute depends on the discriminating power of the component items and accounts for, as well as reflects, the reliability and validity of the instrument. To some extent, however, it depends on the *distribution* of the total scores and on whether the test provides adequate *ceiling* for superior persons in the group. A *normal* distribution of scores, for example, provides maximum discrimination at both ends of the scale (where there are few scores spread out thinly) and less discrimination at the middle part of the scale (where many scores are bunched together); whereas a *rectangular* distribution of scores (that is, an equal number of scores at all points on the scale) provides equal discrimination over the entire range. A *skewed* distribution (where a disproportionate number of scores pile up at one end of the scale) on the other hand, is most discriminating at the end where there are few scores and least discriminating at the opposite end.

An effective test must also have sufficient ceiling to permit the superior individuals in a group to stand out as such. Obviously, if an achievement test is easy enough for the average person in the group to achieve a score of 90 percent, it is virtually impossible to distinguish between more and less knowledgeable students. Maximum discriminability generally prevails when the average score is approximately 50 percent. Adequate ceiling, however, should be provided by including a wide range of items carefully graded in difficulty, rather than depending on a criterion of speed, since the ability to answer questions rapidly also reflects factors basically unrelated to superior competence or aptitude. Difficulty level can be manipulated by varying such factors as abstractness, complexity, familiarity, and degree of understanding required (mere comprehension versus application, interpretation, inference, analysis, or synthesis).

Feasibility

In addition to such theoretical considerations as validity, reliability, representativeness, and discriminating power, various practical matters must be taken into account before one can decide whether a proposed test is feasible. First, how significant is the information it yields, that is, how useful is it in interpreting the pupils' abilities, knowledge, and personality traits and in making educational and vocational decisions? Trivial test data are worthless irrespective of how reliable, valid, or discriminating they may be. A feasible achievement test, for example, should provide differential feedback to both students and teachers about relative strengths and weaknesses in learning and teaching, as well as suggest reasons for these. Otherwise it is useless for diagnostic and remedial purposes. Second, a feasible test should be suitable in form and content for the age range of students for which it is intended. A third practical consideration is the cost of a test and the amount of time required to administer, score, and interpret it. Fourth, how objective is the scoring and how straightforward is the interpretation of the results? Is special training required to score and interpret the test? Does the test manual provide directions for administration and scoring, a table of norms, and guidance for interpreting scores?

THE OBJECTIVE TEST

Objective tests, although difficult and time-consuming to construct, owe their great popularity in education to several factors. First and foremost, perhaps, is the fact that subjectivity and variability in scoring are eliminated. Precise and invariable criteria for scoring—typically a scoring key designating the correct answers—are available in advance. Second, the items are carefully and systematically selected so as to constitute a representative sample of the content to be covered and of the competencies to be evaluated. This implies precise advance specification of educational objectives—both in terms of the particular facts, concepts, principles, and applications which the student is expected to master, and of the ways in which such mastery is supposed to be exhibited. Since the totality of desirable knowledge in a given area obviously cannot be tested, great care must be taken to secure a representative sample of significant (nontrivial) items that is both adequately comprehensive and places the desired relative weight on component topics. Herein lies the other great advantage of objective tests: The brevity of each item and the speed with which it can be answered permits a more comprehensive and systematic sampling of knowledge than is possible by any other means.

An additional advantage in the objective format is the possibility of refining the items, after initial use, for clarity and discriminability and of thus increasing test reliability and validity. Self-evidently, items that are answered correctly by all or most students are too easy to have discriminating power; for opposite reasons the same conclusion applies to items that are answered incorrectly by all or most students. Further, a good item is obviously one that is answered correctly more frequently by the more knowledgeable students, and answered incorrectly more often by the less knowledgeable than by the more knowledgeable students. Items that fail to meet these criteria are either deleted, rewritten less ambiguously, or replaced by other items.

Analysis of the relative frequency with which wrong alternatives are chosen in the multiple-choice format may also reveal either ambiguities in wording or the existence of a prevalent preconception or misconception.[5] If the latter is the case, the item serves a useful diagnostic function and should not be altered. In fact, a multiple-choice item should be deliberately written so as to contain at least one wrong alternative that reflects a common bit of misinformation or a misconception. The adequacy of learning and teaching can then be evaluated just as validly by the good students' greater avoidance of such "plausible but wrong" alternatives as by their greater tendency to choose the correct alternative. On the other hand, if good students choose a particular wrong alternative more frequently than poor students, there are grounds for believing that the item in question is misleading or ambiguous.

Objective tests may be either informal (teacher-made) or standardized (usually produced commercially). Standardized objective achievement tests set out explicitly the conditions of administration, that is, the instructions, the time limit, the allowable help, the permissibility of making calculations or of marking the alternatives, and so on, thereby insuring comparability of scores. Finally, most published standardized tests provide the user with a table of norms based on a large and representative sample. This makes possible the conversion of raw scores into percentile scores or grade equivalents.

Criticisms

In recent years, objective tests have been subjected to vigorous criticism (Black, 1963; M. L. Gross, 1962; B. Hoffmann, 1962), some warranted but much based on misunderstanding of their nature, functions, and inherent limitations. First, despite considerable improvement in this respect over the past decade, many objective tests still measure rote recognition of relatively trivial and disconnected items of knowledge rather than genuine comprehension of broad concepts, principles, and relationships, and ability to interpret facts and apply knowledge.

---

[5]Although objective questions may allow constructed response (for example "8 × 6 = ——" or "What is the product of 8 and 6?"), the increasing availability of test-scoring devices in recent years has been paralleled by a strong shift toward the multiple-choice format, in which the student merely checks the appropriate answer. Not only does such a format allow a rapid mechanical marking, thus saving the teacher hours of labor of questionable value, but following tabulation a number of important statistics can be calculated by the computer—for example, the reliability of the test, the discriminability of each item, the means and spread of test scores, and so on. Although the ability to *recognize* a correct alternative (in the multiple-choice format) does not necessarily imply ability to *recall* it (in the constructed response format), the correlation between the two abilities tends to be reasonably good (Plumlee, 1947; R. W. Tyler, 1934a).

Second, because of unskillful construction of test items, the correct answer is sometimes identifiable by means of unintentional hints, for example, the self-evident implausibility of the wrong alternatives, the use of such words as "always." Both of these deficiencies are easily correctable by using greater care in item construction, by selecting more significant test items, by stressing items that require understanding, thought and insight, by including application and problem-solving items, and by placing greater reliance on delayed retention and transfer retention scores. The multiple-choice format minimizes the role of guessing. It should be noted at this point that unskillfully constructed essay tests and problem-solving tests may also place a premium on regurgitation of rotely memorized knowledge and on rote application of "type problem" solutions.

Third, the correct answer in multiple-choice tests may sometimes be either arbitrary or depend on abstruse hairsplitting. In some instances it may also favor the less knowledgeable or more shallow thinker and penalize the more sophisticated student who takes into account more subtle and penetrating considerations.

Fourth, the great emphasis on time pressure tends to favor the glib, confident, impulsive, and test-wise student, and to handicap the student who either is inclined to be cautious, thoughtful and self-critical, or is unsophisticated about testing. Ideally, a valid test of either scholastic aptitude or academic achievement places greater weight on power than on speed (Yates, 1961); discriminating ability is attained by providing a wide and carefully graded range of difficulty, with ample time for most students to complete the test, rather than by including twice as many items as the average student has time to answer. In our opinion, the current emphasis on speed in most standardized tests of achievement detracts from their validity by placing a premium on factors that are intrinsically unrelated to genuine mastery of subject matter.

Lastly, the limitations of standardized testing must always be borne in mind. For example, multiple-choice tests cannot measure students' ability to spontaneously generate relevant hypotheses, to collect valid laboratory or clinical data, to design an original experiment, or to do creative work. Other kinds of measuring devices, however, are available to test the attainment of these objectives.

INTERPRETATION OF ACHIEVEMENT
TEST SCORES

In general there are three different ways of interpreting achievement test scores. The first method judges a student's performance against the standard of *his own* ability level as determined by his score on an aptitude test, a pretest, a prior achievement test, or an initial achievement test in the course. The second method assesses the adequacy of a student's performance in *relation* to that of his peers; it is necessary both for grouping, pacing, and the individualization of instruction, as well as for making important decisions about his educational and vocational future. As pointed out above, both kinds of assessment are essential and neither one precludes the other. Each of these approaches is concerned with a *relative* standard of performance, but in one case the individual serves as his own standard and in the other his performance is related to group norms.

In some instances, however, an *absolute* standard of performance is indicated which is quite independent of the performance of others or of the individual's relative standing in the group. This is the case, for example, where mastery of a given topic, subject, or skill is a prerequisite for more advanced learnings, and where a certain minimal level of competence is necessary before an individual can be entrusted with certain vocational roles such as life-saver on a beach, physician, pharmacist, secretary, railway engineer, or airplane pilot.

In using the norms of standardized tests, it is important to make sure that they are based on a sample that is both large enough to insure stability and adequately representative of the universe to which they purportedly pertain. The particular norms used must also be relevant in the sense that they are based on groups of individuals who are comparable to the individuals we are testing. For example, in interpreting the achievement test scores of a particular twelfth-grade group in an American high school, we would want to use the norms of American twelfth-graders generally, plus such other differential norms that apply to our group as sex, region, state, urban or rural area, public or private high school. For guidance purposes (for example, grouping, choice of courses, college application), it would be helpful to use the local school norms as well as the cut-off scores employed by various colleges in selecting candidates for admission.

OTHER METHODS OF EVALUATION AND MEASUREMENT

Because of limitations on the kinds of objectives that standardized short-answer tests can measure, other methods of evaluation and measurement are used concomitantly in most educational settings. Thoughtful teachers do not place excessive reliance on standardized objective tests.

Essay or Discussion Questions

Essay examinations, despite their many disadvantages, have a significant place in the evaluation program of a school. They are particularly useful (1) where *spontaneous* recall of information and spontaneous generation of hypotheses are important aspects of the competencies being measured (for example, formulation of diagnostic hypotheses, differential diagnosis), and (2) in less well-established areas of knowledge where there is no single "right answer." In addition, they test a student's ability to organize ideas and marshall evidence, to construct a cogent argument, to evaluate ideas critically, and to express himself clearly and convincingly. Essay-type questions also provide greater scope for original and independent thinking, and give some insight into the cognitive styles, problem sensitivities, and problem-solving strategies of students. On the whole, they are better suited than short-answer questions for measuring students' grasp of the structure of a discipline.

On the other hand, they are much less satisfactory than short-answer tests for measuring knowledge of established concepts, principles, and information in a given subject-matter field, particularly where there is no premium on ability to recall and transform ideas spontaneously. Since only a few questions can be asked on any examination, sampling of content is neither comprehensive nor representative, and scoring tends to be laborious and subjective; hence both reliability and validity are often unsatisfactory. Further, essay examinations encourage bluffing, circumlocution, padding, and discursiveness on the part of students, and tend disproportionately to reward those students who write neatly, excel in the mechanics of English composition (spelling, punctuation, diction, and style), and echo the views and biases of their teachers. Finally, the very ease of constructing essay examinations encourages a rather cavalier and slipshod attitude toward evaluation on the part of those who use them.

On the question of subjective marking, many years ago Falls gave a particular composition to a group of one hundred teachers of English, asking them to grade it on both percentage and grade-level scales. The result (Table 19.1) indicates the enormous variation that will occur when each grader operates with his own set of criteria and standards. Other studies have shown (Hulten, 1925; Childers, 1942) that when the same teacher marks essay questions on two successive occasions the variation in marks awarded to individual students is quite large. In addition, the proposition that the teacher's marking of essay questions is influenced by punctuation, grammatical, and spelling accuracy was recently demonstrated by Marshall (1967); in this study teachers were specifically to grade an historical essay on the adequacy of content alone, and they were apparently not aware that other criteria crept into their assessments.

Many of the aforementioned disadvantages can be mitigated, however, by following a few simple rules. By indicating explicitly the scope and dimensions of the expected answer, much of the ambiguity and vagueness of the global discussion question can be eliminated. As a matter of fact, short essay-type questions that are relatively limited and specific in scope may

TABLE 19.1

THE ESTIMATED GRADE-VALUE AND PERCENTAGE MARKS ASSIGNED TO AN ENGLISH COMPOSITION BY ONE HUNDRED TEACHERS

| | PERCENTAGE MARK | | | | | | | | |
GRADE VALUE	60–64	65–69	70–74	75–79	80–84	85–89	90–94	95–99	*Total*
XV								2	2
XIV									0
XIII							1	2	3
XII					1		2	3	6
XI			2			6	5	2	15
X			1	3	8	4	7	1	24
IX	1		1	1	8	4	4	3	22
VIII			2	2	2	3	4	3	16
VII				2	2	2	1		7
VI	1				1	1		1	4
V	1								1
Total	3		6	8	22	20	24	17	100

Source: Falls, 1928.

exhibit considerable reliability and validity, but by the same token they may also fail to test some of the distinctive competencies that the essay examination is designed to measure. This format, however, is particularly appropriate for problem-solving exercises in such applied fields as medicine, where problems of differential diagnosis, the search for additional needed information, the interpretation of data, and proposed remedies can center on each of several short case presentations. To minimize the strong chance factor in the particular questions that are selected in an essay examination, students may be given some degree of choice in questions.

It is also possible to reduce the subjectivity of scoring by using several readers and by establishing such separate explicit criteria for grading as content, organization, logic, cogency, clarity, and fluency of expression. Halo effect can be minimized by coding students' papers and by scoring, in turn, each question for all students instead of completely grading each student's paper before turning to the next paper. Moreover, where quality of expression rather than substantive content is a major criterion (for example, in English essays) it has been found helpful to provide the marker with a sequence of essays on the same topic illustrating gradations in quality.

Oral examinations typically enjoy the same advantages and disadvantages of the essay examination but, in addition, enable the examiner to probe more deeply when unsure of the student's knowledge or meaning and to cut short irrelevant and discursive answers. In this sense they discourage bluffing. On the other hand, they appear to evoke much more disruptive anxiety than do written examinations and to favor the glib and socially poised individual.

Work Samples

In most areas of education, but particularly in vocational, professional, artistic, and physical training, it is possible to assess the extent to which the objectives of education are actually being attained by directly appraising a performance or work product which clearly reflects the competence being taught. Such work samples include laboratory skills, clinical performance, drawings, themes, research reports, gymnastic or musical performance, the use of tools, art or shop products, typing and stenographic performance, and so on. They constitute much more direct and valid criteria of the competences involved than do short-answer or discussion examinations which can only inferentially measure the same competences. It is obviously much more important to know, for example, how well a student physician can interview, examine, diagnose, and prescribe for an actual patient than how well he can answer questions about the theory and practice of medicine. Such examinations also make possible direct assessments of such traits as flexibility, resourcefulness, perseverance, and creativity. Hence their value largely depends on the extent to which they are able realistically to simulate "real life" conditions of performance.

The most serious disadvantages of these examinations are that they are time-consuming, expensive, and difficult to construct in many areas. It is also difficult to assure breadth and equivalence of sampling. If hospital cases, for example, are used as test material for students in clinical medicine, how adequately can a single case measure a student's ability, and how does one equate cases for difficulty? This argues for the desirability of appraising *all* of a student's work products in a given course of study, for example, all of his laboratory drawings or clinical performances, or of using standardized (for example, televised) case presentations that are uniform for all students.

Scoring presents still another difficulty and is no more reliable and valid than the observational and rating techniques on which it is based. These techniques can be materially improved if the dimensions on or criteria by which the performance is to be judged are specified in advance, if discriminably different points on a rating scale can be both described and quantified, if the ratings of several trained judges are averaged, and if ratings are made concurrently rather than retrospectively. Proper training of the judges includes discussion of the nature of the trait or competence to be rated, making a trial run on ratings, comparing ratings, and deciding how ratings are to be distributed over the scale. Final ratings, of course, are made independently. Halo effect can be minimized by having the rater judge each item on the scale for the entire group before proceeding to the next item.

IMPROVING CLASSROOM EVALUATION AND REPORTING

Any substantial acquaintance with the evaluation procedures used in today's classrooms forces us to admit that the practice of this science is in a pretty crude state. Perhaps cause could be attributed to the fact that many teachers have had little formal training in this area. Thus unprepared, they are easily mesmerized by the apparent (but illusory) accuracy of numerical data resulting from their tests and examinations, while at the same time failing to adequately conceptualize the evaluative process and to design questions which are both comprehensive and reliable. What results is too often only a very partial grasp and utilization of the evaluative data potentially available to the teacher. In this section we look at some specific faults and offer suggestions for improvement.

Using Standardized Tests

Except for reversals here and there, the general trend in today's schools is toward increasingly comprehensive testing programs which make considerable use of standardized tests which have published norms. Aside from reading readiness tests, which are almost universally employed and accepted, teachers too often view these tests as having only nuisance value, and the results as being of interest only to the administrator or guidance counselor. It is a fair guess that a great many teachers could not indicate which tests are given in their schools; needless to say, such teachers make no great use of the results.

However, the standardized test—in addition to its usefulness as an indicator of readiness—can provide educators with a number of external checks on their own evaluations. For example, if children have been receiving arithmetic instruction in a particular school for six years, and during that time have been subjected exclusively to teacher-made tests, the application of a standardized test at that point will allow the school to gauge the general adequacy of its assessment and progress of its students. If, for example, these grade 6 children were to score (on the test norms) at the grade 5 level, then one would want to inquire why this had happened.

Moreover, even though the standardized test is typically not designed to fit a particular text or course, the scores earned on it can be of use in this latter context. For example, since standardized spelling tests—designed for national use[6]—will not necessarily contain precisely the words taught in Miss Jones' fourth-grade class, she will have to construct her own achievement test which adequately samples the words she did teach. Nevertheless, if her test is a reliable and valid measure of the child's spelling ability, one would expect a high correlation between the scores earned on the two tests. A scattergram could be constructed in a very few minutes, yielding—with no further statistical analysis whatsoever—a visual picture of the degree of agreement and the areas of discrepancy. Miss Jones might find, for example, that her own test (confined explicitly to words taught) caused scores to bunch at the high end of the scale, thus failing to distinguish very clearly between good and poor spellers. In this case she might well wonder whether her test adequately measures spelling ability, or whether the better spellers were not wasting a good deal of time on words they already know.

Actually, even in the most extensive testing programs standardized achievement tests will only be available in most subjects at a few designated grade levels, and in some subject areas no standardized tests will be available at all. When an appropriate test is not available the teacher might construct a scattergram between her achievement scores (marks assigned) and MA. Generally speaking, one would again expect a positive relationship to exist and be plainly visible, and if it is not, appropriate questions should again be asked. For example, are the high mental age students doing as well relatively as one might expect? If not, does the test have an unnaturally low ceiling?

Improving Objective Tests

Teachers, in contrast to test constructors, are handicapped by lack of time to construct a good objective test and subject it to even the most elementary statistical checks. It is probably for this reason that teachers frequently resort to "off the top of the head" essay questions which, while they read intelligently, cannot stand up to scrutiny on grounds of reliability, validity, or practical utility. As the following paragraphs suggest, however, much can be done to make better use of objective tests.

Development of Item Bank It has often been recommended, and in this we concur, that the teacher should view the development of a good

---

[6] Such a test will probably have been constructed by administering a list of words of various spelling difficulty to representative samples of students from each grade level, and then determining an average achievement score for each grade (or each month within each grade). In subsequent usage, the child's raw score on the test is matched with an average grade score, thus yielding the grade level of his present achievement.

evaluative test as a long-term project and that he should build upon what he has done the year before, rather than approaching the setting of each new test on an *ad hoc* basis. In his first year the teacher may not have time to produce more than a dozen good items, but having ascertained that these items effectively separate adequate from inadequate performance, they should be retained for use in subsequent years. Early in his career the teacher will want to experiment with a variety of objective test item forms to find one congenial to his own style. The pooling or trading of items among teachers of the same subject is also clearly desirable.

Assessment of Reliability   An early prerequisite for all teachers should be to assess the reliability of their "home-made" tests. If results of studies conducted in the past are still applicable, this is likely to be a shocking though beneficial experience. Perhaps the simplest method is to calculate the "split-half" coefficient and convert it into a total test reliability score. For one unacquainted with the technique—and operating by "cookbook" methods outlined in elementary statistical texts—this might require as much as an hour of labor, but it will be an hour well spent.

To be of full benefit the results of such a calculation should be applied to individual students. Suppose, for example, that a student earns 55 on a test in which the "passing mark" is set at 60; suppose further that the computed "standard error of measurement" is 10. This means that—although one's first inclination is to fail the student—there is actually one chance in six that his "true" score is *above 65,* and about three chances in ten that his "true" score *exceeds 60.* In this event one might want to reconsider or seek additional evidence.

Testing Higher Level Behaviors   In our opinion too many classroom tests still give undue emphasis to items which can be answered on the basis of rote learning. Many teachers are fascinated by sheer knowledge, irrespective of whether or not it represents genuine understanding. Moreover, we have previously observed that even in the "new curricula," problem-solving abilities—one of the professed objectives—seem either neglected or underdeveloped.

It seems clear that a conceptualized hierarchy of behaviors, coupled with some understanding of the processes underlying them, will facilitate the teacher's attempts to construct appropriate items. Specific suggestions for test items have been included in Chapter 2 and in various other places throughout the text. An adequate test of comprehension, for example, requires that the student do more than recite generalizations. Thus he might be asked to select one of several possible rewordings of the generalization, to express the generalization in his own words, to provide an illustration, to identify it in a novel context,[7] or to use it as the basis of new learning (transfer retention test). Other tests, which go beyond mere comprehension, include the use of generalizations in simple applications and problem solving.

Emphasis on Speed We noted earlier that school tests seem more highly speeded than they should be. In the early grades speeded tests are probably useful and justifiable as criteria of achievement in skill areas (reading, arithmetic) where high speed in performing elementary operations seems necessary to the effective utilization of these skills. However, in secondary school and beyond, tests should reflect the much lesser emphasis on speed (and much greater emphasis on power) found in effective adult intellectual performance. Even in the elementary school, some balance between speed and power should be introduced at the first possible opportunity.

Improving Essay Tests

Perhaps the major improvement in respect to essay tests will come with the gradual reduction in their use. At the present time the essay format is often used to obtain information which could be more economically acquired by multiple-choice or short-answer items. Unless the question requires something beyond recall of factual knowledge (for example, describe the five properties of an alloy), it does not really qualify as an essay item even though the student is required to write his answers in sentence or paragraph form.

As indicated earlier, improvement in reliability can be expected if the criteria are clearly delineated and relative emphasis decided in advance of the marking session. Teachers would also profit from examining the results of recent attempts to partially standardize essay questions. Perhaps the best known examples are the so-called Sequential Tests of Educational Progress, which provide examples scored on a dimension of increasing merit.

In his early teaching years the classroom teacher should experiment with a variety of short essay forms for various purposes and should attempt to determine the degree to which the behaviors tested are actually unique to the essay form. If a high correlation obtains between scores on essay tests

---

[7]Much can be learned from Piaget's experiments (for example, the conservation of substance) concerning ways of testing the stability of concepts. In a standard conservation test one can determine whether a child's concept of weight is sufficiently mature that he will conserve the equality of weights when objects are transformed (that is, perceptual conflict introduced). Rotation, translation, or distortion of exemplars from "standard position" provides a good test for many mathematical and scientific concepts.

and scores on objective tests carefully designed to elicit the individual's organization of knowledge, then one must ask what new information the essay test provides. In addition, one can often gauge the individual's ability to organize and marshal ideas by asking for an outline rather than a full treatment of a topic.

Reporting to Parents

The results of an evaluation of the student's progress is of interest to both parents and students. And yet the common vehicle for conveying such information, the report card, is so frequently unintelligible that it has become the object of much sarcasm and lampooning among educational commentators. Those who would abolish the report card in favor of parent-teacher interviews do not really solve the problem, for if the relevant information is not available and coherently organized, extensive verbal camouflage can do little more than confuse.

Actually there are no scientific principles which will allow one to declare in favor of one reporting practice over another, and all that one can hope to do is approach the problem with sufficient common sense that some of the most bizarre and idiosyncratic tendencies, in evidence both among classroom teachers and university professors, will disappear. For example, there is really no way to decide whether a letter grade is better or worse than a numerical mark. Present practice seems to favor letter grades in the primary grades, with a transition to numerical grades at the end of the elementary school and continuing through the high school. One cannot argue, however, that letter grades are therefore only appropriate to the elementary school, since many university undergraduate and graduate departments report only letter grades to students, with apparently adequate results.

Perhaps a major improvement in grading practices will occur when both teachers and professors come to recognize that marks or grades usually have no absolute value but in fact represent a comparison (or relative statement) against some norm. Hence it follows that an adequate communication of achievement should indicate both the *reference group* and the *child's position with respect to this group*. The parents of a grade 4 child may observe that this child has earned a *B* in spelling, and may read from the report card that *B* represents "above average achievement," but the question remains: above average with respect to what group? With the increase in nongraded programs, and the disappearance of a fixed grade reference group, confusion will only increase unless some ingenuity is brought to bear upon the problem. Certainly it should not prove impossible to specify in some intelligible manner the particular reference group to which the child's performance is being related, provided of course that the school is not trying to conceal the nature of its grouping practices from the parents.[8]

The handling of comments concerning the child's assessed aptitude presents certain difficulties. Clearly, an entry beside "arithmetic" to the effect that "Johnny is working up to his capacity" is not very informative, and the school should instead make an *independent* statement about achievement in each subject which satisfies the two criteria listed earlier. However, some overall statement concerning the child's progress vis-à-vis the school's estimate of his relative capacity is probably beneficial in developing realistic expectations. That is, given that Johnny is achieving average marks in a decelerated stream, and the school judges that his present work is commensurate with his capacity, the parent will then possess at least one view of his child's academic potential. When, however, as is frequently the case, reliable capacity estimates are not available, the school might be well advised to confine its remarks to actual achievement.

Teachers should also give thought to the ramifications of certain idiosyncratic marking tendencies. For example, some teachers apparently think it wise to begin the year by awarding relatively low marks, but escalate them progressively throughout the year, presumably to please parents with this spurious evidence of "growth and achievement." The satisfaction which this may give naive parents in the current year is probably more than offset the next year when the marks return to the low initial baseline. Finally, many elementary-school teachers tend to be inordinately generous with marks, apparently feeling that satisfactory performance warrants a mark in the vicinity of 100. One undesirable effect is that a test on which the average score is 95 (out of a possible 100) can hardly be thought to be discriminating at the upper levels of performance. Parents do not always understand the relative nature of grades, and a twenty-point drop in Johnny's average between elementary and secondary school—due entirely to different marking practices—may give rise to unnecessary concern.

TOPICS FOR DISCUSSION AND FURTHER STUDY

1.* In respect to an achievement test which is employed by your supervising teacher or constructed by yourself:

---

[8] We previously noted certain instances in which marks may be thought to be "absolute" in some sense, one of these being where "mastery" tests are employed. For example, the reading program of the first six traditional "grades" could be divided (in a nongraded program) into 25 reading "levels," and the child allowed to proceed to level $n + 1$ after he has "mastered" (earned a minimally acceptable score in a test on) level n. While the mastery of a given unit is thus an "absolute" (rather than a relative) accomplishment, an indirect judgment of relative progress is certainly warranted. Thus the fact that Mary has mastered level 12 should be compared, in a report to parents, to the expected "normal" progress through the sequence of levels.

(a) Compute the reliability;

(b) Determine the standard error of measurement;

(c) Determine the discrepancy between the individual's attained score and his "true" score at various levels of probability.

2. A grade 4 teacher administers a test in history. How can he determine its validity?

3.* Construct a number of multiple-choice and true-false items which attempt to measure behavior at the level of:

(a) Knowledge

(b) Comprehension

(c) Application

(d) Problem solving

Try them out on another prospective teacher and determine possible ambiguities and unintended "hints."

4. Explain in your own words and exemplify with numerical data why an average of raw achievement scores may not be a fair way of arriving at overall class standing. Recall that in some subject areas—for example, mathematics—marks may approach or equal 100; in other areas—for example, English—many teachers rarely award marks over 90.

5.* Examine an essay test administered by a classroom teacher. To what extent does it:

(a) Seek information which could be more adequately obtained by other means;

(b) Test abilities whose expression requires the essay format;

(c) Adequately sample relevant content?

6.* Examine the report card used in a nearby school district. Indicate whether it:

(a) Makes clear the nature of the reference group to which the child is being compared;

(b) Indicates the child's position relative to this group;

(c) Separates performance, effort and aptitude;

(d) Indicates the child's assessed aptitude;

(e) Provides other useful information.

In what ways would you improve upon this communication device?

7. In some schools and universities course marks are distributed from year to year according to the "normal curve" or, alternatively, a fixed percentage of A's, B's, and so on are awarded. What assumptions underlie such a practice? What arguments can be brought against it?

8. Suggest some steps which might be undertaken to standardize marking procedures within and between the elementary and secondary schools. What advantages would this have? What disadvantages?

9. Discuss the place of statements concerning the child's effort and capacity on the report card. In what form should the school's estimate of the child's capacity be divulged to parents and to the child himself? What differences would you advocate in the handling of statements regarding ability?

10. Examine and compare various practices in weighting term tests and final examination marks in arriving at a final course grade. Can any consensus be seen in present practice? Does such a consensus have a plausible rationale?

11.* Construct a number of essay questions appropriate to the age and grade level at which you will be teaching. Draw up a marking guide to indicate the relative weight to be placed on such factors as: substantive content, quality of expression, and accuracy of spelling, punctuation, and grammar. If possible, have two or three teachers use the guide to mark a composition written on one topic. Account for the differences in marks awarded. How can the marking guide be improved?

SUGGESTIONS FOR ADDITIONAL READING

Adams, G., and T. Torgenson. *Measurement and evaluation for the secondary school teacher.* New York: Holt, Rinehart and Winston, Inc., 1956.

Cronbach, L. J. *Essentials of psychological testing* (2d ed.). New York: Harper & Row, Publishers, 1960.

Davis, F. B. *Educational measurements and their interpretation.* Belmont, Calif.: Wadsworth Publishing Company, 1964.

Stanley, J. C. *Measurement in today's schools* (4th ed.). New York: John Wiley & Sons, Inc., 1964.

Thorndike, R. L., and E. Hagen. *Measurement and evaluation in psychology and education* (2d ed.). New York: John Wiley & Sons, Inc., 1961.

Torgenson, T., and G. Adams. *Measurement and evaluation for the elementary school teacher.* New York: Holt, Rinehart and Winston, Inc., 1954.

Tyler, L. E. *Tests and measurements.* Englewood Cliffs, N. J.: Prentice-Hall, Inc., 1963.

GLOSSARY

THIS GLOSSARY CONTAINS ONLY NEW PSYCHOLOGICAL TERMS proposed by the authors in this textbook and its predecessor, or generally accepted psychological terminology which has been used idiosyncratically.

abstract operational stage of cognitive development: that stage in which the individual is capable, *without the aid of concrete empirical props,* of acquiring secondary abstractions and of understanding, using, and meaningfully manipulating both secondary abstractions and the relations between them.

achievement motivation: the motivation to achieve. In school settings it is inclusive of cognitive, affiliative, and ego-enhancement drive.

affiliative drive: concern with achievement as a means of retaining the approval of the superordinate person or group from whom the individual obtains his derived status.

anchoring idea(s): an established relevant idea in cognitive structure to which new ideas are related and in relation to which their meanings are stored in the course of meaningful learning and retention.

anxiety: an actual response or a tendency to respond with fear to any current or anticipated situation which is perceived as a potential threat to self-esteem. In *normal* anxiety the threat is *objectively* dangerous and the fear response is proportionate to the objective degree of threat involved. In *neurotic* anxiety the principal source of the threat inheres in catastrophically impaired self-esteem itself, and the response appears to be disproportionate to the precipitating event.

applied science: a science, such as educational psychology, that is oriented toward practical ends that have social value.

asssimilation: the storing of a newly acquired meaning in linkage with the anchoring idea to which it is related in the course of learning, and its subsequent reduction or loss of dissociability.

603

background propositions: relevant ideas in cognitive structure that bear on a problem-solving task.

cognition: a generic term referring to such higher mental *processes* as representational learning, concept acquisition, propositional learning, meaningful problem solving, thinking, and so on; contrasted to *perception* which involves the generation of an *immediate* content of awareness from stimulus input.

cognitive drive: the desire to acquire knowledge as an end in itself, that is, task-oriented motivation in learning.

cognitive structure: the total content and organization of a given individual's ideas; or the content and organization of his ideas in a particular area of knowledge.

cognitive style: self-consistent and enduring individual differences in cognitive organization and functioning.

combinatorial learning: learning the meaning of a new concept or proposition that cannot be related to any *particular* relevant idea(s) in cognitive structure but can be related to a broad background of *generally* relevant content in cognitive structure.

concept acquisition or learning: learning the meaning of a concept, that is, learning the meaning of its criterial attributes; includes CONCEPT FORMATION and CONCEPT ASSIMILATION.

concept assimilation: the acquisition of new concept meanings through a process of reception learning; the learner is presented with the concept's criterial attributes by definition or context.

concept formation: the acquisition of new concept meanings by a semi-inductive process of discovering their criterial attributes from multiple particular exemplars of the concept.

concrete operational stage of cognitive development: that stage in which the child is capable, *with the aid of concrete empirical props,* of acquiring *secondary* abstractions and of understanding, using, and meaningfully manipulating both secondary abstractions and the relations between them.

connotative meaning: the attitudinal or affective reactions elicited by a concept name.

correlative subsumption: a type of subsumptive or subordinate learning in which the new ideas in the learning task are extensions, elaborations, modifications, or qualifications of an existing relevant idea in cognitive structure.

creative person: an individual possessing a rare and singular degree of originality or creativity in some field of human endeavor that sets him off *qualitatively* from most other persons in this regard.

creative abilities, general: a general constellation of supportive intellectual traits, personality variables, and problem-solving traits (for example, flexibility, problem sensitivity, divergent thinking ability, open-mindedness, venturesomeness, independence of judgment) that help implement the expression of creative potentialities.

creative behavior: an extreme form of problem solving which involves the application of knowldege to uniquely novel or remotely related problems in terms of the individual's own life history. It differs from (common) problem solving in that the individual must draw upon background knowledge which lies outside a defined (or taught) relevant set and must proceed to a solution without the aid of a well-defined strategy.

cultural deprivation or disadvantage: intellectually impoverished surroundings inducing retarded intellectual development and school achievement; found in those lower-class settings providing a paucity of patterned cognitive stimulation and characterized by attitudes of dependency, helplessness and marginality, depressed levels of aspiration, and alienation from the culture at large.

denotative meaning: the distinctive criterial attributes evoked by a concept name as distinguished from the correlated attitudinal or affective reactions it elicits (see CONNOTATIVE MEANING).

derivative subsumption: a type of subsumptive or subordinate learning in which the new ideas in the learning task are supportive or illustrative of an existing relevant idea in cognitive structure.

derived status: a vicarious form of status acquired through dependent identification with a superordinate figure or group.

development (educational): the process by which new educational programs or practices are created and their merit assessed. The first stage in development is *design,* an activity in which the new product is created through an amalgamation of theory, subject matter requirements, and practical wisdom. The second stage is *field testing,* in which the new package is tried on a sample of the anticipated users and the results assessed against stated objectives or conventional standards.

discovery learning: that kind of learning in which the principal content of what is to be learned is not given, but must be discovered by the learner before he can incorporate it into his cognitive structure.

dissociability strength: the extent to which an acquired meaning can be separated or retrieved from the anchoring idea(s) in relation to which it is learned and stored, that is, the extent to which it is retrievable or available as an independent ideational entity.

drive determinant: a biological or psychological need or motive that can selectively increase an organism's responsiveness to particular forms of stimulation by inducing a drive state.

drive reduction: the *immediate* reduction in the level of a drive STATE (or the elevation of selectively generalized response thresholds) following reward, as opposed to the *long-term increase* in the strength of the drive DETERMINANT. For example, awareness of successful learning reduces the drive state induced by cognitive drive for a particular task but increases cognitive drive generally.

drive state: a state of selectively increased motor and perceptual responsiveness to stimulation when a drive *determinant* (that is, biological or psychological need; motive) is operative. It, in turn, is reflective of a selectively generalized lowering of the thresholds of elicitation of those perceptions and responses that can potentially satisfy (reduce) the need or motive in question.

ego-enhancement drive: concern with achievement as a source of primary or earned status.

forgetting: a process of memorial reduction or obliterative assimilation that occurs in the course of storage; as a result of this process, the dissociability strength of an acquired meaning falls below the threshold of availability and the meaning is accordingly no longer retrievable.

immunizing effect of initial practice trial: the facilitating effect which the experience of learning and forgetting on the first trial confers on the second and later trials by making the learner aware of (and thus able to circumvent) negative factors in the learning situation that promote forgetting.

insight: as a *process* of problem solving implies an approach that is oriented toward hypothesis generation and hypothesis testing for the purpose of understanding the significant means-end relationships in a particular problem; as a *product* of problem solving it implies a subjective feeling of pleased discovery and immediate reproductibility and transposability.

integrative reconciliation: a principle of programming learning materials that stresses explicit delineation of similarities and differences between related ideas whenever they are encountered in different contexts.

intelligence: a measurement construct designating general level of cognitive ability.

learning shock: the initial cognitive resistance and confusion generated by exposure to new learning material which raises the threshold of availability *immediately* after learning; the gradual dissipation of learning shock results in an apparent increase in retention at a later testing despite a loss in dissociability strength (the *reminiscence* phenomenon).

logically meaningful material: a learning task that is sufficiently plausible or nonrandom to be nonarbitrarily and substantively relatable to correspondingly relevant ideas that lie within the realm of human learning capability.

maturation: increments in capacity that occur in the demonstrable absence of specific practice experience, that is, increments that are attributable to genic influences and/or incidental experience.

meaning: a differentiated and sharply articulated content of awareness that develops as a product of meaningful symbolic learning, or that may be evoked by a symbol or group of symbols after the latter have been nonarbitrarily and substantively related to cognitive structure.

meaningful learning: the acquisition of new meanings; it presupposes a MEANINGFUL LEARNING SET and a potentially meaningful learning task (that is, a task that can be related in nonarbitrary, substantive fashion to what the learner already knows).

meaningful learning set: a disposition on the part of a learner to relate a learning task nonarbitrarily and substantively to his cognitive structure.

meaningfulness: the relative degree of meaning associated with a given symbol or group of symbols as opposed to their substantive cognitive content.

nonarbitrariness: that property of a learning task (for example, plausibility, nonrandomness) that makes it relatable to cognitive structure on some "sensible" basis.

organizer: introductory material presented in advance of and at a higher level of generality, inclusiveness, and abstraction than the learning task itself; designed to promote subsumptive learning by providing ideational scaffolding or anchorage for the learning task and/or by increasing the discriminability between the new ideas to be learned and related ideas in cognitive structure.

pacing: the rate of introducing new subject matter as determined by the length of the time interval between component task units.

potentially meaningful material: a learning task that can be meaningfully learned both because it is *logically* meaningful and because relevant ideas are present in the *particular* learner's cognitive structure.

practice: repeated exposure to or performance of the learning task.

pre-operational stage of cognitive development: that stage in which the child is capable of acquiring PRIMARY CONCEPTS and of understanding, using, and meaningfully manipulating both primary concepts and the relations between them.

primary concepts: those concepts whose meanings an individual originally learns in relation to concrete empirical experience, that is, those of his concepts whose critical attributes, whether discovered or presented, yield generic meanings during learning when they (the attributes) are *first* explicitly related to the particular exemplars from which they are derived *before* being related alone to his cognitive structure.

primary status: status which an individual earns by virtue of his relative degree of competence or performance ability.

problem-setting propositions: instructions that define the nature, conditions, and objectives of a problem-solving task.

progressive differentiation: the practice of sequencing learning material so that the more inclusive ideas to be learned are presented first and are then progressively differentiated in terms of detail and specificity.

propositional learning: learning the meaning of a new composite idea expresssed in sentence form.

psychological or phenomenological meaning: in contrast to *logical* meaning, the *idiosyncratic* differentiated cognitive content evoked by a given symbol or group of symbols in a *particular* learner; identical with meaning as defined above, that is, a product of meaningful learning.

readiness: the existence of a *developmental* level of cognitive functioning sufficient to make a given learning task possible with reasonable economy of time and effort.

reception learning: that kind of learning in which the entire content of what is to be learned is presented to the learner in more or less final form.

reinforcement: an increase in the availability of an idea or in the probability of response occurrence as a *direct* consequence of a lowering of the threshold of availability or elicitation; believed to occur after reward and drive reduction only in the case of rote verbal learning and stimulus-response learning (for example, conditioning, instrumental learning).

representational or vocabulary learning: learning the meaning of single symbols or learning what they represent; includes "naming" of particular objects and events as well as learning the meanings of concept names.

review: a type of practice characterized by long intervals between exposures to or performances of the learning task.

rote learning: the acquisition of arbitrary, verbatim associations in learning situations where either the learning task cannot be nonarbitrarily and substantively related to cognitive structure or where the learner exhibits a nonmeaningful learning set.

satellization: a form of dependent identification in which the subordinate party obtains vicarious or derived status from the superordinate party provided that he is accepted and intrinsically valued by the latter.

secondary concepts: those concepts whose meanings a given individual does *not* learn in relation to genuine concrete empirical experience, that is, those of his concepts whose criterial attributes yield generic meaning when they (the attributes) are related to cognitive structure *without* being first explicitly related to the particular exemplars from which they are derived.

sensitizing effect of initial practice trial: the ability of the learner on a second or later learning trial to *perceive* (that is, immediately apprehend without the benefit of a meaningful learning process) the meaning of a symbolic expression by virtue of acquiring its meaning on the first learning trial.

sequential dependence: a relationship between units of subject matter appearing earlier and later in which knowledge of the former is essential for learning the latter.

strategy: a set of verbal rules which facilitate problem solving, usually by indicating an order of priority among possible manipulations of background propositions and thereby reducing the element of trial and error required to obtain a solution; a strategy is distinguished from an *algorithm* in that the former generates a series of choice points at which intelligent behavior must be exhibited, while the latter leads to a unique, essentially mechanical, application of one or more propositions.

subordinate or subsumptive learning: learning the meaning of a new concept or proposition that can be subsumed under a relevant, *more* inclusive *particular* idea in cognitive structure; includes *derivative* and *correlative* subsumption.

substantiveness or nonverbatimness: that property of a learning task that permits the substitution of synonymous terms without change of meaning or significant alteration in the content of the task itself.

substrate propositions: propositions undergoing transformation in the course or process of discovery learning or problem solving; includes *problem-setting* and *background* propositions.

superordinate learning: learning the meaning of a new concept or proposition that can subsume relevant and *less* inclusive *particular* ideas in cognitive structure.

task orientation: intrinsic motivation for involvement in a learning task, that is, COGNITIVE DRIVE.

threshold of availability: that critical level of the dissociability strength of a learned idea above which it is retrievable and below which it is not. It can vary as a function of attention, anxiety, competing ideas, criterion of retention, and so on, without any change in dissociability strength itself.

transactional terms: words (for example, conditional conjunctions, qualifying adjectives) that make possible the more efficient juxtaposition and combination of different relatable abstractions into potentially meaningful propositions and their subsequent relationship to established ideas in cognitive structure.

transfer: generally the utilization in another context of learning (for example, propositions, concepts, skills) acquired in one context. *Lateral transfer* refers to the use of learning acquired in one substantive subject-matter area in another subject-matter area or in a nonschool context. *Sequential transfer* refers to the use of earlier-acquired learning at a later point in that series. *Vertical transfer* refers to the application of learning (for example, comprehension of a principle) at one level of the taxonomy to learning (for example, problem solving) at a higher level of the taxonomy.

transfer retention test: a test which measures whether a given segment of knowledge is sufficiently stable, clear, and well-organized to serve as a basis for new sequentially related learning tasks and problem solving.

REFERENCES

Abercrombie, M. L. *Learning to think*. New York: Basic Books, Inc., 1960.

Adams, G., and T. Torgenson. *Measurement and evaluation for the secondary school teacher*. New York: Holt, Rinehart and Winston, Inc., 1956.

Acker, Mary, and Paul McReynolds. The "need for novelty"; a comparison of six instruments. *Psychol. Rec.*, 1967, *17*(2), 177–182.

Adkins, Dorothy C. Measurement in relation to the educational process. *Educ. psychol. Measmt.*, 1958, *18*, 221–240.

Adorno, T. W., Else Frenkel-Brunswick, D. J. Levenson, and R. N. Sanford. *The authoritarian personality*. New York: Harper & Row, Publishers, 1950.

Aiken, H. D. Analytical philosophy and educational development. In *Philosophy and educational development* (George Barnett, Ed.). Boston: Houghton Mifflin Company, 1966, Chapter 1.

Alin, L. H. Experimental studies in verbal versus figural learning and retention. *Acta Psychologica Gothoburgensia. V.* Stockholm, Sweden: Almqvist and Wiksell, 1964.

Allport, G. W. Crises in normal personality development. *Teachers Coll. Rec.*, 1964, *66*, 235–241.

Allport, G. W., and L. Postman. *The psychology of rumor*. New York: Holt, Rinehart and Winston, Inc., 1947.

Almy, Millie, with Edward Chittenden and Paula Miller. *Young children's thinking: Studies of some aspects of Piaget's theory*. New York: Teachers College Press, Columbia University, 1966.

Alper, Thelma G., and S. J. Korchin. Memory for socially relevant material. *J. abnorm. soc. Psychol.*, 1952, *47*, 25–37.

Alpert, A. *The solving of problem situations by preschool children*. New York: Teachers College Press, Columbia University, 1928.

Alpert, R., and R. N. Haber. Anxiety in academic achievement situations. *J. abnorm. soc. Psychol.*, 1960, *61*, 207–215.

611

American Association for the Advancement of Science. *Commission on Science Education Newsletter,* 1967, *3*(3)(a).

American Association for the Advancement of Science. *Science: A process approach.* AAAS Miscellaneous Publication, Sept. 1967(b).

Amidon, E., and N. A. Flanders. The effects of direct and indirect teacher influence on dependent-prone students learning geometry. *J. abnorm. soc. Psychol.,* 1961, *52,* 286–291.

Amos, R. T., and R. M. Washington. A comparison of pupil and teacher perceptions of pupil problems. *J. educ. Psychol.,* 1960, *51,* 255–258.

Anastasi, A. Intelligence and family size. *Psychol. Bull.,* 1956, *53,* 187–209.

Anderson, C. C. A cognitive theory of the non-intellective correlates of originality. *Behavioral Science,* 1966, *11,* 284–294(a).

Anderson, C. C. Psychological contributions to education: A decision concerning second-language learning in the elementary school. *Alberta J. educ. Res.,* 1966, *12*(1)(b).

Anderson, C. C. A theory of nonverbal creativity. University of Alberta, Edmonton, 1968.

Anderson, G. L. Quantitative thinking as developed under connectionist and field theories of learning. In *Learning theory in school situations.* Univer. Minn. Stud. Educ. Minneapolis: University of Minnesota Press, 1949, pp. 40–73.

Anderson, J. E. The limitations of infant and preschool tests in the measurement of intelligence. *J. Psychol.,* 1939, *8,* 351–379.

Anderson, R. C. Learning in discussions: Resumé of the authoritarian-democratic studies. *Harvard educ. Rev.,* 1959, *29,* 201–215.

Anderson, R. C., and R. M. Anderson. Transfer of originality training. *J. educ. Psychol.,* 1963, *54,* 300–304.

Anderson, T. The optimum age for beginning the study of modern languages. *International Review of Education,* 1960, *6,* 298–306.

Andrews, J. M. H. *Public and professional opinion regarding the tasks of the public schools of Alberta.* School of Educational Administration, Faculty of Education, University of Alberta, 1959.

Angell, D., and A. A. Lumsdaine. Prompted plus unprompted trials versus prompted trials alone in paired-associate learning. *Research Report AIR-314-60-IR-129.* Pittsburgh: American Institute for Research, October 1960.

Angell, G. W. The effect of immediate knowledge of quiz results on final examination scores in freshman chemistry. *J. educ. Res.,* 1949, *42,* 391–394.

Annett, M. The classification of instances of four common class concepts by children and adults. *Brit. J. educ. Psychol.,* 1959, *29,* 233–236.

Archambault, R. D. The concept of need and its relation to certain aspects of educational theory. *Harvard educ. Rev.,* 1957, *27,* 38–62.

Armistead, L. M. The effect of stimulus change on an exploratory drive in children. *Dissert. Abstr.,* 1961, *21,* 2190.

Armstrong, H. G. Wastage of ability amongst the intellectually gifted. *Brit. J. educ. Psychol.,* 1967, *37,* 257–259.

Arnsdorf, V. E. An investigation of the teaching of chronology in the sixth grade. *J. exp. Educ.,* 1961, *29,* 207–214.

Asch, M. J. Nondirective teaching in psychology. *Psychol. Monogr.,* 1951, *65,* 4.

Aschner, Mary J., and C. E. Bish (Eds.). *Productive thinking in education.* Washington, D.C.: National Education Association, 1965.

Ash, P. The relative effectiveness of massed versus spaced film presentations. *J. educ. Psychol.,* 1950, *41,* 19–30.

Asher, E. J. The inadequacy of current intelligence tests for testing Kentucky mountain children. *J. genet. Psychol.,* 1935, *46,* 480–486.

Ashmore, H. S. *The Negro and the schools.* Chapel Hill, N.C.: University of North Carolina Press, 1954.

Atkin, J. M., and R. Karplus. *Discovery or invention?* Urbana, Ill.: College of Education, University of Illinois, 1962.

Atkinson, J. W. Motivational determinants of risk-taking behavior. In *Motives in fantasy, action and society* (J. W. Atkinson, Ed.). Princeton, N.J.: D. Van Nostrand Company, Inc., 1958.

Atkinson, J. W. The mainsprings of achievement-oriented activity. In *Learning and the educational process* (J. D. Krumboltz, Ed.). Skokie, Ill.: Rand McNally & Company, 1965.

Auster, D. A comparative study of persuasive techniques in films (abstract). *AV Communication Rev.,* 1966, *14,* 145.

Ausubel, D. P. Prestige motivation of gifted children. *Genet. Psychol. Monogr.,* 1951, *43,* 53–117.

Ausubel, D. P. *Ego development and the personality disorders.* New York: Grune & Stratton, Inc., 1952.

Ausubel, D. P. *Theory and problems of adolescent development.* New York: Grune & Stratton, Inc., 1954.

Ausubel, D. P. Sociempathy as a function of sociometric status in an adolescent group. *Hum. Relat.,* 1955, *8,* 75–84.

Ausubel, D. P. Some comments on the nature, diagnosis, and prognosis of neurotic anxiety. *Psychiat. Quart.,* 1956, *30,* 77–88.

Ausubel, D. P. The use of advance organizers in the learning and retention of meaningful verbal material. *J. educ. Psychol.,* 1960, *51,* 267–272.

Ausubel, D. P. *The psychology of meaningful verbal learning.* New York: Grune & Stratton, Inc., 1963.

Ausubel, D. P. A cognitive structure view of word and concept meaning. In *Readings in the psychology of cognition* (R. C. Anderson and D. P. Ausubel, Eds.). New York: Holt, Rinehart and Winston, Inc., 1965, pp. 58–75(a).

Ausubel, D. P. The effects of cultural deprivation on learning patterns. *Audiovisual Instruction,* 1965, *10,* 10–12(b).

Ausubel, D. P. *The fern and the tiki: An American view of New Zealand national character, social attitudes and race relations.* New York: Holt, Rinehart and Winston, Inc., 1965(c).

Ausubel, D. P. The influence of experience on the development of intelligence. In *Productive thinking in education* (Mary J. Aschner and C. E. Bish, Eds.). Washington, D.C.: National Education Association, 1965, pp. 45–62(d).

Ausubel, D. P. *Maori youth: A psychoethnological study of cultural deprivation.* New York: Holt, Rinehart and Winston, Inc., 1965(e).

Ausubel, D. P. Early versus delayed review in meaningful learning. *Psychol. in Schools,* 1966, *3,* 195–198(a).

Ausubel, D. P. An evaluation of the B.S.C.S. approach to high school biology. *Amer. Biol. Teacher,* 1966, *28,* 176–186(b).

Ausubel, D. P. *Educational psychology: A cognitive view.* New York: Holt, Rinehart and Winston, Inc., 1968.

Ausubel, D. P. *Readings in school learning.* New York: Holt, Rinehart and Winston, Inc. (in press).

Ausubel, D. P., and E. Blake. Proactive inhibition in the forgetting of meaningful school material. *J. educ. Res.,* 1958, *52,* 145–149.

Ausubel, D. P., and D. Fitzgerald. The role of discriminability in meaningful verbal learning and retention. *J. educ. Psychol.,* 1961, *52,* 266–274.

Ausubel, D. P., and D. Fitzgerald. Organizer, general background, and antecedent learning variables in sequential verbal learning. *J. educ. Psychol.,* 1962, *53,* 243–249.

Ausubel, D. P., and H. M. Schiff. A level of aspiration approach to the measurement of goal tenacity. *J. gen. Psychol.,* 1953, *52,* 97–110.

Ausubel, D. P., and M. Youssef. The role of discriminability in meaningful verbal learning. *J. educ. Psychol.,* 1963, *54,* 331–336.

Ausubel, D. P., and M. Youssef. The effect of spaced repetition on meaningful learning. *J. gen. Psychol.,* 1965, *73,* 147–150.

Ausubel, D. P., and M. Youssef. The effect of consolidation on sequentially related, sequentially independent meaningful learning. *J. gen. Psychol.,* 1966, *74,* 355–360.

Ausubel, D. P., E. E. Balthazar, Irene Rosenthal, L. Blackman, S. H. Schpoont, and Joan Welkowitz. Perceived parent attitudes as determinants of children's ego structure. *Child Developm.,* 1954, *25,* 173–183(a).

Ausubel, D. P., Lillian C. Robbins, and E. Blake. Retroactive inhibition and facilitation in the learning of school materials. *J. educ. Psychol.,* 1957, *48,* 334–343(a).

Ausubel, D. P., H. M. Schiff, and E. B. Gasser. A preliminary study of developmental trends in sociempathy: Accuracy of perception of own and others' sociometric status. *Child Developm.,* 1952, *23,* 111–128.

Ausubel, D. P., H. M. Schiff, and M. Goldman. Qualitative characteristics in the learning process associated with anxiety. *J. abnorm. soc. Psychol.,* 1953, *48,* 537–547(a).

Ausubel, D. P., H. M. Schiff, and M. P. Zeleny. Real life measures of academic and vocational aspirations: Relation to laboratory measures and adjustment. *Child Developm.,* 1953, *24,* 155–168(b).

Ausubel, D. P., H. M. Schiff, and M. Zeleny. Validity of teachers' ratings of adolescents' adjustment and aspirations. *J. educ. Psychol.,* 1954, *45,* 394–407(b).

Ausubel, D. P., S. H. Schpoont, and Lillian Cukier. The influence of intention on the retention of school materials. *J. educ. Psychol.,* 1957, *48,* 87–92(b).

Ausubel, D. P., Mary Stager, and A. J. H. Gaite. Retroactive facilitation in meaningful verbal learning. *J. educ. Psychol.,* 1968, *59*(4), 250–255.

Avital, S. M. Higher level thinking in secondary school students' attainment in mathematics. Unpublished doctoral dissertation, University of Toronto, 1967.

Avital, S. M., and Sara J. Shettleworth. *Objectives for mathematics learning: Some ideas for the teacher.* (Bulletin No. 3). Toronto, Ont.: The Ontario Institute for Studies in Education, 1968.

Avital, S. M., Janet Chen, and others. Importance of cueing for mediational processes in a pictorial-verbal learning task. Toronto, Ont.: The Ontario Institute for Studies in Education, 1968.

Ayres, L. P. *Laggards in our schools.* New York: Russell Sage Foundation, 1909.

Back, K. W. Influence through social communication. *J. abnorm. soc. Psychol.,* 1951, *46,* 9–23.

Bahrick, H. P., P. M. Fitts, and R. E. Rankin. Effect of incentives upon reactions to peripheral stimuli. *J. exp. Psychol.,* 1952, *44,* 400–406.

Baker, H. L. High-school teachers' knowledge of their pupils. *Sch. Rev.,* 1938, *46,* 175–190.

Baker, H. V. Children's contributions in elementary school general discussion. *Child Develpm. Monogr.,* 1942, No. 29.

Baker, S. R. A study of the relationship of dogmatism to the retention of psychological concepts: A research note. *J. hum. Rel.,* 1964, *12,* 311–313.

Baldwin, A. L., J. Kalhorn, and F. H. Breese. Patterns of parent behavior. *Psychol. Monogr.,* 1945, *58,* No. 3 (Whole No. 268).

Bandura, A., and R. H. Walters. *Social learning and personality development.* New York: Holt, Rinehart and Winston, Inc., 1963.

Bard, B. Why dropout campaigns fail. *Sat. Rev.,* September 17, 1966.

Barnlund, D. C. A comparative study of individual, majority, and group judgment. *J. abnorm. soc. Psychol.,* 1959, *58,* 55–60.

Barr, A. S., and others. Second report of the Committee on Criteria of Teacher Effectiveness. *J. educ. Res.,* 1953, *46,* 641–658.

Barr, A. S., and others. The measurement and prediction of teaching efficiency. *Rev. educ. Res.,* 1958, *28,* 256–264.

Barr, A. S., and others. Wisconsin studies of the measurement and prediction of teacher effectiveness. *J. exp. Educ.,* 1961, *30,* 5–156.

Barron, F. *Creativity and psychological health.* Princeton, N.J.: D. Van Nostrand Company, Inc., 1963.

Bartlett, F. C. *Remembering.* London: Cambridge University Press, 1932.

Bayley, Nancy. Mental growth in young children. In *39th Yearbook, Nat. Soc. Stud. Educ.,* Part II. Chicago: University of Chicago Press, 1940, pp. 11–47.

Bayley, Nancy. Consistency and variability in the growth of intelligence from birth to eighteen years. *J. genet. Psychol.,* 1949, *75,* 165–196.

Bayley, Nancy. On the growth of intelligence. *Amer. Psychol.,* 1955, *10,* 805–810.

Bayley, Nancy and H. E. Jones. Environmental correlates of mental and motor development: A cumulative study from infancy to six years. *Child Developm.,* 1937, *4,* 329–341.

Bayley, Nancy and M. H. Oden. The maintenance of intellectual ability in gifted adults. *J. Gerontol.,* 1955, *10,* 91–107.

Bayley, Nancy and E. S. Schaefer. *Correlations of maternal and child behaviors with the development of mental abilities: Data from the Berkeley Growth Study.* Monogr. Soc. Res. Child Develpm., Vol. 29, No. 6 (Serial No. 97), Yellow Springs, Ohio: The Antioch Press, 1964.

Beane, D. G. A comparison of linear and branching programmed instruction in plane geometry. *Technical Report* No. 1, Urbana, Ill.: Training Research Laboratory, University of Illinois, July 1962.

Beckmeyer, T. Application of programmed instruction to remedial reading for the deaf (abstract). *AV Communication Rev.,* Winter 1965, *13,* 448–449.

Beggs, D. W., and E. G. Buffie (Eds.). *Independent study.* Bold New Venture Series. Bloomington, Ind.: Indiana University Press, 1965.

Beker, J., L. M. Sundblad, and P. R. Holmes. Changes in junior high school pupils' educational and vocational aspirations during a school desegregation experience. *Proceedings of 75th Annual Convention of the American Psychological Association,* 1967, *2,* 283–284.

Bellack, A. A., and others. *The language of the classroom.* New York: Teachers College Press, Columbia University, 1965.

Bellugi, Ursula and R. W. Brown (Eds.). The acquisition of language. *Monogr. Soc. Res. Child Develpm.,* 1964, *29,* (1), 1–129 (Whole No. 92).

Benne, K. D., and Grace Levit. The nature of groups and helping groups improve their operation. *Rev. educ. Res.,* 1953, *23,* 289–308.

Bentzen, F. Sex ratios in learning and behavior disorders. *Amer. J. Orthopsychiat.* 1963, *33,* 92–98.

Bereiter, C. Psychology and early education. In *Psychology and early childhood education* (D. W. Brison and Jane Hill, Eds.). Monograph Series No. 4. Toronto, Ont.: The Ontario Institute for Studies in Education (in press).

Bereiter, C., and S. Engelmann. *Teaching disadvantaged children in the preschool.* Englewood Cliffs, N.J.: Prentice-Hall, Inc., 1966.

Bereiter, C., and S. Engelmann. An academically-oriented preschool for disadvantaged children: Results from the initial experimental group. In *Psychology and early education* (D. W. Brison and Jane Hill, Eds.). Monograph Series No. 4, Toronto, Ont.: The Ontario Institute for Studies in Education, 1968.

Bergstrom, L. H. School re-organization in Saskatchewan. *Canadian educ. res. Digest,* September 1965, *5,* 248–257.

Berlyne, D. E. Knowledge and stimulus-response psychology. *Psychol. Rev.,* 1954, *61,* 245–254(a).

Berlyne, D. E. A theory of human curiosity. *Brit. J. Psychol.,* 1954, *45,* 180–191(b).

Berlyne, D. E. Recent developments in Piaget's work. *Brit. J. educ. Psychol.,* 1957, *27,* 1–12.

Berlyne, D. E. *Conflict, arousal, and curiosity.* New York: McGraw-Hill, Inc., 1960.

Berlyne, D. E. Emotional aspects of learning. *Annual Review of Psychology.* Palo Alto, Calif.: Annual Reviews, Inc., 1964, pp. 115–142.

Berlyne, D. E. Curiosity in education. In *Learning and the educational process* (J. D. Krumboltz, Ed.). Skokie, Ill.: Rand, McNally & Company, 1965(a).

Berlyne, D. E. *Structure and direction in thinking.* New York: John Wiley & Sons, Inc., 1965(b).

Berlyne, D. E. Conditions of pre-questioning and retention of meaningful material. *J. educ. Psychol.,* 1966, *57,* 128–132.

Berlyne, D. E. Arousal and reinforcement. In *Nebraska Symposium on Motivation*. Lincoln, Neb.: University of Nebraska, 1967, pp. 1–110.

Bernard, Viola W. School desegregation: some psychiatric implications. *Psychiat.*, 1958, *21*, 149–158.

Bernard, W. Psychological principles of language learning and the bilingual reading method.*Mod. Lang. J.*, 1951, *35*, 87–96.

Bernstein, B. Language and social class. *Brit. J. Psychol.*, 1960, *11*, 271–276.

Bernstein, G. Some sociological determinants of perception: An enquiry into subcultural differences. *Brit. J. Sociol.*, 1958, *9*, 159–174.

Bhatnagar, K. P. Academic achievement as a function of one's self-concepts and ego-functions. *Educ. Psychol. Rev.*, 1966, *6*(4), 178–182.

Biddle, B. J. The integration of teacher effectiveness research. In *Contemporary research on teacher effectiveness* (B. J. Biddle and A. J. Ellena, Eds.). New York: Holt, Rinehart and Winston, Inc., 1964, Chapter 1, pp. 1–40.

Biel, W. C., and R. C. Force. Retention of nonsense syllables in intentional and incidental learning. *J. exp. Psychol.*, 1943, *32*, 52–63.

Bigge, M. L. *Learning theories for teachers*. New York: Harper & Row, Publishers, 1964.

Bills, R. E. An investigation of student centered teaching. *J. educ. Res.*, 1952, *46*, 313–319.

Binter, A. R. Two ways of teaching percent. *Elem. Sch. J.*, 1963, *63*, 261–265.

Birkmaier, Emma and D. Lange. Foreign language instruction. *Rev. educ. Res.*, 1967, *37*(2), 186–199.

Birney, R. C. The reliability of the achievement motive. *J. abnorm. soc. Psychol.*, 1959, *58*, 267.

Black, H. *They shall not pass*. New York: William Morrow & Company, Inc., 1963.

Bloom, B. S. *Stability and change in human characteristics*. New York: John Wiley & Sons, Inc., 1964.

Bloom, B. S. *Stability and change in human characteristics*. New York: John of Education and Instructional Programs, University of California at Los Angeles, 1968, *1*(2).

Bloom, B. S., and Lois J. Broder. Problem-solving processes of college students. *Supp. educ. Monogr.*, No. 73. Chicago: University of Chicago Press, 1950, pp. 1–31.

Bloom, B. S., M. D. Engelhart, E. J. Furst, W. H. Hill, and D. R. Krathwohl (Eds.). *Taxonomy of educational objectives: The classification of educational goals. Handbook 1: Cognitive domain*. New York: David McKay Company, Inc., 1956.

Blos, P. *The adolescent personality.*. New York: Appleton-Century-Crofts, 1941.

Blumberg, A., and E. Amidon. Teachers' perceptions of supervisor-teacher interaction. *Administrator's Notebook* 14, May 1964, 1–4.

Bodanskiĭ, F. G. O vozmozhnosti usvoeniya algebraicheskogo sposoba resheniya zadach mladshimi shkol'nikami. (The possibility of learning algebraic solutions of problems by grade school pupils) *Voprosy Psikhologii*, 1967, *13*(3), 120–134.

618

References

Bond, A. De M. *An experiment in the teaching of genetics.* New York: Teachers College Press, Columbia University, 1940.

Bonney, M. E. Sociometric study of agreement between teacher judgments and student choices. *Sociometry,* 1947, *10,* 133–146.

Borg, W. R. *Ability grouping in the public schools.* Madison, Wisc.: Dembar Educational Research Services, 1966.

Bourne, L. E., and R. C. Haygood. Effects of intermittent reinforcement of an irrelevant dimension and task complexity upon concept identification. *J. exp. Psychol.,* 1960, *60,* 371–375.

Bourne, L. E., and R. Pendleton. Concept identification as a function of completeness and probability of information feedback. *J. exp. Psychol.,* 1958, *56,* 413–420.

Bradway, Katherine P., and Clare W. Thompson. Intelligence at adulthood: A twenty-five year follow-up. *J. educ. Psychol.,* 1962, *5,* 1–14.

Braine, M. D. S. The ontogeny of logical operations: Piaget's formulations examined by nonverbal methods. *Psychol. Monogr.,* 1959, *73,* No. 4. (Whole No. 475).

Braine, M. D. S., and Betty L. Shanks. The conservation of a shape property and a proposal about the origin of the conservations. *Canadian J. Psychol.,* 1965, *19,* 197–207.

Briggs, L. J. Two self-instructional devices. *Psychol. Rep.,* 1958, *4,* 671–676.

Briggs, L. J. Prompting and confirmation conditions for three learning tasks employing the subject-matter trainer. In *Student response in programmed instruction* (A. A. Lumsdaine, Ed.). Washington, D.C.: National Academy of Sciences-National Research Council, 1961, pp. 375–387.

Briggs, L. J. Learner variables and educational media. *Rev. educ. Res.,* 1968, *38*(2), 160–176.

Briggs, L. J., and H. B. Reed. The curve of retention for substance material. *J. exp. Psychol.,* 1943, *32,* 513–517.

Brison, D. W. Acceleration of conservation of substance. *J. genet. Psychol.,* 1966, *109,* 311–322.

Brison, D. C. Can and should learning be accelerated? In *Accelerated learning and fostering creativity* (D. W. Brison, Ed.). Toronto, Ont.: Department of Applied Psychology, The Ontario Institute for Studies in Education, 1968.

Brison, D. W., and E. V. Sullivan (Eds.). *Recent research on the conservation of substance.* Educational Research Series No. 2. Toronto, Ont.: The Ontario Institute for Studies in Education, May 1967.

Broadbent, D. E. The well ordered mind. *Amer. educ. Res. J.,* 1966, *3*(4).

Brody, N. Achievement-test anxiety, subjective probability of success in risk-taking behavior. *J. abnorm. soc. Psychol.,* 1963, *66.* 413–418.

Bromer, J. A. A companion of incidental and purposeful memory for meaningful and nonsense material. *Amer. J. Psychol.,* 1942, *55,* 106–108.

Bronfenbrenner, U. The split-level American family. *Sat. Rev.,* October 7, 1967.

Brookover, W. B., S. Thomas and Ann Patterson. Self-concept of ability and school achievement. *Sociol. Educ.,* 1964, *37,* 271–278.

Brooks, N. Language learning: The new approach. *Phi Delta Kappan,* 1966, *47* (7).

Brown, A. F. How administrators view teachers. *Can. educ. and Res. Dig.,* March 1966, *6,* 34–52(a).

Brown, A. F. A perceptual taxonomy of the effective-rated teacher. *J. exp. Educ.,* 1966, *35,* 1–10(b).

Brown, R. G. A comparison of the vocational aspirations of paired sixth grade white and Negro children who attend segregated schools. *J. educ. Res.,* 1965, *58,* 402–404.

Brown, R., and Ursula Bellugi. Three processes in the child's acquisition of syntax. *Harvard educ. Rev.,* Spring 1964, *34,* 133–152.

Brownell, W. A. Observations of instruction in lower-grade arithmetic in English and Scottish schools. *Arith. Teacher,* 1960, *7,* 165–177.

Brownell, W. A., and G. Hendrickson. How children learn information, concepts and generalizations. In *Learning and Instruction: 49th Yearbook Nat. Soc. Stud. Educ.* Part 1. Chicago: University of Chicago Press, 1950, pp. 92–128.

Brownell, W. A., and H. E. Moser. Meaningful versus mechanical learning: A study in grade III subtraction. *Duke Univer. Res. Stud. Educ.,* 1949, No. 8.

Brownell, W. A., and V. M. Sims. The nature of understanding. In *The measurement of understanding: 45th Yearbook Nat. Soc. Stud. Educ.* Part I. Chicago: University of Chicago Press, 1946, pp. 27–43.

Broyler, C. R., E. L. Thorndike, and Ella Woodyard. A second study of mental discipline in high school studies. *J. educ. Psychol.,* 1927, *18,* 377–404.

Bruner, J. S. Going beyond the information given. In *Contemporary approaches to cognition.* Cambridge, Mass.: Harvard University Press, 1957, pp. 41–70.

Bruner, J. S. *The process of education.* Cambridge, Mass.: Harvard University Press, 1960.

Bruner, J. S. The act of discovery. *Harvard educ. Rev.,* 1961, *31,* 21–32(a).

Bruner, J. S. After Dewey what? *Sat. Rev.,* June 17, 1961, 58–59; 76–78(b).

Bruner, J. S. The course of cognitive growth. *Amer. Psychol.,* 1964, *19,* 1–15(a).

Bruner, J. S. Some theorems on instruction illustrated with reference to mathematics. In *Theories of learning and instruction: 63rd Yearbook Nat. Soc. Stud. Educ.* Part I. Chicago: University of Chicago Press, 1964, pp. 306–335(b).

Bruner, J. S. On the conservation of liquids. In J. S. Bruner and others, *Studies in cognitive growth.* New York: John Wiley & Sons, Inc., 1966.

Bruner, J. S., and Rose R. Olver. Development of equivalence transformations in children. *Monogr. Soc. Res. Child Develpm.,* 1963, *28* (Whole No. 86), 125–141.

Bruner, J. S., Rose R. Olver, Patricia M. Greenfield, and others. *Studies in cognitive growth.* New York: John Wiley & Sons, Inc., 1966.

Bryan, G. L., and J. W. Rigney. An evaluation of a method for shipboard training in operations knowledge. *Technical Report* No. 18. Los Angeles: Department of Psychology, University of Southern California, September 1956.

Bryan, Judith F., and E. A. Locke. Goal setting as a means of increasing motivation. *J. applied Psychol.,* 1967, *51* (3), 274–277.

Bullock, H. A. A comparison of the academic achievements of white and Negro high school graduates. *J. educ. Res.,* 1950, *44,* 179–182.

Bumstead, A. P. Distribution of effort in memorizing prose and poetry. *Amer. J. Psychol.,* 1940, *53,* 423–427.

Bumstead, A. P. Finding the best mehod for memorizing. *J. educ. Psychol.,* 1943, *34,* 110–114.

Burack, B., and D. Moos. Effect of knowing the principle basic to solution of a problem. *J. educ. Res.,* 1956, *50,* 203–208.

Burkman, E. *The intermediate science curriculum study (ISCS) program of individualized science instruction for grades seven through nine.* Tallahassee, Fla.: Florida State University, December 1967.

Buros, O. K. (Ed.). *The sixth mental measurements yearbook.* Highland Park, N.J.: Gryphon Press, 1965.

Burt, C. The development of reasoning in children. *J. exp. Pedag.,* 1919, *5,* 68–77.

Burt, C. The inheritance of mental ability. *Amer. Psychol.,* 1958, *13,* 1–15.

Burt, C. Critical notice: The psychology of creative ability. *Brit. J. educ. Psychol.,* 1962, *32,* 292–298.

Burt, C. The genetic determination of differences in intelligence: A study of monozygotic twins reared together and apart. *Brit. J. Psychol.,* 1966, *57*(1 and 2), 137–153.

Burt, C., and Margaret Howard. The relative influence of heredity and environment on assessments of intelligence. *Brit. J. stat. Psychol.,* 1957, *10,* 99–104.

Butler, R. A. Incentive conditions which influence visual exploration. *J. exp. Psychol.,* 1954, *48,* 19–32.

Byers, J. L. A study of the level of aspiration of academically successful and unsuccessful high school students. *Calif. J. educ. Res.,* 1962, *13,* 209–216.

Cambridge Conference on School Mathematics. *Goals for School Mathematics: Report of The Cambridge Conference on School Mathematics.* Boston: Houghton Mifflin, 1963.

Campbell, D. T., and J. C. Stanley. Experimental and quasi-experimental designs for research. In *Handbook on research on teaching* (N. L. Gage, Ed.). Skokie, Ill.: Rand McNally & Company, 1963.

Canadian Council for Research in Education. *Canadian Experience with the Cuisenaire Method.* Ottawa: The Council, 1964.

Canning, R. R. Does an honor system reduce classroom cheating? An experimental answer. *J. exp. Educ.,* 1956, *24,* 291–296.

Cantril, H., and G. W. Allport. *The psychology of radio.* New York: Harper & Row, Publishers, 1935.

Caplehorn, W. F., and A. J. Sutton. Need achievement and its relation to school performance, anxiety and intelligence. *Australian J. Psychol.,* April 1965, *17,* 44–51.

Carbno, W. C., J. W. Soloman, H. H. Russell, and D. S. Abbey. Programmed instruction in remedial arithmetic: A study with underachievers (unpublished report). Toronto: The Ontario Institute for Studies in Education, 1967.

Carey, Susan. The genesis of operational structures: Reply to Piaget's review of J. S. Bruner *et al., Studies in cognitive growth. Contemp. Psychol.,* 1967, *12*(11).

Carlow, C. D. A study of variables within the method of individually guided discovery in secondary school mathematics: The experimental comparison of conceptual structures, consolidation and learner personality with learning, retention, and transfer by ninthgrade college preparatory males (unpublished doctoral thesis). Syracuse, N.Y.: Syracuse University, 1967.

Carlsmith, L. Effect of early father absence on scholastic aptitude. *Harvard educ. Rev.,* 1964, *34,* 3–21.

Carmichael, L., H. P. Hogan, and A. A. Walter. An experimental study of the effect of language on visually perceived form. *J. exp. Psychol.,* 1932, *15,* 73–86.

Carnegie Corporation of New York. Learning to read: The great confusion. *Carnegie Quart.,* 1967, *15*(3).

Carnett, G. S. Is our mathematics inferior? *Math. Teacher,* 1967, *60*(6).

Caron, A. J. Curiosity, achievement, and avoidant motivation as determinants of epistemic behavior. *J. abnorm. soc. Psychol.,* 1963, *67,* 535–549.

Caron, A. J. Impact of motivational variables on knowledge-seeking behavior. In *Productive thinking in education* (Mary Jane Aschner and C. E. Bish, Eds.). Washington, D.C.: National Education Association, 1965.

Carroll, J. B. The analysis of reading instruction: Perspectives from psychology and linguistics. In *Theories of learning and instruction: 63rd Yearbook Nat. Soc. Stud. Educ.* Part I. Chicago: University of Chicago Press, 1964, pp. 336–353.

Carroll, J. B. Psychology: Research in foreign language teaching: The last five years. In *Language teaching: Broader contexts* (R. G. Mead, Jr., Ed.). Northeast Conference on the Teaching of Foreign Languages, Reports of the Working Committees, New York: The Conference, 1966, pp. 12–42.

Carroll, J. B. Review of J. P. Guilford's "The nature of human intelligence" (New York: McGraw-Hill, 1967). *Amer. educ. Res. J.,* March 1968, *5*(2), 249–256.

Carroll, J. B., and Mary L. Burke. Parameters of paired-associate verbal learning: Length of list, meaningfulness, rate of presentation and ability. *J. exp. Psychol.,* 1965, *69,* 543–553.

Carson, A. S., and A. I. Rabin. Verbal comprehension and communication in Negro and white children. *J. educ. Psychol,* 1960, *51,* 47–51.

Carter, D. E. Strategies of instruction. *Child Study Center Bulletin.* Buffalo, New York: State University College, 1967, *3*(3), 51–58.

Carter, Launor F. The computer and instructional technology. In *Current issues in higher education: In search of leaders* (G. Kerry Smith, Ed.). Washington, D.C.: Association for Higher Education, National Education Association, 1967, pp. 253–259.

Carter, L. F., W. Haythorn, J. Lanzetta, and B. Mairowitz. The relation of categorizations and ratings in the observation of group behavior. *Hum. Relat.,* 1951, *4,* 239–254.

Carter, L. J. Interrelationships among memory, rate of acquisition and length of task. *Dissert. Abstr.,* 1959, *19,* 1832.

Carter, R. S. How invalid are marks assigned by teachers? *J. educ. Psychol.,* 1952, *43,* 218–228.

Cartledge, C. J., and E. L. Krauser. Training first-grade children in creative thinking under quantitative and qualitative motivation. *J. educ. Psychol.,* 1963, *54,* 295–299.

Case, D., and J. M. Collinson. The development of formal thinking in verbal comprehension. *Brit. J. educ. Psychol.,* 1962, *32,* 105–111.

Cashdan, S., and G. S. Welsh. Personality correlates of creative potential in talented high school students. *J. Pers.,* 1966, *34* (3), 444–455.

Caspari, E. W. Genetic endowment and environment in the determination of human behavior: Biological viewpoint. *Amer. educ. Res. J.,* 1968, *5*(1), 43–55.

Castenada, A., D. S. Palermo, and B. R. McCandless. Complex learning and performance as a function of anxiety in children and task difficulty. *Child Develpm.,* 1956, *27,* 329–332.

Cattell, R. B. Theory of fluid and crystallized intelligence. *J. educ. Psychol.,* 1963, *54,* 1–22.

Cavan, Ruth S. Negro family disorganization and juvenile delinquency. *J. Negro Educ.,* 1959, *28,* 230–239.

Chall, J. S. *Learning to read: The great debate.* New York: McGraw-Hill, Inc., 1967.

Chansky, N. M. Learning: a function of schedule and type of feedback. *Psychol. Rep.,* 1960, *7,* 362.

Chansky, N. M. Reactions to systems of guiding learning. *Amer. educ. Res. J.,* 1964, *1,* 95–100.

Chapanis, A., and W. C. Williams. Results of a mental survey with the Kuhlmann-Anderson intelligence tests in Williamson County, Tennessee. *J. genet. Psychol.,* 1945, *67,* 27–55.

Childers, L. M. Report of the Research Committee on Examinations. *Proceedings of the 60th Annual Meeting,* National Association of Dental Examiners, 1942, *60,* 77–106.

Christensen, C. M. A note on dogmatism and learning. *J. abnorm. soc. Psych.,* 1963, *66,* 75–76.

Cicirelli, Victor G. Form of the relationship between creativity, IQ, and academic achievement. *J. educ. Psychol.,* 1966, *56*(6), 303–308.

Clark, K. B. Some factors influencing the remembering of prose material. *Arch. Psychol.,* 1940, *36* (Whole No. 253).

Clark, K. B., and M. P. Clark. Racial identification and preference in Negro children. In *Readings in social psychology* (T. M. Newcomb and E. L. Hartley, Eds.). New York: Holt, Rinehart and Winston, Inc., 1947, pp. 169–178.

Clarke, S. T. C. Clear thinking in geometry (unpublished M.Ed. thesis). University of Alberta (Edmonton), 1943.

Cline, V. B., J. M. Richards, and C. Abe. The validity of a battery of creativity tests in a high school sample. *Educ. psychol. Measmt.,* 1962, *22,* 781–784.

Cline, V. B., J. M. Richards, and W. E. Needham. Creativity tests and achievement in high school science. *J. app. Psychol.,* 1963, *47,* 184–189.

Cofer, C. N. A comparison of logical and verbatim learning of prose passages of different length. *Amer. J. Psychol.,* 1941, *54,* 1–20.

Cogan, M. L. The behavior of teachers and the productive behavior of their pupils: I. "Perception" analysis; II. "Trait" analysis. *J. exp. Educ.,* 1958, *27,* 89–105; 107–124.

Cohen, J., and W. Shepler. *Individually prescribed instruction in science (The Oakleaf Project): A status report.* Pittsburgh: Learning and Development Center, University of Pittsburgh, 1967.

Cole, D., and others. The relation of achievement imagery scores to academic performance. *J. abnorm. soc. Psychol.,* 1962, *65,* 208–211.

Coleman, J. S. *The adolescent subculture.* New York: The Free Press, 1961.

Coleman, J. S. Introduction to mathematical sociology. New York: The Free Press, 1964.

Coleman, J. S., and others. *Equality of educational opportunity.* U.S. Department of Health, Education and Welfare. Washington, D.C.: U.S. Government Printing Office, 1966.

Conant, J. B. *Slums and Suburbs.* New York: McGraw-Hill, Inc., 1961.

Conrad, H S., F. N. Freeman, and H. E. Jones. Differential mental growth. In *Adolescence: 43rd Yearbook Nat. Soc. Stud. Educ.* Part I. Chicago: University of Chicago Press, 1944, pp. 164–184.

Conway, J. K. Multiple-sensory modality communication and the problem of sign types. *AV Communication Rev.,* Winter 1967, *15,* 371–383.

Cook, J. O., and M. E. Spitzer. Supplementary report: prompting versus confirmation in paired-associate learning. *J. exp. Psychol.,* 1960, *59,* 275–276.

Cook, W. W., C. H. Leeds, and R. Callis. *The Minnesota Teacher Attitude Inventory.* New York: Psychological Corporation, 1951.

Cooper, Bernice. An analysis of the reading achievement of white and Negro pupils in certain public schools in Georgia. *Sch. Rev.,* 1964, *72,* 462–471.

Cooper, J. C., Jr., and J. H. Gaeth. Interactions of modality with age and with meaningfulness in verbal learning. *J. educ. Psychol.,* 1967, *58,* 41–44.

Corman, B. R. The effect of varying amounts and kinds of information as guidance in problem solving. *Psychol. Monogr.,* 1957, *71,* No. 2 (Whole No. 431).

Cornell, E. L., and C. M. Armstrong. Forms of mental growth patterns revealed by re-analysis of the Harvard growth data. *Child Develpm.,* 1955, *26,* 169–204.

Costanzo, P. R., and M. E. Shaw. Conformity as a function of age level. *Child Develpm.,* 1966, *37,* 967–975.

Costin, F. Dogmatism and learning: A follow-up of contradictory findings. *J. educ. Res.,* 1965, *59,* 186–188.

Coulson, J. E., and H. F. Silberman. Effects of three variables in a teaching machine. *J. educ. Psychol.,* 1960, *51,* 135–143.

Coulson, J. E., and others. Effects of branching in a computer controlled auto-instructional device. *J. appl. Psychol.,* 1962, *46,* 389–392.

Cowan, E. C. The influence of varying degrees of psychological stress on problem-solving rigidity. *J. abnorm. soc. Psych.,* 1952, *47,* 512–519.

Cowen, E. L., M. Zax, R. Klein, L. D. Izzo, and Mary Ann Trost. The relaxation of anxiety in school children to school record, achievement, and behavioral measures. *Child Develpm.,* 1965, *36,* 685–695.

Cox, R. C., and J. M. Gordon. *Validation and uses of the taxonomy of educational objectives: Cognitive domain. A select and annotated bibliography.*

Pittsburgh: School of Education, University of Pittsburgh, 1965. (See also, *Addendum* by R. C. Cox, December 1966.)

Craig, R. C. Directed versus independent discovery of established relations. *J. educ. Psychol.,* 1956, *47,* 223–234.

Craig, R. C. Discovery, task completion, and the assignment as factors in motivation. *Amer. educ. Res. J.,* 1965, *2,* 217–222.

Crandall, V., Rachel Dewey, W. Katkovsky, and Anne Preston. Parents' attitudes and behaviors and grade-school children's academic achievements. *J. genet. Psychol.,* 1964. *104,* 53–66.

Cronbach, L. J. *Essentials of psychological testing.* New York: Harper & Row, Publishers, 1949.

Cronbach, L. J. *Educational psychology.* New York: Harcourt, Brace & World, Inc., 1954.

Cronbach, L. J. *Essentials of psychological testing* (2d ed.). New York: Harper & Row, Publishers, 1960.

Cronbach, L. J. Course improvement through evaluation. *Teachers Coll. Rec.,* 1963, *64,* 672–683.

Cronbach, L. J. Issues current in educational psychology. *Mongor. Soc. Res. Child Develpm.,* 1965, *30* (Serial No. 99), 109–125.

Cronbach, L. J. How can instruction be adapted to individual differences? In *Learning and individual differences* (Robert M. Gagné, Ed.). Columbus, Ohio: Charles E. Merrill Books, Inc., 1967, pp. 23–39(a).

Cronbach, L. J. The logic of experiments on discovery. In *Learning by discovery: A critical appraisal* (L. S. Shulman and E. R. Keislar, Eds.). Skokie, Ill.: Rand McNally & Company, 1967(b).

Cropley, A. J. Creativity and intelligence. *Brit. J. educ. Psychol.,* 1966, *36*(3), 259–266.

Crowder, N. A. Automatic tutoring by intrinsic programming. In *Teaching machines and programmed learning* (A. A. Lumsdaine and R. Glaser, Eds.). Washington, D.C.: National Education Association, 1960, pp. 286–298.

Crutchfield, R. S., and M. V. Covington. Facilitation of creative thinking and problem solving in school children. Paper presented to American Association for the Advancement of Science, Cleveland, Ohio, December 1963.

Cunningham, Ruth. *Understanding group behavior of boys and girls.* New York: Teachers College Press, Columbia University, 1951.

Curry, R. L. The effect of socio-economic status on the scholastic achievement of sixth-grade children. *Brit. J. educ. Psychol.,* 1962, *32,* 46–49.

Dai, B. Some problems of personality development in Negro children. In *Personality in nature, society, and culture.* (C. Kluckhohn and H. A. Murray, Eds.). New York: Alfred A. Knopf, 1949, pp. 437–458.

Davis, A. Child training and social class. In *Child behavior and development.* New York: McGraw-Hill, Inc., 1943, pp. 607–620.

Davis, Allison. Education for the conservation of human resources, *Progressive Educ.,* 1950, *27,* 221–224. Cited in *The social foundations of education* (William Stanley and others, Eds.), 8th ed. New York: Holt, Rinehart and Winston, Inc., 1956, p. 264.

Davis, F. B. *Educational measurements and their interpretation.* Belmont, Calif.: Wadsworth Publishing Co., 1964.

Davis, H. S. *Independent study: An annotated bibliography.* Staff Utilization Project. Cleveland, Ohio: Education Research Council of Greater Cleveland, 1966.

Davis, J. A. *Undergraduate career decisions.* Chicago: Adeline Publishing Co., 1965.

Davis, O. L. Learning about time zones: An experiment in the development of certain time and space concepts (unpublished doctoral dissertation). Nashville, Tenn.: George Peabody College for Teachers, 1958.

Davis, O. L., Jr., and June J. Slobodian. Teacher behavior toward boys and girls during first grade reading instruction. *Amer. educ. Res. J.,* 1967, *4* (3), 261–270.

Day, H. I. Specific curiosity in the classroom. Paper read at annual meeting at Canadian Psychological Association, Montreal, 1966.

Deal., T. N., and P. L. Wood. Testing the early educational and psychological development of children—ages 3–6. *Rev. educ. Res.,* 1968, *38*(1), 12–18.

Dearborn, W. F., P. W. Johnson, and L. Carmichael. Oral stress and meaning in printed material. *Science,* 1949, *110*, 404.

Deb, Maya. Mental work in group and in isolation. *Indian J. Psychol,* 1964, *39* (4), 191–195.

Deese, J. Meaning and change in meaning. *Amer. Psychol.,* 1967, *8*, 641–651.

Degnan, J. A. General anxiety and attitudes toward mathematics in achievers and underachievers in mathematics. *Graduate Research in Education and Related Disciplines,* 1967, *3* (1), 49–62.

Della-Piana, G. M. An experimental evaluation of programmed learning: motivational characteristics of the learner, his responses, and certain learning outcomes. Salt Lake City: University of Utah, 1961.

Della-Piana, G. M., and N. L. Gage. Pupils' values and validity of the Minnesota Teacher Attitude Inventory. *J. educ. Psychol.,* 1955, *46*, 167–178.

De Mille, R., and P. R. Merrifield. Creativity and intelligence. *Educ. psychol. Measmt.,* 1962, *22*, 803–808.

Dembar, W. M., and R. W. Earl. Analysis of exploratory, manipulatory and curiosity behaviors. *Psychol. Rev.,* 1957, *64*, 91–96.

Dennis, W., and Marsena G. Dennis. The effect of restricted practice upon the reaching, sitting and standing of two infants. *J. genet. Psychol.,* 1935, *47*, 21–29.

Denny, J. P. Effects of anxiety and intelligence on concept formation. *J. exp. Psychol.,* 1966, *72*, 596–602.

Deutsch, M. The disadvantaged child and the learning process: Some social psychological and developmental considerations. In *Education in depressed areas* (A. H. Passow, Ed.). New York: Teachers College Press, Columbia University, 1963, pp. 163–179.

Deutsch, M., and others. Some considerations as to the contributions of social, personality and racial factors to school retardation in minority group children. Paper read at meeting of American Psychological Association, Chicago, September 1956.

Deutsche, J. M. *The development of children's concepts of causal relationships.* Minneapolis: University of Minnesota Press, 1937.

Dewey, J. *How we think.* Boston: D. C. Heath and Company, 1910.

d'Heurle, Adma, Jeanne C. Mellinger, and E. A. Haggard. Personality, intellectual, and achievement patterns in gifted children. *Psychol. Monogr.,* 1959, *73,* No. 13 (Whole No. 483).

Dickens, Sara L., and C. Hobart. Parental dominance and offspring ethnocentrism. *J. soc. Psychol.,* 1959, *49,* 297–303.

Dickinson, Elsa. Foreign languages in the elementary schools? *New York State Education,* 1961, *49,* 25–27.

Dienes, Z. P. The growth of mathematical concepts in children through experience. *Educ. Res.,* 1959, *2,* 9–28.

Dienes, Z. P. *An experimental study of mathematics learning.* London: Hutchinson & Co. (Publishers), Ltd., 1963.

Dienes, Z. P. Insight into arithmetical processes. *Sch. Rev.,* 1964, *72,* 183–200.

Diethelm, D., and M. R. Jones. Influences of anxiety on attention, learning, retention, and thinking. *Arch. Neurol. Psychiat.,* 1947, *58,* 325–336.

Di Michael, S. G. The transfer effects of a how-to-study course upon different IQ levels and various academic subjects. *J. educ. Psychol.,* 1943, *34,* 166–175.

Dodwell, P. C. Children's understanding of number and related concepts. *Can. J. Psychol.,* 1960, *14,* 191–205.

Dodwell, P. C. Children's understanding of number concepts: Characteristics of an individual and a group test. *Can. J. Psychol.,* 1961, *15,* 29–36.

Douglass, H. R., and C. Kittelson. The transfer of training in high school Latin to English grammar, spelling and vocabulary. *J. exp. Educ.,* 1935, *4,* 26–33.

Downing, J. What's wrong with i/t/a? *Phi Delta Kappan,* 1967, *48*(6).

Dreger, R. M., and K. S. Miller. Comparative psychological studies of Negroes and whites in the United States. *Psychol. Bull.,* 1960, *57,* 361–402.

Dressel, P., and C. Nelson. Questions and problems in science, *Test Folio No. 1.* Princeton, N.J.: Cooperative Test Division, Educational Testing Service, 1956.

Drevdahl, J. E. Factors of importance for creativity. *J. clin. Psychol.,* 1956, *12,* 21–26.

Drevdahl, J. E., and R. B. Cattell. Personality and creativity in artists and writers. *J. clin. Psychol.,* 1958, *14,* 107–111.

Duel, H. J. Effect of periodic self-evaluation on student achievement. *J. educ. Psychol.,* 1958, *49,* 197–199.

Duncan, C. P. Transfer after training with single versus multiple tasks. *J. exp. Psychol.,* 1958, *55,* 63–72.

Duncan, C. P. Recent research on human problem solving. *Psychol. Bull.,* 1959, *56,* 397–429.

Duncan, C. P. Induction of a principle. *Quart. J. exp. Psychol.,* 1964, *16,* 373–377.

Duncan, F. M., E. I. Signori, and H. Rempel. Authoritarianism and the closure phenomenon. *Percept. Mot. Skills,* 1964, *19,* 663–666.

Duncker, K. On problem-solving. *Psychol. Monogr.,* 1945, *58* (Whole No. 270).

Dunlop, G. M. Further evidence on the control of individual differences in the classroom. *Alberta J. educ. Res.,* 1957, *3,* 104–111.

Dunn, L. M. (Ed.). *Exceptional children in the schools.* New York: Holt, Rinehart and Winston, Inc., 1963.

Durr, W. K. *The gifted student.* New York: Oxford University Press, 1964.

Durrell, D. D. *Improving reading instruction.* New York: Harcourt, Brace & World, Inc., 1956.

Easley, H. The curve of forgetting and the dishtribution of practice. *J. educ. Psychol.* 1937, *28,* 474–478.

Easley, J. A. Is the teaching of scientific method a significant educational objective? In *Philosophy and education* (I. Scheffler, Ed.). Boston: Allyn and Bacon, Inc., 1958.

Easley, J. A. Is the teaching of scientific method a significant educational objec- *Harvard educ. Rev.,* 1959, *29,* 4–11.

Easterbrook, J. A. The effect of emotion on cue utilization and the organization of behavior. *Psychol. Rev.,* 1950, *56,* 183–201.

Eaton, M. T., G. Weathers, and B. N. Phillips. Some reactions of classroom teachers to problem behavior in school. *Educ. Adm. Super.,* 1957, *43,* 129–139.

Ebbinghaus, G. H. *Memory,* 1885. (H. A. Ruger and C. E. Bussenius, Trs.). New York: Teachers College Press, Columbia University, 1913.

Edwards, A. L. Political frames of reference as a factor influencing recognition. *J. abnorm. soc. Psychol.,* 1941, *36,* 34–50.

Edwards, M. D., and Leona E. Tyler. Intelligence, creativity and achievement in a nonselective public junior high school. *J. educ. Psychol.,* 1965, *56,* 96–99.

Eells, K., A. Davis, R. J. Havighurst, V. E. Herrick, and R. W. Tyler. *Intelligence and cultural differences.* Chicago: University of Chicago Press, 1951.

Eglash, A. A group discussion method of teaching psychology. *J. educ. Psychol.,* 1954, *45,* 247–267.

Ehrlich, H. J. Dogmatics and learning. *J. abnorm. soc. Psychol.,* 1961, *62,* 148–149(a).

Ehrlich, H. J. Dogmatism and learning: A five-year follow-up. *Psych. Rep.,* 1961, *9,* 283–286(b).

Eigen, L. D. High-school student reactions to programmed instruction. *Phi Delta Kappan,* 1963, *44,* 282–285.

Eikenberry, D. H. Permanence of high school learning. *J. educ. Psychol.,* 1923, *14,* 463–482.

Ekstrand, B. R. Effect of sleep on memory. *J. exp. Psychol.,* 1967, *75*(1), 64–72.

Elkind, D. The development of quantitative thinking: A systematic replication of Piaget's studies. *J. genet. Psychol.,* 1961, *98,* 37–48.

Elkind, D. Quantity conceptions in college students. *J. soc. Psychol.,* 1962, *57,* 459–465.

Elkind, D. Piaget's conservation problems. *Child Develpm.,* 1967, *38,* 15–27.

Ellis, Dormer. A study of the relationships among scholastic aptitude scores and some measures of academic achievement in the senior grades of secondary schools in Toronto. Metropolitan Toronto Educational Research Council: *Distributed Report No. 12,* December 1965.

Ellis, H. E. *The transfer of learning.* New York: Crowell-Collier and Macmillan, Inc., 1965.

Ellis, J. K. The application of the "taxonomy of educational objectives" to the determination of objectives for health teaching (unpublished doctoral dissertation). East Lansing, Mich.: University of Michigan, 1963.

Endler, N. S., and J. M. Bain. Interpersonal anxiety as a function of social class. *J. soc. Psychol.,* 1966, *70*(2), 221–227.

Endler, N. S., and D. Steinberg. Prediction of academic achievement at the university level. *Personnel and Guidance,* 1963, *4,* 694–699.

Engelmann, S. Cognitive structures related to the principle of conservation. In *Recent research on the acquisition of conservation of substance* (D. W. Brison and E. V. Sullivan, Eds.). Educational Research Series No. 2. Toronto, Ont.: The Ontario Institute for Studies in Education, 1967(a).

Engelmann, S. Relationship between psychological theories and the act of teaching. *J. sch. Psychol.,* 1967, *5*(2), 93–100(b).

Engelmann, S. Teaching formal operations to preschool advantaged and disadvantaged children. *Ontario J. educ. Rec.,* 1967, *9*(3), 193–207(c).

Ericksen, S. C. The zigzag curve of learning. In *Instruction: Some contemporary viewpoints* (L. Siegel, Ed.). San Francisco: Chandler Publishing Company, 1967, pp. 141–180.

Ervin, Susan M. Training and a logical operation by children. *Child Develpm.,* 1960, *31,* 555–563.

Evans, J. L., R. Glaser, and L. E. Homme. An investigation of "teaching machine" variables using learning programs in symbolic logic. Pittsburgh: Department of Psychology, University of Pittsburgh, December 1960(a).

Evans, J. L., R. Glaser, and L. E. Homme. The development and use of a "standard program for investigating programmed verbal learning." Paper presented to American Psychological Association, Chicago, September 1960(b).

Evans, J. L., R. Glaser, and L. E. Homme. A preliminary investigation of variation in the properties of verbal learning sequences of the "teaching machine" type. In *Teaching machines and programmed learning* (A. A. Lumsdaine and R. Glaser, Eds.). Washington, D.C.: National Education Association, 1960, pp. 446–451(c).

Ewert, P. H., and J. F. Lambert. Part II: The effect of verbal instructions upon the formation of a concept. *J. gen. Psychol.,* 1932, *6,* 400–413.

Eysenck, S. B. G., H. J. Eysenck, and G. Claridge. Dimensions of personality, psychiatric syndromes, and mathematical models. *J. ment. Sci.,* 1960, *106,* 581–589.

Falls, J. D. Research in secondary education. *Kentucky Sch. J.,* 1928, *6,* 42–46.

Farber, I. E. Response fixation under anxiety and non-anxiety conditions. *J. exp. Psychol.,* 1948, *38,* 111–131.

Fattu, N. Exploration of interactions among instruction, content, and aptitude variables. *J. teacher Educ.,* 1963, *14,* 244–251.

Fattu, N. The international math survey: A study marred by distorted publicity. *Phi Delta Kappan,* 1967, *48*(10).

Faust, G. W., and R. C. Anderson. Effects of incidental material in a programmed Russian vocabulary lesson. *J. educ. Psychol.,* 58, 3–10.

Faw, V. A psychotherapeutic method of teaching psychology. *Amer. Psychol.,* 1949, *4,* 104–109.

Feather, N. T. The relationship of persistence at a task to expectation of success and achievement related motives. *J. abnorm. soc. Psychol.,* 1961, *63,* 552–561.

Feather, N. T. Effects of prior success and failure on expectations of success and subsequent performance. *J. Pers. Soc. Psychol.,* March 1966, *3,* 287–298.

Feldhusen, J. F., T. Denny, and C. F. Condon. Anxiety, divergent thinking and achievement. *J. educ. Psychol.,* 1965, *56,* 40–45.

Feldhusen, J. F., and H. J. Klausmeier. Anxiety, intelligence, and achievement in children of low, average, and high intelligence. *Child Develpm.,* 1962, *33,* 403–409.

Feshbach, Norma D. Effects of teachers' reinforcement style upon children's imitation and preferences. *Proceedings of the 75th Annual Convention of the American Psychological Association,* 1967, *2,* 281–282.

Festinger, L. The motivating effect of cognitive dissonance. In *Assessment of human motives* (G. Lindzey, Ed.). New York: Grove Press, Inc., 1958, pp. 65–86.

Feibert, M. Sex difference in cognitive style. *Percept. Mot. Skills,* 1967, *24* (3, Part 2), 1277–1278.

Fiedler, F. E. *Leader attitudes and group effectiveness.* Urbana, Ill.: University of Illinois Press, 1958.

Fiedler, F. E. The effect of inter-group competition on group member adjustment. *Personnel Psychol.,* 1967, *20*(1), 33–44.

Fillenbaum, S., and A. Jackman. Dogmatism and anxiety in relation to problem solving: An extension of Rokeach's results. *J. abnorm. soc. Psychol.,* 1961, *63,* 212–214.

Findlay, A. *A hundred years of chemistry* (2d ed.). London: Gerald Duckworth & Co., Ltd., 1948.

Finney, D. J. The statistical evaluation of educational allocation and selection (with discussion). *J. Royal statist. Soc.,* 1962, *125,* Ser. A, 525–564.

Fiske, D. W., and S. R. Maddi. *Functions of varied experience.* Homewood, Ill.: The Dorsey Press, 1961.

Fitch, Mildred L., and others. Frequent testing as a motivating factor in large lecture classes. *J. educ. Psychol.,* 1951, *42,* 1–20.

Fitzgerald, D., and D. P. Ausubel. Cognitive versus affective factors in the learning and retention of controversial material. *J. educ. Psychol.,* 1963, *54,* 73–84.

Flanders, N. A. *Teacher influence, pupil attitudes and achievement.* Minneapolis: College of Education, University of Minnesota Press, 1960.

Flavell, J. H. *The developmental psychology of Jean Piaget.* Princeton, N.J.: D. Van Nostrand Company, Inc., 1963.

Fleischmann, Barbara, Silvia Gilmore, and H. Ginsberg. The strength of nonconservation. *J. exp. child Psychol.,* 1966, *4*(4), 353–368.

Fleming, W. G. Characteristics and achievement of students in Ontario Universities. Report No. II: *Atkinson Study of Utilization of Student Resources.* Toronto, Ont.: Ontario Institute for Studies in Education, 1965.

Flescher, I. Anxiety and achievement of intellectually gifted children. *J. Psychol.,* 1963, *56,* 251–268.

Floch, W. J. An investigation into the effects of three different training methods on the activation and generalization of the concept of conservation of substance in children (unpublished Ed.D. dissertation). Toronto, Ont.: University of Toronto, 1967.

Flory, John, and others. Designing new apparatus for learning. Abstract No. ED 003 732. *Office of Education Research Reports 1956–65, Resumés.* Washington, D.C.: Government Printing Office, 1967, p. 275.

Follettie, J. F. Effects of training response mode, test form, and measure on acquisition of semi-ordered factual materials. *Research Memorandum,* 24. Fort Benning, Ga.: U.S. Army Infantry Human Research Unit, April 1961.

Forehand, G. A. Problems of measuring response to literature. *Clearing House,* February 1966, *40,* 369–375.

Forgus, R. H., and R. J. Schwartz. Efficient retention and transfer as affected by learning method. *J. Psychol.,* 1957, *43,* 135–139.

Forlano, G. *School learning with various methods of practice and rewards.* New York: Teachers College Press, Columbia University, 1936.

Fowler, W. Cognitive learning in infancy and early childhood. *Psychol Bull.,* 1962, *59*(2), 116–152(a).

Fowler, W. Teaching a two-year-old to read: An experiment in early childhood learning. *Genet. Psychol. Monogr.,* 1962, *66,* 181–283(b).

Fowler, W. Effects of early stimulation on the emergence of cognitive processes. Paper delivered to the Conference on Preschool Education sponsored by the Social Sciences Research Council, University of Chicago, February 7, 1966.

Fowler, W. The effect of early stimulation: The problem of focus in developmental stimulation. Paper presented at a Symposium on Heredity and Environment. Annual Meeting of American Educational Research Association, New York, February 16, 1967.

Frankel, E. A comparative study of achieving and under-achieving high school boys of high intellectual ability. *J. educ. Res.,* 1960, *53,* 172–180.

Frase, L. T. Learning from prose material: length of passage, knowledge of results and position of questions. *J. educ. Psychol.,* 1957, *58*(5), 266–272.

Frase, L. T. Some data concerning the mathemagenic hypothesis. *Amer. educ. Res. J.,* 1968, *5*(2), 181–189.

Freeberg, N. E., and D. T. Payne. Parental influence on cognitive development in early childhood: A review. *Child Develpm.,* 1967, *38,* 65–87.

Freedman, J. L. Increasing creativity by free-association training. *J. exp. Psychol.,* 1965, *69,* 88–91.

Freeman, F. N., and C. D. Flory. Growth in intellectual ability as measured by repeated tests. *Monogr. Soc. Res. Child Develpm.,* 1937, *2,* No. 2.

French, E. G., and F. H. Thomas. The relation of achievement motivation to problem solving. *J. abnorm. soc. Psychol.,* 1958, *56,* 45–48.

French, J. W. New tests for predicting the performance of college students with high-level aptitude. *J. educ. Psychol.,* 1964, *55,* 185–194.

Frey, S. H., S. Shimabukuro, and A. B. Woodruff. Attitude change in programed instruction related to achievement and performance. *AV Communication Rev.*, Summer 1967, *15*, 199–205.

Friedlander, B. Z. A psychologist's second thoughts on concepts, curiosity and discovery in teaching and learning. *Harvard educ. Rev.*, 1965, *35*(1), 18–38.

Frutchey, F. P. Retention in high school chemistry. *J. higher Educ.*, 1937, *8*, 217–218.

Fry, E. i/t/a: A look at the research data. *Education*, 1967, *87*(9), 549–553.

Fry, E. G. A study of teaching machine response modes. In *Teaching machines and programmed learning* (A. A. Lumsdaine, and R. Glaser, Eds.). Washington, D.C.: National Education Association, 1960, pp. 469–474.

Fund for the Advancement of Education. *They went to college early*. New York: The Fund, 1957.

Gaarder, A. B., and others. The challenge of bilingualism. In *Foreign language teaching: challenge to the profession* (G. R. Bishop, Jr., Ed.). Princeton, N.J.: Princeton University Press, 1965.

Gage, N. L. (Ed.). *Handbook of research on teaching*. Skokie, Ill.: Rand McNally & Company, 1963.

Gage, N. L. Psychological conceptions of teaching. *Int. J. educ. Sci.*, 1967, *1*, 151–161.

Gage, N. L. Can science contribute to the art of teaching. *Phi Delta Kappan*, 1968, *49*(7), 399–403.

Gage, N. L., and W. R. Unruh. Theoretical formulations for research on teaching. *Rev. educ. Res.*, 1967, *3*, 358–370.

Gagné, R. M. The acquisition of knowledge. *Psych. Rev.*, 1962, *69*, 355–365(a).

Gagné, R. M. Military training and principles of learning. *Amer. Psychol.*, 1962, *17*, 83–91(b).

Gagné, R. M. *The conditions of learning*. New York: Holt, Rinehart and Winston, Inc., 1965.

Gagné, R. M. Educational objectives and human performance. In *Learning and the educational process*. (J. D. Krumboltz, Ed.). Skokie, Ill.: Rand McNally & Company, 1965, pp. 1–24.

Gagné, R. M. Instruction and the conditions of learning. In *Instruction: Some contemporary viewpoints* (L. Siegel, Ed.). San Francisco: Chandler Publishing Company, 1967, pp. 291–313.

Gagné, R. M. Contributions of learning to human development. *Psych. Rev.*, 1968, *3*, 177–191.

Gagné, R. M., and L. T. Brown. Some factors in the programing of conceptual material. *J. exp. Psychol.*, 1961, *62*, 313–321.

Gagné, R. M., J. R. Mayor, Helen L. Garstens, and N. E. Paradise. Factors in acquiring knowledge of a mathematical task. *Psychol. Monogr.*, 1962, *76* (Whole No. 526).

Gagné, R. M., and N. E. Paradise. Abilities and learning sets in knowledge acquisition. *Psychol. Monogr.*, 1961, *75*, No. 14 (Whole No. 518).

Gagné, R. M., and E. C. Smith. A study of the effects of verbalization on problem solving. *J. exp. Psychol.*, 1962, *63*, 12–16.

Gaier, E. L. Selected personality variables and the learning process. *Psychol. Monogr.*, 1952, *66*, No. 17.

Gaier, E. L., and Helen Wamback. Self-evaluation of personality assets and liabilities of Southern white and Negro students. *J. soc. Psychol.*, 1960, *51*,
135–143.

Gaite, A. J. H. A study of retroactive inhibition and facilitation in meaningful
verbal learning (unpublished Ph.D. dissertation). Toronto, Ont.: University
of Toronto, 1968.

Gall, M., and G. A. Mendelsohn. Effects of facilitating techniques and subject-
experimenter interaction on creative problem solving. *J. Pers. soc. Psychol.*,
1967, *5*(2), 211–216.

Gallagher, J. J. *Teaching the gifted child.* Boston: Allyn and Bacon, Inc., 1964.

Garrett, H. E. A developmental theory of intelligence. *Am. Psychol.*, 1946, *1*,
372–378.

Garrett, H. E. *Statistics in psychology and education* (5th ed.). New York: David
McKay Company, Inc., 1958.

Garrett, H. E., A. I. Bryan, and R. E. Perl. The age factor in mental organization. *Arch. Psychol.*, 1935 (Whole No. 175).

Garrison, K. C., and D. G. Force, Jr. *The psychology of exceptional children*
(4th ed.). New York: The Ronald Press Company, 1965.

Garrison, K. C., and J. S. Gray. *Educational psychology.* New York: Appleton-
Century-Crofts, 1955.

Garside, R. F. The prediction of examination marks of mechanical engineering
students at King's College, Newcastle. *Brit. J. Psychol.*, 1957, *48*, 219–220.

Gates, A. I. Recitation as a factor in memorizing. *Arch. Psychol.*, 1917, *7* (Whole.
No. 40).

Gates, A. I., A. T. Jersild, T. R. McConnell, and R. C. Challman. *Educational
psychology* (3d ed.). New York: Crowell-Collier and Macmillan, Inc., 1948.

Gellerman, L. W. The double alternation problem. II. The behavior of children
and human adults in a double alternation temporal maze. *J. genet. Psychol.*,
1931, *39*, 197–226.

Gentile, J. R. The first generation of computer-assisted instructional systems: An
evaluative review. *AV Communication Rev.*, Spring 1967, *15*, 23–53.

George, C. L'anticipation dans la résolution d'une tâche complexe. *Année Psy-
chologique*, 1964, *64*, 83–100.

Gesell, A. *The embryology of human behavior: The beginnings of the human
mind.* New York: Harper & Row, Publishers, 1945.

Gesell, A., and H. Thompson. Learning and growth in identical twin infants.
Genet. Psychol. Monogr., 1929, *6*, 1–124.

Getzels, J. W., and P. W. Jackson. *Creativity and intelligence: Explorations with
gifted students.* New York: John Wiley & Sons, Inc., 1962.

Gerwitz, J. L. Studies in word fluency: Its relations to vocabulary and mental
age in young children. *J. genet. Psychol.*, 1948, *72*, 165–176.

Geyer, M. T. Influence of changing the expected time of recall. *J. exp. Psychol.*,
1930, *13*, 290–292.

Gibby, R. G., and R. Gabler. The self-concept of Negro and white children. *J.
clin. Psychol.*, 1967, *23*(2), 144–148.

Gibby, R. G., Sr., and R. G. Gibby, Jr. The effects of stress resulting from academic failure. *J. clin. Psychol.*, 1967, *23*(1), 35–37.

Gibson, J. J. Social psychology and the psychology of perceptual learning. In *Group relations at the crossroads* (M. Sherif & M. O. Wilson, Eds.). New York: Harper & Row, Publishers, 1953, pp. 120–138.

Gilbert, H. B. On the IQ ban. *Teachers Coll. Rec.*, January 1966, *67*, 282–285.

Glanzer, M. Curiosity, exploratory drive, and stimulus satiation. *Psychol. Bull.*, 1958, *55*, 302–315.

Glanzer, M., and R. Glanzer. Technique for the study of group structure and behavior. II: Empirical studies of the effects of structure in small groups. *Psychol. Bull.*, 1961, *58*, 1–27.

Glaser, R. (Ed.). *Teaching machines and programmed learning. II: Data and directions.* Washington, D.C.: National Education Association, Department of Audiovisual Instruction, 1965.

Glaze, J. A. The association value of nonsense syllables. *J. genet. Psychol.*, 1928, *35*, 255–267.

Gnagey, W. J. The relationship of parental acceptance to the professional attitudes and academic achievement of students in teacher education. Paper read before the American Educational Research Association, February 1966.

Godfrey, Eleanor P. *Audiovisual media in the public schools 1961–64.* Washington, D.C.: Bureau of Social Science Research, December 1965.

Goff, R. M. *Problems and emotional difficulties of Negro children.* New York: Teachers College Press, Columbia University, 1949.

Goldbeck, R. A., and L. J. Briggs. An analysis of response mode and feedback factors in automated instruction. *Technical Report No. 2,* Santa Barbara, Calif.: American Institute for Research, November 1960.

Goldbeck, R. A., V. N. Campbell, and Joan E. Llewellen. Further experimental evidence on response modes in automated instruction. *Technical Report No. 3.* Santa Barbara, Calif.: American Institute for Research, December 1960.

Goldberg, M. L. *Research on the talented.* New York: Bureau of Publications, Teachers College Press, Columbia University, 1965.

Goldman, A. E., and M. Levine. A developmental study of object sorting. *Child Develpm.*, 1963, *34*, 649–666.

Goldman, M. A comparison of individual and group performance for varying combinations of initial ability. *J. Pers. & Soc. Psychol.*, 1965, *1*, 210–216.

Goldman, R. J. The application of Piaget's schema of operational thinking to religious story data by means of the Guttman scalogram. *Brit. J. educ. Psychol.*, 1965, *35*, 158–170.

Gollin, E. S. Organizational characteristics of social judgment: A developmental investigation. *J. Pers.*, 1958, *26*, 139–154.

Goodlad, J. I. Research and theory regarding promotion and nonpromotion. *Elem. Sch. J.*, 1952, *53*, 150–155.

Goodlad, J. I., and R. H. Anderson. *The nongraded elementary school.* New York: Harcourt, Brace & World, Inc., 1959.

Goodlad, J. I., Renata von Stoephasius, and M. Frances Klein. *The changing school curriculum.* New York: The Fund for the Advancement of Education, 1966.

Goodman, M. E. *Race awareness in young children.* Cambridge: Addison-Wesley, 1952.

Goodman, Paul. *Growing up absurd*. New York: Vintage Books, 1956.

Gordon, H. Mental and scholastic tests among retarded children: An enquiry into the effects of schooling on the various tests. *Educ. Pamphlets, Bd. Educ.,* London, 1923, No. 44.

Gordon, K. Class results with spaced and unspaced memorizing. *J. exp. Psychol.,* 1925, *8,* 337–343.

Gough, H. G. Academic achievement in high school as predicted from the California Psychological Inventory. *J. educ. Psychol.,* 1964, *55,* 174–180.

Grant, Eva L. The effect of certain factors in the home environment upon child behavior. *Univer. Iowa Stud. Child. Welf.,* 1939, *17,* 61–64.

Gray, Susan W., and J. O. Miller. Early experience in relation to cognitive development. *Rev. educ. Res.,* 1967, *37*(5), 475–493.

Green, Edward J. Programmed instruction and college and professional education. In *Automated education handbook II. Programmed instruction* (Edith H. Goodman, Ed.). Detroit: Automated Education Center, 1965.

Green, R. F., and B. Berkowitz. Changes in intellect with age. II. Factorial analysis of Wechsler-Bellevue scores. *J. genet. Psychol.,* 1964, *104,* 3–11.

Green, T. F. Teaching, acting and behaving. *Harvard educ. Rev.,* 1964, *34,* 507–524.

Greenberg, H., and D. Fane. An investigation of several variables as determinants of authoritarianism. *J. soc. Psychol.,* 1959, *49,* 195–211.

Greenberg, H., A. L. Chase, and T. M. Cannon. Attitudes of white and Negro high school students in a west Texas town toward school integration. *J. appl. Psychol.,* 1957, *41,* 27–31.

Greenberg, J. W., and others. Attitudes of children from a deprived environment toward achievement-related concepts. *J. educ. Res.,* October 1965, 57–62.

Greenfield, Patricia M. On culture and conservation. In *Studies in cognitive growth* (J. S. Bruner, Ed.). New York: John Wiley and Sons, Inc., 1966, pp. 225–256.

Greenhouse, P. Free recall of categorized and unrelated words under serial or grouped presentation. *Psychonomic Sci.,* 1967, *8*(10), 447-448.

Gregor, A. J. Race relations, frustration and aggression. *Revue Internationale de Sociologie,* 1965, Serie *2*(2), 90–112.

Griffiths, Judith A., Carolyne A. Shantz, and I. E. Sigel. A methodological problem in conservation studies: The use of relational terms. *Child Developm.,* 1967, *38,* 841–848.

Gronlund, N. E. The accuracy of teachers' judgments concerning the sociometric status of sixth-grade pupils. *Sociometry,* 1950, *13,* 197–225; 329–357.

Grooms, R. R., and N. S. Endler. The effects of anxiety on academic achievement. *J. educ. Psychol.,* 1960, *51,* 299–304.

Gropper, G. L. Does "programed" television need active responding? *AV Communication Rev.,* Spring 1967, *15,* 5–22.

Gropper, G. L., and Gerard C. Kress, Jr. Individualizing instruction through pacing procedures. *AV Communication Rev.,* Summer 1965, *13,* 165–182.

Grose, R. F., and R. C. Birney. *Transfer of learning.* Princeton, N.J.: D. Van Nostrand Company, Inc., 1963.

Gross, M. L. *The brain watchers.* New York: Random House, 1962.

Gross, M. M. The effect of certain types of motivation on the "honesty" of children. *J. educ. Res.*, 1946, *40*, 133–140.

Grossack, M. M. Some personality characteristics of southern Negro students. *J. soc. Psychol.*, 1957, *46*, 125–131.

Grote, C. N. A comparison of the relative effectiveness of direct-detailed and directed discovery methods of teaching selected principles of mechanics in the area of physics (unpublished Ed.D. dissertation). Urbana: University of Illinois, 1960.

Grotelueschen, A. D. Differentially structured introductory learning materials and learning tasks. New York: Columbia University, 1967.

Grotelueschen, A. D., and D. O. Sjogren. Effects of differentially structured introductory materials and learning tasks on learning and transfer. *Amer. educ. Res. J.*, 1968, *5*(2).

Gruen, G. E. Experiences affecting the development of number conservation in children. *Child Develpm.*, 1965, *36*, 963–979.

Guilford, J. P. Creativity. *Amer. Psychol.*, 1950, *9*, 444–454.

Guilford, J. P. A system of the psychomotor abilities. *Amer. J. Psychol.*, 1958, *71*, 164–174.

Guilford, J. P. Three faces of intellect. *Amer. Psychol.*, 1959, *14*, 469–479.

Guilford, J. P. Intelligence: 1965 model. *Amer. Psychol.*, 1966, *21*, 20–26.

Guilford, J. P., and R. Hoepfner. Current summary of structure-of-intellect factors and suggested tests. *Reps. psychol. Lab.*, No. 30. Los Angeles: University of Southern California, 1963.

Guilford, J. P., and P. R. Merrifield. The structure of the intellect model: Its uses and implications. *Reps. psychol. Lab.*, No. 24. Los Angeles: University of Southern California, 1960.

Gurnee, H. Group learning. *Psychol. Monogr.*, 1962, *76*, No. 13 (Whole No. 532).

Guthrie, E. R. *The psychology of learning.* New York: Harper & Row, Publishers, 1952.

Gutteridge, M. V. *The duration of attention in young children.* Melbourne: University of Melbourne Press, 1935.

Hadamard, J. S. *An essay on the psychology of invention in the mathematical field.* Princeton, N. J.: Princeton University Press, 1945.

Haggard, E. A. Social status and intelligence: an experimental study of certain cultural determinants of measured intelligence. *Genet. psychol. Monogr.*, 1954, *49*, 141–186.

Hall, C. S., and G. Lindzey. *Theories of personality.* New York: John Wiley & Sons, Inc., 1957.

Hall, J. F. Retroactive inhibition in meaningful material. *J. educ. Psychol.*, 1955, *46*, 47–52.

Hall, V. C. Former student evaluation as a criterion for teaching success. *J. exp. Educ.*, 1965, *34*, 1–19.

Hamilton, Nancy R. Effects of logical versus random sequencing of items in an auto-instructional program under two conditions of covert response. *J. educ. Psychol.*, 1964, *55*, 258–266.

Hammer, E. F. *Creativity: An exploratory investigation of the personalities of gifted adolescent artists.* New York: Random House, Inc., 1961.

Hanson, J. T. Ninth-grade girls' vocational choices and their parents' occupational level. *Vocat. Guid. Quart.,* 1965, *13,* 261–264.

Harlow, H. F. Motivation as a factor in the acquisition of new responses. In *Current theory and research in motivation.* Lincoln: University of Nebraska Press, 1953, pp. 24–49.

Harré, R. Formal analysis of concepts. In *Analysis of concept learning.* (H. J. Klausmeier, Ed.). New York: Academic Press, Inc., 1966.

Harris, D. B. Child development. In *Recent research and developments and their implications for teacher education*: 30th Yearbook American Association of College Teachers of Education. Washington, D. C.: The Association, 1960, pp. 28–44.

Harootunian, B., and M. Tate. The relationship of certain selected variables to problem solving ability. *J. educ. Psychol.,* 1960, *51,* 326–333.

Hart, I. Maternal child-rearing practices and authoritarian ideology. *J. abnorm. soc. Psychol.,* 1957, *55,* 323–327.

Hartshorne, H., and M. A. May. *Studies in the nature of character.* Vol. I. *Studies in deceit.* New York: Crowell-Collier and Macmillan, Inc., 1928.

Hartson, L. Does college training influence test intelligence? *J. educ. Psychol.,* 1935, *27,* 481–491.

Harvey, O. J. Authoritarianism and conceptual functioning in varied conditions. *J. Pers.,* 1963, *31,* 462–470.

Harvey, O. J. Some cognitive determinants of influencibility. *Sociometry,* 1964, *27,* 208–221.

Harvey, O. J., D. E. Hunt, and H. M. Schroder. *Conceptual systems and personality organization.* New York: John Wiley & Sons, Inc., 1961.

Harvey, O. J., M. Prather, B. J. White, and J. K. Hoffmeister. Teacher's beliefs, classroom atmosphere and student behavior. *Amer. educ. Res. J.,* 1968, *5*(2), 151–166.

Hasan, P., and H. J. Butcher. Creativity and intelligence: A partial replication with Scottish children of Getzels' and Jackson's study. *Brit. J. Psychol.,* 1966, *57,* 1–2, 129–135.

Haselrud, G. M., and Shirley Meyers. The transfer value of given and individually derived principles. *J. educ. Psychol.,* 1958, *49,* 293–298.

Haskell, R. I. A statistical study of the comparative results produced by teaching derivations in the ninth grade Latin classes and in the ninth grade English classes of non-Latin pupils in four Philadelphia high schools (unpublished Ph.D. dissertation). University of Pennsylvania, 1923. (Cited in K. C. Garrison, and J. S. Gray. *Educational Psychology.* New York: Appleton-Century-Crofts, 1955.)

Havighurst, R. J., and F. H. Breese. Relation between ability and social status in a mid-western community, III Primary mental abilities. *J. educ. Psychol.,* 1947, *38,* 241–247.

Havighurst, R. J., and L. L. Janke. Relations between ability and social status in a mid-western community, I Ten-year-old children. *J. educ. Psychol.,* 1944, *35,* 357–368.

Havighurst, R. J., and Beatrice J. Neugarten. *Society and education* (2d ed.). Boston: Allyn & Bacon, Inc., 1962.

Havighurst, R. J., and Hilda Taba. *Adolescent character and personality.* New York: John Wiley & Sons, Inc., 1949.

Haywood, H. C., and T. D. Wachs. Size discrimination learning as a function of motivation-hygiene orientation in adolescents. *J. educ. Psychol.,* 1966, *57,* 279–286.

Hebb, D. O. Drives and the C.N.S. (Conceptual Nervous System). *Psych. Rev.,* 1955, *62,* 243–254.

Hebb, D. O. *A textbook of psychology.* Philadelphia: W. B. Saunders Company, 1958.

Heil, L. M., Marion Powell, and I. Feifer. *Characteristics of teacher behavior related to the achievement of children in several elementary grades.* Washington, D.C.: U.S. Department of Health, Education and Welfare, Office of Education, Cooperative Research Branch, 1960.

Heinonen, V. *Differentiation of primary mental abilities.* Jyvaskyla, Finland: Kustantajat Publishers, 1963.

Hendrickson, G., and W. H. Schroeder. Transfer of training in learning to hit a submerged target. *J. educ. Psychol.,* 1941, *32,* 205–213.

Hendrix, Gertrude. A new clue to transfer of training. *Elem. Sch. J.,* 1947, *48,* 197–208.

Hendrix, Gertrude. Prerequisite to meaning. *Math. Teach.,* 1950, *43,* 334–339.

Hendrix, Gertrude. Learning by discovery. *Math Teach.,* 1961, *54,* 290–299.

Herr, D. M. The sentiment of white supremacy: An ecological study. *Amer. J. Sociol.,* 1959, *64,* 592–598.

Herriott, R. E., and Nancy H. St. John. *Social class and the urban school: Impact of pupil background on teachers and principals.* New York: John Wiley & Sons, Inc., 1966.

Hershberger, W. Self-evaluational responding and typographical cueing: techniques for programming self-instructional reading materials. *J. educ. Psychol.,* 1964, *55,* 288–296.

Hess, R. D., Virginia Shipman, and David Jackson. Some new dimensions in providing equal educational opportunity. *J. Negro Educ.,* Summer 1965, *34,* 220–231.

Hibbs, A. R. Science for elementary students. *Teachers Coll. Rec.,* 1961, *63,* 136–142.

Hildreth, G. H. *Introduction to the gifted.* New York: McGraw-Hill, Inc., 1966.

Hilgard, E. R. A perspective on the relationship between learning theory and educational practices. In *Theories of learning and instruction: 63rd Yearbook Nat. Soc. Stud. Educ.,* Part 1. Chicago: University of Chicago Press, 1964, pp. 402–415.

Hilgard, E. R., and G. H. Bower. *Theories of learning.* Des Moines, Iowa: Meredith Publishing Company, 1966.

Hilgard, E. R., R. P. Irvine, and J. E. Whipple. Rote memorization, understanding, and transfer: An extension of Katona's card trick experiments. *J. exp. Psychol.,* 1953, *46,* 288–292.

Hilgard, J. Learning and maturation in preschool children. *J. genet. Psychol.*, 1932, *41*, 36–56.

Hill, D. S. Personification of ideals by urban children. *J. soc. Psychol.*, 1930, *1*, 379–392.

Hill, K. T., and S. B. Sarason. The relation of test anxiety and defensiveness to test and school performance over the elementary school years. *Monogr. Soc. Res. Child Develpm.*, 1966, *31*(2) (Serial No. 104).

Hill, M. C. Research on the Negro family. *Marriage Fam. Living.*, 1957. *19*, 25–31.

Hill, Shirley A. *A study of the logical abilities of children* (doctoral dissertation), Stanford, Calif.: Stanford University, 1961.

Hill, W. F. Activity as an autonomous drive. *J. comp. physiol. Psychol.*, 1956, *49*, 15–19.

Hitt, W. D., and J. R. Stock. The relationship between psychological character-istics and creative behavior. *Psychol. Rec.*, 1965, *15*, 133–140.

Hobson, J. R. Sex differences in primary mental abilities. *J. educ. Res.*, 1947, *41*, 126–132.

Hoffman, B. *The tyranny of testing.* New York: Crowell-Collier and Macmillan, Inc., 1962.

Hofstaetter, P. R. The changing composition of "intelligence": A study in T technique. *J. genet. Psychol.*, 1954, *85*, 159–164.

Holland, J. G. Teaching machines: An application of machines from the labora-tory. In *Teaching machines and programmed learning* (A. A. Lumsdaine and R. Glaser, Eds.). Washington, D. C.: National Education Association, 1960, pp. 215–228.

Holland, J. G., and D. Porter. The influence of repetition of incorrectly answered items in a teaching-machine program. *J. exp. anal. Behav.*, 1961, *4*, 305–307.

Holland, J. L. Creative and academic performance among talented adolescents. *J. educ. Psychol.*, 1961, *52*, 136–147.

Holland, J. L. The prediction of academic and nonacademic accomplishment. *Proceedings of the 1966 Invitational Conference on Testing Problems*, 1967, 44–51.

Holland, J. L., and J. M. Richards, Jr. The many faces of talent: A reply to Werts. *J. educ. Psychol.*, 1967, *58*(4), 205–209.

Hollingshead, A. M. *Elmtown's youth.* New York: John Wiley & Sons, Inc., 1949.

Holloway, H. D. Effects of training on the SRA Primary mental abilities (primary) and the WISC. *Child Develpm.*, 1954, *25*, 253–263.

Holtzman, W. H. Intelligence perspectives 1965: The Terman-Otis memorial lec-tures. In *Intelligence, cognitive style, and personality: A developmental ap-proach.* New York: Harcourt, Brace & World, Inc., 1966. Chapter 1, pp. 1–32.

Holzner, B. The research and development center program in the United States. In *Emerging Strategies and Structures for Educational Change.* Toronto, Ont.: The Ontario Institute for Studies in Education, 1966.

Honzik, Marjorie P. Environmental correlates of mental growth: Prediction from the family setting at 21 months. *Child Develpm.*, 1967, *38*, 337–364.

Hood, H. B. An experimental study of Piaget's theory of the development of number in children. *Brit. J. Psychol.*, 1962, *53*, 273–286.

Hopkins, K. D., O. A. Oldridge, and M. L. Williamson. An empirical comparison of pupil achievement and other variables in graded and ungraded classes. *Amer. educ. Res. J.*, 1965, *2*, 207–215.

Horn, J. L. Intelligence—why it grows, why it declines. *Trans-action*, November 1967, 23–31.

Horn, J. L., and R. B. Cattell. Age differences in fluid and crystallized intelligence. *Acta psychologica*, 1967, *26*(2), 107–129.

Horwitz, M., M. Goldman, and F. J. Lee. *A further study of the effects of power reduction on arousal of hostility.* Office of Naval Research Technical Report, 1956. Cited by M. Horwitz in The veridicality of liking and disliking, in *Person perception and interpersonal behavior* (R. Taguiri and L. Petrullo, Eds.). Stanford, Calif.: Stanford University Press, 1957.

Hovland, C. I. Experimental studies in rote-learning theory: VII. Distribution of practice with varying lengths of list. *J. exp. Psychol.*, 1940, *27*, 271–284.

Hovland, C. I., A. A. Lumsdaine, and F. D. Sheffield. *Experiments in mass communication.* Princeton, N. J.: Princeton University Press, 1949.

Hoyt, K. B. A study of the effects of teacher knowledge of characteristics on pupil achievement and attitudes toward class work. *J. educ. Psychol.*, 1955, *46*, 302–310.

Huang, I. Experimental studies on the role of repetition, organization, and the intention to learn in rote memory. *J. gen. Psychol.*, 1944, *31*, 213–217.

Hudgins, B. B. *Problem solving in the classroom.* New York: Crowell-Collier and Macmillan, Inc., 1966.

Hughes, J. L., and W. J. McNamara. A comparative study of programmed and conventional instruction in industry. *J. appl. Psychol.*, 1961, *45*, 225–231.

Hull, C. L. Qualitative aspects of the evolution of concepts. *Psychol. Monogr.*, 1920, *28* (Whole No. 123).

Hull, C. L. *Principles of behavior.* New York: Appleton-Century-Crofts, 1943.

Hulten, C. E. The personal element in teachers' marks, *J. educ. Res.*, 1925, *12*, 49–55.

Humphrey, L. G. Critique of Cattell's theory of fluid and crystallized intelligence: A critical experiment. *J. educ. Psychol.*, 1967, *58*(3) 129–136.

Hunt, J. McV. *Intelligence and experience.* New York: The Ronald Press Company, 1961.

Hunt, J. McV. The psychological basis for using pre-school enrichment as an antidote for cultural deprivation. *Merrill-Palmer Quart.*, 1964, *10*(3), 209 248.

Hunt, D. E., and B. R. Joyce. Teacher trainee personality and initial teaching style. *Amer. educ. Res. J.*, 1967, *4*(3), 253–259.

Hurst, J. G. A new factor analysis of the Merrill-Palmer with reference to theory and test construction. *Educ. psychol. Measmt.*, 1960, *20*, 519–532.

Husband, R. W. Cooperative versus solitary problem solving. *J. soc. Psychol.*, 1940, *11*, 405–409.

Husén, T. (Ed.). *International study of achievement in mathematics: A compari-*

son of twelve countries (2 vols.). Stockholm: Almqvist & Wiskell; New York: John Wiley & Sons, Inc., 1967.

Inhelder, Bärbel, and J. Piaget. *The growth of logical thinking from childhood to adolescence.* New York: Basic Books, Inc., 1958.

Inhelder, Bärbel, Magali Bovet, and Hermina Sinclair. Developpement et Apprentisage. *Schwizerische Zeitschrift für Psychologie und ihre Anwendungen,* 1967, *26*(1), 1–23.

Irion, A. L., and L. J. Briggs. Learning task and mode of operation variables in use of subject trainer. AFPTRC–TR–57–8, October 1957.

Iscoe, I., M. Williams, and J. Harvey. Modification of children's judgments by a simulated group technique: A normative developmental study. *Child Develpm.,* 1963, *34*, 963–978.

Israel, M. L. Variably blurred prompting: I. Methodology and application to the analysis of paired associate learning. *J. Psychol.,* 1960, *50*, 43–52.

I/T/A Publications, Inc. *The story of i/t/a.* New York, 1965.

Jackson, P. W. *The way teaching is:* Report of the Seminar on Teaching, Association for Supervision and Curriculum Development and The Center for the Study of Instruction. Washington, D.C.: National Education Association, 1966, pp. 7–27.

Jackson, P. W., and Henriette M. Lahaderne. Scholastic success and attitude toward school in a population of sixth graders. *J. educ. Psychol.,* 1967, *58*(1), 15–18.

Jackson, R. W. B., K. F. Preuter, G. E. Flower, and W. G. Fleming. A presentation of the concepts of The Ontario Institute for Studies in Education. In *Emerging strategies and structures for educational change.* Toronto, Ont.: The Institute, 1966.

Jackson, S. The growth of logical thinking in normal and subnormal children. *Brit. J. educ. Psychol.,* 1965, *35*, 255–258.

James, N. E. Personal reference for method as a factor in learning. *J. educ. Psychol.,* 1962, *53*, 43–47.

Janis, I. L., and B. T. King. The influence of role playing on opinion change. *J. abnorm. soc. Psychol.,* 1954, *49*, 211–218.

Janke, L. L., and R. J. Havighurst. Relations between ability and social status in a mid-western community, II Sixteen-year-old boys and girls. *J. educ. Psychol.,* 1945, *36*, 499–509.

Jarolimek, J. The taxonomy: Guide to differentiating instruction. *Social Educ.,* 1962, *26*, 445–447.

Jenkins, J. G., and K. M. Dallenbach. Oblivescence during sleep and waking. *Amer. J. Psychol.,* 1924, *35*, 605–612.

Jenkins, J. G., and W. M. Sparks. Retroactive inhibition in foreign language study. *Psychol. Bull.,* 1940, *37*, 470.

Jenks, Eleanor C. An experimental method to develop creativity in the writing of tenth grade students (unpublished doctoral dissertation). Eugene, Oregon: University of Oregon, 1965. *(Dissert. Abstr.,* 1966, *26*(8), 4501.)

Jennings, F. G. The revolution in education: It didn't start with Sputnik. *Sat. Rev.,* September 16, 1967.

Jensen, A. R. Social class, race and genetics: Implications for education. *Amer. educ. Res. J.,* 1968, *5*(1), 1–42.

Jersild, A. T., and Ruth J. Tasch. *Children's interests.* New York: Teachers College Press, Columbia University, 1949.

John, Vera P. The intellectual development of slum children: Some preliminary findings. *Amer. J. Orthopsychiat.,* 1963, *33*(5), 813–822.

John, Vera P., and L. S. Goldstein. The social context of language acquisition. *Merrill-Palmer Quart.,* 1964, *10,* 265–276.

Johnson, E. S., and C. E. Legg. Why young people leave school. *Bull. nat Assn. sec. sch. Principals,* 1944, *28,* 3–28.

Johnson, F. C. Feedback in instructional television (Abstract). *AV Communication Rev.,* 1962, *10,* 127.

Johnson, G. O. *Education for slow learners.* Englewood Cliffs, N.J.: Prentice-Hall, Inc., 1963.

Jones, H. E. The environment and mental development. In *Manual of child psychology* (2d ed., L. Carmichael, Ed.). New York: John Wiley & Sons, Inc., 1954, pp. 631–696.

Jones, H. E., and H. S. Conrad. The growth and decline of intelligence: A study of a homogeneous group between the ages of ten and sixty. *Genet. psychol. Monogr.,* 1933, *13,* No. 3.

Jones, H. E., and H. S. Conrad. Mental development in adolescence. In *43rd Yearbook Nat. Soc. Stud. Educ.,* Part I. Chicago: University of Chicago Press, 1944, 146–163.

Jones, M. G., and H. B. English. Notational vs. rote memory. *Amer. J. Psychol.,* 1926, *37,* 602–603.

Jones, E. E., and R. Kohler. The effects of plausibility on the learning of controversial statements. *J. abnorm. soc. Psychol.,* 1958, *57,* 315–320.

Joos, L. W. Utilization of teaching machine concept in elementary arithmetic. Baltimore: Board of Education of Baltimore County, 1961.

Judd, C. H. The relation of special training to general intelligence. *Educ. Rev.,* 1908, *36,* 28–42.

Kaess, W., and D. Zeaman. Positive and negative knowledge of results on a Pressey-type punchboard. *J. exp. Psychol.,* 1960, *60,* 12–17.

Kagan, J. Acquisition and significance of sex typing and sex role identity. In *Review of child development research,* Part I (M. L. Hoffman and Lois W. Hoffman, Eds.). New York: Russell Sage Foundation, 1964.

Kagan, J., and P. H. Mussen. Dependency themes on the TAT and group conformity. *J. consult. Psychol.,* 1956, *20,* 19–27.

Kagan, J., L. Pearson, and Lois Welch. Conceptual impulsivity and inductive reasoning. *Child Develpm.,* 1966, *37,* 583–594.

Kagan, J., L. W. Sontag, C. T. Baker, and V. Nelsen. Personality and IQ change. *J. abnorm. soc. Psychol.,* 1958, *56,* 261–266.

Kahl, J. A. *The American class structure.* New York: Holt, Rinehart and Winston, Inc., 1957.

Karlins, M., and H. M. Schroeder. Discovery learning, creativity and the inductive teaching program. *Psychol. Rep.,* 1967, *20*(3), Part I, 867–876.

Karplus, R. The science-curriculum—one approach. *Elec. Sch. J.*, 1962, *62*, 243–252.

Karplus, R., and H. D. Thier. *A new look at elementary school science.* Skokie, Ill.: Rand McNally & Company, 1967.

Katahn, M. Interaction of anxiety and ability in complex learning situations. *J. Pers. & soc. Psychol.*, 1966, *3*(4), 475–479.

Katkovsky, W., Anne Preston, and V. J. Crandall. Parents' attitudes toward their personal achievements and toward the achievement behaviors of their children. *J. genet. Psychol.*, 1964, *104*, 67–82(a).

Katkovsky, W., Anne Preston, and V. J. Crandall. Parents' achievement attitudes and their behavior with their children in achievement situations. *J. genet. Psychol.*, 1964, *104*, 105–121(b).

Katona, G. *Organizing and memorizing.* New York: Columbia University Press, 1940.

Keislar, E. R. Shaping of a learning set in reading. Paper presented to the American Educational Research Association, Atlantic City, N.J., February 1961.

Keislar, E. R., and J. D. McNeil. Teaching scientific theory to first grade pupils by an auto-instructional device. *Harvard educ. Rev.*, 1961, *31*, 73–83.

Keislar, E. R., and J. D. McNeil. A comparison of two response modes in an auto-instructional program with children in the primary grades. *J. educ. Psychol.*, 1962, *53*, 127–131.

Kelly, J. G., J. E. Ferson, and W. H. Holtzman. The measurement of attitudes toward the Negro in the South. *J. Soc. Psychol.*, 1958, *48*, 305–317.

Kelman, H. C., and C. I. Hovland. Reinstatement of the communicator in delayed measurement of opinion change. *J. abnorm. soc. Psychol.*, 1953, *48*, 327–335.

Kempler, H. L. Self-confidence and problem-solving rigidity. *J. clin. Psychol.*, 1962, *18*, 51.

Kendler, H. H., and Tracy S. Kendler. Inferential behavior in preschool children. *J. exp. Psychol.*, 1956, *51*, 311–314.

Kennedy, W. A., and H. C. Willicutt. Praise and blame as incentives. *Psychol. Bull.*, 1964, *62*, 323–332.

Kerfoot, J. F. Reading in the elementary school, *Rev. educ. Res.*, 1967, *37*(2), 120–133.

Kersh, B. Y. The adequacy of "meaning" as an explanation for the superiority of learning by independent discovery. *J. educ. Psychol.*, 1958, *49*, 282–292.

Kersh, B. Y. The motivating effect of learning by directed discovery. *J. educ. Psychol.*, 1963, *53*, 65–71.

Kight, H. R., and J. M. Sassenrath. Relation of achievement motivation and test anxiety to performance in programed instruction. *J. educ. Psychol.*, 1966, *57*, 14–17.

Killian, L. M., and J. L. Haer. Variables related to attitudes regarding school desegregation among white southerners. *Sociometry*, 1958, *21*, 159–164.

King, D. J., and C. N. Cofer. Retroactive interference in meaningful material as a function of the degree of contextual constraint in the original and interpolated learning. *J. gen. Psychol.*, 1960, *63*, 145–148.

Kirk, S. A. *Early education of the retarded child: An experimental study.* Urbana, Ill.: University of Illinois Press, 1958.

Kirkpatrick, J. E. The motivating effect of a specific type of testing program. *Univer. Iowa Stud. Educ.*, 1939, *9*, No. 4, 41–68.

Kittell, J. E. An experimental study of the effect of external direction during learning on transfer and retention of principles. *J. educ. Psychol.*, 1957, *48*, 391–405.

Klare, G. R., J. E. Mabry, and Lenore M. Gustafson. The relationship of patterning (underlining) to immediate retention and to acceptability of technical material. *J. app. Psychol.*, 1955, *39*, 40–42.

Klaus, D. J. The investigation of step size and error rate in programmed instruction. *NAVTRADEVCEN Tech. Rep.*, 1964, No. 1208–1.

Klausmeier, H. J. Effects of accelerating bright older elementary pupils: A follow-up. *J. educ. Psychol.*, 1963, *54*, 165–171.

Klausmeier, H. J., and J. Check. Retention and transfer in children of low, average, and high intelligence. *J. educ. Res.*, 1962, *55*, 319–322.

Klausmeier, H. J., and J. F. Feldhusen. Retention in arithmetic among children of low, average and high intelligence at 117 months of age. *J. educ. Psychol.*, 1959, *50*, 88–92.

Klausmeier, H. J., and W. Goodwin. *Learning and human abilities: Educational psychology* (2d ed.). New York: Harper & Row, Publishers, 1966, Chapter 1.

Klausmeier. H. J., and W. Wiersma. The effects of IQ level and sex on divergent thinking of 7th grade pupils of low, average, and high IQ. *J. educ. Res.*, 1965, *58*, 300–302.

Klausmeier, H. J., J. F. Feldhusen, and J. Check. *An analysis of learning efficiency in arithmetic of mentally retarded children in comparison with children of average and high intelligence.* U.S. Office of Education Cooperative Research Project No. 153. Madison, Wis.: University of Wisconsin, 1959.

Klausmeier, H. J., W. Wiersma, and C. W. Harris. Efficiency of initial learning and transfer by individuals, pairs, and quads. *J. educ. Psychol.*, 1963, *54*, 160–164.

Klein, J. P., J. J. Quarter, and R. M. Laxer. Behavioral counseling of underachievers. Toronto: The Ontario Institute for Studies in Education, 1967.

Klugman, S. F. Cooperative versus individual efficiency in problem solving. *J. educ. Psychol.*, 1944, *35*, 91–100.

Kleinmuntz, B. *Problem solving: Research, method and theory.* New York: John Wiley & Sons, Inc., 1966.

Knoell, D. M. Prediction of teaching success from word fluency data. *J. educ. Res.*, 1953, *46*, 673–683.

Knowlton, J. Q., and L. A. Hamerlynck. Perception of deviant behavior: A study of cheating. *J. educ. Psych.*, 1967, *58*(6), 379–385.

Koch, H. L. The relation of "primary mental abilities" in five- and six-year-olds to sex of child and characteristics of his sibling. *Child Develpm.*, 1954, *25*, 209–223.

Köhler, W. *The mentality of apes.* New York: Harcourt, Brace & World, Inc., 1925.

Kohn, P. M. Serendipity on the move: Towards a measure of intellectual motivation. *Canad. Psychol.*, 1965, *6*, 20–31.

Kohnstamm, G. A. Experiments on teaching Piagetian thought operations. In

Giving emphasis to guided learning (R. J. Ojemann and K. Pritchett, Eds.). Cleveland, Ohio: Educational Research Council of Greater Cleveland, 1966.

Kolb, D. A. Achievement motivation training for underachieving high school boys. *J. Pers. & soc. Psychol.*, 1965, *2*(6), 783–792.

Komisar, B. P. Conceptual analysis of teaching. *High School Journal*, October 1966, *50*, 14–21.

Kooker, E. W., and C. S. Williams. College students' ability to evaluate their performance on objective tests. *J. educ. Res.*, 1959, *53*, 69–72.

Kounin, J. S., and P. V. Gump. The comparative influence of punitive and non-punitive teachers upon children's concepts of school misconduct. *J. educ. Psychol.*, 1961, *52*, 44–49.

Kounin, J. S., P. V. Gump, and J. J. Ryan. Explorations in classroom management. *J. teach. Educ.*, 1961, *12*, 235–246.

Krathwohl, D. R., and others. *Taxonomy of educational objectives: The classification of educational goals. Handbook II: Affective domain.* New York: David McKay Company, Inc., 1964.

Krech, D. The chemistry of learning. *Sat. Rev.*, January 20, 1968.

Kris, Ernst. *Psychoanalytic explorations in art.* New York: International Universities Press, Inc., 1952.

Kristy, Norton F. The future of educational technology. *Phi Delta Kappan*, 1967, *48*, 240–243.

Kropp, R. P., H. W. Stoker, and W. L. Bashaw. Validation of the taxonomy of educational objectives. *J. exp. Educ.*, 1966, *34*(3), 69–76.

Krueger, L. O. The relative effect of interspersing a recall at different stages of learning. *Arch. Psychol.*, 1930, *18* (Whole No. 114), 15–25.

Krueger, W. C. F. The effect of overlearning on retention. *J. exp. Psychol.*, 1929, *12*, 71–78.

Krueger, W. C. F. The optimal effect of recall during learning. *Arch. Psychol.*, 1930, *18* (Whole No. 114), 26–34.

Krug, R. E. Over- and under-achievement and the Edwards Personal Preference Schedule. *J. appl. Psychol.*, 1959, *43*, 133–137.

Krumboltz, J. D. Meaningful learning and retention: practice and reinforcement variables. *Rev. educ. Res.*, 1961, *31*, 535–546.

Krumboltz, J. D., and R. G. Weisman. The effect of overt vs. covert responding to programmed instruction on immediate and delayed retention. *J. educ. Psychol.*, 1962, *53*, 89–92(a).

Krumboltz, J. D., and R. G. Weisman. The effect of intermittent confirmation in programmed instruction. Paper presented to the American Psychological Association, St. Louis, September 1962(b).

Kuhlen, R. G. *The psychology of adolescent development.* New York: Harper & Row, Publishers, 1952.

Kubie, L. S. *Neurotic distortions of the creative process.* New York: The Noonday Press, 1952.

Kurtz, A. K., Jeanette S. Walter, and H. Brenner. The effects of inserted questions and statements on film learning. *Technical Report–SDC. 269–7–16.* Pennsylvania State College, Instructional Films Research Program, September 1950.

Ladd, E. T. Perplexities of the problem of keeping order. *Harvard educ. Rev.,* 1958, *28,* 19–28.

Ladd, F. E. Concept learning in relation to open and closed mindedness and academic aptitude. *Psychol. Rep.,* 1967, *20*(1), 135–142.

Lambert, P. Schedules of reinforcement: Effects on programmed learning. Paper presented to the American Psychological Association, St. Louis, September 1962.

Lambert, P., and others. Experimental folklore and experimentation: The study of programmed learning in Wauwatosa public schools. *J. educ. Psychol.,* 1962, *55,* 485–491.

Lanczos, C. *The variational principles of mechanics.* Toronto, Ont.: University of Toronto Press, 1949.

Lantz, Beatrice. Some dynamic aspects of success and failure. *Psychol. Monogr.,* 1945, *59,* No. 1 (Whole No. 271).

Larson, G. L. Comparison of acquisition, retention, and transfer among three styles of learning, unpublished Ph.D. dissertation). Urbana, Ill.: University of Illinois, 1963.

Lathrop, C. W., and C. A. Norford. Contributions of film introductions and film summaries to learning from instructional films. *Technical Report–SDC.* 269–7–8, Pennsylvania State College, Instructional Films Research Program, November 1949.

Lazare, Sharon. Creativity and curiosity: The overlap. *Child Study,* 1967, *29*(2), 22–29.

Laycock, S. R., and B. C. Munro. *Educational psychology.* Vancouver: The Copp Clark Publishing Company, 1966.

Lee, P. The activation and generalization of conservation of substance (unpublished Ph.D. dissertation). Syracuse, N.Y.: Syracuse University, 1966.

LeFevre, Carol. Inner-city school: As the children see it. *Elem. Sch. J.,* 1966, *67*(1), 8–15.

LeFevre, Carol. Teacher characteristics and careers. *Rev. educ. Res.,* 1967, *37*(4), 433–447.

Lefford, A. The influence of emotional subject matter on logical reasoning. *J. gen. Psychol.,* 1946, *34,* 127–151.

Lehman, H. C. The relationship between chronological age and high level research output in physics and chemistry. *J. Gerontol.,* 1964, *19,* 157–164.

Lesser, G. S. Recent revisions and educational applications of the concepts of intelligence and giftedness. Address at Institute for School Psychologists, University of Wisconsin, 1962.

Lesser, G. S., Rhoda N. Krawith, and Rita Packard. Experimental arousal of achievement motivation in adolescent girls. *J. abnorm. soc. Psychol.,* 1963, *66,* 59–66.

Lessinger, L. M. Test building and test banks through the use of the taxonomy of educational objectives. *California J. educ. Res.,* 1963, *14*(5), 195–201.

Lester, Olive P. Mental set in relation to retroactive inhibition. *J. exp. Psychol.,* 1932, *15,* 681–699.

Levin, G. R., and B. L. Baker. Item scrambling in a self-instructional program. *J. educ. Psychol.,* 1963, *54,* 138–143.

Levine, J., and G. Murphy. The learning and forgetting of controversial material. *J. abnorm. soc. Psychol.*, 1943, *38*, 507–517.

Levonian, E. Opinion change as mediated by an audience-tailored film. *AV Communication Rev.*, July-August 1963, *11*, 104–113.

Levonian, E. Retention of information in relation to arousal during continuously-presented material. *Amer. educ. Res. J.*, 1967, *4*(2), 103–116.

Lieberman, J. Nina. Playfulness and divergent thinking: An investigation of their relationship at the kindergarten level. *J. genet. Psychol.*, 1965, *107*, 219–224.

Lillienfeld, A. M., and B. Pasamanick. The association of maternal and fetal factors with the development of mental deficiency, II Relationship to maternal age, birth order, previous reproductive loss and degree of mental deficiency. *Amer. J. ment. Def.*, 1956, *60*, 557–569.

Lindenbaum, S., and A. Blum. Development of concrete transivity of length: Empirical evidence for the debate. *Proceedings of the 75th Annual Convention of the American Psychological Association*, 1967, *2*, 165–166.

Lindquist, E. F. *Design and analysis of experiments in psychology and education.* Boston: Houghton Mifflin Company, 1953.

Lippitt, R. An experimental study of the effect of democratic and authoritarian group atmospheres. *Univer. Iowa Stud. Child Welf.*, *16*, No. 3. Iowa City, Iowa: University of Iowa, 1940.

Lippitt, R., and R. K. White. An experimental study of leadership and group life. In *Readings in social psychology* (E. E. Maccoby, T. M. Newcomb, and E. E. Hartley, Eds.). New York: Holt, Rinehart and Winston, Inc., 1958, 496–511.

Lipset, S. M. Democracy and working-class authoritarianism. *Amer. sociol. Rev.*, 1959, *24*, 482–501.

Lipson, J. I. An individualized science laboratory. *Science and Children*, December 1966, *4*(4).

Livson, N., and P. H. Mussen. The relation of control to overt aggression and dependency. *J. abnorm. soc. Psychol.*, 1957, *55*, 66–71.

Livson, N., and T. F. Nichols. Social attitude configurations in an adolescent group. *J. genet. Psychol.*, 1957, *91*, 3–23.

Ljung, B. O. *The adolescent growth spurt in mental growth.* Stockholm, Sweden: Almqvist and Wiksell, 1965.

Locke, E. A. Some correlatives of classroom and out-of-class achievement in gifted science students. *J. educ. Psychol.*, 1963, *54*, 238–248.

Locke, E. A. Relationship of task success to task liking: A replication. *Psychol. Rep.*, 1966, *18*(2), 552–554.

Locke, A. E. Further data on relationship of task success to liking and satisfaction. *Psychol. Rep.*, 1967, *20*(1), 246(a).

Locke, A. E. Motivational effects of knowledge of results: Knowledge or goal setting? *J. appl. Psychol.*, 1961, *51*(4, Part I), 324–329(b).

Lombard, J. W. Preparing better classroom tests. *The Science Teacher*, 1965, 33–38.

Long, L., and L. Welch. The development of the ability to discriminate and match numbers. *J. genet. Psychol.*, 1941, *59*, 377–387(a).

Long, L., and L. Welch. Reasoning ability in young children. *J. Psychol.*, 1941, *12*, 21–44(b).

Lord, F. E. A study of spatial orientation of children. *J. educ. Res.*, 1941, *34*, 481–505.

Loretan, J. P. The decline and fall of group intelligence testing. *Teachers Coll. Rec.*, 1965, *67*, 10–17.

Lorge, I. Schooling makes a difference. *Teachers Coll. Rec.*, 1945, *46*, 483–492.

Lorge, I., and others. Solutions by teams and by individuals to a field problem at different levels of reality. *J. educ. Psychol.*, 1955, *46*, 17–24.

Lorge, K. Groupness of the group. *J. educ. Psychol.*, 1955, *46*, 449–456.

Lott, A. J., and Bernice E. Lott. Group cohesiveness, communication level and conformity. *J. abnorm. soc. Psychol.*, 1961, *62*, 408–412.

Lott, A. J., and Bernice E. Lott. Group cohesiveness and individual learning. *J. educ. Psychol.*, 1966, *57*, 61–73.

Lovell, K. A follow-up study of some aspects of the work of Piaget and Inhelder on the child's conception of space. *Brit. J. educ. Psychol.*, 1959, *29*, 104–117(a).

Lovell, K. Jean Piaget's views on conservation of quantity. *Indian psychol. Bull.*, 1959, *4*, 16–19(b).

Lovell, K. A follow-up study of Inhelder and Piaget's "The growth of logical thinking." *Brit. J. Psychol.*, 1961, *52*, 143–153(a).

Lovell, K. *The growth of basic mathematical and scientific concepts in children.* New York: Philosophical Library, Inc., 1961(b).

Lovell, K., and E. Ogilvie. A study of the conservation of substance in the junior school child. *Brit. J. educ. Psychol.*, 1960, *30*, 109–118.

Luchins, A. S. Mechanization in problem solving: The effect of einstellung. *Psychol. Monogr.*, 1942, No. 248.

Luchins, A. S., and Edith H. Luchins. A structural approach to the teaching of the concept of area in intuitive geometry. *J. educ. Res.*, 1947, *40*, 528–533.

Lumsdaine, A. A. Some conclusions concerning student response and a science of instruction. In *Student response in programmed instruction* (A. A. Lumsdaine, Ed.). Washington, D.C.: National Academy of Sciences-National Research Council, 1961, 471–500.

Lumsdaine, A. A. Instruments and media of instruction. In *Handbook of research on teaching* (N. L. Gage, Ed.). Skokie, Ill.: Rand McNally & Company, 1963. Chapter 12, pp. 583–682.

Lumsdaine, A. A., and I. L. Janis. Resistance to "counterpropaganda" produced by one-sided and two-sided "propaganda" presentations. *Public Opinion Quart.*, 1953, *17*, 311–318.

Lundin, R. W., and C. R. Sawyer. The relationship between test anxiety, drinking patterns, and scholastic achievement in a group of undergraduate college men. *J. gen. Psychol.*, 1965, *73*, 143–146.

Lunneborg, Patricia W. Relations among social desirability, achievement and anxiety measures in children. *Child. Develpm.*, 1964, *35*, 169–182.

Lunzer, E. A. Some points of Piagetian theory in the light of experimental criticism. *Child psychol. Psychiat.*, 1960, *1*, 192–202.

Lynn, J. E. *Contract bridge for beginners.* Chicago: Encyclopaedia Britannica, Inc., 1963.

Lyon, D. O. The relation of length of material to time taken for learning and optimum distribution of time. *J. educ. Psychol.,* 1914, *5,* 1–9; 85–91; 155–163.

Lyon, D. O. *Memory and the learning process.* Baltimore: Warwick & York Incorporated, 1917.

McCartin, Sister Rose Amata, and C. E. Meyers. An exploration of six semantic factors at first grade. *Multivariate behav. Res.,* January, 1966, *1,* 74–94.

McClellan, D. C., J. W. Atkinson, R. A. Clark, and E. L. Lowell. *The achievement motive.* New York: Appleton-Century-Crofts, 1953.

McConnell, T. R. Discovery versus authoritative identification in the learning of children. *Univer. Iowa Stud. Educ.,* 1934, *9,* No. 5.

McDonald, F. J. The teacher and the improvement of educational practice. In *Human learning in the school* (J. P. De Cecco, Ed.). New York: Holt, Rinehart and Winston, Inc., 1963.

McDonald, F. J. The influence of learning theories on education (1900–1950). In *Theories of learning and instruction: 63rd Yearbook Nat. Soc. Stud. Educ.,* Part I. Chicago: University of Chicago Press, 1964.

McDonald, F. J. *Educational Psychology.* (2d ed.) Belmont, Calif.: Wadsworth Publishing Co., Inc., 1965.

McGee, H. M. Measurement of authoritarianism and its relation to teachers' classroom behavior. *Genet. psychol. Monogr.,* 1955, *52,* 89–146.

McGeehee, W., and W. D. Lewis. The socio-economic status of the homes of mentally superior and retarded children and the occupational rank of their parents. *J. genet. Psychol.,* 1942, *60,* 375–380.

McGeoch, J. A. Studies in retroactive inhibition: VII. Retroactive inhibition as a function of the length and frequency of the presentation of the interpolated lists. *J. exp. Psychol.,* 1936, *19,* 674–693.

McGeoch, J. A., and A. L. Irion. *The psychology of human learning.* New York: Longmans, Green & Co., Ltd., 1952.

McGeoch, J. A., and G. O. McGeoch. Studies in retroactive inhibition: X. The influence of similarity of meaning between lists of paired associates. *J. exp. Psychol.,* 1937, *21,* 320–329.

McGuigan, F. J., A. D. Calvin, and E. C. Richardson. Manifest anxiety, palmar perspiration-index, and stylus maze learning. *Amer. J. Psychol.,* 1959, *72,* 434–438.

McGuire, C., and others. Dimensions of talented behavior. *Educ. psychol. Measmt.,* 1961, *21,* 3–38.

McKeachie, W. J. Research on teaching at the college and university level. In *Handbook of Research on Teaching* (N. L. Gage, Ed.). Skokie, Ill.: Rand McNally & Company, 1963.

McKee, J. P., and B. F. Leader. The relationships of socio-economic status and aggression to the competitive behavior of preschool children. *Child Develpm.,* 1955, *26,* 135–142.

McNeil, J. D. Programed instruction versus usual classroom procedures in teaching boys to read. *Amer. educ. Res. J.,* 1964, *1,* 113–119.

McNeil, J. D., and E. R. Keislar. Individual differences and effectiveness of auto-instruction at the primary grade level. *Calif. J. educ. Res.,* 1961, *12,* 160–164.

McNeill, D. Developmental psycholinguistics. In *The genesis of language: A psycholinguistic approach* (F. Smith and G. A. Miller, Eds.). Cambridge, Mass.: The M.I.T. Press, 1966.

McNeill, D. Review of J. S. Bruner and others, *Studies in cognitive growth. Contemp. Psychol.,* 1967, *12*(11), 532–533.

McNemar, Olga W. An attempt to differentiate between individuals with high and low reasoning ability. *Amer. J. Psychol.,* 1955, *68,* 20–36.

Maccoby, Eleanor E. (Ed.). *The development of sex differences.* Stanford, Calif.: Stanford University Press, 1966.

Maccoby, N., and F. D. Sheffield. Combining practice with demonstration in teaching complex sequences: Summary and interpretation. In *Student response in programmed instruction* (A. A. Lumsdaine, Ed.). Washington, D.C.: National Academy of Sciences-National Research Council, 1961, pp. 77–85.

MacFarlane, Jean W., Lucille Allen, Marjorie P. Honzik. *A developmental study of the behavior problems of normal children between twenty-one months and fourteen years.* Berkeley, Calif.: University of California Press, 1954.

Mackie, J. B., Anabel Maxwell, and F. T. Rafferty. Psychological development of culturally disadvantaged Negro kindergarten children: A study of the selective influence of family and school variables. *Amer. J. Orthopsychiat.,* 1967, *37*(2), 367–368.

MacKinnon, D. W. The highly effective individual. *Teachers Coll. Rec.,* 1960, *61,* 367–378.

MacKinnon, D. W. The personality correlates of creativity: A study of American architects. In *Proceedings of the XIV International Congress of Applied Psychology* (G. S. Nielsen, Ed.). Copenhagen, 1961.

MacKinnon, D. W. The nature and nurture of creative talent. *Amer. Psychol.,* 1962, *17,* 484–495.

MacKinnon, D. W. Personality correlates of creativity. In *Productive thinking in education* (Mary Jane Aschner and C. E. Bish, Eds.). Washington, D.C.: National Education Association, 1965.

Madsen, K. B. *Theories of motivation.* Cleveland, Ohio: Howard Allen, Inc., 1961.

Maier, N. R. Reasoning in humans. I. On direction. *J. comp. Psychol.,* 1930, *10,* 115–143.

Maier, N. R. Assets and liabilities in group problem solving: The need for an integrative function. *Psychol Rev.,* 1967, *74*(4), 239–249.

Maller, J. B. *Cooperation and competition: An experimental study in motivation.* New York: Teachers College Press, Columbia University, 1929.

Maloney, R. M. Group learning through group discussion: A group discussion implementation analysis. *J. soc. Psychol.,* 1956, *43,* 3–9.

Malpass, Leslie F., and others. Comparison of two automated teaching procedures for retarded children (abstract). *AV Communication Rev.,* Spring 1965, *13,* 102–103.

Maltzman, I., Marigold Belloni, and M. Fishbein. Experimental studies of associative variables in originality. *Psychol. Monogr.*, 1964, *78*, No. 3 (Whole No. 580).

Maltzman, I., L. O. Brooks, W. Bogartz, and S. S. Summers. The facilitation of problem solving by prior exposure to uncommon responses. *J. exp. Psychol.*, 1958, *56*, 399–406.

Maltzman, I., E. Eisman, and L. O. Brooks. Some relationships between methods of instruction, personality variables, and problem-solving behavior. *J. educ. Psychol.*, 1950, *47*, 71–78.

Maltzman, I., E. Eisman, L. O. Brooks, and W. M. Smith. Task instructions for anagrams following different task instructions and training. *J. exp. Psychol.*, 1956, *51*, 418–420.

Maltzman, I., S. Simon, D. Raskin, and L. Licht. Experimental studies in the training of originality. *Psychol. Monogr.*, 1960, No. 493, 1–23.

Mann, J. H. The effect of interracial contact on sociometric choices and perceptions. *J. soc. Psychol.*, 1959, *50*, 143–152.

Mannix, J. B. The number of concepts of a group of E.S.N. children. *Brit. J. educ. Psychol.*, 1960, *30*, 180–181.

Marks, J. B. Interests, leadership and sociometric status among adolescents. *Sociometry*, 1954, *17*, 340–349.

Marks, M. R. Problem solving as a function of the situation. *J. exp. Psychol.*, 1951, *41*, 74–80.

Marks, P. A., and N. Vestre. Relative effects of drive level and irrelevant responses of performance of a complex task. *Psychol. Rev.*, 1961, *11*, 177–180.

Marquart, Dorothy I. Group problem solving. *J. soc. Psychol.*, 1955, *41*, 103–113.

Marsh, G. Effect of overtraining on reversal and nonreversal shifts in nursery school children. *Child Develpm.*, 1964, *35*, 1367–1372.

Marsh, R. W. Research note: A statistical re-analysis of Getzel's and Jackson's data. *Brit. J. educ. Psychol.*, 1964, *34* (Part 1), 91–93.

Marshall, J. C. Composition errors and essay examination grades re-examined. *Amer. educ. Res. J.*, 1967, *4*(4), 375–386.

Maslow, A. H. A theory of human motivation. *Psychol. Rev.*, 1943, *50*, 370–396.

Maslow, A. H. Some theoretical consequences of basic need gratifications. *J. Pers.*, 1948, *16*, 402–416.

Maw, W. H., and E. W. Maw. Children's curiosity as an aspect of reading comprehension. *Reading Teacher*, 1962, *15*, 236–240.

May, Mark A. *Enhancements and simplifications of motivational and stimulus variables in audio-visual instructional materials.* U.S. Office of Education, Project No. 5–0999, Contract No. OE–5–16–006. Hamden, Conn.: Author, 1965.

Mead, Margaret (Ed.). *Cooperation and competition among primitive peoples.* New York: McGraw-Hill, Inc., 1937.

Medley, D. M., and H. E. Mitzel. Some behavioral correlates of teacher effectiveness. *J. educ. Psychol.*, 1959, *50*, 239–246.

Mednick, Martha T., S. A. Mednick, and C. C. Jung. Continual association as a function of level of creativity and type of verbal stimulus. *J. abnorm. soc. Psychol.*, 1964, *69*, 511–515.

Mehler, J. Some effects of grammatical transformations on the recall of English sentences. *Journal of verbal learning and verbal behavior*, 1936, *2*, 346–351.

Meister, M. Cooperation of secondary schools and colleges in acceleration of gifted students. *J. educ. Sociol.*, 1956, *29*, 220–227.

Melton, A. W. (Ed.). *Categories of human learning.* New York: Academic Press, Inc., 1964.

Melton, A. W., and J. McQ. Irwin. The influence of degree of interpolated learning on retroactive inhibition and the overt transfer of specific responses. *Amer. J. Psychol.*, 1940, *53*, 173–203.

Mermelstein, E., and L. S. Shulman. Lack of formal schooling and the acquisition of conservation. *Child Develpm.*, 1967, *38*, 39–52.

Merrifield, P. R., J. B. Guilford, P. R. Christensen, and J. W. Frick. A factor-analytic study of problem solving abilities. *Reps. Psych. Lab.*, No. 22, Los Angeles, Calif.: University of Southern California, 1960.

Merrill, Maud A. Significance of IQ's on the Revised Stanford-Binet Scales. *J. educ. Psychol.*, 1938, *29*, 641–651.

Merrill, M. D. Correction and review on successive parts in learning a hierarchical task. *J. educ. Psychol.*, 1965, *56*, 225–234.

Merrill, M. D., and L. M. Stolurow. Hierarchical preview versus problem oriented review in learning an imaginary science. *Amer. educ. Res. J.*, 1966, *3*, 251–262.

Meyer, Susan R. Report on the initial test of a junior high-school program. In *Teaching machines and programmed learning* (A. A. Lumsdaine and R. Glaser, Eds.). Washington, D.C.: National Education Association, 1960, pp. 229–246(a).

Meyer, Susan R. A test of the principles of "activity," "immediate reinforcement," and "guidance" as instrumented by Skinner's teaching machine. *Dissert. Abstr.*, 1960, *20*, 4729–4730(b).

Meyer, W. J. The stability of patterns of primary mental abilities among junior high and senior high school students. *Educ. psychol. Measmt.*, 1960, *20*, 795–800.

Meyer, W. T., and G. G. Thompson. Sex differences in the distribution of teacher approval and disapproval among sixth-grade children. *J. educ. Psychol.*, 1956, *47*, 385–396.

Meyers, C. E., H. F. Dingman, R. E. Orpet, E. G. Sitkei, and C. A. Watts. Four ability factor hypotheses at three preliterate levels in normal and retarded children. *Monogr. Soc. Res. Child Develpm.*, 1964, *29*, No. 5.

Michael, D. N., and N. Maccoby. Factors influencing verbal learning from films under varying conditions of audience participation. *J. exp. Psychol.*, 1953, *46*, 411–418.

Miezitis, Solveiga A. An exploratory study of divergent production in preschoolers (unpublished Ph.D. dissertation). Toronto, Ont.: University of Toronto, 1968.

Miller, G. A., and Jennifer A. Selfridge. Verbal context and the recall of meaningful material. *Amer. J. Psychol.*, 1950, *63*, 176–185.

Miller, R. H. An exploratory study to develop a method of using electronic data-processing for rapid identification of operational barriers to utilization of selected audiovisual materials (abstract). *AV Communication Rev.*, 1965, *13*, 224.

Millman, J., and M. D. Glock. Trends in the measurement of general mental ability. *Rev. educ. Res.*, 1965, *35*, 17–24.

Milton, O. Two-year follow up: Objective data after learning without class attendance. *Psychol. Rep.*, 1962, *11*, 833–836.

Mitzel, H. Comparison of the effectiveness of individualized with traditional instruction in ninth-grade mathematics. Paper presented to the American Educational Research Association, Atlantic City, N. J., February 1962.

Montgomery, Kay C. The role of exploratory drive in learning. *J. comp. physiol. Psychol.*, 1954, *47*, 60–64.

Moreno, J. L. *Who shall survive?* Washington, D.C.: Nervous and Mental Disease Publishing Company, 1934.

Morphett, M. V., and C. Washburne. When should children begin to read? *Elem. Sch. J.*, 1931, *31*, 496–503.

Morris, D. P., E. Soroker, and G. Buruss. Follow-up studies of shy, withdrawn children. *Amer. J. Orthopsychiat.*, 1954, *24*, 743–754.

Morrisett, L., and C. I. Hovland. A comparison of three kinds of training in human problem solving. *J. exp. Psychol.*, 1959, *58*, 52–55.

Morsh, J. E., and Eleanor W. Wilder. Identifying the effective instructor: A review of the quantitative studies, 1900–1952. *USAF Pers. Train. Res. Cent. Res. Bull.*, 1954, No. AFPTRC–TR–54–44.

Moss, H. A., and J. Kagan. Stability of achievement and recognition seeking behaviors from early childhood through adulthood. *J. abnorm. soc. Psychol.*, 1961, *62*, 504–513.

Moss, J. An experimental study of the relative effectiveness of the direct-detailed and the directed discovery methods of teaching letter-press imposition (unpublished Ed.D. dissertation). Urbana, Ill.: University of Illinois, 1960.

Mowrer, O. H. The psychologist looks at language. *Amer. Psychol.*, 1964, *9*, 660–692.

Mukerji, N. F. Investigation of ability to work in groups and in isolation. *Brit. J. Psychol.*, 1940, *30*, 352–356.

Munn, N. L. Learning in children. *In Manual of child psychology* (L. Carmichael, Ed.). New York: John Wiley & Sons, Inc., 1954, pp. 374–458.

Munro, B. C. Meaning and learning. *Alberta J. educ. Res.*, 1959, *5*, 268–281.

Murray, F. B. Training and the acquisition of the conservation of length in children. *Proceedings of the 75th Annual Convention of the American Psychological Association*, 1967, *2*, 297–298.

Murray, H. A. *Explorations in personality.* New York: Oxford University Press, 1938.

Murstein, B. I. The relationship of grade expectations and grades believed to be deserved to actual grades received. *J. exp. Educ.*, 1965, *33*, 357–362.

Myers, G. C. A study in incidental memory. *Arch. Psychol.*, 1913, *5* (Whole No. 26).

Myers, K. E., R. M. W. Travers, and Mary E. Sanford. Learning and reinforcement in student pairs. *J. educ. Psychol.,* 1965, *56,* 67–72.

Myers, Ruth L., and Louise W. Gates. *Effective listening and cognitive learning at the college level.* Muncie, Ind.: Ball State University, 1966.

Nagge, J. W. An experimental test of the theory of associative interference. *J. exp. Psychol.,* 1935, *18,* 663–682.

Nakamura, C. Y., and G. Boroczi. Effect of relative incentive value on persistence and response speed. *Child Develpm.,* 1965, *36,* 547–557.

National Education Association, Research Division. *The American public school teacher 1960–61.* Research Monograph 1963–M2. Washington, D.C.: The Association, April 1963.

National Education Association, Research Division. Non-graded schools. *Research Memo, 1965–12.* Washington, D.C.: The Association, May 1965.

National Education Association, Research Division. Instructional resources in the classroom. *Research Bulletin,* 1967, *45*(3), 75–77(a).

National Education Association, Research Division. Public school programs and practices. *Research Bulletin,* 1967, *45*(4), 119–120(b).

National Science Teachers' Association, Curriculum Committee. *Theory into action in science curriculum development.* Washington, D.C.: The Association, 1964.

National Society for the Study of Education. Report of the society's committee on arithmetic. *29th Yearbook NSSE,* 1930, pp. 611–619.

Naylor, J. C. and G. E. Briggs. Effects of task complexity and task organization on the relative efficiency of part and whole training methods. *J. exp. Psychol.,* 1963, *65,* 217–224.

Neimark, Edith D., and Nan Lewis. The development of logical problem solving strategies. *Child Develpm.,* 1967, *38,* 107–117.

Nelson, L. D. An assessment of the use of Cuisenaire materials in the teaching of elementary school mathematics. In *Canadian experience with the Cuisenaire method.* Ottawa, Ont.: The Canadian Council for Research in Education, November 1964.

Nelson, V. L. An analytical study of child learning. *Child Develpm.,* 1936, *7,* 95–114.

Neprash, J. A. Minority group contacts and social distance. *Phylon,* 1953, *14,* 207–212.

Newman, E. B. Forgetting of meaningful material during sleep and waking. *Amer. J. Psychol.,* 1939, *52,* 65–71.

Newman, F. M. Questioning the place of social science descriptions in education. *Teachers Coll. Rec.,* 1967, *69*(1).

Newman, S. E. Student versus instructor design of an experimental method. *J. educ. Psychol.,* 1957, *48,* 318–323.

Newstetter, W. K., M. J. Feldstein, and T. M. Newcomb. *Group adjustment: A study in experimental sociology.* Cleveland, Ohio: Western Reserve University, 1938.

Newton, J. M., and A. E. Hickey. Sequence effects in programed learning of a verbal concept. *J. educ. Psychol.,* 1965, *56,* 140–147.

Nichols, R. C. The inheritance of general and specific ability. *National Merit Scholarship Corporation Research Reports,* 1965, *1*(1).

Nisbet, J. Family environment and intelligence. *Eugenics Rev.,* 1953, *45,* 31–40.

Nissen, H. W., K. L. Chow, and J. Semmes. Effects of restricted opportunity for tactual, kinaesthetic and manipulative experiences on the behavior of a chimpanzee. *Amer. J. Psychol.,* 1951, *64,* 485–507.

Northrop, D. S. Effects on learning of the prominence of organizational outlines in instructional films. *Human Engineering Report*–SDC. 269–7–33. Pennsylvania State College, Instructional Films Research Program, October 1952.

Novak, J. D. A model for the interpretation and analysis of concept formation. *J. Res. Sci. Teaching,* 1965, *3,* 72–83.

Nuthall, G. A., and P. J. Lawrence. *Thinking in the classroom.* Wellington, New Zealand: New Zealand Council for Educational Research, 1966.

Nystrand, R. O., and F. Bertolaet. Strategies for allocating human and material resources. *Rev. educ. Res.,* 1967, *37*(4), 448–468.

Oakes, W. F. Use of teaching machines as a study aid in an introductory psychology course. *Psychol. Rep.,* 1960, *7,* 297–303.

Ohnmacht, F. W. Achievement, anxiety, and creative thinking. *Amer. educ. Res. J.,* 1966, *3,* 131–138.

Ojemann, R. H., E. J. Maxey, and B. C. Snider. Further study of guided learning experience in developing probability concepts in grade 5. *Percept. mot. Skills,* 1966, *23,* 97–98.

Ojemann, R. H., and K. Pritchett. Piaget and the role of guided experiences in human development. *Percept. mot. Skills,* 1963, *17,* 927–940.

Ojemann, R. H., and F. R. Wilkinson. The effect on pupil growth of an increase in teachers' understanding of pupil behavior. *J. exp. Educ.,* 1939, *8,* 143–147.

Olson, D. R. Language acquisition and cognitive development. Paper presented to International Conference on Social-Cultural Aspects of Mental Retardation, Nashville, Tenn., June 10–12, 1968.

The Ontario Institute for Studies in Education. *The Dominion Group Test of Learning Capacity* (Intermediate, Form A, Cat. No. 187). Omnibus Edition, 1962.

The Ontario Institute for Studies in Education. *Emerging Strategies and structures for educational change: Conference proceedings.* Toronto, Ont.: The Institute, 1966.

The Ontario Institute for Studies in Education. *New dimensions in curriculum development: 2nd International Curriculum Conference Proceedings.* Toronto, Ont.: The Institute, 1966.

Orpet, R. E., and C. E. Meyers. Six structure-of-intellect hypotheses in six-year-old children. *J. educ. Psychol.,* 1966, *57,* 341–360.

Orr, D. B., H. L. Friedman, and Jane C. C. Williams. Trainability of listening comprehension of speeded discourse. *J. educ. Psychol.,* 1965, *56,* 148–156.

Osborne, A. F. *Applied imagination.* New York: Charles Scribner's Sons, 1957.

Osborne, R. T. Racial differences in mental growth and school achievement: a longitudinal study. *Psychol. Rep.,* 1960, *7,* 233–239.

Osborne, R. T. Factor structure of the Wechsler Intelligence Scale for Children at pre-school level and after first grade: A longitudinal analysis. *Psychol. Rep.* 1965, *16*, 637–644.

Overing, R. L. Studies of learning from compressed visual information. In *Studies related to the design of audiovisual teaching materials* (R. M. W. Travers, and others, Eds.). Final report: May 1966. U.S. Department of Health, Education and Welfare, Office of Education Contract No. 3–20–003, Chapter 7.

Overing, R. L., and R. M. W. Travers. Effect upon transfer of variations in training conditions. *J. educ. Psychol.*, 1966, *57*, 179–188.

Owens, W. A. Age and mental abilities: A longitudinal study. *Genet. psychol. Monogr.*, 1953, *48*, 3–54.

Owens, W. A. Effects of motivating instructions on reaction time in grade school children. *Child Develpm.*, 1959, *30*, 261–268.

Page, E. B. Teacher comments and student performance: A seventy-four classroom experiment in school motivation. *J. educ. Psychol.*, 1958, *49*, 173–181.

Palermo, D. S., A. Castenada, and B. R. McCandless. The relationship of anxiety in children to performance in a complex learning task. *Child Develpm.*, 1956, *27*, 333–337.

Paradowski, W. Effect of curiosity on incidental learning. *J. educ. Psychol.*, 1967, *58*, 50–58.

Partridge, E. D. Guidance of the adolescent. In *Handbook of child guidance* (E. Harms, Ed.). New York: Child Care Publications, 1947.

Pasamanick, B., and H. Knobloch. Early language behavior in Negro children and the testing of intelligence. *J. abnorm. soc. Psychol.*, 1955, *50*, 401–402.

Passow, A. H. The maze of research on ability grouping. In *Grouping in education* (A. Yates, Ed.). New York: John Wiley & Sons, Inc., 1966, Part II, Chapter 4, 161–169.

Patrick, C. Creative thought in artists. *J. Psychol.*, 1937, *4*, 35–73.

Patrick, J. R. Studies in rational behavior and emotional excitement. II: The effect of emotional excitement on rational behavior in human beings. *J. comp. Behav.*, 1934, *18*, 153–195.

Patton, J. A. A study of the effects of student acceptance of responsibility and motivation on course behavior (unpublished doctoral dissertation). East Lansing, Mich.: University of Michigan, 1955.

Pavalko, R. M. Aspirants to teaching: Some differences between high school senior boys and girls planning on a career in teaching. *Sociol. soc. Res.*, 1965, *50*, 47–62.

Peak, Helen. Attitude and motivation. In *Nebraska Symposium on Motivation.* Lincoln, Neb.: University of Nebraska Press, 1955.

Peel, E. A. Experimental examination of some of Piaget's schemata concerning children's perception and thinking, and a discussion of their educational significance. *Brit. J. educ. Psychol.*, 1959, *29*, 89–103.

Penfield, W. The uncommitted cortex. *Atlantic*, July 1964, *214*, 77–81.

Penney, R. K., and B. McCann. The Children's Reactive Curiosity Scale. *Psych. Rep.*, 1964, *15*, 323–334.

Perkins, H. V. Classroom behavior and underachievement. *Amer. educ. Res. J.*, 1965, *2*, 1–12.

Peterson, G. M. An empirical study of the ability to generalize. *J. genet. Psychol.*, 1932, *6*, 90–114.

Peterson, H. A. Recitation or recall as a factor in the learning of long prose selections. *J. educ. Psychol.*, 1944, *35*, 220–228.

Peterson, H. A., M. Ellis, N. Toohill, and P. Kloess. Some meausurements of the effect of reviews. *J. educ. Psychol.*, 1935, *26*, 65–72.

Phillips, B. N., and L. A. D'Amico. Effects of cooperation and competition on the cohesiveness of small face-to-face groups. *J. educ. Psychol.*, 1956, *47*, 65–70.

Phillips, W. B. Counseling Negro students: an educational dilemma. *Calif. J. educ. Res.*, 1959, *10*, 185–188.

Piaget, J. *Judgment and reasoning in the child.* New York: Harcourt, Brace & World, Inc., 1928.

Piaget, J. *The child's conception of the world.* London: Routledge & Kegan Paul Ltd., 1929.

Piaget, J. *The child's conception of physical causality.* New York: Harcourt, Brace & World, Inc., 1932.

Piaget, J. *The psychology of intelligence.* New York: Harcourt, Brace & World, Inc., 1950.

Piaget, J. *The child's conception of number.* New York: Humanities Press, Inc.. 1952.

Piaget, J. *The construction of reality in the child.* New York: Basic Books, Inc., 1954(a).

Piaget, J. Language and thought from the genetic point of view. *Acta Psychol.*, 1954, *10*, 51–60(b).

Piaget, J. Logique et équilibre dans les comportements du sujet. *Études d'Épistémol. génét.*, 1957, *2*, 27–117.

Piaget, J. Development and learning. In *Piaget rediscovered: A report of the Conference on Cognitive Studies and Curriculum Development* (R. E. Ripple and V. N. Rockcastle, Eds.). Ithaca, N.Y.: School of Education, Cornell University, March 1964.

Piaget, J. Review of "Studies in Cognitive Growth" by J. S. Bruner and others. *Contemp. Psychol.*, 1967, *12*(11), 532–533.

Piaget, J., and Inhelder, Bärbel. *L'Image Mentale Chez L'Enfant.* Paris: Presses Universitaires de France, 1966.

Pickrel, E. W. The differential effect of manifest anxiety on test performance. *J. educ. Psychol.*, 1958, *49*, 43–46.

Pierce-Jones, J. Socio-economic status and adolescents' interests. *Psychol. Rep.*, 1959, *5*, 683(a).

Pierce-Jones, J. Vocational interest correlates of socio-economic status in adolescence. *Educ. psychol. Measmt.*, 1959, *19*, 65–71(b).

Piers, Ellen V., Jacqueline M. Daniels, and J. F. Quackenbush. The identification of creativity in adolescents. *J. educ. Psychol.*, 1960, *51*, 346–351.

Pines, Maya. How three-year-olds teach themselves to read and love it. *Harpers,* May 1963, *226*, 58–64.

Pitman, I. J. Learning to read. *J. Royal Soc. Arts,* 1961, *109*, 149–180.

Plumlee, Lynette B. Comparison of problem-types in the comprehensive mathematics test. *College Board Rev.,* 1947, *1*, 17–31.

Poincaré, H. *The foundations of science.* New York: Science Press, 1913.

Polya, E. *How to solve it: A new aspect of mathematical method.* Princeton, N.J.: Princeton University Press, 1945.

Pond, F. L. Influence of the study of Latin on word knowledge. *School Rev.,* 1938, *46,* 611–618.

Popp, Helen, and D. Porter. Programming verbal skills for primary grades. *AV Communication Rev.,* 1960, *8,* 165–175.

Poppleton, Pamela K., and K. Austwick. A comparison of programmed learning and notetaking at two age levels. *Brit. J. educ. Psychol.,* 1964, *34,* 43–50.

Porter, D. Some effects of year-long teaching machine instruction. In *Automatic teaching: The state of the art* (E. Galanter, Ed.). New York: John Wiley & Sons, Inc., 1959, pp. 85–90.

Postman, L., and Virginia L. Senders. Incidental learning and generality of set. *J. exp. Psychol.,* 1946, *36,* 153–165.

Potts, Marion. The effect of second-language instruction on the reading proficiency and general school achievement of primary-grade children. *Amer. educ. Res. J.,* 1967, *4*(4), 366–373.

Pressey, S. L. Some perspectives and major problems regarding "teaching machines." In *Teaching machines and programmed learning* (A. A. Lumsdaine and R. Glaser, Eds.). Washington, D.C.: National Education Association, 1960.

Pressey, S. L. Basic unresolved teaching-machine problems. *Theory into Practice,* 1962, *1,* 30–37(a).

Pressey, S. L. New theory, no "programming," new future. Paper presented to the American Psychological Association, St. Louis, Mo., September 1962(b).

Pressey, S. L. Age and the doctorate—then and now. *J. higher Educ.,* 1962, *33,* 153–160(c).

Pressey, S. L. Two basic neglected psychoeducational problems. *Amer. Psychol.,* 1965, *20,* 391–393.

Pressey, S. L. "Fordling" accelerates ten years after. *J. consult. Psychol.,* 1967, *14,* 73–80(a).

Pressey, S. L. Re-program programing? *Psychol. in Sch.,* July 1967, *4,* 234–239(b).

Price, B. Marian, and B. G. Bell. The relationship of chronological age, mental age, IQ and sex to divergent thinking tests. *J. psychol. Researchers,* 1965, *9,* 1–9.

Probst, C. A. A general information test for kindergarten children. *Child Develpm.,* 1931, *2,* 81–95.

Prothro, E. T. Ethnocentrism and anti-Negro attitudes in the deep South. *J. abnorm. soc. Psychol.,* 1952, *47,* 105–108.

The Provincial Committee on Aims and Objectives in the Schools of Ontario. *Living and Learning: The report of the Provincial Committee on Aims and Objectives in the Schools of Ontario.* Toronto, Ont.: Newton Publishing Company, 1968.

Quimby, Violet. Differences in the self-ideal relationship of an achieved group and an underachieved group. *Calif. J. educ. Res.,* 1967, *18,* 23–31.

Raab, E., and S. M. Lipset. *Prejudice and society.* New York: Anti-Defamation League, B'nai B'rith, 1959.

Radin, Norma, and Constance K. Kamii. The child-rearing attitudes of disadvantaged Negro mothers and some educational implications. *J. Negro Educ.,* 1965, *34,* 138–146.

Randolph, P. H. An experiment in programmed instruction in junior high school (abstract). *AV Communication Rev.,* 1965, *13,* 449.

Rao, V. R. Retroactive inhibition in the learning of sochool material. *J. psychol. Researches,* 1966, *10*(3), 121–129.

Rasmussen, G. R. An evaluation of student-centered and instructor-centered methods of conducting a graduate course in education. *J. educ. Psychol.,* 1956, *47,* 449–461.

Ray, W. E. An experimental comparison of direct-detailed and directed discovery methods of teaching micrometer principles and skills (unpublished Ed.D. dissertation). Urbana, Ill.: University of Illinois, 1957.

Ray, W. S. Originality in problem solving as affected by single–versus multiple –solution training problems. *J. Psychol.,* 1966, *64*(1), 107–112.

Reed, H. B. Distributed practice in addition. *J. educ. Psychol.,* 1924, *15,* 248–249.

Reed, H. B. Meaning as a factor in learning. *J. educ. Psychol.,* 1938, *29,* 419–430.

Reed, H. B. Factors influencing the learning and retention of concepts. I The influence of set. *J. exp. Psychol.,* 1946, *36,* 71–87.

Reed, H. B. Teacher variables of warmth, demand, and utilization of intrinsic motivation related to pupils' science interests: A study illustrating several potentials of variance-covariance. *J. exp. Educ.,* 1961, *29,* 205–229.

Reese, H. W. Manifest anxiety and achievement test performance. *J. educ. Psychol.,* 1961, *52,* 132–135.

Reichard, S., M. Schneider, and D. Rapaport. The development of concept formation in children. *Amer. J. Orthopsychiat.,* 1944, *14,* 156–162.

Reid, J. C., and D. W. MacLennan. Research in instructional television and film. U.S. Office of Education Identification No. OE-34041. Washington, D.C.: Government Printing Office, 1967.

Reid, J. W. An experimental study of "analysis of the goal" in problem-solving. *J. gen. Psychol.,* 1951, *44,* 51–59.

Reidford, Philip. Recent developments in preschool education. In *Psychology and early childhood education* (D. W. Brison and Jane Hill, Eds.). Monograph Series No. 4. Toronto, Ont.: The Ontario Institute for Studies in Education, 1968.

Remmers, H. H. Learning, effort and attitudes as affected by three methods of instruction in elementary psychology. *Purdue Univer. Stud. higher Educ.,* 1933, (21).

Reynolds, J. H. Cognitive transfer in verbal learning. *J. educ. Psychol.,* 1966, *57*(6), 382–388.

Rhine, R. J. The effect on problem solving of success or failure as a function of cue specificity. *Technical Report No. 8,* NR 150–149. Stanford, Calif.: Department of Psychology, Stanford University, 1955.

Richards, T. W., and Virginia L. Nelson. Abilities of infants during the first eighteen months. *J. genet. Psychol.,* 1939, *55,* 299–318.

Ridley, D. R., and R. C. Birney. Effects of training procedures on creativity scores. *J. educ. Psychol.,* 1967, *58*(3), 158–164.

Riesen, A. H. The development of visual perception in man and chimpanzee. *Science.* 1947, *106,* 107–108.

Riessman, F. *The culturally deprived child.* New York: Harper & Row, Publishers, 1962.

Ripple, R. E., and V. N. Rockcastle (Eds.). *Piaget rediscovered: A report of the Conference on Cognitive Studies and Curriculum Development.* Ithaca, N.Y.: School of Education, Cornell University, March 1964.

Ritchie, R. C., and W. H. Worth. Nongraded elementary school programs. *Alberta J. educ. Res.,* 1960, *6,* 176–185.

Robbins, L. N., R. S. Jones, and G. E. Murphy. School milieu and school problems of Negro boys. *Social Problems,* 1966, *13*(4), 428–435.

Robinson, B. W. A study of anxiety and academic achievement. *J. consult. Psychol.,* 1966, *30*(2), 165–167.

Robinson, E. S., and W. T. Heron. Result of variations in length of memorized material. *J. exp. Psychol.,* 1922, *5,* 428–448.

Robinson, F. G. The psychological basis of axiomatic mathematics (unpublished Ph.D. dissertation). University of Alberta, Edmonton, 1959.

Robinson, F. G. *The assignment of educational responsibility.* (Research Study No. 5) Ottawa: Canadian Teachers' Federation, Research Division, 1960.

Robinson, F. G. *Educational research in Canada: An analysis of potential, current status and needed development.* Ottawa, Ont.: Canadian Council for Research in Education, 1965.

Robinson, F. G. Needed curriculum research. In *New dimensions in curriculum development: Proceedings of the Second International Curriculum Conference.* Toronto, Ont.: The Ontario Institute for Studies in Education, April 1966.

Robinson, F. G. Academic psychology and educational practice: A new attempt at fusion. *Ontario Psychol. Assn. Quart.,* 1966.

Robinson, F. G. Review of *Geometry: Kindergarten to grade thirteen: Report of the K-13 Geometry Committee of the Development Division (Ontario Institute for Studies in Education). Ontario J. educ. Res.,* 1967, *10*(1), 67–71.

Robinson, F. G. *School learning: An introduction to educational psychology—Student Guide.* New York: Holt, Rinehart and Winston, Inc. (in press).

Roby, T., E. Nicol, and F. Farrell. Group problem solving under two types of executive structure. *J. abnorm. soc. Psychol.,* 1963, *67,* 550–556.

Roe, Anne. Crucial life experiences in the development of scientists. In *Education and talent* (E. P. Torrance, Ed.). Minneapolis, Minn.: University of Minnesota Press, 1960.

Roe, K. V., H. W. Case, and Anne Roe. Scrambled versus ordered sequence in autoinstructional programs. *J. educ. Res.,* 1962, *53,* 101–104.

Rogers, A. L. The growth of intelligence at the college level. *Sch. & Soc.,* 1930, *31,* 693–699.

Rohman, E. D., and A. O. Wlecke. *Pre-writing: the construction and application of models for concept formation in writing.* U.S. Department of Health, Education and Welfare, Office of Education, Cooperative Research Project No. 2174. East Lansing, Mich.: Michigan State University, 1964.

Rohwer, W. D., Jr., and others. Pictorial and verbal factors in the efficient learning of paired associates. *J. educ. Psychol.,* 1967, *58,* 278–284.

Rokeach, M. *The open and closed mind.* New York: Basic Books, Inc., 1960.

Rosen, B. C. Race, ethnicity, and the achievement syndrome. *Amer. sociol. Rev.,* 1959, *24,* 47–60.

Rosen, B. C. The achievement syndrome and economic growth in Brazil. *Soc. Forces,* 1964, *42,* 341–354.

Rosen, B. C., and R. D'Andrade. The psychosocial origins of achievement motivation. *Sociometry,* 1959, *22,* 185–218.

Rosenfeld, H., and A. Zander. The influence of teachers on aspirations of students. *J. educ. Psychol.,* 1961, *52,* 1–11.

Rosenthal, B. G. Hypnotic recall of material learned under anxiety and non-anxiety producing conditions. *J. exp. Psychol.,* 1944, *34,* 368–389.

Rosenthal, R. Self-fulfilling prophecy. *Psychol. Today,* 1968, *2*(4), 46–51.

Ross, C. C., and L. K. Henry. The relation between frequency of testing and progress in learning psychology. *J. educ. Psychol.,* 1939, *30,* 604–611.

Roth, R. H. Student reactions to programed learning. *Phi Delta Kappan,* 1963, *44,* 278–281.

Rothkopf, E. Z., and Ethel E. Bisbicos. Selective facilitative effects of interspersed questions on learning from written materials. *J. educ. Psychol.,* 1967, *58*(1), 56–61.

Rothkopf, E. Z., and Ester U. Coke. Variations in phrasing, repetition intervals, and the recall of sentence material. *J. verbal Learning verbal Behav.,* February 1966, *5,* 86–91.

Rotter, J. B. Generalized expectancies for internal versus external control of reinforcement. *Psychol Monogr.,* 1966, *80*(1) (Whole No. 609).

Rowlett, J. D. An experimental comparison of direct-detailed and directed discovery methods of teaching orthographic projection principles and skills (unpublished Ed.D. dissertation). Urbana, Ill.: University of Illinois, 1960.

Roy, B. P., and K. K. Sinha. A study of anxiety level and the effects of practice on mental work. *J. psychol. Res.,* 1966, *10*(1), 29–31.

Roy, H. L., J. D. Schein, and D. R. Frisina. New methods of language development for deaf children (abstract). *AV Communication Rev.,* 1965, *13,* 240–241.

Ruja, H. Outcomes of lecture and discussion procedures in three college courses. *J. exp. Educ.,* 1954, *22,* 385–394.

Rusk, B. A. An evaluation of a six-week Headstart program using an academically oriented curriculum: Canton, 1967 (unpublished M.S. thesis). Urbana, Ill.: University of Illinois, 1968.

Rust, M. M. The effect of resistance on intelligence test scores of young children. *Child Develpm. Monogr.,* 1931, (6).

Russell, D. G., and I. G. Sarason. Test anxiety, sex, and experimental conditions in relation to anagram solution. *J. Pers. soc. Psychol.,* 1965, *1,* 493–496.

Russell, H. H. An evaluation of a modern mathematics program. Toronto, Ont.: The Ontario Institute for Studies in Education, 1966.

Ryans, D. G. Some validity extension data from empirically derived predictors of teacher behavior. *Educ. psychol. Measmt.*, 1958, *18*, 355–370.

Ryans, D. G. *Characteristics of teachers.* Washington, D.C.: American Council on Education, 1960.

Ryans, D. G. Some relationships between pupil behavior and certain teacher characteristics. *J. educ. Psychol.*, 1961, *52*, 82–90.

Ryans, D. G. Teacher behavior, theory and research: implications for teacher education. *J. teacher Educ.*, 1963, *14*, 274–293.

Salisbury, B. A study of the transfer effects of training in logical organization. *J. educ. Res.*, 1947, *28*, 241–254.

Samuels, S. J. Attentional process in reading: The effect of pictures on the acquisition of reading responses, *J. educ. Psychol.*, 1967, *58*(6), 337–342.

Sarason, I. G. Test anxiety and the intellectual performance of college students. *J. educ. Psychol.*, 1961, *52*, 201–206.

Sarason, I. G. Test anxiety and intellectual performance. *J. abnorm. soc. Psychol.*, 1963, *66*, 73–75.

Sarason, S. B., and others. *Anxiety in elementary school children: A report of research.* New York: John Wiley & Sons, Inc., 1960.

Sarason, S. B., K. T. Hill, and P. G. Zimbardo. A longitudinal study of the relation of test anxiety to performance on intelligence and achievement tests. *Monogr. Soc. Res. Child Develpm.*, 1964, *29* (Whole No. 98).

Sassenrath, J. M., and C. M. Garverick. Effects of differential feedback from examinations on retention and transfer. *J. educ. Psychol.*, 1965, *56*, 259–263.

Sato, R. Commentary on the international study of achievement in mathematics. *Arith. Teacher*, 1968, *15*(2).

Saugstad, P. Problem-solving as dependent upon availability of functions. *Brit. J. Psychol.*, 1955, *46*, 191–198.

Saugstad, P., and K. Raaheim. Problem-solving, past experience, and availability of function. *Brit. J. Psychol.*, 1950, *51*, 97–104.

Saul, E. V., and C. E. Osgood. Perceptual organization of material as a factor influencing ease of learning and degree of retention. *J. exp. Psychol.*, 1950, *40*, 372–379.

Sax, G. Concept acquisition as a function of differing schedules and delays of reinforcement. *J. educ. Psychol.*, 1960, *51*, 32–36.

Sax, G., and J. P. Ottina. The arithmetic reasoning of pupils differing in school experience. *Calif. J. educ. Res.*, 1958, *9*, 15–19.

Scandura, J. M. Teaching—technology or theory. *Amer. educ. Res. J.*, 1966, *3*(2).

Scandura, J. M., and J. N. Wells. Advance organizers in learning abstract mathematics. *Amer. educ. Res. J.*, 1967, *4*(3), 303–320.

Scanzoni, J. Socialization, n-achievement and achievement values. *Amer. sociol. Rev.*, 1967, *32*(3), 449–456.

Scharf, J. The effect of anxiety, stress instructions and difficulty on verbal problem solving behavior (unpublished doctoral dissertation). New York University, 1964 (*Dissert. Abst.*, 1965, *26*(6), 3481).

Scherer, G. A., and M. Wertheimer. *A psycholinguistic experiment in foreign-language teaching.* New York: McGraw-Hill, Inc., 1964.

Schmeidler, Gertrude R., and others. Motivation, anxiety and stress in a difficult verbal task. *Psychol. Rep.,* 1965, *17,* 247–255.

Schneider, L., and S. Lysgaard. The deferred gratification pattern: a preliminary study. *Amer. sociol. Rev.,* 1953, *18,* 142–149.

The Schools Council for the Curriculum and Examinations. *Mathematics in primary schools: Curriculum Bulletin No. 1.* London: The Council, 1965.

Schpoont, S. H. Some relationships between task attractiveness, self-evaluated motivation, and success or failure (unpublished doctoral dissertation). Urbana, Ill.: University of Illinois, 1955.

Schramm, W. The research on programed instruction. Washington, D.C.: U.S. Department of Health, Education and Welfare, 1964.

Schrupp, M. H., and C. M. Gjerde. Teacher growth in attitudes toward behavior problems of children. *J. educ. Psychol.,* 1953, *44,* 203–214.

Schulman, M. J., and R. J. Havighurst. Relations between ability and social status in a mid-western community. IV Size of vocabulary. *J. educ. Psychol.,* 1947, *38,* 437–442.

Schulz, R. W. The role of cognitive organizers in the facilitation of concept learning in elementary school science (unpublished doctoral dissertation). Lafayette, Ind.: Purdue University, 1966.

Schunert, J. The association of mathematical achievement with certain factors resident in the teacher, in the teaching, in the pupil and in the school. *J. exp. Educ.,* 1951, *19,* 219–238.

Scriven, M. *The methodology of evaluation.* Paper written during author's tenure as director of the Evaluation Project of the Social Science Consortium, supported by a developmental grant from the U. S. Office of Education, 1965 (mimeographed, annotated in Cox and Gordon, 1966).

Sears, Pauline S. Levels of aspiration in academically successful and unsuccessful children. *J. abnorm. soc. Psychol.,* 1940, *35,* 498–536.

Sears, Pauline S. *The effect of classroom conditions on the strength of achievement motivation and work output in children.* Stanford, Calif.: Stanford University Press, 1963.

Sears, Pauline S., and E. R. Hilgard. The teacher's role in the motivation of the learner. In *Theories of learning and instruction: 63d Yearbook Nat. Soc. Stud. Educ.,* Part I. Chicago: University of Chicago Press, 1964.

Sebesta, S. L. Artificial orthography as a transitional device in first-grade reading instruction. *J. educ. Psychol.,* 1964, *55,* 253–257.

Segel, D. *Frustration in adolescent youth.* Washington, D.C.: Federal Security Agency, 1951.

Serra, M. C. A study of fourth grade children's comprehension of certain verbal abstractions. *J. exp. Educ.,* 1953, *22,* 103–118.

Severin, W. The effectiveness of relevant pictures in multiple-channel communications. *AV Communication Rev.,* Winter 1967, *15,* 386–401.

Sexton, Patricia C. Social class and pupil turn-over rates. *J. educ. Sociol.,* 1959, *33,* 131–134.

Shannon, D. C. What research says about acceleration. *Phi Delta Kappan,* 1957, *39,* 70–72.

Shantz, Carolyn U., and C. D. Smock. Development of distance conservation and the spatial coordinate system. *Child Develpm.,* 1966, *37,* 943–948.

Sharpe, J. F. The retention of meaningful material. *Catholic Univer. Amer. Educ. Res. Monogr.,* 1952, *16,* No. 8.

Shaw, M. C. Motivation in human learning. *Rev. educ. Res.,* 1967, *37*(5), 563–582.

Shaw, M. C., K. Edson, and H. M. Bell. Self-concept of bright underachieving high school students as revealed by an adjective check list. *Personnel & Guid. J.,* 1960, *39,* 193–196.

Shaw, M. C., and J. T. McCuen. The onset of academic underachievement in bright children. *J. educ. Psychol.,* 1960, *51,* 103–108.

Shaw, M. E. A comparison of individuals and small groups in the rational solution of complex problems. *Amer. J. Psychol.,* 1932, *44,* 491–504.

Shaw, M. E. Some motivational factors in cooperation and competition. *J. Pers.,* 1958, *26,* 155–169.

Shaw, M. E., and Lilly M. Shaw. Some effects of sociometric grouping upon learning in a second grade classroom. *J. soc. Psychol.,* 1962, *57,* 453–458.

Shay, C. B. Relationship of intelligence to step size on a teaching machine program. *J. educ. Psychol.,* 1961, *52,* 98–103.

Sherif, M., and Carolyn W. Sherif. *Groups in harmony and tension.* New York: Harper & Row, Publishers, 1963.

Sherif, M., and Carolyn W. Sherif. *Reference groups.* New York: Harper & Row, Publishers, 1964.

Sherman, M., and C. B. Key. The intelligence of isolated mountain children. *Child Develpm.,* 1932, *3,* 279–290.

Shuey, A. M. Improvement in scores on the American Council Psychological Examination from freshman to senior year. *J. educ. Psychol.,* 1948, *39,* 417–426.

Shulman, L. S. Review of M. A. Wallach and N. Kogan, *Modes of thinking in young children.* New York: Holt, Rinehart and Winston, Inc., 1965. In *Amer. educ. Res. J.,* 1966, *3*(4), 305–310.

Shulman, L. S., and E. R. Keislar (Eds.). *Learning by discovery: A critical appraisal.* Skokie, Ill.: Rand McNally & Company, 1967.

Shuttleworth, F. K. The cumulative influence on intelligence of socio-economic differentials operating on the same children over ten years. In *39th Yearbook Nat. Soc. Stud. Educ.,* Part II. Chicago: University of Chicago Press, 1940, pp. 275–280.

Siegel, L., and F. G. Macomber. Comparative effectiveness of televised and large classes and of small sections. *J. educ. Psychol.,* 1957, *48,* 371–382.

Sigel, I. E. Developmental trends in the abstraction ability of children. *Child Develpm.,* 1953, *24,* 131–144.

Sigel, I. E., Annemarie Roeper, and F. H. Hooper. A training procedure for acquisition of Piaget's conservation of quantity: A pilot study and its replication. *Brit. J. educ. Psychol.,* 1966, *36*(3), 301–311.

Silberman, H. F. Self-instructional devices and programmed materials. *Rev. educ. Res.,* 1962, *32,* 179–193.

Silberman, H. F., R. J. Malaragno, and J. E. Coulson. Confirmation and prompting with connected discourse material. *Psychol. Rep.,* 1961, *8,* 401–406(a).

Silberman, H. F., and others. Fixed sequence versus branching autoinstructional methods. *J. educ. Psychol.,* 1961, *52,* 166–172(b).

Siller, J. Socio-economic status and conceptual thinking. *J. abnorm. soc. Psychol.,* 1957, *55,* 365–371.

Silverman, R. E., and Millicent Alter. Note on the response in teaching machine programs. *Psychol. Rep.* 1960, *7,* 496.

Silvertsen, D. Goal setting, level of aspiration, and social norms. *Acta Psychologica,* 1959, *13,* 54–60.

Simon, S., E. J. Lotsof, and Helen P. Wycoff. Associative originality training in children. *Psychonomic Science,* 1966, *6*(6), 259–260.

Simpson, E. J. The classification of educational objectives: Psychomotor domain. U.S. Department of Health, Education and Welfare, Office of Education. Vocational and Technical Education Grant Contract No. OE-5-85-104. Urbana, Ill.: University of Illinois, 1966.

Simpson, R. M. Creative imagination. *Amer. J. Psychol.,* 1922, *33,* 234–235.

Sims, V. M. The relative influence of two types of motivation on improvement. *J. educ. Pschol.,* 1928, *19,* 480–484.

Singer, S. L., and B. Stefflre. A note on racial differences in job values and desires. *J. soc. Psychol.,* 1956, *43,* 333–337.

Sjogren, D. D. Achievement as a function of study time. *Amer. educ. Res. J.,* 1967, *4*(4), 337–344.

Skaggs, E. B., and others. Further studies of the reading-recitation process in learning. *Arch. Psychol.,* 1930, *18*(Whole No. 114).

Skeels, H. M. Adult status of children with contrasting early life experiences: A follow-up study *Child Develpm. Monogr.,* 1966, *31,* No. 3 (Serial No. 105).

Skeels, H. M., and E. A. Fillmore. Mental development of children from underprivileged homes. *J. genet. Psychol.,* 1937, *50,* 427–439.

Skeels, H. M., and others. A study of environmental stimulation: An orphanage preschool project. *Univer. Iowa Stud. Child Welf.,* 1938, (4).

Skinner, B. F. *The behavior of organisms.* New York: Appleton-Century-Crofts, 1938.

Skinner, B. F. The science of learning and the art of teaching. *Harvard educ. Rev.,* 1954, *24*(2).

Skinner, B. F. Teaching machines. *Science,* 1958, *128,* 969–977.

Skinner, B. F. Teaching machines. In *Teaching machines and programmed learning* (A. A. Lumsdaine and R. Glaser, Eds.). Washington, D.C.: National Education Association, 1960.

Slamecka, N. J. Studies of retroaction of connected discourse. *Amer. J. Psychol.,* 1959, *72,* 409–416.

Slamecka, N. J. Retroactive inhibition of connected discourse as a function of similarity of topic. *J. exp. Psychol.,* 1960, *60,* 245–249.

Slamecka, N. J. Retention of connected discourse as a function of duration of interpolated learning. *J. exp. Psychol.,* 1962, *63,* 480–486.

Smedslund, J. Transitivity of preference patterns as seen by pre-school children. *Scand. J. Psychol.,* 1960, *1,* 49–54.

Smedslund, J. The acquisition of conservation of substance and weight in children. *Scand. J. Psychol.*, 1961, *2*, 11–20, 71–87; 153–160; 203–210.

Smith, B. O. Critical thinking. In *Recent research developments and their implications for teacher education: 13th Yearbook Amer. Assn. Coll. Teacher Educ.* Washington, D.C.: The Association, 1960, 84–96.

Smith, B. O., and others. *A tentative report on the strategies of teaching.* U.S. Department of Health, Education and Welfare Cooperative Research Project No. 1640. Urbana, Ill.: Bureau of Educational Research, University of Illinois, 1964.

Smith, C. U., and J. W. Prothro. Ethnic differences in authoritarian personality. *Soc. Forces*, 1957, *35*, 334–338.

Smith, H. P. A study in the selective character of American secondary education: Participation in school activities as conditioned by socio-economic status and other factors. *J. educ. Psychol.*, 1945, *36*, 229–246.

Smith, Leone M. Programed learning in elementary school: an experimental study of relationships between mental abilities and performance. *Technical Report* No. 2. Urbana, Illinois: Training Research Laboratory, University of Illinois, August 1962.

Smith, L. M., and F. W. Lutz. Teacher leader behavior and pupil respect and liking. *J. educ. Res.*, 1964, *57*, 434–436.

Smith, M. H., and Ellen Stearns. The influence of isolation on the learning of the surrounding material. *Amer. J. Psychol.*, 1949, *62*, 369–381.

Smith, T. E. The image of high school teachers: self and other, real and ideal (Should teachers be seen and not heard?). *J. educ. Res.*, 1965, *59*, 99–104.

Smith, W., and J. W. Moore. Size-of-step and achievement in programed spelling. *Psychol. Rep.*, 1962, *10*, 287–294.

Smock, C., and B. Holt. Children's reactions to novelty: An experimental study of curiosity motivation. *Child Develpm.*, *33*, 1962, 631–642.

Smuts, R. W. The Negro community and the development of Negro potential. *J. Negro Educ.*, 1957, *26*, 456–465.

Solomon, R. Punishment. *Amer. Psychol.*, 1964, *19*, 239–253.

Solomon, D., L. Rosenberg, and W. E. Bezdek. Teacher behavior and student learning. *J. educ. Psychol.*, 1964, *55*, 23–30.

Sommerfeld, R. E., and N. H. Tracy. A study of selected predictors of success in second-year algebra in high school. Paper presented to American Educational Research Association, Atlantic City, N. J., February 1961.

Sones, A. M., and J. B. Stroud. Review with special reference to temporal position. *J. educ. Psychol.*, 1940, *31*, 665–676.

Sonstroem, Anne M. On the conservation of solids. In J. S. Bruner and others, *Studies in cognitive growth.* New York: John Wiley & Sons, Inc., 1966, pp. 208–224.

Sontag, L. W., C. T. Baker, and V. Nelson. Personality as a determinant of performance. *Amer. J. Orthopsychiat.*, 1955, *25*, 555–563.

Spaulding, R. Achievement, creativity and self-concept correlates of teacher-pupil transactions in elementary schools. Urbana, Ill.: University of Illinois, 1963 (mimeographed).

Speer, G. S. The mental development of children of feeble-minded and normal mothers. In *39th Yearbook Nat. Soc. Stud. Educ.*, Part II. Chicago: University of Chicago Press, 1940, 309–314.

Spence, K. W. The relation of learning theory to the technology of education. *Harvard educ. Rev.*, Spring 1959, *29*, 84–95.

Spielberger, C. D. The effects of manifest anxiety on the academic achievement of college students. *Ment. Hygiene*, 1962, *46*, 420–426.

Spielberger, C. D., and W. G. Katzenmeyer. Manifest anxiety, intelligence, and college grades. *J. consult Psychol.*, 1959, *23*, 278.

Spiker, C. C., and G. Terrell. Factors associated with transposition behavior of preschool children. *J. genet. Psychol.*, 1955, *56*, 143–158.

Spitzer, H. F. Studies in retention. *J. educ. Psychol.*, 1939, *30*, 641–656.

Sprinthall, N. A., J. M. Whitely, and R. L. Mosher. A study of teacher effectiveness, *J. teacher Educ.*, Spring 1966, *17*, 93–106.

Stacey, C. L. The law of effect in retained situations with meaningful material. In *Learning theory in school situations.* University of Minnesota Studies in Education. Minneapolis, Minn.: University of Minnesota Press, 1949, pp. 74–103.

Stanley, J. C. *Measurement in today's schools* (4th ed.). New York: John Wiley & Sons, Inc., 1964.

Steckler, G. A. Authoritarian ideology in Negro college students. *J. abnorm. soc. Psychol.*, 1957, *54*, 396–399.

Stein, J. J. The effect of a pre-film test on learning from an educational sound motion picture. *Technical Report*—SDC 269–7–35. University Park, Penn.: Pennsylvania State University, Instructional Films Research Program, November 1952.

Stendler, Celia B., Dora Damrin, and A. C. Haines. Studies of cooperation and competition: I The effect of working for group and individual rewards on the social climate of children's groups. *J. genet. Psychol.*, 1951, *79*, 173–197.

Stern, G. G. Measuring noncognitive variables in research in teaching. In *Handbook of research on teaching* (N. L. Gage, Ed.). Chicago: Rand McNally & Company, 1963, pp. 398–447.

Stevenson, H. W., and T. Langford. Time as a variable in transposition by children. *Child Develpm.*, 1957, *28*, 365–370.

Stevenson, H. W., and R. D. Odom. The relation of anxiety to children's performance on learning and problem-solving tasks. *Child Develpm.*, 1965, *36*, 1003–1012.

Stevenson, H. W., and E. C. Stewart. A developmental study of racial awareness in young children. *Child Develpm.*, 1958, *29*, 399–409.

St. John, C. W. The maladjustment of boys in certain elementary grades. *Educational Administration and Supervision*, 1932, *18*, 649–672.

Stoddard, G. D. *The dual progress plan.* New York: Harper & Row, Publishers, 1961.

Stodolsky, Susan S., and G. Lesser. Learning patterns in the disadvantaged. *Harvard educ. Rev.*, Fall 1967, *37*(4), 546–589.

Stoker, H. W., and R. P. Kropp. Measurement of cognitive processes. *J. educ. Measmt.*, 1964, *1*, 39–42.

Stolurow, L. M. A comparative study of methods of programming materials for efficient learning in self-instructional devices. Cooperative Research Project No. HEW 661, SAE 8370. Urbana, Ill.: Training Research Laboratory, University of Illinois, June 1961(a).

Stolurow, L. M. *Teaching by machine.* Washington, D.C.: U.S. Office of Education, 1961(b).

Stolurow, L. M. Programed instruction for the mentally retarded (abstract). *AV Communication Rev.,* Spring 1966, *14,* 151–152.

Stolurow, L. M., and C. C. Walker. A comparison of overt and covert response in programmed learning. *J. educ Res.,* 1962, *55,* 421–429.

Stott, L. H., and Rachel S. Ball. Infant and preschool mental tests: Review and evaluation. *Monogr. Soc. Res. Child Develpm.,* 1965, *30,* No. 3 (Serial No. 101). Chicago: University of Chicago Press.

Stouffer, G. A. W., Jr. Behavior problems of children as viewed by teachers and mental hygienists. *Ment. Hygiene,* 1952, *36,* 271–285.

Strayer, Lois C. Language and growth: The relative efficacy of early and deferred vocabulary training studied by the method of co-twin control. *Genet. psychol. Monogr.,* 1930, *8,* 209–319.

Strodtbeck, F. L. Family interaction, values, and achievement. In *Talent and society* (D. C. McClelland, Ed.). Princeton, N.J.: D. Van Nostrand Company, Inc., 1958, pp. 135–194.

Stroud, J. B. The role of practice learning. In *The psychology of learning: 41st Yearbook Nat. Soc. Stud. Educ.,* Part II. Chicago: University of Chicago Press, 1942, pp. 353–376.

Suchman, J. R. *Training children in scientific inquiry.* Urbana, Ill.: College of Education, University of Illinois, 1959.

Suchman, J. R. Inquiry training in the elementary school. *Science Teacher,* 1960, *27,* 42–47.

Suchman, J. R. Inquiry training: Building skills for autonomous discovery. *Merrill-Palmer Quart.,* 1961, *7,* 148–169.

Suchman, J. R. The inquiry process and the elementary school child. Paper presented to a meeting of the American Educational Research Association, Atlantic City, N. J., February 1962.

Sugimura, T. Implicit reinforcement under competitive and noncompetitive situations. *Japanese J. educ. Psychol.,* 1966, *14*(4), 19–23.

Suinn, R. M. A factor modifying the concept of anxiety as an interfering drive. *J. gen. Psychol.,* 1965, *73,* 43–46.

Sullivan, E. V. Acquisition of substance through film modeling techniques. In *Recent research on the conservation of substance* (D. W. Brison and E. V. Sullivan, Eds.). Education Research Series No. 2, Toronto, Ont.: The Ontario Institute for Studies in Education, 1967(a).

Sullivan, E. V. *Piaget and the school curriculum: A critical appraisal.* Toronto, Ont., The Ontario Institute for Studies in Education, 1967(b).

Sullivan, E. V. Piagetian theory and the educational milieu: A critical appraisal. *Canadian J. Behav. Sci.,* Spring 1969 (in press).

Summerfield, A., and H. Steinberg. Reducing interfering in forgetting. *Quart. J. exp. Psychol.,* 1957, *9,* 146–154.

Suppes, P. On the behavioural foundations of mathematical concepts. In *Mathematical learning* (L. N. Morrisett and J. Vinsonhaler, Eds.). Monographs of the Society for Research in Child Development, 1965, *30*(1) (Serial No. 99).

Suppes, P., and Rose Gensberg. Application of a stimulus sampling model to children's concept formation with and without an overt correction response. *J. exp. Psychol.*, 1962, *63*, 330–336.

Swartz, C. A school for human children. New York State University at Stony Brook (Physics Department), undated (mimeographed).

Sweeney, J. R. An experimental study comparing the Cuisenaire method with traditional methods in Grade 1 mathematics. In *Canadian experience with the Cuisenaire method.* Ottawa, Ont.: Canadian Council for Research in Education, 1964.

Swenson, C. H. College performance of students with high and low school marks when academic aptitude is controlled. *J. educ. Res.*, 1957, *50*, 597–603.

Swenson, E. J. Organization and generalization as factors in learning, transfer, and retroactive inhibition. In *Learning theory in school situations.* Univer. Minn. Stud. Educ. Minneapolis, Minn.: University of Minnesota Press, 1949, pp. 9–39.

Symonds, P. M. *What education has to learn from psychology.* New York: Teachers College Press, Columbia University, 1958.

Szuman, S. Comparison, abstraction, and analytic thought in the child. *Enfance,* 1951, *4*, 189–216.

Taft, R. Selective recall and memory distortion of favorable and unfavorable material. *J. abnorm. soc. Psychol.*, 1954, *49*, 23–28.

Tate, M. W., and Barbara Stanier. Errors in judgment of good and poor problem solvers. *J. exp. Educ.*, 1964, *32*, 371–376.

Taylor, C. W. Educational changes needed to develop creative thinking. In *Productive thinking in education* (Mary Jane Aschner and C. E. Bish, Eds.). Washington, D. C.: National Education Association, 1965(a).

Taylor, C. W. (Ed.). *New horizons in creativity.* New York: John Wiley & Sons, Inc., 1965(b).

Taylor, P. Curriculum reform in England. In *Emerging strategies and structures for educational change.* Toronto, Ont.: The Ontario Institute for Studies in Education, 1966.

Teece, J. J. Relationship of anxiety (drive) and response competition in problem solving. *J. abnorm. Psychol.*, 1965, *70*(6), 465–467.

Ter Keurst, A. J. The intrinsic programmed approach to the discovery of concepts in general psychology. *J. exp. Educ.*, 1965, *33*, 351–355.

Terman, L. M., and M. A. Merrill. *Measuring intelligence.* Boston: Houghton Mifflin Company, 1937.

Terman, L. M., and Melita H. Oden. *The gifted child grows up: 25 years follow-up of a superior group.* Stanford, Calif.: Stanford University Press, 1949.

Terman, L. M., and Melita H. Oden. *The gifted group at mid-life.* Stanford, Calif.: Stanford University Press, 1959.

Terman, L. M., and L. E. Tyler. Psychological sex differences. In *Manual of child psychology* (L. Carmichael, Ed.). 2d ed. New York: John Wiley & Sons, Inc., 1954, pp. 1004–1114.

Terrell, G. Manipulatory motivation in children. *J. comp. physiol. Psychol.,* 1959, *52,* 705–709.

Thiele, C. L. *The contribution of generalization to the learning of addition facts.* Contributions to Education, No. 863. New York: Teachers College Press, Columbia University, 1938.

Thisted, M. N., and H. H. Remmers. The effect of temporal set on learning. *J. appl. Psychol.,* 1932, *16,* 257–268.

Thompson, G. G., and C. W. Hunnicutt. The effect of repeated praise or blame on the work achievement of "introverts" and "extroverts." *J. educ. Psychol.,* 1944, *35,* 257–266.

Thompson, R. *The psychology of thinking.* Harmondsworth, Middlesex, England: Penguin Books, 1959.

Thorndike, E. L. *The psychology of arithmetic.* New York: Crowell-Collier and Macmillan, Inc., 1922.

Thorndike, E. L. *The psychology of algebra.* New York: Crowell-Collier and Macmillan, Inc., 1923.

Thorndike, E. L. Mental discipline in high school studies. *J. educ. Psychol.,* 1924, *15.*

Thorndike, E. L. On the improvement of intelligence scores from thirteen to nineteen *J. educ. Psychol.,* 1926, *17,* 73–76.

Thorndike, E. L. *Adult Learning.* New York: Crowell-Collier and Macmillan, Inc., 1928.

Thorndike, E. L. *Human learning.* New York: Appleton-Century-Crofts, 1931.

Thorndike, E. L. *The fundamentals of learning.* New York: Teachers College Press, Columbia University, 1932.

Thorndike, E. L., and others. *The measurement of intelligence.* New York: Teachers College Press, Columbia University, 1926.

Thorndike, R. L. Growth of intelligence during adolescence. *J. genet. Psychol.,* 1948, *72,* 11–15.

Thorndike, R. L. Methodological issues in relation to definition and appraisal of underachievement. *Amer. Psychol.,* 1961, *16,* 46.

Thorndike, R. L. *The concepts of over- and underachievement.* New York: Teachers College Press, Columbia University, 1963.

Thorndike, R. L., and E. Hagen. *Measurement and evaluation in psychology and education* (2d ed.). New York: John Wiley & Sons, Inc., 1961.

Thurstone, L. L. *Primary mental abilities.* Chicago: University of Chicago Press, 1938.

Thurstone, L. L., and Thelma G. Thurstone. *Chicago Test of Primary Mental Abilities,* 1941.

Thurstone, Thelma G. Primary mental abilities, grades 6–9 (1962 revision). Chicago: Science Research Associates, Inc., 1962.

Tiedeman, H. R. A study of retention in classroom learning. *J. educ. Res.,* 1948, *41,* 516–631.

Tizard, J. The effects of different types of supervision on the behavior of mental defectives in a sheltered workshop. *Amer. J. ment. Defic.,* 1953, *58,* 143–161.

Todd, F. G., G. Terrell, and C. E. Frank. Differences between normal and under-achievers of superior ability. *J. appl. Psychol.,* 1962, *46,* 138–190.

Tolor, A., W. L. Scarpetti, and P. A. Lane. Teacher's attitudes toward children's behavior revisited. *J. educ. Psychol.,* 1967, *58*(3), 175–180.

Tomkins, S. S. An experimental study of anxiety. *J. Psychol.,* 1943, *15,* 307–313.

Tomlinson, R. M. A comparison of four presentation methods for teaching complex technical material (unpublished Ed.D. dissertation), Urbana, Ill.: University of Illinois, 1962.

Torgenson, T., and G. Adams. *Measurement and evaluation for the elementary school teacher.* New York: Holt, Rinehart and Winston, Inc., 1954.

Torkelson, G. M., and J. P. Driscoll. Utilization and management of learning resources. *Rev. educ. Res.,* 1968, *38*(2), 129–159.

Torrance, E. P. *Explorations in creative thinking in the early school years: II An experiment in training and motivation.* Minneapolis, Minn.: Bureau of Educational Research, University of Minnesota, 1959.

Torrance, E. P. Eight partial replications of the Getzels-Jackson study. *Res. Memor.,* BER–60–15. Minneapolis, Minn.: Bureau of Educational Research, University of Minnesota, 1960(a).

Torrance, E. P. Gifted children. In *Recent research and developments and their implications for teacher education.* Thirteenth Yearbook, American Association of Colleges for Teacher Education. Washington, D.C.: The Association, 1960, pp. 64–72(b).

Torrance, E. P. *Guiding creative talent.* Englewood Cliffs, N. J.: Prentice-Hall, Inc., 1962.

Torrance, E. P. *Education and the creative potential.* Minneapolis, Minn.: University of Minnesota Press, 1963.

Torrance, E. P. The measurement of creative behavior in children. In *Productive thinking in education* (Mary Jane Aschner and C. E. Bish, Eds.). Washington, D. C.: National Education Association, 1965(a).

Torrance, E. P. *Rewarding creative behavior.* Englewood Cliffs, N. J.: Prentice-Hall, Inc., 1965(b).

Torrance, E. P., K. Yamamoto, D. Schenetzki, N. Palamutlu, and B. Luther. *Assessing the creative thinking abilities of children.* Minneapolis, Minn.: Bureau of Educational Research, University of Minnesota, 1960.

Travers, R. M. W. Towards taking the fun out of building a theory of instruction. *Teachers Coll. Rec.,* 1966, *68,* 49–60.

Travers, R. M. W., and others. *Studies related to the design of audiovisual teaching materials.* U. S. Office of Education, Final Report, Contract No. 3–20–003. Kalamazoo, Mich.: School of Education, Western Michigan University, May 1966.

Traweek, M. W. The relationship between certain personality variables and achievement through programmed instruction. *Calif. J. educ. Res.,* 1964, *15,* 215–220.

Trowbridge, M. H., and H. Cason. An experimental study of Thorndike's theory of learning. *J. gen. Psychol.,* 1932, *7,* 245–248.

Trump, L. J., and D. Baynham. *Guide to better schools: Focus on change.* Skokie, Ill.: Rand McNally & Company, 1961.

Tryon, Carolyn M. The adolescent peer culture. In *Adolescence: 43rd Yearbook Nat. Soc. Stud. Educ.,* Part I. Chicago: University of Chicago Press, 1944.

Tuan, Huei-fen, Chao Li-ju, and Tsao Jihchang. Studies on the methods of memorization used by junior middle school pupils. *Acta Psychologica Sinica*, 1964, *4*, 340–351.

Tuckman, B. W. Group composition and group performance of structured and unstructured tasks. *J. exp. soc. Psychol.*, 1967, *3*(1), 25–40.

Tuddenham, R. D. Jean Piaget and the world of the child. *Amer. Psychol.*, 1966, *21*(3), 207–217.

Tumin, M. M. Readiness and resistance to desegregation: A social portrait of the hard core. *Soc. Forces*, 1958, *36*, 256–263.

Turner, M., and S. S. Dunn. A.C.E.R. prematriculation physics examination: Report No. 2. Hawthorne, Victoria: Australian Council for Educational Research, undated (mimeographed).

Turner, R. L. Characteristics of beginning teachers: Their differential linkage with school-system types. *Sch. Rev.*, 1965, *73*, 48–58.

Tuska, Shirley, and Benjamin Wright. The influence of a teacher model on self-conception during teacher training and experience. *Proceedings of the 73rd annual convention of the American Psychological Association.* Washington, D.C.: The Association, 1965, pp. 297–98.

Twining, P. E. The relative importance of intervening activity and lapse of time in the production of forgetting. *J. exp. Psychol.*, 1940, *26*, 483–501.

Tyler, L. E. *The psychology of human differences.* New York: Appleton-Century-Crofts, 1947.

Tyler, L. E. *Tests and measurements.* Englewood Cliffs, N.J.: Prentice-Hall, Inc., 1963.

Tyler, R. W. What high school pupils forget. *Educ. Res. Bull.*, 1930, *9*, 490–497.

Tyler, R. W. *Constructing achievement tests.* Columbus, Ohio: Ohio State University, 1934(a).

Tyler, R. W. Some findings from studies in the field of college biology. *Science Educ.*, 1934, *18*, 133–142(b).

Tyler, R. W., R. M. Gagné, and M. Scriven. *Perspectives of curriculum evaluation.* Skokie, Ill.: Rand McNally & Company, 1967.

Udry, J. R. The importance of social class in a suburban school. *J. educ. Sociol.*, 1960, *33*, 307–310.

Uhlinger, Carolyn A., and M. W. Stephens. Relation of achievement motivation to academic achievement in students of superior ability. *J. educ. Psychol.*, 1960, *51*, 259–266.

Ullman, C. A. Teachers, peers and tests as predictors of maladjustment. *J. educ. Psychol.*, 1957, *48*, 257–267.

Ulmer, G. Teaching geometry to cultivate reflective thinking: An experimental study with 1239 high school pupils. *J. exp. Educ.*, 1939, *8*, 18–25.

Underwood, B. J. The effect of successive interpolations on retroactive and proactive inhibition. *Psychol. Monogr.*, 1945, *59*, No. 3.

Underwood, B. J. Interference and forgetting. *Psychol. Rev.*, 1957, *64*, 49–60.

Underwood, B. J. Ten years of massed practice on distributed practice. *Psychol. Rev.*, 1961, *68*, 229–247.

Underwood, B. J., and B. R. Ekstrand. Word frequency and accumulative proactive inhibition. *J. exp. Psychol.*, 1967, *74* (2, Part 1), 193–198.

Underwood, B. J., and B. R. Ekstrand. Studies of distributed practice: XXIV Differentiation and proactive inhibition. *J. exp. Psychol.*, 1967, *74*, (4, Part 1), 574–580.

Underwood, B. J., and J. Richardson. The influence of meaningfulness, intralist similarity, and serial position in retention. *J. exp. Psychol.*, 1956, *52*, 110–126.

Uzgaris, I. C. Situational generality of conservation. *Child Develpm.*, 1964, *35*, 831–841.

Van Alstyne, D. *Play behavior and choice of play materials of preschool children.* Chicago: University of Chicago Press, 1932.

Van Buskirk, C. Performance on complex reasoning tasks as a function of anxiety. *J. abnorm. soc. Psychol.*, 1961, *62*, 200–209.

Vandell, R. A., R. A. Davis, and H. A. Clugston. The function of mental practice in the acquisition of motor skills. *J. gen. Psychol.*, 1943, *29*, 243–250.

Van Ormer, E. B. Retention after intervals of sleep and waking. *Arch. Psychol.*, 1932, *21*(137).

Vaughan, G. M., and K. White. Conformity and authoritarianism re-examined. *J. Pers. soc. Psychol.*, 1966, *3*(3), 363–366.

Venezky, R. L. Reading: Grapheme-phoneme relationship. *Education*, May 1967, *87*(9).

Vernon, P. E. Ability factors and environmental influences. *Amer. Psychol.*, 1965, *20*(9), 723–733.

Vick, O. C., and D. N. Jackson. Cognitive styles in the schematizing process: A critical evaluation. *Educ. psychol. Measmt.*, 1967, *27*(2), 267–286.

Vincent, W. S., P. Ash, and L. P. Greenhill. Relationship of length and fact frequency to effectiveness of instructional motion pictures. *Technical Report-SDC.* 269-7-7. University Park, Penn.: Pennsylvania State University, Instructional Films Research Program, November 1949.

Walker, C. C., and L. M. Stolurow. A comparison of overt and covert response in programed learning. *J. educ. Res.*, 1962, *55*, 421–429.

Wallach, Lise and R. L. Sprott. Inducing number conservation in children. *Child Develpm.*, 1964, *35*, 1957–1071.

Wallach, Lise, A. J. Wall, and Lorna Anderson. Number conservation: The roles of reversibility, addition, subtraction, and misleading perceptual cues. *Child Develpm.*, 1967, *38*, 425–442.

Wallach, M. A. Review of E. P. Torrance, *Torrance tests of creative thinking*. *Amer. educ. Res. J.*, 1968, *5*(2), 272–281.

Wallach, M. A., and N. Kogan. *Modes of thinking in young children*. New York: Holt, Rinehart and Winston, Inc., 1965.

Wallas, G. *The act of thought*. New York: Harcourt, Brace & World, Inc., 1921.

Wallon, H. Pre-categorical thinking in the child. *Enfance*, 1952, *5*, 97–101.

Walter, D., Lorraine S. Denzler, and I. G. Sarason. Anxiety and the intellectual performance of high school students. *Child Develpm.*, 1964, *35*, 917–926.

Waly, Patricia, and S. W. Cook. Attitude as a determinant of learning and memory: A failure to confirm. *J. Pers. soc. Psychol.*, 1966, *4*(3), 280–288.

Ward, A. H., and R. A. Davis. Individual differences in retention of general science subject matter in the case of three measurable objectives. *J. exp. Educ.*, 1938, *7*, 24–30.

Ward, A. H., and R. A. Davis. Acquisition and retention of factual information in seventh grade general science during a semester of eighteen weeks. *J. educ. Psychol.*, 1939, *30*, 116–125.

Warner, W. L., and P. M. Lunt. *The social life of a modern community.* New Haven, Conn.: Yale University Press, 1941.

Warner, W. L., and others. *Democracy in Jonesville.* New York: Harper & Row, Publishers, 1949.

Washburne, N. F. Socioeconomic status, urbanism, and academic performance in college. *J. educ. Res.*, 1959, *53*, 130–137.

Waterman, A. D., G. W. Northrop, and L. D. Olson. Motivation and achievement in the elementary school. *Elem. Sch. J.*, 1967, *67*, 375–380.

Watson, G. B. Do groups think more efficiently than individuals? *J. abnorm. soc. Psychol.*, 1928, *23*, 328–336.

Watson, W. S., and G. W. Hartmann. The rigidity of a basic attitudinal frame. *J. abnorm. soc. Psychol.*, 1939, *34*, 314–335.

Wattenberg, W. W., and Clare Clifford. Relation of self-confidence to beginning achievement in reading. *Child Develpm.*, 1964, *35*, 461–467.

Wayson, W. W. Source of teaching satisfaction in slum schools. *Administrator's Notebook*, May 1966, *14*, 1–4.

Webster, S. W. The influence of interracial contact on social acceptance in a newly integrated school, *J. educ. Psychol.*, 1961, *52*, 292–296.

Wechsler, D. *Wechsler Adult Intelligence Scale manual.* New York: Psychological Corporation, 1955.

Wechsler, D. *The measurement and appraisal of adult intelligence* (4th ed.). Baltimore: The Williams & Wilkins Company, 1958, p. 202.

Weiner, B. Need achievement and the resumption of incompleted tasks. *J. Pers. soc. Psychol,* 1965, *1*, 165–168.

Weiner, B. Achievement motivation and task recall in competitive situations. *J. Pers. soc. Psychol.*, 1966, *3*, 693–696(a).

Weiner, B. Motivation and memory. *Psychol. Monogr.*, 1966(b), *80* (18).

Weir, M. W., and H. W. Stevenson. The effect of verbalization in children's learning as a function of chronological age. *Child Develpm.*, 1959, *30*, 143–149.

Weiss, P., M. Wertheimer, and B. Grosbeck. Achievement motivation, academic aptitude, and college grades. *Educ. psychol. Measmt.*, 1959, *19*, 663–666.

Weiss, W., and B. J. Fine. Stimulus prefamiliarization as a factor in ideational learning. *J. educ. Psychol.*, 1956, *47*, 118–124.

Welch, L. The genetic development of the associational structures of abstract thinking. *J. Psychol.*, 1940, *10*, 211–220.

Welch, L., and L. Long. Comparison of the reasoning ability of two age groups. *J. genet. Psychol.*, 1943, *62*, 63–76.

Wellman, B. L. IQ changes of preschool and non-preschool groups during the preschool years: A summary of the literature. *J. Psychol.*, 1945, *20*, 347–368.

Werner, H. *Comparative psychology of mental development.* Chicago: Follett Publishing Co., 1948.

Wertham, F. Psychological effects of school segregation. *Amer. J. Psychother.*, 1952, *6*, 94–103.

Wertheimer, M. *Productive thinking* (enlarged ed., Michael Wertheimer, Ed.). New York: Harper & Row, Publishers, 1959.

Werts, C. E. Sex differences and college attendance. *National Merit Scholarship Corporation Research Report*, 1966, *2*(6)(a).

Werts, C. E. Social class and initial career choice of college freshman. *Sociol. of Educ.*, Winter 1966, *39*, 74–85(b).

Werts, C. E. The many faces of intelligence. *J. educ. Psychol.*, 1957, *58*(4), 198–204.

Westie, F. R. Negro-white status differentials and social distance. *Amer. Sociol. Rev.*, 1952, *17*, 550–558.

Wetherford, R. R., and J. E. Horrocks. Peer acceptance and under- and over-achievement in school. *J. Psychol.*, 1967, *66*(2), 215–220.

Wheeler, L. R. A comparative study of the intelligence of East Tennessee mountain children. *J. educ. Psychol.*, 1942, *33*, 321–334.

White, B. J., and R. D. Alter. Dogmatism and examination performance. *J. educ. Psychol.*, 1967, *58*(5), 285–289.

White, R. W. Motivation reconsidered: The concept of competence. *Psychol. Rev.*, 1959, *66*, 297–333.

White, W. F. Personality determinants of the effects of praise and reproof in classroom achievement. *Proceedings of the 75th annual convention of the American Psychological Association*, 1967, *2*, 323–324.

Whitlock, G. H., L. C. Copeland, and A. M. Craig. Programming versus independent study in learning elementary statistics. *Psychol. Rep.*, 1963, *12*, 171–174.

Wickman, E. K. *Children's behavior and teachers' attitudes*. New York: The Commonwealth Fund, 1928.

Williams, J. D. Teaching arithmetic by concrete analogy. I Miming devices, *Educ. Res.*, 1961, *3*(2 & 3).

Williams, J. D. Teaching arithmetic by concrete analogy. II Structural systems. *Educ. Res.*, 1962, *4*(3).

Williams, J. D. Teaching arithmetic by concrete analogy. III Issues and arguments. *Educ. Res.*, 1963, *5*(2).

Williams, O. A study of the phenomenon of reminiscence. *J. exp. Psychol.*, 1926, *9*, 368–389

Williams, Wilmajean. Academic achievement in a graded school and in a non-graded school. *Elem. Sch. J.*, 1966, *67*, 135–139.

Winick, C. Tendency systems and the effects of a movie dealing with a social problem (abstract). *AV Communication Rev.*, 1964, *12*, 105–106.

Winterbottom, M. M. The relation of need achievement to learning experiences in independence and mastery. In *Motives in fantasy, action and society* (J. W. Atkinson, Ed.). Princeton, N. J.: D. Van Nostrand Company, Inc., 1958.

Wiseman, S. Symposium on the effects of coaching and practice in intelligence tests. IV The Manchester experiment. *Brit. J. educ. Psychol.*, 1954, *24*, 5–8.

Wispé, L. G. Evaluating section teaching methods in the introductory course. *J. educ. Res.*, 1951, *45*, 161–186.

Wittenberg, R. M., and J. Berg. The stranger in the group. *Amer. J. Orthopsychiat.*, 1952, *22*, 89–97.

Wittrock, M. C. Response mode in the programing of kinetic molecular theory concepts. *J. educ. Psychol.*, 1963, *54*, 89–93.

Wittrock, M. C., and T. R. Husek. Effect of anxiety upon retention of verbal learning. *Psychol. Rep.*, 1962, *10*, 78.

Wodtke, K. H. Some data on the reliability and validity of creativity tests at the elementary school level. *Educ. psychol. Measmt.*, 1964, *24*(2), 398–408.

Wodtke, K. H., and B. R. Brown. Social learning and imitation. *Rev. educ. Res.*, 1967, *37*(5), 514–538.

Wohlwill, J. F. A study of the development of the number concept by scalogram analysis. *J. genet. Psychol.*, 1960, *97*, 345–377.

Wohlwill, J. F. Review of Piaget, J., *L'Image Mentale Chez L'Enfant. Contemp. Psychol.*, 1967, *12*(10).

Woodward, J. C. The effect of immediate feedback on learning in social science (abstract). *AV Communication Rev.*, 1965, *13*, 227.

Woodworth, R. S. *Experimental psychology.* New York: Holt, Rinehart and Winston, Inc., 1938, pp. 216–223.

Worcester, D. A. *The education of children of above-average mentality.* Lincoln, Neb.: University of Nebraska Press, 1956.

Wright, J. M., and O. J. Harvey. Attitude change as a function of authoritarianism and punitiveness. *J. Pers. soc. Psychol.*, 1965, *1*, 177–181.

Wright, B., and Barbara Sherman. Love and mastery in the child's image of the teacher. *Sch. Rev.*, 1965, *73*, 89–101.

Wright, Benjamin D., and Shirley A. Tuska. *From dream to life in the psychology of becoming a teacher: Student and first year teachers' attitudes toward self and others.* U.S. Department of Health, Education and Welfare, Office of Education, Cooperative Research Project No. 1503. Chicago: University of Chicago, 1966.

Wulf, F. Über die Veränderung von Vorstelbingen (Gedächtnis und Gestalt). *Psychol. Forsch.*, 1922 *1*, 333–373.

Wyer, R. S., Jr., and R. Bednar. Some determinants of perseverance in achievement-related activity. *J. exp. soc. Psychol.*, 1967, *3*(3), 255–256.

Yamamoto, K. Revised scoring manual for tests of creative thinking: Forms VA and NVA. Minneapolis, Minn.: University of Minnesota Press, 1962.

Yamamoto, K. Role of creative thinking and intelligence in high school achievement. *Psychol. Rep.*, 1964, *14*, 783–789(a).

Yamamoto, K. Threshold of intelligence in academic achievement of highly creative students. *J. exp. Educ.*, 1964, *32*, 401–402(b)

Yamamoto, K. A further analysis of the role of creative thinking in high-school achievement. *J. Psychol.*, 1964, *58*, 277–283(c).

Yamamoto, K. Evaluation of some creativity measures in a high school with peer nominations as criteria. *J. Psychol.*, 1964, *58*, 285–293(d).

Yarmey, A. D. Overt and covert responding in programmed learning. *Ontario J. educ. Res.*, 1964, *7*, 27–33.

Yarrow, Marian R., J. O. Campbell, and L. J. Yarrow. Acquisition of new norms: a study of racial desegregation. *J. soc. Issues*, 1958, *14*, 8–28.

Yates, A. J. Item analysis of Progressive Matrices (1947). *Brit. J. educ. Psychol.*, 1961, *31*, 152–157.

Yates, A. (Ed.). *Grouping in education.* New York: John Wiley & Sons, Inc., 1966.

Young, R. K., W. M. Benson, and W. H. Holtzman. Change in attitudes toward the Negro in a southern university. *J. abnorm. soc. Psychol.,* 1960, *60,* 131–133.

Yudin, L. W. Formal thought in adolescence as a function of intelligence. *Child Develpm.,* 1966, *37,* 697–708.

Yudin, L., and S. L. Kates. Concept attainment and adolescent development. *J. educ. Psychol.,* 1963, *55,* 1–9.

Zagona, S. V., and L. A. Zurcher. The relationship of verbal ability and other cognitive variables to the open-closed cognitive dimension. *J. Psychol.,* 1965, *60,* 213–219.

Zander, A. A study of experimental frustration. *Psychol. Monogr.,* 1944, *56,* (3) (Whole No. 256).

Zillig, M. Einstellung und aussage. *Z. Psychol.,* 1928, *106,* 58–106.

AUTHOR INDEX

677

SUBJECT INDEX